TURBO PASCAL
System Programming

by Michael Tischer

Abacus

A Data Becker Book

Library of Congress Cataloging-in-Publication Data
Tischer, Michael, 1953-
        Turbo Pascal system programming / M. Tischer.
          p.   cm.
        "A Data Becker book"
        Includes index.
        ISBN 1-55755-124-3   :$44.95
        1. Pascal (Computer program language)   2. Turbo Pascal (Computer
program)   3. Systems programming (Computer science)   I. Title.
QA76.73.P2T58   1991
005.265-dc20   91-28922
                                                            CIP

ii

Foreword

This book was written to coincide with the release of Version 6.0 of Turbo Pascal. The new user interface in Version 6.0 marks a milestone in the history of software development. Full mouse support, multiple editor windows, dialog boxes and the macro language included with the editor make this version of Turbo the most complete yet.

Since this is a book on "system programming," the crucial question to ask is:

What's new inside Turbo Pascal that the software developer needs to know so that programs compiled under Version 6.0 will run error-free?

You'll find the answer throughout this book, but here's a short version of the answer: Not much has changed, and most of the programs you may have written for Versions 5.0 and 5.5 of Turbo should port over easily to Version 6.0. Heap handling has changed somewhat in Version 6.0; so programs that use the heap will have problems compiling and running.

Borland has expanded many existing features in Turbo Version 6.0. For example, the integrated assembler lets you create assembly language for 286, 386 and 486 machines within Pascal source code, rather than assembling object code separately. Also, Turbo 6.0 allows you to make function calls just as C programmers do.

Turbo Vision, the object oriented library, offers new scope to programming user interfaces in Pascal. This book contains a basic description of this library. The library itself is so large and complex that a complete description would be beyond the scope of this book.

Turbo Vision provides many object types, object variables and several hundred methods. See Chapter 14 of this book for a quick introduction to object oriented programming according to the CUA standard. The units described in that chapter are a far cry from Turbo Vision, but our units are much easier to develop—especially if you only need a small amount of object oriented programming, and if you don't want to load your program code down with Turbo Vision data.

I hope you have fun and learn a lot as you explore this book.

Michael Tischer   January 1991

Table of Contents:

1. System Programming Basics

Many Pascal programmers start to panic when they hear the words "system programming." This is because system programming is usually associated with assembly language programs. However, you can also implement your own system programming routines in Turbo Pascal.

This chapter contains basic information you'll need throughout this book. You won't have to learn a single assembly language instruction in order to understand the fundamentals of system programming. In addition, this chapter will provide you with enough information on how the Intel 80X86 family of microprocessors work.

In system programming you should know this information since it is an important part of how a Pascal program is converted into a series of assembly language instructions. So, this information will have an effect on how you develop your programs.

The subjects covered in this chapter include the structure of the processor registers, addressing memory with segments and the concept of interrupts. The latter is vital to understanding how a PC works.

1.1   Processor Registers

Every processor uses internal memory locations that are located on the chip itself. This is true whether the processor is an 8086, 6502, a 68000 or a modern RISC processor. These locations are called *processor registers*. The number and size of registers, which are a good indication of how powerful the chip is, will vary from chip to chip. However, the old saying "small is beautiful" is also true, as demonstrated by the 8086/8088. Although these chips have fewer registers than their counterparts, this is sometimes an advantage.

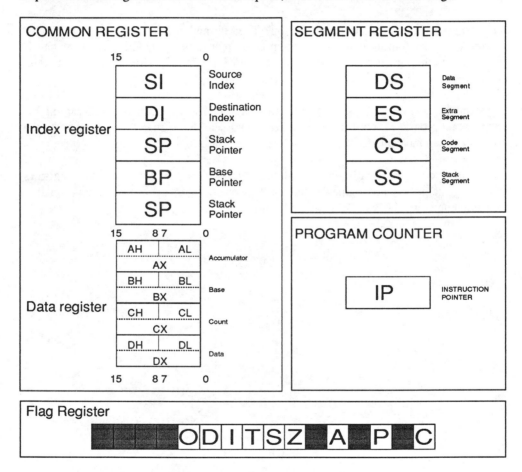

The processor registers of the 8086/8088

The registers of the 8086/8088, shown in the previous figure, perform many functions during the execution of a program. For example, they can be used to store temporary results and partial calculations from mathematical operations. Most assembly language instructions can access memory locations in RAM or ROM, but the processor can execute instructions quicker by using data stored in its own registers. By using registers you can avoid the address and data buses and thereby execute programs faster.

The processor registers can also index addresses, which allows access to other memory locations. This is similar to accessing an array with an index from Pascal.

All 8086/8088 registers are 16-bit, which means that the processors can be considered 16-bit processors. However, the 8088 uses an 8-bit rather than a 16-bit data bus. When the 8088 writes register contents to memory or reads a memory location into a register, it must divide the data into two 8-bit units and send them separately over the data bus. Since the 8086 doesn't have this limitation, it actually executes faster than the 8088.

The 8088 and 8086 chips are no longer considered state of the art. They are the first chips in a line of processors that now include the 80286, the 80386 and the 80486. These chips have better capabilities than their predecessors. However, these capabilities aren't fully explored under the MS-DOS and PC-DOS operating systems. The newer chips are usually run in *real mode*, making them fully compatible with the 8086/8088. The 80286 and its successors have other more powerful operating modes, which can only be accessed under OS/2. These modes will not be discussed in this book.

Throughout this book, the term 8086/8088 refers to the entire 8086 compatible processor family, which includes the 80286, 80386, 80486, and any future additions.

The register figure shows how the individual registers are grouped together and assigned names, similar to variables in Pascal. An assembly language instruction specifies the name of the desired register, which informs the processor of the register that should be accessed. The grouping of the registers is invisible on the processor level and acts only as a visual aid to the user so that he/she can distinguish the different uses of the various registers.

The processor cannot arbitrarily use any register for any operation. Certain registers are dedicated to arithmetic operations, addressing memory or hardware I/O. The following section details the purpose of each register group.

1.1.1 Data Registers

Whether you are programming in Pascal or assembly language, the four data registers (AX, BX, CX and DX) are the most frequently used in system programming. These data registers are used for transferring data and storing arguments for mathematical operations. In addition, certain assembly language instructions access data registers for counting loops and other purposes. Turbo Pascal uses these registers to assign and manipulate variables.

These four data registers play two roles. Either a program can use them as 16-bit registers that can accept values from 0 to 65535 ($0000 to $FFFF) or these registers can be accessed as two 8-bit registers, which correspond to the higher and lower 8-bit halves of the 16-bit register.

These half registers are called H (for HI) and L (for LO). The letters are given as a suffix to the name of the corresponding 16-bit register. Therefore, the AX register is divided into AH and AL (A high and A low), the BX into BH and BL, etc. The 8086/8088 also allows the use of 8-bit variables, with values from 0 to 255 ($00 to $FF). Even though 8-bit operations execute faster than 16-bit operations, they can only be used with values ranging from 0 to 255 ($00 to $FF).

It is important to remember that the half registers can be accessed separately from one another. If you assign a new value to the AX register, the contents of both AH and AL will change. However, you can also manipulate AH by itself. If you do this the contents of AL remain unchanged, but the entire AX register will contain a new value.

A special feature of the 8086/8088 is word format, which is the format used for storing 16-bit values. The low byte contains the least significant memory address value while the high byte contains the most significant address value. So if a program writes the contents of the AX register to memory address Y, the contents of AL will be placed in Y and the contents of AH will be placed in the next memory address (Y+1).

The names of the four data registers weren't simply taken from the first four letters of the alphabet. The letters describe the way certain assembly language instructions use each register:

A X   The *accumulator register* is probably the most frequently used register. It is used during arithmetic operations such as addition, subtraction, multiplication and division for storing operands or results. This register is also used during access through the hardware I/O ports and in processing string instructions.

B X   The *base register* acquired its name from the way it indexes memory addresses starting from a base address, which is similar to the way Turbo Pascal accesses arrays. The BX register can also be used in conjunction with arithmetic instructions.

C X   The *counter register* is used for loop control and moving bits. It can also be used for arithmetic operations just like the other three registers.

D X   The *data register* is important to multiplication operations, during which it is used to store a part of the result. It also serves as an address register for access to expansion cards using I/O instructions. It can also be used for arithmetic operations.

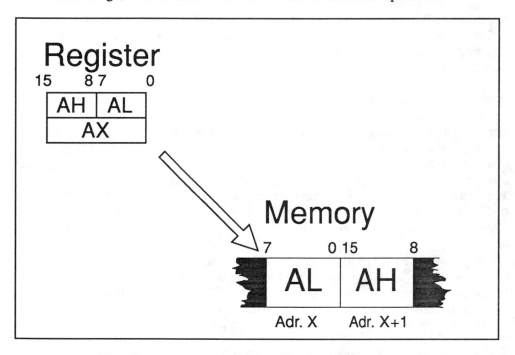

Format of a word in memory

The value of the AX register is determined from the values of the AH and AL registers and vice versa. You can determine the value of the AX register by multiplying the value of the AH register by 256 and adding the value of the AL register.

Example: The value of the AH register is 10, the value of the AL register is 118. The formula for the value of the AX register value is AH*256+AL and when the figures are substituted it is 10*256+118=2678.

1.1.2 Index Registers

We have already seen that one processor register, the BX register, can function as an index register. The 8086/8088 uses five additional registers designed specifically for indexed access to memory. These are the IP, SI, DI, SP and BP registers.

The SP and BP registers are used for addressing the *stack*, a special memory range that we will thoroughly discuss in Section 1.2. Although SP, BP, SI and DI are 16-bit registers, they cannot be divided into two 8-bit registers (see Section 1.1.1). The entire 16-bit register must be accessed at once.

In addition to indexed memory access, SI and DI are also used for *string instructions*, which are important to the 8086/8088. String instructions allow the manipulation of an entire memory range using only one assembly language instruction. This instruction is repeated by the processor as often as necessary until the entire memory range has been processed. Use this method to fill memory ranges with constant values, to compare a range with another, or to copy a range to another without having to set up a loop in your program. This offers an enormous speed advantage over the usual methods of setting up program loops. The reason for this is that the loop already exists at the processor level and does not have to be loaded from memory each time it executes.

The IP register is important to program execution because it always contains the address of the next assembly language instruction to be executed. Because of this, programs are unable to simply load this register with any desired value. This would have the same effect as a jump or a goto statement in a high level language. At the processor level, a jump instruction simply loads the memory address of the jump into the IP register.

Another special feature of the IP register is that it is automatically incremented by the processor. After executing an instruction, the processor increments this register by the length of the instruction (1 to 5 bytes), which then sets it to the next instruction to be executed. This ensures that the program will continue to be executed.

1.1.3 Flag Register

The flag register of the 8086/8088 watches the results of a number of assembly language instructions. It tracks these results in the form of *flags*, which are each equal to one bit of this 16-bit register. As seen in the figure below, however, not all of the bits (or flags) in this register are used when the processor is in real mode.

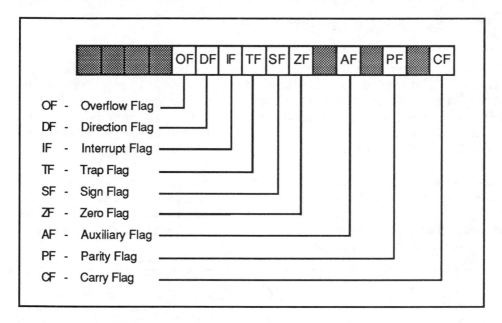

The Flags of the Flag register

Usually arithmetic and comparison instructions will change the status of one of the flags. For example, the Carry flag (C) shows that a value is being carried as the result of addition or subtraction. If after adding the two 8-bit registers AH and CL, the value can no longer be stored in an 8-bit register (i.e., the sum is greater than 255), then this bit would be set. The Zero flag (Z) works in a similar way. For example, when executing a comparison instruction, this flag would be set to 1 when the two operands being compared are identical.

Very few instructions have direct access to the contents of these flags, so you cannot directly determine their values. One exception is the jump instructions that control program flow from one location in memory to another. This allows you to continue program execution at a different memory location if one of the flags has a certain value. If the value you are testing for cannot be found, program execution continues with the next instruction in the sequence. This allows the construction of IF-ELSE statements in assembly language.

You don't have to know the meaning of every flag in order to do your own system programming in Turbo Pascal. For the purposes of our book, only the Carry flag and the Zero flag are important. Turbo Pascal programs can call many operating system routines, which utilize these flags and can return values that inform the calling program whether everything is in order or if an error has occurred.

1.2   Segment Registers

The segment registers are another important register group. Understanding how the segment registers function requires some knowledge of how the 8086/8088 processor addresses memory. If only one 16-bit register was used for addressing memory, the numbers 0 to 65535 could be used, giving a total of 65536 memory locations. Therefore the total number of addressable memory locations would be limited to 64K. This was acceptable a few years ago but today's PC users have applications that require much more memory.

In order to manage more memory, you need to have more bits available for memory addresses. For example 17 bits are required to address 128K; 18 bits for 256K; 19 for 512K; and 20 for one megabyte of addressable memory. You can continue this as far as you wish, but 1 megabyte is the limit for the 8086/8088 processor. Therefore, a 20-bit address is required to access all memory locations.

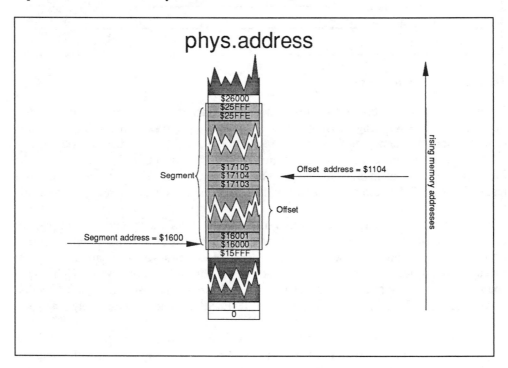

Segment address and offset address functions

Since the 8086/8088 doesn't have 20-bit registers, how can 20-bit addressing be used with 16-bit registers? The developers of the 8086/8088 solved this problem by dividing addressable memory into *memory segments*. When a segment is accessed, the 16-bit base address of the segment (also called the segment address) is moved four bits to the left, and thereby expanded to 20 bits. To reach a specific location within the segment, the 8086/8088 will add an *offset address* to the *segment address*. This value gives the difference between the start of the segment and the desired memory address. The offset address is also a 16-bit value, which limits the number of addressable memory locations within a segment to 65536. So the segment size has been set at 64K.

Theoretically, a segment could begin at any memory address. However, moving the segment address four places to the left makes all segment addresses multiples of sixteen. Segments always begin at an address divisible by sixteen.

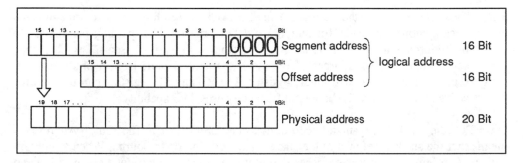

Memory structure using the segment and offset addresses

Using this technique, a segment with segment address 1 begins at memory address 16. Segment 2 begins at 32, etc. When you use hexadecimal notation to represent the segment addresses, you simply add a 0 to the segment address to find the current memory address. Segment $43A8 would start at $43A80, segment $B000 would start at $B0000, etc.

1.2.1 Functions of the Segment Registers

By using 16-bit numbers as segment addresses, the 8086/8088 can address 65536 different segments within 1 megabyte of memory. Only four segments can be active at any given time. Each is represented by one of the four segment registers.

Each register has a different function, which are described below:

C S   This register contains the address of the *code segment*, in which the program code (the executable assembly language instructions) is stored. By joining the CS register with the IP register (index pointer) as the offset address, the 8086/8088 creates a 20-bit address from which the code for the next instruction is read.

D S   The DS register contains the address of the *data segment*, which stores program data such as strings, arrays and jump tables. The 8086/8088 assigns all assembly language instructions, which are associated with data in any way (such as logical and arithmetic instructions), the DS register as the default segment address.

E S   The ES or *extra segment* register is also used for accessing data. Its best application is copying data from one range to another when the amount of data copied is more than 64K and when the source and target ranges are different, non-overlapping segments. The string instructions, which are often used for this type of task, frequently use the ES register. Many programs (including machine code generated from Turbo Pascal) use the ES register as a "catch-all" register, instead of as only a reference to a constant segment. One example application of the ES register might be copying data from one segment to another.

S S   This register acts as the *stack segment*. The stack is used for storing return addresses during subroutine calls, for temporary data storage and for passing parameters to procedures and functions (which can be done with Turbo Pascal). Like the code segment, the offset address of the stack segment is built from a predetermined register, the SP (Stack Pointer) register. The BP and SP registers can be used for addressing the stack. Turbo Pascal frequently uses this capability.

On a PC, the stack is organized according to the LIFO (last in first out) system. This means that the stack is set, within the stack segment, from top to bottom. When a program calls a subroutine, the processor stores the return address at the current stack position and then decrements the stack pointer so that it points to the stack position before the return address. If the subroutine then calls another subroutine, this process is repeated with the subroutine return address added to the stack. When returning from a subroutine call, the processor retrieves the return address from the stack, loads it in the IP register and increments the stack pointer in the SP register so that it points to the previous return address. This will allow you to execute almost any nested subroutine calls without losing all of the necessary return addresses.

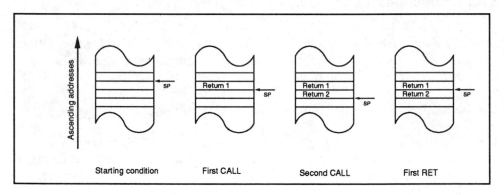

Storing return addresses on the stack

Programs generally access the code, data and stack segments. The individual segments are usually much smaller than 64K. In this case, the segments are arranged end to end in memory so that a given segment starts right after the end of the previous segment. This prevents a waste of valuable memory. The segments will actually overlap, or even be identical in some cases, as shown in the following figure:

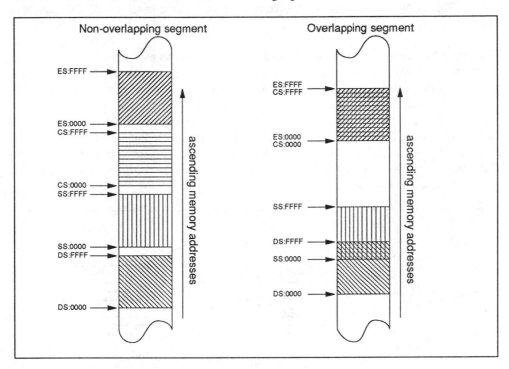

Overlapping and non-overlapping segments

1.2.2 NEAR and FAR Instructions

Memory segmentation requires an ability to distinguish between references to code and variables. This is supported by various assembly language instructions that make NEAR and FAR references. The 8086/8088 refers to variables with a NEAR pointer and calls to program code and subroutines with NEAR calls. The FAR equivalents of these are the FAR pointer and FAR call.

The difference between NEAR and FAR is the inclusion of the segment address in the reference. A NEAR reference omits the segment address. The address is based on the corresponding current segment register. This means that a NEAR call can only be used to call a subroutine located in the same segment as the program making the call. Along the same lines, NEAR pointers can only be used to access data within the currently active data segment. A program cannot leave its own segment with NEAR pointers and NEAR calls.

FAR references do not have this limitation. They use a 16-bit segment address in addition to the offset address to specifically address the segment containing the desired program code or data. This allows access to any variable or program routine in the entire 1 megabyte of addressable memory.

Although FAR references are more powerful, they aren't always used because of the way the processor handles them and the speed with which they are executed. With a NEAR reference, the address of the desired segment is already available in a segment register. With FAR references, the desired segment address must first be found and loaded. This means that NEAR references can be processed much faster than equivalent FAR references. Even though processors are becoming faster, the relative speed difference between NEAR and FAR references will remain significant. So, the proper use of NEAR and FAR references will continue to be very important, even though it increases complexity and can make programs more prone to error.

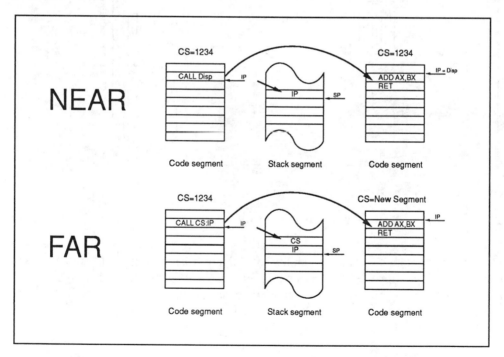

NEAR and FAR references using a subroutine call

1.3   An Introduction to 8086/8088 Interrupts

This section deals with a central concept of PC programming: the use of interrupts in the 8086/8088. Basically, interrupts are the keys to unlocking the operating system functions which control your computer's components, such as the keyboard, monitor, disk drives and printer. Like all PC software, your Turbo Pascal compiler frequently uses these functions.

The term *interrupt* evolved as a description of what happens within the processor. An interrupt will actually "interrupt" the execution of the assembly language program currently being processed in order to call another routine. The new routine that is called after the processor is interrupted is called the *interrupt routine.*

The interrupt routine is an assembly language program that can use all of the assembly language instructions of the processor. The end of an interrupt routine is indicated by the assembly language instruction IRET (Interrupt RETurn). As the name of the instruction implies, control returns to the point in the original program where it was interrupted. This mechanism is very similar to calling a subroutine and then returning to the main program. The difference is that an external device (such as the keyboard) initiates the interrupt rather than an instruction within the program.

A program can be interrupted at any point but must later be continued without any glitches. Therefore, there has to be a way to ensure that the program flow will continue, from the point where it stopped, after the interrupt routine has been executed. The processor does this by storing the return address on the stack so when the IRET instruction appears, the program can go back and continue to execute at the point where it was interrupted. The interrupt handler must also ensure that the contents of the processor registers do not change. This is similar to Pascal program variables changing by themselves without instructions from the program.

However, it is very difficult to ensure that an assembly language routine will not change the contents of any processor register during its execution. There are few assembly language instructions that do not, in some way, manipulate the contents of one or more processor registers. So, the interrupt handler is also responsible for saving the current contents of the processor registers, which it will manipulate, and then restoring these contents immediately before executing the IRET instruction. The 8086/8088 uses the PUSH instructions to store the contents of a register on the stack and the POP instructions to retrieve and reload it.

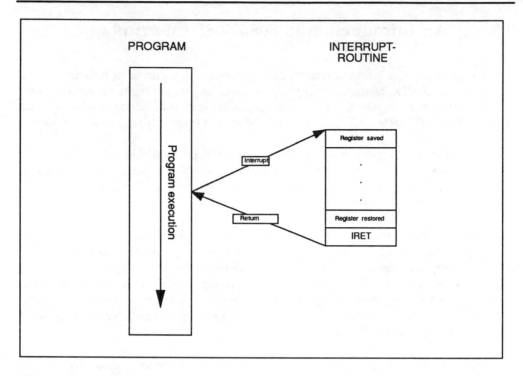

Using an interrupt

1.3.1 Interrupt Vector Table

The 8086/8088 has a total of 256 interrupts available. These are numbered from 0 to 255.

Each interrupt has a corresponding interrupt routine. The *interrupt vector table* specifies the interrupt and the location of its interrupt routine. This table occupies the first 1024 bytes in the addressable memory of a PC. For each interrupt, there is an entry in this table that is a vector corresponding to the starting address of the interrupt routine in memory.

When an interrupt is called, the processor automatically retrieves the starting address of the corresponding interrupt routine from the interrupt vector table and begins executing the routine. The interrupt routine is rarely located in the same code segment as the interrupted program, so the addresses of the interrupt routines are stored as FAR pointers containing the segment address of the proper code segment, as well as the offset address of the routine.

These FAR pointers are stored as *dwords*. A dword consists of two consecutive words and is a 32-bit address. The least significant 16 bits contain the segment address and the most significant 16 bits contain the offset address of the memory location indicated by the pointer. As with single words, the processor switches the most and least significant words. The first 15 bits (the offset address) are stored in the word with the lowest address in memory. The next word in memory will contain bits 16 to 31, the segment address. This is more easily understood visually than verbally. The following figure presents the way a dword is stored in memory:

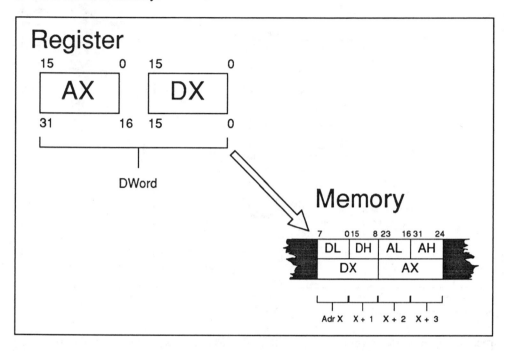

Dword format in memory

Since FAR pointers are used, each entry in the interrupt vector table is 2 words, or 4 bytes. Therefore, the table consists of 1024 bytes and occupies addresses $0000 through and including $3FF.

The number of the interrupt corresponds to the entry number of the interrupt routine in the table. So interrupt number 0 will be table entry 0 and the address of the interrupt routine will be located in addresses $000 to $003. The address of the interrupt routine for interrupt 1 will be in addresses $004 to $007. This process repeats itself all the way up through interrupt number 255 ($FF) at addresses $3FC to $3FF and completes the table.

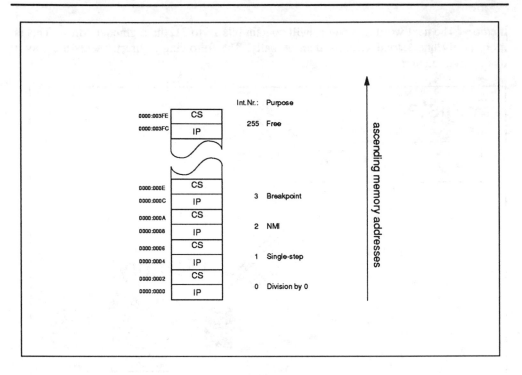

Interrupt vector table structure

Three separate system components within the PC take advantage of the interrupt mechanism: the hardware, the DOS kernel and the ROM-BIOS. They use the system interrupts to generate what are known as software and hardware interrupts. The two subsections that follow describe the characteristics of these two types of interrupts.

1.3.2 Interrupt Types

Interrupts are divided into two types because of the different roles they play for the control of software and hardware. Different types of components place different demands on the system, so the developers of the 8086/8088 established two ways to activate interrupt routines: software interrupts and hardware interrupts.

Software interrupts

A *software interrupt* is an interrupt activated by a special assembly language instruction, the INT instruction. The INT instruction is always used in conjunction with the number of the interrupt to be executed. This allows a program to call a routine when it doesn't know the exact address, but it does know that the routine is accessible as an interrupt routine. The routines in the ROM-BIOS and the DOS kernel can be accessed by any program by using interrupts in this way. Simple functions (e.g., character input/output or file access) can be called directly from the ROM-BIOS and DOS kernel without having to worry about the memory address, availability or structure of the routines.

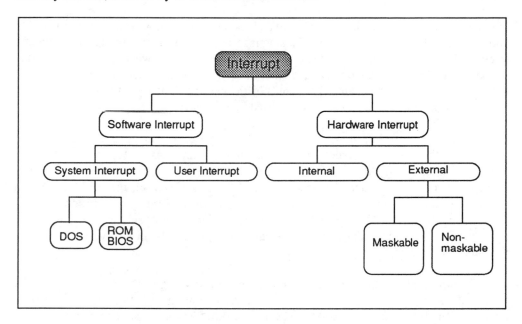

The various types of interrupts

The most important purpose these routines serve is to isolate programs from differences in PC hardware from system to system. The ROM-BIOS and the DOS kernel act as go-betweens so that applications do not have to access hardware directly. This guarantees that a program will have a certain amount of independence from the system differences that can occur because of the countless possible hardware configurations. Programs do not have to consider things like how the ports are configured or what controllers are being used.

Turbo Pascal uses this method by translating commands like WRITELN and READLN to a sequence of assembly language instructions at the processor level. The INT instruction is used to call the corresponding interrupt. But Turbo Pascal does not have a Pascal instruction for every interrupt routine you may need to call. So this book will demonstrate how to call interrupts from Turbo Pascal, as well as discuss the applications of several interrupts and interrupt functions for solving specific problems.

Interrupt functions are similar to Pascal functions in that many require that parameters or arguments be passed to them. These parameters add specific instructions to the functions to which they are passed. Parameters are usually passed through the processor registers. The most frequently used registers are the data registers and the index registers SI, DI and BP. When the interrupt is called, the caller passes the parameters or arguments using these registers. The interrupt routine will then return certain information to various registers.

There are no standards for which register is used with which type of data, since the functions performed by the interrupt routines require literally hundreds of different types of parameters.

In order for interrupt functions to take up as little memory as possible, they must be fast and compact. In this regard, assembly language is the best programming language. An interrupt function expects the parameters to be located in registers where they can be further processed, without first having to move them to other registers or memory locations. Since this greatly depends upon the task performed by the interrupt function and its program code, standardization of parameter transfer is sacrificed for efficiency.

Despite this, there is one standard use of processor registers in parameter transfers to interrupt routines. Many interrupts call several interrupt functions, instead of only one. So, the caller must specify the number of the desired interrupt function in a register. The interrupt functions are numbered starting with 0. The DOS kernel, the ROM-BIOS and system add-ons, such as a mouse interface or the port to EMS memory, will look for this function number in the AH register. Many interrupt functions have subfunctions, which are also numbered starting with 0. The subfunction number must be in the AL register when the interrupt is called.

The interrupt routine returns information through the Carry flag or the Zero flag. All DOS functions use the Carry flag to show whether the operation failed or was successfully executed. The functions of the ROM-BIOS use the Zero flag for the same purpose.

Detailed information on the use of the various processor registers for calling certain interrupt functions can be found in the discussion of each function in subsequent chapters of this book.

As you now see, a software interrupt is somewhat different from the interrupt concept we initially introduced, since the interrupted program is actually calling the interrupt. This is done with the INT instruction, which is intentionally placed in the code by the programmer. However this does not apply to the other interrupt type, the hardware interrupt.

Hardware interrupts

Unlike software interrupts, the *hardware interrupts* are not called with the INT instruction. A hardware interrupt comes directly from a hardware component of the system (such as the keyboard or a disk drive). This is a simple way of making the processor aware of user input, such as keypresses or mouse movement.

The hardware devices use one of the interrupts from $08 to $0F, and the proper interrupt is executed when a device wants to get the processor's attention. As with a software interrupt, the corresponding interrupt routine is then called. The address of this routine is obtained from the interrupt vector table. These entries are initialized by the ROM-BIOS, which also prepares the interrupt handlers to properly respond to the interrupts. Unless you want to program your own interrupt handler you will not come into contact with these interrupts from high level languages or from assembly language. This is usually only necessary for TSR programs, device drivers or other equally ambitious undertakings.

Hardware interrupts originating from the keyboard, disk drives or other peripherals are called *external interrupts*. The two types of external interrupts are those that can be suppressed and those that cannot be suppressed. Pressing a key, for example, is a *maskable interrupt* that can be suppressed with the assembly language instruction CLI (Clear Interrupt Flag). This means that the interrupt call will not be executed and that characters cannot be entered with the keyboard until the suppression is lifted with the STI instruction (Set Interrupt Flag).

The *non-maskable hardware interrupt* cannot be suppressed by the CLI instruction. Among these is the non-maskable interrupt or NMI, which is called when a defective memory chip is found within your PC.

The final type of interrupt is the *internal hardware interrupt*. This type of interrupt is called from one of the processors on the mother board of your PC rather than from some external device. The Timer interrupt, which is executed at regular intervals to allow time measurements, is one example from this category.

The following list gives you an overview of the interrupt assignments for the PC. Not all of the interrupts in the figure will be useful to you in PC programming, and there are many that you will probably never execute.

However, there are also some important interrupts, which can give you access to some powerful functions, that you can program without using assembly language.

With the help of a few tricks, there is a lot you can do with Turbo Pascal. The following chapters will provide you with the necessary instructions and examples.

Interrupt	Address	Purpose
00	000 – 003	CPU: Division by zero
01	004 – 007	CPU: Single <individual> step
02	008 – 00B	CPU: NMI (error in RAM component)
03	00C – 00F	CPU: Breakpoint reached
04	010 – 013	CPU: Numeric overflow
05	014 – 017	Hardcopy
06	018 – 01B	Unknown instruction (80286 and 80386 only)
07	01D – 01F	Reserved
08	020 – 023	IRQ0: Timer (18.2 calls/sec.)
09	024 – 027	IRQ1: Keyboard
0A	028 – 02B	IRQ2: Second 8259 (AT and 80386 only)
0B	02C – 02F	IRQ3: Serial port 2
0C	030 – 033	IRQ4: Serial port 1
0D	034 – 037	IRQ5: Hard disk
0E	038 – 03B	IRQ6: Floppy disk
0F	03C – 03F	IRQ7: Printer
10	040 – 043	BIOS: Video functions
11	044 – 047	BIOS: Determine configuration
12	048 – 04B	BIOS: Determine size of RAM
13	04C – 04F	BIOS: Hard/floppy disk access
14	050 – 053	BIOS: Serial port access
15	054 – 057	BIOS: Cassettes/expanded functions
16	058 – 05B	BIOS: Keyboard query
17	05C – 05F	BIOS: Parallel printer port access
18	060 – 063	ROM-BASIC call
19	064 – 067	BIOS: System boot (Alt+Ctrl+Del)
1A	068 – 06B	BIOS: Time/Date query
1B	06C – 06F	Break key (not Ctrl-C) pressed
1C	070 – 073	Called after every INT 08
1D	074 – 077	Address of the Video Parameter Table
1E	078 – 07B	Address of the Diskette Parameter Table
1F	07C – 07F	Address of graphic hardcopy char. bit map
20	080 – 083	DOS: End program
21	084 – 087	DOS: Call DOS function
22	088 – 08B	Address of the DOS Program End function
23	08C – 08F	Address of the DOS Ctrl-Break function
24	090 – 093	Address of the DOS Error function
25	094 – 097	DOS: Read floppy/hard disk
26	098 – 09B	DOS: Write floppy/hard disk
27	09C – 09F	DOS: End program, remain resident
28–	0A0 –	Reserved for various non-
3F	– 0FF	documented DOS functions
40	100 –	BIOS: Addresses of diskette functions for
40	– 103	XT hard disk BIOS
41	104 – 107	Address of hard disk table #1
42–	108 –	Reserved
45	– 117	
46	118 – 11B	Address of hard disk table #2
47–	11C –	Can be used as desired by

Interrupt	Address	Purpose
49	– 127	application programs
4A	128 – 12B	Real time clock: alarm time reached
4B–	12C –	Can be used as desired by
67	– 19F	application programs
68–	1A0 –	Not used
6F	– 1BF	
70	1C0 – 1C3	IRQ08: Real time clock (AT and 80386 only)
71	1C4 – 1C7	IRQ09: (AT and 80386 only)
72	1C8 – 1CB	IRQ10: (AT and 80386 only)
73	1CC – 1CF	IRQ11: (AT and 80386 only)
74	1D0 – 1D3	IRQ12: (only AT and 80386)
75	1D4 – 1D7	IRQ13: 80287 NMI (AT and 80386 only)
76	1D8 – 1DB	IRQ14: Hard disk (AT and 80386 only)
77	1DC – 1DF	IRQ15: (AT and 80386 only)
78–	1E0 –	Not used
7F	– 1FF	
80–	200 –	Used within the GWBASIC
F0	– 3C3	BASIC interpreter
F1–	3C4 –	Not used, available for use
FF	– 3CF	by application programs

Standard PC interrupts at a glance

1.3.3 Calling Interrupts from Turbo Pascal

The developers at Borland International know the power and usefulness of interrupts. They included two Turbo Pascal procedures that make it easy for the programmer to use the interrupts. They are the INTR procedure and the MSDOS procedure.

The syntax of INTR is as follows:

```
Intr(InterruptNumber : byte, Regs : Registers);
```

The InterruptNumber parameter specifies the number of the interrupt to be called. Values for this parameter range from 0 to 255, so all the available interrupts, including hardware interrupts, can be accessed.

The MSDOS procedure is a variation on the INTR procedure. The syntax is similar:

```
MsDos(Regs : Registers);
```

Unlike INTR, the MSDOS procedure doesn't use an InterruptNumber parameter. This instruction always calls interrupt number $21, which lets the programmer use more than 200 DOS kernel functions.

Both of these procedures use a variable of the REGISTERS type. This is defined in the DOS unit. It serves to store the contents of the processor registers prior to the interrupt call. The interrupt can then use the registers as required. After returning from MSDOS or INTR, the original values of the processor registers can be restored.

REGISTERS creates a record of register names to keep track of all of them. Within the DOS unit REGISTERS is defined as follows:

```
type Registers = record
                    case integer of
                        0 : (AX, BX, CX, DX, BP, SI, DI, DS, ES, Flags : word);
                        1 : (AL, AH, BL, BH, CL , CH, DL, DH : byte);
                    end;
```

The integer variables AX through ES are represented by the Turbo Pascal WORD data type, which corresponds to an unsigned 16-bit value. Similarly, type BYTE represents an unsigned 8-bit value stored in registers AL through DH.

The half registers are just as important as the whole registers when calling interrupts. Two 8-bit variables make up one 16-bit variable. AL and AH occupy the same location in memory as AX, BL and BH occupy the same location as BX. The same holds true for CX (CL/CH) and DX (DL/DH).

The order in which the half registers are specified is important. In memory, the low byte of a word precedes the high byte. You must therefore always declare the L register before the corresponding H register.

If REGS is a variable of type REGISTERS, you can use the various components of these variables to address each processor register:

- Regs.ax,
- Regs.bx,
- Regs.cx,
- Regs.ah,
- Regs.dl, etc.

The InterruptNumber parameter is used to call a specific interrupt. The following line assigns the DL register the value $D3 during the call:

```
Regs.DL := $D3;
```

This format can be used to specify any register. Of course, you must always load values into the registers where the interrupt being called can expect to find them.

The flags from the Flag register are often used instead of, or in addition to, the data and index registers for passing information. DOS functions use the Carry flag, which is set if the function call returns an error.

To help you check the flags, the DOS unit defines a number of constants that reflect the bit values of the individual processor flags:

Constant	Bit Position	Bit Value
FCarry	0	1
FParity	2	4
FAuxiliary	4	16
FZero	6	64
FSign	7	128
FOverflow	11	2048

You can determine whether one of these bits is set by joining the FLAG variable, from the REGISTERS structure, with the corresponding constant by using an AND operator. Let's demonstrate this with an example. The following statement signals an error by setting the BOOLEAN variable ERROR to TRUE if the Carry flag is set:

```
Error := ( ( Regs.Flags and FCarry ) <> 0 );
```

We still need to discuss direct interrupt calls before we can look at interrupt calls in Turbo Pascal. These will be discussed in the next chapter.

2.   Behind the Scenes

In this chapter you'll not only learn about the structure of Pascal programs, but also how they work, how procedures are executed and how variables are stored. You'll discover the special characteristics of the system unit and observe how the heap is organized. We'll investigate these things not just out of curiosity, but because a knowledge of what happens when a Turbo Pascal program is executed will help you understand the material that will be presented in the following chapters.

Without this knowledge, attempting tasks, such as writing TSR programs, temporarily storing Turbo Pascal programs or creating a multitasking unit wouldn't be possible.

2.1   Memory Model

Our look behind the scenes of a compiled program begins with a few questions. Where are all of the individual program elements stored? How does the processor know where to find the program code, the data, the stack and the heap? We must understand the memory model used by Turbo Pascal because its structure will greatly influence the way Pascal programs are translated into machine code.

Turbo Pascal uses only one *memory model*. This is a simple method when compared to C, which may use several. However, using only one memory model will reduce your ability to control the code generation. But it also frees you from the "paralysis of analysis" that often sets in when there are too many programming options to choose.

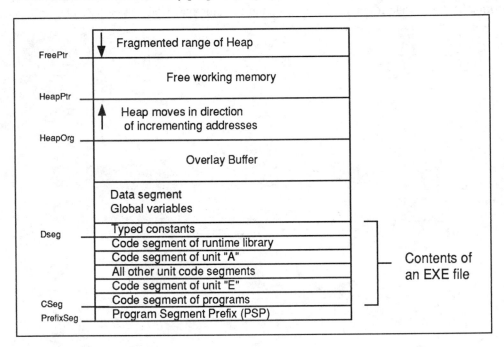

Turbo Pascal memory model

The Turbo Pascal memory model is very different from anything that any other compiler generates. The nearest equivalent may be in Turbo C with the MEDIUM memory model. A Turbo Pascal program contains multiple *code segments*, each of which can occupy the entire 64K or one 8086/8088 memory segment. The main program and each unit are stored in separate code segments. Since a program can have an unlimited number of units, the practical program size is limited by the available memory (up to 1 megabyte). Each program will contain at least two code segments: one for the main program and one for the unit system, which Turbo Pascal automatically includes when it encounters a USES statement.

The individual code segments are listed at the beginning of the Turbo Pascal program after it is loaded into memory by the DOS EXEC loader. The order is determined as follows:

The code segment of the main program is first. The code segments of additional units follow in the reverse order in which they were specified with the USES statement in the program. If the main program contains the statement:

```
Uses Unit1, Unit2, Unit3;
```

then the main program code segment would be followed by the Unit3 code segment, Unit2 code segment and Unit1 code segment. The final code segment is the system unit, which is always last.

There is another structure which precedes the program code segment. This is the *Program Segment Prefix*, or PSP. Instead of being generated by Turbo Pascal, it is generated by the EXEC Loader of each EXE file in memory. DOS places information which it requires for the management of the program into this structure (see the Figure on page 29).

Unlike the (almost) unlimited program size, program data is limited to a single 64K segment. This limit seems almost counterproductive since this segment must be used for global variables, standard constants of the main program and all units. However, 64K is usually enough. If you run out of room in the data segment, you can always use the *heap*, which we'll explain later. Depending on the size of the other program components and the amount of available memory, the heap can provide an additional 100K. The heap is also used for trees, linked lists and other such structures.

The DS register always points to the data segment during program execution so that Turbo always accesses the variables and standard constants. Its address, and therefore the contents of the DS register, are assigned the DSeg variable.

The stack, which is linked to the data segment, is used to store local variables and the return addresses for subroutine calls. Its default size is 16K (16384 bytes), but this can be changed in the integrated development environment using Options / Compiler / Memory. You can also change the stack size within a program by using the compiler directive {$M}. During program execution, the SS register always points to this segment, whose address is given with the predefined variable SSeg.

The contents of the stack pointer changes many times. When the program is started, it points to or after the last byte of the stack segment. This pointer changes each time a subroutine is called and parameters are passed. The pointer will either move towards the beginning or towards the end of the stack segment. You can determine its current value from the variable SPtr, which is defined through the system unit, as are SSeg, DSeg and

CSeg. We'll see how the stack is used to store local variables and for passing parameters to other routines in the following sections.

The heap, which begins at the end of the stack segment, provides memory locations allocated with the New and GetMem statements. If the heap size has not been specified with the compiler directive {$M} or with the menu, using Options / Compiler / Memory, the heap will take the rest of the available 640K of base memory.

If a program works with *overlays*, Turbo Pascal will insert an *overlay buffer* between the stack segment and the heap. Overlays are specified with the USES statement, which creates an overlay unit in the program. The overlay buffer will occupy enough memory to make room for the largest overlay, which ensures that all smaller overlays will also fit.

The PSP

The PSP is a data structure that is placed in memory by the EXEC loader, which is responsible for all EXE and COM programs. The PSP is 256 bytes (16 paragraphs) long and always precedes the code segment of the main program in Turbo Pascal programs. For example, if this main program code segment starts at $3F10, the PSP will begin at $3F00. You won't need to perform this calculation, however, since Turbo Pascal has the segment address of the PSP in a predefined variable, PrefixSeg.

DOS needs the PSP to control a program. The PSP contains information that you may find useful if you ever have to resort to "tricks", or working outside the syntax of Turbo Pascal. Actually, the contents of the PSP are not very mysterious. It has not changed since DOS Version 1.0, even though many changes have happened within the DOS kernel itself.

The first entry in the PSP is a call to interrupt $20, which at one time was used to terminate a program. This has since been replaced by a newer function, which contains the address of the last memory location that DOS has allocated for the program.

The third entry is marked "Reserved", which actually should be interpreted as "undocumented." Many developers have tried to determine the purpose of this entry but only a few have actually succeeded. You shouldn't rely on this entry in your programs because its contents can change with each new version of DOS. We won't describe its purpose here because it doesn't apply to Turbo Pascal.

Memory location 5 in the PSP is a call to the function dispatcher, which is found after interrupt $21 and is used to call the corresponding DOS function. This entry is outdated and no longer useful.

Addr.	Contents	Type
$00	Call interrupt $20	2 BYTE
$02	End address of memory occupied by the program (segment address only)	1 WORD
$04	Reserved	1 BYTE
$05	FAR-CALL to interrupt $21	5 BYTE
$0A	Copy of interrupt vector $22	1 PTR
$0E	Copy of interrupt vector $23	1 PTR
$12	Copy of interrupt vector $24	1 PTR
$16	Reserved	22 BYTE
$2C	Segment address of environment block	1 WORD
$2E	Reserved	46 BYTE
$5C	FCB #1	16 BYTE
$6C	FCB #2	16 BYTE
$80	Number of characters in command line (excluding CR)	1 BYTE
$81	Command line	127 BYTE

Length: 256 Bytes

Program Segment Prefix (PSP) structure

The next three entries are much more important because DOS uses them to store the contents of three interrupt vectors before the start of the program. These three vectors are often taken over by programs during execution. After the program ends they must be restored to their initial values. Interrupt $22 is used to end a program.

This interrupt is called by all the DOS functions that a programmer can use to end a program. Following interrupt $23 is a routine that DOS calls when the user presses <Ctrl><C>. This routine generally will abort the program execution. Interrupt $24 points to a routine called by DOS when a critical error occurs. It generates the "Abort, Retry, Fail?" message.

As you will see later, Turbo Pascal intercepts these last two interrupt vectors so that you can execute your own routines from the system unit instead of from the normal DOS routines. This is how a Turbo Pascal program can, for example, perform I/O checking and prevent a program from being aborted with <Ctrl><C>.

Another reserved field follows the three interrupt vectors. Then following this is the segment address of the environment block. The structure and purpose of the environment block is shown in the next section.

After another undocumented section there are the two *File Control Blocks* (FCBs), which are automatically placed in the PSP by DOS. An FCB is a data structure required by DOS versions before Version 2.0 for file access. With the release of DOS Version 2.0, the FCB functions were replaced by handle functions, which make it easier for programmers to access files and devices. So the use of FCBs is therefore outdated.

The arguments from the command line list some very important information in the last few fields of the PSP. In the buffer starting at $81, the EXEC loader stores all characters, entered on the command line, after the name of the program. Exceptions to this are entries that redirect input or output (> and <), or arguments used when pipelining (|) several commands. The end of the buffer is marked with a carriage return (ASCII code 13). The size of the buffer, which also represents the number of characters it contains, is stored in $80. The carriage return is not counted, since it is appended by the EXEC loader and is not part of the command line.

This is the only way Turbo Pascal can access this information. Before the main program starts, Turbo Pascal reads the number of arguments and stores it as the variable ParamCount. The individual arguments are also available to the program by using the function ParamStr.

Environment block

In addition to the PSP, the EXEC loader places a copy of the *environment block* at the beginning of a program. The environment block, controlled by the command interpreter COMMAND.COM, consists of a collection of ASCII strings that the command processor and other programs can use to obtain certain information, such as the search path for executable programs. Each of these strings usually has the following format:

```
Name=Parameter
```

and is ended with a null character (ASCII code 0). The strings are stored contiguously in memory so that the ending character of one string is following the beginning character of the next. The end of the environment block (which cannot be longer than 32K) is marked by a null end character directly after the ending character of the last string.

Starting with DOS Version 3.0, it is possible to have other strings following the last environment string. The number of additional strings is specified by the word following the last environment string. As of now, DOS has added only one additional string, so this word contains the value 1. This entry contains the complete disk drive and path name of the executed program to which the environment block belongs. This expanded environment block can be used to tell a program the directory from which it was loaded. The program can then use this information to automatically load overlays, configuration files or other important files from this directory without having to ask for the path.

```
1DFE:0000  43 4F 4D 53 50 45 43 3D-43 3A 5C 43 4F 4D 4D 41   COMSPEC=C:\COMMA
1DFE:0010  4E 44 2E 43 4F 4D 00 50-41 54 48 3D 43 3A 5C 3B   ND.COM.PATH=C:\;
1DFE:0020  43 3A 5C 44 4F 53 3B 43-3A 5C 42 41 54 43 48 45   C:\DOS;C:\BATCHE
1DFE:0030  53 3B 45 3A 5C 3B 44 3A-5C 4D 53 43 5C 42 49 4E   S;E:\;D:\MSC\BIN
1DFE:0040  00 49 4E 43 4C 55 44 45-3D 64 3A 5C 6D 73 63 5C   .INCLUDE=d:\msc\
1DFE:0050  69 6E 63 6C 75 64 65 00-4C 49 42 3D 64 3A 5C 6D   include.LIB=d:\m
1DFE:0060  73 63 5C 6C 69 62 00 54-4D 50 3D 64 3A 5C 6D 73   sc\lib.TMP=d:\ms
1DFE:0070  63 5C 74 6D 70 00 50 52-4F 4D 50 54 3D 5B 24 70   c\tmp.PROMPT=[$p
1DFE:0080  5D 00 00 01 00 43 3A 5C-44 4F 53 5C 44 45 42 55   ]....C:\DOS\DEBU
1DFE:0090  47 2E 43 4F 4D 00 00 00-00 00 00 00 00 00 00 00   G.COM..........
```

An environment block in memory (dumped using DEBUG)

The DOS SET and PATH commands are used to manipulate the environment block at the user level. These commands can add new entries to the end of the environment block or change existing entries.

Turbo Pascal can access the information in the environment block because its segment address is stored in offset address $2C of the PSP. The DOS unit provides the functions EnvStr and GetEnv and the global variable EnvCount (the number of entries in the environment block) for this purpose.

The final string, which gives the name and the search path of the executed program, cannot be obtained with these functions. Instead, the system unit function ParamStr, with an argument of 0, will return this information.

2.2 Standard and Non-Standard Constants

Turbo Pascal stores standard constants with all other global variables within the data segment. The only difference between constants and normal variables is that a constant will have a value assigned by the programmer when the program is started. The values of normal variables are not assigned when the program is started. This is also true for the local standard constants used by a procedure or function. These are also stored in the data segment but can only be addressed by the corresponding function or procedure.

Standard constants

Standard constants are not randomly combined with normal variables. Instead, they are found in one large block at the beginning of the data segment. By placing them here, Turbo Pascal saves memory space taken by the EXE file, which was created by the compiled program.

The EXE file must contain everything that needs to be loaded when the program is started. In addition to the program code, this includes the standard constants. These have predefined values that are loaded from the EXE file. The contents of global variables are not defined when the program starts. The EXE file contains references to these variables, but values for these are not loaded into memory. The program simply reserves the required memory space in the data segment after the standard constants.

The earlier versions of Turbo Pascal could handle global data either as pointers, or procedural pointers as typed constants. Otherwise, these versions of Turbo could not solve pointer referencing through compilation, by conveying referenced variable addresses or procedures/functions. You had to rely on global variables, and initialize these variables by hand.

With the introduction of Version 6.0, data and procedural pointers can be configured easily. The variables and routines requiring referencing must be declared within the program code. When specifying procedural pointers, do not use FORWARD to declare the referenced procedure or function. Furthermore, the procedure or function must precede the constant to which it refers.

The following listing gives us an introduction to the methods used by Version 6.0:

```
program TypedConstantPointer;

type BPTR    = ^byte;                        { Pointer to a byte }
     TESTPTR = procedure;              { Pointer to a test procedure }

procedure Test; far;                  { No FORWARD declarations must be }
begin                                 { used before executing the typed }
```

```
   writeln( 'Test executed' );              { constants                    }
end;

{-- Global variables and typed constants --------------------------------}

var x : byte;                                     { reference to XPTR }

const xptr : BPTR = @x;                   { initialize with address X }
      tptr : TESTPTR = Test;          { Initialize with address from Test }

{-- Main program --------------------------------------------------------}

begin
  x := 5;
  writeln( 'X = ', xptr^ );
  tptr;                                              { Call TEST }
end.
```

Non-standard constants

In addition to standard constants, *non-standard constants*, which are declared with the CONST statement, will, in certain cases, occupy memory space. This depends on the variable type because Turbo Pascal only has to reserve memory for constants referenced by pointers. However, this doesn't apply to integers and real numbers. Turbo Pascal can simply use MOV instructions to manipulate numbers in the processor registers or to load them into variables.

String constants

String constants differ from standard and non-standard constants. They must have memory allocated for them because Turbo Pascal accesses string constants with pointers, which can only point to something that physically occupies memory. String constants will pop up in your programs more often than you might expect.

The following are statements that can be used to convey string constants:

```
const Message = 'Hello Turbo Pascal';

writeln( 'StringConstant' );

str - 'Text'
```

These strings must also be available in memory in order to be used.

Unlike standard constants, Turbo Pascal does not place these string constants in the data segment. Instead, they are placed in the code segment directly before the start of the procedure or function that uses them. A string constant used several times in a procedure or

function is only declared once and addressed as needed. The following program listing and
memory dump demonstrate how this is done with Turbo Pascal.

```
program constnt;
const GoodDay    = 'Hello';
      ALongInt   = $11112222;
      ANormalInt = $4711;
      ARealNum   = 1.2345678;
procedure test;
var r: real;
l : longint;
    i : integer;
begin   writeln( GoodDay );
      { cs:001C BF3E01        mov    di,013E   ;normal Writeln sequence    }
      { cs:001F 1E            push   ds                                    }
      { cs:0020 57            push   di                                    }
      { cs:0021 BF0000        mov    di,0000   ; <--- Look!                }
      { cs:0024 0E            push   cs        ;       The string is located }
      { cs:0025 57            push   di        ;       at address CS:0000  }
      { cs:0026 31C0          xor    ax,ax                                 }
      { cs:0028 50            push   ax                                    }
      { cs:0029 9A26069E5F    call   5F9E:0626                            }
      { cs:002E 9AA9059E5F    call   5F9E:05A9                            }
  writeln( ' Turbo ' );
      { cs:0033 BF3E01        mov    di,013E   ;Writeln again             }
      { cs:0036 1E            push   ds                                    }
      { cs:0037 57            push   di                                    }
      { cs:0038 BF0600        mov    di,0006   ;this string is at          }
      { cs:003B 0E            push   cs        ;CS:0006, right behind       }
      { cs:003C 57            push   di        ;the first string           }
      { cs:003D 31C0          xor    ax,ax                                 }
      { cs:003F 50            push   ax                                    }
      { cs:0040 9A26069E5F    call   5F9E:0626                            }
      { cs:0045 9AA9059E5F    call   5F9E:05A9                            }
    writeln( GoodDay );
      { cs:004A BF3E01        mov    di,013E   ;Writeln                   }
      { cs:004D 1E            push   ds                                    }
      { cs:004E 57            push   di                                    }
      { cs:004F BF0000        mov    di,0000   ;Turbo knows that it has    }
      { cs:0052 0E            push   cs        ;already stored this string, }
      { cs:0053 57            push   di        ;so it enters the address   }
      { cs:0054 31C0          xor    ax,ax     ;CS:0000                   }
      { cs:0056 50            push   ax                                    }
      { cs:0057 9A26069E5F    call   5F9E:0626                            }
      { cs:005C 9AA9059E5F    call   5F9E:05A9                            }
  i := ANormalInt;
      { cs:0061 C746F4E803    mov    word ptr [bp-0C],4711 ;load a Word    }
  l := ALongInt;
      { cs:0066 C746F64042    mov    word ptr [bp-0A],2222 ;the two Words  }
      { cs:006B C746F80F00    mov    word ptr [bp-08],1111 ;of a LongInts l. }
  r := ARealNum;
      { cs:0070 C746FA81D9    mov    word ptr [bp-06],D981 ;load a 6 byte  }
```

```
        { cs:0075 C746FC5251      mov     word ptr [bp-04],5152 ;real number       }
        { cs:007A C746FE061E      mov     word ptr [bp-02],1E06                     }
    end;
begin   writeln( GoodDay );
        { cs:0099 BF3E01          mov     di,013E    ;normal Writeln sequence      }
        { cs:009C 1E              push    ds                                       }
        { cs:009D 57              push    di                                       }
        { cs:009E BF8300          mov     di,0083    ;even though Turbo has already }
        { cs:00A1 0E              push    cs         ;stored this string, it is     }
        { cs:00A2 57              push    di         ;stored again at address       }
        { cs:00A3 31C0            xor     ax,ax      ;CS:0083 for the new procedure }
        { cs:00A5 50              push    ax                                       }
        { cs:00A6 9A26069E5F      call    5F9E:0626                                }
        { cs:00AB 9AA9059E5F      call    5F9E:05A9                                }
    writeln( ' Turbo ');
        { cs:00B0 BF3E01          mov     di,013E    ;same as above                }
        { cs:00B3 1E              push    ds                                       }
        { cs:00B4 57              push    di                                       }
        { cs:00B5 BF8900          mov     di,0089    ;this string is also stored   }
        { cs:00B8 0E              push    cs         ;again and the procedure is    }
        { cs:00B9 57              push    di         ;moved up                      }
        { cs:00BA 31C0            xor     ax,ax                                    }
        { cs:00BC 50              push    ax                                       }
        { cs:00BD 9A26069E5F      call    5F9E:0626                                }
        { cs:00C2 9AA9059E5F      call    5F9E:05A9                                }
    test;
end.
```

```
CS:0000 05 48 61 6C 6C 6F 07 20 54 75 72 62 6F 20 55 89  ♦Hello♦ Turbo Uë
CS:0010 E5 B8 0C 00 9A 44 02 0F 00 83 EC 0C BF 3E 01 1E  σ╕    ªD☻* ë∞  ┐>☺▲
CS:0020 57 BF 00 00 0E 57 31 C0 50 9A 26 06 0F 00 9A A9  W┐  ♫W1└P♀&♠  ♀ª
CS:0030 05 0F 00 9A 0E 02 0F 00 DI DL 01 1C 57 BF 06 00  ♣  ♀♫☻  ░╚☺∟W┐♠
CS:0040 0E 57 31 C0 50 9A 26 06 0F 00 9A A9 05 0F 00 9A  ♫W1└P♀&♠  ♀ª♣  ♀
CS:0050 0E 02 0F 00 BF 3E 01 1E 57 BF 00 00 0E 57 31 C0  ♫☻  ┐>☺▲W┐  ♫W1└
CS:0060 50 9A 26 06 0F 00 9A A9 05 0F 00 9A 0E 02 0F 00  P♀&♠  ♀ª♣  ♀♫☻
CS:0070 C7 46 F4 11 47 C7 46 F6 22 22 C7 46 F8 11 11 C7  ╟F⌠◄G╟F÷""╟F°◄◄╟
CS:0080 46 FA 81 D9 C7 46 FC 52 51 C7 46 FE 06 1E 89 EC  F·ü┘╟F⌐RQ╟F■♠▲ë∞
CS:0090 5D C3 05 48 61 6C 6C 6F 07 20 54 75 72 62 6F 20  ]├♣Hello♦ Turbo
```

Memory dump from the start of the code segment of this program

While looking at the above figure, notice the occurrence of the text strings "Hello" and "Turbo". This listing shows that Turbo Pascal doesn't store numerical constants in memory. Instead, the MOV instruction is used to load the variables. The strings are stored in memory. Notice that when a string is used in more than one procedure, it must be stored separately for each procedure. However, if the same string is used several times within the same procedure, it doesn't have to be stored more than once.

At first this may not seem to matter. However, it is unavoidable because of the way the internal *linker* joins the units of the program. Turbo Pascal uses an intelligent linker that places only those procedures, functions and variables in the EXE file that are actually called or used within the program. This means that procedure P2 cannot use string constants from procedure P1, because P1 may never be called and wouldn't appear in the EXE file. So, procedure P2 would be trying to access a string constant that did not exist. This would lead to an "Undefined external" error in the linking procedure.

2.3 Variables

Turbo Pascal places global variables in the data segment and local variables on the stack. But how are variables declared, and in what formats are they stored? We'll answer these questions in this section.

Turbo Pascal divides variable types into groups that are managed in various data formats.

Integer types

Integer variables are divided into types that are represented in binary format using one, two or four bytes. At the processor level these types are Byte, Word and DWORD.

Turbo Pascal uses bytes to store types Byte and ShortInt. The difference between the two is the way the values are interpreted. Since Byte is a data type without a plus/minus sign, any value between 0 and 255 can be represented. In a ShortInt type, bit 7 is the plus/minus sign, so the values that can be represented are -128 through 127.

One difference between variable types with and without signs is in the data types that Turbo Pascal handles with Words. These types are Word and Integer. A Word has a range from 0 to 65535 with no plus/minus sign. Integers range from -32768 to +32767 and have a plus/minus sign.

If larger variables are needed, the data type LongInt must be used. This data type consists of a DWORD (4 bytes) and generally has a sign. The values can range from -2147483648 to 2147483647. Turbo Pascal follows the Intel convention for storage of DWORDS. The lesser valued Word of the LongInt is stored at the lower memory address, and the higher valued Word is stored in the next Word.

Enumerated types

Enumerated types are coded so that the first type is numbered 0, the second is 1, the third is 2, etc. The enumerated type is stored cither as a BYTE when the count is less than 257 different values or as a WORD when more than 257 values are required.

Booleans

Boolean variables are stored as a BYTE. They can have a value of 0 (for FALSE) or 1 (for TRUE). You can understand this definition with the following enumerated type:

```
type boolean = ( FALSE, TRUE );
```

From this statement, the expressions:

```
ord( FALSE )   or   ord( TRUE )
```

will return 0 or 1.

Chars

Chars are stored within a BYTE as 8-bit numbers without plus/minus signs.

Strings

A *string* is a series of characters preceded by a single byte, which gives the current number of characters in the string. This shouldn't be confused with the amount of memory the string requires; this value isn't stored in the string itself.

Since one byte is used to give the length of the string, a string can have up to 255 characters. It will occupy 256 bytes in memory when combined with the length byte. These 256 bytes are always reserved for strings that were declared without a specific length. So, to save memory you should always specify the maximum length of a string whenever possible.

Like Char arrays, strings can be addressed with an index from 0 to the string length. The entry with index 0 returns the current string length. Index 1 returns the first character. This method of storing strings is very efficient. Many programmers use this when developing software with other languages. By accessing the current string length with the index 0, you can perform some tricks that will help increase program execution speed. The following listing shows you how to do this.

```
program stricks;
var str  : string;                      { String with a maximum of 255 characters }
   last : char;
begin
   str := 'Teststring';
   last := str[ ord(str[0]) ];                          { Get last character }
   dec( str[ 0 ] );                        { Remove last character in string }
   inc( str[ 0 ] );                        { Add an exclamation point to the }
   str[ ord(str[ 0 ]) ] := '!';            { end of the string              }
   writeln( str );
end.
```

Notice that you cannot directly use the length byte as the index in the string. Turbo Pascal sees it as a Char, which is the wrong data type for indexing strings. The Ord function can be used to convert a Char to a byte and use it in the index string.

Arrays

Arrays are stored in memory as a series of elements. The lowest numbered element occupies the lowest memory position. The elements follow one another directly, so no memory is lost with unused characters or spaces.

Multidimensional arrays are stored with all elements in one dimension, followed by all elements of the next dimension. In the array:

```
a = array [1..10][1..5] of char
```

the variable A begins in memory with the elements a[1][1] to a[1][5]. Next come elements a[2][1] to a[2][5], then a[3][1] to a[3][5], etc.

Data structures (records)

These are similar to arrays because the individual components are stored without any extra characters or spaces between them. The first element is at the lowest address and the last element is at the highest address. Other structures within a record occupy the same space in memory. These elements are stored the same way as those of a record.

Sets

Turbo Pascal stores *sets* as bit arrays in order to take up as little memory as possible. Each bit represents an element of the set. If the bit is on, then the set contains the corresponding element. Otherwise, it isn't part of the set. The memory requirement is based on the number of elements and the ordinal number of the highest and lowest elements (referred to as Omin and Omax).

The amount of memory needed in bytes can be computed with this formula:

```
MemoryRequired = ( Omax / 8 ) - ( Omin / 8 ) + 1;
```

Pointers

In Turbo Pascal, *data pointers* are typically FAR pointers, which means they consist of a segment address and an offset address. Both addresses are given as Words. The offset address precedes the segment address in memory as described in the Intel standard.

Since the data segment cannot be larger than 64K and the segment address is always available in the DS register, Turbo could use NEAR pointers to access the global data and standard constants in the data segment. However, these pointers are not allowed to access memory regions allocated through the heap. The heap plays an important role in Pascal programming. It is unrealistic to distinguish between data and heap pointers. So Turbo uses FAR pointers so that every memory location in 1 megabyte of memory can be accessed.

The NIL pointer is a very special pointer. It contains the value 0 for both the segment address and the offset address. This points to the first entry of the interrupt vector table, which means this pointer shouldn't be used for referencing data. Pointers to procedures and functions (procedural types) are also stored as FAR pointers. This is done so that Turbo Pascal programs can contain multiple code segments and permits the calling of procedures and functions from other units.

Real types (floating point types)

Standard Turbo Pascal only recognizes the floating point type Real. This can be expanded to three other types with a math coprocessor or an emulation library.

The standard floating point Real type requires six bytes. We won't discuss the format of this data type further because this would require a discussion of mathematical concepts beyond the scope of this book.

Variable alignment

Variable alignment is a technique used by the compiler to position the variables so that the fastest possible access is allowed. To understand this, you must know that the 8086 and compatible processors can access variable types WORD and DWORD (Word and LongInt in Pascal) faster if they begin at an even memory address. Accessing variables at odd memory addresses is slower because the processor must perform more read accesses to the memory in order to load and store the individual bytes of the operands.

This depends on the relationship between the processor and the 16-bit data bus that links it to memory. Systems with an 8088 processor cannot benefit from this alignment since they use an 8-bit data bus and all access to WORDS and DWORDS must be divided into individual bytes.

Turbo Pascal supports variable alignment with Options / Compiler / Align Data. You can choose between BYTE and WORD. In BYTE mode no alignment is performed. Each variable is simply appended behind the previous one. In WORD mode, all variables (whether one or two bytes) are aligned on even memory addresses. When variables are moved to accomplish this, an unused byte between variables is generated.

Within a program you can use the compiler switch {A+} to turn alignment on or {A-} to turn it off for selected variables or groups of variables. The individual elements within structures are not affected by alignment. They remain a continuous series to avoid wasting memory. The same is true for elements of arrays.

The next listing shows how the storage of variables changes when they are aligned. If you compile and run the program both with the alignment on (WORD mode) and alignment off (BYTE mode), you will see how Turbo Pascal moves the variables around.

```
program align;

type structure = record
                  w1 : word;
                  b1 : byte;
                  w2 : word;
                  b2 : byte;
                  l1 : longint;
                  end;

var w1 : word
    b1 : byte;
    w2 : word;
    b2 : byte;
    l1 : longint;

    s: structure;

begin
    writeln;
    writeln( 'Are the variables aligned by WORD?');
    writeln( 'W1: ', not(odd(ofs( w1 ))) );
    writeln( 'B1: ', not(odd(ofs( b1 ))) );
    writeln( 'W2: ', not(odd(ofs( w2 ))) );
    writeln( 'B2: ', not(odd(ofs( b2 ))) );
    writeln( 'L2: ', not(odd(ofs( l1 ))) );

    writeln;
    writeln( Are the components of structure aligned by WORD?');
    writeln( 'S.W1: ', not(odd(ofs( s.w1 ))) );
    writeln( 'S.B1: ', not(odd(ofs( s.b1 ))) );
    writeln( 'S.W2: ', not(odd(ofs( s.w2 ))) );
    writeln( 'S.B2: ', not(odd(ofs( s.b2 ))) );
    writeln( 'S.L2: ', not(odd(ofs( s.l1 ))) );
end.
```

2.4 Procedures and Functions

Procedures and functions are among the most important components of structured programming languages. In this section we'll see how Turbo Pascal procedures are created and called, how local variables are managed and how parameters are passed from the caller.

NEAR or FAR?

The processor doesn't recognize the difference between procedures and functions as they exist in Turbo Pascal. The processor only knows two kinds of subroutines—FAR and NEAR. This distinction is made by the final statement in the subroutine that returns to the routine that called it. This instruction is RET, for RETURN. There are two forms of RET, one with N for NEAR and one with F for FAR. Both forms retrieve the return address from the stack and then continue program execution at this location. The difference is that RETN retrieves only an offset address from the stack and loads it in the IP register. Therefore, the return jump must be to a routine within the same code segment as the subroutine. RETF allows return jumps to routines found in other code segments. This instruction retrieves both an offset address and a segment address from the stack and loads them in the CS register.

In addition to the two RET instructions, the 8086/8088 also recognizes two different CALL instructions. A NEAR call will call a subroutine from the same code segment and a FAR call will call a subroutine from any code segment. FAR calls and returns take more time than the corresponding NEAR operations, so good programming practices will use FAR calls only when absolutely necessary.

The developers at Borland use the following method to distinguish between the two types of subroutines:

Procedures and functions in the main program are NEAR if they are:

- Located in the same code segment as the main program.

- Declared within a procedure or function. These are local routines that will be found within the same code segment as the routine that calls them.

- In the implementation section of a unit. This type can only be called from this unit, so they will be located in the same code segment.

Procedures and functions in the interface section of a unit are FAR, since they can be called from other units (i.e., other code segments) as well as the main program.

Except for one special case, Turbo Pascal can determine whether a routine uses NEAR or FAR operations based on the type of routine. This occurs when calling routines, within a unit, that are executed in the implementation section of the unit. These routines all end with FAR returns, so they must be called with FAR calls. If a NEAR call was used, the system would crash when the processor went to the stack to get the return address and found only the offset address left by the NEAR call. However, there is a way to handle this situation without a FAR call:

```
push cs

call near routine
```

These instructions simulate a FAR call by first putting the address of the current code segment on the stack and then executing a normal NEAR call. The FAR return at the end of the subroutine will then find both the segment address and the offset address it needs. This method will save precious microseconds compared to using a regular FAR call.

The compiler directive {$F+} can also create exceptions to these rules. This will cause all subsequent procedures and functions to use FAR operations. However, this makes sense only when the procedure/function is to be called with a pointer or if you need to use some tricks with assembly language routines. We'll present examples demonstrating this later.

Version 6.0 provided the option of indicating a procedure or function as NEAR or FAR within a procedure/function header, without calling the {$F+} and {$F-} compiler directives. Like the EXTERN statement, the procedure/function header must still be declared as NEAR or FAR. Here are two examples:

```
procedure NearProc( x : integer, s : string); near

function FarFunc( r : real ) : real; far;
```

Later sections of this book contain programs demonstrating explicit FAR declarations in procedures and functions.

The simplest case

In terms of code generation, a procedure with no parameters or local variables is the simplest case. The following program listing shows how such a procedure is converted to machine or assembly language code:

```
program p_std;
procedure test;
begin
  { cs:0000 55          push  bp       ;store BP on the stack      }
  { cs:0001 89E5         mov   bp,sp    ;load BP with SP            }
```

```
{-- the machine code for other Pascal statements would be located here  ---}
end;
{ cs:0003 89EC          mov    sp,bp      ;load SP with old value        }
{ cs:0005 5D            pop    bp         ;retrieve BP from stack        }
{ cs:0006 C3            ret               ;NEAR return to caller         }
begin
   test;              { without this call, test would be removed from the linker }
   { cs:000F E8EEFF       call   TEST       ;NEAR call of Test             }
end.
```

The procedure "test", called by this example, consists only of a begin statement and an end statement. Ideally, the procedure "test" should be converted to one RET instruction. But Turbo Pascal creates four additional statements that work, behind the scenes, with the SP and BP registers.

These additional instructions are the key to working with local variables and to accessing parameters passed from other routines. The following examples will make this clearer. It is unfortunate that Turbo Pascal generates these instructions without being able to tell if they are really necessary.

Local variables

Compared to the previous example, the procedure "test" in the following listing is more complicated. It uses three local variables. The format of these is the same as for global variables. The difference is where Turbo Pascal stores them. Here's an example:

```
program plockvar;
procedure test;
var i : integer;
    b : byte;
    s : string;
begin
 { cs:0006 55            push   bp         ;store BP on stack             }
 { cs:0007 89E5          mov    bp,sp      ;load BP with value from SP    }
 { cs:0009 81EC0401      sub    sp,0104    ;reserve 259 bytes for         }
 {                                         ;variables                     }
 s := 'Hello';
   { cs:000D BF0000        mov    di,0000    ;'Hello' is at CS:0000         }
   { cs:0010 0E            push   cs         ;put this address on the       }
   { cs:0011 57            push   di         ;stack as a FAR pointer        }
   { cs:0012 8DBEFDFE      lea    di,[bp-0103] ;offset address from S to DI}
   { cs:0016 16            push   ss         ;and put on the stack as a     }
   { cs:0017 57            push   di         ;FAR pointer with SS           }
   { cs:0018 B8FF00        mov    ax,00FF    ;maximum length of 255 bytes}
   { cs:001B 50            push   ax         ;as parameter on the stack     }
   { cs:001C 9A21028F5F    call   far StrCopy ;copy 'Hello' to S            }
 i := -15;
   { cs:0021 C746FEF1FF    mov    word ptr [bp-02],FFF1  ;I is at [BP-2]}
 b := 8;
```

```
     { cs:0026 C646FD08         mov      byte ptr [bp-03],08        ;B is at [BP-3]}
end;
   { cs:002A 89EC              mov      sp,bp  ;reload old value of SP and          }
   {                                          ;thereby clean up local variables    }
   { cs:002C 5D                pop      bp     ;retrieve old BP from stack          }
   { cs:002D C3                ret             ;return to caller                    }
begin
   test;          { without this call, test would be removed from the linker }
end.
```

At the start of "test", the contents of the BP register are stored on the stack. This is important compared to the previous example. The next instruction, which changes the value of BP, must be present. It loads the contents of the SP register into BP. This means that both BP and SP will point to the originally stored value of BP. Both registers cannot keep the same value for long because the next instruction decrements SP by 260.

This is the important step for the management of local variables. It reserves 259 bytes of memory on the stack, which is where Turbo Pascal will load the local variables for the procedure "test". At first glance, the stack may not seem like a good place for storing variables. But a closer look will show that it is well suited for the task.

The stack is a place where information is usually not stored for long periods of time. This is evident from the use of the stack for storing return addresses for CALL statements. After this information is retrieved, it is overwritten as soon as the next subroutine is called. Since the contents of the stack are dynamic, it is a good place to store local variables.

Local variables, like return addresses, have a limited time period during which they are useful. They need to exist only as long as it takes to execute the procedure/function that uses them. Although local variables could be stored in the data segment, more memory would be required to make room for all of them. One solution would be to make a large memory pool available for storing local variables. The size of this pool would change according to the number and size of the local variables required by the current function/procedure. However, this would not always work because one procedure/function can call another and they would overwrite the local variables of the other in this memory pool.

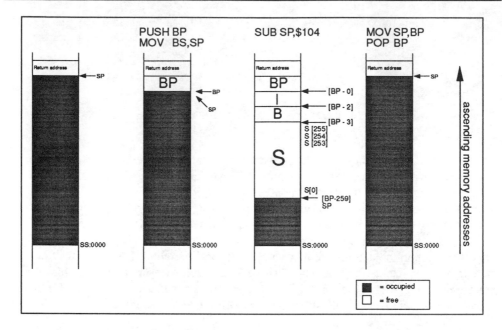

Managing local variables on the stack

When the procedure "test" moves the stack pointer behind the range of its local variables, it ensures that this range will not be overwritten by CALL statements (by the return addresses they store on the stack). Also the range won't be disturbed by local variables loaded from other functions or procedures that are called. If new functions/procedures are called, the stack pointer is again moved behind the additional set of local variables to protect the range from being overwritten. The stack pointer is moved closer to the beginning of the stack with each nested call and at the same time removes any remaining local variables.

At the end of a procedure/function, the stack pointer must be moved back toward the end of the stack to find the proper return address. Turbo Pascal puts the statement for this operation at the end of the procedure/function. First, the SP register is loaded with the value of the BP register. This reassigns the SP register its original value and moves it past the local variables toward the end of the stack. It will point to the location where the original value of BP was stored with the initial PUSH instruction. This value is then retrieved with the POP instruction and the contents of the BP register are restored.

The 80286 and its larger relatives recognize a special instruction for this task called LEAVE, included in the following assembly language code:

```
MOV SP,BP
POP BP
```

Compiled code containing LEAVE will not be compatible with older systems because this instruction won't run in an 8088 machine. However, Version 6.0 includes a global compiler directive {$G} for controlling code generation. {$G+} compiles the code for 286 and higher machines and ends procedures and functions with LEAVE.

The SP register points to the execution of the LEAVE (or equivalent) instructions, as well as the return address of the calling routine. The final RET instruction ends the subroutine and returns program execution to the calling routine.

From this explanation you may conclude that only the SP register is required for managing local variables. So why do we need to access the BP register? The processor dedicates the BP register to the indexed addressing of the stack. Using this register and not the DS register automatically uses the SS register for addressing. The processor uses the BP register as the essential tool for addressing local variables on the stack. The instructions used in the procedure in the example should make this clear.

If you look at the way these instructions are converted to machine code, you'll notice that I starts at address [BP-$2], B starts at [BP-$3] and the string S starts at [BP-$103]. These addresses (the indices to BP) were not selected at random. They reflect the size of each variable and the order in which they were declared with the VAR instruction.

The variable I was the first to be declared. It is a two byte integer. Since address [BP-0] contains the low byte of the original contents of BP, the local variables can only extend to [BP-1]. Since I begins at [BP-2], it will also occupy [BP-1]. B is stored directly in front of I. B requires one byte so it will be at [BP-3]. The last local variable, the string S, requires 256 bytes; so it will start 256 bytes in front of B. Its address is [BP-259].

Using this method, enables you to use deeply nested procedures and functions. Each procedure/function will maintain its own private domain and cannot overwrite that of another.

Most high level language compilers for the PC use the stack for local variables in the same manner. It is well supported by the processor with the necessary assembly language instructions and the use of the BP register for addressing.

Passing parameters

Passing parameters to procedures and functions is also done with the stack. The parameters are loaded on the stack before the procedure/function call. Parameters are processed from left to right, so that the distance between each location of the parameter and the stack pointer increases as you move from left to right.

As with local variables, the transferred parameters are addressed with the BP register. However, parameters have positive offsets. Let's look at the next example.

```
program p_para;
var gi : integer;
procedure test( i : integer; var j : integer );
begin
    { cs:0000 55            push    bp          ;store on stack           }
    { cs:0001 89E5          mov     bp,sp                                 }
  j := i;
    { cs:0003 8B4608        mov     ax,[bp+08] ;get parameter I from stack }
    { cs:0006 C47E04        les     di,[bp+04] ;load the pointer for J in  }
    {                                          ;ES:DI                      }
    { cs:0009 268905        mov     es:[di],ax ;write parameter J there    }
end;
    { cs:000C 89EC          mov     sp,bp       ;restore stack to original }
    { cs:000E 5D            pop     bp          ;condition                 }
    { cs:000F C20600        ret     0006        ;return to caller and remove }
    {                                           ;the arguments passed from the}
    {                                           ;stack                     }
begin
  test( 5, gi );
    { cs:001A B80500        mov     ax,0005     ;put 5 on the stack as     }
    { cs:001D 50            push    ax          ;parameter I               }
    { cs:001E BF3E00        mov     di,offset gi ;pass address of GI as a FAR}
    { cs:0021 1E            push    ds           ;pointer using the stack  }
    { cs:0022 57            push    di                                     }
    { cs:0023 E8DAFF        call    TEST                                   }
end.
```

In this example, two parameters of type Integer are passed to the procedure "test". One is given as a value and the other as a variable. This makes a difference, as the comments in the machine code indicate. Let's see how "test" would be called from the main program.

First, parameter I is put on the stack. This parameter will pass the value 5 to the subroutine. This value is loaded in AX and then placed on the stack with a PUSH instruction. Turbo then gives "test" a local copy. This is a variable that reflects the current value of the parameter but is not the actual value in memory nor is it in any way connected to it. The other parameter is handled quite differently. This is the variable GI. Since it is a variable parameter, "test" must have the ability to change it. It is not enough to simply put the current value on the stack. Turbo Pascal must also have the address so that it can access the value directly.

Although it may not be apparent from the Pascal code, all access to variable parameters within a procedure or function are referenced pointer operations. Turbo Pascal passes a pointer to the actual variable when variable parameters are used. As usual with Turbo Pascal, this is a FAR pointer. The segment address is stored before the offset address on the stack. Since the stack pointer gets closer to the start of the stack segment with each PUSH instruction, this places the offset address before the segment address in memory as specified in the Intel standard.

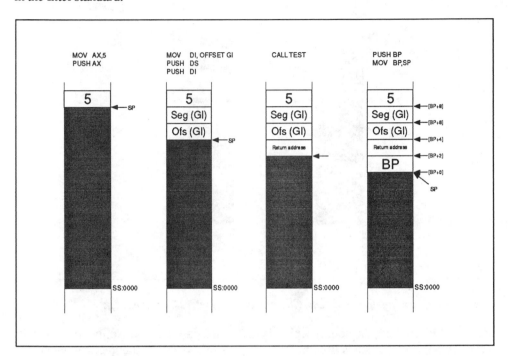

Passing parameters to a procedure/function

The stack is initialized in the usual way with "Test" and then accesses the parameters with the BP register. To load parameter J with the contents of I, the contents of I are first loaded in the AX register. To be able to manipulate the variable for which parameter J stands, the address of this variable must be put on the stack. This is done with a LES instruction, which Turbo always uses for referring to variables with pointers.

A FAR pointer is loaded from the specified memory location by placing the segment address in ES and the offset address in the given register. Index register SI, DI or BX must be used for this purpose, and Turbo Pascal will default to DI as a rule. The ES register is used as the segment register because this is the only register that does not permanently point to a certain segment. ES exists for special uses such as this. After the address has been loaded in this way, "test" can access the passed variable GI.

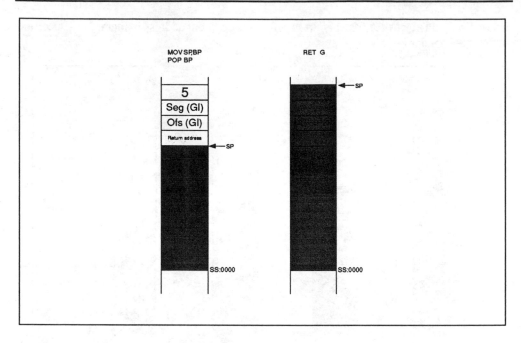

Ending a procedure/function and removing passed parameters from the stack

When "test" is finished, the housekeeping is completed on the stack. Notice that a special form of the RET instruction is used in this case. It is followed with a numerical parameter. This number gives the number of bytes that the processor must increment the contents of the stack pointer after the return to the calling routine. This means the pointer is moved toward the end of the stack. This instruction has the effect of clearing the parameters from the stack at the same time the return jump is executed.

The last example has shown how Turbo Pascal uses variable parameters and integer variables as values. Variable parameters are always passed as pointers regardless of the variable type. When values are passed, the method used for transfer does depend upon the type. The next source code provides an example.

```
program p_para1;
type str8 = string[8];
var gs8   : str8;      gs255 : string;
procedure test( b : byte; l : longint; p : pointer;
               r : real; s8: str8; s255 : string );
begin
{ cs:0000 55            push   bp               ;put on stack               }
{ cs:0001 89E5          mov    bp,sp                                        }
{ cs:0003 81EC0A01      sub    sp,010A          ;reserve 266 bytes on stack }
{ cs:0007 C47E08        les    di,[bp+08]       ;get pointer to parameter S8 }
{ cs:000A 06            push   es               ;from stack put on stack as }
{ cs:000B 57            push   di               ;arg for StrCopy            }
```

```
{ cs:000C 8D7EF7      lea     di,[bp-09]    ;put address of local copy of }
{ cs:000F 16          push    ss            ;S8 ( SS:[BP-9] ) on the       }
{ cs:0010 57          push    di            ;stack                         }
{ cs:0011 B80800      mov     ax,0008       ;copy maximum of 8 bytes       }
{ cs:0014 50          push    ax                                           }
{ cs:0015 9A2102975F  call    StrCopy                                      }
{ cs:001A C47E04      les     di,[bp+04]    ;get pointer to argument       }
{ cs:001D 06          push    es            ;S255 from stack and put on    }
{ cs:001E 57          push    di            ;stack as argument for StrCopy }
{ cs:001F 8DBEF7FE    lea     di,[bp-0109]  ;local copy of S255 begins     }
{ cs:0023 16          push    ss            ;at SS:[BP-$109]               }
{ cs:0024 57          push    di                                           }
{ cs:0025 B8FF00      mov     ax,00FF       ;copy maximum of 255 bytes     }
{ cs:0028 50          push    ax                                           }
{ cs:0029 9A2102975F  call    StrCopy                                      }
{-- here the following Pascal statements can access the transferred    ---}
{-- parameters                                                         ---}
end;
{ cs:002E 89EC        mov     sp,bp         ;restore stack                 }
{ cs:0030 5D          pop     bp                                           }
{ cs:0031 C21800      ret     0018          ;clear args. during return     }
begin
   test( 1, $12345678, nil, pi, gs8, gs255 );
{ cs:003C B001        mov     al,01         ;byte arguments passed as      }
{ cs:003E 50          push    ax            ;WORDs                         }
{ cs:003F B87856      mov     ax,5678       ;load parameter L in DX:AX     }
{ cs:0042 BA3412      mov     dx,1234                                      }
{ cs:0045 52          push    dx            ;and push to the stack from    }
{ cs:0046 50          push    ax            ;there                         }
{ cs:0047 31C0        xor     ax,ax         ;NIL pointer as argument       }
{ cs:0049 31D2        xor     dx,dx         ;P to DX:AX                     }
{ cs:004B 52          push    dx            ;and from there to the stack   }
{ cs:004C 50          push    ax                                           }
{ cs:004D B88221      mov     ax,2182       ;load Pi as 6 byte real        }
{ cs:0050 BBA2DA      mov     bx,DAA2       ;number in DX:BX:AX            }
{ cs:0053 BA0F49      mov     dx,490F                                      }
{ cs:0056 52          push    dx            ;and push to the stack         }
{ cs:0057 53          push    bx                                           }
{ cs:0058 50          push    ax                                           }
{ cs:0059 BF3E00      mov     di,offset gs8 ;put pointer to GS8 on the     }
{ cs:005C 1E          push    ds               ;stack                      }
{ cs:005D 57          push    di                                           }
{ cs:005E BF4700      mov     di,offset gs255 ;put pointer to GS255 on     }
{ cs:0061 1E          push    ds               ;the stack                 }
{ cs:0062 57          push    di                                           }
{ cs:0063 E89AFF      call    TEST                                         }
end.
```

In this example "test" has passed six different parameters: one Byte; one LongInt; one Pointer; one Real; one String eight characters in length; and one standard String that can have up to 255 characters. In the previous example, the synonym Integer was used for all types that Turbo Pascal manages as WORDs. In this example, Byte represents all types managed as BYTEs. These include Char, ShortInt, Boolean, as well as the counter and subrange types.

LongInts and Pointers (both standard and non-standard) are passed so that they are stored on the stack in their normal format. With a LongInt, first the high Word and then the low Word are put on the stack. With Pointers, first the segment address and then the offset address are pushed. Floating point numbers in Real format are also passed directly to the stack, retaining their 6 byte standard format. This means the high Word is pushed first, followed by the middle Words and then the low Word.

Passing strings are different from the other standard types. The caller passes two pointers and Turbo Pascal copies the two strings to two local variables before the first statement in "test" is executed. This is automatic and requires no special code from the programmer. Turbo Pascal reserves only the amount of necessary memory to store these local copies. These are 9 bytes for the variable S8 (starting at [BP-$9]) and 256 bytes for S255 (starting at [BP-$109]).

An internal procedure from the system unit handles the creation of the String copies. This is called the StrCopy procedure, which we will often see. Although an assembly language routine rather than a Pascal procedure, it receives its parameters through the stack in the usual Pascal manner.

There are three parameters: a pointer to the source string, a pointer to the buffer for the local copy and the maximum string length. Before StrCopy copies the source string, it checks its length. If this length is shorter than the specified maximum length, only those characters actually belonging to the string are copied. Here is the listing for this procedure:

```
StrCopy     proc far
            cld                         ;count upwards for string statements
            mov     bx,sp               ;SP to stack address after BX
            mov     dx,ds               ;store DS in DX
            lds     si,ss:[bx+0A]       ;move pointer to Source-String to DS:SI
            les     di,ss:[bx+06]       ;pointer to local copy to ES:DI
            mov     cx,ss:[bx+04]       ;maximum length to CX
            lodsb                       ;length of source string to AX
            cmp     al,cl               ;compare to maximum length
            jbe     kg                  ;less than or equal? yes ---> kg
            mov     al,cl               ;max. length as counter to AL
kg:         stosb                       ;write length byte to local copy
            mov     cl,al               ;move length to be copied to CL
            xor     ch,ch               ;high byte of counter to 0
            rep movsb                   ;copy CX byte of DS:SI to ES:DI
            mov     ds,dx               ;load DX with old value
            ret     000A                ;return to caller and clear stack
StrCopy     endp
```

These examples have demonstrated passing standard variable types. You may be wondering how this works with compound variables such as arrays, records and sets. Turbo Pascal uses one method that covers all three of these types. We will see how this works in the next example which uses six different arrays. The six arrays contain 1, 2, 3, 4, 5 and 6 bytes respectively. The memory they require corresponds directly with the number of entries. Turbo Pascal manages each array by knowing the memory requirements.

```
program p_para2;
type array1 = array [1..1] of byte;
     array2 - array [1..2] of byte;
     array3 = array [1..3] of byte;
     array4 = array [1..4] of byte;
     array5 = array [1..5] of byte;
     array6 = array [1..6] of byte;
var ga1 : array1; ga2 : array2; ga3 : array3;
    ga4 : array4; ga5 : array5; ga6 : array6;
procedure test( a1 : array1; a2 : array2; a3 : array3;
                a4 : array4; a5 : array5; a6 : array6 );
begin
{ cs:0000 55              push    bp          ;put on stack              }
{ cs:0001 89E5            mov     bp,sp                                  }
{ cs:0003 83EC0E          sub     sp,000E     ;reserve space for local copy }
{ cs:0006 C47E10          les     di,[bp+10]  ;get pointer to A3 from stack }
{ cs:0009 06              push    es          ;and then return to stack  }
{ cs:000A 57              push    di                                     }
{ cs:000B 8D7EFD          lea     di,[bp-03]  ;local copy of A3 begins at }
{ cs:000E 16              push    ss          ;[BP-3] on the stack,      }
{ cs:000F 57              push    di          ;put this address on the stack }
{ cs:0010 B80300          mov     ax,0003     ;A3 consists of 3 bytes, put }
{ cs:0013 50              push    ax          ;this on stack as length   }
{ cs:0014 9A0702985F      call    MemCopy     ;create local copy         }
{ cs:0019 C47E08          les     di,[bp+08]  ;get pointer to A5 from stack }
{ cs:001C 06              push    es          ;and return to stack as    }
{ cs:001D 57              push    di          ;parameter for MemCopy     }
{ cs:001E 8D7EF8          lea     di,[bp-08]  ;local copy of A5 starts   }
{ cs:0021 16              push    ss          ;at [BP-8]                 }
{ cs:0022 57              push    di                                     }
{ cs:0023 B80500          mov     ax,0005     ;A5 is 5 bytes             }
{ cs:0026 50              push    ax                                     }
{ cs:0027 9A0702985F      call    MemCopy     ;create local copy         }
{ cs:002C C47E04          les     di,[bp+04]  ;do the same with parameter A6 }
{ cs:002F 06              push    es                                     }
{ cs:0030 57              push    di                                     }
{ cs:0031 8D7EF2          lea     di,[bp-0E]                             }
{ cs:0034 16              push    ss                                     }
{ cs:0035 57              push    di                                     }
{ cs:0036 B80600          mov     ax,0006                                }
{ cs:0039 50              push    ax                                     }
{ cs:003A 9A0702985F      call    MemCopy                                }
   {-- other Pascal statements that access the passed Arrays could be  -}
   {-- located here                                                    -}
```

```
end;
{ cs:003F 89EC            mov     sp,bp       ;restore stack                }
{ cs:0041 5D              pop     bp                                        }
{ cs:0042 C21400          ret     0014        ;clear parameters from stack  }
begin
  test( ga1, ga2, ga3, ga4, ga5, ga6 );
{ cs:004D A03E00          mov     al,[GA1] ;put GA1 on the stack as a byte  }
{ cs:0050 50              push    ax       ;in the form of a Word           }
{ cs:0051 FF363F00        push    [GA2]    ;put GA 2 on the stack           }
{ cs:0055 BF4100          mov     di,offset ga3 ;put pointer to GA3 on      }
{ cs:0058 1E              push    ds            ;the stack                  }
{ cs:0059 57              push    di                                        }
{ cs:005A FF364600        push    [GA4+2]  ;GA4 on stack as a DWORD         }
{ cs:005E FF364400        push    [GA4]                                     }
{ cs:0062 BF4800          mov     di,offset GA5 ;put pointer to GA5 on      }
{ cs:0065 1E              push    ds            ;the stack                  }
{ cs:0066 57              push    di                                        }
{ cs:0067 BF4D00          mov     di,offset GA6 ;put pointer to GA6 on      }
{ cs:006A 1E              push    ds            ;the stack                  }
{ cs:006B 57              push    di                                        }
{ cs:006C E891FF          call    TEST                                      }
end.
```

In this example "test" receives six variables as array type values. The order of the arrays reflects the increasing size of each array. The first parameter is a 1-byte array, the second is a 2-byte array, etc. For our purposes, it is important to understand how Turbo Pascal puts each parameter on the stack when "test" is called from the main program.

The first array, which consists of one byte, is placed in the low byte of a WORD and this WORD is pushed on the stack. The same happens with the second array, which consists of two bytes. Since this already exists as a WORD, it is placed on the stack unchanged. The third array (three bytes) does not go on the stack itself. Instead, a pointer to this array is placed on the stack, similar to the way variable parameters are handled. The next array (four bytes) is again placed directly on the stack. The high Word is pushed before the low Word so that the array will be on the stack in its normal format.

The last two arrays are again passed as pointers. In fact, Turbo Pascal passes all types that are five bytes or larger, as pointers.

The "test" procedure must include those types that are passed as variable parameters, since they require the creation of local copies. As with local copies for Strings, local copies for compound variable types are handled as local variables. Instead of the StrCopy procedure, the internal procedure MemCopy from the system unit is used. This procedure is very similar to StrCopy. It copies a given number of bytes from the source variable to the buffer of the local copy.

Here's a summary of the formats used for passing parameters.

Standard and non-standard variable parameters	POINTER (DWORD)
Char	BYTE in WORD
Boolean	BYTE in WORD
Byte	BYTE in WORD
ShortInt	BYTE in WORD
Integer	WORD
Word	WORD
LongInt	DWORD
Standard and non-standard pointers	POINTER (DWORD)
Real	3 WORDS
Strings	POINTER (DWORD)
Counter and sub-range types	BYTE in WORD or WORD
Compound types with a size of 1 byte	BYTE in WORD
2 bytes	WORD
3 bytes	POINTER (DWORD)
4 bytes	DWORD
4 or more bytes	POINTER (DWORD)

Parameter format during transfer to a procedure/function through the stack

Functions

Functions are similar to procedures in the way they manage local variables and receive parameters. But there is the matter of managing the result of the function and passing it back to the calling routine. The following listing shows how Turbo Pascal handles this:

```
program f_std;
var i : integer;
function test : integer;
begin
  { cs:0000 55              push    bp          ;store BP on the stack          }
  { cs:0001 89E5            mov     bp,sp       ;move contents of SP to BP      }
  { cs:0003 83EC02          sub     sp,0002     ;create room on stack for       }
  {                                             ;function result                }
  test := $4711;
    { cs:0006 C746FE1147    mov     word ptr [bp-02],$4711 ;load function       }
    {                                           ;result                         }
end;
  { cs:000B 8B46FE          mov     ax,[bp-02]  ;function result to AX          }
  { cs:000E 89EC            mov     sp,bp       ;return SP to old value         }
  { cs:0010 5D              pop     bp          ;restore BP                     }
  { cs:0011 C3              ret                 ;and return to caller           }
begin
  i := test;
    { cs:001A E8E3FF        call    TEST        ;call TEST                      }
    { cs:001D A33E00        mov     [I],ax      ;store function result          }
end.
```

The function "test" returns an Integer result. Since Pascal doesn't know exactly when this result will be returned, it creates a local variable to store it. As usual, this is done by subtracting, from the stack pointer, the number of bytes to be reserved. Assigning the value of this variable to the function result is the same as assigning a value to any local variable.

Returning the function result is not done with the stack, but rather with the processor registers. The calling routine can directly place the result in one of these registers. At the end of the "test" function, we see that Turbo Pascal loads the Integer result to the AX register from the local variable before the stack is cleared.

The following listing shows the other registers Turbo Pascal uses for returning this result:

```
program f_regs;
var b : byte;
    l : longint;
    r : real;
    p : pointer;
function fbyte : byte;
begin
  { cs:0000 55          push    bp          ;create stack frame            }
  { cs:0001 89E5        mov     bp,sp                                      }
  { cs:0003 83EC02      sub     sp,0002     ;2 bytes for function result   }
    fbyte := 255;
    { cs:0006 C646FFFF    mov     byte ptr [bp-01],FF ;set function result }
end;
  { cs:000A 8A46FF      mov     al,[bp-01] ;pass function result to AL     }
  { cs:000D 89EC        mov     sp,bp       ;restore stack                 }
  { cs:000F 5D          pop     bp                                         }
  { cs:0010 C3          ret                 ;return to caller              }
function flongint : longint;
begin
  { cs:0011 55          push    bp          ;set stack frame               }
  { cs:0012 89E5        mov     bp,sp                                      }
  { cs:0014 83EC04      sub     sp,0004     ;reserve 4 bytes for LongInt   }
    flongint := $12345678;
    { cs:0017 C746FC7856    mov     word ptr [bp-04],5678 ;load funct. rslt. }
    { cs:001C C746FE3412    mov     word ptr [bp-02],1234                   }
end;
  { cs:0021 C446FC      les     ax,[bp-04] ;load function result in ES:AX  }
  { cs:0024 8CC2        mov     dx,es       ;pass result to DX:AX          }
  { cs:0026 89EC        mov     sp,bp       ;restore stack                 }
  { cs:0028 5D          pop     bp                                         }
  { cs:0029 C3          ret                 ;return to caller              }
function freal : real;
begin
  { cs:002A 55          push    bp          ;Business as usual             }
  { cs:002B 89E5        mov     bp,sp                                      }
  { cs:002D 83EC06      sub     sp,0006     ;Real takes 6 bytes            }
    freal := Pi;
    { cs:0030 C746FA8221    mov     word ptr [bp-06],2182 ;load funct. rslt. }
```

```
  { cs:0035 C746FCA2DA    mov    word ptr [bp-04],DAA2                 }
  { cs:003A C746FE0F49    mov    word ptr [bp-02],490F                 }
end;
 { cs:003F 8B46FA         mov    ax,[bp-06] ;Reals passed to registers }
 { cs:0042 8B5EFC         mov    bx,[bp-04] ;DX:BX:AX                   }
 { cs:0045 8B56FE         mov    dx,[bp-02]                            }
 { cs:0048 89EC           mov    sp,bp                                }
 { cs:004A 5D             pop    bp                                   }
 { cs:004B C3             ret                                         }
function fpointer : pointer;
begin
 { cs:004C 55             push   bp          ;put on stack            }
 { cs:004D 89E5           mov    bp,sp                                }
 { cs:004F 83EC04         sub    sp,0004     ;reserve 4 bytes for pointer }
  fpointer := NIL;
   { cs:0052 31C0         xor    ax,ax     ;NIL = both segment and offset}
   { cs:0054 8946FC       mov    [bp-04],ax ;      portions in ptr. are 0 }
   { cs:0057 8946FE       mov    [bp-02],ax                           }
end;
 { cs:005A C446FC         les    ax,[bp-04] ;returned to register pair }
 { cs:005D 8CC2           mov    dx,es      ;DX:AX as with LongInt     }
 { cs:005F 89EC           mov    sp,bp                                }
 { cs:0061 5D             pop    bp                                   }
 { cs:0062 C3             ret               ;return                   }
 begin
  b := fbyte;
  { cs:006B E892FF        call   FBYTE     ;call function FBYTE       }
  { cs:006E A23E00        mov    [B],al    ;store function result     }
  l := flongint;
  { cs:0071 E89DFF        call   FLONGINT  ;call function FLONGINT    }
  { cs:0074 A33F00        mov    [L],ax    ;function result returned to }
  { cs:0077 89164100      mov    [L|2],dx  ;DX:AX                     }
  r := freal;
  { cs:007B E8ACFF        call   FREAL     ;call function FREAL       }
  { cs:007E A34300        mov    [R],ax    ;low Word to AX            }
  { cs:0081 891E4500      mov    [R+2],bx  ;middle Word to BX         }
  { cs:0085 89164700      mov    [R+4],dx  ;high Word to DX           }
  p := fpointer;
  { cs:0089 E8C0FF        call   FPOINTER  ;call function FPOINTER    }
  { cs:008C A34900        mov    [P],ax    ;return pointer to DX:AX   }
  { cs:008F 89164B00      mov    [P+2],dx                            }
 end.
```

The above listing calls four functions to demonstrate the return of all types of function results. Results are returned using types Byte, LongInt, Real and Pointer. If you retain the proper internal formats, all standard types can be handled in one of the ways shown in this program.

The Byte, which represents Char, Boolean, ShortInt and the Counter and Subrange types, is returned to the low byte of the accumulator register (AL).

The LongInt is passed to register pair DX:AX. The high Word goes to DX and the low Word goes to AX. These registers are also used for returning standard and non-standard pointers. AX receives the offset and DX receives the segment portion of the pointer.

The six bytes that form a Real type are returned to AX, BX and DX. The high Word goes to DX, the middle Word to BX and the low Word to AX.

Fortunately, returning compound types as function results isn't possible. Pascal does not allow for types such as records and arrays to be returned as function results. But what about strings? Read on in the next example.

```
program f_str;
type DosPath = string[64];
var ANewPath : DosPath;      s   : string;
function fpath : DosPath;
begin
 { cs:0007 55            push   bp              ;as usual ...              }
 { cs:0008 89E5          mov    bp,sp                                     }
 { Notice that no memory is reserved for the function result. This is     }
 { because a pointer to the buffer for the function result must be placed }
 { on the stack by the caller.                                            }
  fpath := 'c:\dos';
   { cs:000A BF0000       mov    di,0000        ;String constants 'c:\dos' }
   { cs:000D 0E           push   cs             ;is at CS:0000, put this   }
   { cs:000E 57           push   di             ;address on the stack      }
   { cs:000F C47E04       les    di,[bp+04]     ;get address passed to ES:DI }
   { cs:0012 06           push   es             ;and put on the stack      }
   { cs:0013 57           push   di                                       }
   { cs:0014 B84000       mov    ax,0040        ;max. length for StrCopy is }
   { cs:0017 50           push   ax             ;64 bytes                  }
   { cs:0018 9A2102995F   call   far StrCopy                              }
 end;
 { cs:001D 89EC          mov    sp,bp           ;restore stack            }
 { cs:001F 5D            pop    bp                                        }
 { cs:0020 C3            ret                    ;the passed pointer stays on }
 {                                              ;the stack                }
function fstring : string;
begin
 { cs:0031 55            push   bp              ;the same story           }
 { cs:0032 89E5          mov    bp,sp           ;Turbo copies the string  }
  fstring := 'String Function';
   { cs:0034 BF2100       mov    di,0021        ;constants from memory     }
   { cs:0037 0E           push   cs             ;address CS:0021 to the    }
   { cs:0038 57           push   di             ;calling routine's buffer  }
   { cs:0039 C47E04       les    di,[bp+04]     ;using the StrCopy routine }
   { cs:003C 06           push   es                                       }
   { cs:003D 57           push   di                                       }
   { cs:003E B8FF00       mov    ax,00FF        ;one difference: max. length }
   { cs:0041 50           push   ax             ;for StrCopy is now 256 bytes}
   { cs:0042 9A2102995F   call   far StrCopy                              }
 end;
```

```
{ cs:0047 89EC          mov    sp,bp        ;clear stack                    }
{ cs:0049 5D            pop    bp                                           }
{ cs:004A C3            ret                                                 }
begin
{ cs:0050 55            push   bp           ;the main program acts like     }
{ cs:0051 89E5          mov    bp,sp        ;a procedure                    }
{ cs:0053 81EC0001      sub    sp,0100      ;reserve 256 bytes on the stack}
{                                           ;for the string copy            }
  ANewPath := fpath;
  { cs:0057 8DBE00FF     lea    di,[bp-0100];load offset address of the    }
  { cs:005B 16           push   ss          ;buffer together with SS as a}
  { cs:005C 57           push   di          ;FAR pointer on the stack       }
  { cs:005D E8A7FF        call   FPATH       ;call FPATH                     }
  { cs:0060 BF3E00        mov    di,offset ANewPath                         }
  { cs:0063 1E            push   ds          ;push FAR pointer to            }
  { cs:0064 57            push   di          ;ANewPath to stack              }
  { cs:0065 B84000        mov    ax,0040      ;max. length 64 bytes          }
  { cs:0068 50            push   ax                                         }
  { cs:0069 9A2102995F    call   far StrCopy ;call StrCopy again             }
  s := fstring;
  { cs:006E 8DBE00FF     lea    di,[bp-0100];same as before, only with     }
  { cs:0072 16           push   ss          ;different parameters           }
  { cs:0073 57           push   di                                         }
  { cs:0074 E8BAFF        call   FSTRING                                    }
  { cs:0077 BF7F00        mov    di,007F      ;address of S to stack         }
  { cs:007A 1E            push   ds                                        }
  { cs:007B 57            push   di                                        }
  { cs:007C B8FF00        mov    ax,00FF      ;copy max. 255 bytes           }
  { cs:007F 50            push   ax                                        }
  { cs:0080 9A2102995F    call   far StrCopy ;StrCopy                       }
end.
{ cs:0085 89EC          mov    sp,bp        ;clear string buffer from       }
{ cs:0087 5D            pop    bp           ;stack again                    }
}
```

This listing uses two strings to demonstrate returning strings as function results. One is a standard string with a maximum length of 255 characters and the other is a string of type DosPath, which can have up to 64 characters. This string is returned by the "fpath" function; the "fstring" function returns the standard string.

Both functions are called within the main program and the function results are assigned to the ANewPath and S variables. If you look at the main program you will notice that it initializes the stack like a function or a procedure by storing the contents of the BP register and then loading the stack pointer into this register. This is not unusual for main programs since Turbo Pascal handles the main program as just another procedure that is automatically called when the program is started.

However, it is unusual that Turbo reduces the stack pointer by 256 bytes to make room for local variables before the first Pascal statement is executed. By definition main programs have no local variables, so why is this done? The 256 bytes are needed to assign the results of the functions "fpath" and "fstring" to the variables NewPath and S. This is done with the following expression:

```
ANewPath := fpath;
```

Even though "fpath" is not expecting any parameters, Turbo Pascal loads a parameter on the stack before it is called. This parameter is a pointer to the start of the 256 byte buffer that is reserved at the beginning of the stack. Then function "fpath" is called. It initializes the stack in the usual manner but does not reserve any memory for local variables as we have normally seen.

The returned string is accessed using a pointer instead. This pointer is passed on the stack by the calling routine. This pointer is loaded and placed on the stack as a parameter within "fpath" to return a constant string ('\c:dos') to the caller. This method is part of a sequence of machine instructions during which Turbo Pascal calls the StrCopy procedure (see above) which copies the constant strings to the caller's buffer.

After calling this procedure, "fpath" has fulfilled its task and Turbo Pascal restores the stack to the caller. Notice that "fpath" doesn't remove the pointer from the stack as you would expect. This is not done because the caller still needs this pointer as an argument for its own call of the StrCopy procedure. This call is what actually copies the function result to the assigned variable. This is an indirect way of accomplishing this, since "fpath" could also copy the function result to the variable itself if it were passed a pointer to the variable. This would be much faster.

We can see with the second string function, "fstring", that Turbo Pascal always uses this inefficient method of returning results from string functions. A temporary buffer is created and two copy procedures are used. Obviously, this leaves some room for improvement in future versions of the product.

Now let's summarize the various types of allowed function results and the way each is returned to the process registers.

Type	Register
Char	AL
Boolean	AL
Byte	AL
ShortInt	AL
Integer	AX
Word	AX
LongInt	DX:AX
Standard and non-standard pointers	DX:AX
Real	DX:BX:AX
Counter and sub-region <range?> types	AL or AX, according to size

Function results returned to the processor registers

Ignoring function results

Version 6.0 inserts a new global compiler switch. This switch offers the option of ignoring the results of a function call. The Pascal dialect used in Turbo Pascal has closer ties to the C computing language through this switch, as function results can be acknowledged or ignored at any time.

The {$X} switch defaults to {$X-}, so you must remember to start a program with {$X+} if you want to skip the results of a specific procedure or function, or use a parameter from a different procedure or function.

This directive works only with functions defined within a program, or with another unit specified as the SYSTEM unit. The {$X} directive does not apply to the predefined functions like CHR or ORD, which are used by the SYSTEM unit as well.

The {$X} switch is more useful with the predefined functions like READKEY from the CRT unit, which is often added to program code to pause during execution and wait for a keypress from the user. Earlier versions of Turbo Pascal required a variable declaration in conjunction with READKEY, and the keypress was stored in this variable. This is fine if the results are useful, but a simple Y or N may not be needed by the program. The following example shows a routine without a variable attached to READKEY.

```
program NoFunc;

{$X+}                                        { Ignore function results }

uses Crt;

begin
  write( 'Please press a key to ' +
        'start the program ...' );
  readkey;                                   { No variable declaration needed }
  writeln;
```

```
   writeln( 'End of program' );
end.
```

When this source is compiled, the system ignores the function result, which was placed in registers DX and AX. After this the result is still passed to these registers, since the program code makes no changes to the function as dictated by the entry of the {$X+} switch.

Recursion

Recursions have been one of the great mysteries of Pascal programming. Often, their use seems to originate from irrational rather than rational thinking. Sometimes we're not quite sure how recursions work, but they <u>do</u> work.

You might be disappointed to learn that recursions don't require any special capabilities from the processor. Recursive functions or procedure calls are not that complicated. It doesn't matter to the program whether a procedure calls itself and starts a recursion or if it simply returns to where it was called.

The previous sections on local variable management and parameter transfer have already given us some ideas why this happens. We just have to assemble the pieces of the puzzle.

We'll use a very simple recursive function to help us: the factorial function. This function stems from the study of probabilities and is used to solve problems such as the following:

> "How many different color combinations can you make with three color cards when one card is red, one is green and the third is blue?"

You can solve this problem by simply thinking it through. The first card can occupy any of the three locations. The second card has two alternatives, since one card has already been placed. The last card has only one place it can go. The number of combinations is therefore $3*2*1 = 6$. This calculation is performed by the factorial function. So, the recursive definition for the factorial function FAC is:

```
FAC(n) = n * FAC( n-1 ) with FAC( 1 ) = 1 as the stop condition
```

The following program demonstrates the implementation of a factorial function according to this formula.

```
program fctorial;
var result : longint;
function fac( x : longint ) : longint;
begin
  { cs:0000 55            push   bp       ;set up stack and reserve four   }
  { cs:0001 89E5          mov    bp,sp    ;bytes for the function result   }
```

```
{ cs:0001 89E5          mov    bp,sp      ;bytes for the function result   }
{ cs:0003 83EC04        sub    sp,0004                                     }
  if ( x = 1 ) then
  { cs:0006 837E0600    cmp    word ptr [X+2],0000  ;high Word = 0?        }
  { cs:000A 7512        jne    ELSE                 ;no ---> ELSE          }
  { cs:000C 837E0401    cmp    word ptr [X],0001    ;low Word = 1?         }
  { cs:0010 750C        jne    ELSE                 ;no ---> ELSE          }
    fac := 1            { X = 0, end recursion, return 1                   }
    { cs:0012 C746FC0100 mov   word ptr [bp-04],0001 ;1 as funct. rslt}
    { cs:0015 C746FE0000 mov   word ptr [bp-02],0000 ;in loc. var.         }
    { cs:001B EB20       jmp   END                  ;end function          }
  else                                              { X is not 0           }
    fac := x * fac( x-1 );                  { continue recursion with X minus 1  }
    { cs:001D C44604    les    ax,[bp+04]    ;load X in ES:AX              }
    { cs:0020 8CC2      mov    dx,es         ;and from there to DX:AX      }
    { cs:0022 2D0100    sub    ax,0001       ;calculate X - 1              }
    { cs:0025 83DA00    sbb    dx,0000                                     }
    { cs:0026 52        push   dx            ;and put on stack as          }
    { cs:0027 50        push   ax            ;param. for function call     }
    { cs:0028 E8D6FF    call   FAK           ;Recursion!                   }
    {                                        ;funct. result now in DX:AX   }
    { cs:002B C44E04    les    cx,[bp+04]    ;X to ES:CX                   }
    { cs:002E 8CC3      mov    bx,es         ;from there to BX:CX          }
    { cs:0030 9A0B02975F call  LongMul       ;X times function result      }
    { cs:0035 8946FC    mov    [bp-04],ax    ;store product as             }
    { cs:0038 8956FE    mov    [bp-02],dx    ;function result              }
end;
{ cs:003B C446FC        les    ax,[bp-04]   ;function results to ES:AX     }
{ cs:003D 8CC2          mov    dx,es        ;from there to DX:AX           }
{ cs:003F 89EC          mov    sp,bp        ;restore stack                 }
{ cs:0041 5D            pop    bp           ;POP BP twice is faster than   }
{ cs:0041 5D            pop    bp           ;ADD SP,2                      }
{ cs:0042 C20400        ret    0004         ;return to caller and clear    }
{                                           ;parameter X                   }
begin
  result := fac( 3 );
  { cs:004D B80A00      mov    ax,0003      ;load 3 as LongInt in DX:AX}
  { cs:0050 31D2        xor    dx,dx                                       }
  { cs:0052 52          push   dx           ;and put on stack as a         }
  { cs:0053 50          push   ax           ;parameter                     }
  { cs:0054 E8A9FF      call   FAK          ;call factorial function       }
  { cs:0057 A33E00      mov    [RESULT],ax  ;result from DX:AX to the      }
  { cs:005A 89164000    mov    [RESULT+2],dx ;variable RESULT              }
end.
```

By using the factorial function FAC, the factorial of 3 is calculated within the main program. The call to FAC is performed like any other function call. The argument is placed on the stack, the function is called and the function result is returned to the specified variable.

There isn't a difference between FAC and other functions. The stack is set up and four bytes are reserved for the function result. Then the passed parameter is loaded and checked whether or not it is equal to zero. If so, the function result is returned as 1 and the function and any further recursions are terminated by jumping to the end of the function. Here, the function result is loaded from the local variable to the DX:AX register pair, the stack is restored and the return jump to the calling routine executes.

If parameter X is not equal to 0, then recursion will occur. Parameter X is first loaded into the processor register, decremented by 1 and then placed on the stack. The function then calls itself to begin the recursion. When the recursion is finished, the register pair DX:AX will contain the result of FAC(x-1). This is multiplied by X and placed on the stack.

This may be a little more complex than it appears. The call of FAC(x-1) causes x recursions. Let's take a closer look at how the stack is used during FAC. The BP register gets closer to the start of the stack with each recursive call. So each time FAC is executed, a new set of local variables (which, incidentally, are not used in this particular example) and function results are created. This ensures that FAC will be able to find X unchanged on the stack when it exits from the recursion. If the parameters and local variables were not addressed relative to the moving BP register, the recursions would conflict with each other and end up crashing the computer.

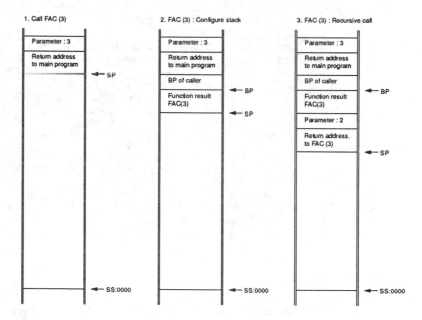

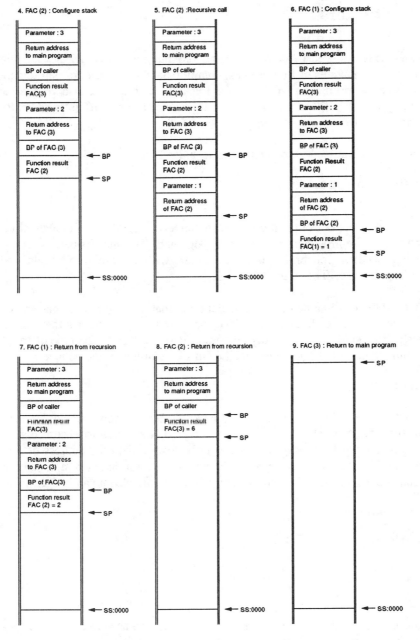

Changing stack contents during the call of FAC(3)

2.5   Pointers

Pointers have always been a vital part of Pascal programming. Whether they are joining list elements or the branches of binary trees, complex data structures are tied together with pointers. When working with DOS or BIOS functions, pointers are also very important in system programming. Whenever you call a function that has buffers or data structures, pointers are needed to reference them.

This section will examine how pointers operate under Turbo Pascal.

Understanding pointers

Although pointers are one of the most basic and important elements of the Pascal language, they tend to confuse programmers, especially beginners. This may be because it is difficult to visualize what a pointer is doing. However, with a little forethought and some experience, pointers will begin to make sense.

The key to understanding pointers is remembering that a pointer never has any contents, such as Char, Integer or Boolean variable types. Pointers hold values that Turbo Pascal interprets as the number of a memory address in RAM or ROM. The type of variable that will be found at this address must be specified in the definition of the pointer. For example:

```
var IP : ^Integer;
```

tells us that IP is a pointer to an Integer variable. Turbo will now assume that the address given in the pointer contains an Integer variable. Turbo helps to ensure that this will always be true by not allowing the pointer to be loaded with the address of a different variable type. The following sequence would produce an error during compiling because the second statement attempts to load the address of a Char variable into an Integer pointer:

```
var IP : ^Integer;
    i  : integer;
    b  : char;
begin
   IP := @i;                 { address of I to IP }
IP := @c;
end;
```

The address in the pointer itself isn't useful unless it can be used to communicate with the variable. This is known as *referencing*. An expression such as:

```
IP^ := 6;
```

is an example of a reference. Verbally, this statement says something like:

"Get the contents of the IP pointer, consider it to be a pointer to an Integer variable, and write the value 6 to this variable."

The following listing will demonstrate the implications of this in Turbo Pascal:

```
program EasyPtr;
var i  : integer;
    ip : ^integer;
    c  : char;
    cp : ^char;
begin
  ip := @i;                                    { IP now points to I }
  { cs:0008 B83E00         mov    ax,offset I ;offset address of I to AX  }
  { cs:000B 8CDA           mov    dx,ds       ;I is in data segment       }
  { cs:000D A34000         mov    [IP],ax     ;store segment and offset   }
  { cs:0010 89164200       mov    [IP+2],dx   ;address in pointer IP      }
  cp := @c;                                    { CP now points to C       }
  { cs:0014 B84400         mov    ax,offset C ;offset address of C to AX  }
  { cs:0017 8CDA           mov    dx,ds       ;C is also in data segment  }
  { cs:0019 A34500         mov    [CP],ax     ;write address of C in DX:AX }
  { cs:001C 89164700       mov    [CP+2],dx   ;in pointer CP              }
  i   := 5;                                    { IP now equals 5          }
  { cs:0020 C7063E000500   mov    word ptr [I],0005 ;direct assignment    }
  ip^ := 6;                                    { now equals 6             }
  { cs:0026 C43E4000       les    di,[IP]     ;contents of IP to ES:DI    }
  { cs:002A 26C7050600     mov    es:word ptr [di],0006 ;6 to [ES:DI]     }
  c   := 'x';
  { cs:002F C606440078     mov    byte ptr [C],'x' ;direct assignment     }
  cp^ := 'u';                                  { making a U out of an X   }
  { cs:0034 C43E4500       les    di,[CP]     ;contents of CP to ES:DI    }
  { cs:0038 26C60575       mov    es:byte ptr [di],'u' ;'x' to [ES:DI]    }
end.
```

This example deals with creating pointers, assigning addresses and referencing variables with the pointers. One Char and one Integer variable are created, along with two pointers called IP and CP. IP points to the Integer variable and CP to the Char variable. Before you can actually access the variables with these pointers, they must be loaded with the addresses of the variables. Before this occurs, the contents of the pointers will be undefined and they will be pointing anywhere in RAM. Since we usually want to avoid writing things to random locations in RAM, you should always initialize a pointer.

The address operator @ is often used for this. It returns the address of a variable. This result can then be assigned to a pointer as long as the variable type and pointer type are compatible. The example uses this method to assign addresses to IP and CP. IP points to I and CP points to C. As we saw in Section 2.3, Turbo Pascal manages pointers independent of the variable type. All pointers are represented by two Words in memory, one which gives the segment address and one which gives the offset address. This can be seen in the way

Turbo Pascal loads the addresses of variables using the register pair DX:AX. The values are assigned to the pointer from here.

After initializing the pointer, I is assigned a value of 5. This doesn't actually require using the pointer. Turbo can load the value directly into the memory location reserved for I. However, referencing the variable I is different. The IP pointer must be used to do this. Turbo loads the address of the variable to be referenced from its pointer into a processor register. This is a very frequently used operation in PC programming, so the 8086/8088 has a special assembly language instruction called LES for this purpose.

LES is always used together with the name of a processor register and the address of the memory location that contains the pointer to be loaded. LES loads the segment portion of the address in ES and the offset portion in the specified register. Turbo Pascal almost always uses the LES instruction with the DI register. This means that the contents of the IP pointer are loaded into the ES:DI register pair.

Turbo Pascal now has the address of the variable to be referenced. By using indexed memory addressing from the DI register, with ES serving as the segment register, the variable can be accessed. Notice the term "word ptr", which Turbo Pascal gives after the MOV instruction that writes the value 6 in the variable being referenced. This means that the MOV instruction is accessing a WORD in memory. As we saw in Section 2.3, Integer variables are stored in WORD format in memory.

This also represents the only difference in the way CP is used. The contents of CP are loaded into ES:DI as above. Instead of "word ptr", Turbo Pascal uses "byte ptr", since Char variables are stored as individual BYTEs in memory. The difference between the two variable types is not in the internal format of the pointer, but rather in the statements that Turbo Pascal creates to access the variables through the pointers.

When referencing a LongInt, Turbo Pascal cannot get by with just one MOV instruction. This variable type uses two WORDs in memory, so Turbo must generate two MOV instructions. This is similar to Real variables, which use 6 bytes in memory. Turbo creates three MOV instructions, each of which loads one of the three WORDs of the Real variable.

We mentioned earlier that Turbo cannot assign the address of a Char variable to an Integer pointer. Actually, the situation isn't so simple. The pointer compatibility rules used by Turbo Pascal have a few loopholes. Turbo allows any assignments to be made within the Integer variable group (Byte, ShortInt, Integer, Word and LongInt); the same is true for pointers. The following listing will demonstrate that Turbo Pascal doesn't do anything to stop you from assigning the address of an Integer or Byte variable to a LongInt pointer.

There are really no negative consequences to doing this, but you must realize that when referencing with this pointer, Turbo will interpret it as a pointer to a LongInt. Therefore, it will write four bytes to memory where perhaps only one or two are actually reserved for the variable. This would result in unintentionally overwriting the corresponding number of following variables, which will usually lead to errors in your program. So, you should watch out for this pitfall.

```
program wrongptr;
var lp : ^longint;
    b  : byte;
    i  : integer;
begin
   lp := @b;                                              { Timber! }
lp^ := $12345678;           { I and the byte after I are both overwritten }
   lp := @i;                                            { Worst case }
lp^ := $12345678;              { the next 2 bytes after I are overwritten }
end.
```

Until now, the pointers we have seen have all been *standard pointers*, which are connected with a specific data type. This tells Turbo Pascal the size and format of the variables that the pointer can access and also which statements to generate when referencing the variables. This is what distinguishes a standard pointer from a *generic pointer*, which is simply a non-standard pointer. So, it is not associated with any particular data type and cannot be used to reference a variable because the format and size of the variable are unknown.

However, generic pointers are still an important part of Turbo Pascal, since many functions (such as GetMem and Ptr) return pointers. These types of pointers cannot be a specific type.

In order to use a generic pointer for referencing a variable within a statement, you can use a type conversion to change the pointer to any desired type. This is easy to do, as demonstrated in the next example. The listing displays the release date of the BIOS version to the screen. Then this information is stored as an ASCII string in the last 16 bytes below the 1 MEG memory limit. The actual length of the string can change with different BIOS versions, so the program searches for the first ASCII character within these 16 bytes.

To access this memory location in ROM, the program uses the PTR function and various type declarations. First, it declares an array containing 16 characters with indices 1 to 16. This array is called BiosDate, and the pointer BDPTR is defined as an array pointer.

To show Turbo Pascal that an array of this type is located at address F000:FFF0, the PTR function is called and the desired segment and offset address components are passed. The result is returned as a generic pointer to the desired memory location. This pointer then undergoes a type conversion to pointer type BDPTR so that it will be recognized as a pointer to an array of type BiosDate. By referencing with this pointer, the base address of the array is returned. The loop counter I is used as an index to access each individual element of the array. From then on, this array at the end of the memory and the one in the data segment or on the stack are identical to Turbo Pascal.

Let's look at a summary of these steps:

ptr($F000, $FFF0) returns generic pointer to memory location F000:FFF0.

BDPTR(ptr($F000, $FFF0)) returns pointer to an array of type BiosDate, which is located at F000:FFF0.

BDPTR(ptr($F000, $FFF0))^[i] returns the Ith character from the array of type BiosDate, which is located at F000:FFF0.

The following program displays the release date of your BIOS on the screen. The date is displayed in MM/DD/YY format.

```
program PtrBios;
type BiosDatum = array[1..16] of char;
     BDPTR     = ^BiosDatum;
var i, j : integer;
begin
  write( 'BIOS Version dated ');
 {-- find first ASCII code -----------------------------------------------}
  i := 1;
  while ( BDPTR(ptr( $F000, $FFF0 ))^[i]<'0' ) or
        ( BDPTR(ptr( $F000, $FFF0 ))^[i]>'9' ) do
   inc( i );                                        { no code, continue search }
              {-- code found, output next 8 characters --------------------}
  for j := 0 to 7 do
     write( BDPTR(ptr( $F000, $FFF0 ))^[i+j] );
  writeln;
end.
```

We will see more of type conversions for generic pointers in the next section, which deals with system programming.

Before we proceed, you should be aware of a potential source of errors while working with pointers. Many Turbo Pascal programmers have spent hours of debugging time because of this trap. The problem has to do with using pointers with the FillChar and Move procedures, which are part of the system unit.

FillChar fills a memory range with a constant character and expects, as the first parameter, a reference to the variable to be filled. Move copies one memory range to another and expects parameters that give references to both memory ranges and the number of bytes to copy.

Both procedures are often used with pointers. This can cause problems if you pass the pointer instead of the address of the variable referenced by the pointer. The results are as follows: with FillChar, the pointer itself and the following bytes will be filled with the constant character; with Move, the memory ranges that begin with the two pointers will be copied. The problem is that these procedures expect to receive this information as non-standard parameters, so Turbo Pascal cannot perform any type checking while compiling. If a pointer is specified, it is handled simply as a variable and its address is passed to the procedure. You can avoid this misunderstanding by referencing the pointers. Here is an example:

```
program MoveFill;
var p1,                                    { Two generic pointers }
    p2 : pointer;
begin
   GetMem( p1, 100 );          { Reserve 100 bytes, address P1 }
   GetMem( p2, 400 );          { Reserve 400 bytes, address P2 }
   FillChar( p1, 100, 'X' );     { This usually causes a crash }
   FillChar( p1^, 100, 'X' );    { This is the correct method }
   Move( p2, p1, 100 );                            { Wrong! }
   Move( p2^, p1^, 100 );                           { Right! }
end.
```

Pointers in system programming

Pointers are important for system programming because many DOS and BIOS functions that use buffers or data structures require pointers. Some functions expect a pointer to be passed when they are called and some return pointers to the calling routine. In either case, a programmer must be thoroughly familiar with the way pointers work and with type conversions in order to achieve the intended result. In this section we will present a practical example of system programming to fully explain these points.

The example revolves around an algorithm that will determine the drive letters of the available DOS drives. Many applications require this kind of routine for tasks such as listing the selection of available disk drives on the screen for a user. Up until Version 3.0, DOS didn't have a function to perform this task. Programmers had to resort to undocumented DOS structures to obtain this information.

The drive letter for each device is available in a DOS data structure called the Drive Parameter Block (DPB). DOS configures this structure for each available drive. As seen in the following figure, a DPB contains much information on each device. For our example, only two fields will be needed. The first field, which contains the device code for the drive, and the last field, which links the individual DPBs with one another in memory.

Addr.	Contents	Type
+$00	Number or device code of the corresponding drive. (0 = A, 1 = B etc.)	1 BYTE
+$01	Subunit of device driver for the drive	1 BYTE
+$02	Bytes per sector	1 WORD
+$04	Interleave factor	1 BYTE
+$05	Sectors per cluster	1 BYTE
+$06	Reserved sectors (for boot sector)	1 WORD
+$08	Number of File Allocation Tables (FATs)	1 BYTE
+$09	Number of entries in root directory	1 WORD
+$0B	First occupied sector	1 WORD
+$0D	Last occupied sector	1 WORD
+$0F	Sectors per FAT	1 BYTE
+$10	First data sector	1 WORD
+$12	Pointer to header of the corresponding device driver	1 PTR
+$16	Media Descriptor	1 BYTE
+$17	Used-Flag ($0FF = no access attempted yet)	1 BYTE
+$18	Pointer to the next DPB (xxxx:FFFF = no moro DPBs to follow)	1 PTR

Length: $1C (28 bytes)

Structure of a Drive Parameter Block (DPB)

To obtain the desired information from the DPBs, you must get into the linked structure. You can gain access to the entire list with the address of the first DPB, since a pointer to the next one is always given as the last entry. But the address of the first DPB is not as accessible. First you must access another internal DOS structure, called the DOS Information Block (DIB). The first field in this structure contains a pointer to the first DPB.

Addr.	Contents	Type
+$00	Pointer to the first Drive Parameter Block (DPB)	1 PTR
+$04h	Pointer to the last DOS buffer	1 PTR
+$08h	Pointer to the clock driver ($CLOCK)	1 PTR
+$0C	Pointer to the console driver (CON)	1 PTR
+$10	Maximum sector length	1 WORD
+$12	Pointer to the first DOS buffer	1 PTR
+$16	Pointer to the Path Table	1 PTR
+$1A	Pointer to the System File Table (SFT)	1 PTR
Length: $1E (30 bytes)		

Structure of the DOS Information Block (DIB)

Once you know the structure of the DPBs and the DIB, you have almost all the information you will need. Now you must find the address of the DIB so you can access it. This can be done with an undocumented DOS function: function number $52. After passing this function number to the AH register, it will return the address of the DIB to register pair ES:BX.

To summarize, the step-by-step procedure for finding a device code is as follows:

• Call function $52.

• Get contents of ES:BX as a pointer to the DIB.

• Get the pointer to the first DPB from the DIB.

• Run through the DPBs until you find the one with $FFFF as the offset address in the "Pointer to the next DPB" field.

While doing this, output the device codes or drive letters in the desired manner.

Translating this plan to Pascal code isn't a simple task. One important part of the method will involve recreating these DOS structures using Pascal records. The address of each field in the Pascal record must correspond exactly with those in the DOS structure; otherwise you will never be able to retrieve the desired information correctly. The structure of such a record is really not difficult, as long as you know the size of each field and the exact number of fields in the DOS structure.

While recreating DOS structures, Pascal programmers will realize that DOS, with a subset of the data types, is supported by Turbo Pascal:

- 1-byte fields correspond to type BYTE.

- 2-byte fields correspond to Integers or Words, depending upon the value of the high bit.

- 4-byte fields can be interpreted as LongInts if they contain numerical information, or as pointers.

When recreating such a data structure, it isn't necessary to assign each field a name and type. Assigning only the fields in which you are interested is sufficient. Then you can fill in the blanks, created by the unnecessary fields, with "dummy variables". This will maintain the proper correspondence between the Pascal record and the DOS structure. Dummy variables are usually an array of type Byte. The array must contain exactly as many elements (and therefore bytes) as the fields you are skipping over in the DOS structure. If DOS returns a pointer to such a data structure, you can use a type conversion to convince Turbo Pascal that the pointer points to a declared Pascal structure. By referencing the pointer, you can then access any field you like.

The following program will help demonstrate these points.

```
program getdrvs;
uses Dos;
procedure GetDrives;
type DPBPTR    = ^DPB;                      { pointer to a DOS Parameter Block }
     DPBPTRPTR = ^DPBPTR;                      { pointer to a pointer to a DPB }
     DPB       = record             { recreation of a DOS Parameter Block }
                    Code  : byte;             { drive code (0=A, 1=B etc. }
                    dummy : array [1..$17] of byte; { not interesting here }
                    Next  : DPBPTR;                  { pointer to next DPB }
                 end;                       { xxxx:FFFF marks last DPB }

var Regs    : Registers;                    { register for interrupt call }
    CurrDpbP : DPBPTR;                         { pointer to DPBs in memory }

begin
   {-- get pointer to first DPB -------------------------------------------}

  Regs.AH := $52;                       { function $52 returns pointer to DIB }
  MsDos( Regs );
  CurrDpbP := DPBPTRPTR( ptr( Regs.ES, Regs.BX ) )^;
   { cs:001C 8B46EE     mov     ax,[bp-12] ;load BX to AX                   }
   { cs:001F 8B56FC     mov     dx,[bp-04] ;load ES to DS                   }
   { cs:0022 89C7       mov     di,ax      ;offset address from AX to DI }
   { cs:0024 8EC2       mov     es,dx      ;segment address from DS to ES}
   { cs:0026 26C405     les     ax,es:[di] ;pointer from ES:DI to ES:AX   }
   { cs:0029 8CC2       mov     dx,es      ;and from there to DX:AX       }
```

```
{ cs:002B 8946E8          mov     [bp-18],ax ;write these pointers to the  }
{ cs:002E 8956EA          mov     [bp-16],dx ;variable CurrDpbP            }

{-- run through each DPB  --------------------------------------------------}

  repeat
     writeln( chr( ord('A') + CurrDpbP^.Code ) );      { output device code  }
     CurrDpbP := CurrDpbP^.Next;                { set pointer to next DPB     }
   until ( Ofs( CurrDpbP^ ) = $FFFF );            { until last DPB is reached }
  end;
begin
   writeln(#13#10'Installed drives: '#13#10);
   GetDrives;
end.
```

The DOS Parameter Block is recreated with a structure called DPB. Only the two fields needed by the program are named. The fields in between are filled with a dummy variable. A pointer of type DPBPTR is defined as a pointer to a DOS Parameter Block.

A repeat of the DOS Information Block isn't included in this program because the information needed from this table (the pointer to the first DPB) is found in the first field. DOS function $52 returns a pointer to the pointer that leads to the first DPB.

A "pointer to a pointer" may sound confusing, but it is not a problem for Turbo Pascal, as shown by the declaration of the DPBPTRPTR type. This type is used after function $52 is called. It loads the address of the first DPB in the pointer CurrDpbP, using the following assignment:

```
CurrDpbP := DPBPTRPTR( ptr( Regs.ES, Regs.BX ) )^;
```

First, a generic pointer is created with the Ptr function using the returned contents of the ES and BX registers. A type conversion is then used to convert this generic pointer into a pointer to a pointer to a DPB. This expression is then referenced and the result is assigned to the variable CurrDpbP.

A pointer is loaded into ES:DI from the memory location referred to by the result of the pointer expression. This register pair will then refer to the start of the DIB. Turbo loads the pointer at the start of the DIB into register pair DX:AX and writes it to the local variable CurrDpbP. This variable will then contain a pointer to the first DPB.

With this pointer, the program enters into a REPEAT-UNTIL loop. In the course of the loop, the DPB referenced by the pointer CurrDpbP is evaluated. The device code of the drive is read and the pointer to the next DPB (located at the end of a DPB) is loaded into CurrDpbP. The loop ends when the offset portion of CurrDpbP contains the value $FFFF. This indicates that the last DPB has been reached. This program is only a small example of what can be done by accessing structures and pointers created by the operating system. The techniques presented in this example will also be used later in the book. Sometimes the structures and data will be more complex, and at other times they will be simpler. The basic principles learned here apply in any case.

WITH statements and pointers

What do WITH statements have to do with pointers? At first glance, they don't seem to do much. The WITH statement is often used to make it easier to address individual data structures (Records) as elements of arrays. Of course it is acceptable to specify a pointer with a WITH statement, as long as the pointer references a record. However, this isn't what we're discussing at the moment.

In this section we will discuss what happens when a WITH statement is converted to assembly language. Pointers play a decisive role in this process. When Turbo Pascal uses a WITH statement to access a data structure and the address of the structure is unknown at the time, the program is compiled and a pointer to the data structure is built. The pointer is stored in a local variable, which is automatically created within the function or procedure. This pointer is loaded into ES:DI in order to access the components of the data structure. The indexed addressing of the DI register creates a direct link to the structure. The following listing shows how this is done.

```
program WithDem1;
type RData = record                          { any desired data record  }
                Field1 : integer;
                Field2 : char;
                   { .
                        .
                        . additional fields can follow here if desired }
             end;
var OneDatum    : RData;                { a data record as global variable  }
    RDataArray : array[1..10] of RData;        { 10 RData in an array  }
    i          : integer;                        { loop counter  }
begin
   with OneDatum do
   { does not generate an assembly language because the address of OneDatum }
   { is already known at the time of compilation                     }
   begin
      Field1 := 1;
      { cs:000B C7063E000100   mov    word ptr [ONEDATUM.FIELD1],1      }
      Field2 := 'a';
      { cs:0011 C606400061     mov    byte ptr [ONEDATUM.FIELD2],'a'    }
   end;
{---- initialize entries from RDataArray using WITH ----}
for i := 1 to 10 do
   with RDataArray[ i ] do
      { cs:0022 A15F00         mov    ax,[I]      ;load index I in AX       }
      { cs:0025 BA0300         mov    dx,0003     ;load size of one record  }
      { cs:0028 F7E2           mul    dx          ;index times record size  }
      { cs:002A 8BF8           mov    di,ax       ;product to DI            }
```

```
      { cs:002C 81C73E00      add    di,offset RDATAARRAY - 3 ;+ base adr.-3}
      { cs:0030 897EFC         mov    [bp-04],di ;pointer to RDataArray[i] in}
      { cs:0033 8C5EFE         mov    [bp-02],ds ;DS:DI to local variable    }
      begin
         Field1 := $4711;
         { cs:0036 C47EFC       les    di,[bp-04] ;WITH pointer to ES:DI  }
         { cs:0039 26C7051147   mov    es:word ptr [di],4711              }
         Field2 := 'x';
         { cs:003E C47EFC       les    di,[bp-04] ;WITH pointer to ES:DI  }
         { cs:0041 26C6450278   mov    es:byte ptr [di+02],'x'            }
      end;
   {- initialize entries from RDataArray using WITH ---------------------- }

   for i := 1 to 10 do
      begin
         RDataArray[i].Field1 := $4711;
            { cs:0059 A15F00      mov    ax,[I]     ;Load AX into index I     }
            { cs:005C BA0300      mov    dx,0003    ;Record size to DX        }
            { cs:005F F7E2        mul    dx         ;Record size * index      }
            { cs:0061 8BF8        mov    di,ax      ;Product to DI            }
            { cs:0063 C7853E001147 mov   word ptr  [di+RDATAARRAY-3],4711    }

         RDataArray[i].Field2 := 'x';
            { cs:0059 A15F00      mov    ax,[I]     ;Load AX into index I     }
            { cs:005C BA0300      mov    dx,0003    ;Record size to DX        }
            { cs:005F F7E2        mul    dx         ;Record size * index      }
            { cs:0061 8BF8        mov    di,ax      ;Product to DI            }
            { cs:0063 C685400078  mov    byte ptr  [di+RDATAARRAY-3],'x'     }
      end;
end.
```

This program revolves around the two global variables OneDatum and RDataArray. The structure of these variables is determined by the data structure RData. OneDatum represents one such structure, while RDataArray is an array with ten such entries.

The various ways of converting the WITH statement are shown within the program. First, WITH is used to access the variable OneDatum. Its address is already known at the time the program is compiled, so Turbo Pascal doesn't need a pointer to access its individual components. Turbo can directly address them within the data segment. In this case, the WITH statement doesn't generate any assembly language. It acts only as a means of accessing the individual components of the variable, without writing a lot of Pascal code.

The access to RDataArray is different. The FOR-NEXT loop runs through each element of the array and addresses each component using a WITH statement. Turbo Pascal doesn't know the address of this data structure at the time of compilation, since index I only exists during the execution of the FOR-NEXT loop. Therefore, Turbo Pascal uses the WITH statement to enter the address of the data structure in a local variable. Since the elements of an array are stored immediately after one another in memory, the address of each can be determined by multiplying the corresponding index by the size of an element of type RData (3 bytes).

This gives Turbo only the offset address of the data structure, relative to the start of the array in memory. The base address of the array must be added to this. Notice that instead of using the actual base address, Turbo uses the base address minus three. This is related to the indexing and the internal storage of the array.

When RDataArray was declared, the elements were assigned index addresses 1 through 10. The first element (with index 1) is located at offset address 0 relative to the start of the array and not at offset address 3. There is no element 0 in the array. So, Turbo must decrement the product of the index and the array element size by 1. This would require an additional assembly language instruction if you didn't automatically subtract the additional bytes when adding on the base address. The following mathematical rules apply for such calculations:

```
Base + ( (Index - 1 ) * 3 ) = Base + ( ( Index * 3 ) - ( 1 * 3 ) ) =
Base + ( ( Index * 3 ) - 3 ) =  Base - 3 + (Index * 3)
```

The two FOR-NEXT loops show how addressing array elements using WITH saves the programmer some typing and leads to efficient assembly language. All ten elements of the array are run through and initialized. The WITH statement isn't used here, so the name of the array and the index of the element being accessed must be given in each case. This means that Turbo must calculate the address of each array element for each access. This generates additional code that unnecessarily takes up time during program execution. So, the WITH statement is highly recommended in these instances.

There are times when the WITH statement could have a negative effect on program speed. This could happen where the address of the data structure to be referenced is already available in a pointer and can therefore be directly given to the local WITH pointer. Moving this pointer does require three assembly language instructions, but this will barely make a difference unless you are striving for maximum execution speed. The next example shows two instances in which Turbo could have saved itself the work with the local WITH variable. If execution speed is more important to you than ease of writing the program, you should do the extra typing required to access individual structure components instead of using the WITH statement.

```
program WithDem2;
type RData = record                              { any desired data record }
              Field1 : integer;
              Field2 : char;
                { .
                  .
                  . additional fields can follow here if desired }
            end;
     RDataPtr = ^RData;                           { pointer to a data record }
var OneDatum : RData;                    { a data record as a global variable }
```

```
procedure test( DP : RDataPtr );
begin
   with DP^ do
   { cs:000E C47E04        les     di,[bp+04] ;pointer passed to ES:DI    }
   { cs:0011 897EFC        mov     [bp-04],di ;and from there to the local }
   { cs:0014 8C46FE        mov     [bp-02],es ;WITH variable               }
     begin
        Field1 := $4711;
        { cs:0017 C47EFC        les     di,[bp-04] ;pointer from WITH var.   }
        { cs:001A 26C7051147    mov     es:word ptr [di],4711                }
        Field2 := 'x';
        { cs:001F C47EFC        les     di,[bp-04] ;pointer from WITH var.   }
        { cs:0022 26C6450278    mov     es:byte ptr [di+02],78               }
     end;
  end;
procedure test1( var Data : RData );
begin   with Data do
   { cs:003B C47E04        les     di,[bp+04] ;pointer passed to ES:DI    }
   { cs:003E 897EFC        mov     [bp-04],di ;and from there store in the }
   { cs:0041 8C46FE        mov     [bp-02],es ;local WITH variable         }
     begin
        Field1 := $4711;
        { cs:0044 C47EFC        les     di,[bp-04] ;pointer from WITH var.   }
        { cs:0047 26C7051147    mov     es:word ptr [di],4711                }
        Field2 := 'x';
        { cs:004C C47EFC        les     di,[bp-04] ;pointer from WITH var.   }
        { cs:004F 26C6450278    mov     es:byte ptr [di+02],78               }
     end;
  end;
begin
   test( @OneDatum );
   test1( OneDatum );
end.
```

This example also uses the data structure RData and the global variable OneDatum. This time, the variable is passed to both the "test" and the "test1" procedures. In the first case, this is done by using the address operator as a pointer and in the second case as a variable parameter. In spite of the different mechanisms used at the Pascal level, the result is the same at the processor level: Turbo passes a pointer to the variable OneDatum to the called procedure. When WITH is used, both procedures use the pointer to access this variable, and in both cases a local WITH variable is created. However, this isn't really necessary. It only makes sense to use this variable if the pointer to the variable is somehow manipulated within the WITH block. While this is theoretically possible, there is really no advantage to it.

A procedure or function can have as many WITH statements following each other as desired. This leads one to believe that Turbo Pascal would reserve the required amount of memory on the stack for the local WITH variables. But this isn't true. Wherever possible, Turbo limits itself to the creation of one such variable that can be used with all WITH statements.

More than one WITH variable will be created only if WITH statements are nested within one another. But this means that multiple WITH variables would have to exist at one time. Otherwise, the same WITH variable is simply overwritten each time it is used.

Pointer arithmetic

Unlike C, Pascal cannot perform pointer arithmetic, which means that pointers cannot be manipulated using addition and subtraction. This is a very useful capability, especially in relation to execution speed.

As an example, consider processing an array with a FOR-NEXT loop, similar to our previous example. To access each array element, the address of the element must be calculated and assigned to a pointer each time the loop is processed. The address is calculated by multiplying the index by the size of the element and then adding the base address of the array.

When you think about this, you realize that each time the loop is processed, the value differs from the previous value only by the element size. An easier way to arrive at the same results would be to set up, before the loop is processed for the first time, a pointer to the first array element. The pointer could then be set to the next array element, each time the loop is executed, simply by adding the element size. This won't cause any problems since Turbo only allows arrays that will completely fit into one memory segment.

With this method, all we have to do is add the element size to the offset portion of the pointer each time through the loop. But Pascal cannot handle pointer arithmetic. Or can it?

Actually it can, with the help of a little trick that allows a program to access the segment address or the offset address within a pointer. Since we know the structure of a pointer in Turbo Pascal, we can recreate it as follows:

```
PtrRec = record                    { recreates structure of a pointer }
           Ofs,                                   { offset address }
           Seg  : WORD;                          { segment address }
         end;
```

This expression makes the offset address available in the form of the component Ofs, which is a normal numerical value that can be manipulated in any of the usual ways.

So the INC instruction is the best way to move the pointer to the next array element because it generates the shortest and fastest assembly language. The SizeOf operator, which can be used with the INC instruction, returns the size of an array element. Putting all of these ideas together into a program would look something like our next example.

```
program PtrMath;
{== type and constant declarations ========================================}
type Infos   = record                                  { the array element }
                 Field1 : integer;
                 Field2 : boolean;
                 Field3 : string[5];
               end;
     InfoPtr = ^Infos;                          { pointer to an Infos record }
     PtrRec  = record                  { recreates the structure of a pointer }
                 Ofs,                                     { offset address }
                 Seg  : WORD;                            { segment address }
               end;
{== global variables =======================================================}
var RData : array [1..100] of Infos;           { the array to be processed }
    i     : integer;                                      { loop counter }
    IP    : InfoPtr;                       { pointer to the current element }
begin
    IP := @RData[1];                           { set pointer to first element }
    for i:=1 to 100 do
      begin
        IP^.Field1 := i;
        IP^.Field2 := TRUE;
        IP^.Field3 := '';

        {-- pointer moves to next element using INC ---------------------- }
        inc( PtrRec( IP ).Ofs, sizeof( Infos ) );
      end;
end.
```

The WITH statement is not used here either. This would only slow down the execution, since the IP pointer already exists and can be used as it is to address the elements.

Even though this method may seem a little obscure at first, it can help speed up program execution. This is because the assembly language that is generated more closely resembles the optimum code, which could otherwise be reached only with assembly language programming. One example of this is the unit for direct manipulation of the screen memory, which is presented in Chapter 6. Through intensive use of this type of pointer arithmetic, the execution is incredibly fast for a Pascal program.

Code pointers

Data pointers in Pascal are rather self-explanatory. But *code pointers* must be explained. You may wonder if they are even necessary. Sometimes they are, as anyone who has ever developed a larger application in Pascal would agree. Sometimes it is useful to be able to call a procedure or a function with a pointer. This often saves having to use a CASE statement to decide which procedure or function to call, based on certain information.

Standard Pascal doesn't have code pointers and these pointers weren't available in Turbo Pascal until Version 5.0. Until then there were some tricks, with INLINE, that could be used. However, with the addition of code pointers to Version 5.0 of Turbo Pascal, Turbo came another step closer to C, which has always supported the use of code pointers.

Turbo describes code pointers as *procedure variables*, even though they work with functions as well as procedures. First, the procedure or function the pointer points to must be defined. The following expression defines PrintFunc as a pointer to a function that receives a string as an argument and returns an integer to the caller:

```
type PrintFunc = function( s : string ); integer;
```

The exact specification of the parameter to be passed and the result to be returned (with functions) is very important. Code pointers in Turbo Pascal are always standardized and the options for type conversions are limited.

When a variable is declared to act as a code pointer to a function or procedure, the function or procedure type must be given. In the next expression, the variable PrintPtr is defined as a code pointer to a function of type PrintFunc:

```
var PrintPtr : PrintFunc;
```

You can then load PrintPtr, with the address of such a function, using a normal variable assignment. The function must be of type PrintFunc. Turbo Pascal keeps track of the function type and the order and names of the parameters, which must also agree with the type declaration. Turbo will only allow functions, such as the following, to be assigned to PrintPtr:

```
function LaserPrint( s : string ) : integer;
```

Unlike loading data pointers, the address operator @ doesn't have to be used. Actually, it must be avoided, because this would cause an error in compilation. The assignment would be completed with:

```
PrintPtr := LaserPrint;
```

Turbo Pascal has additional requirements for procedures and functions called with code pointers. These requirements are related to the internal conversion of these types of calls:

- The procedure/function must be type FAR, since code pointers are always type FAR. This can be done with the compiler directive {$F+} given before the procedure/function declaration. An "invalid procedure reference" message will be returned by the compiler if you attempt to assign a procedure/function address to a code pointer when the procedure/function is not type FAR.

- The procedure/function may not be declared as INLINE. Turbo Pascal doesn't create such routines as independent subroutines. Instead, it inserts the program code in the current location in the program.

- Local procedures and functions defined within a procedure or function are not allowed because they are only available locally.

If you follow all of these rules, calling procedures and functions with code pointers will not cause you any problems. The syntax for this type of call is similar to the one for the normal call using the procedure/function name. Instead of giving the name, the corresponding code pointer is given. Our last example looks like this when the call is done with the code pointer PrintPtr:

```
var result : integer;
begin
   result := PrintPtr( 'test' );
end;
```

Since code pointers aren't different from data pointers internally, they can be used like any other data type in an array or a record. They can also be passed to procedures or functions as parameters. However, you cannot define a code pointer as a standard constant. For unknown reasons, the compiler will return Error 99 (file and procedure types are not allowed here) in this case. This kind of assignment can only be performed at run-time.

The following listing shows a syntax problem encountered with code pointers when trying to determine whether a code pointer is pointing to a certain function.

```
program CPtrAddr;
type GetFnc = function : integer;
var GetPtr : GetFnc;                        { pointer to the Get function }
{$F+} function GetFour : integer;                                   {$F-}
begin   GetFour := 4 end;
 begin
   GetPtr := GetFour;                   { enter address of GetFour in GetPtr }
   writeln( GetPtr );                          { call GetFour with GetPtr }
   if @GetPtr = @GetFour then            { does GetPtr point to GetFour? }
     writeln ('GetFour active');                                   { yes }
   writeln( 'GetPtr is at address ', longint( @@GetPtr ) );
end.
```

GetFnc is declared as a code pointer to a function that requires no argument but returns a result of type Integer to the caller. GetPtr is defined as a variable of this type and loaded with the address of the GetFour function at the start of the program. This function is called using GetPtr and the result is displayed on the screen with Writeln. This shows that, by using code pointers, functions can also be called from the middle of expressions.

The actual problem is found in the next statement. An IF statement is supposed to determine whether the code pointer GetPtr is pointing to the function GetFour. Instinctively, this comparison might be formulated as follows:

```
if GetPtr = GetFour then ...
```

However, this won't work because it results in the specification of a function name within the expression that calls the function. This compares GetPtr with the result of GetFour, which would lead to a compiler error since a code pointer is not compatible with an integer value.

In order to do this type of comparison, Turbo Pascal uses a special syntax where operands are preceded by the address operator @. This tells Turbo Pascal that you want to compare contents of the code pointer GetPtr with the address of GetFour.

But this leads to further difficulties, since the expression @GetPtr would normally give you the address of the variable GetPtr. So, Turbo specifies that the address of the code pointer will be given only if preceded by a double "@", as in the last line of the previous example.

Since special cases such as this may be rare, we will also look at a more common example of the use of code pointers: communication with device drivers. In professional applications, code pointers are often used for this purpose.

This is one way of isolating procedures and functions from the special characteristics of different devices. The following example program defines the structure ProcFuncs, which contains four code pointers. These communicate with the routines that are used to open and close the device and to handle input/output through the device. The variable CallPFs is defined as a global structure containing the pointers to these routines. It is initialized in the main program with pointers to the routines MyOpen, MyClose, MyGet and MyPut, and then it is passed to the procedure CallThem.

This procedure calls the four routines using the code pointers. It represents a typical procedure used by devices that use code pointers to call other procedures and functions. As each of the four My... procedures is called you will see the results displayed on the screen.

```
program ProcPtr;
type ProcFuncs = record
                   Open : function : integer;
                   Close: procedure( Handle : integer );
                   Put  : procedure( DataType : integer; DPointer : pointer );
                   Get  : function( DataType : integer ) : pointer ;
                 end;
var CallPFs : ProcFuncs;    { global structure with pointers to procs/funcs. }
{------------------------------------------------------------------------}
{$F+} function MyOpen : integer;                                    {$F-}
begin   writeln( 'Open function has been called.');   MyOpen := 3; end;
```

```
{----------------------------------------------------------------------}
{$F+} procedure MyClose( Handle : integer );                      {$F-}
 begin
   writeln('Close procedure with Handle ', Handle, ' has been called.' );
 end;
{----------------------------------------------------------------------}
{$F+} procedure MyPut( DataType : integer; DPointer : pointer );  {$F-}
 begin
   writeln('Put procedure with DataType ', DataType, ' has been called.');
 end;
{----------------------------------------------------------------------}
{$F+} function MyGet( DataType : integer ) : pointer ;            {$F-}
 begin
   writeln( 'Get function with DataType ', DataType, ' has been called.' );
   MyGet := NIL;
 end;
{----------------------------------------------------------------------}
procedure CallThem( var PF : ProcFuncs );
var Handle : integer;                    { accepts value returned from Open }
    RetPtr : pointer;                          { value returned from Get }
begin
   Handle := PF.Open;                                  { call Open function }
   { cs:01BC C47E04       les    di,[bp+04] ;pointer to PF to ES:DI       }
   { cs:01BF 26FF1D       call   far es:[di] ;call Open with pointer in PF}
   { cs:01C2 8946FE       mov    [bp-02],ax ;funct. result in local var. }
   RetPtr := PF.Get( 1 );                               { call Get function }
   { cs:01C5 B80100       mov    ax,0001    ;load 1 as parameter in AX  }
   { cs:01C8 50           push   ax         ;and move to stack          }
   { cs:01C9 C47E04       les    di,[bp+04] ;pointer to PF to ES:DI     }
   { cs:01CC 26FF5D0C     call   far es:[di+0C] ;call Get via PF        }
   { cs:01D0 8946FA       mov    [bp-06],ax ;load function result in    }
   { cs:01D3 8956FC       mov    [bp-04],dx ;local variable             }
   PF.Put( 2, RetPtr );                               { call Put procedure }
   { cs:01D6 B80200       mov    ax,0002    ;load parameter 2 in AX and }
   { cs:01D9 50           push   ax         ;from there to the stack    }
   { cs:01DA FF76FC       push   [bp-04]    ;put contents of RetPtr on the}
   { cs:01DD FF76FA       push   [bp-06]    ;stack                      }
   { cs:01E0 C47E04       les    di,[bp+04] ;pointer to PF to ES:DI     }
   { cs:01E3 26FF5D08     call   far es:[di+08] ;call Put with PF       }
   PF.Close( Handle );                              { call Close procedure }
   { cs:01E7 FF76FE       push   [bp-02]    ;put Handle on the stack    }
   { cs:01EA C47E04       les    di,[bp+04] ;pointer to PF to ES:DI     }
   { cs:01ED 26FF5D04     call   es:far [di+04] ;call Close with PF     }
end;
begin
   writeln;
   with CallPFs do                   { initialize structure CallPFs - this }
     begin                           { contains the pointers to the        }
       Open := MyOpen;               { procedures and functions            }
       { cs:020E B81A00   mov    ax,001A           ;store offset and   }
       { cs:0211 BAD05F    mov    dx,5FD0           ;segment address of }
       { cs:0214 A33E00    mov    [CALLPFS.OPEN],ax   ;Open in procedure }
       { cs:0217 89164000  mov    [CALLPFS.OPEN+2],dx ;pointer in CallPFs }
```

85

```
    Close := MyClose;
       { cs:021B B87800    mov    ax,0078                ;store offset and     }
       { cs:021E BAD05F    mov    dx,5FD0                ;segment address of   }
       { cs:0221 A34200    mov    [CALLPFS.CLOSE],ax     ;Close in procedure   }
       { cs:0224 89164400  mov    [CALLPFS.CLOSE+2],dx   ;pointer in CallPFs   }
    Put   := MyPut;
       { cs:0228 B8E700    mov    ax,00E7                ;store offset and     }
       { cs:022B BAD05F    mov    dx,5FD0                ;segment address of   }
       { cs:022E A34600    mov    [CALLPFS.PUT],ax       ;Put in procedure     }
       { cs:0231 89164800  mov    [CALLPFS.PUT+2],dx     ;pointer in CallPFs   }
    Get   := MyGet;
       { cs:0235 B85601    mov    ax,0156                ;store offset and     }
       { cs:0238 BAD05F    mov    dx,5FD0                ;segment address of   }
       { cs:023B A34A00    mov    [CALLPFS.GET],ax       ;Get in procedure     }
       { cs:023E 89164C00  mov    [CALLPFS.GET+2],dx     ;pointer in CallPFs   }
  end;
  CallThem( CallPFs );          { CallThem calls the procedures and functions }
  writeln;
end.
```

The way Turbo Pascal assigns the addresses of the procedures and functions to the code pointers in the CallPFs structure is very interesting. At first we thought the offset addresses were constants and the segment addresses were loaded from the CS register. But actually Turbo Pascal loads the segment addresses as constants too. This must be because the procedures and functions referenced by the pointers could be found in other units and, therefore, in other code segments. The main program cannot get the addresses of these other segments through the CS register. It is interesting that Turbo Pascal makes the situation even more complex by loading both addresses in processor registers DX:AX in order to transfer them from there to the individual code pointers. It seems the processor would not have objected to loading the constants directly into the pointers, which would have saved two statements.

Notice how Turbo Pascal uses the pointers to call the procedures and functions from within the CallThem procedure. The parameters are passed and the results are returned as with any procedure or function. Only the way the CALL statement is used is somewhat different than the usual method. Usually the jump address is given as a constant. In this case, however, it is taken from a code pointer from the data structure which was passed as a variable parameter (and therefore as a data pointer).

Turbo starts this process by loading the pointer to this data structure in ES:DI. The individual pointers can be addressed with ES:[DI], ES:[DI+4], etc. When the CALL statement is executed, the processor gets the FAR address of each routine to be called from the location ES:[DI+x] and then transfers program control to this address.

We have seen how code pointers are very useful for calling procedures and functions for special purposes in special situations. Throughout this book we will encounter their use in several other examples.

2.6　Heap Management

The heap, which has always been important to Pascal, is a memory range that is actively used. Unlike data stored in data segments, the contents of the heap can constantly change. This allows allocation of variable and buffers "on the fly". These allocations are made only at run-time, so the heap is an important tool for working with data structures whose sizes are not known until sometime during the execution of the program. Structures such as trees or linked lists would hardly be possible without the use of the heap. In this section we will discuss how Turbo Pascal manages this important memory range.

By default, Turbo Pascal reserves the entire memory range from the end of the data segment to the end of RAM (up to a maximum of 640K) for the heap. If you want your heap to be smaller, use the menu to select Options / Compiler / Memory Sizes or the compiler directive {$M}. This allows you to specify a minimum heap size, which is useful if you know, at the time of compilation, that a certain minimum amount of memory must be available in the heap. The EXEC Loader at the DOS level will ensure that your program will be started only if this condition is met. If not, the program start is aborted with an appropriate message.

Versions 5.0/5.5 and 6.0 of Turbo manage the heap differently because Version 6.0 drops the old concept of having a fragment list. The next subsection discusses internal heap management in Versions 5.0 and 5.5, while the subsection after discusses the changes to Version 6.0.

2.6.1　Heap Management in Versions 5.0 and 5.5

Turbo Pascal uses three pointers to work with the heap: HeapOrg, HeapPtr and FreePtr. These pointers are declared within the system unit. They are also initialized here before the program is started. HeapOrg points to the start of the heap in memory during the entire program execution. HeapPtr always points to the end of the heap, so its contents will change as memory is allocated and freed. The FreePtr also changes. It points to the so-called Fragment List, which we will soon discuss.

These three pointers are manipulated by the functions Turbo Pascal uses to control the heap. These functions can be grouped into two basic types according to the actions they perform. First there are Mark and Release, which are used to increase and decrease the size of the heap as required. Then there are GetMem and FreeMem, as well as New and Dispose. As we will see in Section 2.7, New and Dispose are simply disguises for internal calls to GetMem and FreeMem. So for now we will limit our discussion to Mark and Release and their counterparts GetMem and FreeMem.

GetMem and FreeMem

Let's look at the way GetMem runs the first time it is called after the program is started. First GetMem must determine whether enough free memory exists between the end of the currently occupied heap and the effective end of the total memory range that can be used as the heap. Usually there will be plenty of memory at this point, since the program has just started and no memory has yet been allocated to the heap. But in the case of programs that require a lot of memory, there may not be enough room left for the heap. In this case, Turbo Pascal will end the program at this point with an error message.

For our purposes, let's assume that sufficient memory is available. The starting address of this memory range is assigned to the variable HeapPtr. When the program is started, this points to the start of the heap, as does HeapOrg. As soon as HeapPtr has the start address of the heap, GetMem increases its value by the number of reserved bytes. This sets HeapPtr to the end of the heap and effectively reserves the memory range between the addresses in HeapOrg and HeapPtr. After this operation, HeapPtr is *normalized*, which means that the segment portion of its address is adjusted so that the offset portion will be between 0 and 15. The same is true for the pointer that is returned to the routine that called GetMem.

Theoretically, each allocated memory range could be an entire segment with a maximum size of 64K. Through normalization, the lower limit is set to 15 bytes. Therefore, calling GetMem can allocate memory blocks with a maximum size of 65521 bytes (65536 - 15).

If additional GetMem calls follow, the contents of HeapPtr are updated each time to point to the end of the newly allocated range. This means that each new range allocated will directly follow the previous range in memory.

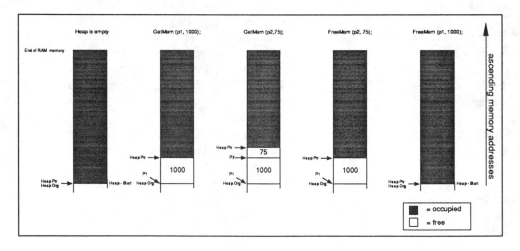

Allocating heap memory with GetMem and FreeMem

Ideally, the individual heap ranges would be freed in reverse order with FreeMem, and the entire heap memory would remain a contiguous block. The HeapPtr would be decremented by the size of the memory range to be freed, approaching the start of the heap in memory. However, this ideal situation is rarely seen in practice. Memory ranges in the middle of the heap are often freed before those at the end. This results in the creation of a useless "hole" in the heap. There must be a way to deal with these holes. Otherwise, a new hole would be created each time FreeMem is called, while GetMem would continue working from the end of the last range in the heap. Soon, GetMem would reach the physical limit of the heap and would not be able to allocate any more memory, even though many unused holes exist between the start and the end of the heap range.

Turbo Pascal solves this problem with a structure called the *Fragment List,* which contains the starting and ending addresses of each unused memory fragment. Actually, the end address is taken as the address of the first byte after the end of the memory fragment. When a range not at the end of the currently occupied heap memory is freed with FreeMem, Turbo creates an entry in the Fragment List. If a range adjacent to a currently existing fragment is freed, Turbo expands the entry for the existing fragment rather than create a new entry in the list.

If there are entries in the Fragment List, GetMem will check there first to see if there is a fragment of memory available that will suit the needs of the calling routine. Ideally, GetMem will find a fragment the exact size of that desired by the calling routine. This would fill in the hole in the heap and the corresponding entry in the fragment list would be removed. As you can imagine, this rarely happens, so GetMem must use fragments that are larger than what is actually needed. This still leaves a hole in the heap but at least it is a smaller hole. With subsequent calls of GetMem, some holes will eventually be completely filled.

Turbo Pascal puts the Fragment List at the end of the heap memory. As mentioned earlier, each entry in the list contains two pointers and therefore occupies eight bytes. Since Turbo Pascal limits the size of the list to one segment, maximum efficiency is achieved, so the list can contain a maximum of 8192 entries (65536/8). One entry is used to indicate the absence of fragmented memory, so a maximum of 8191 fragments can be listed.

The pointer FreePtr points to the start of the Fragment List. This is not a normalized pointer. It contains the base address of the 64K segment at the end of the heap memory as its segment address. Since the end of this segment represents the end of the memory reserved for the Pascal program, the segment address of FreePtr plus $1000 points to the first free byte in memory after the program. The offset portion stored in FreePtr points to the start of the Fragment List within this segment. If no fragments exist, the offset portion of the address is 0. When the first entry in the list is created, the offset address is set to 65528. Each additional entry is made by subtracting 8 bytes, so the list is built from the end of the segment toward the start.

The Fragment List must be accessed and manipulated many times through calls of GetMem and FreeMem. To accomplish this as efficiently as possible, Turbo Pascal doesn't use FAR pointers to access the Fragment List entries. Instead, the DS register is loaded with the segment address, found in FreePtr, while the list is being processed. This allows Turbo to access the entries faster and more efficiently by using NEAR pointers.

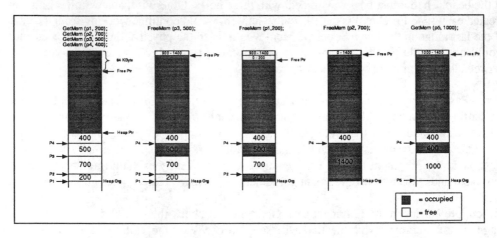

Fragmentation of the heap

There is a serious error that can occur when Turbo Pascal frees memory ranges and attempts to create a new entry in the Fragment List but doesn't have enough room. This could happen if the end of the occupied heap memory has reached the start of the Fragment List. To avoid this situation, the standard constant FreeMin in the system unit determines the size of the memory range that must be held free between the end of the occupied heap memory and the start of the Fragment List. If this limit is broken, calling GetMem will generate a run-time error.

Turbo Pascal initializes this variable with 0, so by default it will have no effect on the program. It really only makes sense to assign a different value if you anticipate that your program will heavily fragment the heap and at the same time require a lot of heap memory. For example, if you want to assure that at least 1000 entries will fit in the Fragment List, you would set FreeMin to 8000 (8 bytes per entry). This would keep 8000 bytes free between the end of the occupied heap memory and the start of the Fragment List.

The following program (HEAP5.PAS) demonstrates the use of the three pointers HeapOrg, HeapPtr and FreePtr to manage the stack and the Fragment List. Because of the changes made to Turbo Pascal 6.0, this program only operates with Turbo Pascal 5.0 or 5.5. If you attempt to compile this source code under Version 6.0, you will receive errors.

To avoid such errors, the beginning of the program contains the instruction {$ifndef VER60}. If the constant VER60 is defined (i.e., if you are compiling this program under

Version 6.0), this source code will compile only the main program and a message stating that you cannot compile this program.

HEAP5.PAS uses GetMem to allocate 5 memory blocks of 256K and then free them in such a way that the heap memory is fragmented. The progression of the program is documented on screen with the display of contents of each pointer and the entries in the Fragment List. Access to the Fragment List is accomplished with several user-defined data types modeled after the internal structure of the Fragment List:

- Type fragentry describes the structure of an entry in the Fragment List using the pointers Start and End.

- The Fragment List is represented with type fragarray as an array with 8191 elements.

- Type fragptr is defined as a pointer to this array.

By converting the non-standard pointer FreePtr to a pointer of type fragptr, the program can access the Fragment List as a normal Pascal array.

```
{****************************************************************************
*   H E A P 5 : Demo of heap management using FreeList, HeapOrg and HeapPtr *
*               for Turbo Pascal 5.0 and 5.5.                              *
**------------------------------------------------------------------------**
*   Author         : MICHAEL TISCHER                                       *
*   Developed on    : 08/01/1989                                          *
*   Last update on  : 06/11/1991                                          *
****************************************************************************}

program heap5;

uses Crt;

{$ifndef VER60}                        { Compile ONLY if not Turbo Ver.6.0 }

{-- Type declarations -----------------------------------------------------}

type hstring = string[4];              { String types for HexStr and HexPtr }
     hpstring = string[9];


     fragentry = record                          { Structure of a fragment entry }
                   Start,
                   REnd   : pointer;
                 end;
     fragarray = array [1..8191] of fragentry;           { fragment list }
     fragptr   = ^fragarray;                     { Pointer to a fragment list }

{-- Global variables ------------------------------------------------------}
```

```
var p1, p2, p3, p4, p5 : pointer;                 { Pointer to the test range }

{*****************************************************************************
*  GetFrags: Determines the entries in a fragment list                      *
**-------------------------------------------------------------------------**
*  Input    : None                                                          *
*  Output   : Number of fragments                                           *
*****************************************************************************}

function getfrags : integer;

begin
  if ( ofs( freeptr^ ) = 0 ) then                    { Offset of FreePtr = 0? }
    getfrags := 0                             { Yes -> No entries available }
  else
    getfrags := (65536 - ofs( freeptr^ )) shr 3;       { Determine entries }
end;

{*****************************************************************************
*  HexStr : Convert a number into a hex string                              *
**-------------------------------------------------------------------------**
*  Input    : HEX = Number to be converted                                  *
*  Output   : String with number in hex notation                           *
*****************************************************************************}

function HexStr( hex : word ) : hstring;

var hstr : hstring;                              { For creating the hex string }
    d,                                             { Value of a hex number }
    b    : byte;                                        { Loop counter }

begin
  hstr := '';                                         { Hex string is empty }
  for b := 1 to 4 do                        { Execute the four hex numbers }
    begin
      d := byte(hex) and 15;          { Determine values of 4 lowest bits }
      if ( d >= 10 ) then                                    { Character? }
        hstr := chr( ord('A')-10+d ) + hstr                      { Yes }
      else                                              { NO -> Number }
        hstr := chr( ord('0')+d ) + hstr;
      hex := hex shr 4;                   { Shift four hex bits to the right }
    end;
  HexStr := hstr;                               { Transfer created string }
end;

{*****************************************************************************
*  HexPtr : Display a pointer in hexadecimal notation                       *
**-------------------------------------------------------------------------**
*  Input    : P = Pointer to be displayed                                   *
*  Output   : String w/ pointer in hex notation                            *
*****************************************************************************}

function HexPtr( p : pointer ) : hpstring;
```

```
var hp : hpstring;

begin
  hp := HexStr( seg( p^ ) );                        { Segment address in hex }
  hp := hp + ':';
  hp := hp + HexStr( ofs( p^ ) );                    { Offset address in hex }
  HexPtr := hp;                                            { Return string }
end;

{**************************************************************************
 *  Wait : Prompt the user to press a key and wait for the keypress.      *
 **----------------------------------------------------------------------**
 *  Input   : None                                                        *
 **************************************************************************}

procedure wait;

var ch  : char;

begin
  write( 'Please press a key...');
  repeat until keypressed;
  ch := ReadKEy;
  if ch = #0 then                                 { Check for extended keycodes }
   ch := ReadKey;
  write( #13 );                                   { Return to beginning of line }
  ClrEol;                                                { Delete entire line }
end;

{**************************************************************************
 *  HeapStatus : Return the pointer to the end of the allocated range, as  *
 *               well as the entries in the fragment list                 *
 **----------------------------------------------------------------------**
 *  Input   : None                                                        *
 **************************************************************************}

procedure HeapStatus;

var  i,                                                  { Loop counter }
     frags : integer;                                { Number of fragments }
     fstart,                                    { Starting address of a fragment }
     fend : pointer;                             { Ending address of a fragment }

begin
  writeln( 'HeapPtr points to           ', HexPtr(HeapPtr) );
  frags := getfrags;
  writeln( 'Fragment list entries        ', frags);
  if ( frags <> 0 ) then
    for i := 1 to frags do
      begin
        fstart := fragptr(freeptr)^[i].Start;
        fend  := fragptr(freeptr)^[i].REnd;
```

```
        writeln( 'Fragment entry    ', i, '':11,
                HexPtr(fstart), ' - ', HexPtr(fend), '  (',
                (longint(seg(fend^ )) shl 4 + ofs(fend^ )) -
                (longint(seg(fstart^)) shl 4 + ofs(fstart^)), ' Byte)' );
      end;
  writeln;
end;

{*************************************************************************
 * M A I N   P R O G R A M                                              *
 *************************************************************************}

begin
  ClrScr;
  writeln( 'The heap begins at         ', HexPtr(HeapOrg) );
  writeln( 'The heap ends at           ',
           HexStr(Seg(FreePtr^)+$1000), ':0000');
  writeln( 'The Heap consists of       ',
           longint(Seg(FreePtr^)+$1000-Seg(HeapOrg^)) shl 4, ' bytes');
  HeapStatus;
  writeln( 'GetMem allocates five ranges with a total of 256 bytes.');
  wait;
  getmem( p1, 256 );
  writeln( 'Range 1                    ', HexPtr( p1 ) );
  HeapStatus;
  wait;
  getmem( p2, 256 );
  writeln( 'Range 2                    ', HexPtr( p2 ) );
  HeapStatus;
  wait;
  getmem( p3, 256 );
  writeln( 'Range 3                    ', HexPtr( p3 ) );
  HeapStatus;
  wait;
  getmem( p4, 256 );
  writeln( 'Range 4                    ', HexPtr( p4 ) );
  HeapStatus;
  wait;
  getmem( p5, 256 );
  writeln( 'Range 5                    ', HexPtr( p5 ) );
  HeapStatus;

  writeln( 'Range 4 cleared - a gap now exists between ranges 3 and 5.' );
  wait;
  freemem( p4, 256 );
  HeapStatus;
  writeln( 'Range 2 cleared - a gap now exists between ranges 1 and 3.' );
  wait;
  freemem( p2, 256 );
  HeapStatus;
  writeln( 'Range 1 cleared - Turbo merges the first two gaps..' );
  wait;
  freemem( p1, 256 );
```

```
   HeapStatus;
   writeln( 'Range 5 cleared - Turbo can now determine the end of the heap.' );
   wait;
   freemem( p5, 256 );
   HeapStatus;
   writeln( 'Range 3 cleared - heap free again.' );
   wait;
   freemem( p3, 256 );
   HeapStatus;
   wait;
   ClrScr;

{$else}                                          { Main Program for TP 6.0 }
begin
   writeln( 'Attention! This program operates only with Turbo Versions 5.0 and ' +
            '5.5.' + #13#10 + '            If you have Turbo Version ' +
            '6.0, call the HEAP6 program.' );
{$endif}
end.
```

Mark and Release

The statements Mark and Release don't work with the heap in a logical way. These statements allow the pointer HeapPtr to be directly manipulated. Mark will return the current contents of the HeapPtr to the calling routine, which tells it where to find the end of the currently occupied heap memory. This pointer, or any other pointer, can then be passed to Release, which loads the pointer into HeapPtr and deletes the Fragment List at the same time. This effectively fills in all of the holes in the heap.

As you can imagine, using Mark and Release in connection with GetMem and FreeMem can have frightening consequences. It can be quite useful, however, in situations where a large number of ranges have been allocated with GetMem. In this case, you can assume that the heap isn't fragmented. You can avoid having to free each range individually with FreeMem by using Mark to determine the contents of HeapPtr, before the first GetMem call, and freeing the allocated ranges by assigning HeapPtr its old value with Release.

Release can also be used to clear the contents of the entire heap by passing it a pointer to the start of the heap. This address is always available from the variable HeapOrg.

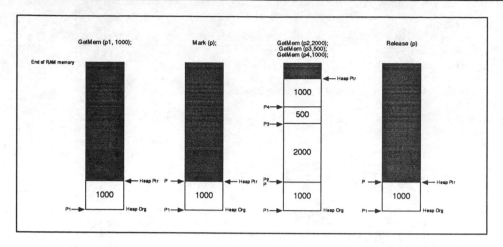

Mark and Release

Before using this somewhat drastic method, remember that not only your program but also other units use the heap and may depend upon the availability of certain allocated heap ranges. For example, the graph unit loads graphic drivers, graphics character sets and internal tables into buffers allocated on the heap. Freeing one of these memory ranges and then overwriting it would almost certainly lead to a program crash.

A new error routine for the heap

Obviously, users expect that professional applications won't suddenly send the message, "heap overflow error" in the middle of their work, which can cause data loss. Programmers must carefully guard against this possibility. Heap overflows are quite possible in the following conditions: if a program uses the heap extensively; a program is large; or if RAM structures, such as device drivers or TSR programs, are present.

To help you deal with this, Turbo Pascal allows you to create your own heap error procedure with the HeapError variable. Since HeapError is a procedure pointer, you can simply assign it the address of this routine at the start of your program.

However, this heap error routine cannot simply be any routine. It must be declared as follows:

```
function HeapError( Size : Word ) : Integer;
```

Like all functions and procedures called with pointers, HeapError must be type FAR. This can be assigned with the compiler directive {$F+}. The HeapError function is called when a memory request from GetMem cannot be fulfilled. The size of the memory range to be allocated is passed as the parameter Size. There are three numerical values that can be returned as the function result. The values have the following meanings:

0   Creates a run-time error and the program crashes.

1   The program is not aborted and the procedure that was originally called (New or GetMem) is passed the value NIL, which allows it (with the proper programming) to recognize the error.

2   Turbo tries again to allocate the requested memory range. This usually isn't successful, in which case the procedure is immediately called again.

Since the HeapError routine is just another normal Pascal function without special attributes, it can be used to notify the user of heap problems, execute automatic backup of data or list actions which may help resolve the problem. In any case, your own error handling routine will be more useful to the user than the normal cryptic error message.

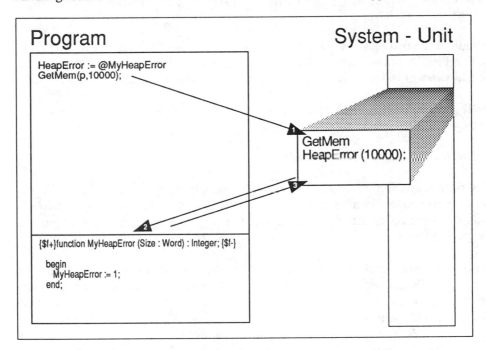

Calling a heap error routine with HeapError

2.6.2 Heap Management in Turbo Pascal 6.0

Version 6.0 still uses the NEW and GETMEM commands for heap memory access, and DISPOSE and FREEMEM for releasing heap memory. However, Version 6.0 allows free memory access without a fragment list or the FreePtr pointer. Instead, Pascal can freely use heap memory similar to memory use from a C compiler.

Every heap range contains a descriptor. This descriptor states the size of this range and points toward the next descriptor. A simple linked list is created from the different descriptors. This list can have the following structure:

```
THeapPtr = ^THeapRec;                          { Pointer to descriptor }
THeap = record                              { describes a free heap entry }
              Next : THeapPtr;              { pointer to next descriptor }
              case integer of                             { length }
               0 : ( Len : pointer );
               1 : ( Bytes : word; Para : word);
              end;
```

The length of the free range, which dictates the size of the descriptor, can be interpreted in two ways: First, as a normalized pointer, which tells us the number of bytes in the range. Second, as two words, from which we can determine the number of paragraphs in the range.

If the HPtr variable is a pointer drawn from a descriptor of type THeapRec, the following equation gives us the length of the free range:

```
longint(HPtr^.Para) * 16 + HPtr^.Byte
```

Version 6.0's heap descriptors operate in multiples of eight. Versions 5.0 and 5.5 of Turbo Pascal allowed you to allocate heaps of one, two and five bytes, but this is not possible in Version 6.0 because of the multiples of eight. Every free memory range requires a descriptor, especially in object-oriented systems like Turbo Vision.

Object-oriented user interfaces require frequent heap access and memory re-allocation for different tasks. These interfaces need the heap and memory for opening, closing and moving windows, and for displaying dialog boxes and file lists on the screen. The smaller the smallest allocatable memory range, the lower the odds of quickly allocating and freeing that memory range. Version 6.0 offers heap allocation in multiples of eight because internal memory access can easily round off numbers to this multiple. Thus, if you want to allocate 12 bytes for a program, the system allocates 16 bytes.

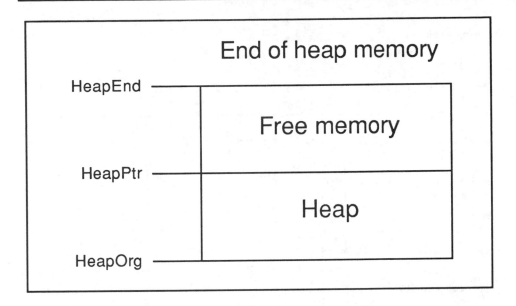

Heap management in Version 6.0 using the HeapOrg, FreeList, HeapPtr and HeapEnd pointers

At maximum, when 7 bytes per heap block are reserved, a 12-byte allocation of all free memory blocks consists of 16 bytes. This refers to all memory blocks from 9 to 16 bytes in length.

If you want to chain groups of free memory blocks, as might occur in a program, the predefined FreeList variable from the SYSTEM unit shows the first link in this chain. The end of the chain is indicated when the pointer in one of the block descriptors contains the same value as the contents of the predefined HeapPtr pointer. This pointer specifies the top boundary of the previously allocated heap memory. If the FreeList pointer points to HeapPtr, then no free block exists below HeapPtr. This means that a memory block must be allocated between HeapPtr and the end of the heap. The heap's end is indicated by the HeapEnd pointer, from which FreePtr gets information about the end of heap.

Here's the HEAP6.PAS program, which demonstrates direct access to the heap in Version 6.0.

```
{*****************************************************************
*  H E A P 6 : Demo of heap management using FreeList, HeapOrg & HeapPtr  *
*              for Turbo Pascal Version 6.0.                     *
**-------------------------------------------------------------**
*  Author         : MICHAEL TISCHER                             *
*  Developed on   :  08/01/1989                                 *
*  Last update on :  06/10/1991                                 *
*****************************************************************}
```

```
program heap6;

uses Crt;

{$ifdef VER60}                          { Compile only if Turbo Ver.6.0 }

{-- Type declarations -------------------------------------------------}

type hstring = string[4];          { String types for HexStr and HexPtr }
     hpstring = string[9];

     THeapPtr = ^THeapRec;                        { Pointer to descriptor }
     THeapRec = record                        { Describes a free heap entry }
                 Next : THeapPtr;          { Pointer to next descriptor }
                 case integer of                            { Length }
                 0 : ( Len : pointer );
                 1 : ( Bytes : word; Para : word );
               end;

{-- Global variables --------------------------------------------------}

var p1, p2, p3, p4, p5 : pointer;                   { Pointer to test range }

{***********************************************************************
*  GetFrags: Determines the number of free blocks below the end of heap  *
**---------------------------------------------------------------------**
*  Input    : None                                                     *
*  Output   : Number of fragments                                      *
***********************************************************************}

function getfrags : integer;

var numfree : integer;                            { Number of free blocks }
    curptr  : THeapPtr;                    { Pointer to current descriptor }

begin
  numfree := 0;                                { Still no free range found }
  curptr := FreeList;                      { Pointer to first free block }

  while ( curptr <> HeapPtr ) do          { End of allocated heap reached? }
    begin                                   { NO -> Still some free blocks }
      inc( numfree );
      curptr := curptr^.next;                { Pointer to next free block }
    end;

  getfrags := numfree;                 { Execute all blocks, return number }
end;

{***********************************************************************
*  HexStr : Convert a number into a hex string                         *
**---------------------------------------------------------------------**
*  Input    : HEX = Number to be converted                             *
```

```
*  Output  : String with number in hex notation                        *
***********************************************************************}

function HexStr( hex : word ) : hstring;

var hstr : hstring;                          { For creating the hex string }
    d,                                           { Value of a hex number }
    b    : byte;                                      { loop counter }

begin
  hstr := '';                                    { Hex string is empty }
  for b := 1 to 4 do                       { Execute the four hex numbers }
    begin
      d := byte(hex) and 15;           { Determine values of 4 lowest bits }
      if ( d >= 10 ) then                                { Character? }
        hstr := chr( ord('A')-10+d ) + hstr                    { YES }
      else                                              { NO -> Number }
        hstr := chr( ord('0')+d ) + hstr;
      hex := hex shr 4;                  { Shift four hex bits to the right }
    end;
  HexStr := hstr;                           { Transfer created string }
end;

{*********************************************************************
*  HexPtr : Display a pointer in hexadecimal notation                  *
**-----------------------------------------------------------------**
*  Input   : P = Pointer to be displayed                               *
*  Output  : String w/ pointer in hex notation                        *
***********************************************************************}

function HexPtr( p : pointer ) : hpstring;

var hp : hpstring;

begin
  hp := HexStr( seg( p^ ) );                   { Segment address in hex }
  hp := hp + ':';
  hp := hp + HexStr( ofs( p^ ) );              { Offset address in hex }
  HexPtr := hp;                                      { Return string }
end;

{*********************************************************************
*  Wait : Prompt the user to press a key and wait for the keypress.    *
**-----------------------------------------------------------------**
*  Input   : None                                                      *
***********************************************************************}

procedure wait;

var ch  : char;

begin
  write( 'Please press a key...');
```

```
  repeat until keypressed;
  ch := ReadKEy;
  if ch = #0 then                         { Check for extended keycodes }
   ch := ReadKey;
  write( #13 );                           { Return to beginning of line }
  ClrEol;                                     { Delete entire line }
end;


{***********************************************************************
* HeapStatus : Return the pointer to the end of the allocated range, as *
*              well as the entries in the fragment list                 *
**-------------------------------------------------------------------**
* Input    : None                                                       *
***********************************************************************}

procedure HeapStatus;

var i,                                              { Loop counter }
    frags : integer;                           { Number of free blocks }
    curptr : THeapPtr;                     { Pointer to current descriptor }

begin
  writeln( 'HeapPtr points to        ', HexPtr(HeapPtr) );
  frags := getfrags;
  writeln( 'Free blocks:            ', frags );
  curptr := FreeList;                       { Pointer to first free block }
  for i := 1 to frags do
    begin
      writeln( 'Fragment entry ', i, ' ':11,
               HexPtr(curptr), ' - ',
               HexStr( seg(curptr^)+curptr^.Para ), ':',
               HexStr( ofs(curptr^)+curptr^.Bytes ), '  (',
               longint( curptr^.Para * 16 ) + curptr^.Bytes,
               ' bytes)' );
      curptr := curptr^.next;               { Pointer to next free block }
    end;
  writeln;
end;


{***********************************************************************
* M A I N   P R O G R A M                                               *
***********************************************************************}

begin
  ClrScr;
  writeln( 'The heap begins at       ', HexPtr(HeapOrg) );
  writeln( 'The heap ends at         ', HexPtr( HeapEnd ) );
  writeln( 'The heap consists of     ',
           longint( ( seg(HeapEnd^)-seg(HeapOrg^) ) * 16 ) +
           ofs(HeapEnd^)-ofs(HeapOrg^) );
  HeapStatus;
  writeln( 'GetMem allocates five ranges with a total of 256 bytes.');
  wait;
```

```
    getmem( p1, 256 );
    writeln( 'Range 1                  ', HexPtr( p1 ) );
    HeapStatus;
    wait;
    getmem( p2, 256 );
    writeln( 'Range 2                  ', HexPtr( p2 ) );
    HeapStatus;
    wait;
    getmem( p3, 256 );
    writeln( 'Range 3                  ', HexPtr( p3 ) );
    HeapStatus;
    wait;
    getmem( p4, 256 );
    writeln( 'Range 4                  ', HexPtr( p4 ) );
    HeapStatus;
    wait;
    getmem( p5, 256 );
    writeln( 'Range 5                  ', HexPtr( p5 ) );
    HeapStatus;

    writeln( 'Range 4 cleared - a gap now exists between ranges 3 and 5.' );
    wait;
    freemem( p4, 256 );
    HeapStatus;
    writeln( 'Range 2 cleared - a gap now exists between ranges 1 and 3.' );
    wait;
    freemem( p2, 256 );
    HeapStatus;
    writeln( 'Range 1 cleared - Turbo merges the first two gaps.');
    wait;
    freemem( p1, 256 );
    HeapStatus;
    writeln( 'Range 5 cleared - Turbo can now determine the end of the heap.' );
    wait;
    freemem( p5, 256 );
    HeapStatus;
    writeln( 'Range 3 cleared - heap free again.' );
    wait;
    freemem( p3, 256 );
    HeapStatus;
    wait;
    ClrScr;

{$else}                             { Main program for TP 5.0 and TP 5.5 }
begin
  writeln( 'Attention! This program operates only with Turbo Version' +
           ' 6.0.    ' + #13#10 + '          Run the HEAP5 program,' +
           'if you have Turbo Pascal 5.0 or 5.5.' );
{$endif}
end.
```

Expanding HeapError

The HeapError function is called in Version 6.0 if memory specified for a heap allocation cannot be found. This function makes no changes, but it is called any time the heap manager must extend beyond the heap range, or when no free or sufficient memory blocks can be found. In this case, the HeapError function is called with a value of 0 in the Size parameter.

The heap manager doesn't read this call as a call for help, but as an indication that the heap has been overstepped. The error code from HeapError is ignored, and the program execution continues as usual.

Executable program systems (e.g., Turbo Vision) can access HeapError for allocating a buffer using the memory between the end of allocated heaps (HeapPtr) and the end of the heaps proper (HeapEnd). This buffer usually contains information which is more important to program execution than to memory storage.

The window buffers used by the Turbo Editor to determine window contents and background windowing are a good example. As soon as the user moves a window to the foreground, the window's contents are restored without completely redrawing the window. One buffer has top priority as the buffer accessed most frequently by the Editor. This buffer is located in the previously unused heap range between HeapPtr and HeapEnd.

However, this buffer can be easily overwritten when the allocated heap section and the HeapPtr variable are reset by a NEW or GETMEM. A program could include an alternate buffer, accessed if the HeapError function is called with a value of zero.

2.7   The System Unit

The *system unit* isn't simply any unit to Turbo Pascal. Its function is quite special, which you might assume since it is automatically linked without any specific USES statement. As we will see by the way it is used, the system unit is more than a collection of procedures and functions that are available for usc by other programs or units.

The system unit seems to have its own intelligence. For example, it can apply the same function to two different data types and generate different program code, depending on the data type. In this sense, Turbo Pascal, under Versions 4.0 and 5.0, is *object-oriented*, which means that the compiler considers the type of each argument that is passed to a procedure or function.

It's also interesting that a number of functions from the system unit don't generate subroutine calls at the assembly language level. Instead, Turbo Pascal converts the call into a sequence of assembly language instructions that handle the task without making a call to a subroutine. This is very similar to INLINE procedures, which enable a programmer to execute a procedure or function in the program code without using a subroutine call.

But that's not all. The actual code that is inserted depends upon the type or even the value of the argument that is passed, assuming this is known at the time the program is compiled. In this sense, the system unit is really less a "unit" and more a part of the compiler.

The following table lists the functions, procedures and "variable references", from the system unit that Turbo Pascal converts directly to a sequence of assembly language instructions:

Abs	DSeg	Length	Pred	SSeg
Addr	Exit	Odd	Ptr	Succ
Chr	Hi	Ofs	Seg	
CSeg	Inc	Ord	SizeOf	
Dec	Lo	Pi	SPtr	

Each function and the series of assembly language instructions to which it is converted will be discussed in the following sections. Each function is described in the context of different calls, various arguments and assignment of the function results to variables. Variables are not initialized when they are passed to functions as arguments. So, these examples wouldn't make sense in the context of a "real" program. We hope this will not confuse you, since these examples are presented for demonstration purposes only.

Abs

The Abs function returns the absolute value of the argument passed to it. The argument must be an Integer type (Byte, ShortInt, Integer, Word, LongInt) or a floating point. If Turbo Pascal already knows the value of the argument at the time of compilation, then the value is a constant and the absolute value can be determined and assigned to the proper variable(s), during the compilation, with MOV instructions. Turbo Pascal also catches range overflows at this time. The following example shows what happens when the absolute value 300 is assigned to a variable of type Byte. Turbo reacts by aborting the compilation and generating an error message.

If the result of the function can only be determined during the program execution, Turbo Pascal generates the code needed to do this and then checks to see if the result is positive or negative. If it is negative, the assembly language instruction NEG is used to change it to a positive number. This happens directly in the program code only with integer expressions. The absolute value of floating point expressions must be calculated with a subroutine call, since it is too complex and too long to insert directly into the program code.

```
{ C_ABS: Sample program to demonstrate assembly language generated by    }
{        Turbo Pascal when the ABS function is called                    }
program C_ABS;
var r : real;
    l : longint;
    i : integer;
    b : byte;
begin
   i := Abs( i * 4 );
   { cs:0008 A14800      mov    ax,[I]     ;load I to AX                  }
   { cs:000B B90200      mov    cx,0002    ;load counter with 2          }
   { cs:000E D3E0        shl    ax,cl      ;AX := AX * 4                  }
   { cs:0010 09C0        or     ax,ax      ;append AX to itself          }
   { cs:0012 7902        jns    0016       ;AX < 0 ?       NO    DDDDD?   }
   { cs:0014 F7D8        neg    ax         ;yes, change sign        3     }
   { cs:0016 A24A00      mov    [I],ax     ;store result      <DDDDDDDY   }
   b := Abs( -5 );
   { cs:0019 C6064A0005  mov    byte ptr [B],05 ;constant!                }
   i := Abs( 32767 );
   { cs:001E C7064800FF7F mov    word ptr [I],7FFF ;ditto                 }
   l := Abs( -1000000 );
   { cs:0024 C70644004042 mov    word ptr [L],4240      ;load low Word    }
   { cs:002A C70646000F00 mov    word ptr [L+2],000F    ;load high Word   }
   r := Abs( PI * 2.0 );
   { cs:0030 C7063E008321 mov    word ptr [R],2183    ;load a 6 byte real }
   { cs:0036 C7064000A2DA mov    word ptr [0040],DAA2 ;constant           }
   { cs:003C C70642000F49 mov    word ptr [0042],490F                     }
  {$ifdef Error }    b := Abs( 3.0 );              { error: Type mismatch }
   b := Abs( 300 );                     { error: Constant out of Range    }
   i := Abs( 322721 );                  { error: Constant out of Range    }
  {$endif}
end.
```

Addr, @-Operator

The Addr function, which is an analog of the @-operator, returns the address of a variable, a standard constant or a procedure/function. Regardless of the argument type, the compiler loads the address in the DX:AX register pair as a FAR pointer. From there, it assigns it to a variable or puts it on the stack if it is to be passed as a parameter to a procedure or function. It is less effective to use this method to assign addresses to variables when the compiler knows the address of the variable prior to compilation. This applies to global variables and absolute variables. The DX:AX register pair can be avoided and the segment and offset addresses can be loaded directly to the assigned variable.

When declaring absolute variables or variables whose addresses are supposed to be obtained through pointers, it is strange that Turbo Pascal also loads the segment address in ES and the offset address in DI or SI. Perhaps this happens because, during future access to the variable, the segment and offset addresses will be needed in these registers anyway.

The code generated also makes a distinction between global variables, stored in the data segment and local variables, stored temporarily on the stack. With global variables, the compiler uses the DS register for the segment address of the variable. The SS register is used for local variables.

The program code will also show that a statement like:

```
p := Addr( p^ );
```

is unusual because it assigns P its own contents. The contents of P are loaded in the register pair DX:AX (by way of DI and ES) and from there to the pointer P. Although this code doesn't have any effect, it is too difficult to eliminate it.

```
{ C_ADDR: Sample program to demonstrate assembly language generated by    }
{         Turbo Pascal when the ADDR function is called                   }
program C_ADDR;
type buf = array[ 1..100 ] of BYTE;
     bp  = ^buf;
var bufptr    : bp;
    globbuf   : buf;
    p         : pointer;
    bios_flag : byte absolute $0040:$0049;
procedure test;
var locbuf : buf;
begin   bufptr := Addr( locbuf );
   { cs:000E 8D469C      lea     ax,[bp-64]     ;offset relative to BP     }
   { cs:0011 8CD2        mov     dx,ss          ;variable is on the stack  }
   { cs:0013 A33E00      mov     [BUFPTR],ax    ;put offset and segment    }
   { cs:0016 89164000    mov     [PUFPTR+2,dx   ;addresses in BUFPTR       }
   bufptr := Addr(globbuf[46]);
   { cs:001A B86F00      mov     ax,offset globbuf + 46; offset address    }
```

```
{ cs:001D 8CDA          mov     dx,ds           ;var. is in data segment  }
{ cs:001F A33E00        mov     [BUFPTR],ax     ;store FAR pointer in      }
{ cs:0022 89164000      mov     [BUFPTR+2],dx   ;BUFPTR                    }
p := Addr( bios_flag );
{ cs:0026 BE4000        mov     si,0040         ;segment address to SI     }
{ cs:0029 8EC6          mov     es,si           ;and store in ES (???)     }
{ cs:002B B84900        mov     ax,0049         ;offset address to AX      }
{ cs:002E 8CC2          mov     dx,es           ;segment address to DX     }
{ cs:0030 A3A600        mov     [P],ax          ;store DX:AX in P          }
{ cs:0033 8916A800      mov     [P+2],dx                                   }
p := addr( bufptr^ );
{ cs:0037 C43E3E00      les     di,[BUFPTR]     ;load ES:DI in BUFPTR      }
{ cs:003B 89F8          mov     ax,di           ;offset address to AX      }
{ cs:003D 8CC2          mov     dx,es           ;segment address to DX     }
{ cs:003F A3A600        mov     [P],ax          ;store together in P       }
{ cs:0042 8916A800      mov     [P+2],dx                                   }
p := addr( p^ );
{ cs:0037 C43E3E00      les     di,[P]          ;contents from P to ES:DI  }
{ cs:003B 89F8          mov     axdi            ;offset address to AX      }
{ cs:003D 8CC2          mov     dx,es           ;segment address to DX     }
{ cs:003F A3A600        mov     [P],ax          ;store all in P next to    }
{ cs:0042 8916A800      mov     [P+2],dx        ;the old                   }

end;

begin
   test;
end.
```

Chr

C programmers working with Pascal for the first time often feel uncomfortable with the distinction between CHAR and INTEGER variable types. However, this doesn't exist in C. Since CHAR and BYTE types are both stored in a byte, why shouldn't it be possible to make direct assignments? Technically, of course, this is possible. But this goes against the philosophy of the Pascal language, which doesn't allow different types to be mixed.

There are a few loopholes that enable you to avoid this limitation. One of these is the Chr function, which can be used to convert the result of an Integer expression to type Char. The following program demonstrates that this really doesn't require any miraculous transformation. The Chr function is used to assign the ASCII character, with code 12, to a Char variable. Since "12" is a constant expression that Turbo Pascal already knows at the time of compilation, the Char variable is simply loaded with the ASCII code of the character. There isn't a faster, more efficient way to do this.

```
{ C_CHR: Sample program to demonstrate assembly language generated by    }
{         Turbo Pascal when the CHR function is called                   }
program C_CHR;
var c : char;
begin
   c := chr( 12 );
   { cs:0008 C6063E000C      mov     byte ptr [C],0C ;constants!         }
end.
```

CSeg, DSeg, SSeg, SPtr

The instructions CSeg, DSeg, SSeg and SPtr give a Turbo Pascal program the option of reading the contents of the CS, DS, SS and SP registers at any time. In this way, the segment address of the main program or a unit, the segment address of the variable segment and the segment address of the stack can be easily determined.

However, the following listing will show that Turbo Pascal does not always generate the optimal code to do this. Even though the processor has nothing against transferring a segment register directly to a memory location (and therefore to a variable), Pascal always takes a detour through the AX register. The desired register is first loaded in AX and from there to the given variable.

This method can only be explained in terms of distinguishing variable assignments and evaluating expressions. Turbo Pascal considers these as two completely different operations:

• Evaluating an expression.

• Assigning the result to a variable or passing the result to a procedure/function.

Turbo Pascal follows this distinction. When an expression is evaluated, the result is always placed in AL, AX or the register pair DX:AX, regardless of type. Then the assignment of this value to a variable follows. The assembly language instruction MOV loads the result from the processor register to the given variable.

```
{ C_SEGS: Sample program to demonstrate the assembly language generated by }
{          Turbo Pascal when the variables CSEG, DSEG, SSEG and SPTR are    }
{          accessed                                                         }
program C_SEGS;
var w : WORD;
begin   w := CSeg;
   { cs:0008 8CC8         mov     ax,cs    ;load DS in AX                    }
   { cs:000A A33E00       mov     [W],ax   ;and from there to the var. W    }
   w := DSeg;
   { cs:000D 8CD8         mov     ax,ds    ;load DX in AX                    }
   { cs:000F A33E00       mov     [W],ax   ;and from there to the var. W    }
   w := SSeg;
   { cs:0012 8CD0         mov     ax,ss    ;load SS in AX                    }
```

109

```
   { cs:0014 A33E00         mov    [W],ax    ;and from there to the var. W  }
   w := SPtr;
   { cs:0017 89E0           mov    ax,sp     ;load SP in AX                 }
   { cs:0019 A33E00         mov    [W],ax    ;and from there to the var. W  }
end.
```

Dec, Inc

The instructions Inc and Dec also do not generate procedure calls. They are converted to individual instructions and, in some instances, just one instruction. This makes them much faster than variable assignments such as:

```
x := x + 1;
```

To evaluate such an expression, Turbo Pascal loads the contents of variable X into a processor register, where it is incremented, and then restores the register contents in the variable.

In this case, Turbo Pascal doesn't take a detour through one of the processor registers. Instead, Turbo takes advantage of the processor instructions of the same name, INC and DEC. These instructions primarily exist to increment and decrement memory locations and processor registers. Turbo Pascal uses them whenever it needs to increment or decrement a variable by 1, when the variable is represented internally as a Byte or a Word. Larger types, such as LongInt, can only be changed with a combination of ADD and ADC instructions. Turbo also uses these instructions when a variable must be incremented or decremented by a value greater than 1.

```
{ C_INCDEC: Sample program to demonstrate assembly language generated by  }
{           Turbo Pascal when the functions INC and DEC are called        }
program C_INCDEC;
var  b : byte;
     i : integer;
     w : word;
     l : longint;
begin
  inc( b );
  { cs:0008 FE063E00        inc    byte ptr [B]  ;increment B              }
  inc( i );
  { cs:000C FF064000        inc    word ptr [I]  ;increment I              }
  inc( w, 5 * 4 );
  { cs:0010 8306420014      add    word ptr [W],0014 ;add to constant      }
  inc( l );
  { cs:0015 8306440001      add    word ptr [L],0001    ;increment low word }
  { cs:001A 8316460000      adc    word ptr [L+2],0000 ;allow for carry-over}
  dec( b );
  { cs:002A FE0E3E00        dec    byte ptr [B]  ;decrement B              }
  dec( i );
  { cs:000C FF064000        dec    word ptr [I]  ;decrement I              }
```

```
     dec( w, 5 * 4 );
     { cs:0032 832E420014     sub     word ptr [W],0014 ;subtract constant    }
     dec( l );
     { cs:0037 832E440001     sub     word ptr [L],0001  ;decrement low Word  }
     { cs:003C 831E460000     sub     word ptr [L+2],0000;compute bit         }
  end.
```

Exit

The Exit statement is used to leave a procedure or function before it is completed or to end
the main program. It is always converted to a jump to the end of the procedure/function or
main program.

```
{ C_EXIT: Sample program to demonstrate assembly language generated by      }
{         Turbo Pascal when the EXIT procedure is called                    }
program C_EXIT;
begin
   exit;
   { cs:001E EB17             jmp     end        ;jump to program end        }
   writeln( 'Unexecutable statement' );
   {                                  end label near                         }
end.
```

Hi, Lo

Turbo Pascal allows the programmer to determine the contents of the high or low byte of a
Word or Integer operand. As we will see in the following listing, these functions can also
be used on the low Word of a LongInt. Access to the high Word isn't possible with this
method.

Turbo Pascal assigns the result of a high/low call to a variable with two MOV instructions.
In this case, however, this does not represent a detour, since the 8086/8088 does not allow
you to load the contents of one memory location directly to another. A processor register
must always be used in between.

```
{ C_HILO: Sample program to demonstrate assembly language generated by      }
{         Turbo Pascal when the functions Hi and Lo are called              }
program C_HILO;
var  w : word;
     l : longint;
     b : byte;
begin   b := hi( $1234 );
     {   cs:0008 C606440012    mov     byte ptr [B],12 ;constant!            }
     b := hi( w );
     {   cs:000D A03F00         mov     al,byte ptr [W+1] ;load high byte of W }
     {   cs:0010 A24400         mov     [B],al           ;and store in B       }
     b := hi( l );
     {   cs:0013 A04100         mov     al,byte ptr [L+1] ;load high byte from }
```

```
  {                                               ;low Word of L        }
  {   cs:0016 A24400          mov      [B],al     ;and store in B       }
  b := lo( $1234 );
  {   cs:0019 C606440034      mov      byte ptr [B],34  ;constant!      }
  b := lo( w );
  {   cs:000D A03F00          mov      al,byte ptr [W]  ;load low byte of W  }
  {   cs:0010 A24400          mov      [B],al     ;and store in B       }
  b := lo( l );
  {   cs:0013 A04100          mov      al,byte ptr [L]  ;load low byte from  }
  {                                               ;low Word of L        }
  {   cs:0016 A24400          mov      [B],al     ;and store in B       }
  end.
```

Length

The Length function can be used to determine the length of a string. As opposed to other languages, such as C, Turbo Pascal can deliver this information rather easily because the first byte of a string (with Index 0) always contains the length. Because of this, an expression such as:

```
  l := s[0];
```

won't be faster than the Length function because both methods merely return the first byte of the string.

When declaring a string constant, Turbo Pascal doesn't store it as a standard constant in the data segment. Instead, the length of the string is instantly returned. In so doing, it is also interesting to note that the Length function doesn't temporarily store the result in a processor register. The length of the string is written directly to the desired variable. This is probably because a statement like:

```
  b := Length( 'Test' );
```

is identical to:

```
  b := 4;
```

for Turbo Pascal, and a processor register isn't required in order to execute the second statement.

```
  { C_LENGTH: Sample program to demonstrate assembly language generated by  }
  {         Turbo Pascal when the LENGTH function is called                 }
  program C_LENGTH;
  var i : integer;
      s : string;
  begin   i := length( 'String' );
     { cs:0008 C7063E000600    mov      word ptr [I],0006 ;constant!        }
```

```
    i := length( s );
    { cs:000E A04000          mov     al,[S]      ;load length from first     }
    {                                             ;string byte to AL          }
    { cs:0011 30E4             xor     ah,ah       ;set high byte to 0         }
    { cs:0013 A33E00           mov     [I],ax      ;and store in I             }
end.
```

Odd

The Odd function is well named. It is used with a Boolean result to tell the calling routine whether the parameter passed (which must be an integer type) is even or odd. The Odd function gets the lowest bit of the operand which determines whether the number is even or odd.

Turbo Pascal checks the contents of this bit by loading the lowest byte of the operand in the AL register. Then all bits in this register are pushed one bit position to the right with the SHR instruction. This moves the lowest bit to the Carry flag, and its value can then be determined with the JB instruction (which jumps if the Carry flag is set). If the bit contains 1, the Odd function returns the value 1 as a result. This is interpreted as TRUE when used with a Boolean type.

If the result of an expression passed to Odd can be evaluated before compiling, Turbo Pascal can return the result as TRUE or FALSE. This avoids having to interpret the expression again at run-time.

```
{ C_ODD: Sample program to demonstrate assembly language generated by         }
{        Turbo Pascal when the ODD function is called                         }
program C_ODD;
var  l : longint;
     i : integer;
     b : byte;
     bo: boolean;
begin   bo := odd( l );
    { cs:0008 A03E00          mov     al,byte ptr [L] ;load low byte from low  }
    {                                                 ;word of L into AL       }
    { cs:000B D0E8            shr     al,1       ;one bit position to the right }
    { cs:000D 7204            jb      0013       ;Carry flag set? YES          }
    { cs:000F B000            mov     al,00      ;NO, even number, load FALSE  }
    { cs:0011 EB02      ZDDD  jmp     0015       ;                             }
    { cs:0013 B001      3     mov     al,01      ;YES, odd number, load TRUE   }
    { cs:0015 A2450     @DD>  mov     [BO],al    ;store result in BO           }
    bo := odd( i );
    { cs:0018 A04200          mov     al,byte ptr [I] ;low byte of I into AL   }
    { cs:001B D0E8            shr     al,1       ;one bit position to the right }
    { cs:001D 7204            jb      0023       ;Carry flag set? YES          }
    { cs:001F B000            mov     al,00      ;NO, even number, load FALSE  }
    { cs:0021 EB02      ZDDD  jmp     0025       ;                             }
    { cs:0023 B001      3     mov     al,01      ;YES, odd number, load TRUE   }
```

```
{ cs:0025 A24500    @DD> mov   [BO],al    ;store result in BO       }
  bo := odd( b );
{ cs:0028 A04400         mov   al,[B]     ;load contents of B into AL }
{ cs:002B D0E8           shr   al,1       ;same as above             }
{ cs:002D 7204           jb    0033                                  }
{ cs:002F B000           mov   al,00                                 }
{ cs:0031 EB02      ZDDD jmp   0035                                  }
{ cs:0033 B001      3    mov   al,01                                 }
{ cs:0035 A24500    @DD> mov   [BO],al                               }
  bo := odd( 17 + 4 );
{ cs:0038 C606450001     mov   byte ptr [BO],01 ;constant!           }
end.
```

Seg, Ofs

The functions Seg and Ofs can be used to return the segment and offset address of a variable, a standard constant or a procedure/function. These two functions have a lot in common with the Addr function, which also returns the address of the operand.

Notice that when accessing absolute variables and variables referenced by a pointer, the segment and offset addresses are loaded in the register pair ES:SI or ES:DI. It's not exactly clear why this happens.

The distinction between local and global variables is also made here. With the Seg function, the SS register is used for local variables while the DS register is used for global variables. With Ofs, the offset address of a global variable is a constant that can be loaded into a register with the MOV instruction. For a local variable, it is always addressed relative to the current contents of the BP register, which will not be known at the time of compilation. Therefore, the LEA instruction must be used to calculate the offset address of the variable relative to the contents of the BP register.

```
{ C_SEGOFS: Sample program to demonstrate assembly language generated by  }
{          Turbo Pascal when the OFS and SEG functions are called         }
program C_SEGOFS;
type buf = array[ 1..100 ] of BYTE;
     bp  = ^buf;
var  w          : word;
     globvar    : integer;
     bios_flag : byte absolute $0040:$0049;
procedure test;
var locvar : integer;
begin   w := Seg( globvar );
{ cs:000E 8CD8           mov   ax,ds      ;DS to AX                  }
{ cs:0010 A33E00         mov   [W],ax     ;and from there to W       }
  w := Seg( locvar );
{ cs:0013 8CD0           mov   ax,ss      ;SS to AX                  }
{ cs:0015 A33E00         mov   [W],ax     ;and from there to W       }
  w := Seg( bios_flag );
```

```
{ cs:0018 BE4000        mov     si,0040    ;segment address of BIOS_FLAG  }
{ cs:001B 8EC6          mov     es,si      ;to ES                         }
{ cs:001D 8CC0          mov     ax,es      ;from there to AX              }
{ cs:001F A33E00        mov     [W],ax     ;and finally to W              }
{                                                                         }
{ this would also work: mov     word ptr [W],0040                         }
w := Ofs( globvar );
{ cs:0022 B84000        mov     ax,offset GLOBVAR;offset address to AX     }
{ cs:0025 A33E00        mov     [W],ax                ;and from there to W }
w := Ofs( locvar );
{ cs:0028 8D46FE        lea     ax,[bp-02] ;figure address relative to BP}
{ cs:002B A33E00        mov     [W],ax     ;and store in W                }
w := Ofs( bios_flag );
{ cs:002E BE4000        mov     si,0040    ;segment address (!) of        }
{ cs:0031 8EC6          mov     es,si      ;BIOS_FLAG to ES               }
{ cs:0033 B84900        mov     ax,0049    ;offset address to AX          }
{ cs:0036 A33E00        mov     [W],ax     ;and store in W                }
{                                                                         }
{ this would also work: mov     word ptr [W],0049                         }
end;
begin
   test;
end.
```

Ord

The Ord function returns the *ordinal value* of an argument. This can be used in connection with all ordinal types. This function is only useful when working with enumerated types and for getting the ASCII code of a Char operand, since the ordinal value of an Integer type is the same as its numerical value.

When using Ord with enumerated types, Turbo Pascal finds that the individual members of an enumerated type are internally managed as successive integer values. So only these integer values need to be returned.

This is similar to what happens with Char types, which are internally represented by the ASCII code of the character. In this case, Turbo Pascal also simply returns the contents of the Char. With Char constants, the ASCII code of the given character is returned.

```
{ C_ORD: Sample program to demonstrate assembly language generated by    }
{        Turbo Pascal when the ORD function is called                    }
program C_ORD;
type Colors = (RED, YELLOW, BLUE);
var  Color    : Colors;
     i        : integer;
     l        : longint;
begin   i := Ord( Color );
{ cs:0008 A03E00        mov     al,[COLOR]  ;get contents of Color         }
{ cs:000B 98            cbw                 ;convert to Integer            }
```

```
    { cs:000C A34000         mov    [I],ax       ;and store in I          }
  i := Ord( RED );
    { cs:000F 31C0           xor    ax,ax        ;internal code for ROT is 0 }
    { cs:0011 A34000         mov    [I],ax       ;store code in I         }
  i := Ord( YELLOW );
    { cs:0014 C70640000100   mov    word ptr [I],0001 ;constant!          }
  i := Ord( BLUE );
    { cs:001A C70640000200   mov    word ptr [I],0002 ;constant!          }
  i := Ord( 'A' );
    { cs:0020 C70640004100   mov    word ptr [I],0041 ;ASCII code for A   }
  i := Ord( l );
    { cs:0026 A14200         mov    ax,[L]       ;load low word of L      }
    { cs:0029 A34000         mov    [I],ax       ;and store as Ord result }
end.
```

PI

From the compiler's point of view, PI is simply a predefined constant in the system unit. Anywhere that PI appears within a listing, Turbo Pascal uses this constant value. The following program shows how this happens.

PI is assigned to a Real number, and Turbo Pascal loads PI as a six byte Real constant into the given variable. This process can't be performed any faster with any other method.

```
  { C_PI: Sample program to demonstrate assembly language generated by Turbo }
  {       Pascal when the constant PI is accessed                            }
  program C_PI;
  var r : real;
  begin
    r := PI;
    { cs:0008 C7063E008221   mov    word ptr [R],2182     ;load Pi as a 6    }
    { cs:000E C7064000A2DA   mov    word ptr [R+2],DAA2   ;byte Real constant}
    { cs:0014 C70642000F49   mov    word ptr [R+4],490F                      }
  end.
```

Pred, Succ

Pred and Succ return the argument that came before (PREDecessor) or the argument that came after (SUCCessor) the argument passed to them. With Integer types, Pred and Succ are equivalent to incrementing or decrementing the argument. In Version 3.0 and lower of Turbo Pascal, these functions are used for this purpose because they are much more efficient than an expression such as:

```
  x := x + 1;
```

In Version 4.0 and up, Inc and Dec are available. These functions are faster than Pred and Succ because they generate just one assembly language instruction instead of three (when used with Bytes and Words). For LongInts, Inc and Dec generate two instructions as opposed to six for Pred and Succ.

The only good remaining application for Pred and Succ is with counter variables. With these types, the compiler knows whether the argument is a constant or an expression that can only be evaluated at run-time. With constants, Turbo Pascal automatically returns the predecessor or successor without having to re-evaluate it during program execution. In this way, range overflows can be detected during compilation, as shown in the last part of the following program.

```
{ C_PRESUC: Sample program to demonstrate assembly language generated by  }
{           Turbo Pascal when the PRED and SUCC functions are called      }
program C_PRESUC;
type Colors = (RED, YELLOW, BLUE);
var Color      : Colors;
     l         : longint;
     b         : boolean;
begin   Color := Pred( BLUE );
   { cs:0008 C6063E0001    mov    byte ptr [COLOR],01  ;constant!          }
   Color := Pred( Color );
   { cs:000D A03E00         mov    al,[COLOR]      ;load current color      }
   { cs:0010 FEC8           dec    al              ;decrement               }
   { cs:0012 A23E00         mov    [COLOR],al      ;and store again         }
   b := Pred( b );
   { cs:0015 A04400         mov    al,[B]          ;get contents of B       }
   { cs:0018 FEC8           dec    al              ;decrement               }
   { cs:001A A24400         mov    [B],al          ;and store again         }
   l := Pred( l );
   { cs:001D C4064000       les    ax,[L]          ;contents of L into ES:AX }
   { cs:0021 8CC2           mov    dx,es           ;from there to DS:AX      }
   { cs:0023 2D0100         sub    ax,0001         ;decrement low word       }
   { cs:0026 83DA00         sbb    dx,0000         ;allow for suppression    }
   { cs:0029 A34000         mov    [L],ax          ;store result             }
   { cs:002C 89164200       mov    [L+2],dx                                  }
   Color := Succ( Color );
   { cs:0030 A03E00         mov    al,[COLOR]      ;load current color       }
   { cs:0033 FEC0           inc    al              ;increment                }
   { cs:0035 A23E00         mov    [COLOR],al      ;and store again          }
   b := Succ( b );
   { cs:0038 A04400         mov    al,[B]          ;load contents of B       }
   { cs:003B FEC0           inc    al              ;increment                }
   { cs:003D A24400         mov    [B],al          ;store                    }
   l := Succ( l );
   { cs:0040 C4064000       les    ax,[L]          ;contents of L to ES:AX   }
   { cs:0044 8CC2           mov    dx,es           ;from there to DX:AX      }
   { cs:0046 050100         add    ax,0001         ;increment low word       }
   { cs:0049 83D200         adc    dx,0000         ;allow for carry          }
   { cs:004C A34000         mov    [L],ax          ;store result             }
   { cs:004F 89164200       mov    [L+2],dx                                  }
{$ifdef ERROR }  Color := Succ( BLUE );
      { Error: Constant out of Range } {$endif}
   end.
```

Ptr

The Ptr function is an interesting example of the intelligence of the Turbo Pascal compiler. It can be used to create a non-standard pointer by combining separate segment and offset addresses.

With this function, Turbo Pascal distinguishes not only between constants and variables, but between different constants. A NIL pointer (segment and offset addresses are both 0) is handled as a special case. Segment and offset addresses are normally handled as constants and loaded into the segment and offset portions of a pointer with the MOV instruction. With a NIL pointer, the XOR instruction is used to set the AX register to 0 and then the contents of AX are loaded as both components of the pointer. Although this method requires one more instruction than the usual way of loading pointers, the MOV instruction works faster with the processor registers than do the normal instructions used to access constants.

```
{ C_PTR: Sample program to demonstrate assembly language generated by Turbo }
{        Pascal when the PTR function is called                             }
program C_PTR;
var p : pointer;
begin   p := ptr( 0, 0 );
   { cs:0008 31C0            xor     ax,ax      ;set AX to 0                 }
   { cs:000A A33E00          mov     [P],ax     ;write 0 to segment and offset }
   { cs:000D A34000          mov     [P+2],ax   ;components of P             }
   p := ptr( 100, 100 );
   { cs:0010 C7063E006400    mov     word ptr [P],0064    ;constants!        }
   { cs:0016 C70640006400    mov     word ptr [0040],0064                    }
   p := ptr( $B000, $0000 );
   { cs:001C C7063E000000    mov     word ptr [P],0000    ;ditto!            }
   { cs:0022 C706400000B0    mov     word ptr [0040],B000                    }
end.
```

SizeOf

The SizeOf function returns the size, in bytes, of the passed variable or variable type. Since this is known at the time of compilation, SizeOf generates a constant and the compiler handles it as such.

```
{ C_SIZEOF: Sample program to demonstrate assembly language generated by  }
{           Turbo Pascal when the SIZEOF function is called               }
program C_SIZEOF;
type buffer = array [1..1000] of byte;
var i : integer;     b : byte;
begin
   i := sizeof( buffer );
   { cs:0008 C7063E00E803    mov     word ptr [I],03E8 ;constant!           }
   b := sizeof( i );
   { cs:000E C606400002      mov     byte ptr [.B],02  ;ditto               }
```

```
{$ifdef ERROR }   b := sizeof( buffer );
      { Error: Constant out of Range } {$endif}
  end.
```

Write and Writeln

Turbo Pascal handles Write and Writeln in a special way. Together with Read and Readln, they represent the only functions in Turbo Pascal that work with a variable number of different arguments. So, the program code that Turbo Pascal generates for these functions is fundamentally different from that generated for passing parameters to other procedures/functions. While the Write and Writeln functions appear to be the same, Turbo Pascal distinguishes between output to standard files and output to text files.

Programmers seldom encounter Write and Writeln when working with files. These functions are usually used for output to the screen. But, to Turbo Pascal, screen output is only a special type of text file. If no file variable was given as the first parameter in a call to Write/Writeln, Turbo Pascal automatically inserts the file variable Output. This is defined in the system unit and is associated with screen output (see Chapter 4 for more information about file variables).

Turbo begins by placing a pointer, to the given file variable, on the stack. This represents the address to which the output of any routine should be sent. It can be a file or a device (printer or screen).

After the file variable, Turbo Pascal processes all arguments from left to right and makes a subroutine call for each argument. Usually each argument would be placed on the stack in its entirety and then processed with a procedure/function call. However, in this case, each argument is processed with a special output routine.

The system unit has a special routine for each type. String, Char, Boolean and Real arguments are handled separately, but there is only one routine for all Integer types (Byte, ShortInt, Integer, Word and LongInt). This routine expects the argument as a LongInt, so all of the smaller types must be expanded to the four byte LongInt format. After this argument has been placed on the stack, it is followed by the output width. This parameter can be specified after the argument, separated by a colon. If no output width is given, Turbo Pascal uses 0 as a default. This means that only as many characters will be output as are necessary to represent the argument.

The output routines for strings, characters, booleans and floating point numbers also expect the output width to be put on the stack after the argument. Turbo also uses 0 in these cases if no value is specified. The output routine for floating point numbers also expects a third parameter, which specifies the number of decimal places. Again, 0 is used as a default if no value is given.

The argument itself is given to the routine in various forms. Characters and booleans are put on the stack as Words. Strings are passed using pointers.

Floating point numbers are stored in their normal six byte format on the stack. All routines have one thing in common: the distance of the passed argument from the stack. This is a responsibility of all procedures/functions. The internal output routines don't disturb the pointer to the file variable, because it must be ready for the next output routine call without having to be put on the stack again.

Only after the last output routine has been called (after the last argument passed to Write/Writeln has been processed), will this pointer be removed from the stack. This is done with a special routine. When this routine is called, it represents the end of the Write/Writeln statement. The first thing this routine does is send the arguments out to the screen. These are found in an internal buffer. Each of the previously called routines converted their arguments to ASCII strings and stored them end-to-end in this buffer, which grew as needed with the output of each routine.

The contents of this buffer are sent to the screen. The routine then deletes the buffer, removes the pointer to the file variable from the stack, and finally returns to the calling routine. The only difference between Write and Writeln is found in this clean-up routine. Writeln inserts a Carriage Return/Linefeed combination at the end of the buffer to mark the end of the line.

The following listing shows examples of how Write and Writeln are used.

```
program writest;
uses Printer;
var  b  : byte;
     i  : integer;
     bo : boolean;
     c  : char;
     r  : real;
begin
   writeln( i:3, b );
   { cs:0012 BF4A02      mov    di,offset OUTPUT ;offset adrs. of Output }
   { cs:0015 1E          push   ds          ;put FAR pointer to Output on  }
   { cs:0016 57          push   di          ;the stack                     }
   { cs:0017 A14000      mov    ax,[I]      ;load I into AX                }
   { cs:001A 99          cwd                ;convert to LongInt            }
   { cs:001B 52          push   dx          ;put on the stack              }
   { cs:001C 50          push   ax                                        }
   { cs:001D B80300      mov    ax,0003     ;load output width             }
   { cs:0020 50          push   ax          ;and put on stack              }
   { cs:0021 9A440E9F5F  call   FIntArg     ;format Integer argument       }
   { cs:0026 A03E00      mov    al,[B]      ;load B into AL                }
   { cs:0029 30E4        xor    ah,ah       ;convert to Word               }
   { cs:002B 31D2        xor    dx,dx       ;Hi Word of LongInt is 0       }
   { cs:002D 52          push   dx          ;put LongInt from DX:AX on the }
```

```
{ cs:002E 50            push    ax        ;stack                      }
{ cs:002F 31C0          xor     ax,ax     ;no width given, then 0     }
{ cs:0031 50            push    ax        ;put on stack as width      }
{ cs:0032 9A440E9F5F    call    FIntArg   ;format Integer argument    }
{ cs:0037 9AB40C9F5F    call    WlnFlush  ;call WritelnFlush          }
{                                         ; - output contents of buffer }
{                                         ; - delete buffer           }
{                                         ; - get pointer to Output from }
{                                         ;   the stack               }
writeln( 'Test ', bo, c );
{ cs:003C BF4A02        mov     di,offset OUTPUT ;offset adrs. of Output }
{ cs:003F 1E            push    ds        ;put address of Output on stack}
{ cs:0040 57            push    di        ;as a FAR pointer           }
{ cs:0041 BF0000        mov     di,0000   ;put address of string to be }
{ cs:0044 0E            push    cs        ;output on the stack as a FAR }
{ cs:0045 57            push    di        ;pointer                    }
{ cs:0046 31C0          xor     ax,ax     ;no width given --> 0       }
{ cs:0048 50            push    ax                                    }
{ cs:0049 9A7C0D9F5F    call    FStrArg   ;format string argument     }
{ cs:004E A04200        mov     al,[BO]   ;load BO into AL            }
{ cs:0051 50            push    ax        ;put on the stack           }
{ cs:0052 31C0          xor     ax,ax     ;no width given --> 0       }
{ cs:0054 50            push    ax                                    }
{ cs:0055 9ABA0D9F5F    call    FBoolArg  ;output Boolean argument    }
{ cs:005A A04300        mov     al,[C]    ;load C into AL             }
{ cs:005D 50            push    ax        ;put on the stack           }
{ cs:005E 31C0          xor     ax,ax     ;no width                   }
{ cs:0060 50            push    ax                                    }
{ cs:0061 9A170D9F5F    call    FCharArg  ;format Char argument       }
{ cs:0066 9AB40C9F5F    call    WlnFlush  ;WritelnFlush, as above     }
writeln( lst, r:8:4 );
{ cs:006B BF4A00        mov     di,offset LST ;offset address of LST  }
{ cs:006E 1E            push    ds        ;put on stack as FAR pointer }
{ cs:006F 57            push    di                                    }
{ cs:0070 FF364800      push    [R+4]     ;put 6 byte Real variable on }
{ cs:0074 FF364600      push    [R+2]     ;the stack                  }
{ cs:0078 FF364400      push    [R]                                   }
{ cs:007C B80800        mov     ax,0008   ;load output width and put on }
{ cs:007F 50            push    ax        ;stack                      }
{ cs:0080 B80400        mov     ax,0004   ;load number of decimal places }
{ cs:0083 50            push    ax        ;and put on the stack       }
{ cs:0084 9AE70E9F5F    call    FRealArg  ;format Real argument       }
{ cs:0089 9AB40C9F5F    call    WlnFlush  ;WritelnFlush, as before    }
write( 'Test' );
{ cs:008E BF4A02        mov     di,offset OUTPUT ;the same story      }
{ cs:0091 1E            push    ds        ;put FAR pointer to Output on }
{ cs:0092 57            push    di        ;the stack                  }
{ cs:0093 BF0000        mov     di,0000   ;put FAR pointer to the string }
{ cs:0096 0E            push    cs        ;on the stack               }
{ cs:0097 57            push    di                                    }
{ cs:0098 31C0          xor     ax,ax     ;no output width            }
{ cs:009A 50            push    ax                                    }
{ cs:009B 9A7C0D9F5F    call    FStrArg   ;format string argument     }
```

```
    { cs:00A0 9AD30C9F5F      call    WFlush    ;this time call WriteFlush    }
    {                                           ;instead of WritelnFlush      }
end.
```

Using Write with a standard file (Writeln is only allowed with text files) is very similar to using Write/Writeln with text files.

Again, Turbo Pascal begins by placing a pointer to the file variable on the stack. The name of this variable must be given to Write as the first argument. The rest of the arguments are again processed from left to right. When variables are called by name, the address of the variable is placed on the stack. If a variable is referenced by a pointer, then the contents of the pointer are put on the stack. An internal routine from the system unit is then called. The same routine is used regardless of variable type. This routine writes the arguments to the file named by the file variable. The file variable also specifies the size of the argument, which tells how many bytes to output. Before returning to the caller, the argument is removed from the stack. The pointer to the file variable is left for future calls.

Each argument is processed in this way. Since this routine writes output directly to a file and doesn't store it in a buffer, there is no need for a clean-up routine. So, the program must remove the pointer to the file variable from the stack by adding 4 to the stack pointer.

```
program writest1;
type Entries = record
                   Name    : string[ 30 ];
                   FstName : string[ 20 ];
                   RefNum  : integer;
                 end;
var FileIn : Entries;
      i,j     : integer;
      fe      : file of Entries;
      fi      : file of Integer;
begin
    write( fi, i, j );
    { cs:0008 BFF800         mov     di,offset FI ;get offset address of FI }
    { cs:000B 1E             push    ds           ;put FAR pointer to FI on }
    { cs:000C 57             push    di           ;the stack                }
    { cs:000D BF7400         mov     di,offset I  ;get offset address of I  }
    { cs:0010 1E             push    ds           ;and put on stack as FAR  }
    { cs:0011 57             push    di           ;pointer                  }
    { cs:0012 9A7005945F     call    Write2File   ;write argument to file   }
    { cs:0017 BF7600         mov     di,offset J  ;get offset address of J  }
    { cs:001A 1E             push    ds           ;put on stack as a FAR    }
    { cs:001B 57             push    di           ;pointer                  }
    { cs:001C 9A7005945F     call    Write2File   ;write argument to file   }
    { cs:0021 83C404         add     sp,0004      ;move FAR pointer to file }
    {                                             ;variable FI from stack   }
    write( fe, FileIn );
    { cs:0024 BFF800         mov     di,offset FE ;get offset address of FE }
    { cs:0027 1E             push    ds           ;put FAR pointer to FE on }
```

```
{ cs:0028 57          push   di              ;the stack               }
{ cs:0029 BF7400      mov    di,offset FileIn;offset of FileIn        }
{ cs:002C 1E          push   ds              ;as a FAR pointer on the }
{ cs:002D 57          push   di              ;stack                   }
{ cs:002E 9A7005945F  call   Write2File      ;write argument to file  }
{ cs:0032 83C404      add    sp,0004         ;move FAR pointer to file }
{                                            ;variable FE from stack  }
   end.
```

Read and Readln

Read and Readln are closely related to Write and Writeln. Instead of writing to a file or device, these statements read data from a file or a device. The syntax used is identical to that of Write/Writeln. The assembly language generated by these statements differs since internal input routines rather that internal output routines are used.

Another difference is the accessing of text files without specifying a file variable. Instead of the standard variable OUTPUT, the file variable INPUT is accessed. INPUT is connected with the keyboard. As with OUTPUT, INPUT is defined and managed by the system unit.

New, Dispose, GetMem and FreeMem

The procedures New and Dispose are used to allocate and free memory on the heap. They're also defined in the system unit. New is different from GetMem in that New can only allocate enough memory to accommodate the variable type referenced by the pointer passed to it as an argument. In Turbo Pascal, GetMem allows you to allocate as much memory as you like on the heap (allowable values range from 1 to 65521 bytes).

You may now be wondering what the difference is between Dispose and FreeMem. Well, a look at the assembly language in the following listing shows us that New and Dispose are really only "disguises". Internally they are converted to calls of GetMem and FreeMem.

GetMem expects the size of the memory block to allocate as an argument. It then returns a pointer to the memory block if sufficient room is available on the heap. GetMem works as a function rather than a procedure.

It is true that there is no memory block size passed when New is called. So, Turbo Pascal allows only standard pointers to be used with New. And since the pointer also tells Turbo the type of the referenced object, it also knows the size of the memory block that will be required. This is automatically passed to GetMem.

FreeMem is the opposite of GetMem. It frees a previously allocated memory range. To do this, it needs the address of the memory range in the form of the pointer returned by GetMem and also the size of the range. This information is provided by the calling routine when GetMem is called. But Dispose doesn't know the size of the memory range, it only has the pointer. Again, Turbo uses the pointer type to determine the size of the memory range to free and passes this to FreeMem.

```
program newtest;
type buffer = array [1..1000] of Word;
var  bufp : ^buffer;
     p    : pointer;
begin
   New( bufp );
   { cs:0008 B8D007        mov    ax,07D0     ;size of a BUFFER in bytes }
   { cs:000B 50            push   ax          ;put on stack as argument  }
   { cs:000C 9A0702965F    call   GetMem      ;call GetMem               }
   { cs:0011 A33E00        mov    [BUFP],ax   ;GetMem returns FAR pointer }
   { cs:0014 89164000      mov    [BUFP+2],dx ;store in BUFP             }
   GetMem( p, 2000 );
   { different statement, same Code!
   { cs:0018 B8D007        mov    ax,07D0     ;2000 bytes to be allocated }
   { cs:001B 50            push   ax                                     }
   { cs:001C 9A0702965F    call   GetMem      ;call GetMem               }
   { cs:0021 A34200        mov    [P],ax      ;FAR pointer from GetMem   }
   { cs:0024 89164400      mov    [P+2],dx    ;store in variable P       }
   Dispose( bufp );
   { cs:0028 FF364000      push   [BUFP]      ;address of allocated block }
   { cs:002C FF363E00      push   [BUFP+2]    ;from pointer BUFP to stack }
   { cs:0030 B8D007        mov    ax,07D0     ;put size of allocated block }
   { cs:0033 50            push   ax          ;on stack                  }
   { cs:0034 9A1F02965F    call   FreeMem     ;call FreeMem              }
   FreeMem( p, 2000 );
   { same here, different statement - same code!
   { cs:0039 FF364400      push   [P]          ;put address of memory block }
     ax,07D0     ;put size of memory block on }
   { cs:0044 50            push   ax          ;the stack                 }
   { cs:0045 9A1F02965F    call   FreeMem     ;call FreeMem              }
end.
```

Unfortunately, it isn't possible to use extended or expanded memory with these statements.

2.8   Development Tools

All of us are familiar with programming errors and bugs. It seems that they're with us every step of the way during program development. Variables with unexpected values, screens with an incorrect appearance, printers sending garbage—these are all relatively harmless problems. It's considerably worse when your computer crashes taking the familiar work environment with it and no amount of pounding on <Ctrl><Break> will bring it back. Of course, this is most likely to happen when you forgot to save your source code before trying to run a program under development. This is why Turbo Pascal has included the ability to catch certain dangerous run-time errors; obviously this will help protect your computer. In the next sections we will see how Turbo handles range checking, I/O checking and stack checking.

Range checking

Range checking is a very helpful tool in the development phase of a program. If you use this option, a program will be stopped with run-time error 201 (Range check error) if the value range of any expression is exceeded. The compiler performs range checking in the following situations:

- When evaluating an expression that returns an ordinal (Char, Boolean, Byte, ShortInt, Integer, Word and LongInt) result that is to be assigned to a variable.

- When evaluating an expression that returns an ordinal result that is to be passed to a procedure or function.

- When indexing arrays and strings.

No checking is done for pointers, since Turbo Pascal cannot perform pointer arithmetic that could cause a pointer to overflow. Turbo Pascal allows pointers to take on any value anyway. Arithmetic routines do check floating point numbers. If a math coprocessor is used, the coprocessor does the range checking.

You can globally toggle the range checking option for ordinal types on and off with Options / Compiler / Range checking. You can also turn this option on and off selectively within a program using the compiler directives {$R+}/{$R-}. Turbo Pascal defaults to no range checking.

Range checking will help you find errors that the Debugger may never find or could find only after a significant amount of time. This is especially true for mistakes in accessing arrays or strings, which are often the cause of strange error messages. If an invalid (meaning "too large") index is used to access an array or a string, you end up running into a memory block that was not allocated to the variable. This often leaves a programmer wondering why a variable that was never accessed suddenly changed its value.

Even though range checking is a powerful tool for finding and preventing errors, the Turbo Pascal manual warns that using range checking will enlarge the .EXE file and significantly slow program execution time. Therefore, you should only use range checking during your testing and switch it off when you compile the final version of your program.

A look at the assembly language generated with range checking demonstrates how much the program grows and how execution is slowed. Turbo calls an additional checking routine before each variable is assigned, before a parameter is passed to a procedure or function, or before an array or a string is accessed.

The developers of Turbo Pascal intended that the range checking feature only be used during development. Otherwise, they would have included more than one single routine to range check all ordinal types. However, this is not the most efficient way of doing range checking, since the ordinal types include Byte, ShortInt, Char, Boolean and LongInt. These types can consist of one to four bytes. Since the checking routine doesn't know the type of variable to be checked, it must work so that it can handle the longest type (LongInt). For the smaller types, this means that they must be expanded to four bytes before the check routine is called. This requires two additional machine language instructions.

The check routine expects the value to be in the DX:AX register pair. DX contains the high Word and AX the low Word. Since the valid range differs from type to type, the check routine must also be passed some information about the valid range of values for the type to be checked. This information is placed in the DI register. This register is usually not used for calculations and must be specially loaded for range checking.

The following example program shows the program code generated with the range checking option switched on. Assignments are made to all of the given ordinal types, the enumerated type CarBrand, and the two string types. Notice that the assembly language instructions CBW and CWD expand the operands to four bytes. CBW stands for "convert Byte to Word". It expands contents of AL into the AH register so that after this operation the entire AX register contains the contents of AL. CWD (convert Word to DWord) works similarly. The contents of AX are expanded to a DWORD in the DX:AX register pair.

```
program RCHECK;
type CarBrand = ( VW, Audi, BMW, Benz, Nissan, Opel,
                  Ford, Volvo, Renault, Peugeot, Fiat );
var CAR : CarBrand;
    l   : longint;
    i   : integer;
    w   : word;
    b   : byte;
    si  : shortint;
    bo  : boolean;
```

```
      s   : string;
      s8  : string[8];
procedure test;
begin
    b       := b - 200;
    { cs:0032 A04800        mov     al,[B]      ;load B into AL                      }
    { cs:0035 30E4          xor     ah,ah       ;convert B to a Word                 }
    { cs:0037 2DC800        sub     ax,00C8     ;subtract 200                        }
    { cs:003A 99            cwd                 ;convert result to LongInt           }
    { cs:003B BF0000        mov     di,0000     ;address of range limits to DI       }
    { cs:003E 9A1C02E15F    call    RCheck      ;call range check routine            }
    { cs:0043 A24800        mov     [B],al      ;O.K., store result                 }
    si      := si * 4;
    { cs:0046 A04900        mov     al,[SI]     ;load SI in AL                       }
    { cs:0049 98            cbw                 ;convert to Integer                  }
    { cs:004A B90200        mov     cx,0002     ;move it over                        }
    { cs:004D D3E0          shl     ax,cl       ;AX := AX * 4                        }
    { cs:004F 99            cwd                 ;convert result to LongInt           }
    { cs:0050 BF0800        mov     di,0008     ;address of range limits to DI       }
    { cs:0053 9A1C02E15F    call    RCheck      ;call range check routine            }
    { cs:0058 A24900        mov     [SI],al                                         }
    l       := l + 100000;
    { cs:005B C4064000      les     ax,[L]      ;load L into ES:AX                   }
    { cs:005F 8CC2          mov     dx,es       ;from there to DX:AX                 }
    { cs:0061 05A086        add     ax,86A0     ;addition low word                   }
    { cs:0064 83D201        adc     dx,0001     ;addition high word                  }
    { cs:0067 BF0500        mov     di,0005     ;address of range limits to DI       }
    { cs:006A 9A1C02E15F    call    RCheck      ;call range check routine            }
    { cs:006F A34000        mov     [L],ax      ;result O.K., store                  }
    { cs:0072 89164200      mov     [L+2],dx                                        }
    bo      := pred( bo );
    { cs:0076 A04A00        mov     al,[BO]     ;load BO into AL                     }
    { cs:0079 FEC8          dec     al          ;decrement (pred)                    }
    { cs:007B 98            cbw                 ;convert to Integer                  }
    { cs:007C 99            cwd                 ;convert to LongInt                  }
    { cs:007D BF1000        mov     di,0010     ;address of range limits to DI       }
    { cs:0080 9A1C02E15F    call    RCheck      ;call range check routine            }
    { cs:0085 A24A00        mov     [BO],al     ;result O.K., store                  }
    CAR     := Succ( CAR );
    { cs:0088 A03E00        mov     al,[KFZ]    ;load KFZ into AL                    }
    { cs:008B FEC0          inc     al          ;increment (succ)                    }
    { cs:008D 98            cbw                 ;convert to Integer                  }
    { cs:008E 99            cwd                 ;convert to LongInt                  }
    { cs:008F BF1800        mov     di,0018     ;address of range limits to DI       }
    { cs:0092 9A1C02E15F    call    RCheck      ;call range check routine            }
    { cs:0097 A23E00        mov     [KFZ],al    ;everything's O.K.                   }
    s[ i ] := 'A';
    { cs:009A A14400        mov     ax,[I]      ;load I into AX                      }
    { cs:009D 99            cwd                 ;convert to LongInt                  }
    { cs:009E BF0000        mov     di,0000     ;address of range limits to DI       }
    { cs:00A1 9A1C02E15F    call    RCheck      ;call range check routine            }
    { cs:00A6 8BF8          mov     di,ax       ;index O.K., move to DI              }
    { cs:00A8 C6854C0041    mov     byte ptr [di+S],41 ;write 'A' in string          }
```

```
    s8[i]  := 'B';
    { cs:00AD A14400        mov    ax,[I]    ;load I into AX              }
    { cs:00B0 99            cwd              ;convert to LongInt         }
    { cs:00B1 BF2000        mov    di,0020   ;address of range limits to DI }
    { cs:00B4 9A1C02E15F    .call  RCheck    ;call range check routine   }
    { cs:00B9 8BF8          mov    di,ax     ;index O.K, move to DI      }
    { cs:00BB C6854C0041    mov    byte ptr [di+S8],42 ;write 'B' in string }
 end;
  begin
  w := w + 1000;
    { cs:00DC A14600        mov    ax,[W]    ;W := W + 1000              }
    { cs:00DF 05E803        add    ax,03E8                               }
    { cs:00E2 31D2          xor    dx,dx     ;high word is 0             }
    { cs:00E4 BFC400        mov    di,00C4   ;address of range limits to DI }
    { cs:00E7 9A1C02E15F    call   RCheck    ;call range check routine   }
    { cs:00EC A34600        mov    [W],ax    ;number O.K., store         }
   i := i - 4711;
    { cs:00EF A14400        mov    ax,[I]    ;I := I - 4711              }
    { cs:00F2 2D6712        sub    ax,1267                               }
    { cs:00F5 99            cwd              ;build LongInt              }
    { cs:00F6 BFCC00        mov    di,00CC   ;address of range limits to DI }
    { cs:00F9 9A1C02E15F    call   RCheck    ;call range check routine   }
    { cs:00FE A34400        mov    [I],ax    ;O.K., store                }
   test;
 end.
```

You will not find the code used to abort the program in case of an error. When a range overflow error is detected, the standard RunError procedure is called. This interrupts the program execution. If no range overflow was detected, the range check routine returns to the calling routine. The operand in the DX:AX register pair can then be processed further.

The use of the DI register is interesting. It contains the offset address of two DWORDS, the upper and lower limits of the valid range for the variable type being checked. The following listing shows that this information is not stored in the data segment with the global variables and standard constants. Instead, it is stored in the code segment directly in front of the procedure that uses the variable, which is also the procedure that calls the check routine.

The check routine gets the address of the code segment of the calling routine from the stack. Since the check routine is a FAR routine, the processor saves the contents of IP and CS for the return jump.

```
check   proc far
        ; Input:  DX:AX      = DWORD to be checked
        ;         CS:[DI]    = Bottom limit
        ;         CS:[DI+4]  = Top limit
        mov    si,sp              ;stack pointer to SI
        mov    es,ss:[si+02]      ;code segment of calling routine to ES
        ; compare DX:AX with the lower limit in ES:[DI]
        cmp    dx,es:[di+02]      ;compare DX with high Word of lower limit
        jg     ober               ;larger? yes --> compare lower limit
```

```
          jl       error             ;smaller? yes --> error
          cmp      ax,es:[di]        ;equal. compare AX with low Word/lower limit
          jb       error             ;smaller? yes --> error
          ; compare DX:AX with upper limit in ES:[DI+4]
uptop:    cmp      dx,es:[di+06]     ;compare DX with high Word of upper limit
          jl       ok                ;smaller? yes --> number O.K.
          jg       error             ;larger? yes --> error
          cmp      ax,es:[di+04]     ;equal. compare AX with low word/upper limit
          ja       error             ;larger? yes --> error
ok:       retf                       ;number O.K., return to calling routine
error:    mov      ax,00C9           ;error message "Range Check Error"
          jmp      runerror          ;interrupt program with run-time error
check    endp
```

The following table shows the address of the range limits for this last Pascal program. Since each entry is eight bytes, the entries are generally spaced eight bytes apart. It is interesting the way Turbo Pascal has optimized the handling of LongInts and string indices. The first two entries in the table show that Turbo Pascal uses the same entry for type BYTE and for string indices, since both must have values between 0 and 255. Another interesting point is that the entry for type LONGINT begins at offset $0005, which almost places it between the entries for BYTE and SHORTINT. There is really no separate entry for this type. Once again, the experience of the Turbo Pascal developers shows through, since this kind of optimization would not have been done by amateurs.

Address	in Memory		Type	Decimal Values	
	Lower	Upper		Lower Limit	Upper Limit
CS:0000	00000000	000000FF	BYTE	0	255
CS:0000	00000000	000000FF	STRING	0	255
CS:0005	80000000	7FFFFFFF	LONGINT	-2147483648	2147483647
CS:0008	FFFFFF80	0000007F	SHORTINT	-128	127
CS:0010	00000000	00000001	BOOLEAN	0	1
CS:0018	00000000	0000000A	KFZ	0	10
CS:0020	00000000	00000008	S8	0	8
CS:00C4	00000000	0000FFFF	WORD	0	65536
CS:00CC	FFFF8000	00007FFF	INTEGER	-32768	32767

It is interesting that each procedure/function has its own range table with entries for all data types used within the procedure/function. As seen in the following program example, Turbo doesn't utilize tables from procedures that have already been compiled. Instead, it creates new entries, even for data types that were already checked for a previous procedure.

At first this may seem rather unnecessary but it is actually unavoidable because of the way the internal linker works to join the program with the various units. Turbo Pascal uses an intelligent linker that only places procedures/functions and variables in the .EXE file if they are actually used in the program. This information isn't always known at the time a program is compiled. For example, procedure P2 cannot use the range entries from procedure P1, because P1 may not actually be called anywhere in the program being compiled and would therefore not appear in the .EXE file.

```
program rcheck1;
var i : integer;
procedure t1;
begin
  i := i + 1;
  { cs:001D A13E00      mov    ax,[I]     ;load I into AX              }
  { cs:0020 40          inc    ax         ;increment                  }
  { cs:0021 99          cwd               ;convert to LongInt         }
  { cs:0022 BF0000      mov    di,0000    ;address of range limits to DI }
  { cs:0025 9A1C02985F  call   RCheck     ;call range check routine   }
  { cs:002A A33E00      mov    [I],ax     ;result O.K., store         }
end;
procedure t2;
begin
  i := i + 1;
  { cs:0038 A13E00      mov    ax,[I]     ;second verse, same as the  }
  { cs:003B 40          inc    ax         ;first                      }
  { cs:003C 99          cwd               ;                           }
  { cs:003D BF2600      mov    di,0026    ;<-- with a different address! }
  { cs:0040 9A1C02985F  call   RCheck     ;                           }
  { cs:0045 A33E00      mov    [I],ax     ;                           }
end;
begin
  i := i + 1;
  { cs:0052 A13E00      mov    ax,[I]     ;one more time!             }
  { cs:0055 40          inc    ax         ;                           }
  { cs:0056 99          cwd               ;                           }
  { cs:0057 BF4C00      mov    di,004C    ;<-- different address!     }
  { cs:005A 9A1C02985F  call   RCheck     ;                           }
  { cs:005F A33E00      mov    [I],ax     ;                           }
  t1;
  t2;
end.
```

Stack checking

A stack overflow is another type of error that often leads to a system crash. It occurs when the Stack pointer tries to exceed the boundaries of the stack during a function/procedure call. This would mean that there isn't enough room on the stack for the local variables of this function. The contents of the Stack pointer jump from 0 to $FFFF and point to the end of the stack segment. Since Turbo Pascal sets up a 16K stack by default and doesn't use the entire stack segment, the pointer points past the boundary of the stack. This wouldn't be so bad if the range after the stack wasn't already being used by the heap.

You don't have to worry about this type of error. It usually only occurs if:

* The stack size was set smaller than the default 16K using the compiler directive {$M} or Options / Compiler / Memory Size.

- Large variable types, especially arrays, are passed to a procedure or function (remember that a local copy of the variable is put on the stack).

- When a recursive function or procedure is used with too many recursions or if too many local variables, parameters and local copies are used.

Stack checking will help you detect these errors while testing your program. By default, stack checking is switched on when you compile. Turbo makes a call to the stack check routine at the start of each procedure or function. The number of bytes needed for local variables and local copies is passed to the stack check function in the AX register. If the stack can satisfy the memory requirement, the stack check routine returns to the calling routine. Otherwise, the stack check routine jumps to the internal routine which generates a run-time error and aborts the program. This process is shown in the following listing.

```
program stkchk;
procedure test;
var a : array [1..100] of word;
    s : string;
begin
  { cs:0000 55            push  bp          ;put on stack              }
  { cs:0001 89E5          mov   bp,sp                                  }
  { cs:0003 B8C801        mov   ax,01C8     ;memory needed for local var. }
  { cs:0006 9A4402935F    call  far StkChk ;call stack check routine  }
  { cs:000B 81ECC801      sub   sp,01C8     ;enough room exists!       }
end;
  { cs:000F 89EC          mov   sp,bp       ;restore stack, delete local }
  { cs:0011 5D            pop   bp          ;variables                 }
  { cs:0012 C3            ret                                          }
begin
  test;
  { cs:001B E8E2FF        call  test        ;call test                 }
end.
```

In this example, the procedure "test" uses two local variables called A (requiring 200 bytes) and S (a standard string requiring 256 bytes). The sum of these two values is placed in the AX register and the required memory (456 bytes) is subtracted from the stack. The local variables are created only after the StkChk routine returns and indicates that there is enough memory on the stack.

But how does the stack check work—how does it know whether the required memory is available? The following listing explains.

```
StkChk  proc    far
        mov     si,sp                   ;move stack pointer (and the
                                        ;number of free bytes) to SI
        sub     si,ax                   ;subtract required number of bytes
        jb      nerror                  ;< 0 ? YES --> error
        sub     si,0200                 ;subtract another 512 bytes
        jb      nerror                  ;< 0 ? YES --> error
        cmp     si,[STACKLIMIT]         ;compare with variable STACKLIMIT
        jb      0257                    ;< STACKIMIT? YES --> error
        ret                             ;O.K., no stack overrun expected
nerror  label   near
        mov     ax,00CA                 ;error code: Stack Overflow
        jmp     runerror                ;create run-time error
StkChk  endp
```

StkChk requires a few more bytes to be free than the calling routine actually requires. There must be at least 512K free after the local variables are created. In addition, StkChk requires that the number of bytes in the standard constant STACKLIMIT from the system unit also be free. This variable was 0 in all of our tests, however, so it had no effect on the result of StkChk. We could not tell whether Turbo Pascal sometimes assigns a different value to this variable or if it is always decided by the programmer.

Stack checking isn't as time consuming as range checking. Since stack checking requires memory overhead, you should always switch the option off with Options / Compiler / Stack checking when you are finished testing. You can also use the compiler directives {$S+} and {$S-} to switch stack checking on and off for individual functions or procedures. This is especially useful for recursive functions/procedures, in which the number of repetitions depends on the data and is not known at compilation time.

I/O checking

Any time a program uses an input/output procedure to access a device or a file there is the danger of an I/O error. The printer may be out of paper, the cable may have come loose from the printer or the disk in the disk drive may be full. There are many possible causes for such errors. To avoid these problems, these errors should be detected as early as possible. Turbo uses the I/O check routine to do this. When I/O checking is on, this routine is called after every call to one of the input/output procedures or functions of the system unit, such as Writeln, Read or Reset. I/O checking is on by default. The program is aborted with a run-time error when an error is found.

This isn't always desirable, however, since a user-friendly application should give the user a chance to fix the error and repeat the operation. A short message, such as "Make sure printer is on" or "Please insert volume xyz", is usually all that is needed. To allow for this, Turbo allows you to turn off I/O checking globally with Options / Compiler / I/O checking. You can also switch I/O checking on for a single statement or procedure with the compiler directive {$I-}.

Error prompts and messages can be added with the IOResult function, which is defined in the system unit. Every input/output statement sets a code, before it finishes, that indicates whether the statement was successfully executed or if an error occurred. IOResult checks the values of this code. The following sample program shows the different ways of using I/O checking.

```
program IoChk;
var TestFile : text;
    AnError  : word;
begin
  Assign( TestFile, 'c:\test.ioc' );
  { cs:0031 BF3E00      mov   di,offset TestFile ;pointer to variable  }
  { cs:0034 1E          push  ds                 ;put TestFile on the  }
  { cs:0035 57          push  di                 ;stack                }
  { cs:0036 BF0000      mov   di,0000     ;pointer to filenames        }
  { cs:0039 0E          push  cs          ;put (CS:0000) on the stack  }
  { cs:003A 57          push  di                                       }
  { cs:003B 9A5D029A5F  call  Assign      ;call Assign procedure       }
  Rewrite( TestFile );
  { cs:0040 BF3E00      mov   di,offset TestFile ;pointer to variable  }
  { cs:0043 1E          push  ds                 ;put TestFile on the  }
  { cs:0044 57          push  di                 ;stack                }
  { cs:0045 9AD2029A5F  call  Rewrite     ;call Rewrite procedure      }
  { cs:004A 9A0E029A5F  call  IOChk       ;call IO Check               }
   {$I-}                             { automatic IO checking disabled  }
  writeln( TestFile, 'Output to TestFile.');
  { cs:004F BF3E00      mov   di,offset TestFile ;pass pointer to file }
  { cs:0052 1E          push  ds                 ;variable             }
  { cs:0053 57          push  di                                       }
  { cs:0054 BF0C00      mov   di,000C    ;put pointer to               }
  { cs:0057 0E          push  cs         ;output string on the stack   }
  { cs:0058 57          push  di                                       }
  { cs:0059 31C0        xor   ax,ax      ;no output width specified    }
  { cs:005B 50          push  ax                                       }
  { cs:005C 9A26069A5F  call  FStrArg     ;format string               }
  { cs:0061 9AA9059A5F  call  WritelnFlush ;output buffer              }
  {                                  ;<-- no call to IOChk here!       }
  AnError := IOResult;
  { cs:0066 9A07029A5F  call  IOResult    ;call IOResult               }
  { cs:006B A33E01      mov   [ERROR],ax  ;store error code            }
  if ( AnError <> 0 ) then writeln( 'ERROR' );
end.
```

Various statements are used here to access a text file with the Testfile variable. No I/O checking is performed on the first statement, which is a call to the Assign procedure. This is because this procedure doesn't access a device or a file. The Rewrite statement is different. This creates a file or empties an existing file. Turbo inserts a call to the I/O check routine after this statement. The I/O check routine only returns to the program if there isn't an error in the execution of Rewrite.

I/O checking is switched off prior to the Writeln statement with the compiler directive {$I-}. As we can see, there is no call to the I/O check routine after this statement. Instead, the program checks for an error itself by using the IOResult function. This function returns an error code. If a value other than 0 is returned, the program will react with an error message.

Let's look at the code generated by the IOChk routine itself.

```
IOChk   proc    far
        cmp     word ptr [INOUTRES],0  ;compare error variable with 0
        jne     AnError                ;<> 0 ---> error
        ret                            ;O.K., no errors
AnError label near
        mov     ax,[INOUTRES]          ;load error code from error variable
        jmp     runerror               ;abort program with run-time error
IOChk endp
```

The internal variable INOUTRES is from the system unit. This is a constant of type WORD. It is apparently where all input/output statements enter their status. This variable is checked by IOChk and its contents are passed to RunError as an error number if it is not 0.

But if the current error code is always found in this variable, why does it have to pertain to a function and not to a reference to this internal variable? A look at the program code for IOResult gives the answer:

```
IoResult proc far
        xor     ax,ax              ;
load AX with 0
        [INOUTRES],ax      ;AX to INOUTRES and INOUTRES to AX
        ret                        ;
return to calling routine
IoResult endp
```

IOResult not only returns the current error status, it also sets INOUTRES to 0. This is also why the Turbo Pascal manual warns that only the first call to IOResult returns the true error code. All subsequent calls would simply return 0.

Another question remains. Why has Turbo Pascal created an internal function to execute only two statements, especially when it uses a time consuming FAR call? The direct conversion of calls to PTR, CHR or INC show that it can't be done any other way.

3. Pascal and Assembly Language

Even though this is a developer's book for Turbo Pascal and not for assembly language, we have included five assembly language modules:

KMBA   This is a link between the keyboard/mouse and the KBM unit (see Chapter 7 for more information).

TRSA   This is for working with the TRS unit (see Chapter 11 for more information).

SWAPA   This is part of the SWAP unit (see Chapter 10 for more information).

MTA   This is the driving force behind the multitasking unit (see Chapter 13 for more information).

KMBTA   This is the expanded version of KBM for working with the multitasking unit.

All five modules are available to handle specific tasks that cannot be coded in Pascal. Their purpose isn't necessarily to increase program execution speed. For example, the two KBM modules could be realized with INLINE statements, although we would prefer not to use this kind of programming.

It's almost as if you were back at the beginning of the 1950s, back before assembly language existed, and programs had to be entered by hand as hex code. The INLINE statements are quite similar to this. The difference is these commands make even less sense than straight hex code, because you first have to use an assembler to enter the commands and then type the assembly code generated from it into your Pascal program. Although there are a few INLINE statements used in this book, there are never more than one or two assembly language instructions for which we already happen to know the hex code.

Turbo Pascal Version 6.0 includes an integrated assembler. This integrated assembler lets you enter assembly language instructions within Pascal procedures and functions. Any assembly language entered in this manner is subject to syntax restrictions presented by Pascal. So, you can have variables declared in the code segment, but these cannot refer to more than one variable name. Assembly language instructions branching to another procedure or function are not allowed, nor are direct accesses between individual routines. These rules are all met by the assembler modules found in this book. These rules are supported by the assembler routines, the TSR, multitasking and SWAP units, because they are deeply rooted in the system, and often are based on DOS programming.

This book contains main program source codes, units and assembly language source, all treated as separate entities and combined through compilation. We recommend that you compile these programs as instructed, and not attempt to modify the Pascal code by adding assembler code. We have found that the integrated assembler actually speeds up some operations, but we still recommend keeping the codes separate from one another. The integrated assembler may be useful for adding short assembly language routines to Pascal code, or it may be the instrument of choice for assembling longer codes.

Not all of you know assembly language nor do all of you have an assembler, which is required for creating object files from the assembler modules listed above. Therefore, the two disks included with the book contain the source code for these assembler modules and assembled object files, which you should copy to a directory on your hard disk along with the corresponding Pascal modules.

3.1   Preparing Assembly Language Programs

You may have had experience linking assembly language routines in Turbo Pascal. If so, you are already familiar with the difference between the Turbo Assembler TASM and Microsoft's MASM. All assembly language modules in this book were coded in MASM format which is compatible with both assemblers.

TASM users must be sure, however, to switch off certain features which are otherwise very helpful in linking assembly language modules with Turbo Pascal programs. These features are:

- The simplified Segment instruction .MODEL TPASCAL, which can be used to name segments and pass their attributes to the Turbo Assembler.

- The ARG instruction, which simplifies receipt of parameters from a called Pascal program.

- The LOCAL instruction, which helps create local variables within an assembly language procedure.

Of course, it is possible to create assembly language modules without using any of these commands, as demonstrated by Microsoft's MASM. Also, instead of producing more efficient program code, these commands only make it easier to create and maintain the assembly language module.

Now that we've discussed compatibility, the rest of the chapter is intended for assembly language programmers who haven't had experience linking assembly language modules with Turbo Pascal programs. In the following sections we will discuss the conventions that must be obeyed in order to successfully integrate an assembly language module with machine code created by Turbo Pascal.

3.2   Linking Modules to Turbo Pascal

Before we start, you should know that almost everything you need to know to create an assembly language module is discussed in Chapter 2. So you've already covered this information if you are reading the chapters in sequential chapter order. The major points are:

- Assembly language modules should be integral parts of a Pascal program and must be oriented toward the basic structure of a Turbo Pascal program (see Section 2.1).

- They must perform their tasks as normal Turbo Pascal procedures and functions (see Section 2.4).

- They usually process variables passed to them by a Turbo Pascal program or are stored there as global variables (Section 2.3).

- In the case of functions, they return the function result to the calling routine through the AX of DX:AX register (Section 2.4).

Tips presented in this chapter for creating your own assembly language modules or for modifying those listed in this book are not discussed in detail. So for examples demonstrating the actual program code and its structure, refer to the sections of Chapter 2 listed above.

Each assembly language module can use exactly one data segment and one code segment. The data segment must be called DATA segment or DSEG and assigned the attributes "segment word public". The code segment is called CODE segment or CSEG, and must have the attributes "segment byte public".

You can create as many variables as you like within the data segment, but none of these can have predefined contents. This means that you cannot create standard constants within the data segment of an assembly language module. But Turbo Pascal allows you to use initialized variables stored in the code segment. But remember that this kind of variable cannot be accessed through the DS register like the others. If you remember this difference while writing your code, you can use standard constants without any problems.

Version 6.0 alleviates these problems, by allowing you to initialize variables in the data segment of an assembler module. Thus, the detour through the code segment is no longer necessary.

All global variables from the data segment in a Turbo Pascal program can be declared as *external* with EXTRN. This allows them to also be accessed from within the program code. However, the opposite is not possible. You cannot make variables, in the assembly language module, available to a Pascal program.

The code segment for the module contains the various procedures, which will either be called from a Pascal program or will be used only within the module. Those that won't be called from Pascal must be declared *public*, by using the command of the same name.

Whether these procedures are type NEAR or FAR is determined by the point of reference within the Pascal program. If they are only called from the IMPLEMENTATION portion of a unit or from a program, then they must be type NEAR. If they are used from the INTERFACE portion of a unit, they must be declared as type FAR. In this way, an assembly language module isn't very different from a normal Pascal procedure.

After successfully assembling the module, it can be linked to the Pascal program with the compiler directive {$L name}, which can be included anywhere in the Pascal program. As a rule, this is placed at the beginning of the program, since the "public" procedures and functions of the module can only be accessed after this compiler directive is executed. Also, a procedure/function declaration similar to the FORWARD statement is required. The EXTERN statement is used, which tells Turbo that the routine is stored externally. This allows the external routine to be accessed as a normal Pascal procedure or function.

This is all you have to do to link an assembly language module. The following chapters will demonstrate how the clever use of linked assembly language modules increases (in some instances dramatically) the potential of Turbo Pascal.

3.3　The Integrated Assembler

Up until now, users have relied on an external assembler or the INLINE statements for linking assembly language routines to Pascal programs. Turbo Pascal 6.0 has an integrated assembler that you can use to include assembly language commands in completely ordinary Pascal procedures and functions.

This may sound like an ideal solution for some. However, this integration doesn't mean peaceful coexistence of Pascal and assembly language. It's more like a marriage of incompatible partners, in the sense that the integrated assembler removes some of the freedom that assembly language programmers had. Although programmers can use the integrated assembler to access Pascal variables, constants, procedures and functions, there are many things they cannot do. For example, programmers cannot create variables using DB, DW and similar related commands. Programmers can't jump back and forth between two routines either: Assembly language allowed this jumping, but Pascal prohibits it. So, while the integrated assembler is a welcome replacement for INLINE statements, it's not always a suitable replacement for external assembly language modules.

We're more interested in the actual implementation of assembly language, rather than the actual syntax of assembly language commands. Here's a short Pascal program with a procedure called FillVideo. The compiled program fills a rectangular area of the screen with characters by directly accessing video RAM. Since such operations appear frequently in video oriented programs, we formulated the routine for the most part with the help of the ASM command in assembly language. FillVideo uses Pascal constants, global (standardized) variables and passing parameters by name. The following is a listing in its original form:

```
{$X+}                                          { ignore function results }

program ASM1;

uses Crt;

const Columns = 80;                      { screen resolution in text mode }
      Rows    = 25;
      vseg : word = 0;                    { segment address of video RAM }

{-----------------------------------------------------------------------}
{-- FillVideo: Fills an area of video RAM with characters ---------------}
{-----------------------------------------------------------------------}

procedure FillVideo ( X1,
                      Y1,
                      VHeight,
                      VWidth  : BYTE;
                      VChars  : char;
```

```
                    VColor  : BYTE );

  begin
    if vseg = 0 then
      asm
              mov   ax,40h
              mov   es,ax
              mov   ax,0B800h
              cmp   word ptr es:[63h],3D4h
              je    @11

              mov   ah,0B0h
        @11:  mov   word ptr vseg,ax
      end;

    {-- Fill loop in assembler (best speed) --------------------------------}

    asm
              cld
              mov   ax,vseg
              mov   es,ax

              mov   al,COLUMNS*2
              mul   Y1
              mov   bl,X1
              shl   bl,1
              xor   bh,bh
              add   ax,bx
              mov   di,ax

              mov   dl,VWidth
              cmp   dl,0
              je    @12
              shl   dl,1
              xor   dh,dh
              neg   dx
              add   dx,COLUMNS*2

              mov   bl,VHeight
              cmp   bl,0
              je    @12
              mov   al,VChars
              mov   ah,VColor
              xor   ch,ch

        @11:  mov   cl,VWidth
              rep   stosw
              add   di,dx
              dec   bl
              jne   @11
        @12:
      end
  end;
```

```
{-- global variables and main program ------------------------------------}

var i      : integer;
    sx, sy : byte;

begin
  Randomize;
  FillVideo( 0, 0, COLUMNS, ROWS, ' ', 7 );
  for i := 1 to 40 do
    begin
      sx := random( COLUMNS - 5 );
      sy := random( ROWS - 3 );
      FillVideo( sx, sy, Random( COLUMNS-sx ) +1, Random( ROWS-sy ) +1,
                 chr( i mod 256 ), random(7)+1 );
      ReadKey;
    end;
end.
```

The compiler must read the assembly language instructions in the program, convert the variables to memory accesses and link these references to constants indicating the instruction at machine level. Global variables and standard constants (e.g., VSEG as stated in the above example) operate as usual, through the data segment. The segment address is kept in the DS register. However, you address the passed parameters and the local variables using the stack because either the caller placed them there, as in a pure Pascal procedure or function, or the Pascal statements within the routine expect to find them there.

A look at the assembled code created by Turbo Pascal makes this clear. The following illustration shows the disassembled machine code of the FillVideo procedure. You can clearly recognize that the procedure, in spite of the two ASM blocks included, is handled like a regular Pascal procedure. So it is placed first on the stack in the customary manner. For this reason, you are able to access the passed parameters and the local variables by using indexed addressing using the BP register.

The compiler converted all accesses to the standardized constants (VSEG) into ordinary read accesses to the data segment, inserting the address of these variables into the appropriate machine language commands. As a result of this procedure, you cannot simply change the contents of the DS register within an ASM block if you are going to access a global variable or standardized constant again afterwards. Although assemblers such as the Turbo Assembler from Borland and the Macro Assembler from Microsoft use the ASSUME command, which could help programmers specify that the data segment can no longer be reached using the DS register, the integrated assembler doesn't have an equivalent command at its disposal.

So, after making a change, you should be sure to load the DS register with its original value before the end of each ASM block, because the compiler assumes that it will also be able to access the data segment after the end of an ASM block using the DS register. If the

DS register no longer points at the data segment at the end of an ASM block, any further program execution could be ruined. This could happen because any subsequent accesses to global variables or standardized constants will be written wildly to the memory. Under the right circumstances, this could damage the interrupt vector table or a TSR program. The same applies to the BP and SS registers, which you also shouldn't change, because the compiler assumes that it can access the local variables and the passed parameters using these registers after the end of the ASM block.

These warnings don't apply to the ES register because you can load it with any values you want within ASM blocks. The same also applies to the AX, BX, CX, DX, DI, SI registers and the Flag register.

Here is the assembly language excerpt we mentioned from the ASM1 program listed earlier:

```
{------------------------------------------------------------------------}
{-- FillVideo: Fills an area of video RAM with characters ---------------}
{------------------------------------------------------------------------}

procedure FillVideo ( X1,
                      Y1,
                      VHeight,
                      VWidth  : BYTE;
                      VChars  : char;
                      VColor  : BYTE );

begin
      { cs:0000 55              push    bp              ;Stack set to       }
      { cs:0001 89E5            mov     bp,sp           ;normal             }
      { cs:0003 31C0            xor     ax,ax           ;No local variables }
      { cs:0005 9A7C02D961      call    61D9:027C       ;Stack check instead}
  if vseg = 0 then
      { cs:000A 833E020000      cmp     word ptr [ASM1.VSEG],0000           }
      { cs:000F 7516            jne     ASM1.33 (0027)                      }
      asm
      { cs:0011 B84000          mov     ax,0040                            }
      { cs:0014 8EC0            mov     es,ax                              }
      { cs:0016 B800B8          mov     ax,B800                            }
      { cs:0019 26813E6300D403  cmp     es:word ptr [0063],03D4            }
      { cs:0020 7402            je      ASM1.29 (0024) ; je @11 -          }
      { cs:0022 B4B0            mov     ah,B0                        |      }
      { cs:0024 A30200          mov     [ASM1.VSEG],ax;   <-------         }
      end;

      {-- Fill loop in assembler (best speed) -------------------------------}
      asm
      { cs:0027 FC              cld                                        }
      { cs:0028 A10200          mov     ax,[ASM1.VSEG]                     }
      { cs:002B 8EC0            mov     es,ax                              }
      { cs:002D B0A0            mov     al,A0           ;Const. COLUMNS*ROWS }
      { cs:002F F6660C          mul     byte ptr [bp+0C] ;[BP+0C] = Y1     }
```

143

```
{ cs:0032 8A5E0E        mov    bl,[bp+0E]        ;[BP+0E] = X1        }
{ cs:0035 D0E3          shl    bl,1                                   }
{ cs:0037 30FF          xor    bh,bh                                  }
{ cs:0039 01D8          add    ax,bx                                  }
{ cs:003B 89C7          mov    di,ax                                  }
{ cs:003D 8A560A        mov    dl,[bp+0A] ;[BP+0A] = Width             }
{ cs:0040 80FA00        cmp    dl,00                                  }
{ cs:0043 7425          je     ASM1.67 (006A)   ;JE @L2               }
{ cs:0045 D0E2          shl    dl,1                                   }
{ cs:0047 30F6          xor    dh,dh            ;as before            }
{ cs:0049 F7DA          neg    dx               ;as before            }
{ cs:004B 81C2A000      add    dx,00A0          ;CONST. COLUMNS*ROWS  }
{ cs:004F 8A5E08        mov    bl,[bp+08]       ;[BP+08] = Height     }
{ cs:0052 80FB00        cmp    bl,00                                  }
{ cs:0055 7413          je     ASM1.67   (006A)                       }
{ cs:0057 8A4606        mov    al,[bp+06]       ;[BP+06] = Character  }
{ cs:005A 8A6604        mov    ah,[bp+04]       ;[BP+04] = Color      }
{ cs:005D 30ED          xor    ch,ch                                  }
{ cs:005F 8A4E0A     -> mov    cl,[bp+0A]       ;[BP+0A] = Width      }
{ cs:0062 F3A5       |  rep    movsw                                  }
{ cs:0064 01D7       |  add    di,dx                                  }
{ cs:0066 FECB       |  dec    bl                                     }
{ cs:0068 75F5       -  jne    ASM1.60   (005F) ;JNE @11              }
    end;
  end;
     { cs:006A 5D          pop    bp                 ;Reset stack      }
        { cs:006B C20C00      ret    000C          ;as before
     }
```

While the compiler in the above example is on the stack, as with an ordinary Pascal procedure or function, this is not always the case with pure assembly language routines. Along with Pascal procedures and functions, which integrate a few assembly language commands into Pascal code using ASM blocks, Turbo Pascal 6.0 is also familiar with pure assembly language routines. They have the keyword ASSEMBLER after them and cannot contain any Pascal instructions other than the procedure or function head. The following MAX routine is a simple example of a pure assembly language routine. You use the MAX routine to calculate the larger of two passed integer values and return it to the caller:

```
program ASM2;

{-- MAX: returns the larger of two INTEGER values ----------------------}

function Max( i1, i2 : integer ) : integer; assembler;
asm
        mov    ax,i1
        cmp    ax,i2
        jae    @11

        mov    ax,i2
    @11:
end;
```

```
{-- global variables and main program ----------------------------------}

var i,
    w1, w2 : integer;

begin
  Randomize;
  for i := 1 to 25 do
    begin
      w1 := random( 32000 );
      w2 := random( 32000 );
      writeln( 'MAX( ', w1:5, ', ', w2:5, ') = ', Max( w1, w2 ) );
    end;
end.
```

As the example above shows, you can also access the passed parameters in pure assembly language routines. From this you can infer that the stack must be configured in some way. Actually, Turbo Pascal also places the various instructions required for addressing local variables and parameters before assembly language routines, provided there are local variables or parameters.

If the procedure or function has local variables or parameters, then the following commands come at the beginning of the procedure:

```
PUSH  BP
MOV   BP,SP
```

while at the end of the procedure there is:

```
MOV   SP,BP
POP   BP
RET   (Pass parameter)
```

If there are both local variables and local parameters, the prolog code is completed by a command, which you use to move the stack pointer to the local variables that come immediately after the saved BP register on the stack. The prolog code of the routine would then be:

```
MOV   BP,SP
SUB   SP,(Size of local variables)
```

while nothing changes in the epilog code. On the other hand, if both local variables and parameters are missing, then no special prolog code is created, and the epilog code will consist only of the RET instruction.

There are some other differences between normal Pascal procedures and functions and pure assembly language routines that are noticeable especially in relation to functions. With normal Pascal functions the function result must always be loaded into an automatically created local variable that you address from an ASM block using the name @RESULT. This is not the case with pure assembly language functions. You are responsible for loading the function result in the registers provided for them before the end of the routine. These registers are described in Section 2.4.

The MAX function in the example above also utilizes this option by loading the function result directly in the AX register, where the caller is expecting it.

There is one last difference between regular Pascal procedures and pure assembly language routines: When pure assembly language routines return value parameters that don't include 1, 2 or 4 bytes or when they return strings, the parameters aren't copied to local variables, which are otherwise automatically created on the stack for this purpose. In this case the programmer has to either create the appropriate local variables and load them with the contents of the parameters, or use the pointers that the caller placed on the stack to access the parameters directly.

4. File Variables

If Pascal didn't have the flexible output procedures, Write and Writeln, we would have to use PRINT, which has several limitations. PRINT cannot accept numerical arguments, is unable to format the output in certain ways and it can't handle several arguments at once, except for strings. Even with strings PRINT can handle only one at a time.

But what happens when you have to send character strings to a device that isn't supported by Write or Writeln? Aside from Read and Readln, Write and Writeln are the only Pascal procedures which can take a variable number of arguments and, regardless of type, convert them into ASCII characters.

Since the normal procedures and functions don't have these capabilities, the programmers at Borland developed Write and Writeln with a concept that enables a program to use these procedures to output information to devices not originally supported. The key to this is the *file variable*, which is declared in the DOS unit. It has the following structure:

```
type TextBuf = array [0..127] of char;
     TextRec = record
                   Handle   : Word;                 { DOS file handle }
                   Mode     : Word;                    { access mode }
                   BufSize  : Word;               { buffer size in bytes }
                   Private  : Word;                   { internal use }
                   BufPos   : Word;            { current index in the buffer }
                   BufEnd   : Word;        { current no. of chars in buffer - 1 }
                   BufPtr   : ^TextBuf;            { pointer to the buffer }
                   OpenFunc : Pointer;         { pointer to Open function }
                   InOutFunc: Pointer;         { pointer to InOut function }
                   FlushFunc: Pointer;         { pointer to Flush function }
                   CloseFunc: Pointer;         { pointer to Close function }
                   UserData : array[1..16] of Byte;         { not used }
                   Name     : array[0..79] of Char;       { file name }
                   Buffer   : TextBuf;            { the standard buffer }
               end;
```

File variable structure in Turbo Pascal

Usually you will not encounter a file variable of type TextRec, since it is substituted by type Text. For example, if you declare the variable DT as a file variable of type Text, Turbo Pascal will reserve enough memory to hold a data structure of type TextRec:

```
var dt : text;
```

The individual fields within it describe the file that is associated with the file variable by Assign and opened with Reset, Rewrite or Append. But at this point Turbo Pascal is still

147

unable to access the individual fields in the file variable because it cannot be sure that dt is not type TextRec. A declaration such as:

```
i := dt.Handle;
```

would fail during compilation because of the strict type checking performed by the compiler. However, an explicit type conversion will achieve the proper results, as shown in the following listing:

```
program afilevar;
Uses Dos;
var dt : text;                        { dt is a file variable of type TextRec }
begin
  with TextRec( dt ) do                         { process dt as TextRec }
    begin
      write( Handle, '   ', Mode );   { output File Handle and Access Mode }
      { .
            .
            . }
    end;
end.
```

You can use file variables to control previously unknown devices or to modify the workings of existing device drivers. But you must understand the function of each field in the file variable. Let's discuss the form of the file variable.

The *file handle*, which is delivered by DOS after the file is opened, is a numerical value that identifies the file to DOS. Turbo gives this number to all DOS function calls that are used to manipulate the file. This is used for performing operations that cannot be done with Turbo but are easy with the proper DOS function. Turbo simply passes this handle directly from the file variable. However, remember that this and all other fields in the file variable contain a valid value only after a successful call of Reset, Rewrite or Append.

The second field contains the access mode of the file. It establishes which operations can be performed on the file using the following constants:

```
const fmClosed = $D7B0;                      { file variable still closed }
      fmInput  = $D7B1;                           { only input allowed }
      fmOutput = $D7B2;                          { only output allowed }
      fmInOut  = $D7B3;                       { input and output allowed }
```

Turbo ensures that no unauthorized write access is performed on a file where input isn't allowed. This is done by aborting the program with run-time error 105 (File not open for output). *Text files*, which are different from standard and non-standard files, can only be read or written, so you will never see a text file, with the value fmInOut in its file variable. This value is only for use with standard and non-standard files, which also uses file variables. However, the TextRec format is unused, so the programmer doesn't have the ability to create and link a special device driver. Therefore, these file types are not addressed in this chapter.

The third field gives the size of the buffer that is reserved for the file variable. Every file has such a buffer. The buffer size, usually 128 bytes, is given in the last field of the file variable. Turbo Pascal uses this buffer for input/output to and from device drivers.

The field labeled "Private" is reserved for internal use. Its purpose cannot be interpreted from its contents.

The use of BufPos and BufEnd, on the other hand, is easily understood. They give the number of bytes to write or the maximum number of bytes to read during a read/write operation. We will discuss these fields again in connection with device drivers.

Turbo Pascal reserves a 128 byte buffer for communication between device drivers and the program code of Write/Writeln or Read/Readln. But, in order to increase speed, it is often useful to define a larger buffer. This buffer is located outside the file variable, so its address must be listed within the file variable. This is the purpose of the BufPtr field, which contains a pointer to the appropriate buffer. Since you can never be sure if an expanded buffer is used for a certain file variable, you should always access the buffer only using this pointer.

After BufPtr there are four other pointers which establish the relationship between the device driver and the file variable. These pointers contain the addresses of four functions that Turbo calls to access the file variable and the corresponding file (or device). These four functions will be the basis of the following discussion, but first we'll finish studying the contents of a file variable.

The next field is called UserData, an Array of 16 bytes. Usually, these 16 bytes remain unused and are reserved for the device drivers that need to store more information than has already been captured in the file variable. You are free to use this field when creating your own device driver.

If a file variable is used to access an actual text file (not a device disguised as a text file), the field Name contains the filename and the full path, as long as one was specified with the Assign statement.

As we mentioned above, the file variable ends at the buffer.

4.1 Device Driver Functions

We may have misled you about device drivers. You should know that a device driver in the form of one compact procedure for handling input and output at the same time does not exist. What we call a device driver actually consists of four functions whose addresses are listed in every file variable. Each of these functions performs a specific task, which you can probably guess from the names of the pointer variables. When a certain operation is to be performed on a file, Turbo Pascal takes the address of the proper function from the file's file variable and calls the function.

Open
: Allows access to a file. It is executed as a result of calling Reset, Rewrite or Append.

InOut
: Handles data transfer between Turbo Pascal and the device associated with the file variable. Depending on the contents of file variable, only read or write accesses may be supported.

Flush
: Only used with file variables that can be written. Calling this procedure indicates the end of an output operation, during which InOut is called at least once.

Close
: Closes the file variable with the standard procedure Close.

All of these functions are called using pointers, so they must be type FAR. This can be done, for example, with the {$F} compiler directive. Each of these functions also returns a type Integer result. This result reflects the status of the operation. Turbo loads it into an internal variable that can be queried with the IOResult function. A result of 0 indicates "everything ok". Any other value indicates that an error has occurred.

Each function receives the file variable as an argument. By passing this variable in the form of a VAR parameter, you can make changes to the contents of this file variable. The functions are described with a type declaration as follows:

```
type DRIVERFCT = function ( var f : TextRec ) : integer;
```

Now let's take a detailed look at how each function works. The Open function is called as soon as a program executes a Reset, Rewrite or Append on a text file. The specified file variable is passed, to the Open function, unchanged.

But before the Open function can be called, its address must be placed in the file variable by the program or the proper unit. You should use a special Assign procedure for files that will be connected to a particular device. This is done with an Assign followed by the name of the device. The file variable should be passed from the calling routine. The standard procedure AssignCrt handles these steps.

The procedure should not only load the OpenFunc field with the address of the Open function, but it should also initialize the other fields. Turbo Pascal only does this by itself if the standard Assign procedure is used. The following program excerpt shows how fields are initialized in an imaginary procedure called AssignPlotter.

```
procedure AssignPlotter( f : TextRec );
begin
  with( f ) do
    begin
      Handle  := $FFFF;
      Mode    := fmClose;
      BufSize := sizeof( Buffer );
      BufPtr  := @Buffer;
      Name[0] := #0;
      OpenFunc := PlotterOpen;
    end;
end;
```

It is important to note that the access mode is given as fmClose so that in case of a Reset, Rewrite or Append call, Turbo Pascal can tell that the file has not yet been opened.

Now, Turbo Pascal calls the Open function. This will then call InOut, Flush or Close, depending on the contents of the Mode field that has since been written to the file variable. Depending on the contents of Mode, different functions will be called. It is easier to define separate functions for input and output than to put both operations into a single function.

Some devices (e.g., the plotter in the example above) perform only input or output so only one set of functions is needed to serve the device. In such cases, the Open function should check to see if an invalid access mode has been entered in the file variable. If so, the program should abort with a run-time error.

OpenPlotter should do this if the value fmInput is found in the Mode field. This would mean that the Reset procedure would be called to prepare the file (or device) to be read.

However, the Open function for a read only device should give an error if fmOutput is found. This would mean that Rewrite or Append would be called to prepare the file/device for a write operation.

After a successful call of the Open function (function result = 0), the other three driver functions can be called in any order. Of the three, the InOut function is the most frequently called. This function is used for data transfer between Turbo Pascal and the device. It is executed by calls to Write/Writeln, Read/Readln, Eof, Eoln, SeekEof and SeekEol. The way it executes its task depends on the contents of the Mode flag within the file variable, which is passed when the function is called.

When dealing with an output function, Mode will contain the value of the constant fmOutput. Then the number of characters listed in the field BufPos will be output from the buffer. This field is then set to 0, so instead of adding new characters to the end of the buffer, the caller will add them to the beginning.

A function result of 0 must also be returned in order for the output to be executed without error. Any other code is interpreted by Turbo Pascal as a run-time error.

If InOut is called for a read operation, the process is somewhat different. First, the field BufSize is evaluated. Its contents determine the maximum number of characters that may be read. The actual number of characters read, which is returned to the field BufEnd, can differ from this when the end of the file is reached or when the device stops delivering characters. If no characters are read and 0 is entered in BufEnd, the subsequent Eof call returns the value TRUE, because Turbo Pascal assumes the end of the file has been reached.

Regardless of the number of characters read, the BufPos field must be reloaded with the value 0 so that Turbo Pascal will take the passed characters from the front of the buffer.

Input and output operations use the Flush function, which is called at the end of Write/Writeln and Read/Readln. The way Flush works also varies with the access mode.

In Input mode (fmInput), the only thing Flush does is set BufEnd and BufPos to 0. All the characters that may still be in the buffer are deleted. This usually doesn't affect the program execution, since Read and Readln take all characters from the buffer anyway. However, your Flush function should perform this task for Turbo Pascal, since this may or may not be critical in future versions.

For character output, Flush has the same meaning as InOut, and can, therefore, point to the same routine. If the InOut function always outputs all characters immediately and doesn't do anything, such as store them in an internal buffer, it is possible to implement Flush as a dummy routine that simply returns 0 as a function result.

Close is always the last function that is called. This function gives the device drive a chance to "clean up" after a file has been closed. Exactly what is done during the clean up depends on what the other driver functions have done. For example, if an internal buffer on the heap was reserved with Open, the Close function is the last chance to free this buffer.

The next section contains a unit which executes output to the screen with Write/Writeln and takes input from the keyboard with Read/Readln. The characters are automatically stored in a log file so that they can be retrieved in case of a system crash or power loss.

4.2   Accessing Log Files

In the PC world, data security may be a neglected topic, discussed only with backup programs. This will definitely change with the growing use of local area PC networks which are prone to different and more frequent errors than a stand-alone PC. Waiting until the end of the week or even the end of the day to backup your data may be too late. A lot can happen during the day and data loss of this magnitude is extremely serious.

This chapter contains an example for creating a device driver in Turbo Pascal that automatically stores all screen and keyboard I/O in a log file. Programs such as this have long been used in mainframe and minicomputer data processing applications, and have proven to be one of the best methods of maintaining data security. Data stored in the log file can be retrieved at any time.

A system such as this also helps data security in another way. Access is denied unless the correct password is supplied, so unauthorized changes to the data cannot be made.

Before we begin to discuss the log unit, we would like to show you the program PROTDEMO.PAS, which is used to demonstrate the action of PROT.PAS.

```
{******************************************************************
 *  ProtDemo : demonstrates the way the PROT unit works - by linking this   *
 *             unit, all screen output is copied to the log file with Write  *
 *             and Writeln                                                   *
 **------------------------------------------------------------------**
 *  Author         : MICHAEL TISCHER                                 *
 *  developed on   : 09/26/1989                                      *
 *  last update    : 09/26/1989                                      *
 ******************************************************************}
program ProtDemo;
uses Prot;                                        { link log unit }
var i    : integer;                               { loop counter }
    IdStr : string[12];                           { ID string }
begin
  {-- For the demonstration, two WRITE and WRITELN statements execute -----}
  {-- and the contents are sent to the screen and to the log file. --------}
  {-- The input is read first with a Readln statement. This data is also  -}
  {-- sent to the log file. -----------------------------------------------}
  write( 'Please enter user ID: ');
  readln( IdStr );
  for i := 1 to 10 do
    begin
      write( 'Turbo Pascal System Programming ' );
      write( i:5, ' -- ' );
      writeln( chr(65+i), chr(66+i), chr(67+i) );
    end;
end.
```

As you can see, the USES statement links the Prot unit with the program, but there are no calls to any procedures or functions from this unit. But there are several Write/Writeln statements and one Readln statement. After executing these, the screen will look similar to this:

```
C:>protdemo
Please enter user ID: MITI
Turbo Pascal System Programming      1 -- BCD
Turbo Pascal System Programming      2 -- CDE
Turbo Pascal System Programming      3 -- DEF
Turbo Pascal System Programming      4 -- EFG
Turbo Pascal System Programming      5 -- FGH
Turbo Pascal System Programming      6 -- GHI
Turbo Pascal System Programming      7 -- HIJ
Turbo Pascal System Programming      8 -- IJK
Turbo Pascal System Programming      9 -- JKL
Turbo Pascal System Programming     10 -- KLM
C:>
```

Screen after the first call of PROTDEMO

There is really no evidence of the log file here, but all input and output, including entry of the user ID, has been stored in the file LOG.DAT within the current directory. This file isn't recreated each time the program is run. Each new I/O will append to the end of the existing file. The log unit also inserts the current date and time prior to the first input/output that is logged.

The following listing shows the contents of the log file after the PROTDEMO program was run on two consecutive days.

```
----------------------------------- Monday,   12/04/1989,  7:12
Please enter user ID: MITI
Turbo Pascal System Programming      1 -- BCD
Turbo Pascal System Programming      2 -- CDE
Turbo Pascal System Programming      3 -- DEF
Turbo Pascal System Programming      4 -- EFG
Turbo Pascal System Programming      5 -- FGH
Turbo Pascal System Programming      6 -- GHI
Turbo Pascal System Programming      7 -- HIJ
Turbo Pascal System Programming      8 -- IJK
Turbo Pascal System Programming      9 -- JKL
Turbo Pascal System Programming     10 -- KLM
----------------------------------- Tuesday,  12/05/1989, 18:25
Please enter user ID: JOO
Turbo Pascal System Programming      1 -- BCD
Turbo Pascal System Programming      2 -- CDE
Turbo Pascal System Programming      3 -- DEF
Turbo Pascal System Programming      4 -- EFG
Turbo Pascal System Programming      5 -- FGH
Turbo Pascal System Programming      6 -- GHI
Turbo Pascal System Programming      7 -- HIJ
```

```
Turbo Pascal System Programming      8 -- IJK
Turbo Pascal System Programming      9 -- JKL
Turbo Pascal System Programming     10 -- KLM
```

Contents of the log file LOG.DAT after running PROTDEMO for two consecutive days

It is interesting that this log file will contain all of the data even though the program PROTDEMO doesn't have any statements for the creation of this file. Simply referencing the PROT unit with the USES statement is enough to send all I/O from Write/Writeln and Read/Readln to the log file.

This happens because of the initialization procedure of the PROT unit. Just like the initialization procedure of the standard units, this is executed before the main program is called. This initialization procedure diverts the Write/Writeln and Read/Readln statements to its own routines which store all characters in the log file. Let's take a look at exactly how this is done.

```
{*******************************************************************
 *  PROT : a unit for logging all input and output through Write/Writeln  *
 *         and Read/Readln to log file.                             *
 **-----------------------------------------------------------------**
 *  Author        : MICHAEL TISCHER                                 *
 *  developed on   : 09/17/1989                                     *
 *  last update    : 09/17/1989                                     *
 *******************************************************************}
unit Prot;
interface
uses Dos;
{-- public constants ----------------------------------------------}
const PROT_NAME : string[80] = 'LOG.DAT';              { name of the log file }
{-- internal section ----------------------------------------------}
implementation
type DRIVERFCT = function ( var f : TextRec ) : integer;
var OldExit    : pointer;              { pointer to original Exit procedure }
    OldOPInOut,                        { pointer to old InOut function of OUTPUT }
    OldOPFlush,                        { pointer to old Flush function of OUTPUT }
    OldIPInOut,                        { pointer to old InOut function of INPUT }
    OldIPFlush : DRIVERFCT;            { pointer to old Flush function of INPUT }
    ProtDat    : text;                       { file variable for log file }
```

As you can see from the unit header, PROT doesn't define any public procedures or functions. Only the standard constant PROT_NAME is public, so that you can give the log file another name in case you use the PROT unit with several different programs. We will discuss the meaning of the various global variables but first let's take a look at the initialization procedure of the unit. This is where most of the action takes place.

```
{*****************************************************************************
 *  ProtInit : Initialization procedure for the PROT unit                   *
 **-------------------------------------------------------------------------**
 *  Input    : none                                                         *
 *  Globals  : OldExit/W, OldOPInOut/W, OldOPFlush/W                         *
 *****************************************************************************}
procedure ProtInit;
const WDays : array [0..6] of string[11] = ( 'Sunday,     ',
                                             'Monday,     ',
                                             'Tuesday,    ',
                                             'Wednesday,  ',
                                             'Thursday,   ',
                                             'Friday,     ',
                                             'Saturday,   '  );

var Year, Month, Day, WeekDay,                                    { date }
    Hour, Minute, Dummy         : word;                           { time }
    dummyStr                    : string;   { file name of log file found }
begin
  {-- create log file if it does not exist, otherwise append data ---------}
  Assign( ProtDat, PROT_NAME );
  dummyStr := FSearch( PROT_NAME, '' );       { search in current directory }
  if ( dummyStr <> '' ) then                              { file found? }
    Append( ProtDat )                               { yes, append new data }
  else                                                     { no, create }
    rewrite( ProtDat );
  {-- write date and time to log file -------------------------------------}
  GetDate( Year, Month, Day, WeekDay );                       { get date }
  GetTime( Hour, Minute, Dummy, Dummy );                      { get time }
  write( ProtDat, '------------------------------------ ',
                  WDays[ WeekDay ],
                  Day:2,
                  '.'                                          );
  if ( Month < 10 ) then write( ProtDat, '0', Month )
                    else write( ProtDat, Month );
  write( ProtDat, '.',
                  Year,
                  ', ',
                  Hour:2,
                  ':'            );
  if ( Minute < 10 ) then write( ProtDat, '0', Minute )
                    else write( ProtDat, Minute );
  writeln( ProtDat, #13#10 );
  {-- divert output through OUTPUT by manipulating the file variable ------}
  with TextRec( Output ) do         { manipulate the file variable OUTPUT }
    begin
      OldOPInOut := DRIVERFCT(InOutFunc);  { store addresses of previous  }
      OldOPFlush := DRIVERFCT(FlushFunc);  { driver functions             }
      InOutFunc := @ProtOPInOut;    { divert driver functions by loading  }
      FlushFunc := @ProtOPFlush;        { new addresses                   }
      {-- the CLOSE function is not changed! -----------------------------}
    end;
  {-- divert input through INPUT by manipulating the file variable --------}
```

```
      with TextRec( Input ) do          { manipulate the file variable INPUT }
        begin
          OldIPInOut := DRIVERFCT(InOutFunc); { store addresses of previous   }
          OldIPFlush := DRIVERFCT(FlushFunc); { driver functions              }
          InOutFunc := @ProtIPInOut;     { divert driver functions by loading }
          FlushFunc := @ProtIPFlush;     { new addresses                      }
          {-- CLOSE function remains unchanged here! ------------------------}
        end;
      OldExit := ExitProc;                      { store current EXIT procedure }
      ExitProc := @ProtExit;            { declare ProtExit as EXIT procedure }
    end;
    {**------------------------------------------------------------------**}
    {** Starting code of Unit                                           **}
    {**------------------------------------------------------------------**}
    begin
      ProtInit;                                            { Initialize Unit }
    end.
```

The previous program excerpt shows the initialization of the unit. The procedure ProtInit is called for the actual initialization. This procedure begins by using the standard procedure FSearch to determine if the log file, whose name is given with the standard constant PROT_NAME, already exists. If not, it is created with Rewrite. If it does exist, it is opened and prepared to accept further characters with Append. The file is opened as a text file since it will hold ASCII characters.

After successfully opening the file, GetDate and GetTime are used to write the current date and time in the log header. Then ProtInit diverts the screen and keyboard I/O from Write/Writeln and Read/Readln.

Now you should know that Turbo Pascal also controls access to the screen and keyboard with an internal file variable. Programs do not usually come into contact with these, because Turbo creates them automatically when input/output procedures are called. For Write and Writeln this file variable is called OUTPUT. This is connected with the screen and can only accept write access. Read and Readln calls use the file variable INPUT, which can only capture characters.

Both are declared within the system unit and are initialized in the initialization section of this unit so that they are ready when the program starts. In order to get the output of these file variables into the log file, the driver functions within the ProtInit unit are diverted to internal functions. This pertains only to InOut and Flush, since the Open function is no longer needed (the file was already opened in the initialization section) and the Close function doesn't need to be diverted.

The old driver functions are not deleted. Their addresses are stored in four global variables of the unit. For OUTPUT, these variables are OldOPInOut and OldOPFlush. The analogs for INPUT are OldIPInOut and OldIPFlush. All four are of type DRIVERFCT <driver function>, which represents a procedural pointer to a function. The pointer is passed as an argument to a file variable and the function returns an INTEGER, just like a regular driver function.

A new EXIT procedure is placed at the end of ProtInit. The current address of the EXIT procedure is stored in OldExit and replaced with the address of ProtExit.

Now each call to Write/Writeln and Read/Readln, which use the file variables INPUT and OUTPUT, will no longer use the original routines from the system unit. Instead, the new routines from the PROT unit are called. Let's see what happens.

```
{******************************************************************************
 * ProtOPInOut: InOut driver function for the file variable OUTPUT.          *
 **-------------------------------------------------------------------------**
 * Input    : F = the file variable Output of type TextRec                   *
 * Output   : the function result of the old driver function                 *
 * Globals  : OldOPInOut/R                                                    *
 ******************************************************************************}
{$F+}                                                         { must be FAR }
function ProtOPInOut( var f : TextRec ) : integer;
begin
  PWrite( f );                                { write characters to log file }
  ProtOPInOut := OldOPInOut( f );             { call the old driver function }
end;
{$F-}
{******************************************************************************
 * ProtOPFlush: Flush driver function for the file variable OUTPUT.          *
 **-------------------------------------------------------------------------**
 * Input    : F = the file variable Output of type TextRec                   *
 * Output   : the function result from the old driver function               *
 * Globals  : OldOPFlush/R                                                    *
 ******************************************************************************}
{$F+}                                                         { must be FAR }
function ProtOPFlush( var f : TextRec ) : integer;
begin
  PWrite( f );                                { write characters to log file }
  ProtOPFlush := OldOPFlush( f );             { call the old driver function }
end;
{$F-}
```

The functions ProtOPInOut and ProtOPFlush are responsible for output through OUTPUT. Both consist of two statements each, which first call the PWRITE function to write the output characters in the log file. So that these two functions don't have to perform the character output themselves, they call the old driver functions by using the global variables that are storing their addresses. The function result is then passed unchanged to the calling routine.

PWrite is not much more extensive than the two new driver functions. All it does is run through the buffer within the file variable and transfers the characters to the log file.

```
{****************************************************************************
*  PWrite : Writes screen output passed through the file variable OUTPUT  *
*           to the log file.                                              *
**----------------------------------------------------------------------**
*  Input   : DatVar = the file variable OUTPUT, as given to the calling  *
*                     routine by Turbo Pascal.                           *
*  Globals : ProtDat/R                                                    *
****************************************************************************}
procedure PWrite( DatVar : TextRec );
var i : integer;                                        { loop counter }
begin
   with DatVar do                       { process the passed file variable }
      for i := 0 to BufPos-1 do                  { process each character }
        write( ProtDat, DatVar.BufPtr^[ i ] );   { and write to ProtDat  }
end;
```

Notice that PWrite also takes output from the Write procedure. It does this without a new or recursive call to ProtOPInOut or ProtOPFlush. The access to this file is not done using the file variable OUTPUT but rather using ProtDat. As a disk file, this file, from the beginning, has completely different driver functions.

The new driver functions for the file variable INPUT work similar to those for OUTPUT. One difference is that the INPUT driver first calls the old driver functions, because these are what return the result that is to be stored in the log file. This happens within the new InOut function and only if the old driver function returns a 0 as the function result.

The new Flush function doesn't output any characters to the log file because it isn't involved in character output, as described above.

```
{****************************************************************************
*  ProtIPInOut: InOut driver function for the file variable INPUT.        *
**----------------------------------------------------------------------**
*  Input   : F = the file variable INPUT of type TextRec                  *
*  Output  : the function result from the old driver function             *
*  Globals : OldIPInOut/R                                                  *
****************************************************************************}
{$F+}                                              { must be type FAR }
function ProtIPInOut( var f : TextRec ) : integer;
var Result : integer;                          { result from ProtIPInOut }
begin
  Result := OldIPInOut( f );              { first call old driver function }
  if Result = 0 then                               { everything o.k.? }
    PRead( f );                        { yes, write characters to log file }
  ProtIPInOut := Result;                    { return result of OldOPFlush }
end;
{$F-}
```

```
{*******************************************************************
*  ProtIPFlush: Flush driver function for the file variable INPUT.  *
**---------------------------------------------------------------**
*  Input    : F = the file variable Input of type TextRec          *
*  Output   : the function result from the old driver function      *
*  Globals  : OldIPFlush/R                                          *
*******************************************************************}
{$F+}                                               { must be FAR }
function ProtIPFlush( var f : TextRec ) : integer;
begin
  if @OldIPFlush <> NIL then              { does a FLUSH function exist? }
    ProtIPFlush := OldIPFlush( f )                  { yes, call }
  else                                                  { no }
    ProtIPFlush := 0;                            {everything o.k. }
end;
{$F-}
```

Notice that the new Flush function uses a dummy procedure in case there is no old Flush function. If the value NIL is found for the pointer to the old Flush function, no attempt is made to call it and a value of 0 is automatically inserted as the function result.

ProtIPInOut is used for logging data from the procedure PRead. In this case, it is the BufEnd field, instead of BufPos, that gives the number of characters returned.

```
{*******************************************************************
*  PRead : Writes input accepted through file variable INPUT into the  *
*          log file.                                                *
**---------------------------------------------------------------**
*  Input    : DatVar = the file variable INPUT as passed to the calling  *
*                      routine by Turbo Pascal.                     *
*  Globals  : ProtDat/R                                             *
*******************************************************************}
procedure PRead( DatVar : TextRec );
var i : integer;                               { loop counter }
begin
  with DatVar do                    { process the passed file variable }
    for i := 0 to BufEnd-1 do              { run through each character }
      write( ProtDat, DatVar.BufPtr^[ i ] );     { and write to ProtDat }
end;
```

The procedure ProtExit is used for closing the log file and reactivating the old driver functions for OUTPUT and INPUT. It is automatically called as the EXIT procedure when the program is finished.

```
{*******************************************************************
*  ProtExit : EXIT procedure for the PROT unit                      *
**---------------------------------------------------------------**
*  Input    : none                                                  *
*  Globals  : OldExit/R                                             *
*******************************************************************}
```

```
{$F+}
procedure ProtExit;
begin
  Close( ProtDat );                                { close the log file }
  ExitProc := OldExit;                    { restore old Exit procedure }
  {-- reactivate the old driver ------------------------------------------}
  with TextRec( Output ) do            { manipulate the file variable OUTPUT }
    begin
      InOutFunc := @OldOPInOut; { here, @ does not return the addresses of }
      FlushFunc := @OldOPFlush; { the variables, but the contents!         }
    end;
  with TextRec( Input ) do             { manipulate the file variable OUTPUT }
    begin
      InOutFunc := @OldIPInOut;
      FlushFunc := @OldIPFlush;
    end;
end;
{$F-}
```

Before ending this discussion, we would like to present a few tips for other applications of the PROT unit. We have seen how PROT works with Write/Writeln and Read/Readln, but procedures such as GotoXY, Window or ReadKey are also used for keyboard and screen I/O. These routines can be included in an expanded form of the PROT unit. Their output will be even easier to include in the log file because each of these routines can simply be diverted by including a routine of the same name in the PROT unit. If you add these procedures, however, you should switch the log format from ASCII to binary. This will make it easier to reconstruct the information later.

If you ever use PROT with a program that has linked the CRT unit, you must include CRT in the USES statement that is executed before PROT starts. This will ensure that the initialization section of CRT is called before PROT. Also CRT diverts the driver functions for INPUT and OUTPUT to its own routines. These routines process input and output faster than those of the system unit. The previous driver functions will become the driver functions from PROT and will not be called by CRT. To ensure that the information will be logged correctly, initialize CRT before PROT, which will store the addresses of the CRT functions as the previous driver functions and then call them.

Refer to Chapter 6 for another demonstration of device drivers. The Window unit presented in that chapter shows how to use a driver to integrate the Write and Writeln procedures into the unit.

5. Direct Hardware Access

You occasionally can't avoid direct access to hardware with Pascal even though it's actually a job for assembly language programming. For example, in Section 11.2, direct access must be made to the video controllers of Hercules and MDA cards in order to distinguish them, and in Section 13.2 where the PC's internal clock is accelerated to achieve faster switching between parallel tasks.

The PC ports, which are the keys to the hardware, act as doors to the various ICs. Ports are the only way to access the components on the mother board (Interrupt Controller, Timer, DMA Controller) and expansion cards. Most chips or cards use many ports rather than a single one. Each port will have a different meaning for a particular device. For example, one port may pass commands to the device while another questions status information. The use of each port varies from chip to chip and must be carefully observed while programming. Be sure to check the technical documentation delivered with your PC or expansion card.

This type of communication is so important to the workings of a PC that the processor has dedicated two machine language commands for this purpose. These commands, which are called IN and OUT, are used for sending/receiving data to and from ports. There are two versions of each command, one for 8 bit ports and one for the newer 16 bit ports.

The number of the port to be addressed must always be given with these commands. Each port has an address between 0 and 65535. As of this time, only port addresses $000 to $3FF have been assigned in PCs. The port assignments are standardized and represent a little-known, but important, indicator of the true compatibility of a PC. The port addresses of the chips are essential to the proper operation of a PC. So these usually will not differ, even on the most exotic PCs. However, the port addresses for other components, such as a real time clock, can differ greatly. Usually, the port addresses of other components are captured by the BIOS. As long as you always use the assigned BIOS interrupt to access the real time clock, you will be protected from this kind of incompatibility.

Although there are many similarities in the port addresses used in the PC/XT and the AT/386, some of the differences are quite significant. These differences are a result of the internal construction of the system not normally visible to the user.

For example, the AT uses two DMA controllers, but the PC/XT uses only one. This allows faster data transfer times between memory and disk drives. The same is true for the Interrupt Controllers. The AT has an advantage over the PC/XT, and is able to use a greater number of expansion cards. The following table will give you an overview of the port addresses used on the PC, XT, AT and 386.

Component	PC/XT	AT and 386
DMA controller (8237A-5)	000-00F	000-01F
Interrupt controller (8259A)	020-021	020-03F
Clock	040-043	040-05F
Programmable Peripheral Interface (PPI 8255A-5)	060-063	none
Keyboard (8042)	none	060-06F
Real time clock (MC146818)	none	070-07F
DMA side register	080-083	080-09F
Interrupt controller 2 (8259A)	none	0A0-0BF
DMA controller 2 (8237A-5)	none	0C0-0DF
Math coprocessor	none	0F0-0F1
Math coprocessor	none	0F8-0FF
Hard disk controller	320-32F	1F0-1F8
Game port (joystick)	200-20F	200-207
Expansion bus	210-217	none
Port 2nd parallel printer	none	278-27F
2nd serial port	2F8-2FF	2F8-2FF
Prototype card	300-31F	300-31F
Network card	none	360-36F
Port for 1st parallel printer	378-37F	378-37F
Monochrome video card and parallel printer port	3B0-3BF	3B0-3BF
Color/Graphic video card	3D0-3DF	3D0-3DF
Floppy disk controller	3F0-3F7	3F0-3F7
1st serial port	3F8-3FF	3F8-3FF

The PC/XT, AT and 386 ports

Although Turbo Pascal has two commands, Port and PortW, for accessing ports, they aren't proper commands because they can be used in many different ways. These commands aren't, as you may think, identical to the machine commands IN and OUT. Both commands can be used for sending and receiving data through a port. The distinction is made by the type of port being addressed. Port is used with 8 bit ports and PortW is reserved for use with 16 bit ports.

The way Turbo converts these commands to IN and OUT commands depends upon how they are used. If the command is on the left side of a declaration, Turbo will interpret this as a request to evaluate the expression on the right side of the equal sign and then send the result to the port. If one of these commands is on the right side of the equal sign, then the contents of the port will be read with the IN machine language instruction. In this way, the command is almost like a function that returns the contents of the port as its result.

The port to be addressed is always given after the command, enclosed in square brackets. The command:

```
port[ 40 ] := $F3
```

will send the value $F3 to port 40, while:

```
writeln( port[ 63 ])
```

will return the contents of port 63.

Let's use a practical example to take a closer look at working with ports. This example does provide substantial background, but it shouldn't be used as a general example for writing test programs to access any port. Doing this could actually damage your hardware. Even reading the contents of certain ports can have a harmful effect on your hardware.

5.1   Keyboard Programming

We will use the Intel 8042 chip found in every AT keyboard for our demonstration. The keyboard controller found in the PC/XT is numbered 8048. Unlike the 8048 (found in PC/XT models), the 8042 is programmable. The BIOS uses the 8042 to perform such tasks as switching the keyboard LEDs on and off to indicate keyboard status.

In addition to this, it's possible to set the *Typematic Rate* of the keyboard. This determines the delay rate and the speed with which the Keyboard controller repeats the character for a key that is pressed and held. This, for example, allows the user to press and hold the cursor keys to move them across an entire page without having to use individual keystrokes to move it each step.

The delay rate before the key starts to repeat can be one quarter, one half, three quarters or one full second. The speed with which the key repeats can be set to values between two and 30 repetitions per second. These two parameters together form the Typematic Rate, which is coded in one byte. The Typematic Rate must be passed to the keyboard controller. This cannot simply be done once by sending the proper byte to the keyboard port. Instead, there must be a regular dialog of information between the program being run and the keyboard.

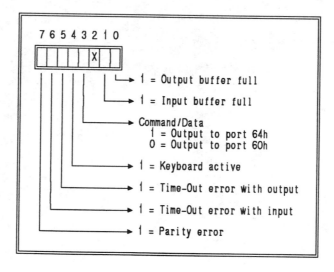

Structure of AT keyboard controller status register

There are actually two keyboard ports involved in this communication. The first, called the *data port*, contains port address $60. The other is called the *status port*, and it is found at port address $64. Its contents determines whether or not the program may access the data port at a given time. The above illustration shows the meanings of the individual bits in the status bytes which can be read through the status port.

A program may only send information to the data port if bit 0 in the status register doesn't contain 1. In this case, there is already information in the data port which must first be read by the system. This happens when a key has been struck and the code for this key is in the data port waiting to be read by the BIOS in order to be processed further.

Bit 1 is also important for our example. By its contents, we can tell if the information needed to set the Typematic Rate has been received by the keyboard controller. As long as this bit contains 1, the information is still at the data port and has not yet been processed by the keyboard. To send a byte to the keyboard, the status port must be queried until bit 0 contains the value 0. This signals that the data port is ready to accept more information. But it is important not to let this query loop run forever. If the data port is not free after a certain amount of time, then something is obviously wrong, and the attempt to send data should end with an error.

In cases where bit 0 is found to contain the value 0 within the given time period, the output byte can be sent to the data port. After this, the status port must again be queried with another loop. This time, it must wait for bit 1 to be set by the controller, indicating that the reply to the byte sent to the data port is ready. Immediately after this, the reply can be read by the data port. You will know the keyboard has accepted the information only if the reply is the code $FA, which represents "Acknowledge".

If the reply is anything else, the operation repeats at least twice. If these additional attempts also fail, then the transfer attempt is aborted. We also need to know what to send the keyboard controller in order to tell it that we want to set the Typematic Rate. The proper command code is $F3. After the keyboard has acknowledged receipt of the "Set Typematic Rate" code, the coded Typematic Rate must follow. The repeat speed and the delay rate are both sent in one byte, occupying the lower 5 bits and the upper 3 bits, respectively. The next two figures show the valid codes for the delay rate and repeat speed.

Code	Delay Rate
00b	1/4 Second
01b	1/2 Second
10b	1/4 Second
11b	1 Second

Code for delay rate

Notice that the delay rate isn't always executed accurately. Variations of +/- 20% aren't unusual, but the user will barely notice a difference.

Code	RpS*	Code	RpS*	Code	RpS*	Code	RpS*
11111b	2.0	10111b	4.0	01111b	8.0	00111b	16.0
11110b	2.1	10110b	4.3	01110b	8.6	00110b	17.1
11101b	2.3	10101b	4.6	01101b	9.2	00101b	18.5
11100b	2.5	10100b	5.0	01100b	10.0	00100b	20.0
11011b	2.7	10011b	5.5	01011b	10.9	00011b	21.8
11010b	3.0	10010b	6.0	01010b	12.0	00010b	24.0
11001b	3.3	10001b	6.7	01001b	13.3	00001b	26.7
11000b	3.7	10000b	7.5	01000b	15.0	00000b	30.0
* Repeats per second							

Codes for number of repeats per second

Even though the relationship between the codes and the corresponding value seems arbitrary, there is a mathematical formula behind it. The binary value of bits 0, 1 and 2 of the code form variable A and the binary values of bits 3 and 4 make up variable B. The formula is:

$$(8 + A) * 2B * 0.00417 * 1/second.$$

You will be able to tell if the Typematic Rate was successfully sent to the keyboard by pressing a key and holding it.

The following program allows you to set the Typematic Rate by entering a value on a command line, when the program is started. Enter a delay rate between 0 and 3 and then the repeat speed, which must be between 0 and 31. If you forget to make an entry, the program shows you what to do with a help text. Within the main program, the components of the Typematic Rate are assembled. This value is passed to the function SetTypm, which uses a local function named SendKb to pass a byte containing the rate.

```
{******************************************************************************
*  FASTKB : Demonstration of port access using the AT keyboard as the        *
*           example device.  The program passes information to the           *
*           keyboard to set the key repeat speed and delay rate.             *
**------------------------------------------------------------------------**
*  Author         : MICHAEL TISCHER                                          *
*  developed on   : 09/23/1989                                               *
*  last update on : 09/23/1989                                               *
******************************************************************************}
program FastKb;
{******************************************************************************
*  SetTypm : sets AT keyboard Typematic Rate                                 *
```

```
**-------------------------------------------------------------------------**
*  Input   : Rate : the Typematic Rate                                       *
*  Output  : TRUE, if the new Typematic-Rate was successfully set,           *
*            otherwise FALSE (communication error or XT keyboard found)      *
*****************************************************************************}
function SetTypm( Rate : byte ) : boolean;
const KB_STATUS_P = $64;                           { keyboard status port }
      KB_DATA_P   = $60;                             { keyboard data port }
      OB_FULL     = 1;               { Bit #0 indicates full output buffer }
      IB_FULL     = 2;          { Bit #1 indicates commands to be processed }
      ACK_SIGNAL  = $FA;           { confirmation of keyboard after receipt }
      SET_TYPEM   = $F3;          { code for command that sets Typematic Rate }
      MAX_TRY = 3;                         { maximum number of retries }

{-- SendKb sends one byte to the keyboard data port -----------[ LOCAL ]---}
function SendKb( what : byte ) : boolean;
var i      : word;                        { loop counter for port query }
    fcount : byte;                                     { error counter }
    ok     : boolean;                        { accepts function result }
begin
  fcount := 0;                                         { no errors yet }
  ok     := FALSE;                        { no successful transmission yet }
  repeat                                               { transfer loop }
    inc( fcount );                           { increment error counter }
    i := 0;                                  { initialize loop counter }
    {-- wait until keyboard input buffer is empty ------------------------}
    repeat
      inc( i );
    until ( i = 32768 ) or ( port[ KB_STATUS_P ] and IB_FULL = 0 );
    port[ KB_DATA_P ] := what;                  { send byte to data port }
    {-- wait until the byte is processed and an answer has been -----------}
    {-- sent to the status port.                            -----------}
    repeat
      inc( i );
    until ( i = 65535 ) or ( port[ KB_STATUS_P ] and OB_FULL = OB_FULL );
    {-- read answer from data port                    -------------}
    {-- ( only an ACKNOWLEDGE indicates successful processing) ------------}
    ok := ( port[ KB_DATA_P ] = ACK_SIGNAL );
  until ( fcount = MAX_TRY ) or ok;
  SendKb := ok;                                  { return function result }
end;
{-------------------------------------------------------------------------}
begin
  inline( $FA );                               { CLI, disable interrupts }
  if SendKb( SET_TYPEM ) then           { send code for "set Typematic Rate" }
    SetTypm := SendKb( Rate )                  { transmission successful }
  else
    SetTypm := FALSE;                       { error during transmission }
  inline( $FB );                                { STI, enable interrupts }
end;
{*****************************************************************************}
{**                            MAIN PROGRAM                               **}
{*****************************************************************************}
```

```
var Delay,                                  { accept the given delay rate }
    Speed,                                  { accept the given repeat rate }
    Fpos1,
    FPos2 : integer;                        { error in string conversion }
    ParErr : boolean;                       { error in parameter transfer }
begin
  writeln( #13#10,'████████████ FASTKB  -  (c) 1989 by MI'+
          'CHAEL TISCHER ████', #13#10 );
  ParErr := true;                           { assume incorrect input for now }
  if ParamCount = 2 then                        { were 2 parameters passed? }
    begin                                                         { YES }
      val(ParamStr(1), Delay, FPos1);   { convert 1st parameter to INTEGER }
      val(ParamStr(2), Speed, FPos2);   { convert 2nd parameter to INTEGER }
      if ((FPos1=0) and (FPos2=0)) then       { error during conversion ?}
        if ((Delay < 4) and (Speed <32)) then       { no, values o.k.? }
          ParErr := false;                   { yes, parameters are o.k. }
    end;
  if ( ParErr ) then                              { parameters o.k.? }
    begin                                                  { no }
      writeln('Call: FASTKB     Delay   Repeat Speed');
      writeln('                         ',#30,'              ',#30);
      writeln('                          |              |');
      writeln('                 ┌─────────────┐ ┌───────────────┐');
      writeln('                 ║ 0 : 1/4 Second ║ ║ 0 : 30.0 W./Sec. ║');
      writeln('                 ║ 1 : 1/2 Second ║ ║ 1 : 26.7 W./Sec. ║');
      writeln('                 ║ 2 : 3/4 Second ║ ║ 2 : 24.0 W./Sec. ║');
      writeln('                 ║ 3 : 1 Second   ║ ║ 3 : 21.8 W./Sec. ║');
      writeln('                 ╠═══════════════╣ ║      .        ║');
      writeln('                 ║ all values ± c 20% ║ ║      .        ║');
      writeln('                 └─────────────┘ ║      .        ║');
      writeln('                                  ║ 28 :  2.5 W./Sec. ║');
      writeln('                                  ║ 29 :  2.3 W./Sec. ║');
      writeln('                                  ║ 30 :  2.1 W./Sec. ║');
      writeln('                                  ║ 31 :  2.0 W./Sec. ║');
      writeln('                                  └───────────────┘');
    end
  else                                          { the parameters are o.k. }
  begin
    if (SetTypm( (Delay shl 5) + Speed )) then       { set Typematic Rate }
      writeln('Typematic rate now set as requested.')
    else
      writeln('ATTENTION! Keyboard controller access error.');
  end;
end.
```

6. Window Management

User friendly interfaces are an essential part of successful programming. Your program solving the most complex problems will be considered a failure if the customers can't understand it. This interface may be the only thing the users will see of your program. Your expertise as a programmer may be judged on the user interface.

IBM published the SAA (System Application Architecture) to provide guidelines on various PC applications and user interfaces. Programs such as Turbo Pascal made a breakthrough by using Pull Down Menus and Windows. The SAA standard supports the use of the mouse, dialog boxes, help buttons and rulers. If you think about what these functions do, you will realize what is involved in their programming. This causes problems for programs like Turbo Pascal which do not contain the routines needed for creating windows, dividing the screen into various regions and other features specified in SAA.

Turbo Pascal does have an advantage over many other languages or development environments in screen output with its routines for character output. These are much faster than the DOS and BIOS functions. Unfortunately, you still can't create windows with these features. After closing, a true window will reveal the screen it was covering. This does not work with WINDOW.

Because of this you should program your own software screen output package. Such software provides both flexibility and speed. Working with windows requires large amounts of data to be transferred between RAM and the screen. You'll have many disappointed users if you rely on the ROM-BIOS functions to do this. However, you cannot completely ignore the BIOS functions. There are many other functions under interrupt $10 than those which perform character output. There are also functions for setting the video mode, cursor position or screen page for display.

Although these are all tasks that can be accomplished by programming the video card, this procedure is not recommended. Each type of video card (from MDA to VGA) would have to be programmed differently. Also, available functions are usually fully preprogrammed and it would be difficult to increase the speed of execution.

For screen output the BIOS functions aren't essential but DOS functions are a requirement. Compared to other screen access options, these functions are very slow and offer only limited control. Even the output cursor position cannot be simply specified since it requires ANSI.SYS. The only time you may want to use the DOS functions is to send program output to a printer or a file, and WriteLn serves this purpose quite well.

6.1 Fundamentals

Another option, besides the DOS and BIOS functions, that is used for accessing the screen is programming the video RAM. Video RAM refers to a special memory area found on the circuit board of a video card that stores the information on the characters or bit map to be sent to the screen in text or graphic mode.

While all types of video cards interpret this information the same way when in text mode, there are dramatic differences in the way the various video cards interpret graphic data. Because of these differences, a special driver is needed. So, in this chapter, we will only discuss screen access in text mode.

The only difference between cards is the location of the video RAM:

- On monochrome cards (MDA, Hercules or monochrome EGA) the video RAM begins at segment address $B000.

- On color cards (CGA, EGA, VGA) the video RAM begins at segment address $B800.

In both cases, the video RAM is a part of the addressable memory. It differs from regular RAM memory only because it is located beyond the 640K limit.

However, this doesn't stop a program from accessing this memory like any other area, since it is still below the 1 megabyte limit of memory addressable to the processor. The only card that may give you problems is the IBM CGA card, which is from the early days of the PC. This card doesn't allow the program and the video controller to simultaneously access the video RAM.

Collisions, producing a snow-like effect on the screen are difficult to avoid without extensive programming because the video controller is continuously updating the screen and accessing the video RAM. Since the old CGA cards are no longer used, we will not discuss this problem.

Now we can explain the various ways to access the video RAM from a Turbo Pascal program. Let's begin by looking at the structure of this memory region. This knowledge is basic to understanding the creation of a window manager.

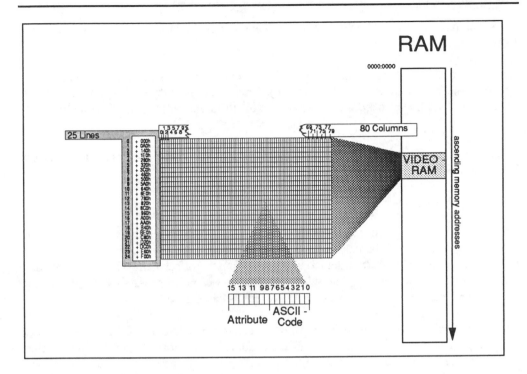

Structure of the video RAM in text mode

A program sees the video RAM, in text mode, as a continuous stream of bytes that are grouped into pairs, which represent a character on the screen. Two bytes are needed because the character and its color are stored separately in one byte each.

The byte with the lower address contains the ASCII code for the character. This determines which of the 256 characters from the ASCII set (for example, the value 32 stands for a space) will appear. The contents of this byte correspond to the number of a code from the ASCII table.

The next byte contains the color of the character. Each individual character can have its own color assignment. This is referred to as the *color byte* with color video cards and the *attribute byte* with monochrome cards. The attribute byte can be used only to change the presentation of the character (i.e., with inverse display or underlining).

The order in which these pairs of bytes are stored determines the order they are displayed on the screen. The very first location in the video RAM (offset address $0000) contains the character that will be displayed in the upper left corner of the screen. This is followed by its color byte. Directly after this is the pair of bytes that describe the character displayed in the second column of the first line on the screen. This is continued for the remaining characters to be displayed in the first line.

Each line on the screen can hold 80 characters and requires 160 ($A0) bytes of video RAM. The first line ends at offset address 159 ($BF). The second line then begins at offset address 160. The second line also requires 160 bytes, so the third line will start at offset address 320 ($140).

Because this pattern repeats itself you can calculate the exact offset address of any character by using the following formula:

```
Offset( Column, Line ) := Line * 160 + Column * 2
```

Remember that the point of reference for this formula is the upper left corner of the screen (coordinates 0/0). Turbo Pascal uses a virtual coordinate system that assigns the upper left corner the coordinates 1/1. In order to quickly calculate the offset addresses, you should use the actual coordinate system. The window manager we will discuss supports the actual coordinate system, found in the video RAM, which is based on 0/0.

The above formula returns the offset position of a character's ASCII code. To determine the color byte of this character, add one byte to this address. This formula is the same whether you are using a 43/50 line switchable EGA or VGA card. The amount of video RAM used will increase but the structure remains the same. The structure changes, however, for EGA or VGA cards that use (non-standard) modes with more than 80 columns per line. In these cases, the factor 160 must be replaced with the number of columns used, multiplied by two.

Unlike monochrome cards, color cards in 80*25 character mode can have up to four screen pages. These pages are spaced 4K apart, starting at segment addresses $B900, $BA00 and $BB00. Even though the segment addresses are different, the structure of the additional screen pages is identical to that of the first, and the formula for calculating the offset addresses is valid.

Only a few programs actually use the other screen pages, since PC applications should be compatible with both color and monochrome video cards. It is easier to limit your work to one screen page and maintain compatibility with monochrome cards, than to program for the possible occurrence of a monochrome card. Therefore, the window manager only uses the first screen page.

In addition to the location and structure of the video RAM, you must also know the meaning of the color and attribute bytes in order to properly display characters. Since colors play a large psychological role in the way we perceive things, your color selections should be as important as the physical layout of your screens.

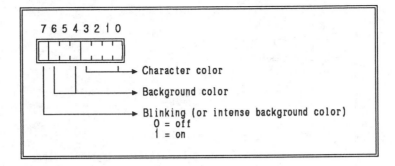

Structure of attribute byte on color video cards

The screen background can be individually selected on both color and monochrome video cards. The lower four bits of the color byte (the LO nibble) contain the code for the foreground and the upper four bits (the HI nibble) contain the code for the background. But using four bits, 16 different colors can be represented for both foreground and background. The following table shows the palette of a color video card.

Decimal	Hex	Binary	Color
0	$00	0000b	Black
1	$01	0001b	Blue
2	$02	0010b	Green
3	$03	0011b	Cyan
4	$04	0100b	Red
5	$05	0101b	Magenta
6	$06	0110b	Brown
7	$07	0111b	Light Gray
8	$08	1000b	Dark Gray
9	$09	1001b	Light Blue
10	$0A	1010b	Light Green
11	$0B	1011b	Light Cyan
12	$0C	1100b	Light Red
13	$0D	1101b	Light Magenta
14	$0E	1110b	Yellow
15	$0F	1111b	White

The color palette of a color video card

The relationship between the color code and a color is fixed only on CGA cards. For EGA and VGA cards, the color codes are only indices to a palette table listing the actual colors. By default the palette table contains colors that correspond to the CGA colors.

Note: You should usually specify only colors 0 through 7 as background colors. Many color cards use a flashing mode when bit 7 of the color byte contains 1, which is the case when a background color with a value greater than 7 is selected.

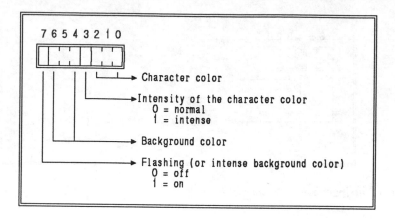

Structure of the attribute bytes on monochrome cards

Monochrome cards can only display different attributes for characters instead of colors. As before, the LO nibble represents the foreground color and the HI nibble represents the background color. However, only certain bit combinations are allowed, and these combinations work the same with all types of video cards from all manufacturers. Bit 3 can be set for a light foreground color, and bit 7 switches the blinking attribute on and off.

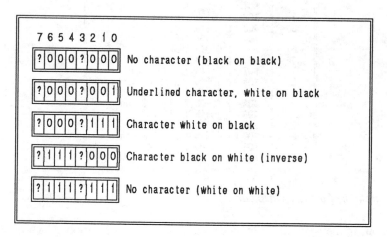

Valid combinations for character and background colors on monochrome video cards

6.2 The Program

This section takes a closer look at the WINDEMO.PAS source code, as well as the WIN.PAS and WIN2.PAS programs which includes our own version of the WIN unit. You'll find descriptions of selected portions of each source code. See your companion diskette for complete source codes for WIN.PAS and WIN2.PAS.

Note: Turbo Pascal provides its own WIN unit. Throughout this book we will be accessing our WIN unit as it appears in this chapter; our WIN unit and the existing Turbo WIN unit are incompatible with one another. Copy the WIN unit Turbo Pascal provides to another disk or directory.

Technically, knowledge of the video RAM structure is all we need to begin programming a window manager. But we also need the programming techniques that can be used to convert this knowledge into Pascal code, which will access the contents of the video RAM as desired.

The video RAM is like a large variable or a buffer that is allocated on the heap. There are many ways to manipulate it.

Basically, the recommended approach involves recreating the contents of the individual locations in the video RAM by using another structure. The following type declaration describes a character/attribute pair as a variant record type called VEL (Video ELement).

```
type VEL     = record                    { describes a character/attribute }
                   case boolean of       { combination in video RAM        }
                      true  : ( Character, Attribute : byte );
                      false : ( Contents            : word );
                   end;
```

This declaration gives the program the option of accessing the character and attribute codes separately or together in the form of a WORD. This dual character reflects the different operations that can be applied to characters in the video RAM.

For example, if a string is output, the character and attribute codes must be processed separately. Although the individual characters will change, the attributes will remain the same for each character in the string. Individual access is also required for an operation such as changing the color of a certain screen region, in which case only the color byte must be manipulated.

Simultaneously accessing character and color bytes is faster than accessing individual components. This type of access is used for operations such as saving a full screen before a window is opened. The part of the screen covered by the new window must be kept in a buffer so that it can be written back to the screen when the overlying window is closed.

Since both the character code and color byte are stored, it is most efficient to do this on the 16-bit level with a single read/write access for each pair.

You should know that a 16-bit access won't be as fast as it would if conventional RAM under 640K is used. The reason for this is that most video cards have 8-bit ports. So, the 16-bit access must be split into two 8-bit operations.

Since this processor uses an 8-bit data bus which must also split the 16-bit data into two 8-bit sections, the same effect will occur with 8088-based machines.

However, for various reasons it still can be productive to use 16-bit access wherever possible:

- This method uses fewer assembly language instructions.

- Execution speed is noticeably faster on ATs and 386-based PCs, which have 16-bit data buses.

- Video cards with 16-bit ports have become more popular.

Turbo Pascal has three different ways to use a structure such as VEL to access the video RAM. The first involves representing the video RAM with a two dimensional array containing components that correspond to VEL. If you are programming for a certain type of video card, the segment address of the video RAM will be known at the time the program is compiled. Therefore, by using ABSOLUTE, you can construct this array from the physical video RAM.

If you only know the location of the video RAM at run time, the array must be referenced with a pointer that has been loaded with the base address of the video RAM. The first listing shows this method.

```
program vio;
type VEL       = record                       { describes a character/attribute }
                   case boolean of        { combination in video RAM         }
                     true  : ( Character, Attribute : byte );
                     false : ( Contents           : word );
                 end;
     VIORAM    = array [0..24,0..79] of VEL;      { recreates the video RAM }
     VIOPTR    = ^VIORAM;                         { pointer to the video RAM }
var  VP        : VIOPTR;                          { pointer into the video RAM }
     Column,
     Row    : byte;
begin
  VP := VIOPTR( ptr( $B800, $0000 ) );          { first page, color cards }
  for Row := 0 to 24 do                         { run through each line }
    for Column := 0 to 79 do                    { run through each column }
      begin
```

```
        VP^[Row, Column].Character  := ord(' ');        { output a space }
        VP^[Row, Column].Attribute := $07; { light char. on dark backgrd. }
      end;
  end.
```

The structure that recreates the video RAM is temporarily called VIORAM. It indexes the columns from 0 to 79 and the lines from 0 to 24. The type VIOPTR is defined as a pointer to this, and the global variable VP is defined as a pointer to this type.

Within the main program, the pointer is loaded with the address of the first screen, for a color card. In this example, this access has been simplified. In a real program, this address would have to be obtained independent of the type of video card. Two FOR loops run through the elements of the array. The elements are accessed using the pointer VP and the line and column indices.

For programmers, this is the best method. Turbo Pascal handles the calculation of the offset addresses of the characters. This also makes it easy to store the entire contents of the video RAM by defining a variable of type VIORAM and using the := operator to assign contents of the video RAM to it. Finally, this makes it easier to recreate the Turbo Pascal coordinate system by using indices from 1 to 25 and 1 to 80.

Although this is the easiest method, it is not the best for speed. While this method has an advantage in processing individual characters, the disadvantage occurs when processing groups of characters, as with windows. In such cases, Turbo Pascal must calculate the address of each new character with every access to the array which considerably slows things down.

This method is also inflexible with the number of columns that can be handled. Variable numbers of lines are easy to deal with by specifying the maximum number of lines available. On VGA cards this would be fifty. But what about variable columns of, say, 80, 96 or 132 characters? This would make it impossible to access the video RAM without redefining the size of the array at run time, which cannot be done with Turbo Pascal.

The MEM command is a second way of approaching this problem. Although this method works near a hardware level, it is better suited for processing groups of characters in video RAM. Since the segment address of this region is known and the offset address of each character to be accessed can be calculated, video RAM can be accessed this way.

```
program vio1;
type VEL      = record                       { describes a character/attribute }
                  case boolean of        { combination in video RAM          }
                    true  : ( Character, Attribute : byte );
                    false : ( Contents            : word );
                  end;
var  VioSeg  : word;                          { segment address of video RAM }
     LLen,                              { length of one screen line in video RAM }
     Column,
     Row    : integer;
begin
   VioSeg := $B800;                                   { first page, color cards }
   LLen   := 80 * 2;                           { length of a screen line }
  for Row := 0 to 24 do                            { process each line }
     for Column := 0 to 79 do                    { process each column }
       begin
         Mem[ VioSeg : Column * 2 + Row * LLen ]     := ord(' ');
         Mem[ VioSeg : Column * 2 + Row * LLen + 1 ] := $07;
       end;
end.
```

In this example, the segment address of the video RAM is kept in a special variable called VioSeg and given, as the segment component for MEM, every time the video RAM is accessed. The offset address is calculated in a loop using the usual formula, which depends on the column and line.

This type of access presents no limits if you want to change the number of columns, since the line length used for the offset address calculation is stored in the variable LLen. This method also allows the use of an offset counter, which can be made in increments of two bytes, to move from character to character in the video RAM. In this way, the character code and attribute byte can be accessed simultaneously, if desired. The MemW command makes it possible to execute a read or write access on a 16-bit Word.

The third method is similar in principle but the internal conversion is a bit faster. Access to the video RAM pointers is accomplished with structures of type VEL.

```
program vio2;
type VEL      = record                  { describes a character/attribute }
                  case boolean of       { combination in video RAM          }
                    true  : ( Character, Attribute : byte );
                    false : ( Contents            : word );
                  end;
     VELPTR  = ^VEL;           { pointer to a screen position in video RAM }
var  VioSeg  : word;                       { segment address of the video RAM }
     VP      : VELPTR;                           { pointer in the video RAM }
     LLen,                                   { length of a line in video RAM }
     Column,
     Row    : integer;
begin
   VioSeg := $B800;                                   { first page, color cards }
```

```
   LLen    := 80 * 2;                                  { length of a line }
  for Row := 0 to 24 do                                { process each line }
    for Column := 0 to 79 do                           { process each column }
      begin
        VP := VELPTR( ptr( VioSeg, Column * 2 + Row * LLen ) );
        VP^.Character  := ord(' ');
        VP^.Attribute := $07;
      end;
end.
```

VELPTR is a pointer to a structure of type VEL. A pointer of this type, called VP, is created as a variable, while the segment address of the video RAM is simultaneously stored in the variable VioSeg.

The PTR function is used to build the address of each character so it can be accessed. The segment portion of the address is taken from VioSeg and the offset portion is calculated with the usual formula. A contiguous region of the video RAM can be easily processed in this way, since we have already seen in Section 2.5 how the offset portion of a pointer can be incremented to allow access to character after character.

This method is faster than the MEM method. It is easier for the processor to load a pointer into a segment register and the corresponding offset register than it is to store the address components into separate variables.

The MEM method is faster when you only want to access one particular character. It can access the character directly, without having to first load its address into a pointer. To optimize the window manager, the MEM method will be used wherever access to single characters or color bytes is required and the pointer method will be used to access entire regions of the video RAM.

Direct access of the video RAM is just one task performed by the window manager, which will be implemented as the WIN unit. At a higher level, it allows you to open several windows. In the Turbo Pascal development environment, the last window opened is the active window for input and output. The windows are organized so that the last window opened is the first to be closed. When the active window is closed, the area of the screen it was covering displays the next active window.

To distinguish windows from the rest of the screen, they can be given *attributes* such as shadows or frames. Also, a window can be moved around the screen or from the background to the foreground to become the active window. The required routines to demonstrate this will be presented in the following pages.

Since there are a total of 39 functions and procedures in the WIN unit, we've divided them into two files, WIN.PAS (which uses the compiler directive $I to link the second part of the unit) and WIN2.PAS.

The start of the WIN unit contains the declarations of the public procedures and functions, followed by the many public constants. The use of each constant will be explained in the text accompanying the various routines.

```
{*******************************************************************************
 *  W I N : This unit contains routines for directly accessing the video   *
 *          RAM and for working with windows.                              *
 **-----------------------------------------------------------------------**
 *  Author        : MICHAEL TISCHER                                        *
 *  developed on  : 03/17/1989                                             *
 *  last update on : 09/21/1989                                            *
 *******************************************************************************}
unit Win;
interface
 uses Dos, Crt;                                                  { link units }
{-- declaration of functions and procedures that can be called from --------}
{-- other programs                                              --------}
 function  VL             ( Offset : integer ) : byte;
 function  VR             ( Offset : integer ) : byte;
 function  VO             ( Offset : integer ) : byte;
 function  VU             ( Offset : integer ) : byte;
 function  WinOpen        ( x1, y1, x2, y2 : byte ) : integer;
 function  WinOpenShadow  ( x1, y1, x2, y2 : byte ) : integer;
 function  WinInFront     ( Key : integer ) : boolean;
 function  WhereX         : integer;
 function  WhereY         : integer;
 function  WinGetChar     ( Column, Line : byte ) : char;
 function  WinGetCol      ( Column, Line : byte ) : byte;
 procedure WinWrite2View  ( Doit : boolean );
 procedure WinPutChar     ( Column, Line : byte; Character : char;
                            WColor : byte );
 procedure WinSetCursor   ( Column, Line : byte );
 procedure WinDefCursor   ( Start, WEnd : byte );
 procedure WinHideCursor;
 procedure WinBlockCursor;
 procedure WinLineCursor;
 procedure WinSetView     ( x1, y1, x2, y2 : byte);
 procedure WinGetView     ( var x1, y1, x2, y2 : byte );
 procedure GotoXY         ( X, Y : integer );
 procedure TextColor      ( Color : byte );
 procedure TextBackground ( Color : byte );
 procedure ClrScr;
 procedure WinClose       ( ReDraw : boolean );
 procedure WinPrint       ( Column, Line, WColor : byte; WOutput : string );
 procedure WinFill        ( x1, y1, x2, y2 : byte; Character : char;
                            WColor : byte );
 function  WinStRep       ( Character : char; Amount : byte ) : string;
 procedure WinFrame       ( x1, y1, x2, y2, WBorder, WColor : byte );
 procedure WinScrollDown  ( x1, y1, x2, y2, Amount, WColor : byte );
 procedure WinScrollUp    ( x1, y1, x2, y2, Amount, WColor : byte );
 procedure WinScrollLeft  ( x1, y1, x2, y2, Amount, WColor : byte );
 procedure WinScrollRight ( x1, y1, x2, y2, Amount, WColor : byte );
```

```
    procedure WinMoveUp        ( Amount : byte );
    procedure WinMoveDown      ( Amount : byte );
    procedure WinMoveRight     ( Amount : byte );
    procedure WinMoveLeft      ( Amount : byte );
    procedure WinMove          ( x, y : byte );
    procedure WinColor         ( x1, y1, x2, y2, WColor : byte );
{-- public constants --------------------------------------------------}
const  {-- the following constants represent the contents of the Video card-}
        MDA       = 0;                          {  MDA and HGC              }
        CGA       = 1;
        EGA       = 2;
        EGA_MONO  = 3;                      { EGA on MDA monitor           }
        VGA       = 4;
        VGA_MONO  = 5;                      { VGA on analog mono monitor   }
        MCGA      = 6;
        MCGA_MONO = 7;                      { MCGA on analog mono monitor  }
        {-- constants for use with the WinFrame procedure -----------------}
        SIN_FR    = 1;                               { single frame   }
        DBL_FR    = 2;                               { double frame   }
        DOT_FR  = 3;                                 { dotted frame   }
        FULL_FR   = 4;                               { full frame     }
        NO_CLEAR    = 255;              { for use with WinScroll procedures }
        WinOpenError = -1;                    { window could not be opened  }
        MAX_COLS    = 132;            { some VGA cards support 132 columns  }
        {-- colors --------------------------------------------------------}
        BLACK        =  0;
        BLUE         =  1;
        GREEN        =  2;
        CYAN         =  3;
        RED          =  4;
        MAGENTA      =  5;
        BROWN        =  6;
        LIGHTGRAY    =  7;
        DARKGRAY     =  8;
        LIGHTBLUE    =  9;
        LIGHTGREEN   = 10;
        LIGHTCYAN    = 11;
        LIGHTRED     = 12;
        LIGHTMAGENTA = 13;
        YELLOW       = 14;
        WHITE        = 15;
```

Some public global variables and standard constants are also defined here. Under certain circumstances they may be helpful to WIN unit users. For example, the variable color is often used. This variable allows the program to determine whether a monochrome or color video card is being used. This variable will contain the value TRUE if a CGA, EGA or VGA card is found or the value FALSE if an MDA or Hercules card is found.

If you want to use the expanded capabilities of an EGA or VGA card to set screen sizes other than the standard 80*25, you will use the variables NumCol and NumLine. These variables list the number of columns and lines used. However, this unit doesn't give you the ability to switch between modes. There is no set way of doing this. Switching modes usually requires using help programs from the manufacturer of the particular video card. If you want your program to use one of these modes, create a batch file that calls the help program and then link this batch file to your program. If WIN detects a greater number of lines or columns than usual during the initialization, the values will be listed in NumLine and NumCol.

All routines in this unit are able to access even coordinates as close to the borders of the screen as possible (131/62).

In addition to the variables, three standard constants are provided. The first is called Write2View. This constant is used because WIN intercepts Write and Writeln commands to ensure that screen output created with these commands is directed to the active window. Just like the Turbo Pascal command WINDOW, the output created with Write and Writeln will orient itself to the coordinates of the window. This can allow actions, such as scrolling the window contents, to write additional lines once the last line in a window has been reached. However, this will only work if Write2View contains the value TRUE. If this constant is set to FALSE, then the borders will not be recognized and window contents will not be scrolled when the last position is reached.

The constants ShadowX and ShadowY are used for opening windows using a shadow. Perhaps you have seen shadowed windows in applications such as Microsoft Works or PC Tools. The shadow is placed on the lower and right sides of the window to visually separate the window from the rest of the screen. ShadowX and ShadowY determine the depth of the shadow in lines and its width in columns.

```
{-- global variables, also accessible to other programs -------------------}
var Color      : boolean;          { TRUE if a color video card is found }
    VioCard,                         { code for the active video card }
    NumLine,                              { number of lines }
    NumCol     : byte;                   { number of columns }
{-- public standard constants ---------------------------------------------}
const Write2View : boolean = TRUE;   { consider visible area when using }
                                     { Write or Writeln commands        }
      ShadowX      : byte = 2;          { width of shadow in columns }
      ShadowY      : byte = 1;          { depth of shadow in lines }
```

The definitions of the public standard constants are followed by many type declarations, which are only used within the unit. These include the structure VEL (mentioned above), which is used to access the elements of the video RAM. The type VELPTR is defined as a pointer to this structure.

The type VELARRAY is used to store screen contents. This is an array of 10,000 elements of type VEL. Since a screen displaying 50 lines of 80 columns only requires 4000 elements of type VEL, you will never have to store 10,000 characters. VELARRAY also helps access the screen buffers that are allocated on the heap and are large enough only to store the required number of characters. Depending on the size of this buffer, routines will access only the first elements of the array. VELARRAY also has a pointer type called VELARPTR.

```
implementation
{-- constants internal to this module ------------------------------------}
const {-- window attributes -----------------------------------------------}
      WIN_SHADOW = 1;                           { Bit 0: window has a shadow }
{-- type declarations, internal to this module --------------------------}
type BPTR      = ^byte;                                { pointer to a byte }
     VEL       = record                   { describes a character/attribute }
                    case boolean of         { combination in video RAM     }
                       true  : ( Character, Attribute : byte );
                       false : ( Contents            : word );
                 end;
     VPTR      = ^VEL;                    { pointer to a character/attribute }
     VELARRAY  = array [0..9999] of VEL;             { window buffer }
     VELARPTR  = ^VELARRAY;                  { pointer to a window buffer }
     WIPTR     = ^WINDES;               { pointer to a window descriptor }
     WINDES    = record                         { window descriptor }
                    Attribute,                      { window attribute }
                    Handle,                  { key to accessing the window }
                    x1, y1,            { the corner coordinates of the window }
                    x2, y2,
                    ViewX1, ViewY1,          { coordinates of the visible area }
                    ViewX2, ViewY2,
                    curc, curr    : byte;{ cursor coordinates before opening }
                    lastwin,                    { link to previous window }
                    nextwin      : WIPTR;       { and to the following }
                    Buffer       : byte;        { window buffer starts here }
                 end;
     PTRREC    = record                            { used to access the }
                    Ofs : word;                    { components of a     }
                    Seg : word;                    { desired pointer     }
                 end;
     HANDLES   = array [0..63] of byte;         { bit field, accepts Handles }
     HANDPTR   = ^HANDLES;                  { pointer to the Handles Array }
```

Type WINDES represents the window descriptor, which contains all the information that WIN needs to control the window. In this unit, the first bit of the window attribute, together with the constant WIN_SHADOW, indicates whether a window will appear with a shadow.

The component Handle assigns an individual identifying number to each window. This information isn't required for normal opening and closing of the window because the "last-opened-first-closed" rule is followed. This information must be available in order to pull any desired window from the background to the foreground and make it the active window.

Information on the location of the windows is stored in the variables X1, Y1, X2 and Y2, which store the coordinates of the upper left and lower right corners of the window.

Wherever a screen region is addressed in the routines of this unit, the region is defined by the coordinates of these corners.

The fields ViewX1, ViewY1, ViewX2 and ViewY2 serve a similar function. They describe the view region, which usually consists of the entire window. Using the correct routine can also assign the visible area to any desired screen region. For example, an intercepted Write or Writeln command can be output to the visible area if the constant Write2View contains the value TRUE.

However, these four variables do not store the visible area of the current window (this is kept in global variables). Instead, these variables refer to the visible area active before the current window was opened/activated. This is required since the routine that opens a window, automatically defines a new visible area that corresponds to the new window. This information is kept in every window descriptor so that the contents of previous visible areas can be restored when the windows are closed.

The structure variables curc and curr perform similar tasks. They record the position of the cursor at the time the current window is opened. After the window is closed, the cursor can be returned to its original position.

The fields lastwin and nextwin establish relationships between window descriptors with a pointer to the most recently opened window and the next window. This allows the window descriptors to be managed as a double linked list. If one of these fields contains the pointer NIL, then either no more windows follow (the window of this window descriptor is therefore the current window) or no other windows precede this window.

As previously mentioned, the contents of a window must be saved whenever a new window is opened. The contents can then be restored after the new window is closed. The buffer used is the part of the window descriptor beginning with the field called Buffer. The size of this buffer depends on the number of characters covered by the new window. The size of the new window is a completely unrelated number, and an array cannot be defined unless the size of the buffer is known at the time of compilation. Instead, the BYTE variable Buffer is used, which serves as the start address of the buffer.

Structures of type WINDES are not defined as global or local variables. Therefore, the amount of room at the end for such a buffer will vary. Instead, they are allocated on the heap with GetMem. This way just enough memory can be reserved to store the components of the structure and the window buffer. The start of the allocated region contains the components of the WINDES structure, followed by the window buffer containing the saved portion of the video RAM.

In addition to WINDES, the previous excerpt also contains a structure called PTRREC, which we have already seen in Section 2.5. It is used to split a pointer in its segment and offset components.

186

An array of type HANDLES accepts the handle (identifying number) assigned to the window. HANDLES is managed internally as a bit array, so that the 64 bytes in the array can represent 256 different handles. The distance of a given bit from the first bit in this array is the number of the handle. If this bit is set, then the handle has already been assigned to a window. A corresponding pointer type called HANDPTR is also defined so that the HANDLE array can be allocated on the heap.

The type declarations are followed by a number of global variables and standard constants used only in the WIN unit. The meaning of each variable is given in the commentary within the program listing.

```
{-- global variables, internal to this module ----------------------------}
var VioSeg      : word;                       { segment address of video RAM }
    Line_Ofs    : integer;               { number of bytes in one line }
    WritelnX,                           { output column for Writeln }
    WritelnY,                            { output row for Writeln }
    vLine,                          { stores the current cursor position}
    vColumn,
    ViewX1,                          { upper left corner of visible area }
    ViewY1,                          { relative to the entire screen    }
    ViewX2,                          { lower right corner of visible area }
    ViewY2      : byte;              { relative to the entire screen    }
   WritelnPtr  : VPTR;         { pointer to output position for WinWriteln }
   FirstWinPtr : WIPTR;            { pointer to first window descriptor }
   CurBufPtr   : VELARPTR;            { pointer to current window buffer }
   HaPtr       : HANDPTR;                    { pointer to Handles Array }
{-- initialized global variables (standard constants) ---------------------}
const NumWin    : integer = 0;                   { number of opened windows }
     CurWinPtr : WIPTR = nil;      { pointer to the last window descriptor }
      WritelnCol: byte = $07;                       { output color for
Writeln }
```

The global variables are initialized with a procedure called WinInit, which is called from the initialization section of the unit and is therefore executed before the program actually starts.

```
{*****************************************************************************
 *  WinInit : Initializes the WIN unit                                      *
 *  Globals : VioCard/W, NumCol/W, NumLine/W, Color/W, VioSeg/W, HaPtr/W   *
 *            Line_Ofs/W                                                     *
 *****************************************************************************}
procedure WinInit;
const VioMode : array [0..11] of byte = ( MDA, CGA, 0, EGA, EGA_MONO, 0,
                                        VGA_MONO,  VGA, 0, MCGA,
                                        MCGA_MONO, MCGA );
     EgaMode : array [0..2] of byte  = ( EGA, EGA, EGA_MONO );
var Regs : Registers;                   { processor regs for interrupt calls }
begin
  VioCard := $ff;                               { no video card found yet }
  {-- test for VGA or MCGA card ---------------------------------------------}
  Regs.ax := $1a00;                          { call function $1A of the }
```

```
      intr($10, Regs);                                { video BIOS           }
      if Regs.al = $1a then                             { VGA or MCGA? }
        begin                                                   { yes }
          VioCard := VioMode[ Regs.bl-1 ];              { get code from table }
          Color := not( ( VioCard = MDA ) or ( VioCard = EGA_MONO ) );
        end
      else                                          { neither VGA nor MCGA }
        begin                                        { test for EGA card }
          Regs.ah := $12;                            { call function $12 }
          Regs.bl := $10;                            { subfunction $10   }
          intr($10, Regs);                            { call video BIOS }
          if Regs.bl <> $10 then                      { EGA installed? }
            begin                                                { yes }
              VioCard := EgaMode[ (Regs.cl shr 1) div 3 ];       { get code }
              Color := VioCard <> EGA_MONO;
            end;
        end;
      {-- get pointer to video RAM ------------------------------------------}
      Regs.ah := 15;                                { get current video mode }
       intr($10, Regs);                           { call BIOS video interrupt }
       if Regs.al = 7 then                           { monochrome mode? }
         VioSeg := $b000                         { yes, video RAM at B000 }
       else                                         { no, color mode }
         VioSeg := $b800;                           { video RAM at B800 }
      if VioCard = $ff then                      { not EGA, VGA or MCGA? }
        begin                                                { yes }
          if Regs.al = 7 then VioCard := MDA
                       else VioCard := CGA;
          NumLine := 25;                          { in 25 line text mode }
          Color := not( ( Regs.al-0 ) or ( Regs.al=2 ) or ( Regs.al=7 ) );
        end
      else                        { if EGA, VGA or MCGA, get number of lines }
        NumLine := BPTR( Ptr( $40, $84 ) )^ + 1;
      NumCol := BPTR( Ptr( $40, $4a ) )^;            { number of columns }
       Line_Ofs := NumCol shl 1;              { offset to start of next line }
      Regs.ah := 5;                            { select current screen page }
       Regs.al := 0;                               { screen page 0 }
       intr($10, Regs);                         { call BIOS video interrupt }
      Regs.ah := 3;                           { get current cursor position }
       Regs.bh := 0;                            { access to screen page 0 }
       intr($10, Regs);                         { call BIOS video interrupt }
      vLine  := Regs.dh;                           { store cursor position }
      vColumn := Regs.dl;
      WinSetView(0, 0, NumCol-1, NumLine-1);    { visible area = entire screen }
      New( HaPtr );                               { allocate Handle Array }
       FillChar( HaPtr^, SizeOf( HaPtr^ ), 0 );    { no Handles assigned yet }
      {-- divert file variable OUTPUT to internal output routine ------------}
      with TextRec( Output ) do             { manipulate the file variable OUTPUT }
        begin
          Handle   := $FFFF;        { Turbo expects this declaration like this }
          Mode     := fmClosed;                    { device still closed }
          BufSize  := SizeOf( Buffer );          { set size and address }
          BufPtr   := @Buffer;                      { of buffer          }
```

```
      OpenFunc := @OutputOpen;                  { address of Open procedure }
      Name[0]  := #0;                           { change name to empty string }
    end;
  Rewrite( Output );                            { initialize file variable }
  {-- Writeln output starting at current cursor position in screen page 0 --}
  WritelnX := vColumn;
  WritelnY := vLine;
  WritelnPtr := GetVioPtr( vColumn, vLine );
end;
  {**---------------------------------------------------------------------**}
  {** Starting code of the unit                                           **}
  {**---------------------------------------------------------------------**}
begin
  WinInit;                                      { call initialization procedure }
  end.
```

The first job for WinInit is to determine the type of the installed video card and to store this as a code in the global variable VioCard. Obtaining this information involves applying various tests.

The first two tests are taken from the expanded BIOS functions available on EGA and VGA cards. First, function $1A, subfunction $00 of the video interrupt is called. This is only available on VGA cards. So if the value $1A isn't returned to the AL register you can assume that no VGA card is installed. If this value is found in AL the function was successfully executed and the BL register will contain a code indicating the type of the active video card. WinInit uses this code as an index to a video table that lists the codes for the various types of video cards.

This table is represented within WinInit by the local standard constant VioMode. There are codes in this table not only for VGA cards, but also for all other types of cards. This is because VGA cards can be used with other cards. So even though a VGA BIOS is found, another type of card may actually be the active card. And since the function $1A returns information only on the active card and not on all installed cards, these codes must be available.

If this test succeeds, the variable color is loaded at the same time. Color can be used if no MDA or EGA card in mono mode was found.

If the first test shows that no VGA card is present, then the second test checks for the presence of an EGA card. This type of card also supports several functions unique to it and VGA type cards. But we already know that no VGA card is present, otherwise the first test would have been positive and the second test would not be run. This test is performed with function $12, subfunction $10, which returns a code indicating the active video card as above. If the BL register contains a value other that $10 after this function is executed, then the function was successful and an EGA card is available. The code returned to the CL register indicates the type of the EGA card and the monitor being used. If the monitor is not monochrome, then the variable color is set to TRUE.

Regardless of whether one of these two tests succeeds, the segment address of the video RAM is obtained next. Function $0F of the BIOS video interrupt is used for this. This function returns the code of the current video mode and is an excellent way to distinguish between color and mono cards. Mono cards have only one video mode (80*25 text mode), which corresponds to code 7. If this code is found, the variable VioSeg is loaded with the address $B000. In all other cases, it is loaded with $B800.

If the type of the active video card still hasn't been determined yet, it is now determined based on the video mode code that is returned. An MDA card is assumed with a video mode of 7. All other video modes are assumed to be CGA cards.

In both cases, the number of lines will be 25. EGA and VGA cards can use more lines, therefore an additional memory location from the BIOS variable region must be read. This is a RAM region which follows directly after the Interrupt Vector Table at segment address $40. This region stores variables that the BIOS uses to perform its tasks, just like any other program. The BIOS is found in a ROM chip, but it must rely on space in RAM to store its variables since this cannot be performed in ROM.

EGA and VGA use free memory locations in this region to store important information. The offset address $84 contains the number of lines on the screen, which is vital for WinInit.

For all other types of video cards, offset address $4A contains the number of columns per line. The contents of this location is also loaded into the variable NumCol, then multiplied by 2 and stored in the variable Line_Ofs.

Next, WinInit uses function $05 of the video BIOS to switch to screen page 0, because all routines in the unit will access this screen page. Another BIOS function, $03, is then called to determine the current cursor position within page 0. This information is loaded into registers DL and DH and written from there to the global variables vLine and vColumn.

The visible area is then defined by calling the procedure WinSetView, which we will look at in detail later. The bit array for the window Handle is also created within WinInit by placing a structure of type HANDLES on the heap. The address of this buffer is stored in the global variable HaPtr. By calling the procedure FillChar, all bits in this array can be set to 0 so that none of the Handles are assigned.

The rest of WinInit diverts the Write and Writeln procedures and initializes the new procedures. Since this is the same process described in Chapter 4, we won't discuss it again.

The Open procedure for the file variable OUTPUT is established as the procedure OutputOpen. This is called by a REWRITE to OUTPUT within WinInit. This routine is found together with the other routines used to divert the output of Write and Writeln in the second part of the WIN unit in the file WIN2.PAS.

```
{*********************************************************************
 *  OutputOpen : Places the contents of OUTPUT file variable into WinInit  *
 *               on the initial call of Write or Writeln.                  *
 **-----------------------------------------------------------------**
 *  Input    : F = OUTPUT file variable of type TextRec            *
 *  Output   : must return 0 by definition (no error)             *
 *  Globals  : none                                               *
 *********************************************************************}

{$F+}                                              { must be FAR }

function OutputOpen( var f : TextRec ) : integer;

begin
  with f do                                { work with file variable }
    begin
      InOutFunc := @WinWriteln;       { set address of the output function }
      FlushFunc := @WinWriteln;           { "Flush" corresponds to "Out" }
      CloseFunc := @WinDummy;              { Close still not considered }
    end;
  OutputOpen := 0;                                  { 0 returned }
end;

{$F-}
```

OutputOpen is responsible for placing the addresses of the driver routines into the file variable (OUTPUT) so that Turbo Pascal can call the correct routine during the execution of Write and Writeln commands.

A close function for OUTPUT isn't necessary. Therefore, the procedure WinDummy has been set up for the corresponding function pointer. This dummy procedure simply returns a function result of 0 to indicate that it executed without an error.

```
{*********************************************************************
 *  WinDummy : called during a Close on the diverted file variable OUTPUT  *
 **-----------------------------------------------------------------**
 *  Input    : F - the file variable OUTPUT of type TextRec       *
 *  Output   : always returns the value 0 (no error)             *
 *  Globals  : none                                               *
 *********************************************************************}
{$F+}                                              { must be FAR }
function WinDummy( var f : TextRec ) : integer;
begin
  WinDummy := 0;                                    { return 0 }
 end;
{$F-}
```

The function WinWriteln is more interesting. This function is called as an In/Out function as well as a Flush function. It takes over the output of text stored in the buffer of the passed file variable OUTPUT. In so doing, the output mode as indicated by the contents of Write2View is considered. If Write2View is TRUE, then the current visible area is used. If it is FALSE, then neither the visible area nor the screen size is considered.

Both modes have a different use for the cursor than is seen with the standard commands. WinWriteln sets the internal output position after the character that was just printed so that the next character will appear right next to it, but the screen cursor isn't set to this same position. This wouldn't be sensible in a windows environment, since the cursor usually points to a certain screen position, but not necessarily to the last character output.

```pascal
{*****************************************************************************
 *  WinWriteln : called by Turbo Pascal during a WRITE or WRITELN command   *
 *               on the file variable OUTPUT                                 *
 **-----------------------------------------------------------------------**
 *  Input    : F = the file variable OUTPUT of type TextRec                 *
 *  Output   : must return the value 0 (no error)                          *
 *  Globals  : Write2View/R, WritelnX/RW, WritelnY/RW, WritelnPtr/RW        *
 *             ViewX1/R, ViewY1/R, ViewX2/R, ViewY2/R                       *
 *****************************************************************************}
{$F+}                                                    { must be FAR }
function WinWriteln( var f : TextRec ) : integer;
var i   : integer;                                      { loop counter }
    ZPtr : BPTR;                        { pointer to the output character }
begin
  with f do                                { process the file variable }
    begin
      ZPtr := BPTR( BufPtr );        { set pointer to the first character }
      if ( Write2View ) then             { consider the view region? }
        begin                      { yes, visible area may be scrolled }
          for i := 1 to BufPos do          { process each character }
            begin
              case Zptr^ of              { evaluate the current character }
                7 : begin                       { BEL : output sound }
                  Sound( 880 );                         { sound on }
                  Delay( 750 );                  { wait 3/4 second }
                  NoSound;                             { sound off }
                end;
                8 : begin            { backspace (BS): one character back }
                  if ( WritelnX = ViewX1 ) then    { to start of line? }
                    begin                  { yes, return to previous line }
                      WritelnX := ViewX2;            { the last column }
                      dec( WritelnY );           { of the previous line }
                    end
                  else                                  { line remains }
                    dec( WritelnX );              { one column back }
                  WritelnPtr := GetVioPtr( WritelnX, WritelnY );
                end;
                10 : begin          { Linefeed (LF): increment output line }
```

```
                    if ( WritelnY = ViewY2 ) then        { last view line? }
                        WinScrollUp( ViewX1, ViewY1+1, ViewX2,
                                     ViewY2, 1, WritelnCol )
                    else            { the visible area need not be scrolled }
                      begin
                        inc( WritelnY );
                        WritelnPtr := GetVioPtr( WritelnX, WritelnY );
                      end;
                  end;
        13 : begin                        { CR: return to start of line }
               WritelnX := ViewX1;
               WritelnPtr := GetVioPtr( WritelnX, WritelnY );
             end;
        else              { output all other characters unprocessed }
          begin
            {-- write character code and attribute to video RAM ----}
            WritelnPtr^.Character := ZPtr^;
            WritelnPtr^.Attribute := WritelnCol;
            {-- set pointer to the next character ------------------}
            inc( PTRREC( WritelnPtr ).Ofs, 2 );
            inc( WritelnX );                   { increment output column }
            if ( WritelnX > ViewX2 ) then        { ViewX2 reached? }
              begin                                           { yes }
                WritelnX := ViewX1;        { to start of the next one }
                if ( WritelnY = ViewY2 ) then      { last view line? }
                  begin                        { yes, scroll visible area }
                    WinScrollUp( ViewX1, ViewY1+1, ViewX2,
                                 ViewY2, 1, WritelnCol );
                    WritelnX := ViewX1;       { continue on left side }
                    WritelnPtr := GetVioPtr( WritelnX, WritelnY );
                  end
                else            { the visible area need not be scrolled }
                  begin
                    inc( WritelnY );
                    WritelnPtr := GetVioPtr( WritelnX, WritelnY );
                  end;
              end;
          end;
      end;
      inc( PTRREC( ZPtr ).Ofs );    { set pointer to next character }
    end;
  end
else              { disregard view region, simply write to video RAM }
  begin
    for i := 1 to BufPos do                  { process each character }
      begin
        case Zptr^ of                  { evaluate current character }
          7 : begin                          { BEL : output sound }
                Sound( 880 );                        { sound on }
                Delay( 750 );                  { wait 3/4 second }
                NoSound;                            { sound off }
              end;
          8 : begin                  { Backspace (BS): back up one char. }
```

```
                          if ( WritelnX = 0 ) then              { start of line? }
                            begin                     { yes, back to previous line }
                              WritelnX := NumCol - 1;               { last column }
                              dec( WritelnY );              { the previous line }
                            end
                          else                                     { line remains }
                            dec( WritelnX );                  { one column back }
                          WritelnPtr := GetVioPtr( WritelnX, WritelnY );
                        end;
                10 : begin           { Linefeed (LF): increment output line }
                        inc( WritelnY );
                        WritelnPtr := GetVioPtr( WritelnX, WritelnY );
                      end;
                13 : begin                        { CR: back to start of line }
                        WritelnX := 0;
                        WritelnPtr := GetVioPtr( WritelnX, WritelnY );
                      end;
                else                  { output all other characters unprocessed }
                  begin
                    {-- write character code and attribute in video RAM ----}
                    WritelnPtr^.Character := ZPtr^;
                    WritelnPtr^.Attribute := WritelnCol;
                    {-- set pointer to next character --------------------}
                    inc( PTRREC( WritelnPtr ).Ofs, 2 );
                    inc( WritelnX );                  { increment output column }
                    if ( WritelnX = NumCol ) then      { end of line reached? }
                      begin                                              { yes }
                        WritelnX := 0;                { jump to the start of the }
                        inc( WritelnY );                          { next line }
                      end;
                  end;
              end;
              inc( PTRREC( ZPtr ).Ofs );     { set pointer to next character }
            end;
          end;
        BufPos := 0;                              { all characters processed }
      end;
   WinWriteln := 0;                                             { return 0 }
  end;
  {$F-}
```

Note: WinWriteln only needs two variables: the integer I, for a loop counter and the pointer ZPtr, which is a running pointer to the output characters in the buffer. The function receives all other information, such as the current output position, from the various global variables of the unit.

Depending on the contents of the standard constant Write2View, two loops are executed which are very similar in structure. They process the characters, which will be output from the buffer, in the file variable. Use a CASE statement to determine if a character is one of the control characters with ASCII codes 7, 8, 10 or 13, or if it is a normal character.

The following description documents the execution of the program section when Write2View contains TRUE. If Write2View is false, the program section is executed in the same way except that the view region, as defined by the variables ViewX1, ViewX2, ViewY1 and ViewY2, isn't considered.

The current output position is obtained from the global variables WritelnX and WritelnY. The variable WritelnPtr also always refers to the current character. This pointer points to the character in video RAM whose coordinates are described by WritelnX/WritelnY. The other meaningful variable for this procedure is WritelnCol, which contains the color to be assigned to the output character.

However, none of these variables are used if the character with ASCII code 7 is sent. This doesn't appear on the screen but instead uses the sound procedure within WinWriteln to sound a tone. After a brief moment, the tone is stopped by NoSound.

The procedure gets slightly more complicated with ASCII code 8, which represents a backspace. First the program determines if the current output column is at the left border of the view region. If so, the output column in WritelnX must be set to the right edge of the visible area and, at the same time, the output line (WritelnY) is decreased by one. However, this doesn't check to see if the upper limit of the visible area is exceeded. This happens because the <Backspace> key is usually not used in a window environment. So this control code is only supported as a matter of form.

If the current output position isn't at the left edge of the visible area, the output column is decreased. In both cases, the pointer WritelnPtr is loaded with the address of the new output position. To do this, WinWriteln uses a function that is called many times within the unit: GetVioPtr. This function uses the usual formula to calculate the address of a character in video RAM and returns this information to the caller as a pointer.

The output line must be incremented if WinWriteln receives ASCII code 10. This code represents a linefeed. If the current output position is already at the lower edge of the visible area, the entire visible area is scrolled up by one line, which removes the top line from view. The procedure WinScrollUp handles this. As input, this procedure causes both the corner coordinates of the region and the number of lines to be scrolled. A color code is also received. This determines what color the empty lines, which are freed, should be painted. WinWriteln passes the current output color from the variable WritelnCol as this parameter.

Position of the output doesn't change if the visible area must be scrolled. Otherwise, WritelnY is incremented and the new output position is loaded into the variable WritelnPtr by calling GetVioPtr.

A linefeed is normally followed by a carriage return, which moves the output position to the beginning of the new line. This is done by loading WritelnX with the contents of ViewX1 and then updating WritelnPtr.

Handling control characters is simple. WinWriteln must do more work when normal ASCII characters are output to the screen. It must enter the character code and its color (from the variable WritelnCol) in the video RAM by referencing the pointer WritelnPtr. Then the output position is moved up to the next character by increasing the offset component of WritelnPtr by two bytes and by incrementing the output column in WritelnX. The next time the video RAM is accessed by WritelnPtr, the next character will automatically be found.

If the right edge of the visible area is exceeded, the output position is continued in the next line, at the left edge of the visible area. If while doing this the bottom line of the visible area is also exceeded, then WinScrollUp is used to scroll the window contents up one line the next time a linefeed is encountered. The new output position is set to the first character in the bottom line of the visible area.

All characters in the output buffer are processed this way. When this is accomplished the function is ended by returning the value 0 (no error).

```
{*****************************************************************************
 *  GetVioPtr  : returns a pointer to a specific character in video RAM    *
 **-------------------------------------------------------------------------**
 *  Input   : Line, Column = coordinates of the character                  *
 *  Output  : pointer to the character in video RAM of type VPTR           *
 *  Info    : starting point is at the upper left corner of the screen     *
 *            (coordinates 0/0)                                            *
 *  Globals : VioSeg/R, NumCol/R                                          *
 *****************************************************************************}
function  GetVioPtr( Column, Line : byte ) : VPTR;
begin
  GetVioPtr := Ptr(VioSeg, (NumCol * Line + Column ) shl 1);
end;
```

Besides GetVioPtr, there is a second function from the WIN unit that is called within WinWriteln. Unlike GetVioPtr, the function WinScrollUp is public so it can be called by other units and programs. This is one of four procedures that is used to scroll part or all of the screen contents in various directions.

As with all of the scrolling procedures, WinScrollUp uses two pointers and a loop to move each line to its new location in the video RAM. To do this, first the number of bytes, that will be moved in each line, is calculated. This information is stored in the local variable Byte2Copy.

Then the two pointers called "frm" and "cpto" are loaded. These represent "copy from" and "copy to" respectively. Using GetVioPtr, the "frm" pointer is loaded with the address of the first character in the first line to be moved. Then "cpto" is loaded with the address of the character n lines above, where n is the number of lines to be scrolled.

After these calculations, the procedure enters a loop that is executed for each line within the region to be scrolled. The Move procedure from the system unit is used to copy the number of bytes noted in Bytes2Copy. The bytes starting with the address in the "frm" pointer are copied starting at the address in "cpto". Then each pointer is set to the start of the next line by adding the length of one complete screen line to the offset component. This value is taken from the global variable Line_Ofs.

After moving each line, the lines that were freed at the bottom of the screen/region are cleared unless the calling routine specified a value of NO_CLEAR for the color of these lines. The procedure WinFill, which we will examine a little later, is used to clear this region.

```
{*************************************************************************
 *  WinScrollUp : scrolls a given screen region up by a given number of lines*
 **--------------------------------------------------------------------**
 *  Input    : x1, y1 = coordinates of the upper left corner          *
 *             x2, y2 = coordinates of the lower right corner         *
 *             Amount = number of lines to be scrolled               *
 *             WColor  = color or attribute of the freed lines       *
 *  Info     : if the constant NO_CLEAR is given as the color, the freed  *
 *             lines are not cleared                                 *
 *  Globals : Line_Ofs/R                                            *
 *************************************************************************}
procedure WinScrollUp( x1, y1, x2, y2, Amount, WColor : byte );
var frm,                                        { copy from ... }
    cpto      : VPTR;                           { ... to        }
    Byte2Copy,                          { number of bytes per line }
    CurLine  : integer;                     { the current line }
begin
  Byte2Copy := (x2 - x1 + 1) shl 1;           { number of bytes }
  frm  := GetVioPtr( x1, y1 );        { pointer to line to be moved }
  cpto := GetVioPtr( x1, y1 - Amount );   { pointer to its new position }
  for CurLine := y1 to y2 do               { process each line }
    begin
      Move( frm^, cpto^, Byte2Copy );              { copy line }
      inc( PTRREC( frm ).Ofs, Line_Ofs );
      inc( PTRREC( cpto ).Ofs, Line_Ofs );
    end;
  if WColor <> NO_CLEAR then                { clear blank lines? }
    WinFill( x1, y2+1-amount, x2, y2, ' ', WColor);         { yes }
end;
```

The procedure WinScrollDown works the same as WinScrollUp. This procedure will scroll down a screen by a given number of lines. As opposed to WinScrollUp, it processes the screen contents from bottom to top, so the offset components of the pointers "frm" and "cpto" must be decremented and not incremented after the copy occurs.

```
{**********************************************************************
 *   WinScrollDown : scrolls any screen region a specific amount down  *
 **------------------------------------------------------------------**
 *   Input    : x1, y1 = upper left corner coordinates of the region   *
 *              x2, y2 = lower right corner coordinates of the region   *
 *              Amount = number of rows by which the region should be scrolled*
 *              WColor = color/attribute for the freed line             *
 *   Info     : if the constant NO_CLEAR is given for WColor, the freed line  *
 *              is not cleared.                                         *
 *   Globals : Line_Ofs/R                                               *
 **********************************************************************}

procedure WinScrollDown( x1, y1, x2, y2, Amount, WColor : byte );

var frm,                                          { copy from ..... }
    cpto     : VPTR;                              { ... to          }
    Byte2Copy,                               { number of bytes per line }
    CurLine  : integer;                           { current line }

begin
  Byte2Copy := (x2 - x1 + 1) shl 1;               { number of bytes }
  frm  := GetVioPtr( x1, y2 );            { pointer to line to be moved }
  cpto := GetVioPtr( x1, y2 + Amount );   { pointer to its new position }

  for CurLine := y1 to y2 do                      { process each line }
    begin
      Move( frm^, cpto^, Byte2Copy );             { copy line }
      dec( PTRREC( frm ).Ofs, Line_Ofs );
      dec( PTRREC( cpto ).Ofs, Line_Ofs );
    end;

  if WColor <> NO_CLEAR then                      { clear blank lines? }
    WinFill( x1, y1, x2, y1+Amount-1, ' ', WColor);     { yes }
end;
```

WinScrollRight and WinScrollLeft work somewhat differently. These two procedures create
a framework for calling the procedure ScrollHori. Depending upon the calling routine, this
procedure will then scroll the screen to the right or left.

```
{**********************************************************************
 *   WinScrollLeft : scrolls a given screen region to the left         *
 **------------------------------------------------------------------**
 *   Input    : see WinScrollUp, WinScrollDown                         *
 *   Globals : none                                                    *
 **********************************************************************}

procedure WinScrollLeft( x1, y1, x2, y2, Amount, WColor : byte );

begin
  ScrollHori( x1, y1, x2, y2, Amount, WColor, TRUE );
end;
```

```
{**************************************************************************
*  WinScrollRight: scrolls a given screen region to the right           *
**----------------------------------------------------------------------**
*  Input   : see WinScrollUp, WinScrollDown                             *
*  Globals : none                                                       *
***************************************************************************}

procedure WinScrollRight( x1, y1, x2, y2, Amount, WColor : byte );

begin
  ScrollHori( x1, y1, x2, y2, Amount, WColor, FALSE );
end;
```

ScrollHori, which is only available within the Win2 source of the WIN unit, processes the
specified screen region line by line and uses the "frm" and "cpto" pointers to move the
contents in the desired direction.

```
{**************************************************************************
*  ScrollHori : scrolls a specified screen region a specified distance from*
*               Column to the left or to the right                      *
**----------------------------------------------------------------------**
*  Input   : x1, y1    = upper left corner coordinate of the region     *
*            x2, y2    = bottom right corner coordinate of the region    *
*            Amount    = number of columns the region should be moved to *
*                        the right or left                              *
*            WColor    = color/attribute of the "clearing" column       *
*            ToTheLeft = TRUE  : region moves to the left               *
*                        FALSE : region moves to the right              *
*  Info    : - If the color constant NO_CLEAR is given, the column left *
*              behind by the movement is not cleared.                   *
*  Globals : Line_Ofs/R                                                 *
***************************************************************************}

procedure ScrollHori( x1, y1, x2, y2, Amount, WColor : byte;
                      ToTheLeft : boolean );

var frm,                                        { copy from...... }
    cpto      : VPTR;                           { ... to          }
    Byte2Copy,                               { number of bytes per line }
    CurLine   : integer;                        { the current line }

begin
  Byte2Copy := (x2 - x1 + 1) shl 1;              { number of bytes }
  frm := GetVioPtr( x1, y1 );
  if ToTheLeft then                        { move the region to the left? }
    cpto := GetVioPtr( x1 - Amount, y1 )                      { yes }
  else                                    { move the region to the right? }
    cpto := GetVioPtr( x1 + Amount, y1 );
  for CurLine := y1 to y2 do                         { execute lines }
    begin
      Move( frm^, cpto^, Byte2Copy );                   { copy line }
      inc( PTRREC( frm ).Ofs, Line_Ofs );
```

199

```
    inc( PTRREC( cpto ).Ofs, Line_Ofs );
  end;

{-- clear free blank columns --------------------------------------------}

if WColor <> NO_CLEAR then                          { delete blank columns? }
  if ToTheLeft then                                 { yes, scroll to left? }
    WinFill( x2-Amount+1, y1, x2, y2, ' ', WColor)
  else                                              { no, scroll to right }
    WinFill( x1, y1, x1+Amount-1, y2, ' ', WColor);
end;
```

We started discussing the scroll procedures because WinScrollUp is called by WinWriteln. There are also a number of other procedures called by the diverted Write/Writeln procedures, that are actually part of the CRT unit but are replaced by new routines here. These procedures/functions are WhereX, WhereY, GotoXY, TextColor, TextBackground and ClrScr.

The new WhereX and WhereY functions return, as usual, the output position of the next Write or Writeln call. This information is obtained from the global variables WritelnX and WritelnY. As opposed to the CRT functions of the same names, these functions relate to base coordinates (0/0) instead of (1/1). This applies throughout the WIN unit.

```
{******************************************************************************
 *   WhereX : returns the output column of the next writeln used by the      *
 *                    OUTPUT file variable                                   *
 **------------------------------------------------------------------------**
 *   Input   : none                                                          *
 *   Output  : see above                                                     *
 *   Globals : WriteLnX/R                                                    *
 ******************************************************************************}

function WhereX : integer;

begin
  WhereX := WritelnX;                                         { return column }
end;
{******************************************************************************
 *   WhereY : returns the output row of the next writeln used by the         *
 *                    OUTPUT file variable                                    *
 **------------------------------------------------------------------------**
 *   Input   : none                                                          *
 *   Output  : see above                                                     *
 *   Globals : WriteLnYX/R                                                   *
 ******************************************************************************}

function WhereY : integer;

begin
  WhereY := WritelnY;                                          { return row }
end;
```

GotoXY can be used to assign a new output position for Write and Writeln. This position would also be based on coordinates (0/0). As opposed to the GotoXY procedure from the CRT unit, the new output position is stored only internally. The position of the screen cursor doesn't change. This is done by the WinSetCursor command, which we will see later.

```
{**************************************************************************
 *   GotoXY : replaces the procedure of the same name from the CRT unit,   *
 *            establishes the output position for the next call of the     *
 *            diverted Writeln procedure                                   *
 **-------------------------------------------------------------------**
 *                                                                         *
 *   Input    : X = output column                                         *
 *              Y = output line                                           *
 *   Info     : the screen cursor is not moved with this procedure as it is *
 *              with the normal GotoXY procedure                          *
 *   Globals : WritelnX/W, WritelnY/W, WritelnPtr/W                        *
 **************************************************************************}
procedure GotoXY( X, Y : integer );
begin
   WritelnX := X;                      { store output position in global variables }
WritelnY := Y;
   WritelnY := Y;
   WritelnPtr := GetVioPtr( x, y );       { create pointer to output position }
   end;
```

The output color for Write and Writeln can be set with the procedures TextColor and TextBackground. These procedures replace those of the same names from the CRT unit. The color information is passed using the variable WritelnCol. Colors can be specified using a code from 0 to 15 or one of the color constants that are defined at the start of the unit.

```
{**************************************************************************
 *   TextColor : sets the foreground color for output from Writeln         *
 **-------------------------------------------------------------------**
 *   Input    : Col = the foreground color (0-15)                         *
 *   Globals : WritelnCol/RW                                              *
 **************************************************************************}
procedure TextColor( Color : byte );
begin
   WritelnCol := ( WritelnCol and $F0 ) or Color;                { insert color }
end;
{**************************************************************************
 *   TextBackground : sets the background color for output from Writeln    *
 **-------------------------------------------------------------------**
 *   Input    : Col = the background color (0-15)                         *
 *   Globals : WritelnCol/RW                                              *
 **************************************************************************}
procedure TextBackground( Color : byte );
begin
   WritelnCol := ( WritelnCol and $0F ) or ( Color shl 4 );     { insert color }
end;
```

All public procedures and functions in the WIN unit expect coordinates to be given in terms of absolute screen position. In many cases, however, it's better to specify coordinates relative to the current visible area and, therefore, also relative to the active window. There are four functions called VL, VO, VR and VU which support this. As a parameter, each of these functions expects an offset to the border of the visible area it represents. This value can be positive or negative.

The result returned by these functions is the absolute screen column or line that is produced by adding the given offset to the border of the region. VO relates to the top line of the visible area, VU to the bottom line, VL to the far left column and VR to the far right column.

```
{***********************************************************************
 *  VL        : returns a coordinate relative to the left border of the   *
 *               current window                                        *
 **-------------------------------------------------------------------**
 *  Input    : Offset = Position of left window border                 *
 *  Output   : absolute column coordinate                              *
 *  Globals : ViewX1/R                                                 *
 ***********************************************************************}
function  VL( Offset: integer ) : byte;
begin
  VL := ViewX1 + Offset;
end;
{***********************************************************************
 *  VR : returns a coordinate relative to the right border of the current  *
 *        window                                                       *
 **-------------------------------------------------------------------**
 *  Input    : Offset = distance from right window border              *
 *  Output   : absolute column coordinate                              *
 *  Info     : if no window is open, the entire screen is used         *
 *  Globals : ViewX2/R                                                 *
 ***********************************************************************}
function VR( Offset : integer ) : byte;
begin
  VR := ViewX2 + Offset;
end;
{***********************************************************************
 *  VO : returns a coordinate relative to the top border of the current   *
 *        window                                                       *
 **-------------------------------------------------------------------**
 *  Input    : Offset = distance from top window border                *
 *  Output   : absolute line coordinate                                *
 *  Info     : if no window is open, the entire screen is used         *
 *  Globals : ViewY1/R                                                 *
 ***********************************************************************}
function VO( Offset : integer ) : byte;
begin
  VO := ViewY1 + Offset;
end;
```

```
{***********************************************************************
 *  VU : returns a coordinate relative to the bottom border of the current  *
 *       window                                                             *
 **-----------------------------------------------------------------------**
 *  Input   : Offset = distance from bottom window border              *
 *  Output  : absolute line coordinate                                 *
 *  Info    : if no window is open, the entire screen is used          *
 *  Globals : ViewY2/R                                                 *
 ***********************************************************************}
function VU( Offset : integer ) : byte;
begin
  VU := ViewY2 + Offset;
end;
```

The WIN unit also uses its own ClrScr procedure. As opposed to the normal procedure, the replacement procedure will clear the entire screen even if more than 80 columns and 25 lines are used. This is done by using the WinFill procedure to fill parts of the screen with a constant character and color.

```
{***********************************************************************
 * ClrScr : clear screen                                               *
 **-----------------------------------------------------------------------**
 *  Input   : none                                                     *
 *  Info    : replaces the procedure of the same name from the CRT unit *
 *  Globals : NumCol/R, NumLine/R, WritelnCol/R                        *
 ***********************************************************************}
procedure ClrScr;
begin
  WinFill( 0, 0, NumCol-1, NumLine-1, ' ', WritelnCol );
end;
```

Like all procedures and functions that manipulate a screen region, WinFill expects the coordinates of the screen region as parameters in a certain order. The coordinates of the upper left corner are given first and the column coordinate is given before the line coordinate. Next are the coordinates for the lower right corner of the region and then the column coordinate is followed by the line coordinate again.

WinFill fills the specified area by using two public procedures/functions from its own unit: WinStRep and WinPrint.

WinStRep creates a string that consists of only one character with a length specified by the calling routine. The repeating character is also passed as a parameter from the calling routine. WinFill calls this function to create a string with a length that corresponds to the width of the region that it wants to fill with the specified character.

Next, WinFill processes each line in the region and outputs the string to each screen line with WinPrint. The entire process results in the specified screen region being filled with the desired character.

```
{*****************************************************************************
 *   WinFill : fills a given screen region with a constant character and    *
 *             its attribute                                                *
 **----------------------------------------------------------------------**
 *   Input   : x1, y1 = coordinates of the upper left corner of the region *
 *             x2, y2 = coordinates of the lower right corner of the region *
 *             Character,                                                    *
 *             WColor  = the character and its attribute                    *
 *   Globals : none                                                         *
 *****************************************************************************}
procedure WinFill( x1, y1, x2, y2 : byte; Character : char; WColor : byte );
var Line : string;                           { stores one line with the character }
begin
   Line := WinStRep( Character, x2-x1+1 );                  { construct a line }
   while y1 <= y2 do                                        { process each line }
     begin
        WinPrint( x1, y1, WColor, Line );                      { output a line }
        inc( y1 );                                  { increment line number }
     end;
end;
{*****************************************************************************
 *   WinStRep : builds a string out of the character to be repeated         *
 **----------------------------------------------------------------------**
 *   Input   : Character = the repeating character                          *
 *             Amount    = number of repetitions, equal to the string length *
 *   Output  : the completed string                                         *
 *   Globals : none                                                         *
 *****************************************************************************}
function WinStRep( Character : char; Amount : byte ) : string;
var Strepstring : string;                        { the string is assembled  }
begin
   StrepString[0] := chr( Amount );
   FillChar( StrepString[1], Amount, Character );
   WinStRep := StrepString;
end;
```

Besides the diverted Write and Writeln procedures, the WinPrint procedure represents a second way to bring characters to the screen. WinPrint is somewhat faster than Write and Writeln because it avoids the internal Turbo Pascal routines. A disadvantage to WinPrint is that it cannot output numerical arguments. There is also no distinction between control characters and normal ASCII characters; all characters are output to the screen unchanged. The visible area also cannot be considered. A string is simply displayed character by character starting at the given screen position. The edge of the screen isn't recognized, so scrolling doesn't occur. Because of its speed, WinPrint should be used when numerical arguments aren't required and when the visible area and control characters can be ignored.

WinPrint uses GetVioPtr to get a pointer to the output position. This is loaded in the variable VioPtr and then the string is processed character by character. Each character is brought to the screen position indicated by VioPtr. The corresponding color byte is loaded with the color code (or attribute) that was passed to WinPrint when it was called.

Next, the offset component of the pointer VioPtr is increased by two bytes so that it points to the next character in the video RAM. This character is processed in the next iteration of the loop, and so on until the end of the string is reached.

A variation of this method for manipulating the screen is used in the procedure WinColor. This function will assign a constant color to a screen region without affecting the characters in the region.

WinColor processes the given screen region line by line and column by column. The address of the processed screen position is always stored in the local variable VioPtr. First this pointer is loaded with the address of the first character of the first line to be processed. It is then incremented by one character to process the rest of the line. At the end of a line, the pointer must be set to the first character of the next line. It would be simple to just call the GetVioPtr function again, but you would be sacrificing speed. The move to the next line can be done faster by incrementing the offset component of VioPtr at the end of a line. However, this time the increment isn't two bytes. Instead, it is the distance between the current address and the start of the next line. This distance, which is constant, is calculated at the start of WinColor and stored in the variable DeltaX.

```
{***********************************************************************
 *  WinColor : fills a given screen region with a constant attribute   *
 *             without affecting the existing characters in the region *
 **-------------------------------------------------------------------**
 *  Input    : x1, y1  = coordinates of the upper left corner of the region  *
 *             x2, y2  = coordinates of the lower right corner of the region *
 *             WColor   = the new color                                *
 *  Globals : Line_Ofs/R                                               *
 ***********************************************************************}
procedure WinColor( x1, y1, x2, y2, WColor : byte );
var VioPtr : VPTR;                            { pointer to the video RAM }
    Line,                             { loop counter for processing lines }
    Column,                         { loop counter for processing columns }
    DeltaX : integer;                        { distance to next line }
begin
  VioPtr := GetVioPtr( x1, y1 );         { set pointer to the first character }
  DeltaX := Line_Ofs - ( (x2-x1) shl 1 ) - 2;       { offset from x2 to x1 }
  for Line:=y1 to y2 do                           { process the lines }
    begin                            { process each column within the line }
      for Column:=x1 to x2 do
        begin
          VioPtr^.Attribute := WColor;             { write color to video RAM }
          inc( PTRREC(VioPtr).Ofs, 2 );               { increase offset by 2 }
        end;
      inc( PTRREC(VioPtr).Ofs, DeltaX );
    end;
end;
```

Sometimes it's necessary to work with individual characters. Procedures such as WinColor and WinFill process entire screen regions. Although it is possible to process individual characters with these procedures, it isn't preferable because of the time involved.

Therefore, the WIN unit has special procedures/functions called WinPutChar, WinGetChar and WinGetCol, for manipulating single characters. These functions do not access the video RAM with pointers. Instead, they use the previously described MEM method.

```
{**************************************************************************
 *   WinGetChar : gets the ASCII code of the character in the given screen *
 *                position                                                 *
 **----------------------------------------------------------------------**
 *   Input   : Line, Column = coordinates of the character                *
 *   Output  : the ASCII code of the character                            *
 *   Globals : VioSeg/R, NumCol/R                                         *
 **************************************************************************}
function  WinGetChar( Column, Line : byte ) : char;
begin
  WinGetChar := chr(Mem[VioSeg : (NumCol * Line + Column ) shl 1]);
end;
{**************************************************************************
 *   WinGetCol : gets the color of the character in the given screen      *
 *               position                                                  *
 **----------------------------------------------------------------------**
 *   Input   : Line, Column = coordinates of the character                *
 *   Output  : the color code of the character                            *
 *   Globals : VioSeg/R, NumCol/R                                         *
 **************************************************************************}
function  WinGetCol( Column, Line : byte ) : byte;
begin
  WinGetCol := Mem[VioSeg : (NumCol * Line + Column ) shl 1 + 1];
end;
{**************************************************************************
 *   WinPutChar : writes a character and its attribute directly to a      *
 *                specified position in video RAM                          *
 **----------------------------------------------------------------------**
 *   Input   : Line, Column = coordinates of the character                *
 *             Character    = the output character                        *
 *             WColor       = its color or attribute                      *
 *   Info    : the reference point is the upper left corner of the screen, *
 *             with coordinates (0/0)                                      *
 *   Globals : VioSeg/R, NumCol/R                                         *
 **************************************************************************}
procedure WinPutChar( Column, Line : byte; Character : char; WColor : byte );
var OfsPos : integer;        { offset position of the character in video RAM }
begin
  OfsPos := (NumCol * Line + Column ) shl 1;     { calculate offset position }
  Mem[ VioSeg : OfsPos ] := ord( Character );        { write character and   }
  Mem[ VioSeg : OfsPos + 1 ] := WColor;              { attribute to video RAM }
end;
```

The cursor is controlled with a series of other procedures. To define the cursor position on the screen, use the procedures called WinSetCursor and WinHideCursor. Three other procedures, WinDefCursor, WinBlockCursor and WinLineCursor, affect the appearance of the cursor.

WinSetCursor uses function $02 of the BIOS video interrupt. This function enables a program to place the cursor at any desired screen location. In addition to the function number in the AH register, the new cursor position is given in the DH and DL registers. WinSetCursor stores the new cursor position in the global variables vLine and vColumn.

```
{*************************************************************************
 *  WinSetCursor : positions the blinking screen cursor                *
 **------------------------------------------------------------------**
 *  Input   : Line, Column = new cursor position                       *
 *  Globals : vLine/W, vColumn/W                                       *
 *************************************************************************}
procedure WinSetCursor( Column, Line : byte );
var Regs : Registers;                     { processor regs. for interrupt call }
begin
  Regs.ah := 2;                           { function number for Set Cursor }
  Regs.bh := 0;                           { access screen page 0 }
  Regs.dh := line;                        { store line }
  vLine   := line;
  Regs.dl := column;                      { store column }
  vColumn := column;
  intr($10, Regs);                        { call BIOS video interrupt }
end;
```

The procedure WinHideCursor uses WinSetCursor. Its job is to hide the blinking cursor so that it is no longer visible on the screen. WinSetCursor moves the cursor to a line beyond the last line displayed. It remains there until a subsequent call of WinSetCursor returns it to visible coordinates.

```
{*************************************************************************
 *  WinHideCursor : removes the cursor from the screen                 *
 **------------------------------------------------------------------**
 *  Input   : none                                                     *
 *  Globals : NumLine/R                                                *
 *************************************************************************}
procedure WinHideCursor;
begin
  WinSetCursor( 0, NumLine + 1 );         { move the cursor beyond the screen }
end;
```

WinDefCursor defines the appearance of the cursor. All video cards have the ability to select the start and end line for the cursor. In this case, "line" doesn't refer to a line of text on the screen but to the individual scan lines of the picture tube in your monitor.

One character is 14 lines high with monochrome cards and the cursor must have values between 0 and 13 for start and end lines. One character is eight lines high and the cursor must have values between 0 and 7 with color cards.

The actual definition of the cursor is done with BIOS function $01 of the video interrupt. This function exists specifically for this purpose. In addition to the function number, the new start line and the new end line are given in the CH and CL registers, respectively.

```
{***********************************************************************
 *   WinDefCursor : defines the appearance of the cursor             *
 **-----------------------------------------------------------------**
 *   Input    : Start = new start line for cursor                    *
 *              End   = new end line for cursor                      *
 *   Globals : none                                                  *
 ***********************************************************************}
procedure WinDefCursor( Start, End : byte );
var Regs : Registers;                    { processor regs. for interrupt call }
begin
  Regs.ah := 1;                          { define function number for Cursor }
  Regs.ch := Start;            { load start and end lines in the registers }
  Regs.cl := End;
  intr($10, Regs);                            { call BIOS video interrupt }
end;
```

The procedures WinBlockCursor and WinLineCursor can be used to create two types of frequently used cursors. The block cursor covers an entire character and the line cursor covers the bottom two lines of a character. The line cursor is standard.

```
{***********************************************************************
 *   WinBlockCursor : sets the cursor to block mode                  *
 **-----------------------------------------------------------------**
 *   Input   : none                                                  *
 *   Globals : Color/R                                               *
 ***********************************************************************}
procedure WinBlockCursor;
begin
  if ( Color ) then                              {color card active? }
    WinDefCursor( 0, 7 )                                      { yes }
  else                                      { monochrome card active }
    WinDefCursor( 0, 13 );
end;
{***********************************************************************
 *   WinLineCursor : sets cursor to line mode                        *
 **-----------------------------------------------------------------**
 *   Input    : none                                                 *
 *   Globals : Color/R                                               *
 ***********************************************************************}
procedure WinLineCursor;
begin
  if ( Color ) then                              {color card active? }
```

```
    WinDefCursor( 6, 7 )                                        { yes }
  else                                            { monochrome card active }
    WinDefCursor( 12, 13 );
end;
```

The procedures WinGetView and WinSetView are used to define visible areas. WinSetView establishes the current visible area and WinGetView returns the corner coordinates of the current visible area.

```
{**************************************************************************
 *  WinSetView : defines a screen region as the view region to which the  *
 *               functions VL, VR, VO and VU will relate                  *
 **----------------------------------------------------------------------**
 *  Input    : x1, y1 = coordinates of the upper left corner of the region *
 *             x2, y2 = coordinates of the lower right corner of the region *
 *  Globals : ViewX1/W, ViewX2/W, ViewY1/W, ViewY2/W                      *
 **************************************************************************}
procedure WinSetView( x1, y1, x2, y2 : byte);
begin
  ViewX1 := x1;                              { store coordinates in the }
  ViewY1 := y1;                              { global View variables    }
  ViewX2 := x2;
  ViewY2 := y2;
end;
{**************************************************************************
 *  WinGetView : returns the current VIEW region                          *
 **----------------------------------------------------------------------**
 *  Input    : x1, y1 = coordinates of the upper left corner of the region *
 *             x2, y2 = coordinates of the lower right corner of the region *
 *  Info     : - the VIEW region defines the region for which the functions *
 *               VL, VR, VO and VU are active                             *
 *             - the passed variables store the coordinates of the VIEW   *
 *               region as noted above                                    *
 *  Globals : ViewX1/R, ViewX2/R, ViewY1/R, ViewY2/R                      *
 **************************************************************************}
procedure WinGetView( var x1, y1, x2, y2 : byte );
begin
  x1 := ViewX1;                              { get coordinates from the }
  y1 := ViewY1;                              { global View variables    }
  x2 := ViewX2;
  y2 := ViewY2;
end;
```

One of the functions used to call WinSetView is WinOpen. This function is used to open a window on the screen. The calling routine passes the coordinates of the window to be opened and then receives a handle that can later be used to pull this window to the foreground in case other windows are opened on top of it. If the window can't be opened because insufficient memory is available on the heap for the window descriptor and the window buffer, the constant WIN_OPEN_ERROR is returned instead of a handle.

The available memory is checked at the start of WinOpen by counting the number of bytes required for the window buffer. This is calculated by multiplying the number of lines by the number of columns that the window will occupy. This total is then multiplied by 2, since each character requires two bytes. The final value is stored in the local variable BufLen.

Next, it must be determined whether the heap has a contiguous memory block large enough to hold the buffer and the window descriptor. This is done by comparing the result of the function MaxAvail with the size of the window descriptor plus the length of the window buffer minus one. If a large enough memory block is available, it is allocated with GetMem, which places the address in the local variable WinPtr.

Then the components of the window descriptor are initialized and the screen contents of the window are stored in the window buffer after the window descriptor. To do this, WinOpen uses the procedure GetScr, which copies a specified screen region to a buffer. The variable CurBufPtr is then loaded with the address of this buffer and the visible area is set with a call to WinSetView.

After the call, the window descriptor is linked with the previous window and the pointer CurWinPtr is set to the new window descriptor.

In the last step, WinOpen finds a free handle in the handle array. This array is searched bit by bit until the first bit set to 0, which represents an unassigned handle, is found. The bit is then set to 1 and its distance from the first bit in the array is passed to the calling routine as the handle.

```
{****************************************************************************
 *   WinOpen : opens a new window                                          *
 **----------------------------------------------------------------------**
 *   Input    : x1, y1 = coordinates of the upper left window corner       *
 *              x2, y2 = coordinates of the lower right window corner       *
 *   Output   : Handle for later access to the window                       *
 *   Info     : if the window can not be opened due to insufficient memory  *
 *              on the heap, the value WinOpenError (-1) is returned as the  *
 *              Handle                                                       *
 *   Globals  : vLine/R, vColumn/R, ViewX1/R, ViewX2/R, ViewY1/R, ViewY2/R  *
 *              NumWin/W, FirstWinPtr/RW, CurWInPtr/RW, HaPtr^/RW            *
 ****************************************************************************}
function WinOpen( x1, y1, x2, y2 : byte ) : integer;
var i, j,                                            { loop counter }
    Key,                                             { stores the Handle }
    BufLen : integer;                           { length of the window buffer }
    WinPtr : WIPTR;                                  { window descriptor }
begin
  BufLen := ( x2 - x1 + 1 ) * ( y2 - y1 + 1 ) shl 1;
  if MaxAvail >= BufLen + SizeOf( WINDES ) - 1 then
    begin              { there is enough memory available on the heap }
      GetMem( WinPtr, BufLen + SizeOf( WINDES ) - 1 );
      WinPtr^.x1      := x1;                          { store window    }
```

```
     WinPtr^.x2      := x2;                        { coordinates in }
     WinPtr^.y1      := y1;                        { window         }
     WinPtr^.y2      := y2;                         { descriptor    }
     WinPtr^.curs    := vColumn;             { also store the current }
     WinPtr^.curz    := vLine;               { cursor position        }
     WinPtr^.ViewX1  := ViewX1;                { store the View       }
     WinPtr^.ViewY1  := ViewY1;                { region coordinates }
     WinPtr^.ViewX2  := ViewX2;                { in the window      }
     WinPtr^.ViewY2  := ViewY2;                { descriptor         }
     WinPtr^.Attribute:= 0;              { window has no attribute yet}
     WinPtr^.LastWin := CurWinPtr;     { link to previous window descriptor }
     WinPtr^.NextWin := NIL;                   { no next window exists yet }
     GetScr( x1, y1, x2, y2, @WinPtr^.Buffer );
     CurBufPtr := VELARPTR(@WinPtr^.Buffer);     { pointer to window buffer }
     WinSetView( x1, y1, x2, y2 );       { the window is the new view region }
     if CurWinPtr <> NIL then                   { did a window already exist? }
       CurWinPtr^.NextWin := WinPtr               { yes, link to new window }
     else                          { no, this is the first and only window }
       FirstWinPtr := WinPtr;                    { set pointer to first window }
     CurWinPtr := WinPtr;                 { set pointer to current descriptor }
     inc( NumWin );                       { increment number of open windows }
     {-- look for a free Handle in the buffer, set HaPtr to it ------------}
     Key := 0;                   { the Handle corresponds to the bit position }
     while (HaPtr^[ Key shr 3 ] and ( 1 shl (Key and 7) )) <> 0 do
       inc( Key );                      { Handle already assigned, test next }
     HaPtr^[ Key shr 3 ] := HaPtr^[ Key shr 3 ] or ( 1 shl ( Key and 7 ));
     WinPtr^.Handle := Key;                    { store Handle in descriptor }
     WinOpen := Key;                       { pass Handle back to caller }
   end
 else                      { not enough memory for window descriptor and buffer }
   WinOpen := -1;
end;
```

The procedure used to close the active window is WinClose. This is the exact opposite of WinOpen. It uses the global variable CurWinPtr as a pointer to the descriptor of the active window and doesn't require the coordinates of the window as parameters. It can simply take this information from the descriptor. The only information it expects from the caller is a boolean parameter that tells whether or not the old screen contents under the window should be restored after the window is closed.

After WinClose has cleared the corresponding bit in the handle array, it evaluates the parameter ReDraw. If this variable contains TRUE, the previous screen contents are copied back to the screen using the PutScr procedure. The preceding visible area is then restored and the cursor is returned to its location.

Next, the old window is made the active window. The pointer CurWinPtr is manipulated and the number of opened windows is decremented. Finally, the memory reserved for the window descriptor and its buffer are cleared. No trace of the window remains.

```
{*******************************************************************************
 *   WinClose : closes the active window                                       *
 **---------------------------------------------------------------------------**
 *   Input    : Redraw = TRUE : the contents of the screen region under the    *
 *                              window are restored to the screen              *
 *   Info     : - the calling routine is responsible for making sure that      *
 *                 at least one window is open before this procedure is called *
 *   Globals  : CurWinPtr/RW, FirstWinPtr/RW, HaPTr^/RW, NumWin/W              *
 *******************************************************************************}
procedure WinClose( ReDraw : boolean );
var WinPtr : WIPTR;                            { pointer to the current descriptor }
begin
   with CurWinPtr^ do
     begin
       {-- the window's Handle is freed ------------------------------------}
       HaPtr^[ Handle shr 3 ] := HaPtr^[ Handle shr 3 ] and
                                             not( 1 shl ( Handle and 7 ));
       if ReDraw then                                    { redraw old screen? }
         PutScr( x1, y1, x2, y2, @Buffer );                        { yes }
       WinSetView( ViewX1, ViewY1, ViewX2, ViewY2 );       { old view region }
       WinSetCursor( curs, curz );                { cursor to previous position }
       WinPtr := CurWinPtr;            { store pointer to current descriptor }
       CurWinPtr := LastWin;            { pointer to previous descriptor }
       if LastWin <> NIL then                    { no more windows open? }
         CurWinPtr^.NextWin := NIL                { yes, no more windows }
       else                                                        { no }
         FirstWinPtr := NIL;                    { pointer points to nothing }
       {-- clear memory allocated to descriptor --------------------------}
       FreeMem( WinPtr, (x2-x1+1) * (y2-y1+1) shl 1 + SizeOf(WINDES) - 1);
       CurBufPtr := VELARPTR(@CurWinPtr^.Buffer); { pointer to window buffer }
       dec( NumWin );                         { decrement number of open windows }
     end;
end;
```

The procedures GetScr and PutScr perform important tasks for WinOpen and WinClose. These two procedures are used to store the contents of a given screen region in a buffer and then recall it to the screen. GetScr, which takes a screen region and stores it, goes through the screen line by line and copies the desired portions to a specified buffer. The lines are consecutively stored in the buffer so that bytes are used more effectively.

Each time this loop is executed, the offset component in the pointer to the buffer is incremented by the number of bytes copied so that it has the proper address for the next line to be copied. The address of the bytes to obtain from video RAM and copy in the buffer is performed, as usual, with GetVioPtr. This is then passed directly to MOVE for the copy operation. PutScr works the same way, except that this procedure uses MOVE to copy from the buffer back to video RAM.

```
{*******************************************************************
 *   GetScr : gets a specified screen region from video RAM and stores it   *
 *            in a buffer                                                    *
 **-----------------------------------------------------------------**
 *   Input    : x1, y1 = coordinates of the upper left corner of the region *
 *              x2, y2 = coordinates of the lower right corner of the region *
 *              BufPtr = pointer to the buffer to which the region will be   *
 *                       copied                                             *
 *   Info     : the individual lines are stored in direct succession in the *
 *              buffer                                                       *
 *   Globals : none                                                         *
 *******************************************************************}
procedure GetScr( x1, y1, x2, y2 : byte; BufPtr : pointer );
var nbytes : integer;                        { number of bytes to copy per line }
begin
  nbytes := ( x2 - x1 + 1 ) shl 1;                          { bytes per line }
  while y1 <= y2 do                                       { process each line }
    begin
      Move( GetVioPtr(x1, y1)^, BufPtr^, nbytes);
      inc( PTRREC( BufPtr ).Ofs, nbytes );
      inc( y1 );                                         { set Y1 to next line }
    end;
end;
{*******************************************************************
 *   PutScr : copies the contents of a buffer back to video RAM             *
 **-----------------------------------------------------------------**
 *   Input    : x1, y1 = coordinates of the upper left corner of the region *
 *              x2, y2 = coordinates of the lower right corner of the region *
 *              BufPtr = pointer to the buffer whose contents are to be      *
 *                       copied to video RAM                                *
 *   Info     : the buffer must be formatted in the way PutScr will deliver it*
 *   Globals : none                                                         *
 *******************************************************************}
procedure PutScr( x1, y1, x2, y2 : byte; BufPtr : pointer );
var nbytes : integer;                        { number of bytes to copy per line }
begin
  nbytes := ( x2 - x1 + 1 ) shl 1;                          { bytes per line }
  while y1 <= y2 do                                       { process each line }
    begin
      Move( BufPtr^, GetVioPtr(x1, y1)^, nbytes);
      inc( PTRREC( BufPtr ).Ofs, nbytes );
      inc( y1 );                                         { set Y1 to next line }
    end;
end;
```

There is a second function, in addition to WinOpen, that the WIN unit can use to open a window. This function is WinOpenShadow and works the same as WinOpen except that the lower and right borders of the window are accented with a shadow. Only the size of the actual window, not the size of the shadow, has to be considered when calling WinOpenShadow. The shadow size is automatically calculated.

The window is opened with WinOpen. The shadow is then created with WinShadow, which is called once for the right edge and once for the lower edge of the window.

```
{***************************************************************************
 *   WinOpenShadow : opens a new window and accents it with a shadow      *
 **-------------------------------------------------------------------**
 *   Input   : x1, y1  = coordinates of the upper left window corner     *
 *             x2, y2  = coordinates of the lower right window corner     *
 *   Info    : - the width and depth of the shadow are specified with the *
 *               global variables ShadowX and ShadowY                     *
 *             - the given coordinates do not include the shadow, so they *
 *               must be chosen so that the window plus the shadow will fit*
 *               on the screen                                            *
 *             - in color mode, the shadow is created by changing the     *
 *               character attribute, whereas in mono mode, the shadow    *
 *               is represented by the character '▓'                      *
 *   Globals : CurWinPTr^/W                                              *
 ***************************************************************************}
function WinOpenShadow( x1, y1, x2, y2 : byte ) : integer;
var  Handle : integer;                           { Handle for the open window }
begin
   Handle := WinOpen( x1, y1, x2 + ShadowX, y2 + ShadowY);
   if ( Handle <> WinOpenError ) then
     begin
       CurWinPtr^.Attribute := WIN_SHADOW;              { window has a shadow }
       WinSetView( x1, y1, x2, y2 );     { shadow is outside the view region }
       WinShadow( x2+1, y1+1, x2+ShadowX, y2+ShadowY, VPTR(ptr(VioSeg,0)) );
       WinShadow( x1+ShadowX, y2+1, x2, y2+ShadowY, VPTR(ptr(VioSeg,0)) );
     end;
   WinOpenShadow := Handle;          { return window Handle to calling routine }
end;
```

WinShadow is dependent upon the type of the currently active video card (mono or color) because the shadow effect cannot be obtained with different colors if a monochrome video card is being used. In mono mode, the shadow is created by filling the shadow region with the character "▓" (code 177).

Color mode is slightly more effective. WinShadow processes all characters in the shadow region and determines their color. The background and foreground colors are then made darker. WinShadow will clear bit 3 in the background color if it is found to be set. However, instead of changing color, this action changes intensity. This bit will usually not be found set, however, because it is used by many cards as a blinking attribute. In this case, the background color is set to black.

The foreground color is handled similarly. Bit 3 also represents an intensity bit. If it is found set, it is cleared, and the character will have a darker foreground color. The foreground color remains unchanged if this bit is not found set.

```
{***************************************************************************
 *  WinShadow : creates a shadow for a specified screen region            *
 **-----------------------------------------------------------------------**
 *  Input    : x1, y1 = coordinates of the upper left shadow corner       *
 *             x2, y2 = coordinates of the lower right shadow corner       *
 *             BufPtr = pointer to the buffer to be manipulated            *
 *  Info     : - in color mode, the shadow is created by changing the      *
 *               character attribute, in mono mode, it is made by filling   *
 *               the shadow region with the character "▓"                   *
 *  Globals : NumCol/R, Color/R, Line_Ofs/R                                *
 ***************************************************************************}
procedure WinShadow( x1, y1, x2, y2 : byte; BufPtr : VPTR );
var Attribute : byte;                        { the attribute to be manipulated }
    Line,                            { loop counter for processing lines }
    Column,                          { loop counter for processing columns }
    DeltaX   : integer;                      { distance to the next line }
begin
  inc( PTRREC( BufPtr ).Ofs, ( y1 * NumCol + x1 ) shl 1 );   { load pointer }
  DeltaX := Line_Ofs - ( (x2-x1) shl 1 ) - 2;        { offset from x2 to x1 }
  if ( Color ) then                                        { color mode? }
    for Line := y1 to y2 do                            { process each line }
      begin                                          { process each column }
        for Column := x1 to x2 do
          begin
            Attribute := BufPtr^.Attribute;         { get character attribute }
            {-- change background color ---------------------------------}
            if Attribute and 128 <> 0 then          { lighter background? }
              Attribute := Attribute and 128          { yes, clear bit 7 }
            else                                    { no, normal background }
              Attribute := Attribute and 15;        { background is now black }
            {-- change foreground color ---------------------------------}
            if Attribute and 8 <> 0 then            { lighter foreground? }
              Attribute := Attribute and (255 - 8);     { yes, clear bit 3 }
            BufPtr^.Attribute := Attribute;   { attribute back to video RAM }
            inc( PTRREC(BufPtr).Ofs, 2 );   { set pointer to next character }
          end;
        inc( PTRREC(BufPtr).Ofs, DeltaX );
      end
  else                                              { no, monochrome mode }
    for Line := y1 to y2 do                            { process each line }
      begin                                          { process each column }
        for Column := x1 to x2 do
          begin
            BufPtr^.Contents := ord( '▓' ) + ( $7 shl 8 );{ set char.&color }
            inc( PTRREC(BufPtr).Ofs, 2 );   { set pointer to next character }
          end;
        inc( PTRREC(BufPtr).Ofs, DeltaX );
      end
end;
```

In addition to shadows, windows can also have different types of frames. The WIN unit uses the WinFrame procedure to create a frame around any specified screen region.

As parameters, this procedure receives the coordinates of the upper left and lower right corners of the frame, the frame type and the frame color. The different frame types are represented by constants that are defined at the start of the WIN unit.

SIN_FR	Creates a frame with a single frame character.
DBL_FR	Creates a frame with two frame characters.
DOT_FR	Creates a frame with ASCII character 177 (▓).
FULL_FR	Creates a frame with ASCII character 219 (█).

Within WinFrame, the frame character is assigned to a local standard constant called RCharacter. This variable is an array with four elements, each of which is a structure of type RStruc. Each frame character is listed in these structures. The constants for the various frame types correspond to the indices to the character sets within RCharacter. This makes it easy to access the required frame character(s).

```
{*************************************************************************
 *  WinFrame : creates one of four frame types around a specified screen  *
 *             region                                                     *
 **---------------------------------------------------------------------**
 *  Input    : x1, y1 = coordinates of the upper left corner of the region  *
 *             x2, y2 = coordinates of the lower right corner of the region *
 *             WBorder = one of the constants EIN_RA, DOP_RA etc.          *
 *             WColor  = color or attribute for the frame character        *
 *  Globals : none                                                        *
 *************************************************************************}
procedure WinFrame( x1, y1, x2, y2, WBorder, WColor : byte );
type RStruc = record                   { describes the characters of a frame }
                UpperLeft,
                UpperRight,
                LowerLeft,
                LowerRight,
                Vertical,
                Horizontal  : char;
              end;
const RCharacter : array[1..4] of RStruc =        { the possible frame types }
        (
        ( UpperLeft  : '┌'; UpperRight : '┐'; LowerLeft  : 'L';
          LowerRight : '⌡'; Vertical   : '|'; Horizontal : '─' ),
        ( UpperLeft  : '╔'; UpperRight : '╗'; LowerLeft  : 'L';
          LowerRight : '╨'; Vertical   : '║'; Horizontal : '=' ),
        ( UpperLeft  : '▓'; UpperRight : '▓'; LowerLeft  : '▓';
          LowerRight : '▓'; Vertical   : '▓'; Horizontal : '▓' ),
        ( UpperLeft  : '█'; UpperRight : '█'; LowerLeft  : '█';
          LowerRight : '█'; Vertical   : '█'; Horizontal : '█' )
        );
var StrepBuf : string;                         { stores a horizontal line }
    Line     : byte;                           { loop counter }
begin
  with RCharacter[ WBorder ] do
    begin
      WinPutChar( x1, y1, UpperLeft, WColor );          { output the four }
      WinPutChar( x2, y1, UpperRight, WColor );         { frame corners   }
```

```
        WinPutChar( x1, y2, LowerLeft, WColor );
        WinPutChar( x2, y2, LowerRight, WColor );
        StrepBuf := WinStRep( Horizontal, x2-x1-1 );    { output the two }
        WinPrint( x1+1, y1, WColor, StrepBuf );         { horizontal     }
        WinPrint( x1+1, y2, WColor, StrepBuf );         { lines          }
        dec( y2 );                                   { calculate last line }
        for Line:=y1+1 to y2 do                        { process each line }
          begin                                        { draw vertical line }
            WinPutChar( x1, Line, Vertical, WColor );
            WinPutChar( x2, Line, Vertical, WColor );
          end;
      end;
    end;
```

In addition to the ones already described, there are also five other procedures for manipulating windows. These procedures are used to move the active window. Four of these procedures, WinMoveUp, WinMoveDown, WinMoveLeft, WinMoveRight move the window in one specified direction. WinMove can be used to place the window anywhere on the screen.

We'll use WinMoveUp as an example since the first four procedures work the same way.

In addition to moving a window, all Move procedures must restore the old contents under the window. The contents of the newly covered screen region must also be saved. This is done by first allocating a buffer that is the same size as the newly covered screen region. GetScr is used to store the contents of the region that will be covered when the window is moved.

The window is then moved, with one of the four Scroll routines, in the desired direction. The contents of the screen region that the window was covering are restored from the window buffer with PutScr. This completes the movement of the window, but the window buffer must now be rearranged to put the contents of the new screen region under the window in the proper order. This is done by moving the part of the window buffer, that is still needed, to its new location within the window buffer and then bringing the contents of the newly covered screen region in from the allocated buffer.

To finish, the window coordinates within the window descriptor and the visible area are passed on. If the screen cursor was located within the window to be moved, it is moved with the window. The output positions for Writeln are passed in the coordinates WritelnX and WritelnY as long as the standard constant Write2View contains TRUE. The allocated buffer is freed and control is then returned to the calling routine.

```
{***************************************************************************
 *   WinMoveUp : moves the active window a given number of lines up         *
 **------------------------------------------------------------------------**
 *   Input    : Amount = number of lines to move the window up              *
 *   Info     : the calling routine is responsible for making sure that the *
 *              window will not be moved off the screen                     *
 *   Globals  : vLine/RW, vColumn/RW, Write2View/R, ViewY1/W, ViewY2/W      *
 *              WritelnY/W                                                  *
 ***************************************************************************}

procedure WinMoveUp( Amount : byte );
var BufPtr : VPTR;                              { pointer to temporary buffer }
    WWidth,                                       { window width in columns }
    WLength,                                     { window length in columns }
    BufLen : integer;               { length of the temporary buffer in bytes}
{-- GetPtr returns a pointer to the start of a line in the ------[ LOCAL ]--}
{-- buffer of the active window                                          --}
function GetPtr( Line : integer ) : pointer;
begin
  GetPtr := @CurBufPtr^[ Line * WWidth ];
end;
{--------------------------------------------------------------------------}
begin
  with CurWinPtr^ do                   { access the active window descriptor }
    begin
      WWidth := x2 - x1 + 1;
      WLength := y2 - y1 + 1;
      BufLen := WWidth * Amount shl 1;
      GetMem( BufPtr, BufLen );                    { allocate temp. memory }
      GetScr( x1, y1-Amount, x2, y1-1, BufPtr );
      WinScrollUp ( x1, y1, x2, y2, Amount, NO_CLEAR );
      PutScr( x1, y2-Amount+1, x2, y2, GetPtr( WLength - Amount ) );
      Move( GetPtr( 0 )^, GetPtr(Amount)^, WWidth * (WLength-Amount) shl 1);
      Move( BufPtr^, GetPtr( 0 )^, BufLen );
      {-- if the cursor was within the window, it must also be moved -------}
      if ( (x1 <= vColumn ) and (x2 >= vColumn ) and
           (y1 <= vLine ) and (y2 >= vLine ) ) then
        WinSetCursor( vColumn , vLine - Amount );
      {-- in Write2View mode, the output position for Write and ------------}
      {-- Writeln must be moved with the window             ------------}
      if ( Write2View ) then                          { in Write2View mode? }
        begin                                                     { yes }
          dec( WritelnY, Amount );                    { pass Write position }
          WritelnPtr := GetVioPtr( WritelnX, WritelnY );
        end;
      dec( y1, amount );                          { update window coordinates }
      dec( y2, amount );
      FreeMem( BufPtr, BufLen );                   { clear allocated buffer }
    end;
  dec( ViewY1, amount );                                { move view region }
  dec( ViewY2, amount );                                { with the window  }
end;
```

```
{*****************************************************************************
 *  WinMoveDown : moves the active window a specified number of lines down  *
 **------------------------------------------------------------------------**
 *  Input    : Amount = number of lines to move the window down             *
 *  Info     : the calling routine is responsible for making sure that the  *
 *             window will not be moved off the screen                      *
 *  Globals  : vLine/RW, vColumn/RW, Write2View/R, ViewY1/W, ViewY2/W       *
 *             WritelnY/W                                                    *
 *****************************************************************************}
procedure WinMoveDown( Amount : byte );
var BufPtr : VPTR;                               { pointer to temp. buffer }
    WWidth,                                   { width of window in columns }
    WLength,                                 { length of window in columns }
    BufLen : integer;                    { length of temp. buffer in bytes }
{-- GetPtr returns a pointer to the start of a line in the ------[ LOCAL ]--}
{-- buffer of the active window                                          --}
function GetPtr( Line : integer ) : pointer;
begin
  GetPtr := @CurBufPtr^[ Line * WWidth ];
end;
{---------------------------------------------------------------------------}
begin
  with CurWinPtr^ do                   { access the active window descriptor }
    begin
      WWidth := x2 - x1 + 1;
      WLength := y2 - y1 + 1;
      BufLen := WWidth * Amount shl 1;
      GetMem( BufPtr, BufLen );                        { allocate temp. memory }
      GetScr( x1, y2+1, x2, y2+Amount, BufPtr );
      WinScrollDown( x1, y1, x2, y2, Amount, NO_CLEAR );
      PutScr( x1, y1, x2, y1+Amount-1, GetPtr( 0 ) );
      Move( GetPtr(Amount)^, GetPtr( 0 )^, WWidth * (WLength-Amount) shl 1);
      Move( BufPtr^, GetPtr( WLength - Amount )^, BufLen );
      {-- if the cursor was in the window, it must also be moved -----------}
      if ( (x1 <= vColumn ) and (x2 >= vColumn ) and
           (y1 <= vLine ) and (y2 >= vLine ) ) then
        WinSetCursor( vColumn , vLine + Amount );
      {-- in Write2View mode, the output position for Write and ------------}
      {-- Writeln must be moved with the window            ------------}
      if ( Write2View ) then                          { in Write2View mode? }
        begin                                                       { yes }
          inc( WritelnY, Amount );                    { pass Write position }
          WritelnPtr := GetVioPtr( WritelnX, WritelnY );
        end;
      inc( y1, amount );                          { update window coordinates }
      inc( y2, amount );
      FreeMem( BufPtr, BufLen );                      { free allocated buffer }
    end;
  inc( ViewY1, amount );                       { move the view region (global }
  inc( ViewY2, amount );                       { variables) with the window   }
end;
```

```
{***************************************************************************
 *  WinMoveRight : moves the active window a specified number of columns  *
 *                 to the right                                           *
 **---------------------------------------------------------------------**
 *  Input   : Amount = number of columns to move the window              *
 *  Info    : the calling routine is responsible for making sure that the *
 *            window will not be moved off the screen                    *
 *  Globals : vLine/RW, vColumn/RW, Write2View/R, ViewX1/W, ViewX2/W     *
 *            WritelnX/W                                                  *
 ***************************************************************************}
procedure WinMoveRight( Amount : byte );
var BufPtr,                                         { pointer to temp. buffer }
    LBufPtr   : VPTR;               { running pointer in the temp. buffer }
    Byte2Copy,                                { number of bytes to copy }
    Line,                   { loop counter for processing the window lines }
    EndLine,                                               { same }
    WWidth,                                    { window width in columns }
    WLength,                                   { window length in columns }
    BufLen    : integer;                { length of temp. buffer in bytes }
{-- GetPtr returns a pointer to a certain character in the ------[ LOCAL ]--}
{-- buffer of the active window                                          --}
function GetPtr( Line, Column : integer ) : pointer;
begin
  GetPtr := @CurBufPtr^[ Line * WWidth + Column ];
end;
{--------------------------------------------------------------------------}
begin
  with CurWinPtr^ do                    { access active window descriptor }
    begin
      WWidth := x2 - x1 + 1;
      WLength := y2 - y1 + 1;
      BufLen := WLength * Amount shl 1;
      GetMem( BufPtr, BufLen );                    { allocate temp. memory }
      GetScr( x2+1, y1, x2+Amount, y2, BufPtr );
      ScrollHori( x1, y1, x2, y2, Amount, NO_CLEAR, FALSE );
      Byte2Copy := ( WWidth - Amount ) shl 1;
      LBufPtr := BufPtr;                { running pointer to start of buffer }
      EndLine := WLength - 1;
      for Line:=0 to EndLine do                         { process each line }
        begin
          PutScr( x1, Line+y1, x1+Amount-1, Line+y1,
                     GetPtr( Line, 0 ) );
          Move( GetPtr( Line, Amount )^, GetPtr( Line, 0 )^, Byte2Copy );
          Move( LBufPtr^, GetPtr( Line, WWidth - Amount )^, Amount shl 1 );
          inc( PTRREC( LBufPtr ).Ofs, Amount shl 1 );
        end;
      {-- if the cursor was in the window, it must also be moved -----------}
      if ( (x1 <= vColumn ) and (x2 >= vColumn ) and
           (y1 <= vLine ) and (y2 >= vLine ) ) then
        WinSetCursor( vColumn + Amount , vLine );
      {-- in Write2View mode, the output position for Write and -----------}
      {-- Writeln must be moved with the window              -----------}
      if ( Write2View ) then                        { in Write2View mode? }
```

```
        begin                                              { yes }
          inc( WritelnX, Amount );                { pass Write position }
          WritelnPtr := GetVioPtr( WritelnX, WritelnY );
        end;
      inc( x1, amount );                     { update window coordinates }
      inc( x2, amount );
      FreeMem( BufPtr, BufLen );                  { free allocated buffer }
    end;
  inc( ViewX1, amount );                     { move view region (global }
  inc( ViewX2, amount );                     { variables) with window   }
end;
{*************************************************************************
 *  WinMoveLeft : moves the active window a specified number of columns   *
 *                to the left                                             *
 **---------------------------------------------------------------------**
 *  Input    : Amount = number of columns to move the window              *
 *  Info     : the calling routine is responsible for making sure that the*
 *             window will not be moved off the screen                    *
 *  Globals  : vLine/RW, vColumn/RW, Write2View/R, ViewX1/W, ViewX2/W     *
 *             WritelnX/W                                                  *
 *************************************************************************}
procedure WinMoveLeft( Amount : byte );
var BufPtr,                                   { pointer to temp. buffer }
    LBufPtr  : VPTR;              { running pointer in the temp. buffer }
    Byte2Copy,                           { number of bytes to copy }
    Line,                   { loop counter for processing each window line }
    EndLine,                                           { same }
    WWidth,                           { window width in columns }
    WLength,                          { window length in columns }
    BufLen   : integer;              { length of temp. buffer in bytes }
{-- GetPtr returns a pointer to a certain character in the ------[ LOCAL ]--}
{-- buffer of the active window                                         --}
function GetPtr( Line, Column : integer ) : pointer;
begin
  GetPtr := @CurBufPtr^[ Line * WWidth + Column ];
end;
{---------------------------------------------------------------------------}
begin
  with CurWinPtr^ do                { access the active window descriptor }
    begin
      WWidth := x2 - x1 + 1;
      WLength := y2 - y1 + 1;
      BufLen := WLength * Amount shl 1;
      GetMem( BufPtr, BufLen );                    { allocate temp. memory }
      GetScr( x1-Amount, y1, x1-1, y2, BufPtr );
      ScrollHori( x1, y1, x2, y2, Amount, NO_CLEAR, TRUE );
      Byte2Copy := ( WWidth - Amount ) shl 1;
      LBufPtr := BufPtr;                 { running pointer to start of buffer }
      EndLine := WLength - 1;
      for Line:=0 to EndLine do                      { process each line }
        begin
          PutScr( x2-Amount+1, Line+y1, x2, Line+y1,
                    GetPtr( Line, WWidth - Amount ) );
```

```
            Move( GetPtr( Line, 0 )^, GetPtr( Line, Amount )^, Byte2Copy );
            Move( LBufPtr^, GetPtr( Line, 0 )^, Amount shl 1 );
            inc( PTRREC( LBufPtr ).Ofs, Amount shl 1 );
          end;
      {-- if the cursor was in the window, it must also be moved -----------}
      if ( (x1 <= vColumn ) and (x2 >= vColumn ) and
           (y1 <= vLine ) and (y2 >= vLine ) ) then
        WinSetCursor( vColumn + Amount , vLine );
      {-- in Write2View mode, the output position for Write and ------------}
      {-- Writeln must be moved with the window          ------------}
      if ( Write2View ) then                        { in Write2View mode? }
        begin                                               { yes }
          dec( WritelnX, Amount );                 { pass Write position }
          WritelnPtr := GetVioPtr( WritelnX, WritelnY );
        end;
      dec( x1, amount );                         { update window coordinates }
      dec( x2, amount );
      FreeMem( BufPtr, BufLen );                    { free allocated buffer }
    end;
  dec( ViewX1, amount );                        { move view region (global }
  dec( ViewX2, amount );                        { variables) with window    }
end;
```

WinMove is an easier method. It starts by saving the complete contents of the active window in a temporary buffer and then restoring the contents of the window buffer to the screen with PutScr.

Next, it puts the screen contents of the new window position in the window buffer of the active window and copies the window contents from the temporary buffer. This completes the movement of the window. After this, the same parameters described above are passed to complete the procedure.

```
{*****************************************************************************
 *   WinMove : moves the current window to a specified screen position       *
 **-----------------------------------------------------------------------**
 *   Input   : x, y : new coordinates of the upper left window corner        *
 *   Info    : the calling routine is responsible for making sure that the   *
 *             window will not be moved off the screen                       *
 *   Globals : vLine/RW, vColumn/RW, Write2View/R, ViewX1/W, ViewX2/W,       *
 *             ViewY1/W, ViewY2/W, WritelnX/W, WritelnY/W                     *
 ****************************************************************************}
procedure WinMove( x, y : byte );
var BufPtr : VPTR;                                  { pointer to temp. buffer }
    DeltaX,                                    { distance between old and new }
    DeltaY,                                    { window positions            }
    WWidth,                                        { window width in columns }
    WLength,                                       { window length in columns }
    BufLen : integer;                          { length of temp. buffer in bytes }
begin
  with CurWinPtr^ do                           { access current window descriptor }
    begin
```

```
         WWidth := x2 - x1;
         WLength := y2 - y1;
         BufLen := ( WLength + 1 ) * ( WWidth + 1 ) shl 1;
         GetMem( BufPtr, BufLen );                      { allocate temp. buffer }
         GetScr( x1, y1, x2, y2, BufPtr );    { copy current window to buffer }
         PutScr( x1, y1, x2, y2, @Buffer );
         DeltaX := x - x1;                              { distance in columns }
         DeltaY := y - y1;                                { distance in lines }
         {-- if the cursor was in the window, it must also be moved -----------}
         if ( (x1 <= vColumn ) and (x2 >= vColumn ) and
              (y1 <= vLine ) and (y2 >= vLine ) ) then
           WinSetCursor( vColumn - x1 + x, vLine - y1 + y );
         {-- in Write2View mode, the output position for Write and ------------}
         {-- Writeln must be moved with the window          -----------}
         if ( Write2View ) then                         { in Write2View mode? }
           begin
             dec( WritelnX, x1 - x );
             dec( WritelnY, y1 - y );
             WritelnPtr := GetVioPtr( WritelnX, WritelnY );
           end;
         x1 := x;                                 { set new window coordinates }
         x2 := x + WWidth - 1;
         y1 := y;
         y2 := y + WLength - 1;
         GetScr( x, y, x2, y2, @Buffer );
         PutScr( x, y, x2, y2, BufPtr );
         FreeMem( BufPtr, BufLen );                     { free allocated buffer }
       end;
     inc( ViewX1, DeltaX );                      { move view region (global }
     inc( ViewX2, DeltaX );                      { variables) with window    }
     inc( ViewY1, DeltaY );
   end;
```

The most complex function in the WIN unit is WinInFront. This function looks through the handle list for a window to place in the foreground making it the active window.

The contents of the window must be obtained and the buffers of every window lying over the desired window must be accessed. Also, the background of this window will change if any window behind it is removed.

It's not easy to access the contents of a specific window. It depends on the location of the window but only a small portion of it may actually be visible on the screen. So, the contents of the desired window must be combined from the window buffers of every window on top of it.

Therefore, WinInFront is slower than the other routines of the WIN unit. It also requires more heap memory. Three buffers the size of the entire video RAM must be allocated and processed during this function. There are also two additional buffers whose size depends upon the size of the windows on screen.

Occasionally, there may not be enough heap memory available to handle all of this. This is why WinInFront is structured as a function that returns a result to notifying the calling routine whether it could complete its task.

The first step is to find the window descriptor whose handle was passed. If the function finds that this window is already in the foreground, it immediately returns to the calling routine with the result TRUE. Otherwise the heap is checked to see if enough memory is available for the five screen buffers. If not, the function is immediately terminated with a result of FALSE.

If enough memory is available, WinInFront continues by entering the necessary data (visible area, cursor position) in the window descriptor of the window being processed. The procedures WinSetView and WinSetCursor are called to place these values in the variables ViewX1, etc.

The window in front of the window being moved will now be followed by a different window. Therefore, it must take the visible area and cursor position which had been stored in the window being moved.

Now the function must obtain the contents of the window being moved. First it places a complete copy of the entire video RAM in the buffer VioCopy. The screen contents remain unchanged in this buffer until the end of the function. The contents of this buffer are copied to other buffers, such as the one indicated by the pointer Design, during the process. The contents of the window being moved will be assembled in the Design buffer by accessing the window buffers of all windows lying on top of it.

WinInFront does this with a local procedure called Put. This procedure works like PutScr but it doesn't copy the contents of the given window buffer to video RAM. Instead, it places the data in a copy of the video RAM and gives the address of this copy to the calling routine. WinInFront also uses a procedure called Get to copy the data from this buffer to another.

After processing all of the windows that overlay the window being moved, the contents of this window can be obtained from the Design buffer. This information is copied to a separate buffer which is also allocated on the heap. The buffer is referenced with the pointer WinNrBuf.

Note: There is now an important difference between windows with and without shadows. For windows with shadows, only the actual window region is copied to WinNrBuf because the shadow depends on what is below the window. The shadow is recreated later behind the window.

The window being moved is deleted from the structure buffer so that only the underlying windows remain. Using this buffer, the function then continues to update the window buffers of the windows that were under the window being moved. Each window is processed in a loop between the window being moved and the window that was previously active.

Within this loop, the current contents of the video RAM are copied from the VioCopy buffer to the structure buffer. Then all windows between the active window and the one being processed are run through a second loop. In this loop, the window being processed is deleted from the structure buffer. At the end of the second loop, the contents of the window that was just processed in the first loop can be obtained from the structure buffer.

Before this happens, the screen contents under this window are copied from the structure buffer to the window buffer and the window contents are placed in the structure buffer. If the window had a shadow, it must be recreated later. The shadow cannot be stored, because its appearance depends upon the screen contents located under the window.

In this way, all windows are processed through the structure buffer. Their backgrounds are stored in the window buffer at the end of each window descriptor. The window being moved is copied as the top window and its new background is stored in the window buffer. If the window had a shadow it would now be recreated.

The window is then moved within the linked list of window descriptors so that its descriptor is at the end of the list. The pointer CurWinPtr is set to the new active window descriptor. The only thing left to do is to bring the contents of the structure buffer to the screen in the foreground and to free all allocated buffers.

```
{************************************************************************
 *  WinInFront : moves a specified window to the foreground            *
 **------------------------------------------------------------------**
 *  Input    : Key = window Handle that is returned by WinOpen or      *
 *                   WinOpenShadow when a window is opened             *
 *  Output   : True, if the window can be moved to the foreground,     *
 *             False, if there is not enough memory to execute the function *
 *  Globals  : Line_Ofs/R, CurWinPtr/RW, FirstWinPtr/RW, NumLine/R,    *
 *             NumCol/R                                                 *
 ************************************************************************}
function WinInFront( Key : integer ) : boolean;
var DummyWD : WINDES;                               { dummy descriptor }
    RunWiP,                        { running pointer through the window list }
    WiP     : WIPTR;                    { pointer to the window being moved }
    TempBuf,                        { temporary buffer to store a window }
    WinBuf,                            { second copy of the video RAM }
    WinNrBuf,                      { contents of the window being moved }
    VioCopy,                  { pointer to buffer with copy of the video RAM }
    WDesn,       { pointer to the buffer in which the window is disassembled }
    Design  : VPTR;                        { pointer to new screen }
    Nr,                         { number of windows to process in the list }
    TempLen,                           { length of temporary buffer }
    VioLen,                          { number of bytes in video RAM }
    AwiLen,                          { length of window to process }
```

```
     i, j    : integer;                                       { loop counters }
{-- the local procedures Get and Put are used to process the various -------}
{-- buffers that recreate the video RAM                       -------}
procedure Get( x1, y1, x2, y2 : byte; VioPtr, BufPtr : pointer );
var nbytes : integer;                          { number of bytes to copy per line }
begin
  nbytes := ( x2 - x1 + 1 ) shl 1;                            { bytes per line }
  inc( PTRREC( VioPtr ).Ofs, (x1 + y1 * NumCol) shl 1 );
  while y1 <= y2 do                                        { process each line }
    begin
      Move( VioPtr^, BufPtr^, nbytes);
      inc( PTRREC( VioPtr ).Ofs, Line_Ofs );
      inc( PTRREC( BufPtr ).Ofs, nbytes );
      inc( y1 );                                        { set Y1 to next line }
    end;
end;
procedure Put( x1, y1, x2, y2 : byte; VioPtr, BufPtr : pointer );
var nbytes : integer;                          { number of bytes to copy per line }
begin
  nbytes := ( x2 - x1 + 1 ) shl 1;                            { bytes per line }
  inc( PTRREC( VioPtr ).Ofs, (x1 + y1 * NumCol) shl 1 );
  while y1 <= y2 do                                        { process each line }
    begin
      Move( BufPtr^, VioPtr^, nbytes );
      inc( PTRREC( VioPtr ).Ofs, Line_Ofs );
      inc( PTRREC( BufPtr ).Ofs, nbytes );
      inc( y1 );                                        { set Y1 to next line }
    end;
end;
{--------------------------------------------------------------------------}
begin
  {-- set the pointer WiP to the window being processed --------------------}
  WiP := FirstWinPtr;                          { WiP points to the first window }
  Nr := 0;                                     { the first window is number 0 }
  while WiP^.Handle <> Key do                       { Handle not yet found? }
    begin                                                          { no }
      WiP := WiP^.NextWin;                          { set pointer to next window }
      inc( Nr );                                     { increment the number }
    end;
  if ( WiP = CurWinPtr ) then                  { is the window already on top? }
    begin                                              { yes, end function }
      WinInFront := TRUE;
      exit;
    end;
  {-- allocate five buffers to store parts of the video RAM or each --------}
  {-- window                                                        --------}
  VioLen := NumLine * NumCol shl 1;            { number of bytes in video RAM }
  if MaxAvail <= VioLen * 5 then               { enough room for all 5 buffers? }
    begin                                                          { no }
      WinInFront := false;                     { return error to the calling routine }
      exit;                                            { exit the function }
    end;
  {-- enough memory is available on the heap, enter cursor position and ----}
```

```
{-- view region in the descriptor of the active window          ----}
DummyWD := Wip^;                                { store the current descriptor }
Wip^.curs    := vColumn;
Wip^.curz    := vLine;
Wip^.ViewX1 := ViewX1;
Wip^.ViewY1 := ViewY1;
Wip^.VicwX2 := ViewX2;
Wip^.ViewY2 := ViewY2;
{-- set cursor position and view region for the new window --------------}
with Wip^.NextWin^ do
  begin
    WinSetView( ViewX1, ViewY1, ViewX2, ViewY2 );
    WinSetCursor( curs, curz );
  end;
{-- enter the data for the window being moved in its current -------------}
{-- successor                                            -------------}
with Wip^.NextWin^ do
  begin
    ViewX1 := DummyWD.ViewX1;
    ViewY1 := DummyWD.ViewY1;
    ViewX2 := DummyWD.ViewX2;
    ViewY2 := DummyWD.ViewY2;
    curs    := DummyWD.curs;
    curz    := DummyWD.curz;
  end;
GetMem( Design,  VioLen);                    { memory for the new screen }
GetMem( WDesn,   VioLen);           { memory for the disassembled window }
GetMem( VioCopy, VioLen);              { memory for the video RAM copy }
{-- copy video RAM contents to buffers VioCopy and Design ----------------}
GetScr( 0, 0, NumCol-1, NumLine-1, VioCopy );
Move( VioCopy^, Design^, VioLen );           { copy of video RAM to Design }
{-- close all windows on top of the window being processed in the --------}
{-- Design buffer                                        --------}
RunWip := CurWinPtr;                     { pointer to current (last) window }
for i:=NumWin-1 downto Nr+1 do                    { process each window }
  with RunWiP^ do
    begin
      Put( x1, y1, x2, y2, Design, @Buffer );
      RunWiP := LastWin;                   { pointer to previous window }
    end;
{-- store contents of window being processed in a separate buffer --------}
{-- (accessed with the pointer WinNrBuf                  --------}
with WiP^ do
  begin
    if ( ( Attribute and WIN_SHADOW ) <> 0 ) then
      begin                       { window has a shadow, do not copy shadow }
        AwiLen := (x2-x1+1-ShadowX) * (y2-y1+1-ShadowY) shl 1;   { buffer }
        GetMem( WinNrBuf, AwiLen );              { allocate memory for window }
        Get( x1, y1, x2-ShadowX, y2-ShadowY, Design, WinNrBuf );
        Put( x1, y1, x2, y2, Design, @Buffer );              { clear window }
      end
    else                          { window has no shadow, copy entire window }
      begin
```

227

```
                AwiLen := (x2 - x1 + 1) * (y2 - y1 + 1) shl 1;     { buffer length }
                GetMem( WinNrBuf, AwiLen );                   { allocate memory for window }
                Get( x1, y1, x2, y2, Design, WinNrBuf );  { copy window to buffer }
                Put( x1, y1, x2, y2, Design, @Buffer );              { clear window }
            end;
      end;
{-- bring each window that was under the window being moved into the -----}
{-- Design buffer and store its contents                            -----}
for i:=Nr+1 to NumWin-1 do                            { process each window }
  begin
    Move( VioCopy^, WDesn^, VioLen );                   { copy video RAM to WDesn }
    RunWiP := CurWinPtr;                        { WiP points to the last window }
    {-- delete the windows above window i in WDesn buffer ----------------}
    for j:=NumWin-1 downto i+1 do
      with RunWiP^ do
        begin
          Put( x1, y1, x2, y2, WDesn, @Buffer );                { delete window }
          RunWiP := LastWin;                     { set WiP to previous window }
        end;
    {-- get the contents under window i from the Design buffer and then --}
    {-- copy window i to the Design buffer                             --}
    with RunWiP^ do
      begin
        Get( x1, y1, x2, y2, Design, @Buffer ); { get screen under window }
        {-- if the window has a shadow, it must be recreated -------------}
        if ( ( Attribute and WIN_SHADOW ) <> 0 ) then
          begin                                      { recreate the shadow }
            TempLen := ( x2-x1+1-ShadowX ) * ( y2-y1+1-ShadowY ) shl 1;
            GetMem( TempBuf, TempLen );              { allocate temp. buffer }
            Get( x1, y1, x2 - ShadowX, y2 - ShadowY, WDesn, TempBuf );
            Put( x1, y1, x2 - ShadowX, y2 - ShadowY, Design, TempBuf );
            WinShadow( x2-ShadowX+1, y1+ShadowY, x2, y2, Design );
            WinShadow( x1+ShadowX, y2-ShadowY+1, x2-ShadowX, y2, Design );
          end
        else                                    { no shadow to reconstruct }
          begin
            TempLen := (x2 - x1 + 1) * (y2 - y1 + 1) shl 1;
            GetMem( TempBuf, TempLen );             { allocate temp. buffer }
            Get( x1, y1, x2, y2, WDesn, TempBuf );
            Put( x1, y1, x2, y2, Design, TempBuf );
          end;
        FreeMem( TempBuf, TempLen );                       { free temp. buffer }
      end;
  end;


{-- store contents under the new window and store the window itself ------}
{-- in the Design buffer                                           ------}
with WiP^ do
  begin
    Get( x1, y1, x2, y2, Design, @Buffer );
    if ( ( Attribute and WIN_SHADOW ) <> 0 ) then
      begin                             { window has a shadow, recreate shadow }
        Put( x1, y1, x2-ShadowX, y2-ShadowY, Design, WinNrBuf );
```

228

```
        WinShadow( x2-ShadowX+1, y1+ShadowY, x2, y2, Design );
        WinShadow( x1+ShadowX, y2-ShadowY+1, x2-ShadowX, y2, Design );
      end
    else                                            { window has no shadow }
      Put( x1, y1, x2, y2, Design, WinNrBuf );
  end;
{-- put the descriptor of the moved window at the end of the linked ------}
{-- list of window descriptors                                    ------}
Wip^.NextWin^.LastWin := WiP^.LastWin;
if WiP = FirstWinPtr then                      { was WiP the first window? }
  FirstWinPtr := WiP^.NextWin  {yes, its successor is now the first window}
else                                       { no, WiP has another successor }
  Wip^.LastWin^.NextWin := WiP^.NextWin;
Wip^.NextWin := nil;                          { no more windows after WiP }
Wip^.LastWin := CurWinPtr;          { the previous top window follows WiP }
CurWinPtr^.NextWin := WiP;                        { now points to WiP }
CurWinPtr := WiP;
CurBufPtr := @Wip^.Buffer;
{-- output the assembled buffer to the screen --------------------------}
PutScr( 0, 0, NumCol-1, NumLine-1, Design );
{-- free the allocated buffers -----------------------------------------}
FreeMem( WinNrBuf, AwiLen );
FreeMem( Design,   VioLen);                      { memory for the new screen }
FreeMem( WDesn,    VioLen);               { memory for the assembled window }
FreeMem( VioCopy, VioLen);               { memory for the copy of video RAM }
WinInFront := TRUE;                                    { everything's o.k. }
end;
```

Obviously, WinInFront isn't simple. However, it is an exception among the many procedures and functions presented in this chapter. Now let's look at a sample application involving the WIN unit.

An example program, WINDEMO, is listed below. In order to keep it from being several pages long, we included only the routines that are commonly accessed. The complete program is on the companion diskette for this book.

```
{********************************************************************
 *  WinDemo : demonstration of the functions and procedures of the   *
 *            WIN unit                                               *
 **-----------------------------------------------------------------**
 *  Author       : MICHAEL TISCHER                                   *
 *  developed on  : 09/20/1989                                       *
 *  last update on : 09/20/1989                                      *
 ********************************************************************}
uses Crt, Win;
const RESVDMEM = 4000;                  { reserve 4000 bytes for windows }
type EColor = record               { colors for the various screen elements }
               TI,                                              { title }
               BG,                                         { background }
               PR,                             { color for PressWin frame }
               PT : byte;                        { color for PressWin text }
```

```
                     end;
     const MonoEColor  : EColor = ( TI : $70; BG : $07; PR : $07; PT : $0F );
           ColorEColor : EColor = ( TI : RED      shl 4 + WHITE;
                                    BG : BLACK    shl 4 + WHITE;
                                    PR : RED      shl 4 + YELLOW;
                                    PT : RED      shl 4 + WHITE      );
     {-- global variables -------------------------------------------------}
     var F       : EColor;                                { screen colors }
         ResvdPtr : pointer;                    { pointer to reserved memory }
     {*********************************************************************
      *  Zoom : opens a window in which the frame grows from the center outward *
      *         until the window has reached its full size                *
      **---------------------------------------------------------------**
      *  Input   : X1, Y1, = coordinates of the window                   *
      *            X2, Y2                                                 *
      *            Frame    = frame type                                 *
      *            WColor   = colors for frame and window contents        *
      *  Output  : none                                                  *
      *********************************************************************}
     function Zoom( x1, y1, x2, y2, Typ, WColor : byte ): integer;
     const WHOA = 5;
     var xr1, yr1,                           { coordinates of the growing frame }
         xr2, yr2 : byte;
         Handle   : integer;                              { window Handle }
     begin
       Handle := WinOpen( x1, y1, x2, y2 );                  { open window }
       if ( Handle <> WinOpenError ) then       { could the window be opened? }
         begin                                           { yes, zoom frame }
           {-- set start coordinates for the frame ---------------------}
           xr1 := VL(0) + ( (x2-x1+1) div 2 );
           xr2 := xr1-1;
           yr1 := VO(0) + ( (y2-y1+1) div 2 );
           yr2 := yr1-1;
           repeat   {-- bring frame step by step to the full size -------------}
             if ( xr1 > x1 ) then dec( xr1 );              { increment ordinates }
             if ( yr1 > y1 ) then dec( yr1 );        { or decrement if the full }
             if ( xr2 < x2 ) then inc( xr2 );        { size has not yet been    }
             if ( yr2 < y2 ) then inc( yr2 );        { reached                  }
             WinFrame( xr1, yr1, xr2, yr2, Typ, WColor );         { draw frame }
             WinFill( xr1+1, yr1+1, xr2-1, yr2-1, ' ', WColor); {delete contents}
             delay( WHOA );                                 { brief pause }
           until (xr1 = x1) and (yr1 = y1) and (xr2 = x2) and (yr2 = y2);
         end;
       Zoom := Handle;                      { return Handle to calling routine }
     end;
     {*********************************************************************
      *  PressWin : opens a window and asks the user to press a key       *
      **---------------------------------------------------------------**
      *  Input   : CENTERED  = TRUE, if the window is to be centered on the *
      *                        screen                                    *
      *  Globals :  ResvdPtr/RW                                          *
      *  Info    :  if the window is not centered, it will appear in the lower *
      *             left corner of the screen                            *
```

```
**********************************************************************}
procedure PressWin( Centered : boolean );
const PWWIDTH = 44;                        { window width in columns }
      PWDEPTH = 5;                         { window height in lines }
var DummyHandle : integer;              { window Handle, not needed }
    CurX,                               { previous cursor position }
    CurY,
    UColumn,                    { coordinates of upper left window corner }
    ULine      : byte;
    A_Key      : char;
begin
  if ( Centered ) then                         { window centered? }
    begin                                               { yes }
      UColumn := ( NumCol - PWWIDTH ) div 2; { calculate start coordinates }
      ULine   := ( NumLine - PWDEPTH ) div 2;
    end
  else                       { no, place in lower left corner of screen }
    begin
      ULine := NumLine - 1 - PWDEPTH;
      UColumn := 2;
    end;
  FreeMem( ResvdPtr, RESVDMEM );                  { free reserved memory }
  DummyHandle := Zoom( UColumn, ULine, UColumn + PWWIDTH-1,
                       ULine + PWDEPTH-1, DBL_FR, F.PR );
  WinPrint( VL(2), VO(2), F.PT, 'Please press any key ...');
  WinSetCursor( VR(-2), VO(2) );
  {-- read the first character from the keyboard buffer and then wait for -}
  {-- a new key to be pressed                                             -}
  while KeyPressed do               { read all keys until none are left }
    A_Key := ReadKey;
  A_Key := ReadKey;                                      { read new key }
  if ( A_Key = #0 ) then                          { expanded key code? }
    A_Key := ReadKey;                     { yes, read second byte as well }
  WinClose( TRUE );                              { close window again }
  GetMem( ResvdPtr, RESVDMEM );                  { allocate memory again }
end;
{**********************************************************************}
procedure demo1;
const MAXWIN    = 100;              { maximum number of opened windows }
      MINWIDTH = 15;                      { minimum width of a window }
      MINDEPTH =  5;                      { minimum height of a window }
      MINYSTART =  1;                          { minimum start line }
      MINXSTART =  0;                          { minimum start column }
var i,                                               { loop counter }
    Num,                            { number of opened windows }
    Handle : integer;                            { window Handle }
    WColor,                      { color for frame and window contents }
    x1, y1,                         { coordinates of the window }
    x2, y2 : byte;
begin
  Randomize;                                   { initialize randomizer }
  Num := 0;                                   { no window open yet }
  repeat
```

```
        x1 := MINXSTART + Random( NumCol-MINWIDTH-1 );      { left window column }
        y1 := MINYSTART + Random( NumLine-MINDEPTH-1 );       { top window line }
        x2 := x1 + MINWIDTH + Random( NumCol-MINWIDTH-x1-1 );      { right side }
        y2 := y1 + MINDEPTH + Random( NumLine-MINDEPTH-y1-1 );   { bottom line }
        Handle := WinOpen( x1, y1, x2, y2 );                   { open window }
        if ( Handle <> WinOpenError ) then                      { successful? }
          begin                                                       { yes }
            inc( Num );                        { increment number of open windows }
            {-- select colors for window frame and contents -------------------}
            if ( Color ) then                              { color possible? }
              WColor := Random( 8 ) shl 4 + WHITE                    { yes }
            else                       { no, choose between INVERSE and NORMAL }
              if ( Random( 2 ) = 1 ) then WColor := $07          { normal }
                                    else WColor := $70;          { inverse }
            {-- fill window, draw frame, etc. --------------------------------}
            WinFrame( VL(0), VO(0), VR(0), VU(0), SIN_FR, WColor );
            WinFill( VL(1), VO(1), VR(-1), VU(-1), ' ', WColor );
            GotoXY( VL(3), VO(0) );
            Write( ' ', Num:3, ' ' );
          end;
      until ( Handle = WinOpenError ) or ( Num = MAXWIN );
      PressWin( TRUE );                          { wait for a key to be pressed }
      {-- close all windows ----------------------------------------------------}
      for i := 1 to Num do
        WinClose( TRUE );            { delete window, restore old background }
    end;
    {**********************************************************************}
    procedure demo2;
    const AWINDOW =   8;                        { number of windows to construct }
          WIDTH   =  40;                           { window width in columns }
          DEPTH   =   9;                           { window height in lines }
          STARTX  =   2;                       { start column of first window }
          STARTY  =   1;                         { start line of first window }
          DELTAX  =   5;                 { distance in columns between windows }
          DELTAY  =   2;                   { distance in lines between windows }
          WHOA    = 250;                                          { pause }
    type Wrip = record
                  BackCol : byte;                          { background color }
                  WriX,
                  WriY    : integer;
                end;
    var Handles   : array[ 1..AWINDOW ] of integer; {Array with window Handles}
        Wrips     : array[ 1..AWINDOW ] of Wrip;    { information for Writeln }
        WiFDummy  : boolean;                     { function result from WinInFront }
        FColor,                                      { frame and window color }
        UColumn,                                         { window position }
        ULine,
        NewFront,                                 { new window now in foreground }
        LastFront,                              { window previously in foreground }
        i         : byte;                                    { loop counter }
        j         : integer;
    begin
      WinFill( VL(0), VO(1), VR(0), VU(0), ' ', $70 );
```

```
  UColumn := STARTX;                      { load start position for first window }
  ULine  := STARTY;
  TextColor( WHITE );
  {-- construct each window -----------------------------------------}
  for i := 1 to AWINDOW do
    begin
      Handles[ i ] := WinOpenShadow( UColumn, ULine, UColumn+WIDTH-1,
                                     ULine+DEPTH-1 );
      if ( Color ) then                              { color capabilities? }
        FColor := ( i mod 8 ) shl 4 + WHITE                      { yes }
      else                           { no, select between INVERSE and NORMAL }
        FColor := $07 shl ( 4 * ( i mod 2 ) );
      WinFrame( VL(0), VO(0), VR(0), VU(0), Random(2)+1, FColor );
      WinFill( VL(1), VO(1), VR(-1), VU(-1), ' ', FColor );
      GotoXY( VL(3), VO(0) );
      Write( ' ', i:3, ' ' );
      WinSetView( VL(1), VO(1), VR(-1), VU(-1) );
      with Wrips[ i ] do                    { enter information in structure }
        begin
          WriX    := VL(0);
          WriY    := VO(0);
          BackCol := FColor shr 4;
        end;
      inc( UColumn, DELTAX );             { calculate start position for }
      inc( ULine, DELTAY );              { next window                  }
    end;
  PressWin( FALSE );                                       { wait for key }
  {-- bring windows from 1 to n to the front -----------------------------}
  for i:=AWINDOW downto 1 do
    WiFDummy := WinInFront( Handles[ i ] );
  PressWin( FALSE );                                       { wait for key }
  {-- continuously place a new window in the foreground and output --------}
  {-- characters to it                                    --------}
  LastFront := AWINDOW;                      { store current foreground window }
  for i := 1 to 50 do                            { do the loop 50 times }
    begin
      repeat                           { make a new window for the foreground }
        NewFront := random( AWINDOW ) + 1;
      until NewFront <> LastFront;     { repeat until a new window is found }
      WifDummy := WinInFront( Handles[ NewFront ] );   { window to front }
      LastFront := NewFront;                   { store new foreground window }
      GotoXY( Wrips[ NewFront ].WriX, Wrips[ NewFront ].WriY );
      TextBackGround( Wrips[ NewFront ].BackCol );
      if ( Color = FALSE ) then                         { Monochrome mode?  }
        TextColor( Wrips[ NewFront ].BackCol xor $7 );
      for j := 1 to 100 + Random( 300 ) do             { output characters }
        write( chr( 32 + j mod 200 ) );
      WinSetCursor( WhereX, WhereY );        { cursor after last character }
      Delay( WHOA );                                      { brief pause }
      Wrips[ NewFront ].WriX := WhereX;      { store current cursor position }
      Wrips[ NewFront ].WriY := WhereY;
    end;
  PressWin( FALSE );                                       { wait for key }
```

```
  {-- close all windows ----------------------------------------------------}
  for i:=1 to AWINDOW do
    WinClose( TRUE );
end;
{****************************************************************************
 *  M A I N   P R O G R A M                                                *
 ****************************************************************************}
begin
  GetMem( ResvdPtr, RESVDMEM );  { allocate RESVDMEM bytes for emergencies }
  if Color then F := ColorEColor                             { set colors }
           else F := MonoEColor;
  {-- prepare screen construction -----------------------------------------}
  TextColor( F.BG and $0F );
  TextBackGround( F.BG shr 4 );
  ClrScr;
  WinFill( 0, 0, VR(0), 0, ' ', F.TI );
  WinPrint( 18, 0, F.TI, 'WINDEMO  -   (c) 1989 by MICHAEL TISCHER' );
  demo1;
  demo2;
  WinFill( 0, 1, VR(0), VU(0), ' ', WHITE );
  WinSetCursor( 0, 0 );
end.
```

Throughout this book there will also be examples of calls to all the other routines presented in this chapter. Many of the following chapters deal with screen output and will refer back to this chapter.

7. Keyboard and Mouse Control

Since introducing the first mouse driven software for PC users, developers have discovered that mouse support has become less a novelty and more a necessity. The publication of the SAA (System Application Architecture) Standard has made the mouse a standard input device. Therefore, users expect to use the mouse in the same way from application to application. Several programs have demonstrated that working with the mouse can be very productive.

Unfortunately, currently there isn't mouse support for Turbo Pascal. The reason for this could be the integrated development environment, which requires a large amount of memory. Adding mouse support to this would probably exceed practical limits.

Microsoft's new Quick Pascal demonstrates this. Its development environment is even more sophisticated than that of Turbo Pascal and it also has full mouse support. The disadvantage in this is that there isn't enough space in memory for both the compiler and the development tools. The compiler must be loaded from disk for every compilation. So the extra speed gained with Turbo Pascal is worth the lack of mouse support.

For most applications, the majority of the problems are caused by memory limitations but result from redesigning the user interface program modules to include mouse support. Supporting a mouse is quite different from a keyboard.

When working with a keyboard, only the code for the key that was pressed must be evaluated. With a mouse, however, there is more information to consider. Moving the mouse alone does not cause any action; but pressing only one of the two (or sometimes three) buttons will invoke an action from the screen object to which the mouse pointer is pointing. This means that any activity involving the mouse must be interpreted in the context of the mouse pointer location.

Even the keyboard interface of a state-of-the-art application can be very demanding. Many programs use special keys which cannot be recognized by the BIOS (and, therefore, not by the Turbo Pascal procedure ReadKey) because they do not generate any keyboard codes. One example of this is the Turbo Pascal Debugger, which allows the user to move the current window or change its size after pressing the <Break> key.

The goal of this chapter is to present the basic concepts of querying the keyboard and the mouse as input devices. This theory is put into practice with an efficient unit that integrates both keyboard and mouse input.

7.1   Theory

Let's begin by looking at the keyboard. The port to this device is generally BIOS interrupt $16. This can be called from a Turbo Pascal program using the INTR statement and Turbo Pascal's ReadKey function supports keyboard input. There are three separate keyboard query functions. When calling them, the function number must be passed in the AH register.

Function $00

>   This function waits until the user presses a key. Function $00 then reads the key, returns the code of this key and removes the key from the keyboard buffer.

Function $01

>   This function can be used to tell a program if there is at least one keystroke in the keyboard buffer. If so, the code of this key is returned without removing it from the keyboard buffer. Turbo Pascal uses this to execute the KeyPressed function.

Function $02

>   This function reads the status of the control keys. It returns a byte to the caller that indicates whether the user is pressing the <Shift>, <Ctrl> or <Alt> key. There is a distinction made between the right and left <Shift> keys. This byte also tells a program whether <Caps Lock>, <Num Lock> or <Insert> are active.

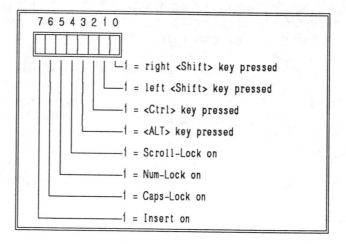

Structure of the Keyboard Status Byte

Functions $00 and $01 can distinguish between normal ASCII codes and *extended keyboard codes*. This last group consists of those keys and key combinations that cannot be represented with an ASCII code. This includes the cursor keys and the function keys as well as all the normal letter and number keys when used with the <Alt> key. If a normal ASCII code is received by function $00 or $01, the AL register will contain the code for this character after the function call is complete. The AH register will contain the Scan Code for the key.

In the AL register, extended keyboard codes are distinguished by the 0 value. AH will contain the extended keyboard code for the key. The following table lists the extended keyboard codes that can be interpreted by the BIOS. Not all of the possible 256 codes are assigned because not all codes can be understood by the BIOS and returned as the function result.

Code	created by pressing...
15	<Enter> + Tab
16–25	<ALT> + Q, W, E, R, T, Y, U, I, O, P
30–38	<ALT> + A, S, D, F, G, H, J, K, L
44–45	<ALT> + Z, X, C, V, B, N, M
71	Home
72	Cursor Up
73	Page Up
75	Cursor Left
77	Cursor Right
80	Cursor Down
81	Page Down
82	Insert
83	Delete
84–93	<Shift> + F1 – F10
94–103	<Ctrl> + F1 – F10
104–113	<ALT> + F1 – F10
115	<Ctrl> + Cursor Left
116	<Ctrl> + Cursor Right
117	<Ctrl> + End
118	<Ctrl> + Page Down
119	<Ctrl> + Home
120–131	<ALT>+ 1, 2, 3, 4, 5, 6, 7, 8, 9, 0
133	F11 (MF II keyboard only)
134	F12 (MF II keyboard only)
135	<Shift> + F11(MF II keyboard only)

Code	created by pressing...
136	<Shift> + F12(MF II keyboard only)
137	<Ctrl> + F11 (MF II keyboard only)
138	<Ctrl> + F12 (MF II keyboard only)
139	<ALT> + F11 (MF II keyboard only)
140	<ALT> + F12 (MF II keyboard only)

Extended keyboard codes

You'll need to go directly to the keyboard hardware if you need to use keys or key combinations that the BIOS doesn't recognize. Each time a key is pressed, the keyboard executes the keyboard interrupt $09. Normally, this points to a routine in the BIOS. This routine reads the code of the key that was pressed from the *keyboard data port* at address $60 and converts it to an ASCII or extended keyboard code. The code is then added to the end of the *keyboard buffer*.

This is accomplished by reading the *scan code* of the key that was pressed. The scan code, which is unrelated to the ASCII character set, represents the number of the key that was pressed. Each key in the keyboard is assigned a number starting with zero. Since the keyboard calls interrupt $09 when a key is pressed and when it is released, there must be a way to distinguish between these two types of information.

Based on this, the keyboard differentiates between make and release codes. Although both of these give the scan code of the key that was pressed, the release code also sets bit 7, so that the code will be between 128 and 256. The maximum number that can be supported is limited to 128 keys. But most keyboards are well under this limit.

The control keys <Shift>, <Ctrl>, etc. are handled as normal keys and don't need special handling. They'll send a make code when pressed and a release code when released. It is up to the BIOS to remember when it receives one of these keys and to act accordingly (i.e., by switching from lowercase to uppercase letters for <Shift>).

Diverting interrupt $09 to enable the BIOS to recognize keys and combinations, which it normally doesn't recognize, will not be demonstrated within the KBM unit. This is used to read the keyboard and mouse.

Mouse reading

A main technical difference between the mouse and the keyboard is that the mouse cannot be read by the BIOS. The BIOS was developed before the development and marketing of the mouse. This is also the reason why a special *mouse driver* must always be used. This device driver can be loaded with a command in the CONFIG.SYS file or it can run as a

TSR program, which remains resident in memory after it is called. An example is MOUSE.COM, which is the driver included with all Microsoft mice.

Microsoft developed the standard for reading a mouse, and the manufacturers of compatible mice have followed this standard. In this case, "compatible" means that the software will react to the mouse the same way it would to a Microsoft mouse.

An interrupt functions as the port between the driver and an application program. This is the mouse interrupt $33. As usual, the various functions of the mouse driver are assigned different function numbers. The specific function is passed in the AX register, not in the AH register as with the BIOS. This allows the use of 16 bit rather than 8 bit function numbers.

Using the *mouse port* has become standard. Initially there were only a few functions available over interrupt $33, but now there is a total of 34. But only a few of these are actually needed to read the mouse. Many of the functions aren't necessary because they relate only to use in the graphic mode; we are focusing on text mode.

The KBM unit presented in the next section uses only nine of these functions.

Function	Task
$0000	Reset mouse driver
$0001	Display mouse pointer
$0002	Remove mouse pointer
$0003	Get mouse pointer position
$0004	Move mouse pointer
$0007	Set horizontal range of movement
$0008	Set vertical range of movement
$000A	Define mouse pointer shape
$000C	Set event handler
$000F	Set pointer speed

Mouse functions used in the KBM unit

Before describing each function, let's discuss two important concepts: determining the mouse position and the appearance of the mouse pointer on screen.

The mouse driver always relates the mouse pointer position to a virtual graphics screen regardless of whether the screen is in text or graphic mode. All mouse functions that either return or receive *mouse coordinates* relate to this virtual mouse screen. Fortunately, converting from this frame of reference to the coordinates of a text screen isn't difficult because eight points in the mouse screen correspond to exactly one column or one line on the text screen.

So, when receiving coordinates from a mouse function, the coordinates must be divided by 8 in order to locate the correct position on the text screen. The best way to do this is to move the value three bit positions to the right.

To move the opposite way, coordinates passed to a mouse function must be multiplied by 8, which is done by moving the value three bits to the left. The shl operator provides a quick way to do this with Turbo Pascal.

The mouse driver actually recognizes two mouse pointers: the *hardware pointer* and the *software pointer*. The hardware pointer is the same as the blinking screen cursor. When the hardware pointer is active, the mouse and mouse driver control the movements of this pointer. However, we don't recommend using this pointer because it may cause confusion in applications where a blinking cursor is used for text input in certain fields.

By using the software pointer, the mouse driver allows you to change this pointer's appearance by setting the *pointer mask* and the *screen mask* with function $000A. The mouse driver uses these two 16 bit values to place the mouse pointer on the screen, with the proper appearance, each time it is moved.

The pointer mask and screen mask are linked to the current screen position in a two step process. Both the character code and the color byte are included for each mask.

The first step is to combine the character and its attribute, as they exist in video RAM, with the screen mask using a binary AND. In the second step, the result is processed further by using an exclusive OR to combine it with the pointer mask. The result of this operation is then written back to video RAM in the current mouse position. This procedure may seem unusual at first but it allows the flexibility of changing the appearance of the mouse pointer:

- The mouse pointer can always be displayed as an independent character with its own color assignment regardless of what character or color it is covering on the screen. To do this, the screen mask is set to 0 in order to clear the character located at the current mouse position. The result of the AND operation on this character and the screen mask is 0. The pointer mask must contain the ASCII code of the mouse pointer and its color. By using the exclusive OR, only these bits are set when combined with 0 from the previous operation and the desired character and color will appear.

- The mouse pointer can always appear as a selected character with a color that depends on the color of the character it covers on the screen. To do this, the screen mask must contain 0 in the LO byte and 255 in the HI byte. This will set the character code to 0 but leave the color unchanged. The pointer mask contains the ASCII code of the pointer character in the LO byte and, for example, the value 255 in the HI byte. When combined, this will invert all color bits and display the character in inverse.

- The character under the mouse pointer can remain and be combined with the mouse pointer by changing colors. To do this, the screen mask must contain the value $00FF while the pointer mask contains 0 in the LO byte and the color of the character in the HI byte.

- The color of the mouse pointer can be created from the color of the character underneath it while the character remains the same. In this case, the screen mask contains the value $FFFF and the pointer mask contains $FF00 to invert this character.

Two examples for combining the current character with the pointer mask and screen mask are shown in the following figure:

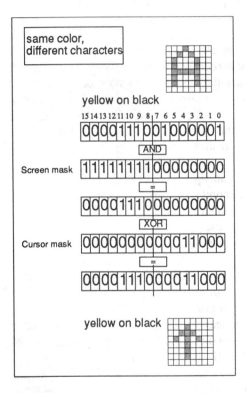
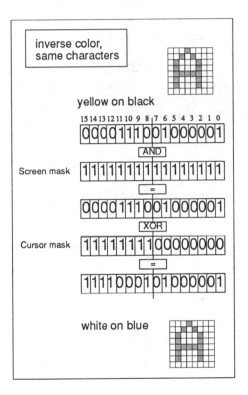

Creating a mouse pointer by combining current character, pointer mask and screen mask

There are a few functions of the mouse driver called from the KBM unit:

Reset mouse driver (function $00)

This function not only resets all parameters to their default values but also allows the user to determine the availability of the mouse driver. The only way to be sure that a mouse driver is installed is if the value $FFFF is found in the AX register after interrupt $33 is called. If any other value is found in this register, you can avoid reading the mouse because either there is no mouse or the proper driver is not installed.

This function also returns the number of mouse buttons to the BX register. PCs can use either a two button or a three button mouse. In your programming, never assume that a two or three button mouse will be connected.

After a successful call of this function, the mouse pointer will be displayed as a software pointer in the middle of the screen. The pointer mask and screen mask have been selected to display the pointer as an inverse character block. The pointer will be placed in screen page 0. But the pointer is not yet actually visible. This can be changed with a call to function $0001.

Display mouse pointer (function $0001)

Other than the function number in the AX register this function doesn't require parameters.

Remove mouse pointer (function $0002)

The mouse pointer will follow the movements of the mouse whether or not it is visible.

Note: Any calls to these two functions must be balanced. For example, two calls to $0002 must be followed by two calls to $0001 to make the pointer visible again.

These functions are called quite often. Unfortunately, the mouse pointer must be switched off prior to every screen output and then switched back on afterwards. This is true at least for direct access to the video RAM, which is done in the WIN unit. The mouse pointer may get overwritten because the mouse driver has no way of determining if any changes have taken place in video RAM.

At first, this may not appear incorrect since the mouse pointer will reappear whenever the mouse is moved. But when the mouse pointer moves, it will rewrite the character, that it was covering, to its previous location. This may not be the same character that was written to the screen from video RAM during the last output.

In some instances the mouse pointer doesn't need to be switched on and off for every output. If a series of screen outputs are to follow in succession, it is acceptable to switch the pointer off before the first output and then back on after the last.

Get pointer position/button status (function $0003)

The position of the mouse pointer can always be determined by calling function $0003; the coordinates will be returned to the CX and DX registers. The CX register provides the horizontal position and the DX register provides the vertical. As mentioned earlier, these values must be divided by 8 to convert them to the screen coordinate system. The upper left screen corner, with coordinates 0/0, is the frame of reference.

This function also returns the current status of the mouse buttons to the BX register. Bit 0 corresponds to the left button and bit 1 for the right button. If a bit is set, then the corresponding mouse button is being depressed by the user.

Move mouse pointer (function $0004)

This function allows the current position of the mouse pointer to be changed. It expects the new coordinates for the mouse pointer to be passed to it in the CX and DX registers. The coordinates must be specified relative to the virtual graphics screen.

Set range of movement (functions $0007 and $0008)

These functions limit the area in which the mouse pointer can move. Function $0007 sets the horizontal limits and function $0008 sets the vertical limits. Both functions expect the lower limit in the CX register and the upper limit in the DX register. If not located within the specified range, the mouse is automatically moved there. After this, the mouse cannot be moved from the defined range.

Define pointer shape (function $000A)

This function sets the pointer mask and the screen mask in order to define the appearance of the mouse pointer. The function number is passed in the AX register. This function also expects the value $0001 as a parameter in the BX register. This tells the function that it will be dealing with the software pointer. The screen mask is passed in the CX register and the pointer mask follows in the DX register.

Set event handler (function $000C)

This is the final important mouse driver function for the KBM unit. This function can be used to eliminate reading the mouse with function $0003 and replace it with an "Event Handler" that can be called by the mouse driver when a mouse event occurs. This method is similar to the way the keyboard is queried, in which interrupt $09 is called when a keyboard event occurs that requires the processor's attention.

Set pointer speed (function $000F)

This function, which is function number $000F, sets the speed of the mouse pointer. It defines the distance the mouse must be moved in order to move the mouse pointer one column or one line across the screen.

This distance is measured in Mickeys (1/200 inch) and is set separately for horizontal and vertical movement. The default is 8 Mickeys horizontal and 16 Mickeys vertical. This function expects the value for horizontal movement to be passed in the CX register and the value for vertical movement in the DX register.

The mouse event handler is not an interrupt. It is called by the mouse driver like a normal subroutine using a FAR CALL. The program itself can determine when this subroutine call should happen. This is because when the event handler is installed, the bits it passes to function $000C determine which events will call the event handler.

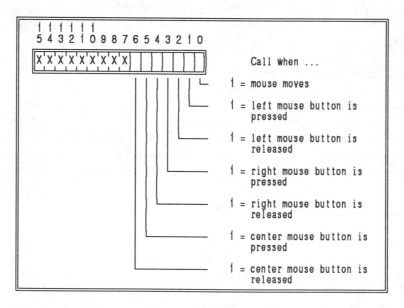

Bit mask specifying the events that will trigger a call to the mouse event handler

The function $000C expects the address of the event handler in the register pair ES:DX. ES contains the segment address and DX contains the offset address. The first call of the event handler can occur immediately after returning from this function.

Each time the handler is called, it is passed information that describes the current status of the mouse. The handler will find this information in the processor registers AX, BX, CX, DX, DI and SI. Like all other processor registers, the contents of these aren't allowed to change as a result of the call to the handler. The contents must be saved and restored after returning to the mouse driver.

The AX register contains the event that triggered the call to the event handler. If this matches one of the events defined in the CX register the event handler is called. Otherwise the call is ignored.

The BX register contains the current status of the mouse buttons. Like function $0003, bit 0 is for the left button and bit 1 is for the right button. The middle button (if present) is represented by bit 2. Another parallel to function $0003 is the contents of the CX and DX registers. These give the current position of the mouse pointer with the horizontal coordinate in CX and the vertical coordinate in DX.

Both registers SI and DI contain information on the movement of the mouse pointer. Specifically, they tell the relative distance from the current mouse position to its position at the time of the last call to the handler. Both distances are given in Mickeys, which means they are related to the movement of the mouse and not to the virtual mouse screen. SI contains the horizontal distance and DI the vertical distance. This information is seldom used by the event handler, however, since it can easily obtain and work with the current position of the mouse pointer from CX/DX.

We still need to discuss why an event handler is needed for the mouse and what role it will play in the KBM unit. This will be addressed in the next section.

7.2   The KBM Unit

You must find a common way of dealing with both types of information and events if you want to integrate the reading of a mouse and keyboard in one program. An effective way of doing this is to orient the program to events that don't differentiate between mouse and keyboard. To do this, a routine is created which stores the next event in a data structure and then returns it to the calling routine. One field in this data structure tells the calling routine what event was captured so it can react accordingly.

These events are taken from several lists of events or *event queues*. Events from the corresponding event handler are added to the end of these event queues. The KBM unit has two queues: one for mouse events and one for keyboard events. Collisions can occur when both queues contain events at the same time. By storing the clock time at which the event occurred, you can determine which occurred first and which should be passed to the calling routine first.

Integrating the proper event handlers and their read routines is one of the most important tasks performed by the KBM unit. Unfortunately, this cannot be accomplished in Turbo Pascal alone, so a small assembler module called KBMA.ASM is also part of the KBM unit.

In this module there are two procedures which form links to the event handlers for the keyboard and mouse. These two procedures are only starting points for the handlers. The actual work is done by Turbo Pascal procedures called from the assembler module.

The KBM unit also provides easy access to the mouse driver functions, which were described in the previous section. The ability to define different screen ranges is also very helpful. These screen ranges represent objects that can be selected by the mouse. When a mouse event is received, the object that was activated and the distance of the mouse pointer from the upper left corner of the object will then automatically be known. This makes it easy to react to the mouse event because the program will know if an input field, the main menu or some other symbol was activated.

Now let's look at the listing for the KBM unit so we can review all the details of how this works. We will also look at the accompanying assembler module. Finally, there is a demo program that shows how the unit can be used.

We will start with the file KBM.PAS, which includes a number of important type declarations.

```
{**************************************************************************
 * K B M : A unit which provides easy access to mouse and keyboard.     *
 **--------------------------------------------------------------------**
 * Author        : MICHAEL TISCHER                                      *
 * developed on   : 06/01/1989                                          *
 * last update on : 09/23/1989                                          *
 **************************************************************************}

unit Kbm;

interface

uses Win, Dos;                                              { link units }

{== Type declarations needed by procedures and functions using this unit ==}

type  KCODE    = word;              { key code, >= 256 : extended key code }
      PTRVIEW  = longint;                        { mouse pointer design }

      MSRANGE  = record                      { describes a mouse range }
                   x1,              { upper left coordinates of the }
                   y1,              { specified range               }
                   x2,              { lower right coordinates of the }
                   y2  : byte;      { specified range               }
                 end;
      RNGARRAY = array [0..99] of MSRANGE;               { range array }
      RNGPTR   = ^RNGARRAY;                      { pointer to range array }

      EVENT = record                { describes mouse or keyboard event }
                EvntCode : integer;                       { event code }
                Time     : longint;                      { time in ticks }

                case byte of                      { keyboard or mouse }
                  0 : { Mouse: ( EV_MOU_...) ---------------------------}
                      ( Rel_Row,                 { mouse pointer position, }
                        RelColumn,               { relative to range       }
                        Abs_Row,                 { mouse pointer position,  }
                        AbsColumn,               { relative to stored screen }
                        Range,                        { mouse range }
                        Buttons : byte );            { button status }

                  1 : { KCode: ( EV_KEY_PRESSED ) ----------------------}
                      ( Key : KCODE );                  { key pressed }

                  2 : { Keys which produce no code: ( EV_KEY_UNKNOWN ) ---}
                      ( ScanCode,                  { scan code returned }
                        Status   : byte );          { control key status }

                  3 : { Status key, no code ( EV_KEY_STATUS ) ------------}
                      ( StateKey : byte );
              end;

      EVENTHANDLER = procedure ( var EvRec : EVENT );
```

247

KCODE

This is the first type defined and is used anywhere a procedure or function encounters key codes. Since this type is created from a word and not a char, it is easier to distinguish ASCII codes and extended keyboard codes. If a KCODE was represented as a char, supplementary information would be required to tell if the KCODE was an ASCII code or an extended keyboard code. Instead, KBM captures all of this information in one word by increasing the value of extended keyboard codes by 256. If the program encounters a KCODE with a code greater than 256, it will know that it is an extended keyboard code.

PTRVIEW

This is used to define the pointer mask and screen mask. It consists of a 16 bit value in a LongInt. We will discuss this in greater detail in connection with the functions MouPtrMask, PtrDifChar and PtrDifCol.

MSRANGE

This type is used for splitting the screen into mouse ranges. It stores the coordinates of the upper left and lower right corners of the range. Type RNGARRAY consists of a collection of up to 100 elements of type MSRANGE. Type RNGPTR is a pointer to such an array.

EVENT

Perhaps the most important type in KBM is type EVENT, which describes the various events. EVENT is defined as a variant record in order to capture the different characters of the possible events. The record contains several fields that more closely describe the nature of each event. The type of event can be taken from the field EvntCode, which is always available. This field can be queried with the help of the EVENT constants that will be presented below.

The field Time is also always present. This gives the time at which the event occurred. The time is not represented in hours, minutes and seconds, but rather as a running value that is incremented 18.2 times per second by the internal PC clock. The value itself isn't actually needed, since it is used only to determine the order in which events occur.

For all types of mouse events, there are six pieces of information stored in the Event structure. These include the coordinates that give the position of the mouse pointer at the time of the event. Abs_Row and AbsColumn give the absolute position of the mouse pointer in relation to the upper left corner of the screen (coordinates 0/0). Rel_Row and RelColumn will relate to the position of the mouse pointer relative to the upper left corner of the range where the mouse pointer is located.

The code number for the range is in the variable Range. If the constant NO_MSRANGE is encountered, then the pointer was not located in any defined range. In this case, RelColumn and Rel_Row will also relate to the upper left corner of the screen.

The variable Buttons gives the status of the mouse buttons. This information is taken, unchanged from the mouse driver, which delivers it to the mouse event handler in the BX register.

An EVENT record contains less information for a keystroke. The variable EvntCode will contain the constant EV_KEY_PRESSED and the code for the key will be listed in the variable Key.

If a key (scan) code is encountered that the BIOS cannot process, then EvntCode will contain the constant EV_KEY_UNKNOWN. The variables ScanCode and Status then contain information about the key. ScanCode will contain the scan code that was received and Status gives the status of the control keys <Alt>, <Shift> and <Ctrl>. The assignment of the bits within this byte corresponds to that assignment given to function $02 of the BIOS keyboard interrupt described at the beginning of this chapter. It only makes sense to evaluate this information if you want to be able to capture keystrokes that cannot be interpreted by the BIOS. This will usually not be necessary. If required you can use this information to divert the keyboard interrupt $09 to your own interrupt handler. ,

The last event is represented by the constant EV_KEY_STATUS. By using the constants KEY_RIGHT_SHIFT, KEY_LEFT_SHIFT, etc. in the StateKey variable, this indicates when a control key has been pressed.

The last public type declared in this unit is EVENTHANDLER. This is a procedural type, or rather a pointer to a procedure, which is passed to an EVENT record in the form of the variable EvRec. Together with the procedure KbmRegisterHandler, this type allows the definition of procedures that can be called from the KBM unit, based on certain events, just as the mouse event handler is called from the mouse driver. EVENTHANDLER will be discussed in more detail later.

```
{== Declaration of functions and procedures which can be called from ======}
{== other programs                                               ======}

procedure KbmRegisterHandler  ( Event : word; Handler : EVENTHANDLER );
procedure KbmDeRegisterHandler( Event : word );
procedure KbmGetEvent         ( var EvRec : EVENT );
procedure KbmPeekEvent        ( var EvRec : EVENT );
procedure KbmReleaseMode      ( KMode : byte );
procedure KbmSetMode          ( KMode : byte );
function  MouPtrMask          ( Character, Color  : word ) : PTRVIEW;
function  PtrDifChar          ( Character : byte ) : word;
function  PtrDifCol           ( Color : byte ) : word;
procedure MouDefinePtr        ( Mask : PTRVIEW );
procedure MouDefRange         ( Amount : byte; BPtr : RNGPTR );
procedure KbmEventWait        ( WaitEvent : integer; var EvRec : EVENT );
procedure MouShowMouse;
procedure MouHideMouse;
procedure MouSetMoveArea      ( x1, y1, x2, y2 : byte );
```

```
procedure MouSetSpeed          ( XSpeed, YSpeed : integer );
procedure MouMovePtr           ( Col, Row : byte );
procedure KbmInit              ( Columns, Lines_ : byte );
procedure KbmEnd;
```

Some public variables are also defined in this unit. One of the most important is the Boolean variable MouAvail. This tells a program whether a mouse is installed. If this variable contains TRUE, then the variables CurRng, CurBut, CurX and CurY will always reflect the status of the mouse. CurRng contains the number of the current mouse range (or the constant NO_MSRANGE). CurBut contains the status of the mouse buttons. CurX and CurY contain the mouse position relative to the upper left corner of the screen.

```
{== Variables needed from within an application program ==================}

var MouAvail : boolean;                     { TRUE when a mouse is available }

   {-- Variables loaded every time the mouse handler is called ------------}

   CurRng,                                       { number of current range }
   CurBut,                                        { mouse button status }
   CurX,                                  { current mouse pointer position }
   CurY  : byte;                          { relative to entire screen      }
```

There are also many public constants that are used to access events and recognize key codes, in addition to other purposes. These begin with the EVENT codes that are used for the variable EvntCode within an EVENT record.

```
{== Constants needed by an application program ============================}

const {------------------------------------------------- Event codes ------}

        EV_NO_EVENT     =    0;                         { no event prepared }
        EV_MOU_MOVE     =    1;                             { mouse moved }
        EV_LEFT_PRESS   =    2;                 { left mouse button pressed }
        EV_LEFT_REL     =    4;                { left mouse button released }
        EV_RIGHT_PRESS  =    8;                { right mouse button pressed }
        EV_RIGHT_REL    =   16;               { right mouse button released }
        EV_KEY_PRESSED  =  256;                             { key pressed }
        EV_KEY_UNKNOWN  =  512;      { key combination that produces no code }
        EV_KEY_STATUS   = 1024;          { Status key, produces no code }

        EV_MOU_ALL      =   31;                         { all mouse events }
        EV_KEY_ALL      = 1792;                       { all keyboard events }
        EV_ALL          = 1823;           { all mouse and keyboard events }
```

If a status key is pressed (EvntCode := EV_KEY_STATUS), the variable StateKey within the EVENT record will contain one of the following constants:

```
{-------------------------------------- Status key codes -------------}

KEY_RIGHT_SHIFT =    1;
KEY_LEFT_SHIFT  =    2;
KEY_CTRL        =    4;
KEY_ALT         =    8;
KEY_SCROLL_LOCK =   16;
KEY_NUM_LOCK    =   32;
KEY_CAPS_LOCK   =   64;
 KEY_INSERT       = 128;
```

Notice that the first four constants concern the keyboard and the last four represent toggle switches. If a bit is set, the key has been pressed and the mode has been turned on.

These constants can also be found in the EVENT variable Status, which can always be read when EvntCode contains the constant EV_KEY_UNKNOWN. Since more than one control key may need to be pressed simultaneously, different KEY_... constants can be combined with an OR operation within Status to form a single value. Different toggle modes may also be active at the same time.

The following constants describe the appearance of the mouse pointer and define parts of the pointer mask and screen mask.

```
{-------------- Constants used for describing mouse pointer --------}

PtrSameChar = $00ff;
PtrSameCol  = $00ff;
PtrInvCol   = $7777;
PtrSameColB = $807f;                     { blinking - same color     }
 PtrInvColB  = $F777;                      { blinking - different
color }
```

A long list of key codes, mostly the extended key codes, follows these constants. These codes are standardized just like the ASCII character set and can, therefore, be used in all of your programs for evaluating extended keyboard codes. Notice that codes with numbers smaller than 256 are normal characters that carry a special meaning.

```
{------------------------------------ Control key codes -----------}

BEL     =    7;                          { Bell character   }
BS      =    8;                          { Backspace key    }
TAB     =    9;                          { Tab key          }
LF      =   10;                          { Linefeed         }
CR      =   13;                          { Return key       }
ESC     =   27;                          { Escape key       }
SPACE   =   32;                          { Space            }
CTRL_A  =    1;                          { CTRL + A         }
CTRL_B  =    2;                          { CTRL + B         }
CTRL_C  =    3;                          { CTRL + C         }
```

```
CTRL_D    =    4;              { CTRL + D          }
CTRL_E    =    5;              { CTRL + E          }
CTRL_F    =    6;              { CTRL + F          }
CTRL_G    =    7;              { CTRL + G          }
CTRL_H    =    8;              { CTRL + H          }
CTRL_I    =    9;              { CTRL + I          }
CTRL_J    =   10;              { CTRL + J          }
CTRL_K    =   11;              { CTRL + K          }
CTRL_L    =   12;              { CTRL + L          }
CTRL_M    =   13;              { CTRL + M          }
CTRL_N    =   14;              { CTRL + N          }
CTRL_O    =   15;              { CTRL + O          }
CTRL_P    =   16;              { CTRL + P          }
CTRL_Q    =   17;              { CTRL + Q          }
CTRL_R    =   18;              { CTRL + R          }
CTRL_S    =   19;              { CTRL + S          }
CTRL_T    =   20;              { CTRL + T          }
CTRL_U    =   21;              { CTRL + U          }
CTRL_V    =   22;              { CTRL + V          }
CTRL_W    =   23;              { CTRL + W          }
CTRL_X    =   24;              { CTRL + X          }
CTRL_Y    =   25;              { CTRL + Y          }
CTRL_Z    =   26;              { CTRL + Z          }
BACKTAB   =  271;              { SHIFT + TAB       }
ALT_Q     =  272;              { ALT + Q           }
ALT_W     =  273;              { ALT + W           }
ALT_E     =  274;              { ALT + E           }
ALT_R     =  275;              { ALT + R           }
ALT_T     =  276;              { ALT + T           }
ALT_Y     =  277;              { ALT + Y           }
ALT_U     =  278;              { ALT + U           }
ALT_I     =  279;              { ALT + I           }
ALT_O     =  280;              { ALT + O           }
ALT_P     =  281;              { ALT + P           }
ALT_A     =  286;              { ALT + A           }
ALT_S     =  287;              { ALT + S           }
ALT_D     =  288;              { ALT + D           }
ALT_F     =  289;              { ALT + F           }
ALT_G     =  290;              { ALT + G           }
ALT_H     =  291;              { ALT + H           }
ALT_J     =  292;              { ALT + J           }
ALT_K     =  293;              { ALT + K           }
ALT_L     =  294;              { ALT + L           }
ALT_Z     =  300;              { ALT + Z           }
ALT_X     =  301;              { ALT + X           }
ALT_C     =  302;              { ALT + C           }
ALT_V     =  303;              { ALT + V           }
ALT_B     =  304;              { ALT + B           }
ALT_N     =  305;              { ALT + N           }
ALT_M     =  306;              { ALT + M           }
F1        =  315;              { F1 key            }
F2        =  316;              { F2 key            }
F3        =  317;              { F3 key            }
```

```
F4          = 318;          { F4 key         }
F5          = 319;          { F5 key         }
F6          = 320;          { F6 key         }
F7          = 321;          { F7 key         }
F8          = 322;          { F8 key         }
F9          = 323;          { F9 key         }
F10         = 324;          { F10 key        }
CDOWN       = 336;          { Cursor Down    }
CHOME       = 327;          { Cursor Home    }
CUP         = 328;          { Cursor Up      }
CPGUP       = 329;          { Page Up        }
CLEFT       = 331;          { Cursor Left    }
CRIGHT      = 333;          { Cursor Right   }
CEND        = 335;          { Cursor Right   }
CPGDN       = 337;          { Page Dn        }
INSERTKEY   = 338;          { INSERT key     }
DELETEKEY   = 339;          { DELETE key     }
SHIFT_F1    = 340;          { SHIFT + F1     }
SHIFT_F2    = 341;          { SHIFT + F2     }
SHIFT_F3    = 342;          { SHIFT + F3     }
SHIFT_F4    = 343;          { SHIFT + F4     }
SHIFT_F5    = 344;          { SHIFT + F5     }
SHIFT_F6    = 345;          { SHIFT + F6     }
SHIFT_F7    = 346;          { SHIFT + F7     }
SHIFT_F8    = 347;          { SHIFT + F8     }
SHIFT_F9    = 348;          { SHIFT + F9     }
SHIFT_F10   = 349;          { SHIFT + F10    }
CTRL_F1     = 350;          { CTRL + F1      }
CTRL_F2     = 351;          { CTRL + F2      }
CTRL_F3     = 352;          { CTRL + F3      }
CTRL_F4     = 353;          { CTRL + F4      }
CTRL_F5     = 354;          { CTRL + F5      }
CTRL_F6     = 355;          { CTRL + F6      }
CTRL_F7     = 356;          { CTRL + F7      }
CTRL_F8     = 357;          { CTRL + F8      }
CTRL_F9     = 358;          { CTRL + F9      }
CTRL_F10    = 359;          { CTRL + F10     }
ALT_F1      = 360;          { ALT + F1       }
ALT_F2      = 361;          { ALT + F2       }
ALT_F3      = 362;          { ALT + F3       }
ALT_F4      = 363;          { ALT + F4       }
ALT_F5      = 364;          { ALT + F5       }
ALT_F6      = 365;          { ALT + F6       }
ALT_F7      = 366;          { ALT + F7       }
ALT_F8      = 367;          { ALT + F8       }
ALT_F9      = 368;          { ALT + F9       }
ALT_F10     = 369;          { ALT + F10      }
CTRL_LF     = 371;          { CTRL + Left    }
CTRL_RI     = 372;          { CTRL + Right   }
CTRL_PGDN   = 374;          { CTRL + PgUp    }
CTRL_HOME   = 375;          { CTRL + Home    }
ALT_1       = 376;          { ALT + 1        }
ALT_2       = 377;          { ALT + 2        }
```

```
        ALT_3    = 378;                    { ALT + 3          }
        ALT_4    = 379;                    { ALT + 4          }
        ALT_5    = 380;                    { ALT + 5          }
        ALT_6    = 381;                    { ALT + 6          }
        ALT_7    = 382;                    { ALT + 7          }
        ALT_8    = 383;                    { ALT + 8          }
        ALT_9    = 384;                    { ALT + 9          }
        ALT_0    = 385;                    { ALT + 0          }
      CTRL_PGUP = 388;                           { CTRL + PgUp
    }
```

The public part of the unit ends with the last constants. Now the part that starts the binding of the object file, created by the assembler module KBMA.ASM, begins. The declaration of constants used only within the module that follows.

```
    implementation

    {$L kbma}                              { add kbma.obj assembler module }

    {== Internal constants =====================================================}

    const NO_MSRANGE    = 255;             { mouse pointer not in range xy }
          EVQ_LEN       = 100;             { length of mouse or keyboard
    queue }
```

There are also some types defined for internal use. You should already be familiar with type PTTREC, from Section 2.5, as a way to split a pointer into its components. Type PTRVREC is similar. This is used to disassemble type PTRVIEW to obtain the pointer mask and screen mask.

Type RNGBUF is used to identify the range where the mouse pointer is currently located. This type recreates the video RAM in a way that uses only one byte for each screen position instead of two, as is actually found in the video RAM. This single byte stores the number of the range to which each screen position belongs. To obtain the current mouse range, all you have to do is get the array index from the current mouse position and then retrieve the range code from the array element with this index. The advantage of using this method to determine the range is that, despite using a high amount of memory, it works faster than comparing the mouse position with all defined ranges in a loop.

Not all of the 10,000 bytes specified in RNGBUF are needed. The reserved memory range must only have as many bytes as there are characters on the screen; this is usually 2000 bytes. RNGBUF is larger because the KBM unit must also support the text modes of EGA and VGA cards, which can display up to 4000 characters. Memory isn't wasted in this range because it is allocated on the heap. The same number of bytes are taken that are actually needed. Access to the range buffer is accomplished with the corresponding pointer type RBPTR.

```
{== Internal type declarations ===========================================}

type  PTRREC   = record                         { used for access to the   }
                   Ofs : word;                  { elements of any mouse    }
                   Seg : word;                  { pointer                  }
                 end;

      PTRVREC  = record                         { used for access to the }
                   ScreenMask : word;           { elements of a PTRVIEW  }
                   PointrMask : word;
                 end;

      RNGBUF   = array [0..10000] of byte;               { range buffer }

      RBPTR    = ^RNGBUF;                        { pointer to a range buffer }

      EVQUEUE  = record                                 { an EvntCode queue }
                   Next,                        { pointer to next event }
                   Last  : integer;             { pointer to last event }
                   Queue : array [1..EVQ_LEN] of EVENT;    { event buffer }
                 end;

      EVQUEUEPTR = ^EVQUEUE;                    { pointer to the event queue }

      EVHANDREC = record              { element in the event handler table }
                    Call    : boolean;            { handler installed? }
                    Handler : EVENTHANDLER;       { procedure pointer }
                  end;
```

Managing mouse and keyboard events in queues is done with type EVQUEUE. This contains the actual EVENT queue as well as the variables Next and Last, which serve as indices to the next and the last elements in the queue. When the queue is initialized, Next and Last both point to the first element. If an element is written to the queue, Last will point to it. Then Last is incremented. If this places it outside the queue array, it is reset to the start of the queue.

Next is handled the same way. If an event is read from the queue, it is taken from the position indicated by Next and then incremented. Next is also set back to the beginning when reaching the end of the queue.

As long as Next and Last contain the same value, the queue is empty. The queue is full if Last stores a new event and then bumps into Next when it is incremented. In this case, Last is not incremented and the last event is overwritten by the next event to be captured. The constant EVQ_LEN gives the length of the event queue. Since the length is so big, the queue probably won't be filled.

The type EVQUEUEPTR is used as a pointer to an event queue.

The last internal data type is the structure EVHANDREC. This stores information on one of the event handlers.

Many internal variables are also required in order to do the work of the KBM unit.

```
{== Internal global variables =============================================}

var  NumRanges,                                        { number of ranges }
     TLine,                                        { number of text lines }
     TCol     : byte;                            { number of text columns }
     BufPtr   : RBPTR;               { pointer to range recognition buffer }
     CurRngPtr: RNGPTR;               { pointer to current range vector }
     BLen     : integer;                   { range buffer length in bytes }
     ExitOld  : pointer;              { pointer to old exit procedure }
     HandTab  : array [1..16] of EVHANDREC;   { table with event handlers }
                                              { for application program   }

     KbQueueP,                                  { queue for keyboard events }
     MouQueueP : EVQUEUEPTR;                     { queue for mouse events }

     OldKbHandler : pointer;                  { address of old int09 handler }

     Time       : longint absolute $40:$6C;         { BIOS tick counter }
     BiosKbFlag : byte absolute $40:$17;         { BIOS keyboard flag }
     CurStatus  : byte;                      { current keyboard status }
```

Three of these variables deserve special mention: HandTab, Time and BiosKbFlag.

HandTab is an array with 16 entries of type EVHANDREC, in which information on the event handlers is stored. The index of each handler corresponds with the bit position of its EV_... constant. Since EV_MOU_MOVE has bit value 1, it is the first element in HandTab. Then there is EV_LEFT_PRESS with bit value 2. However, don't assume that this is going to be a linear correspondence. The next (3rd) element is EV_LEFT_REL, which has a bit value of 4. Mathematically, each element occupies the array position that equals the logarithm of its bit value plus one.

BiosKbFlag and Time are two absolute variables that reference memory locations within the BIOS variable segment. Time is equivalent to the LongInt in the BIOS that stores the current time. BiosKbFlag is the byte in the BIOS that gives the current status of the control keys. This is the same byte that is returned by calling function $02 of the BIOS keyboard interrupt. This information is not obtained with the BIOS function because it must be used within the event handlers for both the keyboard and mouse. It must be retrieved quickly to avoid noticeable delays in the program. Direct access to this variable is a good way to do this.

Following the variables, the two event handlers from the assembler module are declared as external procedures. Although these routines aren't called from the unit itself, their addresses are needed so they can be installed as interrupt handlers or event handlers.

```
{== Declarations of external functions ====================================}

{$F+}                                              { the function is FAR }
procedure NewMouHandler ; external ;             { mouse event handler }
procedure NewKbHandler  ; external ;       { new keyboard handler (Int $09) }
{$F-}                                                { FAR functions
disabled }
```

Procedures and Functions

We've already discussed the KBM unit in detail. Now we come to the procedures and functions.

Let's begin with the starting code that initializes the unit.

```
{**----------------------------------------------------------------**}
{** Starting code of unit                                          **}
{**----------------------------------------------------------------**}

begin
  KbmInit( NumCol, NumLine );                          { initialize unit }
  ExitOld := ExitProc;                   { mark address of Exit procedure }
  ExitProc := @KbmEnd;                   { define KbmEnd as Exit procedure }
end.
```

This begins by calling the KbmInit procedure, which is the actual initialization procedure. The screen size must be passed so that the internal range buffer can be allocated and initialized on the heap. The variables NumCol and NumLine from the WIN unit are used for this. Since the use of these two variables is the only link between the WIN and KBM, WIN is specified in the USES command at the start of KBM.

A new EXIT procedure is also defined in the usual way. In this case, it is called KbmEnd. Let's now look at the initialization procedure KbmInit.

```
{******************************************************************}
{*  KbmInit: initialization procedure                          *}
{**--------------------------------------------------------------}
{*  Input  : Columns = number of screen columns               *}
{*           Lines_  = number of screen lines                 *}
{******************************************************************}

procedure KbmInit( Columns, Lines_ : byte );

var Regs   : Registers;           { processor register for interrupt call }
    i      : byte;                    { loop counter as index in HandTab }
```

```
begin

  {-- install new keyboard handler -------------------------------------}

  CurStatus := BiosKbFlag;                        { load BIOS keyboard status }

  GetIntVec( $09, OldKBHandler );         { Get address of int $09 handler }
  SetIntVec( $09, @NewKbHandler );              { install new handler }

  TLine := Lines_;                        { Store number of columns and }
  TCol  := Columns;                       { rows in global variables    }

  {-- allocate and fill buffer for mouse range --------------------------}

  BLen := TLine * TCol;                   { number of characters on screen }
  GetMem( BufPtr, BLen );                 { allocate internal range buffer }
  KbmIBufFill( 0, 0, TCol-1, TLine-1, NO_MSRANGE );

  Regs.AX := 0;                               { initialize mouse driver }
  Intr( $33, Regs );                          { call mouse driver }
  MouAvail := ( Regs.AX = $ffff );            { mouse available? }

  CurRng := NO_MSRANGE;                       { mouse pointer in no range }
  CurX   := TCol + 1;                     { position outside the screen }

  {-- configure and initialize mouse and keyboard queue ------------------}

  New( KbQueueP );                            { create keyboard queue }
  KbQueueP^.Next := 1;                    { still no event in the queue }
  KbQueueP^.Last := 1;

  New( MouQueueP );                           { create mouse queue }
  MouQueueP^.Next := 1;                   { still no event in the queue }
  MouQueueP^.Last := 1;

  for i := 1 to 16 do            { still no user event handler installed }
    HandTab[ i ].Call := FALSE;

  if ( MouAvail ) then                        { is there a mouse installed? }
    begin                                                           { Yes }
      MouSetMoveArea( 0, 0, TCol-1, TLine-1 );    { set range of movement }

      CurX    := KbmIGetX;                      { load current mouse position }
      CurY    := KbmIGetY;                      { in global variables        }

      {-- install NewMouHandler mouse event handler ---------------------}

      Regs.AX := $000C;         { function number for "Set Mouse Handler" }
      Regs.CX := EV_MOU_ALL;                       { load event mask }
      Regs.DX := Ofs( NewMouHandler );      { offset address of handler }
      Regs.ES := Seg( NewMouHandler );      { segment address of handler }
      Intr( $33,  Regs );                          { call mouse driver }
    end;
end;
```

During this procedure, the current keyboard status is obtained from the proper variable and entered in the global variable CurStatus. This is done to establish a frame of reference that can be used to record any changes within this byte. Then the new handler for the keyboard interrupt $09 is installed by obtaining the address of the current handler with GetIntVec and then using SetIntVec to enter the address of the new handler in the Interrupt Vector Table.

The following program code creates and initializes the internal range buffer. The screen resolution passed by the calling routine is stored in the global variables TLine and TCol and is used to calculate the length of the buffer which is then stored in BLEN. A buffer of the proper size is then allocated on the heap and its address is entered in the global variable BufPtr. Since no mouse ranges have been defined yet, the entire buffer is filled with the range code NO_MSRANGE by calling the internal procedure KbmIBufFill.

Calling function $0000 of the mouse driver determines the availability of the mouse. The variable MouAvail is then loaded with the proper value. Next, the two queues are created on the heap and initialized. The Array HandTab is also initialized. This contains the pointers to the various event handlers of the application program. Since none are currently installed, the Call field will contain FALSE for each entry.

If the presence of a mouse driver is detected with the test described above, the mouse parameters and variables are initialized. The area in which the mouse can move is then set to the entire screen by calling the procedure MouSetArea. The current mouse position is obtained and entered in the variables CurX and CurY.

Finally, a call to function $000C of the mouse driver is used to install the mouse event handler NewMouHandler from the assembler module. The event mask in the CX register contains the constant EV_MOU_ALL, so all types of mouse events will trigger a call to the new mouse event handler. This completes the work of KbmInit. Control is returned to the calling routine and the mouse pointer is still not visible on the screen.

You will have noticed that several other KBM procedures are called within this procedure. We will take a look at each of these now. The first call is to the procedure KbmIBufFill, which stores codes for mouse ranges in the internal range buffer.

```
{*****************************************************************}
{*   KbmIBufFill: stores the range code for a mouse range in the internal  *}
{*               range buffer of this module                       *}
{**-------------------------------------------------------------**}
{*   Input  : x1, y1 = upper left corner of the mouse range        *}
{*           x2, y2 = lower right corner of the mouse range         *}
{*           Code   = the range code                               *}
{*****************************************************************}

procedure KbmIBufFill( x1, y1, x2, y2, Code : byte );

var Index   : integer;                      { points to field being processed }
    Column,                                            { loop counter }
    Row   : byte;

begin
  for Row  :=y1 to y2 do                             { process each line }
    begin
      Index := Row   * TCol + x1;                  { first index of the line }
      for Column:=x1 to x2 do               { process each column in the line }
        begin
          BufPtr^[ Index ] := Code;                       { save code }
          inc( Index );                       { set index to next field }
        end;
    end;
end;
```

In addition to the range code, the corner coordinates of the specified range are also passed to this procedure. The range is then processed top to bottom, from line by line and column by column. The specified range code is entered in each processed array element.

KbmInit isn't the only procedure that calls KbmIBufFill. The procedure MouDefRange, which actually defines the mouse ranges, also calls it. To do this, KbmIBufFill must also know the number of ranges to define and a pointer to the Array that stores each range descriptor.

MouDefRange lists both of these parameters in global variables and fills the entire range buffer with the code NO_MSRANGE to eliminate any leftover range designations. The individual ranges given in the array are then processed in a loop. The code for each range is its index within the range array.

```
{*********************************************************************}
{*   MouDefRange:    enables the assignment of different screen ranges   *}
{*                   which can be recognized as mouse ranges             *}
{**------------------------------------------------------------------**}
{*   Input  : Amount = number of the screen range                       *}
{*            BPtr   = pointer to the array describing the ranges as a   *}
{*                     structure of type MSRANGE                         *}
{*   Info:    - the free remaining screen ranges are assigned the code   *}
{*              NO_MSRANGE                                                *}
{*********************************************************************}

procedure MouDefRange( Amount : byte; BPtr : RNGPTR );

var CurRng,                                    { number of the current range }
    Range : byte;                                      { loop counter }

begin
  CurRngPtr := BPtr;                           { mark pointer to vector and }
  NumRanges := Amount;                         { number of ranges           }
  FillChar( BufPtr^, BLen, NO_MSRANGE );       { all elements = NO_MSRANGE }
  for Range:=0 to amount-1 do                  { process individual ranges }
   with BPtr^[ Range ] do
     KbmIBufFill( x1, y1, x2, y2, Range );

  CurRng := BufPtr^[ CurY * TCol + CurX ];              { send current range }
end;
```

KbmInit also calls the functions KbmIGetX and KbmIGetY. These are used to obtain the current mouse position with function $0003 of the mouse driver. The position is returned as separate X and Y coordinates.

```
{*********************************************************************}
{*   KbmIGetX: returns the text column where the mouse pointer is located  *}
{**------------------------------------------------------------------**}
{*   Output : column of the mouse pointer relative to the text screen      *}
{*********************************************************************}

function KbmIGetX : byte;

var Regs : Registers;                    { processor register for interrupt call }

begin
  Regs.AX := $0003;                 { function number for "Get mouse position" }
  Intr( $33,  Regs );                              { call mouse driver }
  KbmIGetX := Regs.CX shr 3;                  { compute and return column }
end;

{*********************************************************************}
{*   KbmIGetY: returns the text row where the mouse pointer is located    *}
{**------------------------------------------------------------------**}
{*   Output : row of the mouse pointer, relative to the text screen       *}
{*********************************************************************}
```

```
function KbmIGetY : byte;

var Regs : Registers;                    { processor register for interrupt call }

begin
  Regs.AX := $0003;                      { function number for "Get mouse position" }
  Intr( $33, Regs );                              { call mouse driver }
  KbmIGetY := Regs.DX shr 3;                     { compute and return row }
end;
```

The procedures MouShowMouse, MouHideMouse, MouSetMoveArea, MouSetSpeed and MouMovePtr also call functions of the mouse driver. These procedures are convenient interfaces to the mouse driver functions. They pass the function number in the proper register and then call the mouse driver with interrupt $33.

```
{*********************************************************************}
{*  MouShowMouse: makes mouse pointer visible on the screen         *}
{**---------------------------------------------------------------**}
{*  Info: calls to MouShowMouse and MouHideMouse must be balanced  *}
{*********************************************************************}

procedure MouShowMouse;

var Regs : Registers;                    { processor register for interrupt call }

begin
  Regs.AX := $0001;                      { function number for "Show Mouse" }
  Intr( $33, Regs );                             { call mouse driver }
end;


{*********************************************************************}
{*  MouHideMouse: remove the mouse pointer from the screen          *}
{**---------------------------------------------------------------**}
{*  Info: calls to MouShowMouse and MouHideMouse must be balanced  *}
{*********************************************************************}

procedure MouHideMouse;

var Regs : Registers;                    { processor register for interrupt call }

begin
  Regs.AX := $0002;                      { function number for "Hide Mouse" }
  Intr( $33, Regs);                              { call mouse driver }
end;
```

```
{*********************************************************************}
{*  MouSetMoveArea: set the area in which the mouse can move        *}
{**-----------------------------------------------------------------**}
{*  Input  :  x1, y1 = coordinates of the upper left corner of the range  *}
{*            x2, y2 = coordinates of the lower right corner of the range *}
{*  Info:   - these coordinates relate to the text screen and not to the *}
{*            virtual graphics screen of the mouse driver           *}
{*********************************************************************}

procedure MouSetMoveArea( x1, y1, x2, y2 : byte );

var Regs : Registers;                { processor register for interrupt call }

begin
  Regs.AX := $0008;              { function number for "Set vertical limits" }
  Regs.CX := integer( y1 ) shl 3;                    { convert to virtual }
  Regs.DX := integer( y2 ) shl 3;                    { mouse screen        }
  Intr( $33, Regs );                                 { call mouse driver }
  Regs.AX := $0007;            { function number for "Set horizontal limits" }
  Regs.CX := integer( x1 ) shl 3;                    { convert to virtual }
  Regs.DX := integer( x2 ) shl 3;                    { mouse screen        }
  Intr( $33, Regs );                                 { call mouse driver }
end;


{*********************************************************************}
{*  MouSetSpeed: set the relationship between mouse movement and the *}
{*               resulting movement of the mouse pointer            *}
{**-----------------------------------------------------------------**}
{*  Input  : XSpeed = speed in X direction                          *}
{*           YSpeed = speed in Y direction                          *}
{*  Info:   - both parameters are expressed in Mickeys (8 pixels)   *}
{*********************************************************************}

procedure MouSetSpeed( XSpeed, YSpeed : integer );

var Regs : Registers;                { processor register for interrupt call }

begin
  Regs.AX := $000f;       { function number for "Set mickeys to pixel ratio" }
  Regs.CX := XSpeed;
  Regs.DX := YSpeed;
  Intr( $33, Regs);                                  { call mouse driver }
end;


{*********************************************************************}
{*  MouMovePtr: moves the mouse pointer to a new screen position    *}
{**-----------------------------------------------------------------**}
{*  Input  : COL = the new screen column of the mouse pointer       *}
{*           ROW = the new screen row of the mouse pointer          *}
{*  Info:   - the coordinates relate to the text screen and not to the *}
{*            virtual graphics screen of the mouse driver           *}
{*********************************************************************}
```

```
procedure MouMovePtr( Col, Row : byte );

var Regs   : Registers;             { processor register for interrupt call }
    NewRng : byte;                             { range to move mouse to }

begin
  Regs.AX := $0004;      { function number for "Set mouse pointer position" }
  CurX := col;                              { store coordinates    }
  CurY := row;                              { in global variables }
  Regs.CX := integer( col ) shl 3;        { convert coordinates and   }
  Regs.DX := integer( row ) shl 3;        { store in global variables }
  Intr( $33, Regs );                            { call mouse driver }

  CurRng := BufPtr^[ Row * TCol + Col ];                  { get new range }
end;
```

MouDefinePtr is a procedure that calls function $000A of the mouse driver to define the appearance of the mouse pointer in the pointer mask and the screen mask. This procedure doesn't expect the two bit masks as separate parameters but rather as one LongInt of type PTRVIEW. It then splits this parameter into the LO Word and HI Word of type PTRVREC to obtain the pointer mask and screen mask, which it passes to the mouse driver.

```
{********************************************************************}
{*  MouDefinePtr: passes the pointer mask and screen mask to the mouse  *}
{*               driver, which then define the appearance of the mouse  *}
{*               pointer                                            *}
{**--------------------------------------------------------------**}
{*  Input  : Mask = the pointer mask and screen mask as one parameter of  *}
{*               type PTRVIEW                                       *}
{*  Info:     - the parameter mask is created by the MouPtrMask procedure  *}
{*            - the upper 16 bits of Mask represents the screen mask,  *}
{*              the lower 16 bits represent the pointer mask         *}
{********************************************************************}

procedure MouDefinePtr( Mask : PTRVIEW );

var Regs : Registers;                  { processor register for interrupt call }

begin
  Regs.AX := $000a;          { function number for "Set text pointer type" }
  Regs.BX := 0;                              { create software pointer }
  Regs.CX := PTRVREC( Mask ).ScreenMask;       { low word is AND mask }
  Regs.DX := PTRVREC( Mask ).PointrMask;       { high word is XOR mask }
  Intr( $33, Regs);                             { call mouse driver }
end;
```

MouDefinePtr uses this unusual method because of the way the function MouPtrMask creates the pointer mask and screen mask. This function is set up so that it can give its result directly to MouDefinePtr. Since a function cannot return two parameters as its result, the pointer mask and screen mask must be combined into one value. Both Words are easily accommodated by one LongInt.

```
{***************************************************************}
{*  MouPtrMask: creates the pointer mask and screen mask from the bit   *}
{*              for the character and the color                 *}
{**-----------------------------------------------------------**}
{*  Input  : Character = bit mask for pointer mask and screen mask      *}
{*                         character                            *}
{*           Color     = bit mask for pointer mask and screen mask color *}
{*  Output : pointer mask and screen mask as one value of type PTRVIEW  *}
{*  Info:    the constants PtrSameChar, PtrSameCol, PtrSameColB,        *}
{*           PtrInvCol and PtrInvColB as well as the results of the     *}
{*           functions PtrDifChar and PtrDifCol can be passed as the    *}
{*           color and character                                *}
{***************************************************************}

function MouPtrMask( Character, Color  : word ) : PTRVIEW;

var Mask : PTRVIEW;                    { the pointer/screen mask to be created }

begin
  PTRVREC( Mask ).ScreenMask := ( ( Color and $ff ) shl 8 ) +
                                ( Character and $ff );
  PTRVREC( Mask ).PointrMask := ( Color and $ff00 ) + ( Character shr 8 );
  MouPtrMask := Mask;                        { return mask to calling routine }
end;
```

MouPtrMask expects two parameters as its arguments. These determine the character and color of the mouse pointer. Don't worry about specifying these because you can pass any of several constants or the results of the functions PtrDifChar and PtrDifCol to the function.

These two functions are used if the mouse pointer will appear as a given character or color on the screen. This character or color must be passed to PtrDifChar or PtrDifCol and the function result passed on with the call to MouPtrMask.

```
{***************************************************************}
{*  PtrDifChar: creates the character component of the screen mask and  *}
{*              pointer mask                                    *}
{**-----------------------------------------------------------**}
{*  Input  : ASCII code of the character to represent the mouse pointer *}
{*  Output : pointer and screen masks for this character        *}
{*  Info:    the result is further processed by the MouPtrMask procedure *}
{***************************************************************}

function PtrDifChar( Character : byte ) : word;

begin
  PtrDifChar := Character shl 8;
end;
```

```
{***************************************************************************}
{*  PtrDifCol: creates the color component of the pointer mask and screen *}
{*            mask                                                         *}
{**-----------------------------------------------------------------------**}
{*  Input  : color of the character that will represent the mouse pointer *}
{*  Output : pointer and screen masks for this color                      *}
{*  Info:    the result is further processed by the MouPtrMask procedure  *}
{***************************************************************************}

function PtrDifCol( Color : byte ) : word;

begin
  PtrDifCol := Color shl 8;
end;
```

The constant PtrSameChar can be given as the character. This won't change the character under the mouse pointer.

The color can be specified with the constants PtrSameCol, PtrInvCol, PtrSameColB or PtrInvColB as well as the result of the function PtrDifCol. These constants have the following effects:

PtrSameCol

> The mouse pointer takes the same color as the character that previously occupied the position.

PtrInvCol

> The mouse pointer inverts the color of the character below.

PtrSameColB

> The mouse pointer keeps the color of the character below but begins to blink.

PtrInvColB

> The color of the character below is inverted and it begins to blink.

Let's look at the following program lines to see how these different functions and constants work together.

```
MouDefinePtr( MouPtrMask( PtrSameChar, PtrInvCol ) );
                                                { same character, inverted }
MouDefinePtr( MouPtrMask( PtrDifChar( 24 ), PtrSameCol ) );
                                                { up arrow, same color }
MouDefinePtr( MouPtrMask( PtrSameChar, PtrDifCol( $0E ) ) );
                                                { same character, yellow on black }
```

While a program that uses the KBM unit will probably use procedures, such as MouDefRange or MouDefinePtr, for access to the event handlers, an interrupt handler within KBM isn't allowed. This isn't necessary because these handlers produce EVENT records that can be queried by other procedures. Before continuing, let's take a quick look at the two handlers for keyboard and mouse events in the KBM unit.

The keyboard handler is called KbHandler. Like the mouse handler, it is called from the assembler module. Instead of replacing the BIOS handler, KbHandler merely expands it. There is also a call to the old BIOS handler within the assembler module. Similar to the BIOS handler, KbHandler also reacts to the make and release codes generated by the keyboard at the data port after executing interrupt $09. This code is passed to KbHandler by the calling routine.

```
{*****************************************************************************}
{*   KbHandler : called by the Int09 handler (NewKbHandler in the          *}
{*               assembler module) when a key is pressed                    *}
{**-----------------------------------------------------------------------**}
{*   Input  : KbPort = code read from keyboard port $60                     *}
{*****************************************************************************}

procedure KbHandler( KbPort : byte );

var EvRec  : EVENT;                        { EVENT record to be created }
    Regs   : Registers;                       { processor register }
    NewKbS : byte;                            { new keyboard status }

begin
  EvRec.Time := Time;                             { get clock time }
  Regs.AH := 1;                           { determine if a key has been }
  intr( $16, Regs );                        { converted to a key code    }
  if ( Regs.Flags and FZERO = 0 ) then
    begin                          { yes, character now in keyboard buffer }
      Regs.AH := 0;                         { load character from keyboard }
      intr( $16, Regs );                     { buffer via the BIOS        }
      if ( Regs.AL = 0 ) then EvRec.Key := Regs.AH + 256
                         else EvRec.Key := Regs.AL;
      EvRec.EvntCode := EV_KEY_PRESSED;                  { set event code }
      KbmPutQueue( KbQueueP, EvRec );             { place event in queue }
    end
  else                                { keystroke produced no key code }
    begin
      NewKbS := BiosKbFlag;                 { get status of control keys }
      if ( CurStatus <> NewKbS ) then          { status change? }
        begin
          if ( CurStatus < NewKbS ) then            { was a bit set? }
            begin                               { yes, save event }
              EvRec.StateKey := CurStatus xor NewKbS;   { isolate flag }
              if ( EvRec.StateKey <> KEY_INSERT ) then    { not INSERT? }
                begin                           { no, create EVENT }
                  EvRec.EvntCode := EV_KEY_STATUS;
```

267

```
                    KbmPutQueue ( KbQueueP, EvRec );        { put event in queue }
                end;
            end
        end
    else                                                    { no, no status change }
        if ( KbPort < 128 ) then                                     { make code? }
        begin                                               { yes, create event }
            EvRec.EvntCode := EV_KEY_UNKNOWN;                     { unknown code }
            EvRec.ScanCode := KbPort;                             { pass scan code }
            EvRec.Status   := NewKbs;           { load status in EVENT record }
            KbmPutQueue ( KbQueueP, EvRec );               { put event in queue }
        end;
        CurStatus := NewKbS;                         { store new keyboard status }
    end;
end;
```

KbHandler first obtains the current clock time and stores it in the EVENT record that will be added to the event queue. By calling BIOS keyboard interrupt function $01, the handler determines if a keystroke is waiting in the BIOS keyboard buffer. If the function returns with a deleted Zero Flag a character is waiting. This means that the BIOS has received a make code and converted it to the proper ASCII code or extended keyboard code. This code is then read by function $00 of the BIOS keyboard interrupt and placed in the Key field of the local EVENT record. At the same time, a check is made to see if the code is an extended keyboard code. If so, the code is increased by 256.

The constant EV_KEY_PRESSED, loaded in the EvntCode field of the EVENT record, identifies the event. The EVENT record is then placed in the keyboard queue by calling the procedure KbmPutQueue. This completes the work of the handler.

If an ASCII or extended keyboard code wasn't recognized either the keystroke created a status change that must be recorded in EV_KEY_STATUS or the keystroke could not be interpreted by the BIOS. This creates an EVENT of type EV_KEY_UNKNOWN.

KbHandler distinguishes between these two cases by comparing the current BIOS keyboard status with the status that was stored the last time it was called. A status change occurred if status values differ. The bit that has changed within the status byte is then isolated. An event of type EV_KEY_STATUS is created only if a mode change has occurred (such as NUM LOCK, SCROLL LOCK, etc.). The INSERT mode is handled as an extended keyboard code.

If no status change occurred, an event of type EV_KEY_UNKNOWN is created if the make code was 127 or less.

The mouse handler MouEventHandler has fewer options. It creates an event only if a mouse movement occurs that changes the position of the pointer in relation to the virtual mouse screen, but not in relation to the text screen. In some cases, the mouse handler may be called in response to a number of events, not just one.

Like KbHandler, MouEventHandler is called from the assembler module, which passes certain event information. Not all information, however, given to the assembler module by the mouse driver is passed on to MouEventHandler. The relative mouse movements in the processor registers DI and SI are not passed on. The mouse position is converted to the coordinate system of the text screen within the assembler module, which makes it easier for MouEventHandler to process.

These coordinates are used to determine the code number of the mouse range where the mouse pointer is located. This is stored in the local variable NewRng. If this range isn't defined (code = NO_MSRANGE) the coordinates are loaded without changes into the local variables NewC and NewR. Otherwise, the coordinates are set relative to the upper left corner of the current range and the distance to this point is stored in NewC and NewR.

The handler then runs through a loop that processes the lower five bits of the event mask representing the events EV_MOU_MOVE; EF_LEFT_PRESS; EV_RIGHT_PRESS; EV_LEFT_REL; and EV_RIGHT_REL. If one of these bits is set and the conditions mentioned above regarding the movement of the mouse pointer do not apply, the corresponding mouse event is created. The event code is the current bit mask for the event flag which corresponds to the event constants.

Finally, the global variables CurX, CurY, CurBut and CurRng are updated and the procedure is ended.

```
{*******************************************************************}
{*  MouEventHandler: called by mouse driver via the assembler routine  *}
{*              kbma when a mouse event occurs                        *}
{**---------------------------------------------------------------**}
{*  Input  : EvFlags  = the event mask                               *}
{*           ButState = current status of mouse buttons              *}
{*           X, Y     = current position of mouse pointer in relation to *}
{*                      the text screen                              *}
{*******************************************************************}

procedure MouEventHandler( EvFlags, ButState, x, y : integer );

var NewC,                      { new coordinates of mouse pointer }
    NewR,                      { relative to new range            }
    NewRng : byte;             { range number where the }
    EvData : EVENT;            { new event occurred     }
    Ticks  : longint;          { stores the current clock time }
    i,                         { loop counter }
    Mask   : integer;          { bit mask }

begin
  Ticks := Time;                            { get time }
```

```
    NewRng   := BufPtr^[ y * TCol + x ];                      { get range }
    if ( NewRng = NO_MSRANGE ) then                           { no range? }
      begin                           { yes, coordinates relate to entire screen }
        NewR := y;
        NewC := x;
      end
    else                 { no, coordinates relate to upper left corner of range }
      begin
        NewR := y - CurRngPtr^[ NewRng ].y1;
        NewC := x - CurRngPtr^[ NewRng ].x1;
      end;


    {-- capture each event separately as an EVENT record --------------------}

    Mask := 1;                                     { start with event bit 0 }
    with EvData do                                 { create event record }
      begin
        Time       := Ticks;                       { load data in the event record }
        Buttons    := ButState;
        Range      := NewRng;
        Rel_Row    := NewR;
        RelColumn  := NewC;
        Abs_Row    := y;
        AbsColumn  := x;
      end;

    for i:=0 to 4 do                               { look at each bit in EvFlag }
      begin
        if not((EvFlags and Mask = 0) or
               ((Mask = EV_MOU_MOVE) and ((x = CurX) and (y = CurY)))) then
          begin
            EvData.EvntCode := Mask;                      { store event code }
            KbmPutQueue( MouQueueP, EvData );    { put event record in queue }
          end;
        Mask := Mask shl 1;                              { process next event bit }
      end;

    {-- store new mouse data in global variables --------------------------}

    CurX := x;                                     { new mouse position }
    CurY := y;
    CurBut := ButState;                            { store status of mouse buttons }
    CurRng := NewRng;                              { store new mouse range }
  end;
```

Both the keyboard handler and mouse handler in the KBM unit use the procedure
KbmPutQueue to add EVENT records to the end of these queues. This procedure fills the
queue with the same method described for building an EVQUEUE structure.

```
{**********************************************************************}
{*   KbmPutQueue : adds an EVENT record to the end of an event queue   *}
{**-------------------------------------------------------------------*}
{*   Input  : Qp   = pointer to the queue of interest                  *}
{*            EvRec = the EVENT record to be added to the queue        *}
{*   Info:    if there is no more room in the event queue, the procedure *}
{*            overwrites the last event                                *}
{**********************************************************************}

procedure KbmPutQueue( Qp : EVQUEUEPTR; EvRec : EVENT );

var NewLast : integer;                                { new last entry }

begin
  with Qp^ do                               { process the specified queue }
    begin
      Queue[ Last ] := EvRec;               { copy EVENT record to queue }
      NewLast := Last + 1;                   { number of new last entry }
      if ( NewLast > EVQ_LEN ) then         { wrap around to end of queue }
        NewLast := 1;
      if ( NewLast <> Next ) then                              { overflow }
        Last := NewLast;                          { no, set last entry }
    end;
end;
```

KbmGetQueue is similar to KbmPutQueue. This procedure retrieves the next event from a queue. If an event isn't in the queue when the procedure is called the constant EV_NO_EVENT is entered in the EvntCode field of the EVENT record. The value MAXLONGINT is also entered in the Time field. This is a constant, defined by Turbo Pascal, that is equal to the largest value that can be stored in type LongInt. In a moment, the reason for this will be clear.

```
{**********************************************************************}
{*   KbmGetQueue : reads the next event from the mouse or keyboard queue *}
{**-------------------------------------------------------------------*}
{*   Input  : Qp   = pointer to the queue of interest                  *}
{*            EvRec = variable that stores and EVENT record            *}
{*   Info:    if no event is in the queue at the time of the function  *}
{*            call, the function returns the constant EV_NO_EVENT and   *}
{*            loads the Time field with the value MAXLONGINT           *}
{**********************************************************************}

procedure KbmGetQueue( Qp : EVQUEUEPTR; var EvRec : EVENT );

begin
  with Qp^ do                               { process the specified queue }
    begin
      if ( Next = Last ) then                         { no event in queue? }
        begin                                                       { No }
          EvRec.EvntCode := EV_NO_EVENT;                     { no event }
          EvRec.Time := MAXLONGINT;                       { invalid time }
```

```
            end
        else                        { there is at least one element in the queue }
          begin
            EvRec := Queue[ Next ];              { get EVENT record from queue }
            if ( Next = EVQ_LEN ) then Next := 1        { set EvNext to next }
                              else inc( Next );    { queue element       }
          end;
      end;
  end;
```

The difference between KbmPeekQueue and KbmGetQueue is that the EVENT isn't removed from the queue. These two functions are similar to functions $00 and $01 of the BIOS keyboard interrupt. The first function removes a character from the keyboard buffer and the second simply queries the buffer without changing the contents.

```
{*********************************************************************}
{*  KbmPeekQueue : reads the next event from the mouse or keyboard queue  *}
{*                 without removing the event from the queue              *}
{**-----------------------------------------------------------------*}
{*  Input  : Qp    = pointer to the queue of interest                *}
{*           EvRec = variable that stores an event record            *}
{*  Info:    if no event is in the queue when the function is called, *}
{*           the function returns event type EV_NO_EVENT and loads the *}
{*           Time field with the value MAXLONGINT                     *}
{*********************************************************************}

procedure KbmPeekQueue( Qp : EVQUEUEPTR; var EvRec : EVENT );

begin
    with Qp^ do                              { process the specified queue }
      begin
        if ( Next = Last ) then              { no element in the queue? }
          begin                                            { No }
            EvRec.EvntCode := EV_NO_EVENT;             { no event }
            EvRec.Time := MAXLONGINT;               { invalid time }
          end
        else                            { there is an element in the queue }
          EvRec := Queue[ Next ];            { get EVENT record from queue }
      end;
end;
```

These procedures cannot be called directly. The KBM unit contains two special procedures called KbmGetEvent and KbmPeekEvent that are used for reading events. These two procedures are similar to the BIOS functions previously mentioned. KbmGetEvent removes an event from the queue and KbmPeekEvent examines but doesn't change the queue contents.

KbmGetEvent uses a loop to read the mouse and keyboard queues with KbmPeekQueue until an event is present in the queue. When a mouse or keyboard event is found, it is removed from the queue with KbmGetQueue. This is why KbmPeekQueue returns the largest possible time value when an event isn't found in the queue.

Since this time will never be reached, real events that occur will always take precedence because they have a lower time value.

```
{****************************************************************}
{*   KbmEventWait: waits for the occurrence of a certain keyboard or mouse *}
{*              event                                             *}
{**-------------------------------------------------------------**}
{*   Input  : WAIT_EVENT = bit mask that specifies the desired event  *}
{*            EV_REC     = event record in which information on the event *}
{*                         will be returned.                      *}
{*   Info:    - WAIT_EVENT can be specified by combining the various *}
{*              event constants EV_MOU_MOVE, EV_LEFT_PRESS etc. with a *}
{*              logical OR                                         *}
{*            - the procedure will only return when one of the specified *}
{*              events occurs. Non-specified events that occur in the *}
{*              meantime are ignored                              *}
{*            - this procedure can be called recursively, so that an event *}
{*              handler can also access KbmEventWait.             *}
{****************************************************************}

procedure KbmEventWait( WaitEvent : integer; var EvRec : EVENT );

var CurEvent : EVENT;                    { stores the current event index }
    Index    : byte;                     { in the event handler table     }

begin
  repeat                                      { wait for specific event }
    KbmGetEvent( CurEvent );                       { get event code }

    {-- call handler of application program ----------------------------}

    Index := KbmIGetIndex( CurEvent.EvntCode );   { get index from table }
    if ( HandTab[ Index ].Call ) then           { handler installed? }
     HandTab[ Index ].Handler( CurEvent );            { yes, call }

  until ( CurEvent.EvntCode and WaitEvent <> 0 );
    EvRec := CurEvent;                    { pass event to calling routine }
end;
```

You may wonder why two different queues are used since these two procedures combine the contents of both queues. Obviously using one queue would save time while reading for events because you would only have one queue to check. Since each event would already be in chronological order, the time the events occurred would not have to be compared.

If one of the event handlers is executing, it's possible that a call to the other, which will momentarily lock up the program, will follow. This can make it difficult to manage the queue, because events could begin to overlap. Strategies for avoiding these types of problems are discussed in Chapter 13, which deals with the creation of a multitasking unit. Therefore it is better to use two separate queues with the KBM unit.

The procedures KbmGetEvent and KbmPeekEvent return the desired event to the calling procedure. The procedure KbmEventWait can be used to wait for a specific type of event. This procedure is very similar to KbmGetEvent, but in addition to an EVENT record, it also receives a bit mask that describes the type of event that should be returned. This additional parameter can be passed as an EV_... constant or as several of these constants combined with a logical OR. When events are combined in this way KbmEventWait will return to the caller as soon as any one of the specified events is encountered.

When reading for events, the procedure KbmEventWait should precede KbmGetEvent because this is where the actual call to the event handler takes place. After receiving an event, KbmEventWait will pass the index of the corresponding event code in the array to the handler using KbmGetEvent. The index is used to check if an event handler exists for the event. If so, then the proper handler is called and the event is passed to it.

The function KbmIGetIndex, available only to routines of the KBM unit, is used to get the index from the event handler table HandTab. When passed by the bit mask of the event, it returns the corresponding index (the dual logarithm described above). You can calculate this value by counting the number of bit positions moved in order to reach bit position 0.

```
{*****************************************************************************}
{*   KbmIGetIndex : uses an event mask to retrieve the corresponding index *}
{*                  from the event handler table                           *}
{**-----------------------------------------------------------------------*}
{*   Input  : MASK = the event mask                                        *}
{*   Output : Index between 1 and 16                                       *}
{*****************************************************************************}

function KbmIGetIndex( Mask : word ) : byte ;

var i : byte;                                          { stores the index }

begin
  i := 1;
  while ( Mask <> 1 ) do                    { event bit still not in bit 0 ? }
    begin                                                           { No }
      Mask := Mask shr 1;                 { move mask one bit to the right }
      inc( i );                                        { increment index }
    end;
  KbmIGetIndex := i;                                        { return index }
end;
```

This function isn't called from KbmEventWait. It is also called through the procedures KbmRegisterHandler and KbmDeRegisterHandler. These procedures activate and deactivate the handlers. KbmRegisterHandler receives two parameters:

- The event constants that describe the event type and lead to the call of the proper handler.

- The name of the event handler. This is a variable of type EVENTHANDLER.

The same event handler can be specified with a number of different events. But only one of the event constants can be given as the first parameter. Combining the event constants isn't allowed in this case.

```
{*******************************************************************}
{*   KbmRegisterHandler : registers an application program's handler   *}
{*                   for a certain event                            *}
{**---------------------------------------------------------------**}
{*   Input   : EVENT   = the event mask                            *}
{*             HANDLER = the handler to be called                  *}
{*******************************************************************}

procedure KbmRegisterHandler( Event : word; Handler : EVENTHANDLER );

var i : byte;                                { index in event handler table }

begin
  i := KbmIGetIndex( Event );                           { get index }
  HandTab[ i ].Call := TRUE;                           { call handler }
  HandTab[ i ].Handler := Handler;          { store pointer to handler }
end;
```

To deactivate a handler, the procedure KbmDeRegisterHandler must be called. The only parameter expected by this procedure is the event constant that was used to register the handler with KbmRegisterHandler.

```
{*******************************************************************}
{*   KbmDeRegisterHandler : removes an application program's handler for  *}
{*                   a certain event                              *}
{**---------------------------------------------------------------**}
{*   Input   : EVENT = the event mask                             *}
{*******************************************************************}

procedure KbmDeRegisterHandler( Event : word );

begin
  HandTab[ KbmIGetIndex( Event ) ].Call := FALSE;      { do not call the  }
end;                                                   { handler any more }
```

KbmSetMode and KbmReleaseMode are the final two procedures of the KBM unit that can be called by other programs. They allow you to activate or deactivate the toggle keys,

(<Scroll Lock>, <Num Lock> and <Caps Lock>) on the keyboard, from a program without actually pressing the keys.

This is accomplished by setting or clearing the proper bits in the BIOS keyboard flag. Usually the BIOS would first know of this change the next time interrupt $09 is called from the keyboard or the next keyboard read. The procedure calls function $02 of the BIOS keyboard interrupt after manipulating the keyboard flag. This also updates the status of the keyboard LEDs on AT and 386 machines.

```
{**************************************************************************}
{*   KbmReleaseMode : clears one of the keyboard modes (SCROLL LOCK,     *}
{*                    NUM LOCK or CAPS LOCK)                             *}
{**----------------------------------------------------------------------*}
{*   Input  : KMode = one of the codes KEY_SCROLL_LOCK, KEY_CAPS_LOCK or *}
{*                    KEY_NUM_LCOK                                       *}
{*   Info   : on ATs and 386 machines, this procedure automatically      *}
{*            updates the keyboard LEDs to reflect the status change -    *}
{*            this does not work on XTs                                  *}
{**************************************************************************}

procedure KbmReleaseMode( KMode : byte  );

var Regs : Registers;               { processor register for interrupt call }

begin
  BiosKbFlag := BiosKbFlag and ( KMode xor $FF );            { clear bit }
  Regs.AH := $02;                          { read BIOS keyboard status so    }
  intr( $16, Regs );                       { BIOS recognizes the mode change }
end;

{**************************************************************************}
{*   KbmSetMode : turns on one of the keyboard modes (SCROLL LOCK,       *}
{*                NUM LOCK or CAPS LOCK)                                 *}
{**----------------------------------------------------------------------*}
{*   Input  : KMode = one of the codes KEY_SCROLL_LOCK, KEY_CAPS_LOCK or *}
{*                    KEY_NUM_LCOK                                       *}
{*   Info   : on At and 386 machines, this procedure also updates the     *}
{*            keyboard LEDs to reflect the mode change -                  *}
{*            this does not work on XTs                                  *}
{**************************************************************************}

procedure KbmSetMode( KMode : byte  );

var Regs : Registers;               { processor register for interrupt call }

begin
  BiosKbFlag := BiosKbFlag or KMode;                          { set bit }
  Regs.AH := $02;                          { read BIOS keyboard status so    }
  intr( $16, Regs );                       { BIOS recognizes the mode change }
end;
```

Your programs won't be able to access the procedure KbmEnd, which is called to end a program linked to the KBM unit with a USES command. This procedure is defined as the EXIT procedure in the initialization part of the unit. Its purpose is to deactivate the event handlers for the mouse and keyboard. For the mouse event handler, this is done by calling function $0000 of the mouse driver, which resets the mouse. This also automatically deactivates the event handler.

The keyboard handler KbHandler is deactivated by again entering the address of the original handler in the proper interrupt vector in the Interrupt Vector Table.

The memory blocks allocated on the heap for the two event queues are also freed. However, theoretically, this isn't necessary. The heap is automatically cleared when the program is ended. It is usually a good idea to have programs clean up after themselves.

```
{**************************************************************************}
{*   KbmEnd: called to end use of the functions and procedures of the   *}
{*           mouse module                                               *}
{**--------------------------------------------------------------------**}
{*   Info:   - this procedure does not have to be explicitly called from *}
{*             the application program since the procedure KbmInit defines *}
{*             it as the Exit procedure                                  *}
{**************************************************************************}

{$F+}                        { must be FAR to be called as Exit procedure }

procedure KbmEnd;

var Regs : Registers;        { processor register for interrupt call }

begin
  MouHideMouse;                     { hide mouse pointer from screen }
  Regs.AX := 0;                          { reset mouse driver }
  Intr( $33, Regs);                      { call mouse driver }

  Dispose( KbQueueP );            { dispose of keyboard queue }
  Dispose( MouQueueP );              { dispose of mouse queue }

  FreeMem( BufPtr, BLen );              { free allocated memory }
  SetIntVec( $09, OldKBHandler );   { restore old keyboard handler }
  ExitProc := ExitOld;         { re-install old exit procedure }
end;

{$F-}                                    { disable FAR procedure }
```

Before discussing the demo program KBMDEMO.PAS, we need to look at the assembler module KBMA.ASM. This contains the new interrupt handler for interrupt $09 and the event handler for the mouse. Each of these is responsible for calling the corresponding Pascal routines. The module saves the processor registers and loads the parameter to be added on the stack. Also, it must ensure that the DS register is loaded with the segment address of the proper Turbo Pascal data segment. The handlers cannot assume that this register always points to the correct Turbo Pascal segment. This is definitely true for the mouse handler, and it leaves no room for doubt when applied to the new keyboard handler.

Also, note the different commands used to end the two handlers. The keyboard handler is a true interrupt handler and can only end with the IRET command. The mouse handler is a FAR procedure so it can end with a normal RET command.

```
;****************************************************************************;
;*                          K B M A . A S M                               *;
;*------------------------------------------------------------------------*;
;*    Task           : Assembler module for the KBM unit                  *;
;*------------------------------------------------------------------------*;
;*    Author         : MICHAEL TISCHER                                     *;
;*    developed on   : 06/01/1989                                          *;
;*    last update    : 06/03/1989                                          *;
;*------------------------------------------------------------------------*;
;*    assembly       : TASM KBMA       or                                 *;
;*                     MASM KBMA;                                          *;
;*                     ... KBM unit will access assembled OBJ file         *;
;****************************************************************************;

;== Data segment ===========================================================

DATA    segment word public

extrn  OldKbHandler : dword         ;Address of old Int 09 handler

DATA    ends

;== Program ================================================================

CODE    segment byte public         ;Program segment

        assume CS:CODE               ;CS points to the code segment. Contents
                                     ;of DS, SS and ES are unknown

public      NewMouHandler            ;gives the Turbo Pascal program the
public      NewKbHandler             ;option of supplying the address of the
                                     ;assembler handler

extrn       MouEventHandler : near   ;Turbo Pascal event handler to be called
extrn       KbHandler       : near   ;Keyboard handler to be called

;--------------------------------------------------------------------------
;-- NewMouHandler: Event handler first called by the mouse driver, used for
;--                calling the Turbo Pascal MouEventHandler procedure
;-- Call from TP : Not allowed!

NewMouHandler proc far

            push ax                  ;Get processor registers
```

```
            push bx
            push cx
            push dx
            push di
            push si
            push bp
            push es
            push ds

            ;-- Place arguments for calling the Turbo Pascal function -------
            ;-- onto the stack
            ;-- Call:
            ;--    MouEventHandler (EvFlags, ButStatus, x , y : integer );

            push ax              ;Place event flags on the stack
            push bx              ;Place mouse button status on the stack

            mov  di,cx           ;Place horizontal coordinate in DI
            mov  cl,3            ;Loop counter for coordinate number

            shr  di,cl           ;Divide DI (horizontal coord.) by 8
            push di              ;and place on the stack

            shr  dx,cl           ;Divide DX (vertical coord.) by 8
            push dx              ;and place on the stack

            mov  ax,DATA         ;Move segment address of data segment
            mov  ds,ax           ;AX into the DS register

            call MouEventHandler ;Call the Turbo Pascal procedure

            ;-- Get needed registers from stack ----------------------------

            pop  ds
            pop  es
            pop  bp
            pop  si
            pop  di
            pop  dx
            pop  cx
            pop  bx
            pop  ax

            ret                  ;Return to mouse driver

NewMouHandler endp

;-------------------------------------------------------------------------
;-- NewKbHandler: New keyboard handler, called by interrupt 09h to call the
;--               Turbo Pascal KbHandler procedure
;-- Call from TP :Not allowed!

NewKbHandler proc far
```

```
        sti                     ;Enable interrupt call
        push ax                 ;Get processor registers
        push bx
        push cx
        push dx
        push di
        push si
        push bp
        push es
        push ds

        in   al,60h             ;Read scan code from keyboard and
        xor  ah,ah              ;push onto stack as argument for
        push ax                 ;calling KbHandler

        mov  ax,DATA            ;Segment address of data segment AX
        mov  ds,ax              ;Place AX in the DS register

        assume ds:data

        pushf                   ;Simulate interrupt call to old
        call [OldKbHandler]     ;interrupt handler

        ;-- Place arguments needed for calling Turbo Pascal function ----
        ;-- on the stack
        ;-- Call:
        ;--    KbHandler( KbPort : byte );

        call  KbHandler         ;Call Turbo Pascal procedure

        assume ds:nothing

        ;-- get needed registers from stack ----------------------------

        pop  ds
        pop  es
        pop  bp
        pop  si
        pop  di
        pop  dx
        pop  cx
        pop  bx
        pop  ax

        iret                    ;Return to interrupted program

NewKbHandler endp

;-----------------------------------------------------------------------

CODE    ends                    ;End of code segment
        end                     ;End of program
```

The demo program KBMDEMO.PAS illustrates the use of the many procedures and functions of the KBM unit. It centers around a window that records all incoming events. This allows you to see exactly which events are triggered by the mouse and keyboard. Depending on what kind of keyboard you have, there may be several EV_KEY_UNKNOWN events, especially if you press and hold the <Shift> or <Ctrl> keys. The keyboard continues to send the make code for these keys but it is only recognized as a status change the first time the code is received.

KBMDEMO starts by declaring a structure with the screen colors. Two standard constants of this type are created. These store the colors that will be used during the program execution for mono and color mode. This method was already used in the WIN unit to orient the program to the available video system.

```
{***********************************************************************
*   KbmDemo: demonstrates the functions and procedures for reading the   *
*            mouse and keyboard contained in the KBM unit                *
**-------------------------------------------------------------------**
*   Author        : MICHAEL TISCHER                                    *
*   developed on   : 06/20/1989                                        *
*   last update on : 02/23/1990                                        *
***********************************************************************}

uses Kbm, Win;

{-- Type declarations ------------------------------------------------}

type Colors = record                          { colors for text output }
               TI,                                           { title }
               BL,                                       { info line }
               BG,                                { screen background }
               FR,                                    { border color }
               MO  : byte;                 { window color during movement }
             end;

{-- typed constants --------------------------------------------------}

const MonoColors  : Colors = ( TI : $78; BL : $70; BG : $07;
                               FR : $70; MO : $0F );

      ColorColors : Colors = ( TI : RED   shl 4 + WHITE;
                               BL : CYAN  shl 4 + YELLOW;
                               BG : BLUE  shl 4 + WHITE;
                               FR : CYAN  shl 4 + WHITE;
                               MO : RED   shl 4 + YELLOW );

{-- global variables -------------------------------------------------}

var ev     : EVENT;                          { stores current event }
    Handle : integer;              { window handle for the event window }
    i      : integer;                            { loop counter }
    F      : Colors;
```

The screen is assembled in the main program. Then the procedure Mover is declared as the event handler for all events of type EV_KEY_STATUS by calling KbmRegisterHandler. This procedure will then be called whenever the program encounters an event of this type with the KbmEventWait procedure. This means that Mover will be called whenever the user presses <Shift>, <Ctrl> or <Num Lock>.

After this handler is registered, the main program enters a loop that will only end if the <Enter> key is pressed. KbmEventWait is called, and all types of events are entered in the global variable ev. The type of event is evaluated with a case statement and the event information from the EVENT record is displayed on screen.

The screen is cleared and the program ends after <Enter> is pressed.

```
{**************************************************************************
*  Mouse: display mouse events in the event window                       *
**----------------------------------------------------------------------**
*  Input   : Name = name of the event (9 characters)                     *
*            Ev   = event record with event data                         *
**************************************************************************}

procedure Mouse( Name : string; Ev : EVENT );

begin
  with Ev do                                  { display mouse event data }
    write( Name, ' | Pos.: (', AbsColumn:2, '/',
           Abs_Row:2, ') Rng.: ', Range:3,
           ' Buttons: ', Buttons );
end;

{**************************************************************************
*                       M A I N   P R O G R A M                          *
**************************************************************************}

begin
  {-- Define mouse area and appearance of mouse pointer ------------------}

  MouSetMoveArea( 0, 1, 79, 23 );
  MouDefinePtr( MouPTrMask( PtrDifChar( 24 ), PtrInvCol  ));;

  {-- Create screen and event window -------------------------------------}

  WinHideCursor;                                           { hide pointer }
  if Color then F := ColorColors                           { set colors }
           else F := MonoColors;

  WinFill ( VL( 0), VO( 1), VR( 0), VU( 0), #250, F.BG );
  WinFill ( VL( 0), VO( 0), VR( 0), VO( 0), ' ', F.TI );
  WinFill ( VL( 0), VU( 0), VR( 0), VU( 0), ' ', F.BL );
  WinPrint( VL(22), VO(0), F.TI, 'KBMDEMO - (c) 1989 by Michael Tischer');
  WinPrint( VL( 2), VU(0), F.BL,
```

```
              '└'#16' = End    |  Break = Move window');
Handle := WinOpenShadow( VL(10), VO( 5), VR(-4), VU(-5) );
WinFill ( VL(01), VO(01), VR(-1), VU(-1), ' ', F.FR );
WinFrame( VL( 0), VO( 0), VR(0), VU(0), DBL_FR, F.FR );
WinPrint( VL(10), VO( 0), F.FR, '═══════════╤');
WinPrint( VL(10), VU( 0), F.FR, '═══════════╧');
WinPrint( VL( 3), VO( 1), F.FR, ' Time   |   Event    | Description ');
WinPrint( VL( 0), VO( 2), F.FR, '╟───────────────┼───────────────┤' );
WinPrint( VL(23), VO( 2), F.FR, WinStRep('─', 42 ) );
WinPrint( VR( 0), VO( 2), F.FR, '╢' );
for i := 3 to 13 do
  WinPrint( VL(10), VO( i), F.FR, '|             |');
WinSetView( VL( 1), VO( 3), VR(-1), VU(-1) );
GotoXY( VL(0), VO(-1) );
TextColor( F.FR and $0F );
TextBackGround( F.FR shr 4 );
MouShowMouse;                                      { show mouse pointer }

{-- Call Mover procedure when a status (toggle) key is pressed ----------}

KbmRegisterHandler( EV_KEY_STATUS, Mover );

{-- Event loop -----------------------------------------------------------}
repeat
  KbmEventWait( EV_ALL, ev );                      { accept all events }
  MouHideMouse;                                    { hide mouse pointer }
  with ev do                              { process event structure }
    begin                          { convey event and display event data }
      writeln;
      write( Time:8, ' | ' );
      case EvntCode of
        EV_KEY_PRESSED :                          { a key code was received }
          begin
            write( 'KEY      | Code : ', Key:3 );
            if ( ( Key >= 32 ) and ( Key <=255 ) ) then
              write( ' (''', chr( Key ), ''')' )
            else
              if ( Key > 255 ) then
                write( ' (extended key code)'        );
          end;

        EV_KEY_UNKNOWN :        { a scan code was received that could not }
          begin                 { be converted to a keyboard code        }
            write( 'SCANCODE | Code : ', ScanCode:3 );
            write( ' (no key code generated)' );
          end;

        EV_KEY_STATUS :                          { status (toggle) key pressed }
          begin
            write( ' STATUS  |   Status key : ' );
            case StateKey of
              KEY_RIGHT_SHIFT : write( 'right Shift key');
              KEY_LEFT_SHIFT  : write( 'left Shift key');
```

283

```
                    KEY_CTRL          : write( 'Ctrl key');
                    KEY_ALT           : write( 'Alt key');
                    KEY_SCROLL_LOCK   : write( 'Scroll Lock' );
                    KEY_NUM_LOCK      : write( 'Num Lock');
                    KEY_CAPS_LOCK     : write( 'Caps Lock');
                 end;
               end;

            {-- Mouse events ------------------------------------------------}

            EV_MOU_MOVE    : Mouse( 'M_MOVE   ', ev );
            EV_LEFT_PRESS  : Mouse( 'M_LEFT_P ', ev );
            EV_RIGHT_PRESS : Mouse( 'M_RIGHT_P', ev );
            EV_LEFT_REL    : Mouse( 'M_LEFT_R ', ev );
            EV_RIGHT_REL   : Mouse( 'M_RIGHT_R', ev );

         end;
       MouShowMouse;
     end;
  until  ( (ev.EvntCode = EV_KEY_PRESSED)  and  (ev.Key = CR) );
  MouHideMouse;                                       { hide mouse pointer }
  WinClose( TRUE );                                   { close window }
  WinSetCursor(0, 0);
  WinFill( VL(0), VO(1), VR(0), VU(0), ' ', $7 );
end.
```

Pressing the <Shift><Break> or the <Ctrl><Break> keys (depending on your system) while the main program is reading events produces surprising results. Not only does the event window change colors but no more events will be displayed—even if you continue to press keys or move the mouse. The program will only react to the cursor keys now, which can be used to move the event window to a new location.

Once you press the <Enter> key, the event window will return to its previous color and continue to display new events.

Stopping the program with <Break> in order to move the window is a mechanism you may recognize from programs like the Turbo Pascal debugger. This process executes every time the keyboard must be read.

This program accomplishes this by registering a handler for the event EV_KEY_STATUS and is the type of event generated when the <Break> keys are pressed. This handler calls the procedure Mover which takes over any further keyboard queries and allows the window to be moved.

```
{**************************************************************************
*  Mover: called by KbmEventWait when a status (toggle) key is pressed    *
**----------------------------------------------------------------------**
*  Input   : EvRec = event that led to the call of this procedure         *
**************************************************************************}

{$f+}              { must be FAR because it is called by a procedure pointer }

procedure Mover( var EvRec : EVENT );

const InMover : boolean = FALSE;                         { Mover already active? }

var Ev      : EVENT;                                  { used for reading events }
    Column,                           { coordinates of upper left corner of window }
    W_Row   : byte;

begin
  if ( (EvRec.StateKey = KEY_SCROLL_LOCK) and not( InMover ) ) then
    begin                      { SCROLL LOCK pressed, not already in Mover }
      InMover := TRUE;                                  { Mover now active }
      KbmReleaseMode( KEY_SCROLL_LOCK );               { release SCROLL LOCK }
      Column  := VL(0) - 1;                    { calculate coordinates of   }
      W_Row   := VO(0) - 3;                    { upper left corner of window }
      MouHideMouse;                                    { hide mouse pointer }
      WinColor( Column, W_Row, VR(1), VU(1), F.MO );   { invert window }
      MouShowMouse;                            { display mouse pointer again }
      repeat                                                { input loop }
        KbmEventWait( EV_KEY_PRESSED, Ev );              { wait for a key }
        MouHideMouse;                                { hide mouse pointer }
        case Ev.Key of                                       { read key }
          CUP : if W_Row <> 1 then            { window already in top line? }
                  begin                                      { no, move up }
                    WinMoveUp( 1 );
                    dec( W_Row );
                  end;

          CLEFT : if ( Column <> 0 ) then          { window in left border? }
                    begin                                  { no, move left }
                      WinMoveLeft( 1 );
                      dec( Column );
                    end;

          CRIGHT : if ( Column < 12 ) then        { window in right border? }
                     begin                               { no, move right }
                       WinMoveRight( 1 );
                       inc( Column );
                     end;

          CDOWN : if ( W_Row < 8 ) then         { window in bottom border? }
                    begin                         { no, move down one line }
                      WinMoveDown( 1 );
                      inc( W_Row );
                    end;
```

```
        end;

        MouShowMouse;                              { display mouse pointer again }
      until ( Ev.Key = CR );          { repeat until the Enter key is pressed }
      MouHideMouse;                                     { hide mouse pointer }
      WinColor( Column, W_Row, VR(1), VU(1), F.FR );   { make window normal }
      MouShowMouse;                              { display mouse pointer again }
      EvRec.EvntCode := EV_NO_EVENT;                { suppress original key }
      InMover := FALSE;                                      { not in Mover }
    end;
  end;

  {$f-}
```

Mover starts by checking the event to see if the <Shift><Break> or <Ctrl><Break> keys were pressed and if Mover is already active. The procedure cannot be called again if it is already active.

If the key was <Break> and Mover is not already active a call to KbmReleaseMode frees the Break mode again. Then the event window changes color as defined in the color structure. The read loop that follows evaluates all keys pressed and continues until <Enter> is pressed. If a cursor key is encountered one of the WinMoveXXXX procedures is used to move the window, providing it isn't already at an edge of the screen.

After <Enter> is pressed, the window returns to its normal color and control is returned to the calling routine. The event constant EV_NO_EVENT is entered in the EvntCode field of the EVENT record that is passed back so that the <Break> key is not output to the event window.

Using event handlers from other programs is a powerful technique. Another use of event handlers is to create a macro recorder. With every event of type EV_KEY_PRESSED, the key could be compared with a specified key which triggers the recording of the subsequent series of keys. All keys could be recorded until the key code signaling the end of the recording is received.

There are also many other ways to use event handlers to make the KBM unit an even more powerful and flexible tool for reading the mouse and keyboard.

8.   Using GOTO with Turbo Pascal

Although it is sometimes necessary, using GOTO can create some frustrating problems.

The Turbo Pascal GOTO command can only be used within a procedure or function. It often can be avoided by using IF-THEN-ELSE. It would be better to have a GOTO command that can work outside a single procedure or function. While Pascal has no such command, the C language has two functions, SETJMP and LONGJMP, for this purpose.

Being able to use a GOTO this way is very helpful for jumping out of deeply nested loops or recursions if there is an error that requires program termination or termination of the current operation. Without the ability to directly react to the error with a GOTO, each function or procedure must notify its calling routine of the error until the notification reaches the top level and can be processed. Programming a mechanism to handle all of this is rather complex. Using a procedure-external GOTO would be more efficient.

Let's look at a *parser*—a program that automatically interprets and converts character strings. Parsers are useful in applications such as the Turbo Pascal compiler. They can work themselves into deeper and deeper recursions while processing the source text. If an error is found within the lower levels of a recursion, the parser execution must end with an error message. It would be too complicated to resolve this level by level, recursion by recursion, until you reached the top level of the program where the error could be handled.

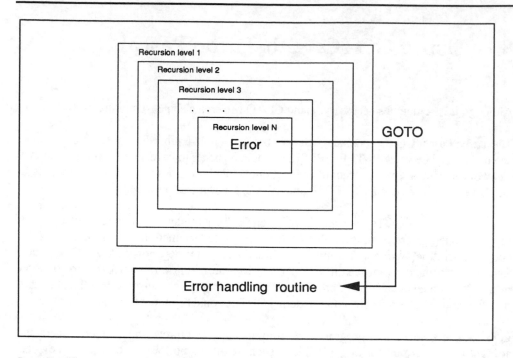

Reaction to an error within nested recursions calls using a procedure-external GOTO

The procedure-external GOTO is also useful for quickly exiting from errors encountered during access to external devices, such as printers or disk drives.

8.1   The FARJMP Unit

Unfortunately, procedure-external GOTOs cannot be performed with the Pascal GOTO command, which only works within a given function or procedure. It would take major revisions deep within the source code of the Turbo Pascal compiler to make this possible.

Since this isn't very practical, we'll present a procedure-external GOTO that can be executed with the help of two procedures similar to those found in the run time library of a C compiler. Before we look at these two procedures, which make up the FARJMP unit, refer to this example program to see how they work.

This example accesses an external device and uses the most direct way to exit to the error handling routine when errors occur. Here is the listing for FJDEMO.PAS.

```
{***********************************************************************
*   FJDEMO : Demonstrates the use of the procedures SetJmp and LongJmp from *
*            the FARJMP unit.                                          *
*            A typical program execution is simulated. Data is loaded from  *
*            a file into memory where it is processed and then written back *
*            to the file. During one of the three times the data is   *
*            processed, an error occurs. The program moves to the error     *
*            handling routine using LongJmp.                           *
**-------------------------------------------------------------------**
*   Author        : MICHAEL TISCHER                                    *
*   developed on  : 06/24/1989                                        *
*   last update on : 02/26/1990                                       *
***********************************************************************}

program FJDEMO;

uses FarJmp;                                          { add FarJmp unit }

const ErrMes : array [1..3] of string =
  ( '(LoadFile) : File not found       ',
    '(EditFile) : Incorrect file format',
    '(SaveFile) : Write access not possible' );

var ErrJmp  : JMPBUF;                        { jump buffer for error case }
    ErrCode : integer;                { error code on return from SetJmp }
    ErrProc : integer;                { procedure that simulates an error }


{***********************************************************************
*   LoadFile : Load a file                                            *
***********************************************************************}

procedure LoadFile;

begin
  if ErrProc = 2 then LongJmp( ErrJmp, 1 );
```

```
end;

{******************************************************************************
*  EditFile : Edit the file just loaded                                       *
******************************************************************************}

procedure EditFile;

begin
  if ErrProc = 0 then LongJmp( ErrJmp, 2 );
end;

{******************************************************************************
*  SaveFile: Save the edited file                                             *
******************************************************************************}

procedure SaveFile;

begin
  if ErrProc = 1 then LongJmp( ErrJmp, 3 );
end;

{******************************************************************************
*  Process: Control program execution                                         *
******************************************************************************}

procedure Process;

begin
  LoadFile;
  EditFile;
  SaveFile;
end;

{******************************************************************************
*                        M A I N   P R O G R A M                              *
******************************************************************************}

begin
  Randomize;                           { select processing step in which the }
  ErrProc := Random( 2 );              { error should occur                   }

  writeln('FJDEMO - (c) 1989 by Michael Tischer'#13#10);
  ErrCode := SetJmp( ErrJmp );
  if ( ErrCode = NOJMP ) then                              { call LongJmp? }
    Process                                      { no, execute program }
  else                          { LongJmp was called, an error has occurred }
    writeln( 'Error during ', ErrMes[ ErrCode ], '!' );
end.
```

A procedure-external GOTO, implemented with the FARJMP unit, uses two steps. The first step is the SetJmp function call at the point in the program to which the GOTO will return.

Note: You cannot simply enter a call to this function at the corresponding location in the code. Only after this call has been executed at run time is the location known so that a jump can later be made. This is because the address of the proper program line and other parameters can only be established at run time.

In this example, SetJmp is called from the main program. The function must receive a variable of type JMPBUF. This is declared in the FARJMP unit. SetJmp stores the information required to execute the GOTO in the variable ErrJmp.

When called, SetJmp returns the code NOJMP to indicate the program reached its destination without error. A code other than NOJMP is found if the program returns to this line from a GOTO by the LongJmp procedure.

The code is evaluated to distinguish between a normal SetJump call and the return through a LongJmp. The code is then loaded in the global variable ErrCode. If it doesn't equal NOJMP, then the error code is passed to the routine that called SetJmp. This code represents an index in the array ErrMes which contains the various error messages in the form of strings.

If the program determines that the call wasn't made using LongJmp, the procedure Process is called. This controls the subsequent program flow by calling three procedures that load a file, process and then save the data.

These three procedures are actually dummies. Their sole responsibility is to produce an error and use LongJmp to jump to the error handling routine. The variable ErrProc determines which of these three procedures generates the error. The main program will randomly select which variable will generate the error.

By calling LongJmp, the program execution is transferred to the point stored by SetJmp, in the variable JMPBUF. In this program line, LongJmp returns to the point where the function result of SetJmp was previously assigned to the variable ErrCode. This time the error code is passed and does not equal -1 which represents NOJMP.

It may not be clear why a variable of type JMPBUF must also be passed with a call to LongJmp. The FARJMP unit could use an internal variable to keep this information. However, you wouldn't be able to choose between different jump lines simply by creating several variables of this type and calling SetJmp to load each with a different jump location.

No assembler routines are involved although it seems like there is some detailed internal programming involved in keeping track of jumping back and forth. To use SetJmp and LongJmp, you must know the following three things (more information is in Chapter 2):

- How the procedures and functions are arranged internally.

- The way parameters are passed.

- The way function results are returned.

The trick with SetJmp and LongJmp isn't in saving the address of a program line and then going to that line with the Assembler command JMP. The important thing is to return the stack to its original condition after a return jump with LongJmp. A number of return addresses, parameters and local variables collect on the stack as a result of previous subroutine calls. If these aren't removed, there could be a stack overrun during calls to subsequent procedures or functions.

To remove these return addresses, parameters and local variables, the SP register is needed. After LongJmp is executed, this register must point to the stack position it did before the SetJmp call. The BP register must also be restored to its original value. If this isn't done, the reactivated procedure or function won't be able to access its local variables or parameters. This is accomplished in the FARJMP unit.

The constant NOJMP and the structure JMPBUF are declared in the header and the interface part of the unit. The contents of JMPBUF represents the contents of the processor registers CS, IP, BP and SP.

```
{*********************************************************************
 * F A R J M P : A unit that implements a procedure-external GOTO using    *
 *               two procedures - SETJMP and LONGJMP.                      *
 **-----------------------------------------------------------------**
 * Author          : MICHAEL TISCHER                                       *
 * developed on     : 06/24/1989                                           *
 * last update on   : 02/26/1990                                           *
 *********************************************************************}

unit FARJMP;

interface

{-- public constants -------------------------------------------------}

const NOJMP = -1;                    { return did not occur via a LongJmp call }

{-- public type declarations ----------------------------------------}

type JMPBUF = record                 { this type stores the information }
```

```
                  BP,                    { required for the return jump    }
                  SP,
                  CS,                    { the order must not be changed! }
                  IP  : word;
               end;
```

```
{-- declaration of functions and procedures that can be called by ---------}
{-- other applications                                          ---------}
```

```
function  SetJmp ( var JB : JMPBUF ) : integer;
procedure LongJmp( JB : JMPBUF; RetCode : integer );
```

```
implementation
```

SetJmp must be called before LongJmp because it is the first of the two procedures from this unit to be executed. SetJmp's job is to save the return address to the calling routine, the contents of the BP register at the time it is called and the contents of the SP register before it is called. It saves this information in the JMPBUF structure that is passed to it. Some of this information can only be obtained from the stack, so the structure of the stack at the time SetJmp is called is included as a comment.

```
{***********************************************************************
*  SetJmp : sets the point in the program to which the LongJmp procedure  *
*           will jump                                                     *
**---------------------------------------------------------------------**
*  Input   : JB : a data structure of type JumpBuf which contains the     *
*                 information needed for the jump                         *
*  Output  : NOJMP if the return occurs from this function -              *
*            any other value indicates the return jump was via LongJmp    *
***********************************************************************}
```

```
function SetJmp( var JB : JMPBUF ) : integer;
```

```
type WordP  = ^word;                               { pointer to a word }
```

```
begin
```

```
    {---- when this program line is reached the stack has this structure ----}
    {                                                                        }
    {  |                                     |       [ SP + $0C ]            }
    {  |-------------------------------------|                               }
    {  |  Address of the JMPBUF structure    |                               }
    {  |- that was passed when SetJmp was   -|                               }
    {  |  called (FAR pointer)               |       [ SP + $08 ]            }
    {  |-------------------------------------|                               }
    {  |  return address to calling routine  |                               }
    {  |- as a FAR pointer                  -|       [ SP + $04 ]            }
    {  |-------------------------------------|                               }
    {  |  contents of the BP register at the |                               }
    {  |  time this procedure was called     | <--- BP  [ SP + $02 ]        }
```

```
{  |--------------------------------------------------|              }
{  |   reserved memory for storing the                |              }
{  |   function result                                | <--- SP  [ SP + $00 ]  }
{  |--------------------------------------------------|              }
{  |                                                  |              }
{  |                                                  |              }
{--------------------------------------------------------------------}
```

```
{- store the return address of the calling routine, the former contents -}
{- of the BP register                                                   -}

JB.BP := WordP( ptr( SSeg, Sptr+2) )^;
JB.IP := WordP( ptr( SSeg, Sptr+4) )^;
JB.CS := WordP( ptr( SSeg, Sptr+6) )^;

{- SP must point to the position on the stack where LongJmp will store --}
{- the new contents of the BP register and the return address         --}

JB.SP := Sptr + 12 - 6 - 6;

  SetJmp := NOJMP;                    { show that this is not a LongJmp call }
end;
```

On top of the stack is a pointer to the JMPBUF structure that is passed to SetJmp when it is called. Since this parameter is given as a variable and not as a value, Turbo Pascal passes a pointer to the structure rather than the structure itself. After this pointer is the return address of the calling routine which was placed on the stack by the processor when the CALL command was executed. Next are the contents of the BP register at the time the procedure was called. In Chapter 2 we mentioned that every Turbo Pascal procedure or function automatically saves the contents of the BP register on the stack so that you can retrieve the contents of this register unchanged. The final stack element is an automatically created local variable that will accept the function result. The stack pointer points to the start of this variable on the stack.

The return address to the calling routine and the prior contents of the BP register can only be obtained by reading their values from the stack. This is not a problem since the structure and the contents of the stack are known and Turbo Pascal can get the segment address and the current offset address of the stack from the SP register.

All three cases start by creating a generic pointer to the desired stack location using the Ptr function. Since one Word is read from the stack in each case, the pointer is converted to type WordP. This type was declared within the function specifically for this purpose. The desired information can be read from the stack by referencing this pointer.

The SP register is handled differently than the CS, IP and BP registers. LongJmp will later be called by this JMPBUF structure. It expects the component SP to contain the address where it should put the return address and the original contents of the BP register on the stack.

Before the call to SetJmp, SP points 12 bytes beyond the position it will contain during the execution of SetJmp. The SP register must be assigned the value Sptr+12-6-6 since LongJmp needs 2x6 bytes on the stack.

After SetJmp loads the values into each component of the JMPBUF structure, it returns the constant NOJMP as its function result to indicate a SetJmp call and then returns to the calling routine.

```
{********************************************************************
*  LongJmp : a procedure-external GOTO that continues program execution  *
*            at the program from which SetJmp was called                 *
**----------------------------------------------------------------**
*  Input   : JB      : jump buffer containing the address of the program  *
*                      line given by SetJmp - this is where program       *
*                      execution will be continued                        *
*            RetCode : function result returned by the subsequent SetJmp  *
*                      call                                               *
********************************************************************}

procedure LongJmp( JB : JMPBUF; RetCode : integer );

type WordP  = ^word;                              { pointer to a word }

begin
   {--- when this program line is reached, the stack has this structure ----}
   {                                                                        }
   {  |                                    |                                }
   {  +------------------------------------+                                }
   {  | address of the JMPBUF structure    |                                }
   {  +-| that was passed when this procedure -|                           }
   {  | was called (FAR pointer)            |       [ SP + $10 ]            }
   {  |                                    |                                }
   {  +------------------------------------+                                }
   {  | RetCode parameter that was passed   |                                }
   {  | when this procedure was called      |       [ SP + $0E ]            }
   {  +------------------------------------+                                }
   {  | return address to calling routine   |                                }
   {  +-|                                  -|                               }
   {  | as a FAR pointer                    |       [ SP + $0A ]            }
   {  +------------------------------------+                                }
   {  | contents of the BP register at the  |                                }
   {  | time this procedure was called      | <--- BP  [ SP + $08 ]         }
   {  +------------------------------------+                                }
   {  | local copy of passed JmpBuf structure |                              }
   {  |      Component  IP                  |       [ BP - $02 ]            }
   {  +--                               -- |                               }
   {  |                                    |                                }
   {  |      Component  CS                  |       [ BP - $04 ]            }
```

```
{    ┌────                          ─┐                              }
{    │                               │                              }
{    │   Component  SP               │          [ BP - $06 ]        }
{    ├────                          ─┤                              }
{    │                               │                              }
{    │   Component  BP               │ <--- SP  [ BP - $08 ]        }
{    ├────                          ─┤                              }
{    │                               │                              }
{                                                                   }
{-------------------------------------------------------------------}
```

```
{-- manipulate the return address of the calling routine of the stack ---}
{-- in order to return to the caller of SetJmp                        ---}


WordP( ptr( SSeg, JB.SP   ) )^ := JB.BP;
WordP( ptr( SSeg, JB.SP+2 ) )^ := JB.IP;
WordP( ptr( SSeg, JB.Sp+4 ) )^ := JB.CS;


{-- load the passed return code in the AX register to simulate the ------}
{-- function result of SetJmp                                     ------}

inline( $8b / $46 / $06 );                              { mov ax,[bp+6] }

inline( $8b / $ae / $fa / $ff );                        { mov bp,[bp-6] }

{ mov    sp,bp        ;the compiler generates these commands          }
{ pop    bp           ;automatically in order to restore the stack    }
{ ret    6            ;                                                }
end;


{**-------------------------------------------------------------------**}
{** Starting code of the unit                                        **}
{**-------------------------------------------------------------------**}

begin                                 { no initialization is required }
end.
```

As in SetJmp, the stack is also manipulated in LongJmp, so the contents of the stack before the function call are listed.

At the top section of the stack for LongJmp is a pointer to the JMPBUF structure that was passed as a parameter. With SetJmp, only a pointer to this structure was placed on the stack because the parameter was passed as a variable. In this case, LongJmp receives this parameter as a value. Since it exceeds the maximum limit of 4 bytes for compound types, Turbo Pascal doesn't pass the structure on the stack but instead passes a pointer to LongJmp.

The error code to be returned comes after this pointer. This is followed by the return address of the calling routine and the original contents of the BP register. Also included is a local copy of the passed JMPBUF structure. This is created before the execution of the first Pascal command in LongJmp.

It is LongJmp's responsibility to take the address of the original SetJmp caller and the contents of its BP register from the passed JMPBUF structure and put them on the stack. This automatically brings Turbo Pascal back to the original caller after the procedure ends. However, this information can't be written to the current position on the stack. It must be entered at the position indicated by the JMPBUF component SP.

The original contents of BP are entered at this location, followed by the return address to the routine that called SetJmp. This operation moves the stack pointer six bytes closer to its destination. This represents the first six bytes in the expression "Sptr+12-6-6".

Before it is finished, LongJmp must ensure that the stack pointer points to the previously entered information. This is not yet true, since SP is now pointing to the local copy of the JMPBUF structure.

To take care of this, LongJmp uses a command, created by Turbo Pascal at the end of every procedure or function. In this sequence, Turbo Pascal sets SP to its old value by loading this register with the current contents of the BP register. The second step is to retrieve the original contents of BP from the stack. This is accomplished with the help of the first Inline command at the end of the LongJmp procedure. The desired location for the SP register is loaded from the JMPBUF structure into BP and from there into SP.

The second Inline command is used to help LongJmp simulate a function. The function result is the error code that is returned to the caller of SetJmp. If LongJmp were a true function, it would require the calling routine to have a variable or an expression to accept the function result. However, LongJmp doesn't return to its caller, so it must be set up as a procedure.

The second Inline command is used to load the "function result" (the error code) into the AX register. This is where the caller of SetJmp retrieves the function result.

LongJmp is ended with a RET 6 command. This doesn't return to the calling routine but only removes the passed parameter, which consists of 6 bytes, from the stack. This represents the second 6 bytes in the expression:

```
Sptr+12-6-6;
```

Even though a few tricks are needed to use the FARJMP unit, it performs the desired task.

9. More Memory for your Programs

Even though the capabilities of the PC hardware systems continue to expand, some applications haven't kept up with these changes because of memory limitations. Often the reason for this is the PC operating system itself. This operating mode, known as Real Mode, limits the amount of memory addressable by the processor to 1,048,576 locations, or 1 megabyte. A large amount of this must be reserved for the ROM BIOS, the video RAM, and other system expansions. This leaves only 640K for the actual RAM memory.

Very little consideration was given to future expansion when PCs were shipped with 64K or 128K of RAM. A PC with 256K was considered extravagant. The developers of MS-DOS probably were not alone in the belief that "no one will ever need more memory than 256K." However, as computers became more widely used in office and business environments, users quickly realized that their systems were running out of RAM (even with 640K). Now in the 1990s, memory has become a true limit for many users, especially in graphic or desktop publishing applications.

Two solutions to the memory problem have been developed: EMS (Expanded Memory Specification) according to the LIM standard, and extended memory. So, as a programmer you must learn how to use the various types of memory expansions if your program needs more RAM than is available. Unfortunately, programmers have discovered that neither of these offer a simple solution to memory limitations.

Even if your PC has an expansion card with 4 megabytes of memory, you cannot simply add this to the heap so that your Turbo Pascal programs can use it. This is because only parts of this memory can be accessed at once; the entire region isn't visible to your program. You must use techniques enabling you to work with extra memory but which may be unfamiliar.

Even though these two types of extra memory are fairly common, you cannot assume that every computer is able to use them. It's important to establish the type and amount of extra memory that your program requires before beginning development. If you're developing an application for a client, you'll need to know what types of hardware will be available before beginning. There's also the question of how much extra memory is available: 512K, 1 meg or even 8 megabytes. Typically the only time you can determine this information is when the program boots.

There are several factors to determine whether to use extended memory or EMS. They both have their strengths and weaknesses. Since each type of memory is accessed differently, it is very difficult to incorporate the use of both types of memory in one program.

9.1   Accessing Extended Memory

Extended memory is the continuation of RAM beyond the 1 megabyte limit. This divides the RAM into two regions which separates the ROM BIOS and the system expansions from each other.

While the conventional RAM below the 640K limit can be addressed by DOS, this isn't possible for extended memory. It exceeds the memory access limit of real mode; the 8086 and other chips of this family are confined to this limit. The 640K limit can be exceeded in Virtual Protected Mode. This mode is supported in 80286 and subsequent chips. DOS cannot run in this mode. The two modes, especially in addressing memory, are significantly different. This makes it possible to expand the addressable memory to 16 megabyte in Protected Mode.

The processor must briefly be switched from Real Mode to Protected Mode to access extended memory. This is why extended memory can only run on AT and 386 systems that support Protected Mode. PCs and XTs cannot use extended memory. You shouldn't write your program to use extended memory if it has to run on a PC or XT. You can, however, use Expanded Memory, which is also available to PCs and XTs.

Even extended memory may not be the best choice for ATs. Switching between Real Mode and Protected Mode takes time because the microprocessor does not have the ability to switch itself back from Protected Mode to Real Mode.

The BIOS, which controls access to extended memory, must be changed in order to return to the original operating mode. This involves a reset, which is executed through the keyboard controller.

PC systems that have a 386 processor don't have this problem. This chip completely supports extended memory. If, from the beginning, you know that your application will only run on 386 machines, then extended memory is clearly the best choice.

With the proper driver, extended memory can easily emulate expanded memory. This allows it to be used with many commercial software packages. To satisfy all the PC and XT users, commercial software developers generally support expanded memory rather than extended memory.

Extended memory is often installed directly on the motherboard, which usually has space for up to 8 megabytes. Extended memory can also be installed on an expansion card. There are many of these cards on the market. *Above Board* from Intel is perhaps the most popular.

The BIOS offers two functions, which are obtained using interrupt $15, for accessing extended memory. This interrupt was actually designed as a port to cassette tape drives. However, these routines became obsolete as disk drives quickly replaced cassette drives.

When the AT was introduced, the cassette routines were discarded and interrupt $15 was reassigned as a port to some new BIOS functions. But the name *cassette interrupt* remains.

One of the two functions for accessing extended memory is $88, which returns the size of the extended memory in Kbytes. It's called by passing the function number to the AH register. The result is returned to the AX register. If a result of 0 is returned no extended memory is installed and attempts to access this memory will fail.

It's also possible to receive a 0 if extended memory is installed but is being used by a device driver or a TSR program. Cache programs often use this memory to store sectors from a disk so they can be accessed without reading the disk again. This allows the access time of a hard disk to be tripled. RAM disks, such as the device driver VDISK (included with MS-DOS), also use extended memory.

Since an application that uses extended memory cannot immediately determine if a device driver or a TSR program is using the same memory, there can be conflicts over which one will use it. These conflicts usually end in a system crash and could possibly destroy data on your hard disk. This happens because the conflicting programs can overwrite data in extended memory, which could then be copied back to your hard disk. Unfortunately, the BIOS doesn't contain a memory manager for extended memory that can allocate and free given regions. Therefore, the competing programs must ensure that no collisions occur.

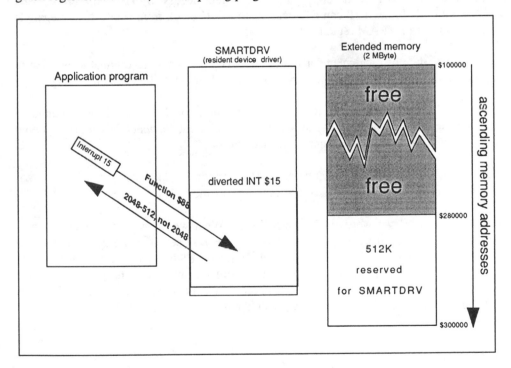

Reserving memory regions in extended memory

If you use cache programs, such as PC TOOLS, you may already be familiar with the following simple but effective trick. Reserve the required memory region at the end of the extended memory and protect it from being overwritten by diverting BIOS function $88 to a routine of your own. It returns the size of the portion that is still free instead of returning the actual size of the extended memory.

This tells other programs the extended memory, below what is occupied and above 1 megabyte (which is where extended memory starts by definition), is free to use. This prevents any collisions. Of course, not all TSR programs and device drivers handle the extended memory this way. For example, some programs take the memory required right from the start of extended memory, without protecting itself by diverting interrupt $15. Fortunately, it's possible for other programs to detect the presence of a RAM disk. But this is not true for all TSR programs and device drivers since a different test mechanism must be developed for each one. In some cases, it isn't even possible to test for the presence of the program. So, your program should inform users of this problem and give the appropriate instructions.

Another function of BIOS interrupt $15 is available for accessing Extended RAM. This is function $87. Although it allows copying memory regions above the 1 megabyte limit, each call to this function can copy only 64K. Direct access to extended memory isn't possible with this function. It can only read up to a 64K block from above the 1 megabyte limit and copy it to a RAM region below.

The block can then be manipulated and, if desired, copied back to its original location or to some other location in extended memory by using another call to function $87.

However, this isn't a simple function to call because the BIOS must be switched to Protected Mode. Let's take a closer look at this operating mode, which has helped open up the full capabilities of the 80286 and successive chips.

What distinguishes Protected Mode from Real Mode is not so much the processor commands but rather the method used for addressing memory.

Pointers consist of two words in Protected Mode. What we know as a segment address doesn't exist. Instead of the physical address of a memory segment, we get an index to a table known as the *descriptor table*. This table lists each segment, its location in memory, access privileges and size. This allows much more flexibility for the processor, since segment addresses can now begin at any location. Segment sizes can be assigned from 1K to 64K. Each entry in this segment table is called a *segment descriptor*. The following table shows its structure.

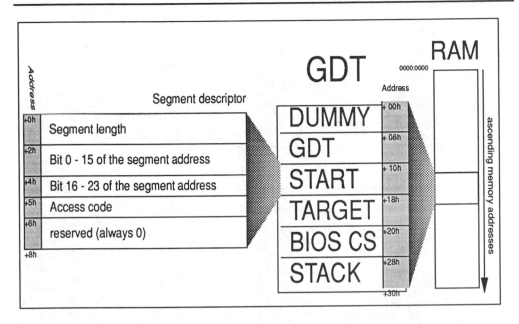

Structure of a segment descriptor in Protected Mode of the 80286 and subsequent processors

Notice that the base address of the segment within a segment descriptor is given as a 24-bit linear address and not as the usual segment/offset pair.

This allows a total of 16 megabytes to be addressed. For example, if a segment begins at the 1 megabyte limit, it will have the address $100000. Lower addresses are found in conventional RAM, video RAM or the ROM BIOS.

The processor recognizes several segment tables, the most important of which is the Global Descriptor Table (GDT). This table must exist, with a total of six entries, in memory and be initialized before function $87 is called.

Function $87 expects to receive a pointer to this table in register pair ES:DI. Also, the AH register must contain the function number and the CX register must contain the number of words to copy. Notice that the use of words means that only memory blocks with an even number of bytes can be copied. So, it is important to keep one extra byte free in the buffer in the data segment or on the heap in case the data to be copied has an uneven length and one extra byte must be copied. If you are working with data structures, you can easily get around this problem by adding a dummy field, which consists of one byte, to the end of the structure.

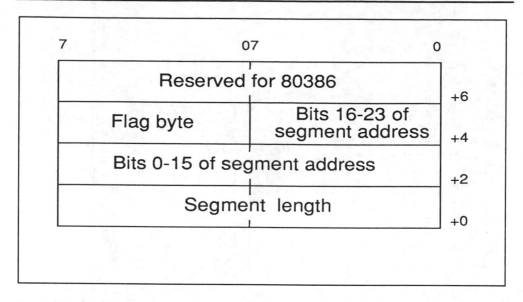

7	07	0	
Reserved for 80386			+6
Flag byte	Bits 16-23 of segment address		+4
Bits 0-15 of segment address			+2
Segment length			+0

Structure and order of the segment descriptor as expected by function $87

Of the six segment descriptors in the GDT, only the Start and the Target descriptors must be initialized before calling function $87. Start describes the memory segment from which you want to copy data and Target describes the data segment to which the data will be copied. Both must begin with the first byte of the corresponding memory block and must be at least large enough to hold the entire block to be copied. The access code is the value $92 which allows the BIOS to read and describe the segment.

With this background information, you should now be able to follow the workings of the EXT unit, which creates an efficient interface with extended memory.

```
{*******************************************************************
* E X T : a unit for accessing "Extended Memory" above the 1 meg memory  *
*          limit                                                    *
**---------------------------------------------------------------**
* Author        : MICHAEL TISCHER                                  *
* developed on   : 05/12/1989                                      *
* last update on : 02/27/1990                                      *
*******************************************************************}

unit EXT;

interface

uses DOS;

{----- declaration of global variables that can be read by other ----------}
{----- programs and units                                  ----------}
```

```
var ExtAvail : boolean;                          { Extended Memory available? }
    ExtStart : longint;   { start address of Extended Memory as linear add. }
    ExtLen   : integer;              { size of Extended Memory in kilobytes }

{-- declaration of functions and procedures that can be called by other ---}
{-- programs or units                                              ---}

function  ExtAdrConv( Adr : pointer ) : longint;
procedure ExtRead    ( ExtAdr : longint;  BuPtr : pointer;  Len : word );
procedure ExtWrite   ( BuPtr : pointer;  ExtAdr : longint;  Len : word );
```

The interface between your program and this unit consists of three global variables, two procedures and one function. All have the prefix "Ext" as part of their names to distinguish them as part of this unit. Each of the three variables are initialized before the program starts.

They are assigned the following values:

ExtAvail If TRUE, extended memory is available. If FALSE, either memory is not installed beyond the 1 megabyte limit or not available at all. Extended memory is occupied by other programs.

ExtStart Contains the linear start address of the extended memory (if it exists). Normally, this address is $100000, but it will be greater if a RAM disk of type VDISK is installed above the 1 megabyte limit. Here, as in the rest of the unit, the data type LongInt is used to store linear memory addresses. Although this type consists of four bytes, one byte more than is actually needed to represent a linear address, it offers the advantage of predefined arithmetic operations.

ExtLen Stores the size of the free extended memory in kilobytes.

What the Ext routines do will be explained in a moment. First, look at the data structures declared at the beginning of the implementation section of the unit.

```
implementation

{-- data structures for accessing the Extended RAM ----------------------}

type SDES = record                                      { segment descriptor }
               SLngth    : word;              { length of segment in bytes }
               AdrLow    : word;      { bits 0 to 15 of the segment address }
               AdrHigh   : byte;      { bits 16 to 23 of the segment address }
               Attribute : byte;                       { segment attribute }
               Res       : word;                      { reserved for 80386 }
            end;
```

```
     GDT  = record                                 { Global Descriptor Table }
              Dummy  : SDES;
              GDTS   : SDES;
              Start  : SDES;                               { copy from ... }
              Target : SDES;                               { ... to        }
              Code   : SDES;
              Stack  : SDES;
            end;

    LI = record                        { used to access the components of a }
           LoWord : word;              { LongInts that represents a 32 bit  }
           HiByte : byte;              { linear address                     }
           dummy  : byte;
         end;
```

To create the GDT required by function $87, first type SDES is declared. This type duplicates the structure of a segment descriptor. Type GDT is a structure that incorporates the six required segment descriptors.

The third type, LI, works with function $87 less directly. It supports the entry of linear addresses, in the form of a LongInt, into each segment descriptor. The LongInt is divided into a LO word and a HI byte, which is taken as the LO byte of the HI word. The HI byte of the HI word is removed because only three lower bytes, or 24 bits, are required to represent a linear address. In order for Turbo Pascal to allow a LongInt to be converted to a structure of type LI, LI must be the same size as a LongInt, or four bytes. Therefore, the highest byte is declared as a dummy variable.

The global variables just described are declared in the procedure ExtGetInfo. This procedure, inaccessible to external units and programs, is called during the initialization section of the EXT unit before the actual program start. Its most important and complex job is to determine whether a RAM disk created by VDISK already exists at the beginning of extended memory.

```
{******************************************************************************
 *  ExtGetInfo : obtains the start address and size of Extended RAM in       *
 *               consideration of any RAM disk which may be found            *
 **------------------------------------------------------------------------**
 *  Input   : none                                                           *
 *  Output  : none                                                           *
 *  Globals : ExtAvail/W, ExtStart/W, ExtLen/W                               *
 ******************************************************************************}

procedure ExtGetInfo;

type BOOT_SECTOR = record                          { boot sector of a RAM disk }
                     dummy1   : array [1..3] of byte;
                     Name     : array [1..8] of char;
                     BpS      : word;
                     dummy2   : array [1..6] of byte;
```

```
                    Sectors : word;
                    dummy3   : byte;                    { makes length even }
                end;

    var BootSec  : BOOT_SECTOR;                    { stores boot sector }
        LastOne  : boolean;                        { marks end of loop }
        Regs     : Registers;        { processor registers for interrupt call }

    begin
      {-- obtain size of Extended Memory, thereby establishing if Extended ----}
      {-- Memory is even available                                       ----}

      Regs.ah := $88;          { function no. for: "get size of Extended RAM" }
      intr( $15, Regs );                            { call cassette interrupt }
      if ( ( ( Regs.Flags and FCarry ) <> 0 ) or ( Regs.AX = 0 ) ) then
        begin                              { no Extended RAM available }
          ExtAvail := FALSE;
          ExtLen   := 0;
          ExtStart := 0;
          exit;                                        { return to caller }
        end;

      ExtAvail := TRUE;                        { Extended Memory available }
      ExtLen   := Regs.AX;            { Extended RAM available, store size }

      {-- search for RAM disks of type VDISK ------------------------------}

      ExtStart := $100000;                            { start at 1 meg }
      LastOne := FALSE;                               { assume RAM disk }
      repeat                                          { query loop }
        ExtRead( ExtStart, @BootSec, SizeOf( BootSec ) );
        with BootSec do
          begin
            if ( Name[1] = 'V' ) and            { 'VDISK' must be found }
               ( Name[2] = 'D' ) and            { in boot sector       }
               ( Name[3] = 'I' ) and
               ( Name[4] = 'S' ) and
               ( Name[5] = 'K' )
            then             { boot sector found, set address after RAM disk }
              inc( ExtStart, longint( Sectors ) * BpS )
            else
              LastOne := TRUE;                    { no more RAM disks found }
          end;
      until LastOne;

      {-- subtract size of RAM disks from total Extended Memory --------------}

      dec( ExtLen, integer( (ExtStart - longint($100000)) shr 10) );
    end;
```

A RAM disk can be identified by a specific data structure, called the *boot sector*, which precedes the RAM disk in memory. DOS expects to find a boot sector in the first sector of any storage medium, including hard disks and floppy disks. RAM disks are handled like any other storage medium so the boot sector will always precede a RAM disk in memory.

The type BOOT_SECTOR recreates the structure of a boot sector within the ExtGetInfo procedure. This type doesn't include all fields in a boot sector, which is actually 512 bytes long. Only the fields between the start of the boot sector and the last specified field are defined. All other fields are represented by dummy variables. The fields we are concerned with include Name, BpS and Sectors. You'll soon see how these fields help search for a RAM disk.

Before the procedure searches for boot sectors, the size of the extended memory is obtained with BIOS function $88. If the Carry Flag is set after the function call the function is not supported by the installed BIOS. This indicates a PC/XT with a 8086/8088 or V20 processor.

These types cannot use extended memory. A value of 0 returned to the AX register also indicates that no extended memory is available. The global variable ExtAvail is then set to FALSE and the procedure is ended with the EXIT command.

Otherwise, the size of the extended memory is stored and the search for RAM disks above the 1 megabyte memory limit begins. Since several RAM disks can be installed and, therefore, several boot sectors may be found, the search takes place in a loop. In this loop, the procedure ExtRead is called. This loads a memory block, the size of a BOOT_SECTOR, from the address ExtStart in extended memory into the variable BootSec.

The contents of this variable, and therefore the contents of the assumed boot sector, are then examined. The letters "VDISK" in the name field of the boot sector indicate a RAM disk. If this character string is found, the boot sector probably belongs to a RAM disk. Although unlikely, it's possible that another program has written this character string to this location in extended memory.

If a RAM disk is found, usable memory for the program begins after the RAM disk. So, ExtGetInfo must also determine the size of the RAM disk. This information can also be found in the boot sector in the fields BpS and Sectors. BpS indicates the number of bytes per sector in this particular RAM disk and Sectors gives the total number of sectors in the RAM disk. The previous start address stored in ExtStart must be increased by these two factors in order to place the start of the available extended memory after the RAM disk.

If more than one RAM disk exists, subsequent disks will always be located consecutively in memory. This means that the search for the next RAM disk can simply be continued at this memory location. The search loop is ended when a boot sector matching the search criteria isn't found. The variable ExtStart will then contain the desired start address of the free extended memory. The difference between this value and the actual start of extended memory at 1 megabyte must be subtracted from the total installed extended memory.

```
{*************************************************************************
*  ExtAdrConv : converts a pointer to a 32 bit linear address that is   *
*               returned in the form of a LONGINT                       *
*-----------------------------------------------------------------------*
*  Input   : Adr = the pointer to be converted                          *
*  Output  : the converted address                                      *
*************************************************************************}

function ExtAdrConv ( Adr : pointer ) : longint;

type PTRREC = record                            { used to access the }
                 Ofs : word;                     { components of the  }
                 Seg : word;                     { desired pointer    }
              end;

begin
  ExtAdrConv := longint( PTRREC( Adr ).seg ) shl 4 + PTRREC( Adr ).ofs;
end;
```

The function ExtAdrConv, which plays an important role within the EXT unit, is used to convert a pointer to a linear address. This is important for copying memory blocks between conventional and Extended RAM because BIOS function $88 also expects the addresses of memory blocks in conventional RAM in the form of linear addresses.

The given pointer is separated into its segment and offset components and converted to a linear address. This is done in the CPU in Real Mode simply by moving the segment address four bits to the left and adding the offset address.

The procedures ExtWrite and ExtRead will usually handle calling this function for you so you won't need to use ExtAdrConv.

```
{*************************************************************************
*  ExtCopy : copies data between two specified buffers within the 16 meg *
*            of addressable memory available to the 80286/386/486.       *
**----------------------------------------------------------------------**
*  Input   : Start = address of the start buffer as 32 bit linear address *
*            Target= address of the target buffer as 32 bit linear address *
*            Len   = number of bytes to copy                            *
*  Info    : - the number of bytes to copy must be an even number       *
*            - this procedure is intended only for use within this unit  *
*************************************************************************}

procedure ExtCopy( Start, Target : longint; Len : word );

var GTab : GDT;                             { Global Descriptor Table }
    Regs : Registers;             { processor registers for interrupt call }
    Adr  : longint;                      { for conversion of addresses }

begin
  FillChar( GTab, SizeOf( GTab ), 0 );                { all fields to 0 }
```

```
{-- build segment descriptor of the start segment ----------------------}

GTab.Start.AdrLow    := LI( Start ).LoWord;
GTab.Start.AdrHigh   := LI( Start ).HiByte;
GTab.Start.Attribute := $92;
GTab.Start.SLngth    := Len;

{-- build segment descriptor of the target segment --------------------}

GTab.Target.AdrLow    := LI( Target ).LoWord;
GTab.Target.AdrHigh   := LI( Target ).HiByte;
GTab.Target.Attribute := $92;
GTab.Target.SLngth    := Len;

{-- copy memory blocks with the help of function $87 of the cassette ----}
{-- interrupt $15                                                    ----}

Regs.AH := $87;                    { function number for 'copy memory' }
Regs.ES := seg( GTab );                          { address of GDT }
Regs.SI := ofs( GTab );                          { to ES:SI       }
Regs.CX := Len shr 1;              { number of words to copy to CX }
intr( $15, Regs );                             { call function }
if ( Regs.AH <> 0 ) then                          { error? }
  begin                           { yes, AH contains error code }
    writeln('Error while accessing extended RAM (', Regs.AH,')!');
    RunError;                     { stop program with run time error }
  end;
end;
```

Since ExtCopy calls the BIOS function $87 and creates the required segment descriptor in the GDT, it is the most important procedure of the unit.

It isn't important to ExtCopy whether memory blocks should be copied to or from conventional or extended RAM. ExtCopy expects only two LongInts, which represent the start and target buffers and contain the number of bytes to be copied. This number is converted to words before calling the BIOS function.

The Global Descriptor Table is represented within ExtCopy by the variable GTab. This variable is type GDT. ExtCopy first sets all fields in this structure to 0 before initializing the start and target descriptors. In both cases, a type conversion is used to convert the addresses to LI structures. This is done by separating the address into a LO word and a HI byte. The information is then entered in the proper fields in the segment descriptor, which also contains the length of a segment and the access code, or *segment attribute*.

Now everything is ready for a call to function $87. Each register is loaded and BIOS interrupt $15 is called. The contents of the AX register will indicate if the operation was successful or if an error occurred through the following error codes:

0	successful operation
1	parity error in extended memory
2	something wrong with GDT at the time of the function call (since ExtCopy creates a correct GDT this code should never appear)
3	Protected Mode could not be properly installed

In the version we have seen, ExtCopy stops the program execution, by calling the procedure RunError, if any of these errors are encountered. This procedure, which is used for handling errors, can be easily modified.

```
{*********************************************************************
 *  ExtRead : reads a given number of bytes from Extended Memory to main  *
 *            memory                                                  *
 **-----------------------------------------------------------------**
 *  Input   :  ExtAdr = source address in Extended RAM (linear address)  *
 *             BuPtr  = pointer to the target buffer in main memory  *
 *             Len    = number of bytes to copy                      *
 *  Info    : only even numbers of bytes can be read!               *
 *********************************************************************}

procedure ExtRead( ExtAdr : longint;  BuPtr : pointer;  Len : word );

begin
  ExtCopy( ExtAdr, ExtAdrConv( BuPtr ), len );
end;

{*********************************************************************
 *  ExtWrite : writes a given number of bytes from main memory to Extended  *
 *             Memory                                                 *
 **-------------------------------------------       -----------------**
 *  Input   :  BuPtr  = pointer to the source buffer in main memory  *
 *             ExtAdr = target address in Extended RAM (linear address)  *
 *             Len    = number of bytes to be copied                 *
 *********************************************************************}

procedure ExtWrite( BuPtr : pointer;  ExtAdr : longint;  Len : word );

begin
  ExtCopy( ExtAdrConv( BuPtr ), ExtAdr, len );
end;
```

ExtCopy is called by the procedures ExtRead and ExtWrite, which act as the interfaces between an application program and extended memory. ExtRead reads a memory block from extended memory and copies it to conventional RAM and ExtWrite copies from conventional RAM to extended memory. Both procedures must receive, as LongInts, the buffer addresses in extended memory.

The memory blocks in conventional RAM are referenced with normal (non-standard) pointers. If it's easier for you, these procedures can be modified to accept non-standard

311

variable parameters instead of the pointers. You won't have to use the "@" operator when using a variable to specify addresses in conventional RAM. You must always use the referencing symbol "^" after a pointer if the pointer only points to the buffer instead of representing it.

The initialization section is the last part of the EXT unit.

```
{**-------------------------------------------------------------------**}
{** Starting code of the unit                                        **}
{**-------------------------------------------------------------------**}

begin
  ExtGetInfo;                { obtain availability and size of extended memory }
end.
```

After frequent calls to function $87, your system clock may run slower. All interrupts must be suppressed while the processor is operating in Protected Mode. This includes the Timer interrupt, which produces the signal that drives the internal real time clock.

The program EXTDEMO is an example of working with the procedures, functions and variables of the EXT unit. The main program starts by answering these two questions:

• Is extended memory installed?

• Where does it begin and how big is it?

The procedure CheckExt determines whether extended memory is installed. It runs through the extended memory kilobyte by kilobyte and copies a 1K buffer called WriteBuf to each position in extended memory. The contents of this buffer are selected randomly each time the procedure is executed.

Next, this buffer is copied from extended memory to the buffer, ReadBuf, in conventional RAM. The contents of this buffer are compared to those of WriteBuf. An error message appears if any differences are encountered.

Extended memory itself will usually operate without any problems. If an error does occur, it's more likely to be a parity error during the call to function $87 in ExtCopy than any error during CheckExt. This demonstration program is a good example for your own experiments with extended memory.

```
{*****************************************************************************
 *  ExtDemo: demonstrates the operation of the functions and procedures of  *
 *           the EXT unit for accessing Extended Memory                     *
 **-------------------------------------------------------------------**
 *  Author          : MICHAEL TISCHER                                       *
 *  developed on     : 05/18/1989                                           *
```

```
*  last update on   : 02/27/1990                                              *
********************************************************************************}

program ExtDemo;

uses Ext;

{-- global variables ---------------------------------------------------}

var RdLen    : integer;                      { size of the RAM disk in kilobytes }

{*******************************************************************************
*  CheckExt : checks for errors in the free Extended RAM                       *
*******************************************************************************}

procedure CheckExt;

var AdrTest   : longint;                            { address of test block }
    i, j      : integer;                               { loop counter }
    WriteBuf,                                          { test blocks }
    ReadBuf   : array [1..1024] of byte;
    PError    : boolean;                   { turn pointer to memory error on }

begin
  Randomize;                              { initialize random number generator }
  AdrTest := ExtStart;
  for i := 1 to ExtLen do                 { process the memory in 1K blocks }
    begin
      for j := 1 to 1024 do               { fill block with random number }
        WriteBuf[ j ] := Random( 255 );

      write(#13, AdrTest );              { output address of checked 1K block }

      {-- write to WriteBuf and then copy to ReadBuf ---------------------}

      ExtWrite( @WriteBuf, AdrTest, 1024 );
      ExtRead( AdrTest, @ReadBuf, 1024 );

      {-- establish identity of WriteBuf and ReadBuf ---------------------}

      for j := 1 to 1024 do
        if WriteBuf[j] <> ReadBuf[j] then    { buffer contents identical  }
          begin                                      { no, error! }
            writeln( ' Error! Memory location ', AdrTest + longint(j-1) );
            PError := TRUE;
          end;

      inc( AdrTest, longint( 1024 ) );      { set AdrTest to next 1K block }
    end;
  writeln;
  if not( PError ) then                                        { error? }
    writeln( 'everything o.k!' );                              { no }
end;
```

```
{*****************************************************************************
*  M A I N   P R O G R A M                                                   *
*****************************************************************************}

begin
  writeln( #13#10'EXTDEMO - (c) 1989 by Michael Tischer'#13#10);
  if ExtAvail then                              { is Extended RAM available? }
    begin                                                             { yes }
      RdLen := integer( (ExtStart - longint( $100000 ) ) shr 10 );
      if ( RdLen = 0 ) then                     { are RAM disks installed? }
        begin                                                          { no }
          writeln( 'No RAM disks installed. ');
          writeln( 'The free Extended RAM begins at the ',
                   '1 MB memory limit. ');
        end
      else                                      { yes, RAM disks found }
        begin
          writeln( 'One or more RAM disks occupy ', RdLen,
                   ' K of extended RAM.');
          writeln( 'The free extended RAM begins ', RdLen,
                   ' K after the 1 meg memory limit.');
        end;
      writeln( 'The extended RAM consists of ',
               ExtLen, ' KB.');
      writeln( #13#10'The extended RAM is now being checked',
               ' for errors...'#13#10);
      CheckExt;
    end
  else
    writeln( 'There is no extended RAM installed in your computer!');
end.
```

9.2   Expanded Memory Specification (EMS)

The Expanded Memory System is the other method for adding memory above the 640K limit. This type of memory is the result of the LIM standard set by three leading companies in the PC world. The acronym LIM represents the first letter of each of these companies: Lotus, Intel and Microsoft.

Expanded Memory System offers a way to make extra memory available for computers with 8086/8088 processors. Several application packages, including Turbo Pascal, have needed a way to use extra memory.

Since EMS must reside below the 1 megabyte limit, it is slightly more difficult to install and use than extended memory.

The built-in intelligence that EMS cards have, in addition to the actual RAM, allow you to insert portions of up to 8 megabytes of installable EMS memory below the 1 megabyte limit. The inserted portion of memory is visible in the *page frame*, a 64K memory block that acts as a window for accessing EMS. Where the page frame is located depends upon the system configuration and the resulting BIOS expansions. There will always be a free 64K block at some location between segment addresses \$C000 and \$EFFF that the EMS card can use as a page frame.

Since this region will always be below the 1 megabyte limit, it can be accessed with normal FAR pointers. This is useful to Turbo Pascal developers, because, as detailed in Section 2.3, FAR pointers are used by Turbo Pascal to access data in memory.

Inserting portions of EMS through the page frame can be compared to the screen display of a spreadsheet program. The page displayed on the screen may be only one page of a very large spreadsheet. Also, just as different parts of a spreadsheet can be displayed by pressing a key, the EMS card allows different locations in expanded memory to be displayed in the page frame.

The entire EMS memory is divided into 16K EMS pages. So, a contiguous 64K block of EMS doesn't have to be manipulated within the page frame. The page frame can hold four of these 16K blocks and each of them can come from a different EMS location.

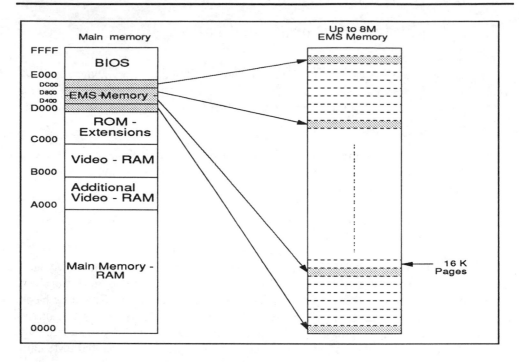

Accessing EMS according to the LIM Standard

An application program can determine which EMS pages to place in the page frame by using the EMM (Expanded Memory Manager) functions.

This is a device driver that must be installed in the CONFIG.SYS file with a DEVICE command in order to work with EMS. Interrupt $67 is used as the interface to the functions of the EMM. Like the BIOS functions, these functions are also assigned a series of function numbers that must be passed in the AH register to call a function.

We can describe the functions required to access EMS by presenting the EMS unit, which creates an interface to EMS memory. As with EXT, which can be used to access extended memory, the EMS unit doesn't provide any help for setting up your own application programs to access EMS.

```
{*****************************************************************************
 *    E M S : a unit that can be used as an interface between a program and  *
 *          the Expanded Memory Manager (EMM) - this allows access to EMS    *
 *          memory                                                           *
 **-----------------------------------------------------------------------**
 *   Author        : MICHAEL TISCHER                                         *
 *   developed on  : 06/09/1989                                             *
 *   last update on : 06/09/1989                                            *
 *****************************************************************************}
```

```
unit Ems;

interface

uses Dos;

{-- declaration of functions and procedures that can be called from  ------}
{-- other programs                                                   ------}

function  EmsGetFreePage   : integer;
function  EmsGetPtr        ( PhysPage : byte ) : pointer;
function  EmsAlloc         ( Amount : integer ) : integer;
procedure EmsMap           ( Handle, LogPage : integer; PhysPage : byte );
procedure EmsFree          ( Handle : integer );
procedure EmsRestoreMapping( Handle : integer );
procedure EmsSaveMapping   ( Handle : integer );

{-- constants, public -------------------------------------------------}

const {------------------------------------------- EMS error codes ------}

      EmsErrOk        = $00;   { everything o.k., no error              }
      EmsErrSw        = $80;   { error in EMM (software)                }
      EmsErrHw        = $81;   { EMS hardware error                     }
      EmsErrInvHandle = $83;   { invalid EMS handle                     }
      EmsErrFkt       = $84;   { invalid function called                }
      EmsErrNoHandles = $85;   { no more handles free                   }
      EmsErrSaResMap  = $86;   { error while saving or restoring Mapping }
      EmsErrToMany    = $87;   { more pages were requested than are     }
                               { physically available                  }
      EmsErrNoPages   = $88;   { more pages requested than are free     }
      EmsErrNullPages = $89;   { null page requested                    }
      EmsErrLogPInv   = $8A;   { logical page does not belong to handle }
      EmsErrPhyPInv   = $8B;   { invalid physical page number           }
      EmsErrMapFull   = $8C;   { Mapping memory region is full          }
      EmsErrMapSaved  = $8D;   { Mapping already saved                  }
      EmsErrMapRes    = $8E;   { attempt to restore Mapping without     }
                               { previously saving it                  }
```

The declarations of the public functions and procedures of the EMS unit are in the interface section. There are also a number of constants declared that represent the EMS error codes. Each EMS function expects a function number in the AH register and each function returns its result to this register as a status code. Only code 0 signifies that an error hasn't occurred and that the function is complete. All other codes represent errors.

After any function or procedure from the EMS unit is called, this error code can be obtained from the global variable EmsError. This variable, like other global variables, gives the caller information on the status of the EMS and the EMM. All variables, procedures and functions have the prefix "Ems" as part of their names to indicate their origin in the EMS unit.

```
{-- global variables accessible to other programs ------------------------}

var EmsInst      : boolean;         { contains TRUE if EMS memory is available }
    EmsPages     : integer;                    { total number of EMS pages }
    EmsVersion,                    { EMS version number (32 = 3.2, 40 = 4.0) }
    EmsError     : byte;                        { stores EMM error number }
```

The variable EmsInst will indicate whether or not EMS memory is available.

This variable is Boolean type and contains TRUE if EMS memory is available and a corresponding EMM is found. The total number of installed EMS pages is given in the variable EmsPages. Notice that this value doesn't necessarily have to correspond to the total number of EMS pages available, since some pages may have been allocated to TSR programs, the operating system or device drivers. The actual number of available EMS pages can only be obtained with a function that we will see in a moment.

The variable EmsVersion returns the EMS version number. To understand its meaning, you must know that EMS memory and its management (like most PC hardware) has been enhanced over time. This has led to increased capabilities for the EMM and EMS hardware. EMS Version 4.0 is the most recent, supporting more powerful hardware, but is compatible with all its predecessors, such as 3.2, which are still in use. This allows you to insert any part of EMS memory into almost any desired location below the 1 megabyte limit. It also allows you to protect EMS from being deleted by a reset, which is a significant advantage when using RAM disks.

All three EMS variables are loaded by an initialization procedure before the actual program start. This procedure is automatically called without any formal calls from your programs. You can determine whether there is EMS memory available for your program immediately after the program start.

The initialization procedure is called EmsInit. It first establishes if an EMM is available and if EMS memory is installed. It does this with an equally unconventional and effective method that is based on the EMM. The EMM is a character device driver, a type which DOS normally uses to access devices such as the keyboard, screen or a printer.

The EMM has little in common with the keyboard, the screen or a printer because it doesn't work with a device. Also, the requirements for managing memory expansion are very different from those used for accessing a keyboard or the screen.

Note: You may have considered establishing the EMM as a TSR program. However, a device driver is always installed from CONFIG.SYS and requires less memory than a TSR program.

The EMM must conform to one of the expectations DOS requires of a device driver. It must begin with a structure that identifies it as a device driver and contain the information that DOS needs to work with it.

The name of the device that the driver manages is in a character driver. This is how devices, such as CON, NUL and LPT, obtain their names. The EMS drivers are always called "EMMXXXX0". If you find a device of this name, you can be sure it contains the EMM. Unfortunately, DOS doesn't enable programs to search for a specified device name. You must find another way to locate the EMS driver.

The key to the EMM is interrupt $67, which allows access to all of the EMM functions. Since the corresponding interrupt handler is found within the EMM, the entry for interrupt $67 in the Interrupt Vector Table must point within the EMM. Device drivers must always consist of only one memory segment. This segment address, located in the Interrupt Vector Table, will point to the start of the EMM in memory.

The EMM starts at offset 0 with a header. This header contains the identifying device name at offset 10. This is what allows EmsInit to determine whether an EMM is available.

```
implementation

{-- constants internal to this program ------------------------------------}

const EMS_INT = $67;                  { interrupt vector for accessing the EMM }

{-- global variables internal to this module ----------------------------}

var EmsFrameSeg : word;               { segment address of the EMS page frames }

{***********************************************************************
 *  EmsInit : Initializes the unit                                     *
 ***********************************************************************}

procedure EmsInit;

type EmmName  = array [1..8] of char; { name of the EMM from driver header }
     EmmNaPtr = ^EmmName;                    { pointer to name in driver header }

const Name : EmmName = 'EMMXXXX0';                      { name of EMS driver }

var Regs  : Registers;                { processor registers for interrupt call }

begin
  {-- start by determining if EMS memory and the proper EMM are installed -}

  Regs.ax := $35 shl 8 + EMS_INT;                { get interrupt vector with }
  msdos( Regs );                                 { DOS function $35          }

  EmsInst := ( EmmNaPtr(Ptr(Regs.ES,10))^ = Name ); { compare driver name }
```

```
    if ( EmsInst ) then                          { is an EMM installed? }
      begin                                                    { yes }

        {-- get total number of EMS pages ----------------------------------}
        Regs.AH := $42;                { function no. for "get number of pages" }
        intr( EMS_INT, Regs );                                { call EMM }
        EmsPages := Regs.DX;                       { store total number of pages }

        {-- get segment address of EMS page frame --------------------------}
        Regs.AH := $41;  { Function no. for "get segment add. of page frame" }
        intr( EMS_INT, Regs );                                { call EMM }
        EmsFrameSeg := Regs.BX;                        { store segment address }

        {-- get version number of EMM --------------------------------------}
        Regs.AH := $46;              { function no. for "get EMM version number" }
        intr( EMS_INT, Regs );                                { call EMM }
        EmsVersion := ( Regs.AL and 15 ) + ( Regs.AL shr 4 ) * 10;

        EmsError := EmsErrOk;                           { no errors yet }

      end;
  end;
```

EmsInit first defines the type EmmName, which reflects the structure of the name field in the driver header. A pointer to this type is also declared. The standard constant of this type, called Name is then declared. This contains the name of the EMM driver.

In the program code, the DOS function $35 is called. This is used to obtain the contents of an entry in the Interrupt Vector Table. This is where we get the memory address to which the EMM interrupt $67 will point. DOS returns this address to the ES:BX register pair. The segment address, which is used in the next statement, is now important.

Note: Although the Turbo Pascal procedure GetInVec could be used, this wouldn't be worthwhile in this case. Only the segment address and not a complete pointer to the driver is required.

Now the segment address is combined with the offset 10 to create a non-standard pointer with the PTR function. A type conversion turns this into a pointer of type EmmNaPtr, which points to a driver name in memory.

This pointer is referenced and then compared with the contents of the standard constant Name, which is the name of the EMM. This expression utilizes Turbo Pascal's ability to compare complete arrays within an expression and to assign a boolean result to a variable of type Boolean. So, the contents of the 8 bytes at address ES:10 are compared with the standard constant Name. If they match, Turbo Pascal assigns the value TRUE to the variable EmsInst, indicating that an EMM was found.

If an EMM is found, EmsInst continues with the initialization. Then the total number of EMS pages is obtained. EmsInst can do this with EMM function $42. The only parameter required is the function number. It returns the total number of EMS pages to the DX register. This number is stored in the global variable EmsPages.

Next, the procedure gets the segment address of the page frame. This represents the base address for all access to EMS memory. You can use function $41, which returns the desired address to the BX register, to do this. This information is stored in the variable EmsFrameSeg. This variable is accessible only to the procedures and functions of the EMS unit.

The last thing EmsInst does is get the version number of the EMM. A special function, $46, is available for this as well. This function returns the EMM version number to the AL register. The LO nibble represents the part of the version number after the decimal and the HI nibble represents the part before the decimal. The value 32 represents Version 3.2 and the value 40 represents Version 4.0.

```
{*******************************************************************
*   EmsGetPtr : returns a pointer to one of the four physical pages of the  *
*               EMS page frame                                     *
**---------------------------------------------------------------**
*   Input    : PhysPage = number of the physical page             *
*   Output   : pointer to this page                               *
********************************************************************}

function EmsGetPtr( PhysPage : byte ) : pointer;

begin
  EmsGetPtr := ptr( EmsFrameSeg, PhysPage shl 14 );
end;
```

The function EmsGetPtr performs a simple but important operation. It provides a way for an application program to get a non-standard pointer to the beginning of one of the four pages in the page frame. Remember that the pages are numbered 0 to 3.

You can use the function EmsGetFreePage to determine the number of free EMS to be reserved by your program. This function doesn't receive any parameters. It returns the number of free pages to the calling routine as the function result.

```
{****************************************************************************
*  EmsGetFreePage : gets the number of free EMS pages (1 page = 16K)      *
**----------------------------------------------------------------------**
*  Output   : the number of free pages                                    *
****************************************************************************}

function EmsGetFreePage : integer;

var Regs : Registers;                    { processor registers for interrupt call }

begin
  Regs.AH := $42;                        { function no. for "get number of pages" }
  intr( EMS_INT, Regs );                                          { call EMM }
  EmsGetFreePage := Regs.BX;                    { return number of free pages }
end;
```

Internally, EmsGetFreePage uses EMM function $42, which returns the desired information to the BX register.

The first step in actually working with EMS memory is to call the function EmsAlloc, which is used to allocate EMS pages to your program. The logic of this process is similar to allocating heap memory with the Turbo Pascal functions New or GetMem.

```
{****************************************************************************
*  EmsAlloc : allocates a given number of EMS pages                       *
**----------------------------------------------------------------------**
*  Input    : Amount = number of pages to allocate                        *
*  Output   : handle for later access to the allocated pages              *
*  Info     : if an error occurs, the variable EmsError will contain a    *
*             value not equal to 0 (an error code) after the function call *
****************************************************************************}

function EmsAlloc( Amount : integer ) : integer;

var Regs : Registers;                    { processor registers for interrupt call }

begin
  Regs.AH := $43;                           { function no. for "allocate pages" }
  Regs.BX := Amount;                       { number of pages is passed to BX }
  intr( EMS_INT, Regs );                                        { call EMM }
  EmsAlloc := Regs.DX;                         { the handle is passed to DX }
  EmsError := Regs.AH;                                            { error? }
end;
```

EmsAlloc must be located beyond the number of desired pages. This value is passed without changes on the EMM function $43, which actually allocates the EMS pages. Along with the usual error code, this function returns a handle to the DX register. This handle, which is important for later access to the allocated pages, is a numeric value that points to the allocated pages within the EMM, serving as an identifier. EmsAlloc returns this handle, as the function result, to the calling routine. This guarantees that the caller is able to access the allocated pages and free them again later.

Although the EMS functions/procedures we have listed until now probably won't have errors and it isn't necessary to query EmsError after calling them, there are still a few things that can go wrong with EmsAlloc. Perhaps the desired number of pages aren't available or all handles have already been assigned. Even if errors rarely occur it's always advisable to query the error status after calling this function.

A call to EmsMap will usually follow the allocation of EMS pages with EmsAlloc. Before accessing any allocated page, it must first be loaded into one of the four pages in the page frame. EmsMap performs this task using EMM function $44.

The first parameter EmsMap expects is the handle that was returned by the previous call to EmsAlloc. Next comes the logical page number, which starts at zero, or the number of the page that will be loaded in the page frame. For example, the pages allocated with a call of EmsAlloc (5) would be numbered from 0 to 4. The third parameter is the physical page. This represents one of the four physical pages in the page frame where the logical page will be loaded. This parameter must be from 0 to 3 because the page frame has four physical pages.

In addition to loading new pages into the page frame, this procedure can be used to force previously loaded pages out of the page frame. Any changes made to these pages while they were in the page frame aren't lost. They are automatically stored back in EMS memory and will be available the next time the page is loaded in the page frame.

```
{**********************************************************************
* EmsMap : loads one of the allocated logical pages into one of the 4    *
*          physical pages of the EMS page frame                          *
*--------------------------------------------------------------------**
*  Input   : Handle   = handle that identifies the allocated page        *
*            LogPage  = number of the logical page to be loaded          *
*            PhysPage = the physical page number                         *
*  Info    : if an error occurs, the variable EmsError will contain a    *
*            value other than 0 (error code) after the function call     *
**********************************************************************}

procedure EmsMap( Handle, LogPage : integer; PhysPage : byte );

var Regs : Registers;              { processor registers for interrupt call }

begin
  Regs.AH := $44;                { function no. for "map expanded memory page" }
  Regs.DX := Handle;                    { load the parameters in the registers }
  Regs.BX := LogPage;
  Regs.Al := PhysPage;
  intr( EMS_INT, Regs );                                        { call EMM }
  EmsError := Regs.AH;                                          { error? }
end;
```

323

Allocated EMS pages are released by calling EmsFree. This procedure must be called by a program because the allocated pages aren't automatically freed after the program ends. This distinguishes EMS memory from memory such as the heap, which Turbo Pascal automatically frees after a program ends. If you don't call this procedure, the allocated pages will remain reserved until the next system reset and subsequent programs may not be able to take full advantage of EMS.

The handle must be passed when calling EmsFree so that the EMM knows which EMS pages to free. The number of pages don't have to be given, since the EMM saves this value internally with the handle and it will automatically free all pages associated with the given handle. This also invalidates the handle so that it can no longer be used when calling EmsMap or the other EMS procedures or functions.

```
{****************************************************************************
 *   EmsFree : frees EMS pages previously allocated with EmsAlloc          *
 **----------------------------------------------------------------------**
 *   Input   : Handle = the handle under which the pages were allocated    *
 *   Info    : if an error occurs, the variable EmsError will contain a    *
 *             value other than 0 (error code) after the function call     *
 ****************************************************************************}

procedure EmsFree( Handle : integer );

var Regs : Registers;            { processor registers for interrupt call }

begin
  Regs.AH := $45;               { function number for "release handle & EMS" }
  Regs.DX := Handle;                    { load parameter in the register }
  intr( EMS_INT, Regs );                           { call EMM }
  EmsError := Regs.AH;                                { error? }
end;
```

The next two procedures are required for using EMS memory for TSR programs.

Since the program that was interrupted may also be using EMS, do not change EMS contents. After the TSR program is finished, a program will expect the EMS memory to look the same as it did before the TSR program started. This is especially true with the arrangement and contents of the logical pages found in the four physical pages in the EMS page frame. These cannot be changed.

Therefore, the procedure EmsSaveMapping must be called when a TSR program is activated. This stores a "snapshot" of the current page frame contents. The TSR program can then use EmsMap to load its own EMS pages into the page frame. Before returning to the interrupted program, EmsRestoreMapping must be called to restore the page frame to its original contents.

Both procedures expect a handle, from a previous call of EmsAlloc, as an argument. It is important that the pages belonging to this handle haven't already been freed with EmsFree, which would render the handle invalid.

Don't forget to pass the same handle in both cases so that the EMM will know which mapping to restore.

```
{***************************************************************************
* EmsSaveMapping : saves a mapping of the current logical EMS pages in     *
*                  the four physical pages of the EMS page frame           *
**----------------------------------------------------------------------**
* Input  : Handle = the handle under which the pages were allocated        *
* Info   : if an error occurs, the variable EmsError will contain a        *
*          value other than 0 (error code) after the function call         *
***************************************************************************}

procedure EmsSaveMapping( Handle : integer );

var Regs : Registers;              { processor registers for interrupt call }

begin
  Regs.AH := $47;                  { function number for "save mapping" }
  Regs.DX := Handle;               { load the parameter in the register }
  intr( EMS_INT, Regs );                              { call EMM }
  EmsError := Regs.AH;                                 { error? }
end;

{***************************************************************************
*  EmsRestoreMapping : retrieves a mapping previously saved with the       *
*                  procedure EmsSaveMapping                                *
**----------------------------------------------------------------------**
* Input  : Handle = the handle under which the pages were allocated        *
* Info   : if an error occurs, the variable EmsError will contain a        *
*          value other than 0 (error code) after the function call         *
***************************************************************************}

procedure EmsRestoreMapping( Handle : integer );

var Regs : Registers;              { processor registers for interrupt call }

begin
  Regs.AH := $48;                  { function number for "restore mapping" }
  Regs.DX := Handle;               { load parameter in the register }
  intr( EMS_INT, Regs );                              { call EMM }
  EmsError := Regs.AH;                                 { error? }
end;
```

After this, the main program is called when the unit is linked and before the actual program start. It calls the procedure EmsInit which was previously described.

```
{**--------------------------------------------------------------------**}
{** Starting code of the unit                                          **}
{**--------------------------------------------------------------------**}

begin
  EmsInit;                                              { initialize the unit }
end.
```

The following demo program will demonstrate the EMS unit. This program shows how the various procedures and functions work. This demo doesn't cover the Ems function calls, which should be clear from the previous descriptions. Instead, it focuses on the way the pages in the page frame are accessed after the desired pages have been allocated and loaded.

This example uses EMS memory to store screen pages like those used in Chapter 6. In text mode, each page consists of 4000 characters. Four of these screen pages are stored in each available EMS page. Although 64 bytes are lost per page with this method, it is still less than the amount that would be lost if the screen pages had to be stored one after another.

The second part is where the program actually uses four screen pages per EMS page. This section processes all screen pages and displays them by copying them to video RAM.

```
{***********************************************************************
 * EmsDemo: demonstrates the use of the functions and procedures of the  *
 *          EMS unit, used to access Expanded Memory according to the LIM *
 *          standard                                                      *
 **--------------------------------------------------------------------**
 * Author       : MICHAEL TISCHER                                         *
 * developed on  : 05/12/1989                                            *
 * last update on : 05/12/1989                                           *
 ***********************************************************************}

program EmsDemo;

uses Dos, Crt, Ems;                                     { bind units }

{***********************************************************************
 * FillAndPrint : fills the EMS pages found and prints them to the screen  *
 **--------------------------------------------------------------------**
 * Input    : none                                                        *
 * Output   : none                                                        *
 ***********************************************************************}

procedure FillAndPrint;

type ScreenPage = array [1..2000] of word;    { structure of a screen pg. }
     Page  = array[1..4] of ScreenPage;       { 4 screen pgs. per EMS pg. }
     PAPTR = ^Page;                      { pointer to one pg. with 4 screen pgs. }

var i, j, k,                                            { loop counters }
    Amt,                                         { number of pages to process }
```

```
Handle   : integer;        { handle for accessing the allocated EMS pgs. }
PageBase : PAPTR;              { pointer to first EMS pg. in page frame }
VioSeg,                            { segment address of video RAM }
FillWord : word;                          { the fill word }
Regs     : Registers;      { processor registers for interrupt call }

begin
  {-- get pointer to video RAM -----------------------------------------}
  Regs.ah := 15;                             { get current video mode }
  intr($10, Regs);                         { call BIOS video interrupt }
  if Regs.al = 7 then                         { monochrome mode? }
    VioSeg := $b000                      { yes, video RAM at Bd00 }
  else                                        { no, color mode }
    VioSeg := $b800;                     { video RAM at B800 }

  PageBase := EmsGetPtr( 0 );                { pointer to first page }

  {-- allocate all available EMS pages ---------------------------------}
  Amt := EmsGetFreePage;          { get number of pages to be processed }
  Handle := EmsAlloc( Amt );           { allocate all available pages }
  if ( EmsError <> EmsErrOK ) then                { error? }
    begin
      writeln( 'Error while allocating EMS pages!');
      exit;
    end
  else
    begin
      {-- process each EMS page and store 4 screen pages containing a -----}
      {-- constant character in each                              -----}

      for i := 0 to Amt-1 do                   { outer loop for EMS pages }
        begin
          EmsMap( Handle, i, 0 );  { EMS page to page #0 of the page frame }
          if ( EmsError <> EmsErrOK ) then               { error? }
            begin
              writeln( 'Error while mapping an EMS page!');
              exit;
            end;
          for j:= 1 to 4 do                { 4 screen pages per EMS page }
            begin
              Write( #13, 'EMS page: ', i+1:2, ' , Screen page: ',
                     i * 4 + j:2 );
              FillWord := ( i * 4 + j ) + $700;  { character and attribute }
              for k := 1 to 2000 do           { process each screen page }
                PageBase^[j][k] := FillWord;   { enter char. and attribute }
            end;
        end;

      {-- copy each screen page from EMS memory to video RAM one after --- }
      {-- the other                                            --- }

      for i := 0 to Amt-1 do                      { outer loop for EMS pages }
        begin
```

327

```
          EmsMap( Handle, i, 0 );   { EMS page to page #0 of the page frame }
          if ( EmsError <> EmsErrOK ) then                          { error? }
            begin
              writeln( 'Error while mapping an EMS page!');
              exit;
            end;
          for j := 1 to 4 do                { 4 screen pages per EMS page }
            begin                           { copy screen page to video RAM }
              Move( PageBase^[j][1], ptr( VioSeg, 0 )^, 4000 );
              GotoXy( 1, 1 );
              Write( '  EMS page: ', i+1:2, ', Screen page: ',
                     i * 4 + j:2, '  ' );
              delay( 200 );                               { short pause }
            end;
        end;
    end;

  EmsFree( Handle );                             { free all allocated pages }
  if ( EmsError <> EmsErrOK ) then                          { error? }
    writeln( 'Error while freeing the allocated EMS pages!');
  end;
```

This excerpt from the listing shows the most important parts of the program, the procedure FillAndPrint, which creates the individual screen pages.

Three types are defined for this purpose:

ScreenPage

is a reconstruction of a screen page from video RAM. Each individual character position is represented by a word that stores both the character and its attribute. It would be easier to manipulate the characters and attributes if they were stored in separate bytes, but this would be unnecessary in this example.

Page   describes the contents of one EMS page as an array with four screen pages.

PAPTR   is a pointer to type Page, and therefore also to an EMS page and its four screen pages.

There are also a number of variable definitions. Their meaning should be clear from the program comments.

FillAndPrint starts by getting the segment address of the video RAM. Refer to Section 6.2 for more information on using this method. It also distinguishes between the two video modes to identify color and monochrome systems. Next, the variable PageBase is loaded with the memory address of the first EMS page.

Although PageBase is a standard pointer, it requires no type conversion because the function EmsGetPtr returns a non-standard pointer, which is compatible with all standard pointers by definition.

In the next step, all available EMS pages are allocated. This is accomplished by obtaining the number of non-reserved pages with the function EmsGetFreePage and loading the result in the variable Amt. The actual allocation is done by calling EmsAlloc and passing the variable Amt as the argument. The EMS handle that is returned is stored in the variable Handle.

As a precaution, the procedure checks for errors in EmsError after the call to EmsAlloc. The procedure is ended if an error is detected. If the requested number of EMS pages were successfully allocated, the procedure enters a loop that processes all reserved pages. In this loop, each page is loaded as the first page of the page frame by calling EmsMap and another error check is performed.

If the page was correctly loaded into the page frame, each screen page within the page is processed in another loop. A brief message will appear on the screen and a FillWord is calculated. The FillWord is used for the character and attribute codes for all characters in the screen page being filled.

Another loop is used to actually fill the page. All 2000 elements of an array of type ScreenPage are processed. Each array element is accessed with the pointer PageBase, that is initially loaded with the address of the first page in the page frame. It therefore always points to the EMS page of interest, which is loaded as the first page of the page frame. By referencing this pointer, Turbo Pascal sees the first page in the page frame as a variable of type Page, the elements of which can be accessed in the normal way. In this case, it doesn't matter to Turbo Pascal that it is dealing with a special memory region.

After all screen pages are filled, each EMS page and screen page is processed once again. In this case, each screen page is copied to video RAM with the MOVE procedure. This displays each page on the screen. A short pause is executed between each screen page using the DELAY command.

This completes the work done by FillAndPrint. After all allocated pages are once again free, the procedure returns to its caller, the main program of EmsDemo. The main program outputs the status information stored in the public EmsXXXX variables from the EMS unit. FillAndPrint is called only if the existence of EMS memory has been confirmed.

```
{****************************************************************************
* M A I N   P R O G R A M                                                  *
****************************************************************************}

begin
  ClrScr;
  writeln( #13#10'EMSDEMO - (c) 1989 by Michael Tischer'#13#10);
  if EmsInst then                               { is EMS memory installed? }
    begin                                                            { yes }
      writeln( 'EMS Version Number: ', EmsVersion div 10, '.',
               EmsVersion mod 10 );
      writeln( 'There are ', EmsPages*16, ' K of EMS memory available in ',
               EmsPages, ' EMS pages.');
      writeln( 'There are ', EmsPages-EmsGetFreePage,
               ' pages already allocated.'#13#10 );
      writeln( 'As an example of the use of EMS memory for storing ',
               'statistical data,' );
      writeln( 'each EMS page will be loaded with 4 screen',
               'pages, which will later be');
      writeln( 'copied to video RAM.');
      If EmsGetFreePage <> 0 then
        begin
          writeln;
          FillAndPrint;                                   { execute demo }
          ClrScr;
        end;
    end
  else                                          { no, no EMS driver found }
    writeln( 'There is no EMS memory installed!' );
end.
```

This program also serves as a good starting point for experimenting with the uses of EMS. In this example, the term "screen pages" can be substituted with any type of statistical or status data that can be stored in EMS memory. It may become more difficult if you want to manage data of different sizes with EMS pages. But once you understand the principles of working with EMS, you will be able to do this in less time and with less work.

10. Exec Without Using Extra Memory

A programmer was once asked by a company to develop a user interface, similar to today's widely available Norton Commander or XTREE, for in-house use. However, only a few people in the company understood electronic data processing and only the owner's son was learning Pascal programming in school.

Although the project started well, the programmer made a serious error when he postponed writing the section of the program which accessed user applications until the end of the project. By that time it was too late to add this section; the program had already become so large there wasn't enough free memory remaining for the execution of other programs using the Turbo Pascal Exec procedure. Even though tests indicated there was still 220K of free memory, this wasn't enough for "memory hogs" like Microsoft Word, Lotus 1-2-3 or dBASE. In this chapter, we will show you how to solve this problem.

10.1 The SWAP Unit

This solution is based on writing a new Exec procedure which removes the complete Turbo program from memory and places it in a file or in EMS memory. This makes memory available for calling the indicated program. After program execution ends, the Turbo program is again loaded into the memory and the Turbo program execution can continue as usual.

However, the implementation of this idea was more difficult than it first appeared. Since the task can only be performed through assembler routines, we will first demonstrate how to use the new Exec procedure. Then we will explain the SWAP unit, whose assembly language section is extremely complicated.

When you wish to join all these codes together to make a functional program, remember to assemble the SWAPA.ASM source code in TASM using the /MX command line option; compile the SWAP.PAS source code; then compile the SWAPDEMO.PAS source code.

There isn't actually a "new" Exec procedure. Instead there are two functions which can be accessed through the SWAP unit. These functions, which are called ExecPrg and ExecCommand, differ from each other in one small respect. ExecPrg is used for the execution of EXE and COM programs whose name and path are known in the current memory medium. ExecCommand, however, can also be used for calling batch files and resident DOS commands, because the command processor is started and the program name or command is passed to it. Because of this, ExecCommand is more flexible because the command processor independently searches for a file with the .BAT, .EXE or .COM extension and extends this search to the directories which were contained in the PATH command. This capability isn't usually available with the Exec procedure in Turbo. Because of this, the program to be executed has less available memory and requires more time to bring the program into execution because the command processor must first be loaded and started.

A string which contains the name of the command or program to be executed and the parameters to be passed at the start of the program start must be passed to both functions. As a result, both functions return a code which indicates whether the function completed its task effectively or an error occurred. The example program SWAPDEMO.PAS demonstrates how the two functions work by using the example of ExecCommand.

```
{****************************************************************
*   SWAPDEMO : demonstrates the use of the functions ExecCommand and   *
*              ExecPrg from the SWAP unit                              *
**------------------------------------------------------------**
*   Author       : MICHAEL TISCHER                              *
*   developed on  : 06/14/1989                                  *
*   last update on : 03/01/1990                                 *
****************************************************************}

program SwapDemo;

{$M 16384, 0, 655360}                     { allocate all of memory for Turbo }

uses Crt, Dos, Swap;                          { include the three units }

{****************************************************************
*                     M A I N   P R O G R A M                    *
****************************************************************}

var ComSpec : string;                          { command processor path }
    ErrCode : byte;                       { error code of ExecCommand }
begin
  writeln;
  writeln('         SWAPDEMO - (c) 1989 by Michael Tischer     ');
  writeln;

  writeln('This is a demonstration of the SWAP unit. Setting the heap');
  writeln('size to 655,360 in the $M compiler directive ensures that');
  writeln('Turbo Pascal allocates all available memory before the');
  writeln('program starts.');
  writeln;
  writeln('On calling the EXEC procedure from Turbo, no other program');
  writeln('can be called, demonstrated by the following test call.');
  writeln;
  write( 'Exec(''\COMMAND.COM'', ''/cdir *.*'') ');

  ComSpec := GetEnv( 'COMSPEC' );             { get command processor path }
  Exec( ComSpec, '/cdir *.*' );                    { display directory }
  if ( DosError <> 0 ) then                              { error ? }
    begin                                          { yes, as expected }
```

```
         TextColor( $0 );
         TextBackground( $F );
         write( '<--- Error, no memory!');
         TextColor( $7 );
         TextBackground( $0 );
         writeln;
         writeln;
         writeln('Now the new EXEC COMMAND procedure will execute, which ');
         writeln('places most of the memory on disk or in EMS memory. ');
         writeln;
         writeln( 'ExecCommand( ''dir *.*'' ) ');

         ErrCode := ExecCommand( 'dir *.*' );
         writeln;
         if ( ErrCode = SwapErrOk ) then
           writeln('Everything O.K. SwapDemo terminated. ')
         else
           write('Error');
           case ErrCode of                          { read & act on error code }
             SwapErrStore    : writeln(' during memory storage!');
             SwapErrNotFound : writeln(': program not found!');
             SwapErrNoAccess : writeln(': access denied!');
             SwapErrNoRam    : writeln(': program too large!');
           end;
       end;
     end;
   end.
```

With the compiler directive $M and the value 655360 assigned for the heap size, the above demonstration program automatically reserves the total available memory for itself. It then calls the normal Turbo Pascal Exec procedure but this fails because all memory is allocated. The call to ExecCommand is different. Here the program call can be performed since enough space is available through the storage of the memory content. The DIR command is called to display all the files in the current directory.

A call from ExecCommand may fail for various reasons. The function result that is returned should be read after the function call. This is supported by various constants which are defined within the INTERFACE section of the SWAP unit. These constants all start with the "SwapErr" prefix, followed by an error designation. SwapErrOK, which has a special status, indicates that ExecPrg or ExecCommand executed without problems. The significance of the other error constants can be seen in the above demonstration program, which reads the error code after calling ExecCommand and displays an error message.

From a viewpoint of execution speed, storing the program in EMS memory is preferable to creating a SWAP file. The two functions create a SWAP file only if EMS memory wasn't installed in the first place, or if there is not enough EMS memory available. These functions cannot access extended memory, but if your computer has EMS you can use this area of memory with the help of a small trick.

First you must create a RAM disk in the extended memory with sufficient memory to store a program. For example, you can use the device driver VDISK, which is included in most implementations of DOS. If the EMS memory cannot be accessed, you must manipulate the constant SwapPath which indicates the path within the SWAP unit where the SWAP file should be created before the first call of one of these two Exec functions. Enter the path designation (the root directory of the RAM disk) into this constant. If the RAM disk has the device name E, use the statement:

```
SwapPath := 'e:\'
```

With the device driver VDISK, the two Exec functions create their SWAP file within extended memory. Usually SwapPath points to the root directory of drive C: (normally the specifier for a hard disk drive).

If your programs occupy a lot of memory, the two Exec functions must store data to disk, which increases the time between program executions. So, use the compiler option $M to limit the size of the memory allocated for your program as much as possible. The smaller heap and stack require fewer bytes of memory.

If you install your own *interrupt handler* in your Turbo program, be sure to replace this handler with the old routine before calling ExecCommand or ExecPrg. Otherwise, this handler may be started during the execution of the called program, but the code is no longer in memory because it was overwritten by the called program. This can lead to a system crash. After the end of ExecCommand and ExecPrg you can re-install your interrupt handler.

Turbo also redirects some interrupts to its own routines. However, you don't have to worry about these interrupts because the SWAP unit automatically replaces them with the old interrupt handler before the execution of the indicated program and installs them again before returning to the caller.

Now let's discuss the internal structure of the SWAP unit and its corresponding assembler module SWAPA.ASM. Before dividing the program code into more understandable segments, we'll look at the use of a comprehensive assembler module.

The problem is related to the program itself. When the SWAP unit stores the Turbo program, it overwrites a part of itself. Up to the moment when the program to be executed is loaded into the memory area, this isn't a problem. However, you cannot reload the Turbo Pascal program after the entire program code was overwritten by another program.

Storing the memory only after the end of the SWAP unit and releasing it for the program to be called won't be very effective because this memory is preceded by the complete code of the main program, and perhaps even the program codes for some units which would continue to occupy a fair part of the memory area. There is also the problem of accessing data. This area is overwritten since the data segment and the stack are located after the SWAP unit. The assembly language code generated by Turbo Pascal constantly accesses the data segment and the stack; a system crash is almost inevitable.

An assembler routine which stores stack, data and variables must be used within the program code. This routine must be independent of the data segment and the Turbo stack. One problem would be solved, but the problem of freeing as much memory as possible isn't yet solved. Even an assembler routine is a part of the SWAP unit and, because of this, is located somewhere in the middle of the Turbo Pascal program.

The only solution to this problem involves copying the assembler routine to the beginning of the Turbo Pascal program. Actually, the assembler routine is copied past the end of the PSP, which is the location where the code segment of the main program usually begins. Only the 256 bytes of the PSP and the memory space for the assembler routine must remain reserved, which combined requires less than 1K of memory. The rest of the memory can be freed and overwritten by the program that is loaded.

The assembler routine cannot be copied directly following the end of the PSP because the program code located there can't be overwritten. This is because the program code may be called later as part of the main program. So, the assembler routine must be stored with the rest of the program and then reloaded later. However, this isn't easy because while the Turbo Pascal program is being reloaded, the assembler routine will overwrite itself. So, the assembler routine isn't simply copied to the beginning of the memory, but exchanged byte for byte with the program code previously located there.

After the exchange of the program code, the program code from the beginning of the main program is now located where the assembler routine was previously. Its memory is now occupied by the assembler routine. So, the routine can limit itself to storing the area between its own end and the end of the memory reserved for the program. To prevent the replacement of the exchange routine itself, which would cause a system crash, there is a *label* at the end of the assembler module which marks the end of the area to be exchanged.

The relocated program code, which starts to write the rest of the program into a file or the EMS memory, is called after the exchange. The indicated program is started with the DOS Exec function and the memory area is then loaded again. The assembler module cannot access Pascal routines because it assumes that these have been overwritten by the called program. After the assembler module section, which was loaded after PSP, is exchanged for the program code originally located there, the memory returns to its original status. The Exec function returns to its caller.

This overview of the Exec functions hides the fact that a problem lies in the details required to make the Exec functions successfully return to their original caller. The individual programming steps will be explained on the basis of the listing for the SWAP unit and the assembler module SWAPA.ASM.

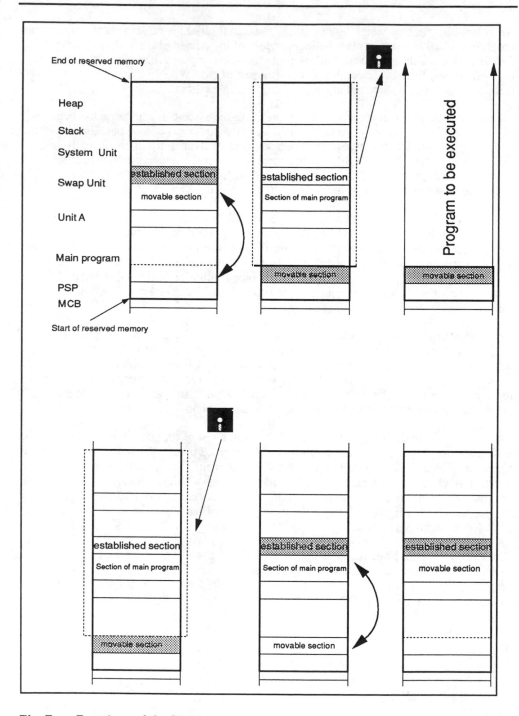

The Exec Functions of the SWAP unit

To illustrate the correct chronology of the SWAP unit execution, the individual procedures and listing sections aren't presented in the order in which they appear in the program listing. Instead, they are shown in the sequence in which they are activated after a call of ExecPrg or ExecCommand. We will begin with the introductory part of the Pascal unit SWAP.

```
{*********************************************************************
*   S W A P : A unit which makes available an alternative Exec procedure   *
*             for calling any program from a Turbo Pascal program. Unlike  *
*             the normal Exec procedure, the Turbo program is stored in EMS *
*             memory or hard disk before the new program is executed. This  *
*             saves memory for the execution of the new program.            *
**-----------------------------------------------------------------**
*   Author          : MICHAEL TISCHER                                 *
*   developed on    : 06/09/1989                                      *
*   last update on  : 03/01/1990                                      *
*********************************************************************}

unit swap;

interface

uses DOS, Ems;

{-- Declaration of functions and procedures which can be called   ---------}
{-- from another program                                          ---------}

function ExecPrg    ( Command : string ) : byte;
function ExecCommand( Command : string ) : byte;

{-- Constants, public -----------------------------------------------------}

const SwapPath : string[ 80 ] = 'c:\';

        {----------------------- Error codes of ExecPrg & ExecCommand ------}

        SwapErrOk       = 0;                      { no error, everything O.K. }
        SwapErrStore    = 1;        { Turbo Pascal program could not be stored }
        SwapErrNotFound = 2;                            { program not found }
        SwapErrNoAccess = 5;                  { access to program denied }
        SwapErrNoRAM    = 8;                        { not enough memory }

implementation

{$L swapa}                                { include assembler module }

{-- Declaration of procedures from SWAPA assembler module -----------------}

function SwapOutAndExec( Command,
                         CmdPara : string;
                         ToDisk  : boolean;
                         Handle  : word;
                         Len     : longint ) : byte ; external;
```

337

```
function InitSwapa : word ; external;

{-- Global variables, internal to this module ----------------------------}

var Len : longint;                        { number of bytes to be stored }
```

The beginning of the SWAP unit lists declarations which were discussed earlier with the ExecPrg and ExecCommand functions: the SwapErr... constants and the typed constant SwapPath. Here the compiler directive $L links the assembly language module SWAPA, and two external declarations provide the interface between Pascal and assembly language.

The variable Len is defined as the single global variable of the SWAP unit. It indicates the number of bytes to be stored—the distance between the end of the assembler module, after being moved behind the PSP, and the end memory reserved for the program. Since this parameter doesn't change during program execution, but is required by every call of ExecCommand or ExecPrg, the unit initializes Len before the actual Pascal program starts.

```
{**------------------------------------------------------------------**}
{** Starting code of the unit                                       **}
{**------------------------------------------------------------------**}

begin
  {-- Calculate the number of bytes to be stored ------------------------}

  {$ifdef VER60}                                        { for Version 6.0 }
  Len := ( longint(Seg(HeapPtr^)-(PrefixSeg+$10)) * 16 ) -
  InitSwapa + Ofs(HeapPtr^);
  {$else}                                     { for Versions 5.0 and 5.5 }
  Len := ( longint(Seg(FreePtr^)+$1000-(PrefixSeg+$10)) * 16 ) - InitSwapa;
  {$endif}
end.
```

The expression used by Len during the initialization is complicated. First the distance between the beginning of the program (i.e., the first byte in the code segment of the main program) and the last byte reserved for the program is calculated. Its address, as shown in Section 2.6, can be calculated with the segment address of the predefined pointer FreePtr, to which the value $1000 must be added. This occurs in the first part of the expression with:

```
Seg(FreePtr^)+$1000
```

The segment address, which starts the code segment of the main program, can be reached through the predefined variable PrefixSeg. This variable indicates the segment address of the PSP, at the end of which the main program is immediately connected. Since the PSP contains 256 bytes (16 paragraphs), the main program's segment address can be obtained with the expression:

```
PrefixSeg+$10.
```

If the segment addresses resulting from this expression are subtracted from each other, the result is the number of paragraphs between the start of the main program and the end of the heap. If this number is multiplied by 16, the result will be the number of bytes between the two points. Then subtract the size of the assembler module, which was moved to the beginning of the main program. This value is returned by the function InitSwapa from the assembler module which is called at the end of the expression.

The expression used under Turbo Pascal 6.0 differs from the calculations under Turbo Pascal 5.0 and 5.5 only in the end address of the program. In Version 6.0, because of the altered heap management, Turbo Pascal doesn't even recognize the FreePtr pointer. Instead, Version 6.0 uses the HeapEnd pointer to describe the heap end. This pointer doesn't even appear in the above expression for Turbo Pascal 6.0, because using it would gather the entire heap, including the part that is unallocated.

You could hardly prevent this under Turbo Pascal 5.0 and 5.5, because the fragment list is kept at the end of the heap so that you had to save the entire heap. Since Turbo 6.0 doesn't have a fragment list, you can stop saving the heap at the end of the upper limit of the allocated region, which is described by the HeapPtr pointer used in the expression above.

Within the SWAP unit the initialization is preceded by the function ExecCommand, which consists of only two commands.

```
{*********************************************************************
*  ExecCommand : Executes a program as if its name was indicated in the  *
*                user interface of DOS.                              *
**-----------------------------------------------------------------**
*  Input    : Command = String with the name of the program to be executed  *
*                       and the parameters which are to be passed in the    *
*                       command line.                                *
*  Output   : One of the error codes SwapErr...                      *
*  Info     : Since the call of the program occurs through the command  *
*             processor, this procedure permits the execution of resident  *
*             DOS commands (DIR etc.) and batch files.               *
*********************************************************************}

function ExecCommand( Command : string ) : byte;

var ComSpec : string;                            { command processor path }

begin
  ComSpec := GetEnv( 'COMSPEC' );                { get command processor path }
  ExecCommand := NewExec( ComSpec, '/c'+ Command ); { execute prg/command }
end;
```

First ExecCommand determines the path of the command processor COMMAND.COM. This is stored within the Environment in the variable COMSPEC, whose contents can be determined with the help of the predefined function GetEnv. The path and filename are passed, by ExecCommand, to the function NewExec. This function coordinates the storage of the memory and the call of the indicated program within the SWAP unit. Two parameters must be passed to it: the name of the program to be executed and the parameters which will be passed to this program with the command line.

Since ExecCommand should not only permit the calling of EXE and COM files, but also the execution of batch files and resident DOS commands, it always gives the name of the calling program as the command processor. Through NewExec, it passes the /c parameter as an argument, followed by the name of the program or the command to be called. The /c parameter ensures that instead of expecting input from the keyboard, the command processor executes the command that follows the /c parameter and then returns to the caller.

The ExecPrg function, which also uses the NewExec function, is more comprehensive.

```
{**************************************************************************
 *  ExecPrg : Executes a program through NewExec whose name and extension *
 *            must be specified.                                          *
 **----------------------------------------------------------------------**
 *  Input : Command = String containing the name of the program to be    *
 *                    executed, as well as the parameters passed to the   *
 *                    command line.                                       *
 *  Output : One of the SwapErr... error codes                           *
 *  Info   : This procedure can execute EXE and COM programs, but not batch *
 *           files or resident DOS commands. The program's path and       *
 *           extension must be provided since no search is made through    *
 *           the PATH command for the program.                           *
 **************************************************************************}

function ExecPrg( Command : string ) : byte;

const Text_Sep : set of char = [ ' ',#9,'-','/','>','<',#0,'|' ];

var i        : integer;                        { index in source string }
    CmdLine,                                   { accepts command }
    Para     : string;                         { accepts parameter }

begin
  {-- Isolate the command from the command string -----------------------}

  CmdLine := '';                               { clear the string }
  i := 1;                { begin with the first letter in the source string }
  while not ( (Command[i] in Text_Sep) or ( i > length( Command ) ) ) do
    begin                                { character is not Text_Sep }
      CmdLine := CmdLine + Command[ i ];            { accept in string }
      inc( i );                  { set I to next character in the string }
    end;

  Para := '';                                  { no parameter detected }

  {-- search for next "non-space character" -----------------------------}

  while (i<=length(Command)) and ( (Command[i]=#9) or (Command[i]=' ') ) do
```

```
    inc( i );

  {-- copy the rest of the strings into the para string ------------------}

  while i <= length( Command ) do
    begin
      Para := Para + Command[ i ];
      inc( i );
    end;

  ExecPrg := NewExec( CmdLine, Para );   { execute command through NewExec }
end;
```

Before the call of NewExec, ExecPrg must separate the program name and the arguments, which were passed to it as a string during the call. It tests this string for the current character, through which the typical constant separator is defined. In it are all the characters, which according to DOS rules, cannot appear in a filename. As soon as ExecPrg encounters one of these characters, it has reached the end of the filename in the string. All characters that follow are considered arguments and are gathered into a string that is passed to NewExec as second parameter.

NewExec contains the call of the assembler module in the form of the SwapOutAndExec function, which stores the memory and calls the indicated program. Since the assembler module cannot use the various Pascal procedures and functions, NewExec takes over many tasks for the assembler module.

```
{******************************************************************************
* NewExec : Controls current Turbo Pascal program's memory, and the          *
*           call for the program indicated.                                   *
**-------------------------------------------------------------------------**
* Input : CmdLine = String containing name of the program to be called       *
*         CmdPara = String containing command line parameters for the        *
*                   program to be called                                      *
* Output : One of the SwapErr... error codes                                 *
******************************************************************************}

function NewExec( CmdLine, CmdPara : string ) : byte;

var Regs,                            { processor register for interrupt call }
    Regs1    : Registers;
    SwapFile : string[ 81 ];                  { name of the temporary Swap-file }
    ToDisk   : boolean;               { store on disk or in EMS-memory ? }
    Handle   : integer;                            { EMS or file handle }
    Pages    : integer;                      { number of EMS pages required }

begin
  {-- Test if storage is possible in EMS memory --------------------------}

  ToDisk := TRUE;                                          { store on disk }
  if ( EmsInst ) then                              { is EMS available? }
```

```
      begin                                                   { Yes }
        Pages   := ( Len + 16383 ) div 16384;    { determine pages needed }
        Handle := EmsAlloc( Pages );                   { allocate pages }
        ToDisk := ( EmsError <> EmsErrOk );    { allocation successful ? }
        if not ToDisk then
          EmsSaveMapping( Handle );                      { save mapping }
      end;

   if ToDisk then                                  { store in EMS memory? }
     begin                                                { no, on disk }

       {- Open temporary file in SwapPath with attributes SYSTEM & HIDDEN --}

       SwapFile := SwapPath;
       SwapFile[ byte(SwapFile[0]) + 1 ] := #0;{ conv. string to DOS format }
       Regs.AH := $5A;          { function number for "create temp. file" }
       Regs.CX := Hidden or SysFile;                     { file attribute }
       Regs.DS := seg( SwapFile );         { address of SwapPath to DS:DX }
       Regs.DX := ofs( SwapFile ) + 1;
       MsDos( Regs );                            { call DOS interrupt $21 }
       if ( Regs.Flags and FCarry = 0 ) then           { file opened? }
         Handle := Regs.AX                           { yes, note handle }
       else                        { no, terminate function prematurely }
         begin
           NewExec := SwapErrStore;   { error during storage of the program }
           exit;                                { terminate function }
         end;
     end;

   {-- Execute program through assembler routine ----------------------}

   SwapVectors;                               { reset interrupt vectors }
   NewExec := SwapOutAndExec( CmdLine, CmdPara, ToDisk, Handle, Len );
   SwapVectors;                     { install Turbo-Int-Handler again }

   if ToDisk then                             { was it stored on disk? }
     begin                                                    { yes }
       {-- close temporary file and delete it --------------------------}

       Regs1.AH := $3E;              { function number for "close file" }
       Regs1.BX := Regs.AX;                   { load handle into BX }
       MsDos( Regs1 );                        { call DOS interrupt $21 }

       Regs.AH := $41;               { function number for "erase file" }
       MsDos( Regs );
     end
   else                                      { no, storage in EMS memory }
     begin
       EmsRestoreMapping( Handle );             { restore mapping again }
       EmsFree( Handle );            { release allocated EMS memory again }
     end;
 end;
```

NewExec's most important task is to prepare for the memory storage and to decide whether the memory should be written into a temporary file or into the EMS memory. To do this, the function uses, among other items, the functions and procedures from the EMS unit.

If EMS memory is available, which can be determined by looking at the contents of the EmsInst variable, NewExec calculates the number of EMS pages required to store the memory. A call of EmsAlloc indicates whether this amount of pages is still available. If it is, the storage to EMS begins. If the calling program itself utilizes this memory extension, the procedure EmsSaveMapping, which stores the current condition between logical EMS pages and the four physical pages in EMS page frame, is called.

The storage is made to a temporary file if no EMS or not enough EMS pages are available. The name of this file is not preset by the SWAP unit because DOS offers a special function through function $5A, which automatically generates the filename without prompting the user for the creation of temporary files. Only the path in which the temporary file should be created must be passed to this function. For this task the processor registers DS and DX are used. During the call of the function they must contain the address of a buffer in which the name is stored.

A Pascal string can't be passed because DOS expects the string in another format. The length byte at the beginning of the string is not required by DOS, but a character with the ASCII code 0 as end mark is required. NewExec performs the required conversions by assigning the variable SwapPath to the variable SwapFile and attaching the required null byte to its end. The address of the first character in SwapFile is passed to the DOS function, instead of the address of SwapFile, which skips the introductory length byte.

During the call, the DOS function $5A expects a numerical value in the CX register, which provides the attribute of the file to be created. NewExec selects the Hidden and SysFile attributes to hide the file as a system file. This ensures that the file won't be visible to a user during the directory listing.

It is possible that DOS can't create a temporary file because the selected directory is already full or an invalid directory was indicated in the SwapPath variable. The function $5A returns with the Carry flag set and NewExec delivers the error code SwapErrStore to the user without calling the assembler module.

If function $5A successfully executes, the caller receives a file *handle*, which is passed as an identification code during all later accesses to the file. The work needed to be done before the actual call of SwapOutAndExec is almost completed. Only Turbo internal interrupt handlers must be deactivated, which can be done with the SwapVectors routine. Then the assembler routine SwapOutAndExec is called and is followed by the new call of SwapVectors to activate the various interrupt handlers again.

After the call of SwapOutAndExec some "housecleaning" functions must still be performed, depending on whether the storage is a temporary file or in the EMS.

In the first instance, the temporary file must be deleted again after being closed with the DOS function $3E. Even though only the file handle must be provided, function $41 needs both the complete path and filename in order to delete the file. This is available from the SwapFile variable because the function $5A, when it was called, attached the filename to the end of the buffer. An error status isn't provided after the call of both functions because an error shouldn't occur here.

During the storage into EMS, two tasks must be considered. The first is to release the EMS memory again and the second is to restore the previously stored mapping of the logical EMS pages and the pages in the EMS page frame. For both tasks the EMS unit provides the procedures EmsFree and EmsRestoreMapping.

We will now leave the Pascal portion of the SWAP unit and turn to the assembler part contained in the SWAPA.ASM file. Two functions are important here. SwapInit, which is called by the initialization routine of SWAP and SwapOutAndExec, which is where the call occurs within the function NewExec. First let's look at the beginning of the assembler module where the variables of the module are declared.

```
;***********************************************************************;
;*                         S W A P A . A S M                          *;
;*-------------------------------------------------------------------*;
;*       Task        : Assembler module for the SWAP unit             *;
;*-------------------------------------------------------------------*;
;*       Author      : MICHAEL TISCHER                                *;
;*       developed on :  06/01/1989                                   *;
;*       last update  :  02/28/1990                                   *;
;*-------------------------------------------------------------------*;
;*       assembly     : TASM - /MX SWAPA                              *;
;*                      ... bind to the SWAP unit                     *;
;***********************************************************************;

;== Constants =========================================================

STACK_LEN equ 64                ;Number of words in the internal stack

;== Structures ========================================================

ExecStruc struc                 ;Data structure for EXEC function
EsSegEnv  dw ?                  ;Segment address of environment blocks
EsCmdPAdr dd ?                  ;Pointer to command line parameters
EsFCB1Adr dd ?                  ;Pointer to FCB #1
EsFCB2Adr dd ?                  ;Pointer to FCB #2

ExecStruc ends

;== Data segment ======================================================
```

```
DATA    segment word public

extrn  PrefixSeg : word          ;Segment address of PSP in Turbo variables

DATA    ends

;== Program ======================================================

CODE       segment byte public    ;Program segment

public     SwapOutAndExec         ;Gives a Turbo Pascal program the
                                  ;ability to pass the address of
                                  ;the assembler handler
public     InitSwapa              ;Initialization procedure
```

Various declarations are encountered here, such as the size of the internal stack, which is active during the storage of the memory, and the ExecStruc structure, which accepts information that the DOS EXEC function requires in order to call the selected program.

The data segment doesn't accept variables in this module, but only contains an Extrn declaration of the PrefixSeg variable, which is contained in the System unit and reflects the segment address of the PSP.

At the beginning of the code segment, the two procedures InitSwapa and SwapOutAndExec are declared as public so they can be called from the Pascal part of the SWAP unit. Following this are the variables which are part of the memory area that is moved to the beginning of the main program. Since these variables are needed during the execution of the program code which was moved there, they cannot be stored in the data segment since it will be stored with their help and later overwritten by the called program.

All variables are stored under the label CodeStart, which marks the beginning of the area within the assembler module that is moved to the beginning of the main program.

```
;== Variables in code segment ====================================

CodeStart  equ this byte          ;Code begins here which is copied to
                                  ;the Turbo program

;-- Variables needed by the Swap routines for uploading and downloading ----

CoStAddr   dd ?                   ;Orig. address of PARA(CodeStart)
CoStLen    dw ?                   ;Number of words swapped w/ CoStAddr
StackPtr   dw ?                   ;Gets old stack pointer
StackSeg   dw ?                   ;Gets old stack segment
TurboSeg   dw ?                   ;Segment address - Turbo code segment

;-- Variables needed for program configuration and command execution -------
```

```
NewStack      dw STACK_LEN dup (?)        ;New stack
EndStack      equ this word               ;End of stack

Command       dd ?                        ;Pointer to command
CmdPara       dd ?                        ;Pointer to command line parameters
ToDisk        db ?                        ;True when disk swapping occurs
Handle        dw ?                        ;Disk or EMS handle
Len           dd ?                        ;Number of bytes saved

FCB1          db  16 dup ( 0 )            ;FCB #1 for PSP
FCB2          db  16 dup ( 0 )            ;FCB #2 for PSP
CmdBuf        db 128 dup ( 0 )            ;Commands following prg. name
PrgName       db  64 dup ( 0 )            ;Program name
ExecData      ExecStruc < 0, CmdBuf, FCB1, FCB2 >   ;Data structure for EXEC

OldPara       dw ?                        ;Number of previously reserved paragraphs
FrameSeg      dw ?                        ;Segment address of EMS page frame
Error_Code    db 0                        ;Error code for caller

TerMes        db 13,10,13,10
              db  "┌────────────────────────────────────────────┐",13,10
              db  "║ SWAP : Stored Turbo Pascal program could     ║",13,10
              db  "║        not be reloaded back into memory.     ║",13,10
              db  "║        Program execution terminated!         ║",13,10
              db  "└────────────────────────────────────────────┘"
              db 13,10,13,10,"$"
```

The first block of variables contains the information that is required for copying the program code to the beginning of the code segment. This process is called *downloading* because the program code is moved to a memory location with a lower address. So, *uploading* signifies the copying of the program code to its original address.

Also, an entire series of other variables and buffers are required (i.e., the memory area for the internal stack, which is marked by the NEWSPEAK variable). The variables Command, CmdPara, ToDisk, Handle and Len reflect the various parameters that the Pascal function NewExec passes to the assembler routine SwapOutAndExec. These variables will be discussed in more detail in the following section.

The Block variable, which follows the variables FCB1, FCB2, CmdBuf, PrgName and ExecData, accepts the information that the DOS function EXEC needs in order to load and start the indicated program. We will discuss this in more detail with the call of this function.

Located before the beginning of the program code, the final variables serve different purposes. Although the TerMes variable is rarely used, it is an important variable when the module needs to access it. TerMes contains an error message which the assembler module sends to the display screen only when the stored memory cannot be loaded again after the execution of the program. Since SwapOutAndExec can't return to the Pascal program, the program execution is terminated when this error message is displayed.

We will now jump from the beginning of the assembler module to the end. The InitSwapa function is called within the initialization portion of the SWAP unit. Its task is to return the number of bytes, in the portion that is moved, to the caller. Simultaneously, it stores this value, converted to words, in the CoStLen variable, which is later accessed during the uploading and downloading of the program code.

```
;----------------------------------------------------------------------------
;-- InitSwapa : Computes the number of bytes/words allocated for a program
;--             swap with the start of the Turbo program in memory
;-- Input       : none
;-- Output      : number of bytes
;-- Pascal call : function InitSWapa : word;
;-- Info        : This procedure must be called before the
;--               first call to SwapOutAndExec!

InitSwapa   proc near

            assume cs:code, ds:data

            mov    bx,offset CodeStart    ;AX points to start of code
            and    bx,0FFF0h              ;Round off at start of paragraph
            mov    ax,offset CodeEnd      ;BX points to end of code
            sub    ax,bx                  ;Compute number of bytes
            inc    ax                     ;Convert CX to words
            shr    ax,1
            mov    CoStLen,ax             ;Mark number of words to be swapped
            shl    ax,1                   ;Convert to bytes

            ;-- Return contents of AX as function result

            ret                           ;Return to caller

InitSwapa   endp

;----------------------------------------------------------------------------

CODE        ends                 ;End of code segment
            end                  ;End of program
```

At the beginning of the procedure, the ASSUME command informs the assembler that the CS register points to the code segment during the call of the procedure and the DS register contains the segment address of the data segment. During access to the CoStLen variable, which is defined within the code segment, the assembler automatically creates a *segment override* to the CS register. This results in the processor accessing the CS register, instead of the DS register, during the address creation.

The portion of the assembler module that will be moved is marked by the two labels CodeStart and CodeEnd. The number of bytes to be moved is the difference between the two offset addresses. Since the program portion which is moved must start at a location that is divisible by 16, the offset address of CodeStart is rounded before the subtraction with an AND command to the previous paragraph start. The number of bytes to be moved include the distance between the paragraph start and the actual address of CodeStart.

The procedure itself is already located behind the label CodeEnd and isn't relocated. This isn't necessary because InitSwapa is only called once before the start of the program, and then is no longer required.

The SwapOutAndExec procedure, which is the interface between the Pascal and the assembler portion of the unit isn't moved either. It immediately precedes the InitSwapa procedure within the listing.

```
;-------------------------------------------------------------------------
;-- SwapOutAndExec : Swaps the current program to EMS memory or hard disk
;--                  and starts another program using the DOS EXEC function
;-- Call from Turbo: SwapOutAndExec( Command,
;--                                  CmdPara : string;
;--                                  ToDisk  : boolean;
;--                                  Handle  : word;
;--                                  Len     : longint );
;-- Info          : The Command and CmdPara parameters must be configured
;--                  as strings in DOS format.

SwapOutAndExec proc near

ACommand    equ dword ptr [bp+16]   ;Constants for accessing the
ACmdPara    equ dword ptr [bp+12]   ;specified arguments
AToDisk     equ  byte ptr [bp+10]
AHandle     equ  word ptr [bp+ 8]
ALen        equ dword ptr [bp+ 4]
ARG_LEN     equ 16                  ;Lengths of arguments

            assume cs:code, ds:data

            push bp                 ;Enable access to the arguments
            mov  bp,sp
```

NewExec passes various parameters to SwapOutAndExec, which it addresses like any normal Pascal procedure or function through the BP register and the stack. There are two pointers to the two strings which NewExec obtains from its caller. In the first of the two is the name of the program that will be called; in the second is the parameter, in ASCII form, which will be passed to the program.

The next parameter is of the Boolean type and indicates if memory occurs in a temporary file or in the EMS. As the name "ToDisk" implies, the value TRUE represents memory on disk.

Regardless of ToDisk's contents, a handle is required as identification for access to either the EMS memory or the temporary file. In both cases this handle is represented as a word so it can be passed to SwapOutAndExec as a parameter whose interpretation depends on the value in ToDisk. The last parameter is passed to SwapOutAndExec from the caller. It is the number of bytes to be stored, in the form of a LongInts.

To make addressing these various parameters easier, the procedure defines various textmacros, in which the addresses of the individual parameters are given relative to the contents of the BP register. With these textmacros, various parameters are accessed within the procedure. First the program name is copied from its storage place to the PrgName variable in the code segment. If the program name is longer than 64 bytes, which shouldn't happen, only the first 64 bytes are copied.

```
          ;-- Copy program name to buffer in code segment ----------------

          mov    dx,ds              ;Mark DS
          push   cs                 ;Set ES to CS
          pop    es

          lds    si,ACommand        ;DS:SI points to command buffer
          mov    di,offset PrgName  ;ES:DI points to PrgName
          cld                       ;Increment on string instructions
          lodsb                     ;Read length of Pascal string
          cmp    al,64              ;More than 64 characters?
          jbe    CmdCopy            ;No ---> CmdCopy

          mov    al,64              ;Yes ---> Copy a maximum of 64 characters

CmdCopy:  xor    ah,ah              ;Set Hi-Byte to 0 length and
          mov    cx,ax              ;load into the counter
          rep movsb                 ;Copy string
```

During the next step, the second string with the parameters is copied into the CmdBuf variable within the code segment. However, the DOS EXEC function expects this buffer in a special format, since it copies it without changes to the end of the PSP, which is placed in front of the called program in memory. The first byte accepts the length of this string. Remember that a maximum length, here 126 bytes, cannot be exceeded. The EXEC function also requires that a carriage return character be attached at the end of the buffer.

```
          ;-- Copy command line in buffer in code segment ----------------

          lds    si,ACmdPara        ;DS:SI points to CmdPara buffer
          mov    di,offset CmdBuf   ;ES:DI points to CmdBuf
          lodsb                     ;Read length of Pascal string
```

349

```
                cmp    al,126          ;More than 126 characters?
                jbe    ParaCopy        ;No ---> ParaCopy

                mov    al,126          ;Yes ---> Copy maximum of 126 characters

    ParaCopy:   stosb                  ;Store length as first byte
                xor    ah,ah           ;Set Hi-Byte to 0 length and
                mov    cx,ax           ;load into the counter
                rep movsb              ;Copy string

                mov    al,0dH          ;Add carriage return
                stosb
```

The DOS EXEC function also expects two File Control Blocks (FCBs), which it copies into the memory locations designated for this purpose, in the PSP. Up to DOS Version 2.0, DOS copied the first two parameters passed to a program into this FCB, which DOS assumed was a filename. Although none of today's popular programs access this information, SwapOutAndExec also loads the first two parameters into the FCBs provided to preserve compatibility with the old DOS programs.

```
        ;-- Transfer filename from command line to FCBs -----------------

                push   cs               ;Transfer CS to DS
                pop    ds

                mov    si,offset CmdBuf+1 ;DS:SI points to CmdBuf + 1
                mov    di,offset FCB1   ;ES:DI points to FCB #1
                mov    ax,2901h         ;Function no.:"Transfer filename to FCB"
                int    21h              ;Call DOS interrupt

                mov    di,offset FCB2   ;ES:DI now points to FCB #2
                mov    ax,2901h         ;Function no.: "Transfer filename to FCB"
                int    21h              ;Call DOS interrupt

                mov    ds,dx            ;Move old value into DS
```

SwapOutAndExec isn't concerned with the structure of the FCBs and the evaluation of the parameter from the command line. For this task DOS uses the function $29, sub-function $01 which enters a filename into an FCB. Within SwapOutAndExec, two calls of this function must occur. During its call, the function expects the address of the FCBs in the ED:DI register pair. The variables (or buffer) with the names FCB1 and FCB2 are located in this register.

The register pair DS:SI must point to the filename that will be sent to the FCB. Before the first call of the function $29, these two registers are loaded with the addresses of the CmdBuf variable, which was copied at the beginning of the procedure from the parameter string.

Instead of returning the register pair DS:SI, unchanged to the caller, function $29 loads this register pair with the address of the parameters within the command line following the one just processed. So, the two registers don't have to be loaded again for the second call of this function. Only the DI register contains a new value with the offset address of FCB2.

In the last step of moving the program code, SwapOutAndExec loads the parameter, passed by NewExec and not yet processed, into the variables within the code segment.

```
;-- Transfer remaining parameters to variables ------------------

les    ax,ALen          ;Change length
mov    word ptr Len + 2,es
mov    word ptr Len,ax

mov    al,AToDisk        ;Change disk flag
mov    ToDisk,al

mov    ax,AHandle        ;Change handle
mov    Handle,ax

push   ds                ;Push DS onto the stack
```

Preparations are made for moving the program after the remaining parameters are transmitted. This is done by loading the various registers with the addresses of the program parts to be switched.

```
;-- Exchange variables and program code between labels CodeStart -
;-- and CodeEnd with the contents of the PSP code segment

mov    ax,PrefixSeg      ;ES:DI points to start of Turbo
add    ax,10h            ;program following PSP
mov    TurboSeg,ax       ;Mark addr. of Turbo code segment
mov    es,ax
xor    di,di

push   cs                ;Set DS to CS
pop    ds
assume cs:code, ds:code

mov    si,offset CodeStart    ;DS:SI points to CodeStart
and    si,0FFF0h              ;Round off at start of paragraph

mov    cx,CostLen             ;Get number of words to be swapped
mov    word ptr CoStAddr,si       ;Mark address of
mov    word ptr CoStAddr + 2,ds   ;PARA(Codestart)

mov    dx,es             ;Mark target segment in DX
cld                      ;Increment on SI/DI string instructions

;-- Swap loop -----------------------------------------------
```

```
dl_loop:   mov   ax,[si]        ;Load word from assembler module
           mov   bx,es:[di]     ;Load word from Turbo Pascal program
           stosw                ;Write assm. module word to Turbo program
           mov   [si],bx        ;Write Turbo program word to assm. module
           inc   si             ;Set SI to next word
           inc   si             ;(increment SI through STOSW)
             loop  dl_loop           ;Use all words
```

The address of the main program is determined through the PrefixSeg variable, defined in the System unit with the 16 paragraphs added. This value is not only loaded into the E register but also stored in the TurboSeg variable because it will be needed later. As start offset in this segment, the DI register is loaded with the value 0 in order to move the program code from the assembler module directly behind the PSP.

The registers DS:SI are loaded with the start address of the program code to be moved (i.e., the address of the label CodeStart). This address is also stored in the CoStAddr variable because it will be needed later for the uploading of the program code. As previously mentioned during the description of the InitSwapa procedure, the offset address of CodeStart is rounded off to a paragraph start. The reason for this will become clear immediately after the copy process is completed.

Before the beginning of the downloading, the number of words to be exchanged is loaded into the CX register. During the call of InitSwapa, this information is stored in the CostLen variable and can be read without any difficult calculations.

The actual downloading is rather simple. The two memory areas to be exchanged are processed in ascending order and exchanged one word at a time. Then the DI and SI registers, which acted as indices, are incremented by two in order to point to the next word. After the completion of the loop, the program code is located between the labels CodeStart and CodeEnd at the beginning of the main program and the code stored there is located between the two labels in the code segment of the SWAP unit.

However, moving the program code isn't sufficient because this changes the location of the program code within its own segment. While it originally started at the offset address CodeStart, within the code segment of the SWAP unit, it is now located starting at offset address 0 in the code segment of the main program. Because of this, all commands that refer to the offset address of the program code (and the variables) within the code segment must be modified. This includes all Jump commands and the references to variables within machine language commands, such as MOV.

Since it would take a lot of time to examine the individual commands within the program code and to individually enter the new offset addresses into the individual commands, SwapOutAndExec uses a trick. During the call of the StartSwap procedure, which controls the execution of the program code that was moved, the procedure ensures that the displaced program code retains its original offset position within the code segment. The CS register isn't loaded with the segment address of the main program because the offset address of the program code is 0 relative to this address. Instead, the CS register is supplied with a smaller value which is selected so that the CodeStart label in the new segment continues to be located at the normal offset address.

The offset address of CodeStart, which is the distance between the beginning of the segment and the label and converted to paragraphs, is subtracted from the segment address of the main program. For example, if the CodeStart label is at the offset address 128, within the code segment of the SWAP unit, then there are eight paragraphs between the start of the code segment and this label. Therefore, the CS register, during the call of StartSwap, shouldn't be loaded with the segment address of the main program, but with this address minus 8. So, CodeStart is also located at the offset address 128, within its new segment.

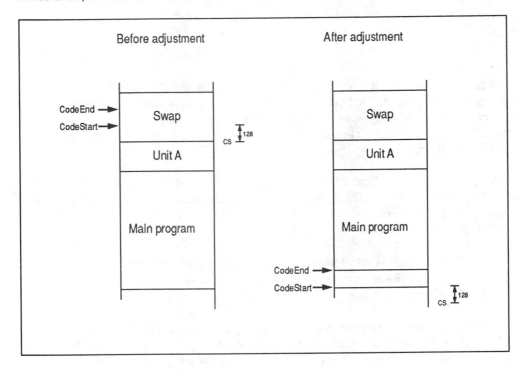

Adjustment of the Segment addresses during the call of StartSwap

Although this process has worked so far, you cannot assume that CodeStart is located at an offset address that is divisible by sixteen. This is absolutely necessary in order for this to work. Therefore, at the proper places in the program code, the offset address of CodeStart is rounded off to the beginning of the preceding paragraph. This copies between 0 and 15 more bytes than are necessary to the beginning of the main program. But this prevents having to adjust the offset addresses within the program code.

```
;-- Adapt segment address of code segment before calling the ---
;-- StartSwap procedure so that variable references to the code
;-- segment remain unchanged

mov    ax,offset CodeStart ;Compute number of paragraphs between
mov    cl,4                ;CodeStart and the start of the
shr    ax,cl               ;segment, and get segment address in
sub    dx,ax               ;DX

push   cs                  ;Return address to BACK label
mov    ax,offset back      ;Move onto the stack
push   ax

push   dx                  ;Push segment address onto stack
mov    ax,offset StartSwap ;Move offset address onto stack
push   ax

retf                       ;FAR-RET to StartSwap
```

The above command sequence demonstrates our explanations on adjusting the segment address into the program. First the offset address of CodeStart is loaded into the AX register and converted into paragraphs. It doesn't have to be rounded to the beginning of the preceding paragraph because this is done automatically with the division by shifting four bit positions to the right.

The value obtained is subtracted from the segment address of the main program, which at this moment is still in the DX register. To pass the program execution to the procedure StartSwap, its offset address and the newly calculated segment address is brought on the stack as it would occur during a FAR CALL command.

Before this, the Return Jump address for the SwapOutAndExec procedure is brought to the stack so that StartSwap can later return with a simple FAR Return command to SwapOutAndExec.

The RETF command, which appears after StartSwap's address is loaded to the stack, leads to the call of StartSwap. This happens because the computer reads the last two words from the stack and considers them as a Return Jump address to the caller. This automatically loads the desired address as a new segment address into the CS register and the offset address of StartSwap into the IP register.

Now let's discuss the execution SwapOutAndExec in more detail. The address of the label Back, which immediately follows the FAR Return command that leads to the call of StartSwap, was brought to the Stack after the address of StartSwap. After its completion, StartSwap is automatically returned to this program location with a FAR Return command. At this time the execution of the program to be called is already completed and StartSwap has loaded the previously stored program code into memory again.

```
back:           ;----------------------------------------------------------------
                ;-- Returns original program to main memory and executes the
                ;-- program.
                ;-- Registers have the following contents:
                ;--    DS:SI = End of assembler code following the PSP
                ;--    ES:DI = End of Turbo code in the SWAP unit
                ;--    CX    = Number of words
                ;----------------------------------------------------------------

                assume cs:code, ds:nothing

                std                       ;Decrement string instructions by SI/DI

                ;-- Swap back loop ----------------------------------------------

ul_loop:        mov    bx,es:[di]         ;Get byte from old memory range
                mov    ax,[si]            ;Get byte from current memory range
                mov    [si],bx            ;Byte from old memory rng to current rng
                dec    si                 ;Set SI to previous word
                dec    si
                stosw                     ;Byte from current memory rng to old rng
                loop   ul_loop            ;Repeat until memory ranges are exchanged
```

After the return from StartSwap, the uploading of the program code still must be performed. This concludes SwapOutAndExec's work and restores the memory to its original appearance.

This occurs within a loop which processes, in reverse order, the memory area that will be exchanged, which prevents any problems in case the program code to be moved overlaps with the memory area from the beginning of the main program. However, this can only occur if the distance between the beginning of the main program and the beginning of the program code to be moved is smaller than the length of this code. Although this is almost impossible, you should check this to be sure.

Again, the two memory areas are addressed through the register pairs ES:DI and DI:SI. But this time the registers are loaded with the various addresses, not by SwapOutAndExec, but by StartSwap. This is related to the fact that required information is inside the variables in the moved program code. Since SwapOutAndExec will return it to the original position, this procedure doesn't have access to the different variables. So, it must delegate this task to the StartSwap procedure.

Once the program code is uploaded, the SwapOutAndExec routine finishes its work. The original contents of the DS and the BP registers are again loaded from the stack and then the function result from the error variable Error_Code is transferred to the AX register that will be passed to the caller. During the terminating RET command, the parameters passed by NewExec are deleted and the stack is returned to its original condition. The ARG_LEN constant that is used is defined at the beginning of SwapOutAndExec and mirrors the number of bytes which NewExec stores as parameters on the stack.

```
        pop    ds                  ;Pop DS off of stack
        assume ds:data

        pop    bp                  ;Pop BP

        ;-- MOV SP,BP must not be given, since SP doesn't change

        xor    ah,ah               ;Place error code in AX
        mov    al,Error_Code

        ret ARG_LEN                ;Return to caller, clear arguments
                                   ;from stack

SwapOutAndExec endp
```

We now come to the StartSwap procedure, which takes over the control of the various activities within the program code that will be moved. This procedure follows the variables in the code segment. No parameters are passed to the procedure by SwapOutAndExec because all the required information is in the different variables that were moved with it to the beginning of the main program.

```
;--------------------------------------------------------------------
;-- StartSwap : Coordinate swapping of Turbo Pascal program

StartSwap  proc far

        assume cs:code, ds:nothing

        ;-- Store current stack and initialize new stack ----------------

        cli                        ;Suppress interrupts
        mov    StackPtr,sp         ;Mark current stack
        mov    StackSeg,ss
        push   cs                  ;Install new stack
        pop    ss
        mov    sp,offset EndStack - 2
        sti                        ;Re-enable interrupts

        push   cs                  ;Set DS to CS
        pop    ds
        assume cs:code, ds:code
```

Since the stack of the Turbo program will later be moved with the rest of the memory, StartSwap first installs a new stack. To be able to activate the old stack later, the contents of the CS and the SP registers are stored in the StackPtr and StackSeg variables. A new stack will simultaneously be installed when new contents are later assigned to them. The NEWSPEAK variable makes the memory area for the new stack available. Since the stack for the 8086/8088 "grows" from the top toward the bottom, the stack pointer is set to the end of the stack, which is marked by the EndStack label.

Then the DS register is loaded with the contents of the CS register. Because of this, the relocated variables can be addressed as usual with the DS register, without the assembler creating a special segment override. This is passed to it through the ASSUME instruction.

```
            ;-- Overwrite unnecessary memory -------------------------------

            cmp    ToDisk,0         ;Write to EMS memory?
            je     Ems              ;Yes ---> Ems

            call   Write2File       ;No ---> Write to file
            jnc    ShrinkMem        ;No error ---> ShrinkMem

            mov    Error_Code, 1    ;File output error?
            jmp    short GetBack     ;return to Turbo

Ems:        mov    ah,41h           ;Pass segment address of the page frame
            int    67h              ;Call EMM
            mov    FrameSeg,bx       ;Place result in variables

            call   Write2Ems        ;Write program to EMS
```

Next the memory area is moved. Through the ToDisk variable, StartSwap determines whether the storage should be made to EMS or disk. For storage on a disk, it calls the Write2File procedure. If an error occurred during the execution, the Write2File procedure signals with the contents of the carry flags during the return to StartSwap. In this case StartSwap loads the error code 1 into the error variable of the same name and returns, without performing its job, to SwapOutAndExec.

During the storage in EMS, the segment address of the EMS page frame is determined. To do this, StartSwap uses the EMS function $41, which returns the desired information in the BX register. This address is stored in the FrameSeg variable. For storing the memory, StartSwap uses, for the EMS, a utility procedure named Write2Ems which will be described later with Write2File.

After moving the memory, nothing will prevent the release of the memory that is no longer needed. So that you understand the functional operation of this part of the program, we have included a brief explanation of the memory allocation of DOS.

The Memory Allocation of DOS

As an operating system, DOS has the task of managing the operations of the computer. These operations include memory devices, display screen, keyboard and RAM memory. Programs cannot simply occupy RAM memory areas but must request it from DOS, just as the memory areas of the Turbo Pascal heap must be allocated.

For this purpose, DOS provides these three functions:

- $48   To allocate the RAM memory.
- $49   To release the allocated RAM memory.
- $4A   To change the size of a previously allocated memory block.

All three functions operate on paragraphs and not on a byte basis. This requires that an allocated memory area must always be a size divisible by 16 and that DOS always starts at a memory address that is divisible by 16. Only in this way can DOS guarantee that the beginning of an allocated memory area always coincides with the beginning of a segment.

These three functions cannot determine the size of the memory area reserved by DOS before the Turbo program loads and executes. This information is required by StartSwap if the memory reserved for the Turbo program should again need the original size after the execution of the program. This is the most important requirement for reloading the stored memory.

The information about the size of the allocated memory area cannot be discovered through the DOS functions, but is already in memory near the Turbo program. DOS places, in front of every memory area allocated with the function $48a, a data structure for the administration of this memory area. This is called a *Memory Control Block* but is only addressed by its acronym MCB.

Since the memory allocated for our Turbo Pascal program starts with the PSP, the applicable MCB immediately precedes the PSP. Since an MCB always consists of 16 bytes, its segment address can be calculated through the segment address of the PSP from the PrefixSeg variable. So, it is PrefixSeg 17.

Addr.	Content	Type
$00	ID ("Z" = last MCB, "M" = more to follow)	1 BYTE
$01	Segment address of the PSP	1 WORD
$03	Number of paragraphs in the allocated memory	1 WORD
$05	unused	11 BYTE

A Memory Control Block in the memory

In the first field of the MCB one of the creators of MS-DOS, Mark Zbikowski, built a legacy for himself. This field always contains one of his initials: "M" indicates that this MCB is followed by other MCBs and "Z" indicates that this is the last MCB in memory.

The segment address of the PSP of the program is in the second field. It is only important if the allocated memory area is the Environment Block of a program, which creates a connection between Environment and PSP. This field points to the memory area itself if the memory area is a PSP.

The third field in the MCB, which accepts the information about the size of the memory area in paragraphs, is important. Since the next MCB begins immediately after the end of the allocated memory area, the field contains the distance to the next MCB minus 1. This provides a chained list of the MCBs which is ended by an MCB with the letter "Z" in the first field.

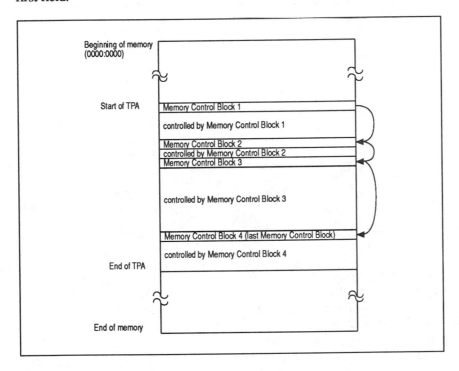

Chaining allocated memory areas through their MCBs

With information about the existence, arrangement and construction of the MCBs, StartSwap can determine the size of the allocated memory areas, even when DOS isn't really willing to offer this information.

Back to the SWAP unit. To determine the size of the reserved memory area, StartSwap loads the segment address of the PSP from the TurboSeg variable into the AX register. It then subtracts the value 17 from it and obtains the segment address of the MCB. From the memory location 3, within this segment, it loads the desired information and enters it into the OldPara variable.

Then it limits the size of the reserved memory area by calling the function $4A. In the ES register it passes the segment address of the allocated memory and also the segment address of the PSP. The number of available paragraphs is passed in the BX register. Since StartSwap wants to reduce, not extend, the reserved memory space, the error condition doesn't have to be checked after the call of DOS function $4A. The memory reduction always executes without error.

```
                ;-- Provide number of currently allocated paragraphs ------------

ShrinkMem: mov     ax,TurboSeg         ;Segment address of Turbo code segment
           sub     ax,11h             ;Allocate 10 paragraphs for PSP and 1
                                       ;for MCB
           mov     es,ax              ;ES now pointer to Turbo prog. MCB
           mov     bx,es:[3]          ;Get number of paragraphs allocated
           mov     OldPara,bx         ;and place in variable

                ;-- Calculate the number of paragraphs needed and reduce   --
                ;-- memory requirements by this amount                     --

           inc     ax                 ;AX now points to the PSP
           mov     es,ax              ;for function call to ES
           mov     bx,CostLen         ;Number of words needed by Swap routine
           add     bx,128+7           ;Recalculate and round off PSP
           mov     cl,3               ;Divide by 8 words (per paragraph)
           shr     bx,cl

           mov     ah,4Ah             ;Function number for "change size"
           int     21h                    ;Call DOS interrupt
```

Once the excess memory is released, the call of the indicated program through the DOS EXEC function can be started. This function has the number $4B, subfunction $00, and during the call expects two pointers in the register pair ES:BX and DS:DX. ES:BX must point to the EXEC parameter block, a data structure whose format was formed by the assembler structure ExecStruc and whose declaration can be found at the beginning of the assembler module.

The first information stored there is the segment address of the environment block which is placed in front of the program to be called. The second field stores a pointer to the command line buffer, which the EXEC function copies, before the start, to the PSP of the called program. Also, the last two fields are pointers. They accept the addresses of the two FCBs, which are copied to the PSP of the called program.

The code segment already contains the structure in the form of the ExecData variable, which should be passed to the DOS EXEC function. ExecData in the first field contains the value 0 which provokes DOS to precede the called program with the same environment block that was also assigned to the Turbo program. The three pointers occupy the addresses of the CmdBuf, FCB1 and FCB2 variables, which were already initialized by SwapOutAndExec.

These pointers are obviously affected by the relocation of the program code because the buffer to which they point is moved to the beginning of the main program. Since the segment address within the three pointers is altered, they must be individually re-adjusted.

For this reason, StartSwap loads the segment address of the code segment into the segment portions of the three pointers.

The address of the strings must be passed to the second pointer of the DOS EXEC function. It contains the name and the path of the program to be executed. This information is copied, by SwapOutAndExec, into the PrgName buffer. So, the address of the buffer is passed to the DOS EXEC function in the register pair DS:DX.

```
;-- Execute specified command line using the EXE function ------

mov     bp,ds               ;Store DS

mov     ax,cs               ;Set ES and DS to CS
mov     es,ax
mov     ds,ax

;-- Enter segment address of code segments in the pointer -----
;-- to the EXEC structure

mov     word ptr ExecData.EsFCB1Adr + 2,ax
mov     word ptr ExecData.EsFCB1Adr + 2,ax
mov     word ptr ExecData.EsCmdPAdr + 2,ax

mov     bx,offset ExecData   ;ES:BX point to parameter block
mov     dx,offset PrgName     ;DS:DX point to command string

mov     ax,4B00h            ;Function number for "EXEC"
int     21h                 ;Call DOS interrupt
mov     ds,bp               ;Move DS
jnc     ReMem               ;No error ---> ReMem

mov     Error_Code,ah       ;Note ErrorCode
```

After the function call a test is made on the basis of the carry flags if the program could be executed. If this flag is set, an error occurred and the AH register contains an error code. If this happens, the error code is stored in the variable of the same name and later returned to the NewExec.

Regardless of whether or not an error occurred after the call of the DOS EXEC function, the reloading of the memory is prepared. First the memory must be brought back to its old size, for which the function $4A must be called again. For the desired size, the number of paragraphs which was previously determined through the MCB and stored in the OldPara variable, is passed to it.

```
                 ;-- Return memory to original size -----------------------------

ReMem:      mov     ax,TurboSeg         ;Set Turbo code segment address
            sub     ax,10h             ;to start of PSP
            mov     es,ax              ;and load into ES
            mov     bx,OldPara         ;Old number of paragraphs

            mov     ah,4Ah             ;Function number for "change size"
            int     21h                ;Call DOS interrupt
            jnc     GetBack            ;No error ---> GetBack

            jmp     Terminate          ;Error in ReMem --> End program
```

After the function, a test is made to determine if the allocated memory can be expanded to its old size. This test is performed because there are various reasons why this may not be possible. For example, the called program may have been a TSR program that made itself resident in memory and doesn't even consider releasing the reserved memory. Some programs can be directly removed from memory. However, programs that allocate additional memory using DOS function $48 may "forget" to use DOS function $49 to release this additional memory before the program ends.

In both cases the function $4A returns with a set carry flag to the caller. This signals the error. StartSwap must terminate program execution with an error message because the relocated memory couldn't be reloaded. This makes returning to the Pascal portion of the SWAP unit impossible.

If the memory could be enlarged, the relocated memory is reloaded. The GctFromFile procedure is called if the relocation was made to a disk, but if the EMS was used, the GetFromEms procedure is called. After the successful call of these procedures, StartSwap has almost completed its assignment. It reactivates only the old stack and prepares the various processor registers for the uploading of the program code before returning to SwapOutAndExec.

```
                 ;-- Return to program -------------------------------------------

GetBack:    cmp     ToDisk,0           ;Write to EMS memory?
            je      Ems1               ;Yes ---> Ems1

            call    GetFromFile        ;No, reload as file
            jnc     CloseUp            ;No error ---> CloseUp

            jmp     Terminate          ;Read error, end program

Ems1:       call    GetFromEms         ;Get Turbo Pascal program from EMS memory

                 ;-- Restore old stack -------------------------------------------

CloseUp:    cli                        ;Suppress interrupts
            mov     ss,StackSeg
```

```
        mov    sp,StackPtr
        sti                        ;Re-enable interrupts

;-- Prepare registers for swap ----------------------------------

        push   cs                  ;Push DS to CS
        pop    ds
        assume cs:code, ds:code

        mov    cx,CoStLen          ;Number of words to be swapped
        mov    di,cx               ;Move number of words to DI
        dec    di                  ;Decrement by one word
        shl    di,1                ;Double it
        mov    si,di               ;move to SI
        add    di,word ptr CostAddr     ;DI+offset addr. of Swap routine
        mov    es,word ptr CostAddr + 2 ;ES gets old CS of Swap routine
        mov    ds,TurboSeg         ;Seg addr. of start of code

        ret                        ;Return to SwapOutAndExec

StartSwap  endp
```

During our discussion of the assembler module SWAPA, we overlooked the four procedures used by StartSwap to store the memory either on Disk or EMS and then later reload it. These four procedures are: Write2Ems, Write2File, GetFromFile and GetFromEms.

Write2Ems writes the program in a large loop, in 16 Kbyte blocks to the EMS. Not only is the memory processed, but a new logical EMS page is brought into the first physical page in the page frame that will be loaded with the saved memory contents. Within this loop more information must be controlled than can be stored in the various processor registers. For this reason, information must be stored in a variable which precedes the procedure in the code segment. This variable is called HiWLen and accepts the Hi-Word of the number of bytes that will be stored. The register assignment within the loop reveals the procedure itself.

```
;------------------------------------------------------------------------
;-- Write2Ems : Write program to be swapped to EMS memory
;-- Input     : BX = Segment address of EMS page frame
;--             DS = Codesegment

EMS_PLEN   equ 16384               ;Length of an EMS page

HiWLen     dw    ?                  ;Remaining Hi-Word length

Write2Ems  proc near

        push   ds                  ;Push DS onto stack
        cld                        ;Increment on string instructions
        mov    es,bx               ;ES points to the page frame
```

```
              mov    bp,word ptr Len          ;Move Lo-Word length to BP
              mov    ax,word ptr Len + 2      ;Move Hi-Word length to AX
              mov    HiWLen,ax                ;and then to variable

              mov    dx,Handle                ;Move EMS Handle to DX
              xor    bx,bx                    ;Start with first logical page

              assume cs:code, ds:nothing

              jmp short WriECalc              ;Jump in the loop

    WriELoop: ;-- Register allocation within this loop ----------------------
              ;
              ;  AX          = Times this, times that
              ;  BX          = Number of logical EMS pages to be addressed
              ;  CX          = Number of bytes to be copied in this execution
              ;  DX          = EMS handle
              ;  ES:DI       = Pointer to first page in EMS page frame (Target)
              ;  DS:SI       = Pointer to first word to be copied      (Start)
              ;  HiWLen:BP   = Number of bytes remaining to be copied

              mov    ax,4400h                 ;Function number for illustration
              int    67h                      ;Call EMM

              mov    si,offset CodeEnd        ;Offset for Swapping
              xor    di,di                    ;Write to the start of the EMS page
              mov    ax,cx                    ;Move number to AX
              rep movsb                       ;Copy memory

              sub    bp,ax                    ;Remainder of written bytes
              sbb    HiWLen,0                 ;Decrement

              inc    bx                       ;Increment number of logical page

              mov    ax,ds                    ;Starting segment to AX
              add    ax,EMS_PLEN shr 4        ;Increment by written paragraphs
              mov    ds,ax                    ;and move to DS

    WriECalc: mov    cx,EMS_PLEN              ;Write EMS_PLEN bytes
              cmp    HiWLen,0                 ;More than 64K?
              ja     WriELoop                 ;Yes ---> WriELoop
              cmp    bp,cx                    ;No ---> More than EMS_PLEN bytes?
              jae    WriELoop                 ;Yes ---> Continue writing
              mov    cx,bp                    ;No ---> Write remainder
              or     cx,cx                    ;No more bytes to write?
              jne    WriELoop                 ;No ---> WriELoop

    WriERet:  pop    ds                       ;Pop DS off of stack
              ret                             ;Return to caller

    Write2Ems endp
```

The procedure GetFromEms, which reloads the memory, works like Write2Ems. It processes the EMS pages, brings them into the first page of the EMS page frame and copies their contents from there to the RAM memory. The register assignment within the loop is almost identical to Write2Ems.

```
;--------------------------------------------------------------------
;-- GetFromEms : Get the swapped program from EMS memory
;-- Input    : DS = Code segment

GetFromEms proc near

        push  ds                    ;Push DS onto the stack
        cld                         ;Increment on string instructions

        mov   bp,word ptr Len       ;Move Lo-Word length to BP
        mov   ax,word ptr Len + 2   ;Move Hi-Word length to AX
        mov   HiWLen,ax             ;and from there to variable

        mov   dx,Handle            ;Move EMS handle to DX
        xor   bx,bx                ;Start with first logical page

        mov   ds,FrameSeg          ;DS points to the page frame
        push  cs                   ;Set ES to the code segment
        pop   es

        assume cs:code, ds:nothing

        jmp short GetECalc          ;Jump to the loop

GetELoop: ;-- Register allocation within this loop ----------------------
        ;
        ; AX       = times this, times that
        ; BX       = Number of logical EMS pages to be swapped
        ; CX       = Number of bytes to be copied in this execution
        ; DX       = EMS handle
        ; DS:SI    = Pointer to first page in EMS page frame (Start)
        ; ES:DI    = Pointer to target address in memory
        ; HiWLen:BP = Number of bytes still to be copied

        mov   ax,4400h             ;Function number for illustration
        int   67h                  ;Call EMM

        mov   di,offset CodeEnd     ;Offset for Swapping
        xor   si,si                ;Write to the start of the EMS page
        mov   ax,cx                ;Move number to AX
        rep movsb                  ;Copy memory

        sub   bp,ax                ;Remainder of written bytes
        sbb   HiWLen,0             ;Decrement

        inc   bx                   ;Increment number of logical page
```

```
                mov     ax,es                   ;Move starting segment to AX
                add     ax,EMS_PLEN shr 4       ;Increment by written paragraphs
                mov     es,ax                   ;and move it to ES

GetECalc:       mov     cx,EMS_PLEN             ;Write EMS_PLEN bytes
                cmp     HiWLen,0                ;More than 64K?
                ja      GetELoop                ;Yes ---> GetELoop
                cmp     bp,cx                   ;No ---> More than EMS_PLEN bytes?
                jae     GetELoop                ;Yes ---> Continue writing
                mov     cx,bp                   ;No ---> Write remainder
                or      cx,cx                   ;No more bytes to write?
                jne     GetELoop                ;No ---> GetELoop

GetERet:        pop     ds                      ;Pop DS off of stack
                ret                             ;Return to caller

GetFromEms endp
```

During output, Write2File also processes the memory, in steps whose size is determined by the constant NUM_WRITE, into the temporary file. If this size is small, the output loop must be executed more frequently. The DOS function $40, which is called for the output to the file, doesn't necessarily increase in speed with an increase in block size. In our example, the selected block size was 2048, because it corresponds to the size of a cluster in hard disk units with a capacity of up to 32 MBytes and represents a type of closed unit which can be quickly processed by DOS. Unlike the EMS procedures, all information within the output loop of Write2File can be captured in the processor registers. So variables in memory aren't required.

```
;--------------------------------------------------------------------------
;-- Write2File : Write the program to be swapped to a file
;-- Returns    : Carry-Flag = 1 : Error

Write2File proc near

NUM_WRITE   = 2048                       ;Bytes to be written per execution
                                         ;to power of 2 (max. 2^16)

                assume cs:code, ds:code

                push    ds               ;Push DS onto stack
                mov     bp,4000h         ;Function number for "Write"
                mov     bx,Handle        ;Load file handle

WriFStart:  mov     di,word ptr Len      ;Move Lo-Word length to DI
                mov     si,word ptr Len + 2  ;Move Hi-Word length to SI
                mov     dx,offset CodeEnd    ;Write offset address
                jmp     short WriFCalc       ;Compute no. of bytes to be written

WriFLoop:   ;-- Register allocation within this loop -----------------
                ;
                ;  AX          = times this, times that
                ;  BX          = DOS file handle
```

```
;   CX          = Number of bytes to be read/written
;   DS:DX       = Address at which they should be read/written
;   DI:SI       = Number of bytes still to be copied
;   BP          = Number of DOS function to be called

            mov     ax,bp                   ;Load DOS function number
            int     21h                     ;Call DOS interrupt
            jc      WriFEnd                 ;Error ---> WriFEnd
            mov     ax,ds                   ;Starting segment to AX
            add     ax,NUM_WRITE shr 4      ;Increment by written paragraphs
            mov     ds,ax                   ;and move to DS
            sub     di,cx                   ;Decrement remainder of
            sbb     si,0                    ;written bytes

WriFCalc:   mov     cx,NUM_WRITE            ;Write NUM_WRITE bytes
            cmp     si,0                    ;More than 64K?
            ja      WriFLoop                ;Yes ---> WriFLoop
            cmp     di,cx                   ;No ---> More than NUM_WRITE bytes?
            jae     WriFLoop                ;Yes ---> Continue writing
            mov     cx,di                   ;No ---> Write remainder
            or      cx,cx                   ;No more bytes to write?
            jne     WriFLoop                ;No ---> WriFLoop

WriFEnd:    pop     ds                      ;Reload DS
WriFRet:    ret                             ;Return to caller

Write2File endp
```

While Write2Ems and GetFromEms represent two separate procedures, Write2File and GetFromFile work together. Their only difference is the DOS functions that are called inside the loop. In Write2File the function $40 is called, while GetFromFile uses the function $3F for reading in the data. Since the function number can be easily passed parameters with a processor register, GetFromFile accesses the code of Write2File by jumping into this procedure to pass the function number for "read" in the BP register.

Before doing this, it sets the file pointer to the beginning of the file with DOS function $42 so that reading proceeds from the front to the back in Write2File.

```
;-------------------------------------------------------------------------
;-- GetFromFile : Return the swapped program to memory
;-- Returns     : Carry-Flag = 1 : Error

GetFromFile proc near

            assume cs:code, ds:code

            push   ds                ;Push DS onto the stack

            ;-- Move file pointer to the start of file ----------------

            mov    ax,4200h          ;DOS function number
```

```
        mov     bx,Handle           ;Load file handle
        xor     cx,cx               ;CX:DX gives its position
        mov     dx,cx
        int     21h                 ;Call DOS interrupt
        jc      WriFRet             ;Error ---> WriFRet

;-- Load file into memory with the help of Write2File -----

        mov     bp,3F00h            ;Function number for "Read"
        jmp     WriFStart           ;Jump to Write2File

GetFromFile endp
```

We conclude our discussion of the assembler module with the Terminate label. At various locations, StartSwap jumps to this label when the relocated memory cannot be reloaded. This prevents a return to the Pascal module.

With the help of DOS function $09 the error message TerMes, which is defined within the variable area in the code segment, is displayed. As in function $09, a dollar sign marks the end of the string output. After this text is displayed, the program is terminated through the DOS function $4C and the return code 1 is passed in the AL register. This usually indicates poor execution and can be sensed with the batch variable ERRORLEVEL, during the call of the Turbo Pascal program within a batch file.

The program code, which was copied by StartSwap into the code segment of the main program, also ends after Terminate. Then there are only the procedures SwapOutAndExec and InitSwapa.

```
;-------------------------------------------------------------------------
;-- Terminate : The system can't return to the original Turbo Pascal
;--             program. The program ends with an error code.

Terminate  label near

        ;-- Display error message -----------------------------------

        push    cs                  ;Set DS to CS
        pop     ds
        mov     dx,offset TerMes ;DS:DX points to the error message
        mov     ah,9                ;Function number for "Display string"
        int     21h                 ;Display DOS interrupt

        mov     ax,4C01h            ;End program with error code
        int     21h


;=========================================================================

CodeEnd    equ this byte            ;Copy code from the start of the Turbo
                                    ;Pascal program to this point
```

11. TSR Programming

Terminate and Stay Resident (TSR) programs are used on most PC systems today. These programs are usually short utility programs. Even though TSR programs have contributed to the success of the PC and the MS-DOS operating system, many users consider them "outlaw" computer applications. Since TSRs don't always follow the rules, some users and developers do not consider TSRs true PC applications.

DOS itself is to blame for these outlaw programs because it has a single task structure. TSR programs are an attempt to make the PC "execute" more programs at a time. Most often a TSR program is activated by pressing a key or key combination. This temporarily suspends the currently executing application while the TSR executes. When you are done using the TSR, you can deactivate it, and you'll be able to continue using the original application which was suspended.

There are several technical problems in getting TSR programs to run under DOS. But the fact that hundreds of commercial TSR programs are available prove that these problems can be solved.

In the first section of this chapter we'll discuss the little sisters of the TSRs, the ISRs (Interrupt Service Routines). They are as efficient and useful as TSR programs, but perform their work undercover and do not interact with the user. ISRs are easier to develop than TSRs and provide an appropriate introduction to this material. To put it another way, an ISR is a sub-group of the TSR programs. Many developers consider ISRs to be part of the TSR family.

True TSR programs which remain in the background and wait for the user to activate them are discussed in the second section.

11.1   ISR and TSR Basics

ISR (Interrupt Service Routines) and TSR programs appear in many different forms. Sometimes they appear as cache programs, sometimes as calculator applications or macro generators and sometimes (unfortunately) as computer viruses. Although these applications differ, each shares a similar basic structure.

It's not enough to simply place these programs in memory and wait until they are activated by the user. The program must be integrated with the system and remain there undetected until a specific signal invokes the program. These signals or *interrupt calls* are the medium through which the different components of the system can communicate. This communication could include the hardware reporting a keystroke, or an application program searching for a file using DOS commands. Interrupts are always involved and must be intercepted if the program participates in system processes.

A TSR program or an ISR program redirects one or more interrupts to its own routines by changing the entries in the Interrupt Vector Table. Since the program usually shouldn't replace the interrupt handler, its own interrupt handler acts as an interface between triggering the interrupt and the receiver, which is designed similar to the original interrupt handler. The TSR's interrupt handler only examines the information passed from the caller through the processor registers, and sends this information <u>unchanged</u> to its predecessor. If the TSR changed the processor registers in any way, these changes would interfere with system operation.

For example, by attaching itself to the BIOS interrupt $17, a TSR printer driver can easily convert the character set of the PC to the character set of the printer currently connected to the system. This interrupt acts as an interface between the application and the printer routines in BIOS. The function number is passed to BIOS in the AH register. Using this value, the ISR program's interrupt handler determines whether a character should be displayed during the call. If so, it can load the code from the proper register and then replace it with another code. By passing the two items of information to the original BIOS interrupt, the program modifies the output without affecting the application.

During the call of the previous interrupt handler, a TSR program or an ISR program cannot always assume that it receives the original handler in the BIOS or DOS. Other TSR programs may have attached themselves to the handler before this TSR program, and these are called instead of the BIOS or DOS handler. As long as they pass the interrupt call to the previous interrupt handler, the interrupt signal will reach the correct address, even if the information passed was modified in the interim by several ISR or TSR programs. The following illustration shows a group of these interrupt handlers attached to the BIOS printer interrupt, forming a chain.

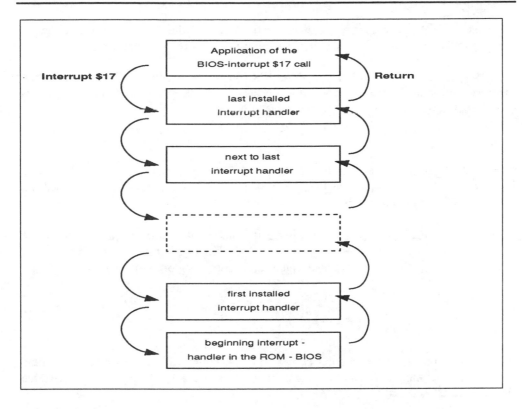

Chained ISR programs

The CLOCK program listed in this section is a simple example of an ISR program. After the user calls it, this program displays the time on the screen. The location of the time display defaults to the upper right corner of the screen. If you prefer having the time display at another position on the screen, you can indicate this when calling CLOCK from the DOS prompt. You can use the following options to control the time display:

/rddd   Specifies the screen row at which you want the time display to appear. The ddd parameter is a decimal number representing the screen row.

/cddd   Specifies the screen column at which you want the time display to appear. The ddd parameter is a decimal number representing the screen column.

/oddd   Specifies the color. The ddd parameter is a decimal number representing a color code between 0 and 255.

/tddd   Specifies the number of *ticks* that should elapse before the program refreshes the time display. CLOCK usually refreshes the time display once every second. If the screen scrolls (e.g., because of entering DOS commands from the system prompt), the time disappears from the screen and returns only at the beginning of the next second. You can control the clock's refresh rate on the screen with the following parameter: A tick is a time unit which corresponds to 18.2^-1 seconds.

Like every good TSR and ISR program, CLOCK can also be deactivated and removed from memory, releasing the memory originally allocated for the program. To do this, CLOCK is called from the DOS prompt without parameters:

```
clock
```

The CLOCK program automatically recognizes that it was already installed and removes itself from memory. A subsequent call re-installs CLOCK in memory. Then another call will remove it. This cycle can be repeated endlessly.

If you call CLOCK using parameters after it is installed in memory, you can control the display mode. The parameters are passed to CLOCK and the time can be displayed at another screen location or another color can be used, depending on the parameter.

For example:

```
clock /r24 /c0 /o244 /t3
```

displays the time in the lower left corner (line 24, column 0) of the screen. The time appears in white numbers on a red background (color code 244) and is refreshed every three ticks (about 1/6 second).

CLOCK is based on interrupt $1C, which is called 18.2 times per second by the timer (an integrated circuit on the main circuit board of the computer). This provides the cyclical signal which is the basis of every time measurement. However, instead of calling interrupt $1C, the timer triggers hardware interrupt $08, which usually points to a special interrupt routine in the ROM BIOS. During every call it increments an internal time counter from which the actual time can be calculated in hours, minutes and seconds, after some conversions. Hardware interrupt $08 also performs other tasks. For example, these other tasks include switching off the motor in the disk drive if no access has occurred within a certain period of time.

To offer other programs the capability of using the cyclical signal of the timer, the BIOS interrupt handler calls interrupt $1C before its termination. The BIOS initializes it during the system boot in such a way that it points directly to an IRET assembly language instruction. This interrupt can then be redirected by any program to its own handler without affecting the system.

How CLOCK makes use of this capability will be demonstrated in the following source code listing.

```
{****************************************************************************
*   Clock : A TSR program, which after its call displays the current time   *
*           permanently on the screen.                                      *
**------------------------------------------------------------------------**
*   Author         : MICHAEL TISCHER                                        *
*   developed on   : 08/12/1989                                             *
*   last update on : 08/13/1989                                             *
****************************************************************************}

program Clock;

{$S-}                                              { no stack checking }
{$M 1048,0,0}                                      { 1K stack, no heap }

uses Dos, Crt;

type Time = array[1..8] of record      { accepts time string for video RAM }
                             TChar : char;
                             TColr : byte;
                           end;
     TZ   = ^Time;                                 { pointer to time string }

     PSP  = record                                         { creates PSP }
              dummy : array [0..$2b] of byte;
                                      { fields which are not significant here }
              EnvSeg : word;              { segment address of the environment }
            end;
     PSPP = ^PSP;                                         { pointer to PSP }
```

CLOCK begins with two compiler directives which disable stack checking and limit the heap and stack memory requirements within the program. The heap is eliminated from this program, and the stack is reduced to a minimum size of 1,024 bytes. The limitation of stack and heap memory ensures that Turbo Pascal allocates as little RAM for the program as possible. This minimum allocation helps keep a maximum amount of RAM open for other programs, since the TSR occupies the stack and heap memory whether it is active or not. If a TSR or an ISR occupies a lot of memory, there may not be enough memory free for operating other applications.

The two compiler directives are followed by various type declarations needed by CLOCK. The time type defines the array in which CLOCK stores the current time. Its construction follows the structure of the video RAM in text mode so that CLOCK can copy the time directly into video RAM without accessing a BIOS or DOS function. Every character's attribute is stored, along with the eight characters used in constructing the time on the screen.

Also, a part of the PSP appears in a structure of the same name. It allows easy access to the segment address of the environment block. This access is needed when deactivating the program to release the memory originally reserved for the environment block. TZ and PSPP are additional pointers used for defining the PSP.

This declaration is followed by various typed and untyped constants. The untyped constants define the number of interrupts to be redirected, the default position of the time display on the screen and the default color of the time display.

```
const TimeInt        = $1C;                    { the interrupts to be redirected }
      DefaultTColr = $70;                                { default color }
      DefaultLine = 0;                         { standard output position }
      DefaultCol = 72;

      PrgID       : string  = 'CLOCK_PAS V1.0';    { identification string }
      TickCount : byte    = 18;                          { tick count }
      Correction1 : byte   = 5;                   { correction counter 1 }
      Correction2 : byte   = 31;                  { correction counter 2 }
      ShowBefore : boolean = FALSE;                    { construct time }
```

PrgId is defined as a typed constant of type string. It is used later during the search in memory for an already installed copy of CLOCK. TickCount, Correction1 and Correction2 are counters used in tracking the passage of time. Their importance becomes more obvious as we turn to the description of the interrupt handler for interrupt $1C. ShowBefore indicates that the time should be displayed after a certain number of ticks, rather than once a second. ShowBefore is set to TRUE if the user includes the parameter /t when calling CLOCK from the DOS prompt.

The constants are followed by the program's global variables. OldTimer accepts the address of the interrupt handler which, until the installation of CLOCK, was hidden behind this interrupt. A different kind of pointer contains the variable VideoPtr, which points to the physical position in video RAM into which the time is copied.

```
var OldTimer       : pointer;           { pointer to the old interrupt handler }
    VideoPtr       : pointer;  { pointer to the output position in video RAM }
    ShowInterval : byte;        { display frequency when ShowBefore = TRUE }
    ShowTime       : byte;         { tick counter when ShowBefore = TRUE }
    TimeStr        : time;                                { time string }
```

The variables ShowInterval and ShowTime are only important if the time is displayed before the end of a second and the ShowBefore variable contains the value TRUE. ShowInterval accepts the number of ticks, after which the time display must be reconstructed. ShowTime acts as the counter for the ShowInterval variable. The TimeStr variable stores the time string, whose content is reflected by the time. The PriTime procedure, which is called on various occasions during program execution, copies the time information into video RAM for display on the screen.

```
{****************************************************************************
*   PriTime : displays the current time on the screen                      *
**------------------------------------------------------------------------**
*   Input   : none                                                         *
*   Global  : VideoPtr/R, TimeStr/R                                        *
****************************************************************************}

procedure PriTime;

begin                                             { write time string into }
  Move( TimeStr, VideoPtr^, sizeof( TimeStr ) );  { video RAM              }
end;
```

The NextSecond procedure updates the time by one second. Like a mechanical counter, this procedure increments the time within the time string starting at the one second column. Once the one second column goes past a count of 9, NextSecond resets the one second column to 0 and carries the 1 over to the column indicating tens of seconds. The procedure continues up to the column denoting tens of hours. All numbers are then converted to ASCII format.

At first this process seems complicated. It may appear easier to increment the second counter on every call, then convert the data into hours, minutes and seconds later on. This method would be faster than the procedure used in our example, but the results would require conversion to an ASCII string to permit display. Since the display process includes this time-consuming step, the algorithm used in NextSecond is actually superior in execution speed over the other method.

This algorithm must execute quickly, because for every second of processor time, these operations are taken from the current application. This style of programming concentrates on easing the programmer's work instead of execution speed, and isn't very effective. A system's performance can easily be affected by a poorly coded, frequently called interrupt handler.

```
{****************************************************************************
*   NextSecond : increments the current time in the variable TimeStr       *
*               by one second                                              *
**------------------------------------------------------------------------**
*   Input   : none                                                         *
*   Global  : TimeStr/RW                                                   *
****************************************************************************}

procedure NextSecond;

begin
  Inc( TimeStr[8].TChar );                          { increment one second }
  if ( TimeStr[8].TChar > '9' ) then                          { overflow? }
    begin                                                           { yes }
      TimeStr[8].TChar := '0';                    { set one second to zero }
      Inc( TimeStr[7].TChar );                      { increment ten second }
```

375

```
if ( TimeStr[7].TChar = '6' ) then                    { minute finished? }
 begin                                                            { yes }
  TimeStr[7].TChar := '0';                      { set ten second to zero }
  Inc( TimeStr[5].TChar );                      { increment one minute }
  if ( TimeStr[5].TChar > '9' ) then                        { overflow? }
   begin                                                          { yes }
    TimeStr[5].TChar := '0';                    { set one minute to zero }
    Inc( TimeStr[4].TChar );                    { increment ten minute }
    if ( TimeStr[4].TChar = '6' ) then                       { new hour? }
     begin                                                        { yes }
      TimeStr[4].TChar := '0';                  { set ten-minute to zero }
      Inc( TimeStr[2].TChar );                    { increment one hour }
      if ( TimeStr[1].TChar = '2' ) and ( TimeStr[2].TChar = '4' ) then
       begin                                                  { new day }
        TimeStr[1].TChar := ' ';
        TimeStr[2].TChar := '0';
       end
      else                                                 { no new day }
       if ( TimeStr[2].TChar > '9' ) then      { overflow of one hour? }
        begin
         TimeStr[2].TChar := '0';                     { one hour to zero }
         if ( TimeStr[1].TChar = ' ' ) then     { reached 10 o'clock? }
          TimeStr[1].TChar := '1'                                { yes }
         else                                          { no, 20 hour }
          TimeStr[1].TChar := '2';
        end;
     end;
   end;
 end;
end;
```

The new interrupt handler for interrupt $1C is stored in the NewTimer procedure. This procedure must be equipped with the reserved word Interrupt to allow activity as an interrupt handler. The reserved word interrupt instructs the Turbo Pascal compiler to generate a slightly different program code than usual at the beginning and end of the procedure. Before the stack is configured, all processor registers are stored on the stack. This ensures that these registers can be restored in the application that was executing before the interrupt call. In addition, the DS register must be loaded with the segment address of the Turbo Pascal data segment, since you cannot assume that the DS register points to this segment during entry to the interrupt handler.

```
CLOCK.NEWTIMER: begin
  cs:009F 50          push    ax        ;store processor registers
  cs:00A0 53          push    bx        ;on the stack
  cs:00A1 51          push    cx
  cs:00A2 52          push    dx
  cs:00A3 56          push    si
  cs:00A4 57          push    di
  cs:00A5 1E          push    ds
  cs:00A6 06          push    es
```

```
cs:00A7 55              push    bp          ;construct the stack as
cs:00A8 89E5            mov     bp,sp       ;usual

cs:00AA B8E062          mov     ax,DATA     ;load segment address of the
cs:00AD 8ED8            mov     ds,ax       ;data segment to DS

;-- assembly language which converts some Pascal commands within the procedure

CLOCK.148: end;
cs:0110 89EC            mov     sp,bp       ;reset the stack
cs:0112 5D              pop     bp

cs:0113 07              pop     es          ;return the registers from the stack
cs:0114 1F              pop     ds          ;again
cs:0115 5F              pop     di          ;changes to the registers
cs:0116 5E              pop     si          ;are passed to the caller
cs:0117 5A              pop     dx          ;because of this
cs:0118 59              pop     cx
cs:0119 5B              pop     bx
cs:011A 58              pop     ax
cs:011B CF              iret                ;interrupt routine termination
```

Program code generated by Turbo Pascal at the beginning and end of an interrupt procedure

Even with the stack available, it cannot be assumed that the register pair SS:SP points to the program stack. Turbo doesn't load these registers with the address of the Turbo Pascal stack because both "normal" Pascal programs and TSRs access the same interrupt procedures. The routines in CLOCK could be included in a separate program to permanently display the current time on the screen during the execution of this program. In this particular case, Turbo cannot load the SS and SP registers with the program stack address during entry to the interrupt procedure because the stack's contents would be overwritten. This inevitably leads to a program crash.

The procedure always uses the active stack because Turbo doesn't access the SS and SP registers during entry to the interrupt procedure. There should be no problems if this interrupt procedure involves an application's stack. However, if a DOS function was interrupted during execution, and the DOS stack is therefore active, problems may develop because the DOS stack is rather small. Dangerous consequences could result if too many variables and buffers are stored on the stack during the interrupt procedure, or during the procedures and functions called by the interrupt procedure.

There shouldn't be any problems in the preceding case because stack use is minimal in the NewTimer and NextSecond procedures. However, the {$S-} compiler directive must be included because Turbo always expects considerably more bytes in the stack than are required. It is important to prevent the termination of the Turbo interrupt handle. The {$S-}

compiler directive prevents a return to the interrupted program by generating a run-time error.

Before executing the first command from the interrupt procedure, Turbo stores the processor registers on the stack. The registers and parameters which were passed can then be addressed. This is very practical, since the contents of the registers can be read and changed. To use this capability, each processor register must be listed as a parameter during the procedure declaration.

A declaration sequence must be used which corresponds to the commands generated by Turbo for register storage. A typical declaration of this type reads as follows:

```
procedure Name( Flags, CS, IP, AX, BX, CX, DX, SI, DI, DS, ES, BP : word ):
interrupt;
```

This declaration allows access to the processor registers stored by Turbo, the return address to the caller through the CS:IP registers, and the flag register. This information was automatically stored on the stack by the processor during the interrupt call. Compared with the information stored by Turbo, this data is handled as if they are normal parameters.

The names assigned to the individual parameters (or registers) in the example above are symbolic names. You can use any name. If your interrupt procedure doesn't access all registers, only the registers accessed need to be listed. To ensure that the position of individual parameters agrees with the processor registers stored on the stack, you cannot omit parameters at random. They can only be omitted at the beginning of the list, if they precede the first access by the interrupt procedure. All subsequent registers must be indicated so that Turbo can properly address them.

For example, if your interrupt procedure accesses the CX, SI and BP registers, all the registers must be listed in the procedure declaration as parameters that follow the CX register. This is because only the first of the three registers is stored on the Turbo stack. In this case, the declaration must be:

```
procedure Name( CX, DX, SI, DI, DS, ES, BP : word ): interrupt;
```

The CLOCK interrupt procedure NewTimer uses even fewer processor registers. It can handle parameter declarations since it doesn't access any registers. As the timer calls NewTimer 18.2 times per second, NewTimer introduces a new second after every 18.2 calls by calling the NextSecond procedure. However, this isn't easy. NewTimer can, with the help of a counter, count the 18 calls until it has to introduce the next second. But how will it count the missing 0.2 calls remaining until the beginning of the next second?

Even though this isn't technically possible, it would introduce an error if a new second is introduced after only 18 calls. So NewTimer must use a trick for time measurement. In addition to the actual call counter TickCount, NewTimer maintains two correction counters which are named Correction1 and Correction2.

```
{*************************************************************************
*   NewTimer : the new timer interrupt, which is called 18.2 times per   *
*              second from the timer chip.                               *
**---------------------------------------------------------------------**
*   Global  : TickCount/RW, Correction1/RW, Correction2/RW, TimeStr/R,   *
*             VideoPtr/R, ShowBefore/R, ShowTime/RW, ShowInterval/R      *
*************************************************************************}

procedure NewTimer; interrupt;

begin
 dec( TickCount );                                    { register call }
 if ( TickCount = 0 ) then                   { 18 ticks already elapsed? }
   begin                                                        { yes }
     TickCount := 18;                     { 18 ticks until the next second }
     dec( Correction1 );                  { decrement correction counter 1 }
     if ( Correction1 = 0 ) then                        { correction due? }
       begin                                                    { yes }
         Correction1 := 5;          { 5*18 ticks until the next correction }
         inc( TickCount );              { 19 ticks until the next second }
         dec( Correction2 );          { decrement correction counter 2 }
         if ( Correction2 = 0 ) then                { correction due? }
           begin                                                { yes }
             Correction2 := 31;    {31*5*18 ticks until the next correction }
             inc( TickCount );         { 20 ticks until the next second }
           end;
       end;
     NextSecond;                          { increment time by one second }
     PriTime;                             { display time on the screen }
     ShowTime := ShowInterval;             { delay cyclical output   }
   end
 else                                       { no new second started }
   if ( ShowBefore ) then           { display time in cyclic intervals? }
     begin                                                      { yes }
       dec( ShowTime );                     { decrement cycle counter }
       if ( ShowTime = 0 ) then               { time for output? }
         begin                                                  { yes }
           PriTime;                       { display time on the screen }
           ShowTime := ShowInterval;         { reset cycle counter }
         end;
     end;
end;
```

To determine if it has reached the value 0, the counter TickCount decrements and is tested for every call of the procedure. If it has reached zero, 18 ticks have passed and a new second must be introduced through the NextSecond procedure. Before this happens, TickCount is again set to a value of 18 and the correction counter Correction1 is decremented. This counter always counts down from five. When it reaches the value 0, 90 (5*18) calls of

NewTimer have elapsed. Within this time period, NewTimer increments the time by 5 seconds.

Actually, NewTimer was exactly one tick too fast, since 5*18.2 results in 91, not 90. For this reason, the counter TickCount in this example increments from 18 to 19. So instead of being introduced after 18, the next second is introduced after 19 ticks. So, the tick "lost" in the last 5 seconds is regained.

If a second corresponded to exactly 18.2 ticks, we could design a perfect clock program easily. In reality, however, NewTimer must allow exactly 18.20648193 calls until a second has passed. Even after the correction occurring every 5 seconds, NewTimer is still slightly ahead of its time. But this deviation is so small that it becomes noticeable only after 2,790 (31*5*18) calls, when the timer is "fast" by one tick. To compensate for this, NewTimer contains a correction counter which is initialized with a value of 31 and is decremented only when the first correction counter reaches 0. When it has reached this value, TickCount is again incremented and the next second is initiated only after 20 ticks. This mechanism keeps the deviation below 2 seconds per day.

The correction mechanisms operate only when TickCount has reached the value 0, after its decrementing at the beginning of the procedure. If this doesn't occur, NewTimer hasn't fulfilled its assignment. This may have happened because the call to CLOCK indicated the /t parameter, displaying the time before the arrival of the next second. NewTimer tests this status with the ShowBefore variable which contains the value TRUE in this example. If this occurs, the ShowTime counter is decremented and the PriTime procedure displays the time when ShowTime contains a value of 0. Then ShowTime is again loaded with the number of ticks stored in the ShowInterval variable, which must elapse until the next time display.

Through the study of PriTime, NextSecond and NewTimer you are now familiar with the three procedures required for the actual time display after the installation and termination of CLOCK. All other procedures and functions help with installation and deactivation only, without affecting CLOCK's display.

The Help procedure is one of this group. Help displays information about CLOCK on the screen. This procedure is activated when the user enters the name CLOCK and the -h or /h parameter from the DOS prompt.

```
{***************************************************************************
*  Help : display help information on screen with data about call and     *
*         application of CLOCK                                            *
**----------------------------------------------------------------------**
*  Input :  none                                                          *
***************************************************************************}

procedure Help;

const HelpText : array [1..16] of string = (
 'call: CLOCK [/h] [/c] [/r] [/o] [/t]',
 '',
 '/h = Display help (this) screen',
 '/c = Screen column of time display (0 to 79,    Default = 72)',
 '/r = Screen row of time display    (0 to 24,    Default =  0)',
 '/o = Color of time output          (0 to 255,   Default = inverted)',
 '/t = Internal clock, tick interval (1 to 9      Default = 1)',
 '     Without this parameter, the time is displayed every new',
 '     second.',
 '',
 'INSTALLATION      - The first execution of the CLOCK program installs it.',
 'DE-INSTALLATION   - Subsequent execution with out any parameters. ',
 'CHANGE PARAMETERS - Subsequent execution with parameters.',
 '',
 'All parameters are expected in decimal notation.',
 '' );

var i : integer;

begin
  for i := 1 to 17 do                          { process the lines  }
    writeln( HelpText[i] );                     { and display them   }
end;
```

The GetPtr function is called when an already installed copy of the CLOCK should be removed from memory, or when the user assigns CLOCK a new screen color or screen position. It is the responsibility of GetPtr to create a pointer that points to a specific variable in the already installed CLOCK program.

```
{***************************************************************************
*  GetPtr : returns a pointer to a variable in the already installed      *
*           CLOCK program in memory.                                       *
**----------------------------------------------------------------------**
*  Input :   Addrss  = Address of the addressed variable in the current   *
*                      version of CLOCK                                   *
*            PSPSEG  = Segment address of the PSP in the installed         *
*                      CLOCK program                                      *
*  Output : pointer to this variable in the installed program             *
***************************************************************************}

function GetPtr( Addrss : pointer; PSPSeg : word ) : pointer;
```

```
begin
  GetPtr := ptr( PSPSeg + ( Seg(Addrss^)-PrefixSeg ) , Ofs(Addrss^) );
end;
```

To help you visualize how this function works, think of a situation in which CLOCK is installed and then recalled. At that particular moment, there are two identical CLOCK programs in memory: One that is already installed and resident in memory, and another just started. Aside from residing at two different addresses, the two programs are identical.

Although the individual segments of the two programs are at different addresses, the distances of the variables to the beginnings of their segments and the distances to the different segments are identical. This also implies that the distance of a variable from the start of the program in memory is identical for both programs. If this distance and the beginning of the already installed CLOCK copy in memory is known, a pointer to any variable in this program can be constructed.

GetPtr accepts this task by creating a pointer to the variable in the current program and the segment address of the PSP of the already installed CLOCK copy. During the creation of this pointer, it first calculates the distance between the segment of the variable and the PSP of the current program, which marks the start of the program in memory. This distance is added by GetPtr to the segment address passed from the PSP of the already installed program. The offset address of the variable, relative to the beginning of the segment, is identical in both programs and therefore can be stored unchanged in the pointer.

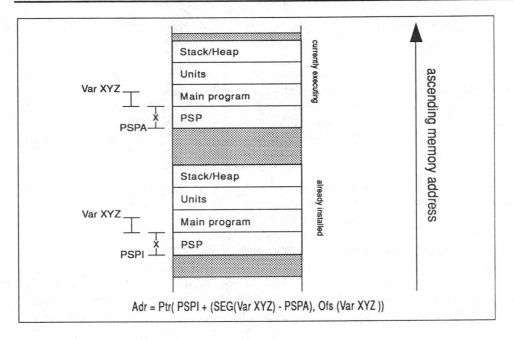

Determining the variable address of an installed CLOCK program

While a caller of GetPtr can easily determine the address of the addressed variable through the address operator @, the segment address indicating the program start of an already installed CLOCK copy isn't easily accessible. There isn't even a guarantee that the program was already installed. Using the YetInstalled procedure searches memory for an existing copy of the CLOCK program.

YetInstalled uses a string which the caller has passed to identify an existing program. In its search, YetInstalled looks for a constant string. It's best to use a typed string constant in this case, such as the PrgID variable. YetInstalled expects this string as a variable (not as a value parameter) so that Turbo passes the address of this string and doesn't store a local copy on the stack.

The address of this string is as important as the string's content. Since this string must be located within the memory allocated for the installed CLOCK program and at the same location in the current version of the program, it would be very time-consuming to search the entire memory for this string. YetInstalled accesses the GetPtr function to obtain a pointer to the string in memory. Instead of searching randomly through all the memory segments, YetInstalled follows the individual memory blocks, which were reserved through DOS function $48.

In Chapter 10 we mentioned that DOS placed an MCB (Memory Control Block) in front of every allocated memory block, through which the individual areas of memory were chained together. If you followed this chain, you would pass through every allocated memory area and would eventually run into the CLOCK program, provided it is already resident.

To follow the chain, you must first find the entrance (i.e., the address of the first MCB). Although this information isn't easily released by DOS, an undocumented DOS function can be used (see Section 1.3.3 for more information). Here we use function $52, which passes the address of the DIB (DOS Information Block) to the ES:BX register pair. A pointer with the segment and offset address of the first MCB in memory is located immediately preceding this data structure, at register pair ES:BX-4.

YetInstalled reads this address and then checks all the MCBs in memory starting with the first one. This search continues until it finds the string or completes a search of all the MCBs without finding the string. It finds the string in memory where the string and the current copy of CLOCK are located. YetInstalled recognizes this by comparing the address of the PSP in the memory area to be searched with its own PSP address from the PrefixSeg variable.

Once the search loop ends, the YetInstalled procedure returns either the segment address of the PSP in the program it found, or the value 0 if it could not find CLOCK in memory.

```
{****************************************************************************
 *  YetInstalled : determines if the program is already installed in        *
 *                 memory.                                                   *
 **------------------------------------------------------------------------**
 *  Input : IDStr = the identification string                               *
 *  Output : the segment address of the PSP of the program found, or 0      *
 *           if the program was not found.                                  *
 ****************************************************************************}

function YetInstalled( var IDStr : string ) : word;

type MCB        = record                                    { creates an MCB }
                    IdCode : char;   { "M" = another MCB follows, "Z" = end }
                    PSP : word;                  { Segment address of the PSP }
                    Paras : word;  { number of paragraphs in controlled area }
                  end;
     MCBPTR     = ^MCB;                               { pointer to an MCB }
     MCBPTRPTR = ^MCBPTR;                   { pointer to a pointer to an MCB }
     STRPTR     = ^string;                         { pointer to a string }

var Regs       : Registers;           { processor register to an interrupt call }
    CurMCB     : MCBPTR;                       { pointer to current MCB }
    PSPFound : word;       { segment address of the PSP of the program found }
    Ende       : boolean;                          { last MCB reached? }
    StPtr      : ^string;                  { pointer to ID string in memory }

begin
  {-- determine pointer to first MCB in memory ---------------------------}
```

```
    Regs.AH := $52;                    { function $52 returns address of the DIB }
    MsDos( Regs );
    CurMCB := MCBPTRPTR( ptr( Regs.ES, Regs.BX-4 ) )^;

    {-- search the MCBs in memory -------------------------------------------}

    Ende     := FALSE;
    PSPFound := 0;                                        { the program was not found }

    repeat
       {-- Determine if the ID string was passed, and if it exists in memory --}
       {-- at the same location as this program                             --}

       if ( STRPTR( GetPtr( @IDStr, CurMCB^.PSP ))^ = IDStr ) and
          ( CurMCB^.PSP <> PRefixSeg ) then
         PSPFound := CurMCB^.PSP;                          { found a copy in memory }

       if ( CurMCB^.IDCode = 'Z' ) then            { is current MCB the last? }
          Ende := TRUE                                     { yes, search ended }
       else                          { no, set pointer CurMCB to next MCB in memory }
          CurMCB := ptr( Seg(CurMCB^) + CurMCB^.Paras + 1, 0 );
    until ( PSPFound <> 0 ) or Ende;

    YetInstalled := PSPFound;              { PSPFound <> 0 ---> program found }
  end;
```

YetInstalled is followed by the GetVal and InitVal procedures, described later in this chapter.

YetInstalled is called with the CheckAndInit procedure, which is responsible for evaluating the arguments from the command line. CheckAndInit installs the program in memory, deactivates an already installed copy of the program or sends new parameters to the installed copy, based on these arguments.

Since CheckAndInit only works on the program if an invalid or unknown parameter wasn't detected, it defines the Boolean variable Install, which is set to TRUE if all the parameters are recognized. The parameter reading itself occurs in a loop which reads each parameter with the help of the function ParamStr (found in the System unit). A parameter is only valid if it begins with a minus sign or slash, followed by one of these letters: H, C, R, O or T. The routine is not case sensitive, so it doesn't matter whether the user enters parameters as uppercase letters or lowercase letters.

All parameters up to the /h parameter must be followed by numbers in decimal notation. These numbers are converted into binary format by the GetVal procedure and assigned to their respective variables. CLOCK simultaneously tests the parameter to ensure that the values included in the parameter lie within an allowable value range. If the values are outside the limits set, the CheckandInit procedure displays an error message and Install is set to FALSE.

```
{****************************************************************************
 *  CheckAndInit: reads the arguments in the command line and initializes   *
 *               various global variables.                                  *
 **------------------------------------------------------------------------**
 *  Input : None                                                            *
 *  Global : column/W, line/W, TColr/W, ShowBefore/W, ShowTime/W, VideoPtr/W *
 ****************************************************************************}

procedure CheckAndInit;

type PP  = ^pointer;                                   { pointer to pointer }
     PB  = ^byte;                                         { pointer to byte }
     PBO = ^boolean;                                   { pointer to Boolean }

var TimePtr  : TZ;                                  { pointer to time string }
    Regs     : Registers;              { processor registers for interrupt call }
    CurPtr   : pointer;            { pointer to current handler for timer int }
    PrgSeg,                     { PSP segment of already installed CLOCK copy }
    VioSeg   : word;                   { segment address of the video RAM }
    line,                                            { output row of time }
    column,                                       { output column of time }
    TColr,                                              { color of time }
    i        : byte;                                    { loop counter }
    Install  : boolean;                             { install program? }
    Parameter : string;              { a parameter from the command line? }

begin
  Install := TRUE;                              { in doubt for the user ... }

  line   := DefaultLine;                           { set a default value }
  column := DefaultCol;
  TColr  := DefaultTColr;

  {-- process arguments in the command line and evaluate        --------}

  for i := 1 to ParamCount do
    begin
      Parameter := ParamStr(i);                       { get parameter I }
      if ( Parameter[1] <> '/' ) and ( Parameter[1] <> '-' ) then
        begin                     { parameter not started by '-' or '/' }
          writeln( 'Unknown Parameter: ', Parameter );
          Install := FALSE;                                { note error }
        end
      else                 { first character of parameter is '-' or '/' }
        case UpCase(Parameter[2]) of                { read parameter code }
          'H' : begin
                  Help;                      { output auxiliary display }
                  Install := FALSE;             { do not install program }
                end;

          'C' : begin              { parameter /C determines output column }
                  Install := GetVal( Parameter, column, 0, 79 );
                end;
```

```
         'R' : begin;                  { parameter /R determines the output row }
                 Install := GetVal( Parameter, line, 0, 24 );
               end;

         'O' : begin                   { parameter /O defines the output color }
                 Install := GetVal( Parameter, TColr, 0, 255 );
               end;

         'T' : begin                    { /T for the cyclical output of time }
                 Install := GetVal( Parameter, ShowInterval, 1, 9 );
                 ShowBefore := TRUE;            { display time cyclically }
                 ShowTime := 1;                 { display time immediately }
               end;
      else
        begin
          writeln( 'Unknown Parameter: ', Parameter );
          Install := FALSE;                               { note error }
        end;
     end;
  end;

if ( Install = TRUE ) then                      { were the parameters O.K.? }
  begin                                                           { yes }
    {-- set pointer VideoPtr to output position in the video RAM --------}
    Regs.ah := 15;                        { determine current video mode }
    intr($10, Regs);                         { call BIOS video interrupt }
    if Regs.al = 7 then                              { monochrome mode? }
      VioSeg := $b000                        { yes, video RAM at B000 }
    else                                              { no, color mode }
      VioSeg := $b800;                           { video RAM at B800 }
    VideoPtr := Ptr( VioSeg, ( column + line * 80 ) shl 1 );

    {-- determine if the program was already installed ------------------}

    PrgSeg := YetInstalled( PrgID );                    { search memory }
    if ( PrgSeg = 0 ) then                    { program not yet installed? }
      begin                                             { no, install }
        InitTime( TColr );                      { initialize time string }
        GetIntVec( TimeInt, OldTimer );    { get old interrupt handler }
        SetIntVec( TimeInt, @NewTimer );      { install new handler }
        PriTime;                           { display time on the screen }
        writeln( 'CLOCK is installed.' );
        writeln( 'Re-execution will de-install the program.');
        keep( 0 );                 { terminate program, but remain resident }
      end
    else                                    { program is already installed }
      if ( ParamCount = 0 ) then            { no parameters, remove program? }
        begin                                                     { yes }
          {-- determine if the CLOCK program in memory was already ------}
          {-- overwritten by another TSR program              ------}

          GetIntVec( TimeInt, CurPtr );   { get address of current handler }
```

```
                if ( CurPtr = GetPtr( @NewTimer, PrgSeg ) ) then
                  begin { CLOCK is still current Int-Handler, reinstall }
                    SetIntVec( TimeInt, PP( GetPtr( @OldTimer, PrgSeg ))^ );

                  {-- release environment block of the old clock using DOS  --}
                  {-- function $49                                          --}

                    Regs.AH := $49;                       { DOS function number }
                    Regs.ES := PSPP( ptr( PrgSeg, 0) )^.EnvSeg;
                    MsDos( Regs );

                  {-- release old CLOCK program from memory      ----------}

                    Regs.AH := $49;                       { DOS function number }
                    Regs.ES := PrgSeg;    { segment address of allocated memory }
                    MsDos( Regs );

                    writeln( 'CLOCK has been de-installed.' );
                  end
                else    { another TSR-program has redirected the timer interrupt }
                  writeln( 'CLOCK can not be de-installed because another ',
                           'TSR-program has been installed after it.' );
              end
          else                  { write new parameters into already installed copy }
            begin
              writeln( 'Parameter passed to already installed ',
                       ' CLOCK.');
              inline( $FA );                              { disable interrupts }
              PP( GetPtr( @VideoPtr, PrgSeg ) )^ := VideoPtr;
              PBO( GetPTr( @ShowBefore, PrgSeg ) )^ := ShowBefore;
              PB( GetPTr( @ShowInterval, PrgSeg ) )^ := ShowInterval;

              {-- get pointer to TimeStr variable in installed CLOCK      ---}
              {-- and enter new color into the array                      ---}

              TimePtr := GetPtr( @TimeStr, PrgSeg );
              for i := 1 to 8 do
                TimePtr^[i].TColr := TColr;

              inline( $FB );                              { re-enable interrupts }
            end;
        end;
    end;
```

If the parameters that were passed are valid, the pointer VideoPtr to the display position in video RAM is created after the completion of the evaluation loop. Since the coordinates and the offset address are known and stored in the column and line variables, only the segment address of the video RAM must be calculated separately. Function $0F of the BIOS video interrupt indicates through a returned video code whether a monochrome or a color video card is installed and in use. This process was discussed in Chapter 6.

A call of the YetInstalled procedure determines whether a copy of the program has already been installed. If not, preliminary tasks begin for installing the program. The current time is passed to the time variable by the InitTime procedure. Then the address of the current handler of interrupt $1C is determined and stored in the OldTimer variable. After that the program installs the NewTimer handler by passing its address to the correct memory location within the Interrupt Vector Table. From this moment on, the interrupt procedure NewTimer is called 18.2 times per second.

Turbo Pascal communicates with DOS functions during both of these tasks using the GetIntVec and SetIntVec procedures.

Before the program ends, a message and the time appear on the screen using PriTime so that the time disappears one second after the program terminates. The program must be terminated by the Keep procedure instead of ending in the usual way. As its name implies, Keep maintains CLOCK in memory.

After calling YetInstalled, if the CheckAndInit routine determines that a copy of CLOCK is already installed, its future operation depends on the parameters passed in the command line during the call. If the user enters the name CLOCK without parameters, an existing CLOCK is removed from memory. This is only possible if another TSR program hasn't already redirected interrupt vector $1C to its own routines. At its end this routine will usually call the preceding interrupt handler and CLOCK's NewTimer procedure. This call produces a system crash as soon as CLOCK is removed from the memory and is replaced with another program.

Because of this, the current contents of the interrupt vector for interrupt $1C is read and tested to see if it still points to the CLOCK program in memory. If it does, the process of disabling CLOCK begins.

First the address of the original interrupt handler (installed in the OldTimer variable in the deactivated version of CLOCK) is determined. Access to this variable is only possible after calling the GetPtr function and referring to the pointer that was returned.

The second step is to release the memory currently occupied by CLOCK. The segment address of the released memory must be passed to DOS function $49 in the ES register. This function must be called twice because DOS allocates two memory blocks for every program starting the program through function $48. The first memory block accepts the environment and corresponding strings. Its segment address is in the EnvSeg field, within the PSP of the CLOCK program about to be deactivated. Also, this information is determined by referencing a pointer returned by the GetPtr function.

The second memory block contains the program itself, comprising memory from the beginning of the PSP to the end of the heap. Its segment address was already returned from the YetInstalled function and is passed directly to DOS function $49.

If the program is neither re-installed, nor is an installed copy removed from memory, the screen position and color parameters are passed to the existing CLOCK application. This process continues in the same manner for all parameters. The GetPtr function determines a pointer to the variable, which is then converted to a typed pointer by the type conversion. The variable can be referenced, read or changed through this pointer.

Before this happens the CLI assembly language instruction (placed into the program code by an INLINE statement) disables the interrupts. This prevents the triggering of interrupt $1C before all variables could be written into their corresponding memory locations within the installed CLOCK. After this process ends, the program executes the STI assembly language instruction, which allows interrupt access to the processor.

In addition to Help, PriTime, GetPTr and YetInstalled, CheckAndInit also calls the InitTime procedure and the GetVal function. These are listed below.

```
{*************************************************************************
*  GetVal : converts a numeric value within a parameter string         *
*           into binary notation and tests the validity in the         *
*           framework of the indicated value range                     *
**--------------------------------------------------------------------**
*  Input : Parameter = Parameter string with number after third character *
*          Variable  = Variable which stores the binary value          *
*          Min       = lower limit of value range (>=0)                *
*          Max       = upper limit of value range (<256)               *
*  Output : TRUE, if the number could be converted and is in the indicated *
*           value range, otherwise FALSE                               *
*  Info    : during an error, an error message is displayed automatically *
*  Global  : None                                                      *
*************************************************************************}

function GetVal( Parameter : string; var Variable : byte;
                 Min, Max : byte ) : boolean;

var error   : integer;                  { error variable for Val procedure }
    StrCopy : string;                      { copy of the parameter string }

begin
  StrCopy := Parameter;                      { store parameter string }
  Parameter[1] := ' ';       { replace the first two characters with spaces }
  Parameter[2] := ' ';
  Val( Parameter, Variable, error );             { convert ASCII to binary }
  if ( error <> 0 ) then                        { no conversion possible? }
    begin                                                        { yes }
      writeln( 'Invalid Parameter: ', StrCopy );
      GetVal := FALSE;                                          { error! }
    end
  else                             { number OK, but in value range? }
    if ( Variable >= Min ) and ( Variable <= Max ) then
      GetVal := TRUE                           { in value range, all OK }
    else                                        { outside the value range }
```

```
      begin
        writeln( 'Parameter outside the value range (', Min,
                 ' - ', Max, ') : ', StrCopy );
        GetVal := FALSE;
      end;
end;
{****************************************************************************
 *  InitTime : Initializes the variable TimeStr with the current time       *
 *             and a constant color.                                        *
 **------------------------------------------------------------------------**
 *  Input : color = Output color of the time                                *
 *  Global : TimeStr/W                                                      *
 ****************************************************************************}

procedure InitTime( color : byte );

var i          : byte;                                      { loop counter }
    Hour,                                          { variable for current time }
    Minute,
    Second,
    Hundredth : word;

begin
  {-- determine current time, convert to ASCII and store in TimeStr   ------}

  GetTime( Hour, Minute, Second, Hundredth );                  { get time }
  if ( Hour < 10 ) then                                  { before 10 AM? }
    TimeStr[ 1 ].TChar := ' '          { yes, first digit in string is empty }
  else                                                            { no }
    TimeStr[ 1 ].TChar := chr( Hour div 10 + ord('0') );    { ten hours }

  TimeStr[ 2 ].TChar := chr( Hour   mod 10 + ord('0') );    { one hour }
  TimeStr[ 4 ].TChar := chr( Minute div 10 + ord('0') );   { ten minutes }
  TimeStr[ 5 ].TChar := chr( Minute mod 10 + ord('0') );   { one minute }
  TimeStr[ 7 ].TChar := chr( Second div 10 + ord('0') );   { ten seconds }
  TimeStr[ 8 ].TChar := chr( Second mod 10 + ord('0') );   { one second }

  TimeStr[3].TChar := ':';                { colon separates hours from minutes }
  TimeStr[6].TChar := ':';                { and minutes from seconds          }

  for i := 1 to 8 do                       { store output color in TimeStr }
    TimeStr[i].TColr := color;
end;
```

The main program for CLOCK is very brief. It contains two Writeln statements and the CheckAndInit call. Once this procedure is completed, the program ends. However, it doesn't return directly to the main application if CLOCK was called for the first time—CLOCK is installed in memory first.

```
{****************************************************************************
 *  M A I N   P R O G R A M                                                 *
 ****************************************************************************}
```

```
begin
  writeln( #13#10, 'CLOCK - permanent time display on the screen' );
  writeln( '(c) 1989 by MICHAEL TISCHER'#13#10 );
  CheckAndInit;                         { read arguments, initialize and install }
end.
```

Even though CLOCK performs its task well without slowing foreground applications too much, you may have noticed that this program does have some drawbacks. One of these problems involves the stack (more on this later in this chapter).

CLOCK is a very self-centered program. After executing its own interrupt handler, it doesn't call the previously installed handler. Instead, it automatically returns to the interrupted program once the interrupt procedure finishes execution. Any TSR programs installed before CLOCK will not operate properly once CLOCK is installed.

Also, the technique used by CLOCK for display affects programs that operate in graphic modes or use several screen pages. Since CLOCK doesn't notice the switch between text mode and graphic mode, it also displays its output within the graphic mode to video RAM. This produces undesirable results because video RAM in graphic mode interprets data differently than video RAM in text mode. If other screen pages are activated through the BIOS video interrupt functions, the clock completely disappears from the screen. This occurs because CLOCK continues to send its output to the first screen page, even when a completely different page is displayed on the screen.

These problems can be solved. However, some assembly language instructions must be included in the program code using INLINE statements. For example, the stack problem can be solved by storing the contents of the SS and SP register in variables and initializing these registers with the address of the Turbo stack at the beginning of NewTimer. However, you must ensure that NewTimer is called only after the program ends, instead of during the execution of Keep, which requires the Turbo stack.

CLOCK can be modified to cooperate with previously installed TSR programs by calling the old interrupt handler within the interrupt procedure NewTimer, whose address is stored in the OldTimer variable. During this execution, the processor must be emulated by storing the contents of the flag registers on the stack during an interrupt call. Then the interrupt handler is called like a FAR procedure. Both can be simulated by using two assembly language instructions, which are included in the program using INLINE statements:

```
inline( $9C );                    { store flag register on the stack }
inline( $FF / $1E / OldTimer );            { call old handler }
```

You can place these two statements either at the beginning or the end of the NewTimer interrupt procedure.

The problems affecting the graphic mode and various screen pages can also be solved if the current application uses the BIOS video functions instead of directly accessing the video card. Interrupt $10 can easily be intercepted by CLOCK through an additional interrupt procedure, and can determine whether the caller wishes to specify a new graphic mode by placing function number $00 in the AH register. In this case, the code number of the video mode must be tested in the AL register and, during entry into graphic mode, a flag must be set to prevent access to video RAM in PriTime. This flag is cleared again when the caller specifies text mode during a call to this BIOS function.

The problem affecting the various screen pages can be solved in the same way because the executing program also must use a certain function of video interrupt $10. Within the new handler for this interrupt, the function can also be intercepted and the VideoPtr pointer can be loaded with the address of the screen position in this page, depending on the selected screen page. During the redirection of interrupt $10, don't forget to call the old interrupt handler within the new interrupt procedure so that the assignment from the caller is executed and your interrupt handler doesn't represent the final station of the interrupt call.

Even though it works quite well and could serve as a basic framework for the creation of a ISR application which intercepts other interrupts and thereby controls printer output, keyboard input or screen output, CLOCK can easily be improved. With a knowledge of system programming, there are few limits to your creativity.

11.2   Developing a TSR

ISR programs can be triggered by internal sources. TSRs such as SideKick®, however, are directly activated by the user by pressing a predetermined key combination called the *hotkey*. The application which was executing in the foreground is "frozen" until the user has finished using the TSR program and has returned the TSR to the background.

These characteristics of a TSR program create some problems. For example, how should the TSR program react to the activation of its hotkeys, and how should it move to the foreground while suspending the currently executing application?

Besides these general problems, a closer examination reveals many other questions. Once called, the TSR program must store the complete screen contents. This means that it must store all the information needed to restore the screen to its original state once the interrupted application is returned to the foreground. A solution must also be found for the problem that occurs when the foreground application is interrupted by a TSR program during the call of a DOS function. Since DOS was intended to be a single task system, it assumes that only one application will be active. So, calling a simple DOS function within a TSR program can cause a system crash.

These problems can be solved, even though DOS isn't designed to accommodate TSR programs. However, Pascal cannot do it alone. An assembler module must be created to implement required interrupt handlers and routines (see Chapter 3). The assembler module TSRA.ASM, which will appear later in this chapter, is a part of the TSR unit which also appears in this section. The TSR unit relieves you of much of the work involved in developing TSR programs, and which protects your TSR program from the previously mentioned problems.

With the help of only five functions and procedures, this unit covers all assignments which occur during the creation, installation and deactivation of TSR programs. Only one procedure call is required to convert your program into a TSR program, make it resident in memory and ensure that it will be called when the user presses the selected hotkey.

The three programs must be prepared in the following order to create an executable program:

- Assemble the TSRA.ASM source code using MASM or TASM. This assembly creates a file named TSRA.OBJ.

- Compile the TSR.PAS source code using Turbo Pascal (make sure that the TSRA.OBJ file created by assembling TSRA.ASM can be easily accessed by the compiler).

- Compile the TSRDEMO.PAS source code using Turbo Pascal (make sure that the TSR.TPU file generated by compiling TSR.PAS is easily accessible to the compiler).

Before discussing the development of this unit we will demonstrate how to use the TSR unit through a demonstration program called TSRDEMO. This program contains most of the capabilities found in a typical TSR program. We gave TSRDEMO a simple assignment. After the user presses the hotkey, TSRDEMO opens a window on the screen and displays the contents of the current disk directory. After displaying the last file name, this window closes again and the execution of the interrupted application continues.

```
     File    Edit    Run    Com┌══════ TSRDEMO - (c) 1989 by MICHAEL TISCHER ══════┐
                          ═════║IBMBIO.COM    08/09/1985  12:00     7820  RHS--A ║
       Line 772   Col 76  Inse║IBMDOS.COM    08/09/1985  12:00    27760  RHS--A ║
│      BYTEP = ^byte;         ║COMMAND.COM   08/09/1985  12:00    23210  -----A ║
│                             ║12311986      12/30/1986  15:40        0  ---V-A ║
│begin                        ║DOS           12/30/1986  15:40        0  ----D- ║
│  {-- The information is writ║MPLAN         01/24/1990  14:12        0  ----D- ║
│  {-- key_mask and scan_code ║DUMP.BAT      01/25/1990   9:45      556  -----A ║
│                             ║PCTOOLS       12/29/1989  15:18        0  ----D- ║
│   WORDP(TsrGetPtr( @key_mask║PASC_EXE      05/03/1989  12:01        0  ----D- ║
│   BYTEP(TsrGetPtr( @scan_code║123          01/24/1990  15:09        0  ----D- ║
│end;                         ║TEMPO2        06/21/1989  11:34        0  ----D- ║
│{**************************║FL            01/25/1990  11:36        0  ----D- ║
│ *  TsrRemove : removes previo║TEMPO3       06/25/1989  11:34        0  ----D- ║
│ **_____║CHART         01/25/1990  13:44        0  ----D- ║
│ *                          ║    Please press a key ...                      ║
│ *  Input : none            ╚════════════════════════════════════════════════╝
│ *  Output : TRUE if the TSR pl
│ *           not be removed because of another TSR overlaid in memory.       *│
│ *  Info    : TsrRemove may only be called after calling TsrYetInstall,      *│
│ *            indicating whether a copy of this program is already installed* │
│ *  Global : OldTsrPSP/R                                                     *│
│────────────────────────── Watch ────────────────────────────────────────────│
│                                                                              │
└──────────────────────────────────────────────────────────────────────────────┘

  F1-Help  F5-Zoom  F6-Switch  F7-Trace  F8-Step  F9-Make  F10-Menu
```

TSRDEMO in action

If you like this program, you can easily enhance it so that it displays various directories, or even performs file maintenance on the files in these directories (copy, delete, move). You may even want to create your own TSR user interface similar to the Norton Commander or XTREE, based on the TSRDEMO source code listed here and on the companion diskettes which accompany this book.

```
{***************************************************************************
*    TSRDEMO - demonstrates the creation of TSR programs with the help    *
*              of the TSR unit.                                           *
**-----------------------------------------------------------------------**
*    Author          : MICHAEL TISCHER                                    *
*    developed on     : 09/05/1989                                        *
*    last update on   : 03/03/1990                                        *
****************************************************************************}

program tsrdemo;

{$M 2048, 8000, 8000}                              { 2K stack and 8K heap }
{$I-}                                                  { no I/O checking }

uses dos, tsr, crt, win;

{-- typed and untyped constants ------------------------------------------}

const MyId : TsrIdStr = 'TSRDEMO-PAS';          { identification string }
const DEFAULT_MASK    = LSHIFT + RSHIFT;                     { default
activation }
```

The beginning of TSRDEMO shows that the TSRDEMO uses the TSR unit and the WIN unit described earlier in this book (see Chapter 6), as well as the CRT and DOS units. The WIN unit accesses to the screen while TSRDEMO displays the disk directory. As in CLOCK, the size of the stack and the heap are limited. However, unlike CLOCK, the program must allocate some heap memory. This is because the WIN unit heap memory is used for allocating memory used for storing screen contents.

The 8,000 bytes indicated for the heap may be too much for some systems, and can be reduced if memory allocation problems occur.

TSRDEMO also supports the mechanisms used by CLOCK for installation, deactivation and configuration. For this reason TSRDEMO also has an identification string which determines whether a copy of the program is already installed in memory. This string, which is called MyId, is a string of type TsrIdStr. This type is defined by the TSR unit and represents a string with a maximum length of 20 characters. This greatly reduces memory requirements (a standard string can be up to 255 characters long), and therefore allocates 20 bytes in memory, regardless of the string's actual length.

Another constant, called DEFAULT_MASK, defines the hotkeys of the program. The combination of the left and right <Shift> keys are used for the default hotkey combination, but other keys or key combinations can also be assigned by entering the proper parameters when starting the program.

These introductory declarations are followed by the TSR procedure. This procedure is called by the TSR unit after the user presses the hotkey. At the time of this call, the TSR unit has already completed the required preliminary work for executing the TSR program:

- The screen contents were stored and the system changes to 80x25 text mode, regardless of the previously active video mode.

- The Turbo stack and the Turbo data segment are installed.

- The program is allowed access to all DOS functions and the Turbo Pascal procedures/functions that contain DOS calls, regardless of the problem of re-entry to DOS.

The TSR procedure can act like a normal Pascal procedure, which is executed in the context of a normal application. It can call the procedures and functions from the System unit and other units; allocate memory on the heap; and access devices, files and directories.

Only one condition must be met for a procedure to be called by the TSR unit as a TSR procedure. It must be a FAR procedure, so that it can be called through a procedure pointer. This requirement is easily met by preceding the declaration with the {$F+} compiler directive.

```
{********************************************************************
*  MyTsr : TSR procedure called when the user activates the TSR    *
**--------------------------------------------------------------**
*  Input : none                                                    *
********************************************************************}

{$F+} procedure MyTsr;                                    {$F-}

type Colors = record                        { colors for text output }
             TI,                                        { title }
             FR,                               { color of frame }
             DN,                           { color for file name }
             BT,                         { color for "activate key" }
             ER,                 { color for error window and frame }
             EM : byte;                   { color for error message }
           end;

const Attribute : array[1..6] of char = 'RHSVDA';        { file attribute }

const MonoColors  : Colors = ( TI : $0F; FR : $70; DN : $70;
                               BT : $78; ER : $07; EM : $0F );
      ColorColors : Colors = ( TI : RED   shl 4 + WHITE;
                               FR : BLUE  shl 4 + LIGHTCYAN;
                               DN : BLUE  shl 4 + WHITE;
                               BT : BLUE  shl 4 + YELLOW;
                               ER : RED   shl 4 + YELLOW;
```

397

```
                              EM : RED  shl 4 + WHITE       );

    var i, j,                                              { loop counter }
        WinLen    : integer;                            { length of window }
        key       : char;
        Handle    : integer;               { handle for access to window }
        Dir_Srch : SearchRec;              { for FindFirst and FindNext }
        DT        : DateTime;                 { date and time of a file }
        F         : Colors;                          { display color }

    begin
      {-- construct window for directory display ----------------------------}

      if Color then F := ColorColors                       { set colors }
               else F := MonoColors;
      if TsrShowScreen then WinLen := 15          { select window length }
                       else WinLen := 23;
      Handle := WinOpen( 30, 0, 79, WinLen+1 );           { open window }
      WinFrame( VL(0), VO(0), VR(0), VU(0), DBL_FR, F.FR );    { draw frame }
      WinFill( VL(1), VO(1), VR(-1), VU(-1), ' ', F.DN );     { erase window }
      WinSetView( VL(1), VO(1), VR(-1), VU(-1) );          { set view range }
      WinPrint( VL(5), VO(-1), F.TI, ' TSRDEMO - (c) 1989 by MICHAEL TISCHER ');
      TextBackground( F.DN shr 4 );                    { set output color }
      TextColor( F.DN and $0f );
      GotoXY( VL(0), VO(0) ); { screen position of upper left corner of window }

      WinHideCursor;                                       { hide cursor }

      {-- display files in the current directory ----------------------------}

      i:=1;
      FindFirst( '*.*', AnyFile, Dir_Srch );               { find first file }
      while ( DosError <> 18 ) do                    { found another file ? }
        begin                                              { yes, display }
          if ( DosError <> 0 ) then                  { path not found ? }
            begin                                               { yes }
              Handle := WinOpen( VL(3), VO(5), VL( 44 ), VO(12) );
              WinFrame( VL(0), VO(0), VR(0), VU(0), SIN_FR, F.ER );
              WinFill( VL(1), VO(1), VR(-1), VU(-1), ' ', F.ER );
              WinPrint( VL(3), VO(2), F.EM, 'A T T E N T I O N !');
              WinPrint( VL(3), VO(4), F.EM,
                        'No access to current drive.');
              WinPrint( VL(3), VO(5), F.EM, 'Strike key ...');
              key := ReadKey;                                { get key }
              if key = #0 then                       { extended key code? }
                key := ReadKey;                 { yes, read second byte }
              WinClose( TRUE );                      { close window again }
              DosError := 18;                            { end of loop }
            end
          else                                     { another file was found }
            begin
              write( Dir_Srch.name, '':12-length(Dir_Srch.name) );
```

```
                {-- display date and time of the file -------------------------}

                UnpackTime( Dir_Srch.Time, DT );              { unpack date and time }
                if Dt.Month < 10 then write( '  0', DT.Month )
                            else write( '   ', DT.Month:2 );
                if Dt.Day < 10 then write( '/0', DT.Day )
                            else write( '/', DT.Day:2 );
                write( '/', DT.Year, ' ' );

                write( DT.Hour:2, ':' );
                if Dt.Min < 10 then write( '0', DT.Min )
                            else write( DT.Min:2 );

                write( Dir_Srch.Size:8, ' ' );               { display file size }

                {-- output the file attributes --------------------------------}

                for j := 1 to 6 do       { test bits 0 to 5 in the attribute byte }
                  begin
                    if ( ( Dir_Srch.Attr and 1 ) = 1 ) then        { bit set? }
                      write( Attribute[j] )                 { yes, display code }
                    else                                              { no }
                      write( '-' );
                    Dir_Srch.Attr := Dir_Srch.Attr shr 1;       { check next bit }
                  end;

                writeln;

                {-- if the window is full, or no additional files were ----------}
                {-- found, the program prompts the user to press a key ----------}

                inc( i );                              { increment line number }
                FindNext( Dir_Srch );                      { search for next file }
                if ( i = WinLen ) or ( DosError <> 0 ) then
                  begin
                    TextBackground( F.BT shr 4 );            { set display color }
                    TextColor( F.BT and $0f );
                    write( ' Please press a key ...' );
                    key := ReadKey;                               { read key }
                    if key = #0 then                      { extended key code? }
                      key := ReadKey;                     { yes, read second byte }
                    write( #13 );          { move cursor to beginning of the line }
                    TextBackground( F.DN shr 4 );            { set display color }
                    TextColor( F.DN and $0f );
                    i := 1;                              { return to first line }
                  end;
              end;
          end;
        WinClose( TRUE );                                  { close window again }
      end;
```

The TSR procedure is introduced by the declaration of a structure named Colors, which stores the colors in which the individual objects (e.g., file names, messages for the user) are displayed on the screen. To produce the correct results with both monochrome and color systems, separate color sets are defined with the typed constants MonoColors and ColorColors for the two types of video cards.

The beginning of MyTsr defines which color palette is used. The F variable is loaded with one of the two palettes. The choice depends on the content of the Color variable which is imported when the WIN unit is included during compilation. As its name suggests, the Color variable contains the value TRUE if a color card is installed, and FALSE if an MDA (a Monochrome Display Adapter) or a Hercules card is installed.

This test is followed by a call to the TsrShowScreen function found in the TSR unit. This function restores the stored screen contents belonging to the interrupted application. This happens because when the TSR procedure executes, the screen is already in 80x25 text mode, but is empty. TsrShowScreen can perform only if the screen was in text mode before the TSR program was activated. In this case it restores the old screen contents and returns the value TRUE.

However, if the screen was in graphic mode before the user pressed the hotkey, TsrShowScreen returns the value FALSE to the caller Inside MyTsr. The returned values determine the length of the window in which the current directory will be displayed. If the screen content could be restored, the window occupies only the upper half of the screen. Otherwise, the window extends from the first screen line to the last screen line.

MyTsr now follows the usual procedure calls included in the WIN unit, which contribute to the construction of a screen window. The window is opened, surrounded by a frame and cleared.

The FindFirst and FindNext procedures from the DOS unit process the current directories. If an error occurs (e.g., drive not ready), a window containing an error appears. After the user presses any key, the TSR procedure ends and control returns to the interrupted program.

Since the procedure displays the individual data items in the window by calling Write and Writeln, the first few entries would scroll up and out of sight if more file names are in the current directory than there are available lines in the directory window. To solve this problem, the procedure operates in a manner similar to the DIR command in /P mode. The window fills with as many new entries as will fit in the window, and the procedure prompts the user to press a key to continue.

After the program displays the last data entry, the directory window is closed without restoring the original screen contents. This is unnecessary because after the procedure ends, the TSR unit (which copied the original screen contents during the restoration to video RAM) becomes active again.

After installing the program, MyTsr is the only procedure which is still active as a TSR application. All the other procedures and functions within TSRDEMO perform the installation, deactivation and transmission of new parameters to an already installed program.

The CheckKey function performs an important task involving the /K parameter used to specify hotkeys. CheckKey allows the user to start the program after installation using a key combination other than the default key combination. Several of these parameters are available. The total of the indicated control keys determines the key combination which must be pressed to start TSRDEMO.

CheckKey places the /K parameter in an array which consists of eight elements of type StatRecord. The array stores the name of the parameter and its bit value. The latter information can be read from the constants LSHIFT, RSHIFT, CTRL etc., whose definitions lie within the TSR unit. The following example configures TSRDEMO for activation by pressing the <Ctrl> key:

```
>TSRDEMO /KCTRL
```

As the typed constant KnownKeys shows, the TSR unit allows you to start the TSR program using the <Alt> key, the <Ctrl> key, both <Shift> keys pressed simultaneously, the <Break> key, the <Num Lock> key, the <Caps Lock> key and the <System Request> key. These keys are suitable for this purpose since they aren't used by MS-DOS or by most applications, so they can easily be used with TSR programs.

Every TSR program should contain a function such as CheckKey, which allows the user to specify which key or key combination should start the TSR program. A conflict can easily occur if several TSR programs use the same key combination. When such a conflict takes place, usually only the most recently installed TSR program remains accessible. This happens because this program first receives the message of the keystroke from the interrupt handler chain, but doesn't pass this message to the following interrupt handlers. Instead, it takes control of program execution.

```
{*************************************************************************
*  CheckKey : checks the command line for a /K parameter                *
**---------------------------------------------------------------------**
*  Input : MASK      = existing keyboard template                       *
*          PARAMETER = parameter string                                 *
*  Output : TRUE if the parameter was OK, otherwise FALSE               *
*  Info    : In case of error a message is displayed                    *
*************************************************************************}

function CheckKey( var KMask : integer; Parameter : string ) : boolean;

type StatKeyName = string [8];               { name of a status key }
     StatRecord  = record                    { describes a status key }
                     Name : StatKeyName;                      { name }
                     Bit  : integer;                         { value }
                   end;
```

```
const KnownKeys : array [1..8] of StatRecord =
     (
        ( Name : '/KLSHIFT'; Bit : LSHIFT ),        { names of the     }
        ( Name : '/KRSHIFT'; Bit : RSHIFT ),        { various control }
        ( Name : '/KCTRL' ; Bit : CTRL   ),         { keys and bit     }
        ( Name : '/KALT'   ; Bit : ALT    ),        { values used as   }
        ( Name : '/KSYSREQ'; Bit : SYSREQ ),        { parameters for   }
        ( Name : '/KBREAK' ; Bit : BREAK  ),        { TSRDEMO          }
        ( Name : '/KNUM'   ; Bit : NUM    ),
        ( Name : '/KCAPS'  ; Bit : CAPS   )
     );

var i : integer;                                    { loop counter }

{-- local procedure, converts strings into upper case letters -------------}

procedure StrUp( var Str : string );

var i : byte;

begin
  for i := 1 to length( Str )                        { process string }
    do Str[i] := UpCase( Str[i] );                   { convert letters }
end;


{-------------------------------------------------------------------------}

begin
  StrUp( Parameter );                    { convert string to upper case letters }
  Parameter[1] := '/';              { place slash at beginning of the parameter }

  {-- search KnownKeys array for parameter -------------------------------}

  i := 1;                                 { start search with the first entry }
  while ( i < 9 ) and ( KnownKeys[i].Name <> Parameter ) do
   inc( i );                              { not found yet - try next element }

  if ( i <> 9 ) then                                  { parameter found? }
    begin                                                        { yes }
      KMask := KMask or KnownKeys[i].Bit;        { set bit in the template }
      CheckKey := TRUE;                                   { return TRUE }
    end
  else                                               { unknown parameter }
    begin
      writeln( 'Unknown parameter: ', Parameter );
      CheckKey := FALSE;
    end;
end;
```

The CheckKey function is called by the CheckPara procedure, which is responsible for reading the command line parameter, installing the program and removing the program. It recognizes two different kinds of parameters, which are represented by the HercPage and KMask variables.

If the /K parameter is detected while reading arguments from the DOS prompt, CheckKey is called. The parameter is passed to the KMask variable. Its individual bits represent a certain control key. CheckKey sets the bit corresponding to the name of the control key during the evaluation of the passed parameter. After processing all arguments, the various bits in the mask reflect the individual control keys which must be simultaneously pressed to activate the TSR program.

In addition to the /K parameter, CheckPara also recognizes the /H parameter, which must be followed by either the number 0 or 1. This parameter indicates the number of the screen page which the TSR unit stored during activation of the TSR program. This screen page remains in effect for subsequent TSR activation. This information is important only to Hercules cards and programs that operate in Hercules graphic mode. Most TSR programs cannot sense which Hercules screen page is currently in use because this setting isn't controlled by BIOS functions. In addition, the corresponding hardware register cannot be read, and this register contains the number of the active screen page.

Normally the TSR unit accesses the first screen page, which is the correct choice for most applications. Some other programs (e.g., Microsoft Word) use the Hercules graphic mode and the second screen page. So if you were installing TSRDEMO for use on a system including both a Hercules card AND Microsoft Word, we recommend the following call:

```
TSRDEMO /H1
```

The number of the Hercules graphic page is stored in the TSR unit's typed constant TsrHercPage. During installation of the program, CheckPara loads this parameter with the value from the /H parameter, or the default value if this parameter is omitted.

```
{*****************************************************************************
 *  CheckPara : analyzes the parameter from the command line               *
 **-----------------------------------------------------------------------**
 *  Input : none                                                           *
 *****************************************************************************}

procedure CheckPara;

type INTP = ^integer;

var i        : byte;                                    { loop counter }
    Install  : boolean;                            { were parameters OK? }
    KMask,                                  { template for activating control keys }
    HercPage : integer;                         { graphic page for Hercules }
    Parameter : string;                         { stores the current parameter }

begin
```

```
Install   := TRUE;                          { assume correct parameters }
HercPage := TsrHercPage;                      { store default setting }
KMask    := 0;                                { no key selected yet }

{-- read and process arguments from the command line -------------------}

for i := 1 to ParamCount do
  begin
    Parameter := ParamStr(i);                         { get parameter I }
    if ( Parameter[1] <> '/' ) and ( Parameter[1] <> '-' ) then
      begin                      { parameter not preceded by '-' or '/' }
        writeln( 'Unknown parameter: ', Parameter );
        Install := FALSE;                                 { store error }
      end
    else                    { first character in parameter is '-' or '/' }
      case UpCase(Parameter[2]) of               { read parameter code }
        'H' : begin
                if ( length(Parameter) <> 3 ) or
                   (( Parameter[3] <> '0' ) and ( Parameter[3] <> '1' ))
                  then begin
                    writeln( 'Invalid parameter: ', Parameter );
                    Install := FALSE;           { error, do not install }
                  end
                else                            { 0 or 1 indicated }
                  HercPage := ord(Parameter[3]) - ord('0');
              end;

        'K' : begin
                Install := CheckKey( KMask, Parameter );
              end;
        else
          begin
            writeln( 'Unknown parameter: ', Parameter );
            Install := FALSE;                             { store error }
          end;
      end;
  end;

if ( Install = TRUE ) then                        { were parameters OK? }
  begin
    if KMask = 0 then                             { no key selected? }
      KMask :=  DEFAULT_MASK;                     { no, use default }

    if ( TsrYetInstalled( MyId ) ) then     { program already installed? }
      begin                                                   { yes }
        if ( ParamCount = 0 ) then         { no command line parameter? }
          begin                  { no, remove program from memory again }
            if TsrRemove then
              writeln( 'TSRDEMO program now removed from memory.')
            else
              writeln( 'TSRDEMO program already installed, ',
                       'but cannot be removed from memory.');
          end
```

```
        else              { write new parameter into already installed copy }
          begin
            writeln( 'New parameter accepted into TSRDEMO program.');
            TsrNewKey( KMask, NOKEY );
            INTP ( TsrGetPtr( @TsrHercPage ) )^ := HercPage;
          end;
      end
      else                                { if not yet installed, install }
        begin
          writeln( 'TSRDEMO program now installed.');
          writeln;
          writeln( 'If you didn''t enter any /K options, the default');
          writeln( 'hotkey combination is <Left SHIFT><Right SHIFT>');

          TsrHercPage := HercPage;           { store Hercules graphic page }
          WinSetCursor( WhereX, WhereY );    { set cursor for program end }
          TsrInstall( KMask, NOKEY , MyTsr );
        end;
    end;
  end;
```

After reading the parameter, CheckPara ensures that all parameters are valid by checking the contents of the Install variable. If so, this variable contains the value TRUE and governs the installation/deactivation of the program. A test is made to determine whether the KMask variable still contains the value 0, through which it was initialized before the evaluation of the command line parameters. If so, a /K parameter wasn't encountered and KMask is loaded with the constant DEFAULT_MASK, which specifies the default hotkey combination (left <Shift> and right <Shift>).

The additional program code closely resembles the corresponding section in the CLOCK program listed in Section 11.1. TSRDEMO can also determine whether the program was previously installed. The TsrYetInstalled function is called, which is identical to the YetInstalled function in the CLOCK program. Since it is part of the TSR unit, it doesn't have to be placed directly in your TSR programs.

The identification string MyId is passed to TsrYetInstalled as a parameter. When TsrYetInstalled determines that TSRDEMO is already installed (based on MyId), it returns TRUE. If so, CheckPara uses the ParamCount function to test whether TSRDEMO received parameters from the user from the DOS prompt. If not, the TsrRemove disables the already installed TSRDEMO and removes it from memory.

As in CLOCK, this is only possible if the interrupt handler of the TSR program wasn't overlaid by other TSR programs in the meantime. Therefore, TsrRemove returns a function result of type boolean to the caller, which indicates if the program could be deactivated. CheckPara displays a message on the screen, depending on the function result.

If the program is already installed but parameters were included in the most recent call, this indicates that the user wants to assign the already installed program a new hotkey, or wants it to operate with another Hercules screen page. In order to give the Hercules graphic card a new parameter, we will use a method that was presented in the CLOCK program. A pointer to the variable which was addressed within the installed program is determined, and the variable is referenced through this pointer. The CLOCK program used a function GetPtr. Here it is called TsrGetPtr and is available through the TSR unit.

Unlike GetPtr, only the address of the addressed variable is passed, and not the segment address of the PSP in the installed program. This information is also requested by TsrGetPtr, but this function receives it from a variable that is integral to the unit. This variable is initialized through the call of the TsrYetInstalled function. Notice that with the TsrHercPage variable, a variable is addressed which is in an included unit, rather than within the TSR program itself. This doesn't affect TsrGetPtr; the correct pointer will still be returned.

The TSR unit includes a function called TsrNewKey, which allows you to define a new hotkey without accessing the TsrGetPtr function. Two parameters must be passed to this function: the mask for the control keys and a scan code. The TSR unit can be activated by other keys on the keyboard used in conjunction with the specified control keys. For example, a program can be activated by pressing the key combination <Alt><A>.

TSRDEMO uses the constant NOKEY instead of a scan code, which is defined by the TSR unit. This constant tells the called function that TSRDEMO can only be activated by pressing control keys; normal keys cannot be included.

We also encounter the NOKEY constant during the installation of the program, which occurs in the Tsr unit through the TsrInstall procedure. The control key mask and the scan code must be passed to it as the first parameter. Also, CheckPara only indicates the KMask variable and uses the constant NOKEY for the scan code.

TsrInstall expects a pointer to the TSR procedure within the program (i.e., the procedure through which the execution of the program is started after pressing the hotkey) as the third parameter. CheckPara provides the procedure MyTsr for this parameter.

The call of the install procedure is also the last statement within CheckPara because, instead of returning to the caller, TsrInstall simultaneously installs the various interrupt handlers, terminates program execution and makes the program resident. Since CheckPara oversees the evaluation of the command line parameters and the installation/deactivation of the program, almost no tasks remain for the main program. It is therefore a very short program.

```
{*****************************************************************************
*                        M A I N   P R O G R A M                           *
*****************************************************************************}

begin
  writeln( #13#10, 'TSRDEMO - (c) 1989 by MICHAEL TISCHER' );
```

```
    CheckPara;                                          { check for parameter }
    WinSetCursor( WhereX, WhereY );          { set cursor behind last output }
  end.
```

From the application of the TSR unit through the TSRDEMO program, we now turn to
the TSR unit itself. It consists, as previously mentioned, of an assembler section and a
Pascal section. The assembler code is located in the TSRA.ASM file. The Pascal code is
located in the TSR.PAS file. Since TSR.PAS performs the most work and only delegates
tasks, which it cannot perform, to the assembler module, we'll start by examining
TSR.PAS.

At the beginning of the TSR unit you will find the usual declarations of the public types,
procedures, functions and variables. You've read explanations for most of these in this
description of TSRDEMO.

```
{*****************************************************************************
 *   TSR : A unit for the creation of TSR programs in Turbo Pascal.         *
 **-----------------------------------------------------------------------**
 *   Author          : MICHAEL TISCHER                                      *
 *   developed on     : 09/01/1989                                          *
 *   last update on   : 03/02/1990                                          *
 *****************************************************************************}

unit TSR;

{$S-R-}                                    { no stack or range checking here }

interface

uses DOS, CRT;                                     { use the DOS and CRT unit }

{-- Type declarations required for the call of the public P/F ------------}

type TsrIdStr    = string[20];                     { identification string }
     TsrProcedure = procedure;        { TSR procedure of the main program }

{-- public procedures and functions -------------------------------------}

function  TsrYetInstalled( var IDStr    : TsrIdStr ) : boolean;
function  TsrGetPtr      (     address  : pointer ) : pointer;
function  TsrRemove                                : boolean;
function  TsrShowScreen                            : boolean;
procedure TsrInstall     (     KeyState : word;
                               CurKey   : byte;
                               Call     : TsrProcedure );
procedure TsrNewKey      (     NewStatus : word;
                               NewScan   : byte );

{-- global variables and typed constants, public ------------------------}

const TsrHercPage : integer = 0;    { Hercules page for graphic mode (0/1) }
```

In the listing, these declarations are followed by a long chain of constants. These constants represent the keyboard's scan codes, which can be used with the various control keys as hotkeys. Usually you wouldn't encounter these scan codes during Pascal programming because they only control internal communication between the keyboard and BIOS keyboard interface, and are converted by it into ASCII codes and extended keyboard codes. Within the TSR unit these codes must be accessed because a series of key combinations, which are permitted as hotkeys, aren't recognized by BIOS and, therefore, aren't converted into ASCII or extended keyboard codes. So, testing these keys through the BIOS isn't possible, and action must be taken on the hardware of the keyboard.

If you consider the various constants and compare the sequence of the codes with the position of the keys on the keyboard, you will find that the scan code simply counts the keys of the keyboard from left to right and from top to bottom. The keyboard only sends the BIOS the number of the key, which the BIOS must convert into a keyboard scan code.

```
{-- public constants ------------------------------------------------}

    {-- scan codes of various keys ----------------------------------}

const SC_ESC            = $01;     SC_Y              = $2C;
      SC_1              = $02;     SC_X              = $2D;
      SC_2              = $03;     SC_C              = $2E;
      SC_3              = $04;     SC_V              = $2F;
      SC_4              = $05;     SC_B              = $30;
      SC_5              = $06;     SC_N              = $31;
      SC_6              = $07;     SC_M              = $32;
      SC_7              = $08;     SC_COMMA          = $33;
      SC_8              = $09;     SC_PERIOD         = $34;
      SC_9              = $0A;     SC_SLASH          = $35;
      SC_0              = $0B;     SC_SHIFT_RIGHT    = $36;
      SC_UNDERSCORE     = $0C;     SC_PRINT_SCREEN   = $37;
      SC_APOSTROPHE     = $0D;     SC_ALT            = $38;
      SC_BACKSPACE      = $0E;     SC_SPACE          = $39;
      SC_TAB            = $0F;     SC_CAPS           = $3A;
      SC_Q              = $10;     SC_F1             = $3B;
      SC_W              = $11;     SC_F2             = $3C;
      SC_E              = $12;     SC_F3             = $3D;
      SC_R              = $13;     SC_F4             = $3E;
      SC_T              = $14;     SC_F5             = $3F;
      SC_Z              = $15;     SC_F6             = $40;
      SC_U              = $16;     SC_F7             = $41;
      SC_I              = $17;     SC_F8             = $42;
      SC_O              = $18;     SC_F9             = $43;
      SC_P              = $19;     SC_F10            = $44;
      SC_UE             = $1A;     SC_NUM_LOCK       = $45;
      SC_PLUS           = $1B;     SC_SCROLL_LOCK    = $46;
      SC_RETURN         = $1C;     SC_CURSOR_HOME    = $47;
      SC_CONTROL        = $1D;     SC_CURSOR_UP      = $48;
      SC_A              = $1E;     SC_CURSOR_PG_UP   = $49;
      SC_S              = $1F;     SC_NUM_MINUS      = $4A;
```

```
SC_D              = $20;    SC_CURSOR_LEFT    = $4B;
SC_F              = $21;    SC_NUM_5          = $4C;
SC_G              = $22;    SC_CURSOR_RIGHT   = $4D;
SC_H              = $23;    SC_NUM_PLUS       = $4E;
SC_J              = $24;    SC_CURSOR_END     = $4F;
SC_K              = $25;    SC_CURSOR_DOWN    = $50;
SC_L              = $26;    SC_CURSOR_PG_DOWN = $51;
SC_OE             = $27;    SC_INSERT         = $52;
SC_AE             = $28;    SC_DELETE         = $53;
SC_GREATERTHAN    = $29;    SC_SYS_REQUEST    = $54;
SC_SHIFT_LEFT     = $2A;    SC_F11            = $57;
SC_BACKSLASH      = $2B;    SC_F12            = $58;
```

In addition to the scan codes, the bit values of each control key have been captured and represented as symbolic constants. These constants were already used within TSRDEMO in the CheckKey procedure.

```
{-- bit values for the control keys -------------------------------}

const LSHIFT =     1;                           { left SHIFT key }
      RSHIFT =     2;                          { right SHIFT key }
      CTRL   =     4;                                { CTRL key }
      ALT    =     8;                                 { ALT key }
      SYSREQ = 1024;               { SYS-REQ-key ( AT keyboard only ) }
      BREAK  = 4096;                              { BREAK key }
      NUM    = 8192;                                { NUM key }
      CAPS   = 16384;                             { CAPS key }

      NOKEY  = 128;                 { control keys only, no scan code }
```

The storage and restoration of the screen context are especially important during the activation of the TSR program and the return of the interrupted program. This is demonstrated by the numerous constants, types and internal global variables that have been defined for this purpose.

```
implementation

{$L tsra}                                  { include assembler module }

{-- constants, modular internal -------------------------------------}

const MONO_ADR_REG   = $3b4;    { addresses of the various ports for }
      MONO_DATA_REG  = $3b5;    { direct access to the video card    }
      LP_RESET_LATCH = $3bb;
      LP_TRIGGER     = $3ba;
      LP_SET_LATCH   = $3b9;
      MONO_STATUS    = $3ba;
      MONO_CONTRL    = $3b8;
      VGA_GC_ADR     = $3ce;
      VGA_GC_DATA    = $3cf;
      VGA_SQ_ADR     = $3c4;
```

```
        VGA_SQ_DATA    = $3c5;
        HERC_CONF      = $3bf;

{-- Type declarations, module internal -----------------------------------}

type VioSaveBuf  = array [$0000..$3fff] of byte;     { 16K from video RAM }
     VSPtr       = ^VioSaveBuf;          { pointer to the physical video RAM }
     Video_Cards = ( MDA, CGA, HERC, EGA, VGA, UNKNOWN );
     PSP         = record                                    { forms the PSP }
                     dummy  : array [0..$2b] of byte;{insignificant fields }
                     EnvSeg : word;    { segment address of the environment }
                   end;
     PSPPTR      = ^PSP;                                    { pointer to PSP }
     HiLo        = record     { division of a word into high and low byte }
                     LoByte,
                     HiByte : byte;
                   end;


{-- global variables, modular internal -----------------------------------}

var {------- variables for storing and restoring the screen content -------}

     Video_Card : Video_Cards;                        { the current video card }
     VideoMode,                           { number of the original video mode }
     ScrLines,                     { number of display lines (<>0 : EGA, VGA) }
     VideoPage  : byte;                  { number of original display page }
     InGraphc   : boolean;                       { is a graphic mode active? }
     CurStartEnd,                 { start and end line of the blinking cursor }
     CurPos     : word;                           { position of the cursor }
     PalRegs    : array [1..17] of byte;           { VGA palette register }
     DACRegs    : array [1..768] of byte;        { VGA DAC color register }
     SaveBuf    : VioSaveBuf;                  { buffer for storing video RAM }
     VioPtr     : VSPtr;                            { pointer to video RAM }

     {----------------------- Variables for the DOS context change --------}

     TsrStackSeg,                         { stack segment of this program }
     TsrStackOFs,                         { stack pointer of this program }
     TsrDTAOfs,                     { address of the DTA of this program }
     TsrDTASeg,
     TsrPSP,                       { PSP segment address of the active program }
     OldTsrPSP  : word;    { segment address of an already installed copy }
     TsrProc    : TsrProcedure;     { TSR procedure from the main program }

{-- Declaration of external routines from the assembler module ------------}

procedure key_mask                              ; external;
procedure scan_code                             ; external;
procedure TsrAInit( KeyState : word;
                    CurKey   : byte )           ; external;
function  TsrRestoreVec                  : boolean; external;
```

A series of procedures and functions are involved in the storage and restoration of the screen contexts. They originate in the two procedures SaveVideoContext and RestoreVideoContext, which are immediately called before the activation (SaveVideoContext) and after the termination of the TSR program (RestoreVideoContext). This ensures that the screen is returned to its original form when the interrupted program resumes execution.

The GetVideoData procedure determines what type of video card is installed, and whether it is in text or graphic mode. The video card type is stored by GetVioMode in the global variable Video_Card, which is of type Video_Cards. It is a counter variable which includes MDA, Hercules, CGA, EGA and VGA video cards. The information about the current video mode is stored in the global variable InGraphc, which is of type boolean. TRUE indicates that the card found is in graphic mode.

The path through which GetVideoData gets this information is very involved, and contains many tests which are tailored to each video card.

First, all general information accessible to every program through BIOS video interrupt $10 is collected. This information comprises the number of the current video mode, the number of the current screen page, the current cursor position and the format of the cursor. The information is stored in the global variables VideoMode, VideoPage, CurStartEnd and CurPos.

The first test concentrates on checking for a VGA card. VGA cards enhance video interrupt $10 by including some functions that are only available during the installation of such a card. One of these functions is function $1A, sub-function $00. If after its call, the function number, previously passed in the AH register, is now in the AL register, it can be assumed that a VGA card is installed. This isn't the only use of this function; it also returns a code in the BL register, which provides information about the active video card. This could be another video card, because an additional video card other than a VGA card may be installed in the system.

GetVideoData uses the returned information as an index to an array named VGAVioTab, in which the video card codes are stored.

If the AL register doesn't contain the value $1A after calling function $1A, there is no VGA BIOS or VGA card installed. The search for the installed video card continues with the call of a BIOS function, found only in EGA and VGA cards. Since TSR has already determined that a VGA card isn't available, a positive response in this test indicates that the computer has an EGA card.

The task of function $12, sub-function $10 in this connection is insignificant. This function is only important when the value $10 remains in the BL register following the

411

function call. If this is true, the function call failed, which indicates that there is no EGA BIOS or EGA card.

If the first two tests confirm that an EGA or VGA card is installed, we can gather still more information about these video cards. First there is the number of the screen lines. EGA cards can produce 43 lines in text mode and VGA cards produce 50 lines. This information is obtained from a memory location in the variable area of the BIOS, which immediately follows at the end of the interrupt vector table and begins at segment address $40.

Whether the installed card is in graphic mode can be determined from the number of the current video mode, which was revealed at the beginning of the procedure by a call of BIOS function $0F. A value greater than seven corresponds to one of the graphic modes supported only by the EGA and VGA cards. If such a mode is active, the InGraphc variable is set to TRUE and the VioPtr pointer receives the address A000:0000. This is the base address of the bit planes, which contain pixel information for the extended graphic modes. The VioPtr pointer is very important for storage and later restoration because it points to the beginning of the video RAM in memory.

If the video mode value is less than seven, the InGraphc variable is loaded with the value FALSE, which indicates that the video card is in the text mode. That is not always true, because code numbers 4, 5 and 6 may also instruct EGA and VGA cards to emulate the CGA graphic modes. However, these modes can be handled as text modes by screen memory. So, it is proper, from a programming viewpoint to set the InGraphc variable to FALSE. With code numbers less than seven, video RAM is in the video mode and always at segment address B800:0000. This address is then loaded into the VioPtr variable.

The only remaining candidates are the MDA, CGA and Hercules cards. It's easy to differentiate between the two monochrome cards and the CGA card by testing a memory location in the BIOS variable area, which is used by ROM BIOS to store the base address of the video controller. You should know that the various video cards are controlled through programmable video controllers, which have various registers and can be accessed through two ports. The first port is the address port. The number of the addressed register is sent to this port. Over the second (data) port you can read the registers with a read access, or write a new value to the registers.

Read access to all registers is only possible on a VGA card, while the other cards permit the reading of only a few specific registers.

Since MDA, CGA and Hercules cards have identical video controllers, the BIOS can program them with identical routines. A difference may occur only through the port number of the data and address register, which in monochrome cards can be reached through port $3B4 and in CGA cards through port $3D4. If the memory location named above in the BIOS variable area contains the value $3B4 (here represented by the constant MONO_ADR_REG), you can be sure that either an MDA or a Hercules card is installed.

412

In this case, you must then differentiate between the two cards. This isn't easy, because the information isn't stored by the BIOS. The two cards differ internally in a few small respects, and one of these respects must be used to differentiate between them.

Within the status register of both cards, there is one bit that only changes its content during the creation of the display by the Hercules card. This happens because it reproduces the color of the point which the electronic beam touches during the drawing of the screen. If this point is on, the bit (bit 7) contains the value 1. If this point is off, bit 7 contains the value 0.

To have a comparative value, the content of this bit is determined and then a loop is executed. This loop executes a maximum of 32,768 times, tests the current content of this bit and compares the contents with the previously determined value. If the content of this bit remains unchanged after 32,768 executions, this indicates the presence of an MDA card. In this case, the InGraphc variable should remain unset because MDA cards cannot display graphics.

If the test indicates that the video card installed is a Hercules card, it must then be determined which mode is enabled (text or graphics). This must be done because, in addition to an 80x25 text mode, the Hercules cards can also produce a 720x348 high-resolution graphic mode. The IsHercInGraph function determines the current graphic mode, passing the result to the InGraphc variable.

The video RAM for both cards in text mode appears at address B000:0000. Hercules graphic mode in page 0 starts at this same address (B000:0000). Hercules graphic mode in page 1 begins at address B800:0000.

During the description of TSRDEMO it was mentioned that a program cannot read the current graphic page of the Hercules card. So, the procedure must rely on the TsrHercPage variable.

If it is determined during the test of the video controller's port address that a CGA card is installed, VioPtr is loaded with the address B800:0000 (the base address of the video RAM for CGA cards). If the card is in graphic mode, this is determined by the code number of the current video mode. The codes 4, 5 and 6 represent one of the three graphic modes of this card.

```
{*********************************************************************
*  GetVideoData : determines the characteristic data for the current   *
*                 video card and for the current video mode.           *
**-----------------------------------------------------------------**
*  Input : none                                                        *
*  Global : Video_Card/W, VideoMode/W, VideoPage/W, ScrLines/W, VioPtr/W *
*           InGraphc/W,                                                 *
*********************************************************************}
```

```
procedure GetVideoData;

const VGAVioTab : array [0..12] of Video_Cards =
                 ( UNKNOWN, MDA     , CGA     , UNKNOWN, EGA     ,
                   EGA,     UNKNOWN, VGA     , VGA     , UNKNOWN,
                   CGA,     CGA,     CGA                        );

var Regs    : Registers;              { processor registers for interrupt call }
    i       : integer;                              { loop counter }
    Status  : byte;                             { MDA-/Hercules status port }

begin
  Video_Card := UNKNOWN;                             { card still unknown }

  Regs.AH := $0f;              { function number for "video mode determined" }
  Intr( $10, Regs );                              { BIOS video interrupt }
  VideoMode := Regs.AL and $7f;            { store mode, turn off bit 7 }
  VideoPage := Regs.BH;                            { store screen page }

  Regs.AH := $03;              { function number for "load cursor position" }
  Intr( $10, Regs );              { get information on current screen page }
  CurStartEnd := Regs.CX;         { store start and end line of cursor }
  CurPos      := Regs.DX;                  { store cursor position }

  Regs.AX := $1a00;                         { function 1Ah ( VGA only ) }
  Intr( $10, Regs );
  if ( Regs.AL = $1a ) then                  { is this function available? }
    begin                         { yes, VGA, code of current card in BL }
      if ( Regs.BL <> $ff ) then                  { video card known? }
        Video_Card := VGAVioTab[ Regs.BL ]     { yes, get code from table }
    end
  else                                      { not VGA, is it an EGA? }
    begin
      Regs.ah := $12;                              { call function $12, }
      Regs.bl := $10;                              { sub-function $10  }
      intr($10, Regs);                             { call video BIOS }
      if Regs.bl <> $10 then                       { EGA installed? }
        Video_Card := EGA;                                  { yes }
    end;

  {-- determine if the EGA or VGA card is in graphic mode ----------------}
  if ( Video_Card = EGA ) or ( Video_Card = VGA ) then
    begin
      ScrLines := Mem[ $40 : $84 ];         { get number of screen lines }
      if ( VideoMode > 7 ) then                        { in graphic mode? }
        begin                                                  { yes }
          InGraphc := TRUE;
          VioPtr   := Ptr( $a000, $0000 );
        end
      else                                        { no, in text mode }
        begin
          InGraphc := FALSE;
```

414

```
              VioPtr    := Ptr( $b800, $0000 );
          end;
      end;

  if ( Video_Card = UNKNOWN ) then               { video card still unknown? }
    if ( MemW[ $0040:$0063 ] = MONO_ADR_REG ) then      { monochrome card? }
      begin                                   { yes, must be MDA or Hercules }
        VioPtr := Ptr( $b000, $0000 );

        {-- The program distinguishes between an MDA and a Hercules card   -}
        {-- through bit 7 in the CRT status register, because this bit     -}
        {-- changes its content continuously only with Hercules-cards      -}

        Status := port [ MONO_STATUS ] and $80;       { read CRT status port }
        i := 0;
        while ( port[ MONO_STATUS ] and $80 = Status ) and ( i < 32767 )
          do inc( i );

        if ( i = 32767 ) then                          { did the bit change? }
          Video_Card := MDA                                       { no, MDA }
        else                                    { yes, must be Hercules card }
          begin
            Video_Card := HERC;
            InGraphc := IsHercInGraph;               { test for graphic mode }
            if InGraphc then              { Hercules card in graphic mode? }
              VioPtr := Ptr( $b000 + $800 * TsrHercPage, 0 ); {yes,pg. addr.}
          end;
      end
    else                                                     { must be CGA }
      begin
        Video_Card := CGA;
        InGraphc   := ( VideoMode >= 1 ) and ( VideoMode <= 6 );
        VioPtr     := Ptr( $b800, $0000 );
      end
  end;
```

After finding a Hercules card, the auxiliary procedure GetVideoData uses the function IsHercInGraph to determine whether this card is in text mode or graphic mode. However, the registers of the card can't be read, which would reveal the current mode. So, we must use some more complex methods to obtain the desired information.

The algorithm used within IsHercInGraph is based on a simple feature of the Hercules card. The *light pen* support offered by the Hercules card has been used less frequently over the years. The Hercules card has three special light pen registers which are supported by two registers in the video controller. When the user presses the light pen button, these registers store the offset position of the electron beam in the video RAM, signalling the current position of the light pen on the screen.

The trick is to simulate the pressing of this button at the end of the screen construction, and then read the stored offset position from the two video controller registers. This offset will

415

be much greater in graphic mode than in text mode, because graphic mode needs more bytes than text mode.

This process is rather complicated, but it works.

```
{****************************************************************************
 *   IsHercInGraph : tells the caller if the Hercules graphic card is in    *
 *                   graphic or text mode                                   *
 **------------------------------------------------------------------------**
 *   Input  : none                                                          *
 *   Output : TRUE = graphic mode active, FALSE = text-mode                 *
 *   Info   : The number of the active screen page                         *
 *            cannot be determined !                                        *
 ****************************************************************************}

function IsHercInGraph : boolean;

var LpPos : record                  { offset position of the light pen in video RAM }
              case boolean of
                TRUE  : ( LoB, HiB : byte );            { position as 2 bytes }
                FALSE : ( LpWord : integer );           { position as 1 word }
              end;

begin
  port[ LP_RESET_LATCH ] := 0;          { reset the light pen latch register }

  {-- wait first for the start, then the end of the vertical return -------}
  {-- of the electron beam                                          -------}

  while ( port[ LP_TRIGGER ] and $80 <> 0 ) do ;            { start }
  while ( port[ LP_TRIGGER ] and $80 = 0 ) do ;            { end }

  {-- wait for next start of the vertical return and then simulate the ----}
  {-- activation of the light pen to determine its position, which    ----}
  {-- indicates the size of the video RAM and therefore the video mode ----}

  inline ($fa);                                 { cli, suppress interrupts }

  while ( port[ LP_TRIGGER ] and $80 <> 0 ) do ;        { wait for start }
  port[ LP_SET_LATCH ]:=0;                       { store light pen position }

  inline ($fb);                                 { sti, re-enable interrupts }

  {-- read light pen position from video controller registers $10 and $11 -}

  port[ MONO_ADR_REG ] := $10;         { read high byte light pen position }
  LpPos.HiB := port[ MONO_DATA_REG ];
  port[ MONO_ADR_REG ]:=$11;           { read low byte light pen position }
  LpPos.LoB := port[ MONO_DATA_REG ];

  IsHercInGraph := ( LpPos.LpWord ) > ( 45 * 87 );
end;
```

416

We now come to the SaveVideoContext procedure, which controls the saving of the screen context. It first calls the GetVideoMode procedure. After its execution, it can determine the type of active video card through the global variable named Video_Card, and adjust its activities accordingly.

When a VGA card is active, SaveVideo Context saves the 16 palette registers and the 256 DAC color registers, which are very important in creating the color signals. The attribute byte, which follows every character in video RAM in text mode, does not include an absolute color code for VGA cards. Instead, this byte represents an index to one of 16 8-bit *palette registers*. The color code still isn't found in these registers because their content is interpreted by the video controller of the VGA card as an index to one of the entries in a color table, which has 256 entries. The individual entries, which are viewed as a DAC color register, each contain a color code in the form of a 24-bit value. This code is composed of three 8-bit portions specifying the red, green and blue segments of the color.

Since the TSR program and the VGA BIOS can change the contents of these registers during execution, SaveVideoContext saves this information before the TSR program can execute. It can use the sub-functions $09 and $17 of video function $10, which the VGA BIOS provides for this purpose. The contents of the various registers are loaded into the global variables PallRegs and DACRegs, which act as buffers for this task.

The EGA card also uses palette registers, which indicate the color value instead of containing an index to the DAC color table (EGA cards do not use DAC registers). Unfortunately, these registers cannot be saved within SaveVideoContext—they can only be written, not read. Do not allow your TSR program to manipulate these registers while an EGA card is being used.

The storage of the palette and DAC color registers are followed in SaveVideoContext by the storage of the screen context. EGA and VGA cards in graphic mode require special treatment because the structure of video RAM in high-resolution graphic mode differs from any other video cards. This isn't surprising since these cards require up to 256K of video RAM. However, this cannot be stored in the 64K normally reserved for video RAM, which starts at segment address $B000.

EGA and VGA cards are subdivided by video RAM into four bit planes, which all start at segment address $A000. Depending on the availability of RAM on the card, each bit plane can include up to 64K. The two cards for this memory area in text mode and in the CGA compatible graphic modes are in the memory segment starting at segment address $B800, even though the video RAM is always physically at segment address $A000.

Since there are four areas of memory which must be addressed through the same segment address, access to individual bit planes is very complicated and always involves programming various video controllers and video registers. An entire book could easily be devoted to this subject, but space and time prohibit more details in this book. Therefore, instead of discussing the details of this programming, we will present an outline of the execution.

The entire video RAM cannot be stored because up to 256K would be required, and this much memory probably wouldn't be available while an application is executing in the foreground. However, we don't have to worry about this because only the part of the video RAM that is overwritten in the text mode must be stored. This is a total of 16K; each of the four possible 2000 character screen pages only requires 8K. The remaining 8K are overwritten because the pixel patterns of each character in text mode are loaded into video RAM so that the EGA and VGA cards can claim 8K there.

Since these 16K are distributed to three different bit planes, they must be individually addressed and part of their contents saved in the SaveBuf buffer provided for this purpose.

The ASCII codes of the characters, which are written in the video RAM starting at segment address $B800 in text mode, are stored on the first bit plane (bit plane number 0). The ASCII codes are stored sequentially in this bit plane, separate from attribute bytes. These are stored in the second bit plane (bit plane number 1). The video RAM is divided into ASCII codes and attribute bytes, with both at the beginning of their bit planes. Then the four screen pages follow at 1K intervals.

Therefore, the first 4K from bit plane number 0 are copied to the beginning of the buffer SaveBuf. This buffer stores all bytes which could be overwritten, during the manipulation of the video RAM in text mode, with ASCII codes. The second 4K in SaveBuf are occupied by the 4,000 attribute codes from bit plane number 1. The remaining 8K are loaded with the first 8K from bit plane number 2. This happens because in this bit plane, BIOS stores the bit patterns of the characters during the switch to text mode.

After storing the bit planes, the SetVioMode procedure makes the switch to text mode, which then uses the function $00 of the video BIOS. As code number of the video mode, the value $83 is passed for EGA and VGA cards as the video mode code number. This value corresponds to CGA video mode 3 (80x25 character text). By setting bit 7 in this code, the EGA and VGA BIOS is instructed not to delete the contents of video RAM during the switch to text mode. If you didn't send this instruction, the entire 256K would be deleted in one stroke.

Since the bit patterns from the graphic mode form a very jumbled image in text mode, the ClrScr procedure clears the text screen immediately after the switch.

Storing the screen context in EGA/VGA text mode and CGA/Hercules graphic modes is much easier to implement than EGA/VGA graphic mode. The video RAMs in these modes contain continuous groups of bytes. Depending on the video card, these groups can start at segment address $B000 or $B800.

It's also easier to copy the first 16K from these memory areas to the SaveBuf buffer because the VioPtr pointer represents a pointer of the type VioSaveBuf. This describes a 16K buffer and is also represented by the SaveBuf variable. The statement:

```
VioSaveBuf := VioPtr^
```

copies 16K from the video RAM into the SaveBuf buffer.

The switch to text mode, which in these cards also involves the deletion of the various screen pages, also occurs when calling the SetVioMode procedure. You must differentiate between the monochrome and the color cards because both use a different code number for the 80x25 character text mode.

At the end of SaveVideoContext, screen page 0 is enabled to ensure that no other video page is displayed on the screen.

```
{*************************************************************************
 *  SaveVideoContext : stores the current video context and switches the   *
 *                     video card into the 80*25-character text mode.      *
 **---------------------------------------------------------------------**
 *                                                                        *
 *  Input : none                                                          *
 *  Info  : The video context can be restored with ResetVideoContext.     *
 *  Global : PalRegs/W, DACRegs/W                                         *
 *************************************************************************}

procedure SaveVideoContext;

var Regs : Registers;              { processor registers for interrupt call }

begin
  GetVideoData;        { determine type of video card and other information }
  if ( Video_Card = VGA ) then                        { is a VGA installed? }
    begin               { yes, store color palette and DAC color register }
      Regs.AX := $1009;             { store 16 palette and overscan registers }
      Regs.DX := Ofs( PalRegs );             { addresses of buffers to ES:DX }
      Regs.ES := Seg( PalRegs );
      intr( $10, Regs );

      Regs.AX := $1017;                  { store DAC register from buffer }
      Regs.BX := 0;                  { start with the first palette register }
      Regs.CX := 256;                        { load all 256 registers }
      Regs.DX := Ofs( DACRegs );        { address of the buffer to ES:DX }
      Regs.ES := Seg( DACRegs );
      intr( $10, Regs );
    end;

  if (( Video_Card = EGA ) or ( Video_Card = VGA )) and InGraphc then
    begin                              { store parts of the 4 bit planes }

      {-- In text mode the character codes from the video RAM starting at -}
```

```
{-- segment address $B800 are stored in the first bit plane. For     -}
{-- this reason, the first 4K of this bit plane are stored.          -}

    portw[ VGA_GC_ADR  ] := $0005;                    { set read mode 0 }
    portw[ VGA_GC_ADR  ] := $0004;              { activate bit plane #0 }
    move( VioPtr^, SaveBuf[0], $1000 );

    {-- The attribute codes of the character in text mode are stored in -}
    {-- bit plane #1. Therefore, store the first 4K from this bit plane -}
    {-- in the SaveBuf buffer.                                          -}

    portw[ VGA_GC_ADR  ] := $0104;              { activate bit plane #1 }
    move( VioPtr^, SaveBuf[$1000], $1000 );

    {-- The patterns of self-defined characters are stored in bit plane -}
    {-- #2 and since this bit pattern occupies up to 8K, the first 8K   -}
    {-- from bit plane #2 are stored.                                   -}

    portw[ VGA_GC_ADR  ] := $0204;              { activate bit plane #2 }
    move( VioPtr^, SaveBuf[$2000], $2000 );

    SetVioMode( $83 );         { activate 80*25-character text screen, but }
                               { do not erase video RAM ( the bit planes ) }
      ClrScr;                                              { clear screen }
    end
  else                                         { text screen must be saved }
    begin
      SaveBuf := VioPtr^;                 { copy 16K from video RAM in buffer }
      if ( Video_Card = MDA ) or ( Video_Card = HERC ) then
        SetVioMode( 7 )                          { activate monochrome mode }
      else
        SetVioMode( 3 );
    end;

  Regs.AX := $0500;                          { move screen page 0 to the screen }
  Intr( $10, Regs );
end;
```

Besides the GetVideoData procedure in SaveVideoContext, the SetVioMode procedure is also called to activate a new video mode. Since it only makes a call to function $00 of the video BIOS, this procedure is rather short. It's helpful to delegate this task to one of your own procedures, because it's needed for saving the video context <u>and</u> restoring the video context with RestoreVideoContext.

```
{********************************************************************************
 *  SetVioMode : sets a new video mode                                        *
 **----------------------------------------------------------------------------**
 *  Input : MODENR = number of the video mode                                 *
 ********************************************************************************}

procedure SetVioMode( ModeNr : byte );
```

```
  var Regs : Registers;                { processor registers for interrupt call }

begin
  Regs.AX := ModeNr;                      { AH = 0, AL = mode number }
  Intr( $10, Regs );
end;
```

The opposite of the SaveVideoContext procedure is the RestoreVideoContext procedure. This procedure copies the screen context into video RAM, enables the original video mode and returns all the other parameters, which are part of the video context, to their original status.

For example, for EGA and VGA graphic modes, this means that the contents of the SaveBuf buffer are again copied into the various bit planes, where the original video mode must be restored with a call of SetVioMode.

Copying the stored screen context in text mode and CGA/Hercules graphic modes are just as easy as saving the data with SaveVideoContext.

In this case, however, the call becomes:

```
  SaveBuf := VioPtr^;
```

For VGA cards, it's necessary to re-load the palette and DAC color registers with their original values. Function $10 once again provides a routine. Sub-functions $02 and $12 bring the contents of these registers from the PalRegs and DACRegs buffers to their original locations.

RestoreVideoContext handles both EGA and VGA cards which were displaying more than 25 lines in text mode when the user started the TSR program. A call of sub-function $12 of video BIOS function $11 restores the EGA card to 43 line mode and the VGA card to 50 line mode.

The procedure ends with the call of several standard video BIOS functions, which restore the cursor to its original place and format. In addition, the screen page which was encountered during the call of SaveVideoContext is re-activated.

```
{********************************************************************
 *  RestoreVideoContext : restores original video mode and all parameters  *
 *                        stored during the call of SaveVideoContext.       *
 **----------------------------------------------------------------**
 *                                                                  *
 *  Input  : none                                                   *
 *  Global : Video_Card/R, VideoPage/R, CurStartEnd/R, CurPos/R,    *
 *           VioPtr/R, SaveBuf/R, PalRegs/R, DACRegs/R              *
 ********************************************************************}
```

```
procedure RestoreVideoContext;

var Regs : Registers;                    { processor registers for interrupt call }
begin
  if (( Video_Card = EGA ) or ( Video_Card = VGA )) and InGraphc then
    begin                                    { EGA and VGA in graphic modes }
      SetVioMode( $80 or VideoMode );             { activate old video mode }

      portw[ VGA_GC_ADR  ] := $0005;                      { set write mode 0 }
      portw[ VGA_GC_ADR  ] := $ff08;     { load bit mask register with $ff }

      {-- copy the first 4K from the buffer SaveBuf to bit plane #0 -------}

      port[ VGA_SQ_ADR  ] := $02;         { erase bit planes #1-#3 through }
      port[ VGA_SQ_DATA ] := $01;         { the map mask register          }
      move( SaveBuf[0], VioPtr^, $1000);

      {-- copy the second 4K from the buffer SaveBuf to bit plane #1 ------}

      port[ VGA_SQ_ADR  ] := $02;         { erase bit planes #0, #2 and #3 }
      port[ VGA_SQ_DATA ] := $02;         { through the map mask register  }
      move( SaveBuf[$1000], VioPtr^, $1000 );

      {-- copy the stored 8K from bit plane #2 to their original places----}

      port[ VGA_SQ_ADR  ] := $02;      { erase the bit planes #0, #1 and #3 }
      port[ VGA_SQ_DATA ] := $04;      { through the map mask register      }
      move( SaveBuf[$2000], VioPtr^, $2000 );

      port[ VGA_SQ_ADR  ] := $02;               { re-activate all bit planes }
      port[ VGA_SQ_DATA ] := $0f;               { and set default values     }
    end
  else                                    { other cards or VGA/EGA text mode }
    begin
      if ( Video_Card = HERC ) and InGraphc then      { Hercules graphic? }
        PutHerc2Graph                    { yes, set card to graphic mode again }
      else                      { all other video cards in text or graphic mode }
        SetVioMode( VideoMode );                     { restore old video mode }
      VioPtr^ := SaveBuf;               { copy 16K from buffer in video RAM }
    end;

{-- restore palette and DAC color register of the VGA card -------------}

if ( Video_Card = VGA ) then                          { VGA card installed? }
  begin                         { yes, reload palette and DAC color register }
    Regs.AX := $1002;                     { load 16 palette and overscan reg. }
    Regs.DX := Ofs( PalRegs );             { address of the buffers to ES:DX }
    Regs.ES := Seg( PalRegs );
    intr( $10, Regs );

    Regs.AX := $1012;                       { load DAC register from buffer }
    Regs.BX := 0;                      { begin with the first palette register }
```

```
        Regs.CX := 256;                              { all 256 registers loaded }
        Regs.DX := Ofs( DACRegs );            { address of the buffers to ES:DX }
        Regs.ES := Seg( DACRegs );
        intr( $10, Regs );
      end;


  {-- activate original screen page, position cursor and restore screen ---}

  if ( ( Video_Card = EGA ) or ( Video_Card = VGA ) ) and
       ( ScrLines > 25 ) and ( InGraphc = FALSE ) then
    begin                                      { switch to the 43/50-line mode }
      Regs.AX := $1112; { function number for "activate 8*8 character set" }
      Regs.BL := 0;                             { load first character table }
      intr( $10, Regs );
    end;

  Regs.AH := 5;                           { function number for "set screen page" }
  Regs.AL := VideoPage;
  Intr( $10, Regs );

  Regs.AH := 1;                             { function number for "define cursor" }
  Regs.CX := CurStartEnd;                          { load start and end line }
  Intr( $10, Regs );

  Regs.AH := 2;                               { function number for "set cursor" }
  Regs.BH := VideoPage;                                    { page addressed }
  Regs.DX := CurPos;                                      { cursor position }
  Intr( $10, Regs );
end;
```

Regardless of the video card and the active video mode when SaveVideoContext is called, RestoreVideoContext sets all video cards to their original operating modes by calling the SetVioMode procedure. Only the Hercules card cannot be reset to graphic mode in this manner. The video BIOS doesn't recognize this mode. Unlike the EGA and VGA cards, the Hercules card doesn't have its own video BIOS.

This mode must be reset through direct programming of the registers. This task is performed for RestoreVideoContext by the PutHerc2Graph procedure.

```
{*******************************************************************************
*  PutHerc2Graph : returns the Hercules graphic card to graphic mode         *
**-------------------------------------------------------------------------**
*                                                                           *
*  Input : none                                                             *
*  Info  : - The Hercules card can be set into text mode using video        *
*             BIOS function $00.                                            *
*          - Of the two graphic pages the Hercules card is re-activated     *
*             by the page whose number is in the TsrHercPage variable.      *
*******************************************************************************}

procedure PutHerc2Graph;
```

```
   const CrtRegs : array[0..11] of byte =              { values for CRT register }
             ( 53,  45,  46,   7,  91,   2,  87,  87,   2,   3,   0,   0 );

   var i : integer;                                            { loop counter }

   begin
     port[ HERC_CONF ] := 1 + ( TsrHercPage * 2 );              { switch pages on }

     port[ MONO_CONTRL ] := $02;                   { switch display construction off }

     for i:= 0 to 11 do                            { process the CRT registers }
       begin
         port[ MONO_ADR_REG ]  := i;               { display the register number }
         port[ MONO_DATA_REG ] := CrtRegs[ i ];    { send value to data port }
       end;

     port[ MONO_CONTRL ] := $0A + (TsrHercPage * $80);  { screen structure on }
   end;
```

In addition to routines needed for the storage and restoration of the screen context, the TSR unit includes an entire series of routines for installing, activating and deactivating TSR programs.

First we will encounter two functions which may appear familiar to you from the CLOCK program, TsrGetPTr and TsrYetInstalled.

```
{*****************************************************************************
 *   TsrGetPtr : returns a pointer to a variable in the already installed    *
 *               TSR program in memory.                                      *
 **------------------------------------------------------------------------**
 *   Input : ADDRESS = address of the variable addressed in the              *
 *                     currently executing version of the program           *
 *   Output : pointer to this variable in the installed program             *
 *   Info   : Before the first call of this function it must be determined   *
 *            whether a copy of the TSR is already resident in memory, using *
 *            the TsrYetInstalled function.                                  *
 *   Global : OldTsrPSP/R                                                     *
 *****************************************************************************}

function TsrGetPtr( address : pointer ) : pointer;

begin
   TsrGetPtr := ptr(OldTsrPSP + ( Seg(address^)-PrefixSeg ), Ofs(address^));
end;

{*****************************************************************************
 *   TsrYetInstalled : determines if a copy of the program is already        *
 *                     installed as TSR program.                             *
 **------------------------------------------------------------------------**
 *   Input : IDStr = Identification string                                   *
 *   Output : TRUE if the program is already in memory, otherwise FALSE      *
```

```
*  Global : OldTsrPSP/W                                                      *
*************************************************************************}

function TsrYetInstalled( var IDStr : TsrIdStr ) : boolean;

type MCB       = record                                      { creates an MCB }
                   IdCode : char;    { "M" = another MCB follows, "Z" = end }
                   PSP : word;                        { segment address of the PSP }
                   Paras : word; { number of paragraphs in controlled area }
                 end;
     MCBPTR    = ^MCB;                                    { pointer to an MCB }
     MCBPTRPTR = ^MCBPTR;                      { pointer to a pointer to an MCB }
     STRPTR    = ^TsrIdStr;                        { pointer to an ID string }

var Regs     : Registers;              { processor registers for interrupt call }
    CurMCB   : MCBPTR;                           { pointer to current MCB }
    PSPFound : word;          { segment address of PSP of the program found }
    EndIt    : boolean;                            { last MCB reached }

begin
  {-- determine pointer to first MCB in memory ---------------------------}

  Regs.AH := $52;                        { function $52 returns address of the DIB }
  MsDos( Regs );
  CurMCB := MCBPTRPTR( ptr( Regs.ES, Regs.BX-4 ) )^;

  {-- process individual MCBs in memory ----------------------------------}

  EndIt    := FALSE;
  PSPFound := 0;                                  { the program was not yet found  }

  repeat
    {-- Determine if memory controlled by MCB has the ID string at the  ---}
    {-- same location as this program and it is not the current program.---}

    if (STRPTR( Ptr(Seg(IDStr)-PrefixSeg+CurMCB^.PSP, Ofs(IDstr)))^ = IDStr)
       and ( CurMCB^.PSP <> PRefixSeg ) then
      PSPFound := CurMCB^.PSP;                           { found a copy in memory }

    if ( CurMCB^.IDCode = 'Z' ) then           { is the current MCB the last? }
      EndIt := TRUE                                   { yes, end search }
    else                        { no, set pointer CurMCB to next MCB in storage }
      CurMCB := ptr( Seg(CurMCB^) + CurMCB^.Paras + 1, 0 );
  until ( PSPFound <> 0 ) or EndIt;

  OldTsrPSP := PSPFound;                   { store segment address of the program }
  TsrYetInstalled := ( PSPFound <> 0 );  { PSPFound <> 0 --> found program }
end;
```

The TSR program is installed by calling the TsrInstall procedure. This procedure is responsible for storing the address of the TSR procedure, to be called, into the global

variable TsrProc, calling the procedure TsrAInit from the assembler module and ending the
program through the Keep procedure.

```
{**************************************************************************
*  TsrInstall : Installs the TSR and makes it resident in memory.        *
**----------------------------------------------------------------------**
*  Input : KEYSTATE = Control key status which invokes the TSR program   *
*          CURKEY   = Scan code of the key which is used with the        *
*                     control keys for activation of the TSR             *
*          CALL     = TSR procedure to be called                         *
*  Info  : - The procedure does not return to the caller, but            *
*            terminates the program execution.                           *
*          - The NOKEY constant can be used instead of CURKEY, which     *
*            allows program activation by pressing correct control keys. *
*  Global : TsrProc/W                                                    *
***************************************************************************}

procedure TsrInstall( KeyState : word; CurKey : byte; Call : TsrProcedure );

begin
  TsrProc := Call;                            { store procedure to be called }
  TsrAInit( KeyState, CurKey );                { initialize assembler module }
  Keep(0);                                        { make program resident }
end;
```

The TsrRemove function deactivates an already installed TSR program. It is more complex
than TsrInstall and uses an assembler routine to reset the various interrupt vectors to the
original interrupt handler, if subsequent TSRs and interrupt handlers could not perform this
task. If the old handler could be reactivated, the assembler routine returns the value TRUE
to TsrRestoreVec, and TsrRemove releases the memory which DOS had allocated as the
program was loading.

TsrRemove can only be called if a previous call to TsrYetInstalled has shown that the TSR
program is already installed in memory. Otherwise TsrRemove will not find the segment
address of the old program's PSP in the global variable OldTsrPSP. TsrRemove needs this
information before it can release the memory.

```
{**************************************************************************
*  TsrRemove : removes previously installed copy of the TSR from memory  *
**----------------------------------------------------------------------**
*  Input : none                                                          *
*  Output : TRUE if the TSR program could be removed and FALSE if it could *
*           not be removed because of another TSR overlaid in memory.    *
*  Info   : TsrRemove may only be called after calling TsrYetInstall,    *
*              indicating whether a copy of this program is already installed*
*  Global : OldTsrPSP/R                                                   *
***************************************************************************}

function TsrRemove : boolean;
```

```
  var Regs : Registers;                { processor registers for interrupt call }

begin
  if TsrRestoreVec then               { reinstall the old interrupt handler }
    begin                                        { everything OK }
      {-- release environment block of the program to be deactivated ------}
      {-- through DOS function $49                                  ------}

      Regs.AH := $49;                                  { DOS function number }
      Regs.ES := PSPPTR(ptr(OldTsrPSP, 0))^.EnvSeg;
                                        { load segment address from PSP }
      MsDos( Regs );

      {-- release memory of the old program ----------------------------}

      Regs.AH := $49;                                  { DOS function number }
      Regs.ES := OldTsrPSP;          { segment address of allocated memory }
      MsDos( Regs );
      TsrRemove := TRUE;                         { program could be removed }
    end
  else                          { program was overlaid by another TSR program }
    TsrRemove := FALSE;
end;
```

The TsrInit procedure is automatically called before the program starts. TsrInit supplies context information, which is needed when the user invokes the TSR program. This information includes the address of the Turbo stack, the segment address of the PSP and the address of a data area named DTA. The abbreviation DTA stands for Disk Transfer Area, which is a buffer used by DOS in the directory search. This search provides data about each file.

When the user activates the TSR program, the DTA must also be redirected from the interrupted program to the TSR program to prevent DOS from writing its information into the DTA of the interrupted program. If this redirection does not take place, information may be overwritten or destroyed.

All the information found by TsrInit is stored in global variables for later recall during the context change to the TSR program. The address of the Turbo stack is written into the TsrStackSeg and TsrStackOfs variables. The segment address of the PSP is in the TsrPSP variable, and the address of the DTA is passed to the TsrDTASeg and TsrDTAOfs variables.

```
{**********************************************************************
 *  TsrInit : Called automatically before the start of the program. TsrInit *
 *            stores information needed for activation of the TSR program.  *
 **------------------------------------------------------------------------**
 *  Input : none                                                          *
 *  Global : TsrPSP/W, TsrDTAOfs/W, TsrDTASeg/W, TsrStackSeg/W,           *
 *            TsrStackOfs/W                                               *
 **********************************************************************}
```

```
    procedure TsrInit;

    var Regs : Registers;               { processor registers for interrupt call }

    begin
      TsrStackSeg := SSeg;                             { store Turbo stack }
      TsrStackOfs := SPtr;

      TsrPSP := PrefixSeg;                   { store segment address of the PSP }

      {-- get address of the DTA and store -----------------------------------}
      Regs.AH := $2f;                     { function number for "get DTA address" }
      MsDos( Regs );
      TsrDTASeg := Regs.ES;                       { segment address of the DTA }
      TsrDTAOfs := Regs.BX;                       { offset address of the DTA }
    end;


    {**------------------------------------------------------------------------**}
    {** Starting code of the unit                                            **}
    {**------------------------------------------------------------------------**}

    begin
      TsrInit;
    end.
```

The TsrShowScreen function and the TsrNewKey procedure were already mentioned in the description of the TSRDEMO program. TsrNewKey loads a new hotkey into the already installed TSR program. This routine then operates in a similar manner as the installation routine of TSRDEMO, in which the variables in the already installed copy are addressed by the TsrGetPtr function. The variables key_mask and scan_code, which are accessed inside TsrNewKey, are components of the assembler module's code segment rather than normal variables. Therefore, key_mask and scan_code cannot be referenced easily. The TSR unit can only determine the addresses of these variables by using a trick. This is required because Turbo Pascal usually forbids access to variables that are housed in the code segments.

The addresses of the two variables can only be reached by the TSR unit if they are declared as external procedures at the beginning of the unit (which they are not), along with the routines from the assembler module. Since the @ operator specifies the addresses of external procedures, TsrNewKey can access the two variables as it would any normal variable.

```
    {**************************************************************************
    *   TsrNewKey : Places a new key code for TSR activation into an already  *
    *               installed copy of the TSR program                        *
    **----------------------------------------------------------------------**
    *   Input : NEWSTATUS = new template for status keys                     *
    *           NEWSCAN   = new scan code                                    *
    *   Info  : Can only be called after calling TsrYetInstalled,            *
    *             which indicated that a copy of the program is installed.    *
    *   Global : OldTsrPSP/R                                                 *
```

```
************************************************************************}

procedure TsrNewKey( NewStatus : word; NewScan : byte );

type WORDP = ^word;
     BYTEP = ^byte;

begin
  {-- The information is written into the assembler module variables   --}
  {-- key_mask and scan_code                                           --}

  WORDP(TsrGetPtr( @key_mask ))^  := NewStatus;
  BYTEP(TsrGetPtr( @scan_code ))^ := NewScan;
end;
```

The TsrShowScreen function returns the contents of video RAM previously stored during the call of SaveVideoContext, to the screen. This can only occur if the video card was in text mode before the TSR program was activated. So, the function returns the value FALSE to the caller if it determines that the TSR program was activated while the system was in graphic mode.

In any other case, it copies the complete contents of SaveBuf into video RAM and returns the value TRUE.

```
{***********************************************************************
 *   TsrShowScreen : if possible, returns video RAM contents to the screen.  *
 **-----------------------------------------------------------------------**
 *   Input : none                                                         *
 *   Output : TRUE if the video card was in text mode while the TSR was   *
 *            active, otherwise FALSE                                     *
 *   Global : Video_Card/R, VioPtr/R, SaveBuf/R                           *
 ***********************************************************************}

function TsrShowScreen : boolean;

var Result : boolean;

begin
  if ( Video_Card = MDA ) or ( Video_Card = CGA ) then
    Result :- TRUE                          { always TRUE for MDA and CGA }
  else    { for HERC, EGA and VGA only if before the TSR call in text mode }
    Result := ( InGraphc = FALSE );
  if Result then                                    { display possible? }
    VioPtr^ := SaveBuf;                { yes, copy buffer to video RAM }
  TsrShowScreen := Result;
end;
```

The TsrStart procedure of the TSR unit cannot call a TSR program, but it's still important in executing the TSR. This procedure is called by the assembler module as soon as the user presses the hotkey to invoke the TSR. In addition to storing the screen context and calling the TSR procedure, TsrStart also executes various context change operations not performed by the TSRA.ASM assembler module.

These operations include, among other things, the installation of three interrupt handlers, which become active only during the execution of the TSR program. Before the TSR program completes its execution, the original handlers are restored for the return to the interrupted program.

The first two are interrupt vectors $1B and $23, which are called when the user presses <Ctrl><Break>. Since the standard handler triggers the end of the program, these interrupt handlers must be redirected to their own handler. This is required so that the TSR program cannot be interrupted when the user presses <Ctrl><Break>. If the TSR could be interrupted in this manner, you wouldn't be able to return to the interrupted program.

Both interrupt handlers are redirected to the interrupt procedure DummyHandler, which doesn't do anything. This prevents the TSR from accidental interruption. Pressing the <Ctrl><Break> key combination during the execution of the TSR procedure has no effect on the TSR.

The third interrupt handler, interrupt $24, is assigned to DOS and points to the critical error handler. This routine is called by DOS when a fatal error occurs. You may be familiar with one of the standard fatal error messages:

```
Abort, Retry, Ignore?
Abort, Retry, Fail?
```

During program execution, Turbo Pascal redirects this interrupt to one of its own interrupt handlers. Instead of sending the error message to the screen, this interrupt handler stores the error code passed by DOS. After the procedure containing the error ends execution, IOResult tests the error and directs the system to the appropriate action.

At the end of the TSR program, the Keep procedure replaces the Turbo handler with the original handler. Because of this, a new handler must be installed during the execution of the TSR procedure. This ensures that the TSR program won't be interrupted by errors which might prevent the return to the interrupted program. The handler that is used is called CritErrHandler and will be discussed in more detail later in this chapter.

In addition to the installation of the interrupt handler, the TsrStart procedure must also perform other tasks. These include the installation of the internal DTA and the change of the PSP from the interrupted program to the TSR program. Both redirections must be reversed before control returns to the interrupted program. Because of this, TSRStart determines the current address of the DTA and the PSP. Only then does it determine a new DTA address and inform the DOS of the location of the current PSP.

DOS functions are currently available for all of these tasks, but there's a problem. The functions for access to the PSP are undocumented, and Microsoft isn't certain whether it will make these functions available in future versions of DOS. However, the functions needed here aren't at risk of extinction, since they have already survived many version changes in MS-DOS and PC-DOS. The DOS functions needed are available in Version 4.0.

After changing the current PSP and the DTA, SaveVideoContext is then called. This is followed by the call of the TSR procedure using the procedure pointer in the global variable TsrProc. A call to RestoreVideoContext restores the screen to its original state. The PSP and the DTA are redirected to the interrupted program, and the interrupt handlers for interrupts $1B, $23 and $24 are reset. The procedure ends and the system returns to the assembler module. These are followed by the context change to the interrupted program and the return to that program.

```
{*******************************************************************
 *  TsrStart : Called by the assembler portion of the unit, when the user    *
 *             wants to activate the TSR by pressing the proper keys.         *
 **---------------------------------------------------------------------**
 *  Input : none                                                    *
 *  Global : TsrPSP/R, TsrDTAOfs/R, TsrDTASeg/R, TsrProc/R          *
 *******************************************************************}

procedure TsrStart;

var Regs        : Registers;          { processor registers for interrupt call }
    DTASeg,                           { address of the DTA in interrupted program }
    DTAOfs,
    PSP         : word; { segment address of PSP in the interrupted program }
    OldCritErr,                        { pointer to old critical error handler }
    OldBreak,                              { pointer to old break handler }
    OldCBreak   : pointer;             { pointer to old Ctrl-Break handler }

begin
  {-- replace Ctrl-Break and critical error handler ----------------------}
  GetIntVec( $23, OldCBreak );
  SetIntVec( $23, @DummyHandler );
  GetIntVec( $1b, OldBreak );
  SetIntVec( $1b, @DummyHandler );
  GetIntVec( $24, OldCritErr );
  SetIntVec( $24, @CritErrHandler );

  {-- get segment address for the PSP of the interrupted program ----------}
  Regs.AH := $51;                              { function number for "get PSP" }
  MsDos( Regs );
  PSP := Regs.BX;                        { store segment address of the PSP }

  {-- get address of the DTA for the interrupted program ------------------}
  Regs.AH := $2f;                    { function number for "get DTA-address" }
  MsDos( Regs );
  DTASeg := Regs.ES;                            { segment address of the DTA }
```

431

```
        DTAOfs := Regs.BX;                              { offset address of the DTA }

        {-- set PSP of the program ----------------------------------------------}
        Regs.AH := $50;                            { function number for "set PSP" }
        Regs.BX := TsrPSP;                      { segment address of the Turbo PSP }
        MsDos( Regs );

        {-- set DTA of the program ----------------------------------------------}
        Regs.AH := $1a;                            { function number for "set DTA" }
        Regs.DX := TsrDTAOfs;                        { pointer to DTA to DS:DX }
        Regs.DS := TsrDTASeg;
        MsDos( Regs );

        {-- prepare for call of the TSR procedure -------------------------------}
        SaveVideoContext;                                   { store screen context }
        TsrProc;                                             { call TSR procedure }
        RestoreVideoContext;                                    { restore screen }

        {-- activate DTA of the interrupted program again ----------------------}
        Regs.AH := $1a;                            { function number for "set DTA" }
        Regs.DX := DTAOfs;                            { pointer to DTA to DS:DX }
        Regs.DS := DTASeg;
        MsDos( Regs );

        {-- reset PSP of the interrupted program -------------------------------}
        Regs.AH := $50;                            { function number for "set PSP" }
        Regs.BX := PSP;                   { segment address of the original PSP }
        MsDos( Regs );

        {-- restore old Ctrl-Break and critical interrupt handler --------------}
        SetIntVec( $23, OldCBreak );
        SetIntVec( $1b, OldBreak );
        SetIntVec( $24, OldCritErr );
      end;
```

Before turning to the assembler module, we will present two interrupt handlers, which are installed during the execution of the TSR procedure to control interrupts $1B, $23 and $24.

```
{**************************************************************************
*   DummyHandler : new interrupt handler for interrupts $1b and $23.      *
**----------------------------------------------------------------------**
*   Input : none                                                          *
*   Info  : Only active during the execution of TSR program!              *
**************************************************************************}

procedure DummyHandler; interrupt;

begin
end;

{**************************************************************************
*   CritErrHandler : new interrupt handler for critical error interrupt $24 *
```

```
**--------------------------------------------------------------------**
*  Input : none                                                       *
*  Info  : Only active during the execution of the TSR program!       *
*********************************************************************}

procedure CritErrHandler( Flags, CS, IP, AX, BX, CX ,
                          DX, SI, DI, DS, ES, BP : HiLo ); interrupt;

begin
  AX.LoByte := 3;                      { terminate the DOS function where }
end;                                   { error occurred with error
}
```

As its name suggests, nothing happens in the DummyHandler for interrupts $1B and $23. The interrupt handler loads the AL register with the value 3 in the procedure CritErrHandler and returns the change to the caller.

CritErrHandler can access the AL register but not the entire AX register (AH and AL). This occurs because of a procedure declaration, in which individual registers are designated as parameters of the type HiLo. This type, defined at the beginning of the unit, reflects the format of the register as a word, and permits access to the low and high bytes of the register.

In this case, the AL register is loaded with the value 3 because, during the return from the interrupt handler, DOS expects a code which indicates what action to take. For example, the interrupt handler could instruct DOS to re-execute an operation which failed, or to terminate the execution of the TSR procedure. The CritErrHandler selects the most sensible option and instructs DOS, through code 3, that the function call should be declared a failure if an error occurs. The caller should be informed by setting the carry flags and loading an error code into the AH register. The called Turbo procedure or function recognizes the error and stores it as an internal error variable. This internal error variable can be accessed using the IoResult function.

The {$I-} compiler directive disables the automatic I/O checking for the TSR procedure. This ensures that Turbo doesn't automatically terminate the procedure with a run-time error after detecting a problem. This would be the same as termination in DOS and, in this case, the TSR program would prevent re-entry to the interrupted application.

The three interrupt handlers defined by the Pascal portion of the unit are only active during the execution of the TSR procedure. In addition to these three, the assembler module TSRA.ASM defines other interrupt handlers which remain permanently active after the installation of the TSR program. These permanent handlers are the keys to accessing the TSR program and suspending the executing application.

The interrupt handlers aren't located at the beginning of the assembler module. Instead, the data segment of the module contains these handlers. When the TSR unit is included in an application, the data segment information moves into the data segment of the TSR program. This segment contains references to different variables rather than variables themselves. These variables are defined by both the System unit (PrefixSeg) and the TSR unit (OldTsrPSP).

```
;**********************************************************************;
;*                      T S R A . A S M                            *;
;*------------------------------------------------------------------*;
;*    Task        : Makes some routines and interrupt handler available *;
;*                  for the TSR-Unit.                               *;
;*------------------------------------------------------------------*;
;*    Author      : MICHAEL TISCHER                                 *;
;*    developed on : 4/9/1989                                       *;
;*    last update  : 3/2/1990                                       *;
;*------------------------------------------------------------------*;
;*    assembly     : MASM TSRA;   or                                *;
;*                   TASM TSRA                                       *;
;**********************************************************************;


;== data-segment ============================================================

DATA        segment word public     ;Turbo data segment

;-- References to variables in the pascal portion of the unit --------------------
  —

extrn       TsrStackOfs : word      ;Stack pointer of the Turbo program
extrn       TsrStackSeg : word      ;Stack segment of the Turbo program
extrn       OldTsrPsp   : word      ;Segm. addr. of the installed copy
extrn       PrefixSeg   : word      ;Segm addr. of the PSP in current program

DATA        ends                    ;End of the data segment
```

The variable declarations can be found in the code segment instead of the data segment listed above.

The data is followed by two constants, KB_PORT and MAX_WAIT. KB_PORT reflects the number of keyboard data ports through which the scan codes of pressed keys can be sensed. MAX_WAIT is a delay counter needed when the assembler module registers hotkey activation, but cannot do what the user wants done when these keys are pressed. This may occur because access to the hard disk drive or floppy disk drive is in progress, and cannot be interrupted for any reason.

Once this access ends, the system allows execution of the TSR program after no more than the number of ticks contained in MAX_WAIT. Here MAX_WAIT contains a value of 6, so the latest the activation can execute the TSR is a third of a second after the user presses the hotkeys. If this time limit is exceeded, pressing the hotkeys has no effect. The user must then press the hotkeys again to invoke the TSR.

You can set MAX_WAIT to a higher value, but it creates a time lag that will be noticeable to the user. The user barely detects a third of a second delay. However, with a larger value for MAX_WAIT, a much longer time period would elapse between pressing the hotkeys and the appearance of the TSR program. This may cause some confusion because the average user won't know for sure if the TSR program will appear on the screen soon, or if pressing the hotkeys had no effect on the TSR. We recommend that you don't change the default value for MAX_WAIT.

The declaration of the two constants is followed by the code segment, which takes up part of the module listed below. At its beginning is an extrn declaration of the procedure TsrStart, found in the TSR unit. It is called within the module to start the TSR program (see the descriptions of the TSR unit and the TsrStart routine which appeared earlier in this section).

The TsrAInit and TsrRemoveVec procedures are declared as public, and are accessible from the Pascal portion of the TSR unit. The key_mask and scan_code variables are also public. Even though they do not represent procedures, these variables must be declared as public to permit access from the Pascal portion of the TSR unit.

```
;== program =======================================================

CODE        segment byte public    ;the Turbo code segment

            assume cs:CODE, ds:DATA

;-- External declarations of procedures from the Pascal part of the unit ----

extrn       TsrStart : near

;-- Public declarations of internal functions ------------------------------

public      TsrAInit                ;Allows calls from the Turbo program
public      TsrRestoreVec
public      key_mask
public      scan_code
```

These declarations are followed by different variables. Instead of being stored in the data segment, as they normally are, these variables are stored in the code segment because they are generally accessed within the various interrupt handlers of the module. However, it cannot be assumed that the DS register points to the data segment of the TSR program during their call. Consequently, this doesn't guarantee that access to the variables in this segment will occur without problems.

During the execution of the interrupt handlers, the CS register points to the code segment of the TSR unit. If this were not the case, the interrupt handlers couldn't be executed. This pointer allows access to the different variables through the CS register, without having to load the DS register with the segment address of the TSR data segment.

The first variables are key_mask and scan_code, which were discussed earlier in reference to the TsrNewKeys procedure found in the Pascal portion of the TSR unit. They are followed by the recur variable, which prevents the user from repeatedly activating the TSR program. When the TSR is in the foreground, this flag is set to 1. So while the hotkeys are being pressed, the interrupt handler can tell that the program is already active, thus preventing repeated activation.

TSR activation should be blocked during hard disk or floppy disk access. A handler sets the in_bios variable to 1 during the execution of the corresponding BIOS function. When the user presses the hotkey, the TSR cannot be invoked until the BIOS function finishes the disk access.

In this case, the is_waiting variable is set to 1 and serves as a flag whose contents reveal whether the activation of the TSR program is still pending. How much time has elapsed since the activation of the hotkeys can be determined through the wait_count variable, which is immediately set to 0 when the hotkey is pressed. However, this activation must be delayed. The wait_count variable increments with each tick of the internal clock, indicating the time elapsed since the user pressed the hotkeys.

The daptr_ofs and daptr_seg variables which follow the wait_count variable contain a pointer to a very special flag. These variables store the segment and offset address of the DOS Indos flag. Since this flag indicates whether a DOS function is being executed at any time, Indos is vital to invoking the TSR program. The TSR program can only be activated if DOS isn't currently executing one of its own functions. Otherwise, the re-entry problems mentioned earlier would crash the system on the return to the interrupted DOS function.

The address of the DOS Indos flag is followed by four additional pointers, which store the addresses of the original interrupt handler of the redirected interrupts. The variable names reveal which interrupt is permanently redirected by the assembler module during the installation of the TSR program: Interrupts $0C (keyboard), $13 (BIOS floppy disk/hard disk access) and $1C (timer). Interrupt $28 divides up processor time between DOS background programs (e.g., the DOS print spooler PRINT.COM).

The last two variables within the code segment store the address of the stack in the interrupted program. Since we cannot assume that the stack of the interrupted program offers enough space for execution of the TSR procedure, a switch is made in the Turbo stack before the activation of the TSR program. This stack must be restored before the system returns to the interrupted program.

```
;-- Interrupt handler variables (accessible to code segment only) -

key_mask   dw ?                   ;Hotkey template for BIOS keyboard flag
scan_code  db ?                   ;Hotkey scan code
recur      db 0                   ;Prevents recursive TSR calls
in_bios    db 0                   ;Indicates BIOS disk interrupt activity
```

```
    is_waiting db 0                    ;Is program waiting for activation?
    wait_count dw 0                    ;For how many Ticks has it been waiting?

    daptr      equ this dword          ;Pointer to the DOS Indos flag
    daptr_ofs  dw 0                    ;Offset address
    daptr_seg  dw 0                    ;Segment address

    ;-- The following variables store the old addresses of the
    ;-- interrupt handler, which are replaced by a new interrupt handler

    int9_ptr   equ this dword          ;Old interrupt vector 9h
    int9_ofs   dw 0                    ;Offset address of the old handlers
    int9_seg   dw 0                    ;Segment address of the old handlers

    int13_ptr  equ this dword          ;Old interrupt vector 13h
    int13_ofs  dw 0                    ;Offset address of the old handlers
    int13_seg  dw 0                    ;Segment address of the old handlers

    int1c_ptr  equ this dword          ;Old interrupt vector 1Ch
    int1c_ofs  dw 0                    ;Offset address of the old handlers
    int1c_seg  dw 0                    ;Segment address of the old handlers

    int28_ptr  equ this dword          ;Old interrupt vector 28h
    int28_ofs  dw 0                    ;Offset address of the old handlers
    int28_seg  dw 0                    ;Segment address of the old handlers

    ;-- Variables which store the information about the interrupted program -

    iprg_ss    dw 0                    ;SS and SP of the interrupted program
    iprg_sp    dw 0
```

The variables are followed by the TsrAInit procedure, which is called by the Pascal portion of the unit during the installation of the program. Since this procedure can only be called from within the unit, but not from another unit or program, it is type NEAR. Over the stack, the hotkey is passed to it in the form of a bit mask and scan code for the control keys. The two arguments are referenced in the usual manner with two constants, and stored in the corresponding variables.

Next the address of the Indos flag is determined. DOS function $34 and the existence of this flag were once undocumented features, but now they are common knowledge to PC system programmers.

Next is the installation of the various interrupt handlers for the interrupts $09, $13, $1C and $28. The addresses of the current handler is loaded and stored in the specified variable. The DOS function $35 is also used by the Turbo Pascal procedure GetInVec to determine the contents of an interrupt vector. The individual interrupts are then loaded with the addresses of the new interrupt handler from the assembler module, which uses DOS function $25. This is also known to Turbo Pascal and is used by the SetIntVec procedure. Now

TsrAInit completes its assignment and returns to the caller while clearing the two passed arguments from the stack.

```
;-------------------------------------------------------------------------
;-- TSRAINIT: Installs the various interrupt handlers required for the
;--          activation of the program.
;-- call from Turbo: procedure TsrInit( KeyState : word;
;--                                      CurKey   : byte );
;-- Info          : If CurKey >= 128, it is not used for the testing
;--                  of the activation

TsrAInit    proc    near

KeyState    equ [ BP + 6 ]          ;Constants for access to parameters
CurKey      equ [ BP + 4 ]

            push bp                 ;Store BP on the stack
            mov  bp,sp              ;Transmit SP to BP

            mov  ax,KeyState        ;Load KeyState parameter from the stack
            mov  key_mask,ax        ;and store

            mov  al,CurKey          ;Get CurKey parameter from the stack
            mov  scan_code,al       ;and store

            ;-- Determine address of the Indos flags ----------------------

            mov  ah,34h             ;Funct. no.: Get address of Indos flag
            int  21h                ;Call DOS interrupt
            mov  cs:daptr_ofs,bx    ;Store address in the corresponding
            mov  cs:daptr_seg,es    ;variable

            ;-- Get the addresses of the redirected interrupt handlers -----

            mov  ax,3509h           ;get interrupt vector 9h
            int  21h                ;call DOS interrupt
            mov  cs:int9_ofs,bx     ;Store address of the handler in the -
            mov  cs:int9_seg,es     ;variable

            mov  ax,3513h           ;Get interrupt vector 13h
            int  21h                ;Call DOS interrupt
            mov  cs:int13_ofs,bx    ;Store address of the handler in the -
            mov  cs:int13_seg,es    ;variable

            mov  ax,351Ch           ;Get interrupt vector 1Ch
            int  21h                ;Call DOS interrupt
            mov  cs:int1c_ofs,bx    ;Store address
            mov  cs:int1c_seg,es

            mov  ax,3528h           ;Get interrupt vector 28h
            int  21h                ;Call DOS interrupt
            mov  cs:int28_ofs,bx    ;Store address
```

```
                  mov   cs:int28_seg,es

                  ;-- Install the new interrupt handler --------------------

                  push  ds                  ;Store data segment
                  mov   ax,cs               ;Pass CS to AX and then to DS
                  mov   ds,ax

                  mov   ax,2509h            ;Funct. no.: Set interrupt 9h
                  mov   dx,offset int09     ;DS:DX stores address of the handler
                  int   21h                 ;Call DOS interrupt

                  mov   ax,2513h            ;Funct. no.: Set interrupt 13h
                  mov   dx,offset int13     ;DS:DX stores address of the handler
                  int   21h                 ;Call DOS interrupt

                  mov   ax,251Ch            ;Funct. no.: Set interrupt 1Ch
                  mov   dx,offset int1c     ;DS:DX stores address of the handler
                  int   21h                 ;Call DOS interrupt

                  mov   ax,2528h            ;Funct. no.: Set interrupt 28h
                  mov   dx,offset int28     ;DS:DX stores address of the handler
                  int   21h                 ;Call DOS interrupt

                  pop   ds                  ;Return DS from the stack
                  pop   bp

                  ret   4                   ;Back to caller and delete parameter
                                            ;from stack

TsrAInit   endp
```

TsrRestoreVec does the opposite of TsrAInit. It installs the original interrupt handlers for the various interrupts and prevents activation of the TSR program. It only completes this step after it has determined that all interrupt vectors still point to the handlers in the already installed program, and have not been redirected to other interrupt handlers by other TSR programs. However, remember that instead of obtaining the address of the original handler from the installed program, TsrRestoreVec obtains the address of the original handler from the already installed program. In addition, the GetPtr function accesses the segment address of this program, contained in the OldTsrPSP variable.

```
;------------------------------------------------------------------------
;-- TSRRESTOREVEC : is called during the deactivation of a TSR program to
;--                 load the interrupt vectors with their original content.
;-- call from Turbo: function TsrRestoreVec : boolean;
;-- Return : TRUE, if all interrupt vectors still point to the
;--                installed copy of the program
;--                (and only then are the interrupt vectors reset)
;-- Info            : the variable OldTsrPSP from the Pascal code must
;--                point to the PSP of the program to be deactivated
```

```
TsrRestoreVec proc near

            mov   di,ds             ;Store DS in DI

            ;-- Determine address of the code segment of the TSR unit    ----
            ;-- in the version of the program which will be deactivated ----

            mov   ax,cs             ;Code segment to AX
            sub   ax,PrefixSeg      ;Subtract segment address of the PSP
            add   ax,OldTsrPSP      ;Add seg.addr. of PSP in the old program
            mov   dx,ax             ;and load to DX

            ;-- Test if all interrupt vectors modified by the program ---
            ;-- still point to the installed program                  ---

            mov   ax,3509h          ;Get interrupt vector 9h
            int   21h               ;Call DOS interrupt
            mov   ax,es             ;Pass segment address to AX
            cmp   ax,dx             ;and compare
            jne   another_tsr       ;Not equal? ---> ANOTHER_TSR

            mov   ax,3513h          ;Get interrupt vector 13h
            int   21h               ;Call DOS interrupt
            mov   ax,es             ;Pass segment address to AX
            cmp   ax,dx             ;and compare
            jne   another_tsr       ;Not equal? ---> ANOTHER_TSR

            mov   ax,351ch          ;Get interrupt vector 1ch
            int   21h               ;Call DOS interrupt
            mov   ax,es             ;Pass segment address to AX
            cmp   ax,dx             ;and compare
            jne   another_tsr       ;Not equal? ---> ANOTHER_TSR

            mov   ax,3528h          ;Get interrupt vector 28h
            int   21h               ;Call DOS interrupt
            mov   ax,es             ;Pass segment address to AX
            cmp   ax,dx             ;and compare
            jne   another_tsr       ;Not equal? ---> ANOTHER_TSR

            ;-- All interrupt handlers are at the expected locations! ---
            ;-- Load the original addresses of the various interrupt
            ;-- handlers from the old program and activate again.

            cli                     ;No interruptions now
            mov   es,dx             ;Pass segment address to ES

            mov   ax,2509h          ;Restore interrupt 09h
            lds   dx,es:int9_ptr    ;DS:DX point to old interrupt handler
            int   21h               ;Reset vector

            mov   ax,2513h          ;Restore interrupt 13h
            lds   dx,es:int13_ptr   ;DS:DX point to old interrupt handler
            int   21h               ;Reset vector
```

```
        mov   ax,251ch            ;Restore interrupt 1ch
        lds   dx,es:int1c_ptr     ;DS:DX point to old interrupt handler
        int   21h                 ;Reset vector

        mov   ax,2528h            ;Restore interrupt 28h
        lds   dx,es:int28_ptr     ;DS:DX point to old interrupt handler
        int   21h                 ;Reset vector

        sti                       ;Turn on interrupts again
        mov   ds,di               ;Load DS with old value
        mov   al,1                ;Return TRUE

        ret                       ;Back to caller

another_tsr: ;-- Another TSR program has overlaid one or more of the -------
             ;-- handlers: Deactivation impossible !

        mov   ds,di               ;Reset DS
        xor   al,al               ;Return FALSE

        ret

TsrRestoreVec endp
```

The various interrupt handlers installed by the call of the TsrAInit procedure are responsible for the activation of the TSR program. The new handler for interrupt $09 appears in the foreground. The keyboard triggers this call when the user presses or releases a hotkey. It is responsible for detecting the hotkeys.

```
;-- The new interrupt 09h handler (keyboard) -----------------------------

int09       proc far

            assume cs:code, ds:nothing, es:nothing

            sti                   ;Enable interrupts
            push ax               ;Store AX on the stack
            in   al,KB_PORT       ;Get scan code from the keyboard port

            pushf                 ;Call the old handler with the command
            call int9_ptr         ;Simulate INT 9h

            cli                   ;Suppress interrupts
            cmp  recur,0          ;Is the TSR program already active?
            jne  ik_end           ;Yes: back to caller of int. 9

            ;-- Determine if the hotkey was activated -------------------

            cmp  al,128           ;Release code?
            jae  ik_end           ;Yes, do not test
```

```
                cmp    scan_code,128       ;Test the scan code?
                jae    no_scan             ;NO ---> NO_SCAN

                cmp    al,scan_code        ;Was the scan code activated?
                jne    ik_end              ;No, additional tests not necessary

    no_scan:    push   ax                  ;Store DS and AX on the stack
                push   ds

                mov    ax,0040h            ;Segment address of the BIOS segment to AX
                mov    ds,ax               ;and from there to DS
                mov    ax,ds:[17h]         ;Load BIOS keyboard flag
                and    ax,key_mask         ;Leave the bits from KeyMask
                cmp    ax,key_mask         ;Compare with KeyMask
                pop    ds                  ;Restore DS and AX
                pop    ax

                jne    ik_end              ;No Hotkey ---> IK_END

                ;-- Determine if the TSR program can now be activated

                cmp    in_bios,0           ;BIOS disk interrupt active?
                jne    not_now             ;Yes --> delay activation

                ;-- The hotkey was activated, test if DOS is active -------------

                push   ds                  ;Store DS and BX on the stack
                push   bx
                lds    bx,daptr            ;DS:BX now point to the Indos flag
                cmp    byte ptr [bx],0     ;DOS function active?
                pop    bx                  ;Get BX and DS from the stack again
                pop    ds
                jne    not_now             ;DOS function active --> NOT_NOW

                ;-- DOS not currently active, activate TSR program -------------

                call   start_tsr           ;Start the TSR program

    ik_end:     pop    ax                  ;Restore the content of the AX register
                iret                       ;Return to the interrupted program

    not_now:    ;-- The TSR program cannot be activated now, set flag ----
                ;-- for later activation                              ----

                mov    is_waiting,1        ;Program waits for activation
                mov    wait_count,0        ;Set time counter to 0
                jmp    ik_end              ;Back to interrupted program

    int09       endp
```

At the beginning of its execution, the new keyboard handler loads the code, passed by the keyboard, from the data port. The handler then simulates a call of the original interrupt handlers. BIOS processes the information concerning the pressed or released key, after which this information can be converted into an ASCII or extended keyboard code. Also, the BIOS accesses the keyboard port, which hasn't lost its contents even after being read by the interrupt handler or the TSR program.

After the return to the keyboard handler of the TSR program, the recur flag tests whether the TSR program is already active. If so, the keyboard codes aren't tested but an immediate return is made to the program whose execution was interrupted by the call of interrupt $09. If the TSR program is inactive, a test is performed if keyboard code was a release code. This is the designation of the scan codes in which bit 7 is set. Bit 7 indicates that the key whose scan code lies in bits 0 through 6 was released. Since activation of the TSR program is always associated with pressing keys rather than releasing keys, release codes mean that further tests can be omitted and an immediate return jump can be made to the interrupted program.

However, if a make code (a code in the area between 0 and 127) was received, a test is performed if this code corresponds to the hotkey of the program. The test is only required if TsrAInit hasn't passed the value NOKEY for the hotkey. This indicates that the activation occurs only through the control keys; other keys aren't involved. If the content of scan_code agrees with the code received from the keyboard, a test is made with the variable in the BIOS variable area, if the control keys, which were assigned to the hotkey through the key_mask variable, are started. If so, the user has activated the hotkey and it must be determined whether it is possible to activate the TSR program.

The content of the in_bios variable is checked to prevent an activation of the TSR program during floppy disk or hard disk access. If this flag contains a value that is unequal to 0, access occurs and TSR activity must be postponed. If the value 0 is detected in the in_bios variable, the Indos flag is tested to prevent interrupting a DOS function during execution. If this flag also contains the value 0, the TSR program can be activated by a call to the start_tsr procedure, because a DOS function isn't executing. The executing program is interrupted, but the interrupt handler invokes the TSR program instead of returning control to the current program. Only after the TSR program is terminated is the return made to the interrupted program, which isn't aware of its brief suspension any more than it noticed the interruption by the timer or the keyboard interrupt.

If the hotkey was activated without placing the TSR program in the foreground, the is_waiting flag, which contains the value 1, is loaded into the not_now label, which indicates pending activation of the TSR program. At the same time, the tick counter wait_count is set to 0, so that the elapsed time indicates that the TSR program is already waiting.

The new timer interrupt handler increments the wait_count counter, while passing program execution to the original handler.

```
;-- The new interrupt 1Ch handler (timer) ----------------------------------

int1c     proc far

          inc  wait_count       ;Increment wait counter
          jmp  int1c_ptr        ;Jump to old handler
                                ;Do not get register from stack
int1c     endp
```

The new handler does more for interrupt $13, through which DOS (and some application programs) accesses the disk and hard disk drives. Unlike interrupt $09, this is a software interrupt rather than a hardware interrupt. This is called in a program through the execution of the INT instruction.

During the call of the new handler, the in_bios flag is incremented and all other handlers are notified that, at the moment, an access to mass storage is in progress. Then the call of the original handler, which executes the access, occurs. Its return is followed by the decrementing of the previously incremented flag. This doesn't ensure that the access to the devices is terminated because the functions of these BIOS interrupts can call each other. This creates a recursion and in_bios may not contain the value 0 after its decrementation.

If, after the flag has been decremented, the new handler finds this value, the activation of the TSR program is again possible. It must be determined whether, in the meantime, the user has tried unsuccessfully to activate the TSR program. This test is only performed after the handler is sure that the Indos flag contains the value 0 and that DOS would not object to the activation of the TSR program. If this criteria is met, the procedure that activates the TSR program is called, assuming that too much time hasn't elapsed since the activation of the hotkeys.

```
;-- The new interrupt 13h handler (BIOS disk interrupt) --------------

int13     proc far

          inc  in_bios          ;Increment BIOS flag
          pushf                 ;Call the old interrupt handler
          call int13_ptr        ;Simulate over INT 13h
          pushf                 ;Store result of function

          dec  in_bios          ;BIOS disk interrupt inactive
          jne  dbend            ;Recursive call? Yes --> dbend

;-- If the Indos flag contains the value 0, a test can be ------
;-- performed to determine if program is waiting for activation

          push ds               ;Store DS and DI for access to the
          push di               ;Indos flag on the stack
          lds  di,[daptr]       ;Address of the flag to DS:DI
          cmp  byte ptr [di],0  ;Flag is 0?
          pop  di               ;Restore register
```

```
          pop  ds
          jne  dbend              ;Unequal to 0 ---> no test

          call active             ;Is the program waiting for activation?

dbend:    popf                    ;Get function result from stack
          ret  2                  ;Back to caller, but do not get flag
                                  ;Register from stack
int13     endp
```

The handler for interrupt $13 isn't terminated with an IRET instruction like the other handlers. This is because the BIOS handler that was called returns the status of the operation through the carry flag in the flag register. This information would be lost through the execution of the IRET instruction because the previously stored flag register is again loaded from the stack. The handler cannot be terminated with a FAR RET instruction because this would leave the flag register on the stack. Through the indication of the parameter 2 behind the RET instruction, it is assured that the processor returns to the caller and then clears the flag register from the stack.

Since the flag register was used for storing the function result, the content of this register is stored on the stack immediately after the call of the original handler. The next DEC instruction would destroy the information stored there because it sets the Zero flag according to its results. The flag register is restored immediately before the return to the caller to prevent the routine from making any changes.

The last interrupt handler in the assembler module is dedicated to interrupt $28. DOS calls this interrupt when it can spare processor time and wants to allocate it to the background programs. Whether or not this interrupt is used depends on the test of the Indos flag, which contains the value 1 when a program isn't being executed and the command processor is waiting for input. Since the TSR program can be activated, another capability must be used to discover the situation.

The redirection of interrupt $28 is one way to do this because, while the command processor waits for an input, it always calls this interrupt. The new handler then calls the old handler and tests, by using the active procedure, if the TSR program is waiting for its activation. Before this it ensures that an access isn't being performed to the hard disk or floppy disk. This shouldn't happen, but "making sure is being secure".

```
;-- The new interrupt 28h handler (DOS not busy ) --------------------

int28     proc far

          pushf                   ;Call the old interrupt handler
          call int28_ptr          ;simulate through INT 28h

          cmp  in_bios, 0         ;BIOS disk interrupt currently active?
          jne  id_end             ;Yes --> back to caller
```

```
            ;-- BIOS disk interrupt inactive, test for hotkey -------------

            call active             ;Does the program wait for activation?

 id_end:    iret                    ;Back to interrupted program

 int28      endp
```

The active procedure, which can be called from several locations within the various handlers, first checks if the TSR program is waiting for its activation. If it is, this procedure compares the tick counter with the constant MAX_WAIT. Then, only if no additional ticks occurred since the activation of the hotkeys, as recorded in MAX_WAIT, the program is activated. The is_waiting flag is again set to 0. Then a fluid passage occurs to the start_tsr procedure, which follows inside the program listing immediately after the active procedure and is responsible for activating the TSR program.

If too much time has passed since the hotkeys were pressed, the TSR program won't be activated. Before the return to the caller, the is_waiting flag is again set to 0, which signals that the TSR program will no longer wait for its activation.

```
;--------------------------------------------------------------------------
;-- ACTIVE: is called when the TSR program can be activated
;--         to determine if it is waiting for its activation

active      proc near

            cmp  is_waiting,0       ;Is the TSR program waiting?
            je   curend             ;No, return

            cmp  wait_count,MAX_WAIT;Waited too long already?
            jbe  start_it           ;NO ---> start execution

            mov  is_waiting,0       ;Yes, do not activate

curend:     ret                     ;Back to caller

start_it:   mov  is_waiting,0       ;No call waiting

            ;-- Direct transfer to StartTsr -------------------------------

active      endp

;-- START_TSR: Activate the TSR-program ---------------------------------

start_tsr   proc near

            mov  recur,1            ;Set TSR recursion flag

            ;-- Perform context change to Turbo program ---------------
```

```
              cli                      ;No interrupts now
              push ds                  ;Store DS and AX on current stack
              push ax
              mov  iprg_ss,ss          ;Store current stack segment
              mov  iprg_sp,sp          ;and stack pointer

              mov  ax,DATA             ;Segment address of the Turbo data segments
              mov  ds,ax               ;to AX and from there to DS
              assume ds:data

              mov  ss,TsrStackSeg      ;Activate the stack of the Turbo program
              mov  sp,TsrStackOfs
              sti                      ;Activate interrupts again

              push bx                  ;Store processor registers on Turbo stack
              push cx
              push dx
              push bp
              push si
              push di
              push es

;-- Store 64 words from DOS stack ----------------------------

              mov  bx,ds               ;Store DS in BX
              mov  cx,64               ;Loop counter
              mov  ds,iprg_ss          ;Set DS:SI to the end of the DOS stack
              mov  si,iprg_sp

tsrs1:        push word ptr [si]       ;Store word from DOS stack on the Turbo
              inc  si                  ;stack and set SI to the next stack word
              inc  si                  ;
              loop tsrs1               ;Process all 64 words

              mov  ds,bx               ;Return DS from BX

;-- If the hotkey was stored in the keyboard buffer, it must be
;-- removed from it

              mov  ah,1                ;Function 01: is key ready ?
              int  16h                 ;Call BIOS keyboard interrupt
              je   emptybuf            ;NO ---> EMPTYBUF

              xor  ah,ah               ;Read character from keyboard buffer
              int  16h

emptybuf:     call TsrStart            ;Call Start procedure in Pascal code

;-- restore DOS stack again ------------------------------

              mov  cx,64               ;Loop counter
              mov  ds,iprg_ss          ;Load DS:SI with the end address of
```

```
                mov   si,iprg_sp       ;the DOS stack
                add   si,128           ;Set SI to the beginning of the DOS stack
        tsrs2:  dec   si               ;SI to the preceding stack-Word
                dec   si
                pop   word ptr [si]    ;Word from Turbo stack to DOS stack
                loop  tsrs2            ;Process all 64 words

                pop   es               ;Restore registers again from
                pop   di               ;Turbo stack
                pop   si
                pop   bp
                pop   dx
                pop   cx
                pop   bx

                cli                    ;Suppress interrupts
                mov   ss,iprg_ss       ;Set stack pointer and stack segment of the
                mov   sp,iprg_sp       ;interrupted program again

                pop   ax               ;Get AX and DX from DOS stack
                pop   ds
                assume ds:nothing

                mov   recur,0          ;Reset TSR recursion flag
                sti                    ;Interrupts permitted again

                ret                    ;Back to caller

    start_tsr   endp
```

The recur flag in the start_tsr procedure is set to protect the keyboard handler from additional calls to activate the program. The context change to the TSR program then occurs step by step. The current stack is stored and the data segment of the TSR program is passed to the DS register. Since the DS and AX registers are involved in these two operations, but the various register must be returned unchanged, to the caller, the two registers are stored on the stack of the interrupted program.

The Turbo stack is then initialized and the various processor registers are stored on this stack. The last 64 words of the stack of the interrupted program are also stored there. This stored data cannot be destroyed when starting a program from the DOS level and the TSR program calls a DOS function.

After stack data storage the hotkey is removed from the keyboard buffer by the BIOS keyboard routines, provided the hotkey was converted by BIOS into an ASCII or extended key code. This prevents the key from being sent to the TSR program as soon as the system reads the keyboard. This is followed by the call of the TsrStart procedure from the Pascal part of the unit. TsrStart calls the actual TSR procedure in turn and returns to the assembler module after the program ends.

The context change back to the interrupted program initiates by the reloading of the stored 64 stack words. The various processor registers are read from the stack and the original stack is restored again. From it the registers AX and DS are loaded. These registers were stored in the beginning and after the resetting of the recur flag; a return is made to the caller and the interrupted program. The process is finally completed.

12. Configuring Turbo Programs

Creativity programs that can be configured to fit the user's personal needs have always presented problems. The developer has a number of choices. The easiest option is to write the program according to the exact specifications of the user. However, simply doing this can cause problems, since the user may want to run the program on different systems with different capabilities. Consequently, this limits the marketability of the program. The second option is to give the user the finished source code and let the user configure and compile the program. However, this solution defeats the purpose of hiring contract programmers.

The best solution is to write a configuration or installation program. This program could prompt the user for information about the user's system (e.g., video card and monitors) and store this information in an ASCII file (e.g., CONFIG.SYS) or in the main program itself.

We were impressed with the Turbo Pascal installation program TINST.EXE, which provides a framework for configuring Turbo Pascal without generating a separate configuration file. Instead, it writes the configuration data directly into the TURBO.EXE file, which contains a portion of the program code for the integrated environment of Turbo Pascal.

Since we couldn't understand how the information moved through the EXE file to the program, this process confused us for a long time. However, when we did finally learn how TINST works, the solution is simple. The EXE file only contains the executable program as it is loaded into memory. There is some additional information in the EXE file that changes some bytes in the program as it loads. These bytes alter certain memory segments in the program. But usually the program in the EXE file isn't coded in any special way, nor is the data stored in a compressed format.

The EXE file contains the complete program code and the variables. However, only the variables that are loaded with a value at the beginning of the program are included. The uninitialized variables aren't included in the EXE file because they would only occupy space for no logical reason. This is why Turbo Pascal stores its initialized variables (the typed constants) at the beginning of the data segment and, consequently, preceding any variables which haven't been initialized. Since an EXE file loads into memory sequentially, the typed constants can be inserted at the end of the program. These constants can be stored as a separate item from the EXE file.

Since the typed constants are stored in the EXE file in the order they will appear in memory, they are suitable for storing configuration data. If their location within the EXE file is known, their initial values can be preset and changed by the user by manipulating the proper memory locations. Once the program starts, various typed constants represent the configuration data selected by the user.

The configuration data must be stored in the typed constants to allow program configuration. This can easily be done. However, there must be a way for the configuration program to determine the addresses of the typed constants within the EXE file and to manipulate these addresses while they are still in the EXE file. This is difficult because the positions of the various constants depend mainly on the position of the program. Also, since the configuration program is an independent program, these constants may not be recognized by the configuration program.

A *debugger* can be used to determine the addresses of the various typed constants, which the user can then enter manually in the configuration program. Not only is this tedious, but it also depends on whether the user has any knowledge of assembly language programming. This process must be repeated even for the smallest change in the program, because the position of the constants would also change.

One solution is to generate a separate constant file, sometimes called a MAP file. MAP files contain the data needed for configuration by EXE files instructed to search for MAP files. A MAP file is actually a text file, just like a Pascal source code or word processor file. You can read and edit a MAP file using your Turbo Pascal editor or any editor that reads ASCII text files. However, editing a MAP file by hand is also time-consuming work.

12.1   Reading MAP Files

To avoid having to manually read MAP files, we recommend giving this task to a program specifically designed for it. This section lists this type of program. This program can find the addresses of various typed constants, but cannot access them. The TPINST unit listed later in this chapter performs this write access. This writing program shows you how to access the typed constants within the EXE file, and how to create configuration programs similar to Turbo Pascal's own TINST.EXE program.

Access to the typed constants isn't enough by itself, since the configuration data must be available for interaction with the user. Because of this, the TPINST unit also includes routines for the construction and control of pulldown menus, alphanumeric input fields and color selection boxes, which you may recognize if you have used TINST recently. Color selection is an important criterion for the user when shopping for programs, because personal preferences vary. In addition, a program designed for use with a color system may not work well on a system using a CGA video card and a monochrome monitor. Therefore, some allowances may be needed for adapting a program to a hybrid system of this type.

Although these features can't take all the work out of creating a configuration program, they do provide the necessary tools for creating such a program. All you need to do is combine the various routines and decide on the data needed for the menus, dialog boxes, etc.

The first step in creating a configuration program with the tools presented here is using the TPIC program, listed on the following pages, to process the program. TPIC determines the addresses of all typed constants in this program and creates a file which represents a Pascal fragment that can be inserted in the source code of the configuration program in one of two ways:

- Directly in the source.

- Using the {$L} compiler directive.

The file generated by TPIC consists of a series of constant definitions which are untyped constants. They represent the addresses of the various typed constants from the program to be configured within the EXE file. Every constant contains the name of the typed constant that it represents, preceded by the prefix "TPIC_". The constant file itself is always stored by TPIC under the name of the program to be configured and equipped with a file extension of .TCA.

The following illustration shows a typed constant file DEMO.TCA as created by TPIC. The initial number gives the first address, while subsequent numbers represent the offsets from this first address (i.e., $0000B equals $0208B):

```
{ Names and addresses of typed constants in file
DEMO.PAS after compilation }
const TPIC_DSEG_START              =     8320; { $02080 }
      TPIC_CURRENTDOUBLED          =       11; { $0000B }
      TPIC_CURRENT_FRAME           =      269; { $0010D }
      TPIC_FRAME_LINE_T            =       10; { $0000A }
      TPIC_KEY                     =      271; { $0010F }
      TPIC_NORMAL_FRAME            =      268; { $0010C }
      TPIC_OUTHEADER               =       84; { $00054 }
      TPIC_OUTHEADERW              =        7; { $00007 }
      TPIC_OUTHIW                  =        5; { $00005 }
      TPIC_OUTNORMW                =        3; { $00003 }
      TPIC_OUTPUT_FRAMEW           =        9; { $00009 }
      TPIC_TEXTHEADER              =       12; { $0000C }
      TPIC_TEXTHEADERW             =        6; { $00006 }
      TPIC_TEXTHIW                 =        4; { $00004 }
      TPIC_TEXTNORMW               =        2; { $00002 }
      TPIC_TEXT_FRAMEW             =        8; { $00008 }
      TPIC_UPPR                    =      270; { $0010E }
```

The constant file DEMO.TCA created by TPIC

These constants are passed to the configuration program by the routines from the configuration unit TPINST, which is responsible for accessing the typed constants within the EXE file. They access the constant names, but not the actual constant addresses within this file.

We recommend including the constant file in the source code during compilation with the {$L} compiler directive only. This makes the constant file more adaptable to changes in the program to be configured. Otherwise, in order to move the typed constants, you must create a new constant file within the EXE file, which is included in the configuration program and must be compiled. It is easier if you can just load the constants from the TCA file every time you compile, rather than update the source code every time you want to make changes to the configuration.

The constant file shown above was created by TPIC while compiling the DEMO.PAS program listed in this chapter. We included this as an example of creating a configuration program. DEMO.EXE is the program on which we'll be performing configuration experiments. In other words, DEMO will be our guinea pig for demonstrating the configuration tools listed in this chapter.

Here we used the DEMO program instead of any other application. For clarity, any features which didn't need configuring were omitted. What remains is a program that divides the screen into two halves (upper and lower). These halves are assigned the names output window and text window. Both windows have frames, titles and similar texts.

The titles of the windows and the frame and color types used by all elements on the screen are defined by various typed constants, whose names are listed in the illustration above. Later, these constants can be accessed by the user using the configuration program DINST.

Here's the listing for DEMO.PAS. Notice that this program uses the WIN unit created in Chapter 6 of this book, <u>not</u> the WIN unit supplied with Turbo Pascal by Borland International. Make sure that the WIN unit you created in Chapter 6 is within easy reach of the compiler.

```pascal
{*********************************************************************
* DEMO : Demo program for TPIC and TPINST. The DINST program supplies  *
*        configuration data for this program.                         *
**-----------------------------------------------------------------**
* Author         : MICHAEL TISCHER                                    *
* developed on    : 07/08/1989                                        *
* last update on  : 03/05/1990                                        *
*********************************************************************}

program demo;

{-- Inclusion of the required units ------------------------------------}

uses crt,                              { Turbo Pascal CRT unit }
     win;        { Turbo Pascal System Programming window unit ( Chapter 5 )}

{-- Typed constants which can be changed by DINST ----------------------}
const TextNormW     : byte        = 003;      { normal color text window }
      OutNormW      : byte        = 122;    { normal color output window }
      TextHiW       : byte        = 098;    { color marking text window }
      OutIliW       : byte        = 023;   { color marking output window }
      TextHeaderW   : byte        = 112;    { color headline text window }
      OutHeaderW    : byte        = 123;   { color headline output window }
      Text_FrameW   : byte        = 004;      { color frame text window }
      Output_FrameW : byte        = 007;    { color frame output window }
      Frame_Line_T  : boolean     = true;               { frame type }
      CurrentDoubled : boolean    = true;     { current frame doubled }
      TextHeader    : string[ 70 ] = 'text window';        { text title }
      OutHeader     : string[ 70 ] = 'output window';    { output title }


{-- Global variables --------------------------------------------------}

var Normal_Frame,                         { attribute for normal frame }
    Current_Frame : byte                  { buffer for centered string }

begin
  lnum := ( SWidth - Length( was ) ) div 2 ;  { determine number of spaces }
  CStng := WinStRep( #32, lnum ) + was;          { insert leading spaces }
  CStng := CStng + WinStRep( #32, SWidth - Length( CStng ) ); { end spaces }
  Center := CStng;                                { return result }
end;
```

```
{*****************************************************************************
* M A I N   P R O G R A M                                                    *
*****************************************************************************}

begin
  {-- Initialization ---------------------------------------------------------}

    Uppr := true;                                      { upper window now active }
    ClrScr;                                                     { clear screen }
    WinHideCursor;                                                { hide cursor }

  {-- set frame attribute for window ---------------------------------------}

    if Frame_Line_T then                                           { line frame? }
      begin                                                               { yes }
        Normal_Frame := SIN_FR;                  { set attribute for normal frame }
        if CurrentDoubled then          { display current frame as double? }
          Current_Frame := DBL_FR        { yes, set attribute for double frame }
        else                              { no, set attribute for simple frame }
          Current_Frame := SIN_FR
      end
    else
      begin                             { no, block frame but no line frame }
        Normal_Frame := DOT_FR;                 { set attribute for normal frame }
        if CurrentDoubled then          { display current frame as double? }
          Current_Frame := FULL_FR        { yes, set attribute for full frame }
        else                              { no, set attribute for dot frame }
          Current_Frame := DOT_FR
      end;

  {-- construct first window -----------------------------------------------}

    WinColor( 0, 0, 79, 10, TextNormW );              { set color for TextNormW }
    WinFrame( 0, 0, 79, 10, Current_Frame, Text_FrameW );     { window frame }

    WinPrint( 1, 1, TextHeaderW, Center( 78, TextHeader ) );
    WinPrint( 2, 4, TextNormW, ' This is normal text in the text window');
    WinPrint( 2, 7, TextHiW,' This is highlighted text in the text window');

  {-- construct second window ----------------------------------------------}

    WinColor( 0, 11, 79, 24, OutNormW );              { set color for OutNormW }
    WinFrame( 0, 11, 79, 24, Normal_Frame, Output_FrameW );   { window frame }

    WinPrint( 1, 12, OutHeaderW, Center( 78, OutHeader ) );
    WinPrint( 2, 17, OutNormW, ' This is normal text in the output window' );
    WinPrint( 2, 22, OutHiW, ' This is highlighted text in the output window');

  {-- Loop : wait for activation of key and change of active        ---}
  {-- window until the user presses the ESC key                     ---}

    repeat                                                    { start of loop }
```

456

```
   repeat until keypressed;                              { wait for keypress }
   while keypressed do        { read all characters in the keyboard buffer }
      Key := readkey;
   if ( Key <> #027 ) then         { key is not ESC, so program does not end }
     begin

        {-- change active output window ----------------------------------}

        if Uppr then                          { upper window active until now? }
          begin                                 { yes, change frame attribute }
            WinFrame( 0, 0, 79, 10, Normal_Frame, Text_FrameW );
            WinFrame( 0, 11, 79, 24, Current_Frame, Output_FrameW );
          end
        else                                 { no, upper window active until now }
          begin                                    { change frame attribute }
            WinFrame( 0, 0, 79, 10, Current_Frame, Text_FrameW );
            WinFrame( 0, 11, 79, 24, Normal_Frame, Output_FrameW );
          end;
        Uppr := not Uppr;                          { activate other window }

     end;

   until ( Key = #027 );                     { user pressed ESC, end program }

   WinLineCursor;                              { switch on default cursor }
   ClrScr;                                              { clear screen }
   GotoXY( 0, 0 );          { move cursor to upper left corner of screen }
 end.
```

Before demonstrating how the constants from the TCA file described above become the typed constant addresses from the DEMO.PAS program, let's look at how TPIC obtained these addresses.

The keys to this is the MAP file. The command line version of the Turbo Pascal compiler (TPC.EXE) provides information about the assembly language program it created. TPC.EXE recognizes three types of MAP files, which are distinguished by the information they store and the parameter that controls their creation when the user calls TPC.

/GS Instructs the compiler to create a simple MAP file in which only the starting and ending addresses of the various program segments and their length are recorded. The names, precedence and sequence of the segments depend on the way in which the compiler converts the high level language program into assembly language. There are differences between various higher level languages and the available compilers.

/GP Instructs the compiler to create a MAP file in which the program segments and all public symbols and their addresses are recorded. Which symbols are public according to a higher level language compiler and, therefore, must be listed in this files, differs from one compiler to another. In addition to variables and typed constants, TPC also includes procedures and functions which are declared within a program.

/GD   Instructs the compiler to create a MAP file which contains all the information generated by /GP mode, as well as the starting address of the program and the offset addresses of all the program lines.

All three types of MAP files are stored as unformatted ASCII text. This means the programmer can access them using an editor or a word processing application. The interpretation of such a file by the program is more difficult than it would be if the file consisted of binary groups of data.

There's no problem in reading the data, as the TPIC program shows. TPIC receives its information about the positions of the typed constants from one of these MAP files.

Since TPIC cannot assume, during its call, that a MAP file is available for the source code about to be compiled, it creates its own file of this type and then calls the TPC command line compiler. TPIC passes the /GP parameter to TPC.EXE. This instructs the compiler to create a MAP file containing the addresses of all public constants. It uses the ExecPrg function from the SWAP unit (see Chapter 10) to accomplish part of this task. This ensures that the compiler reserves enough memory during execution.

After the program compiles successfully, TPIC generates a MAP file of the DEMO program, as shown in the following illustration:

```
Start   Stop    Length  Name        Class

00000H  00389H  0038AH  DEMO        CODE
00390H  00E4EH  00ABFH  WIN         CODE
00E50H  00EBBH  0006CH  DOS         CODE
00EC0H  014D2H  00613H  CRT         CODE
014E0H  01EFAH  00A1BH  SYSTEM      CODE
01F00H  0228BH  0038CH  DATA        DATA
02290H  0628FH  04000H  STACK       STACK
06290H  06290H  00000H  HEAP        HEAP


  Address           Publics by Value

0000:0000         CENTER
0000:0174         @
0039:003C         WINPUTCHAR
0039:008B         WINSETCURSOR
0039:00CC         WINDEFCURSOR
0039:00FD         WINHIDECURSOR
0039:0119         WINLINECURSOR
0039:0144         WINSETVIEW
0039:016C         CLRSCR
0039:0199         GOTOXY
```

```
0039:01CD        WINSTREP
0039:0212        WINPRINT
0039:029D        WINFILL
0039:0302        WINFRAME
0039:0457        WINCOLOR
0039:0809        WINSCROLLUP
0039:0AB5        @
00E5:0000        MSDOS
00E5:000B        INTR
00EC:0000        @
00EC:016D        TEXTMODE
00EC:0182        WINDOW
00EC:01C2        CLRSCR
00EC:01DC        CLREOL
00EC:01F0        INSLINE
00EC:01F5        DELLINE
00EC:0215        GOTOXY
00EC:0241        WHEREX
00EC:024D        WHEREY
00EC:0259        TEXTCOLOR
00EC:0273        TEXTBACKGROUND
00EC:028B        LOWVIDEO
00EC:0291        HIGHVIDEO
00EC:0297        NORMVIDEO
00EC:029E        DELAY
00EC:02C6        SOUND
00EC:02F3        NOSOUND
00EC:02FA        KEYPRESSED
00EC:030C        READKEY
00EC:032E        ASSIGNCRT
01F0:0002        TEXTNORMW
01F0:0003        OUTNORMW
01F0:0004        TEXTHIW
01F0:0005        OUTHIW
01F0:0006        TEXTHEADERW
01F0:0007        OUTHEADERW
01F0:0008        TEXT_FRAMEW
01F0:0009        OUTPUT_FRAMEW
01F0:000A        FRAME_LINE_T
01F0:000B        CURRENTDOUBLED
01F0:000C        TEXTHEADER
01F0:0054        OUTHEADER
01F0:009C        WRITE2VIEW
01F0:009D        SHADOWX
01F0:009E        SHADOWY
01F0:00D0        OVRCODELIST
01F0:00D2        OVRHEAPSIZE
01F0:00D4        OVRDEBUGPTR
01F0:00D8        OVRHEAPORG
01F0:00DA        OVRHEAPPTR
01F0:00DC        OVRHEAPEND
01F0:00DE        OVRLOADLIST
01F0:00E0        OVRDOSHANDLE
```

```
01F0:00E2          OVREMSHANDLE
01F0:00E4          HEAPORG
01F0:00E8          HEAPPTR
01F0:00EC          FREEPTR
01F0:00F0          FREEMIN
01F0:00F2          HEAPERROR
01F0:00F6          EXITPROC
01F0:00FA          EXITCODE
01F0:00FC          ERRORADDR
01F0:0100          PREFIXSEG
01F0:0102          STACKLIMIT
01F0:0104          INOUTRES
01F0:0106          RANDSEED
01F0:010A          FILEMODE
01F0:010B          TEST8087
01F0:010C          NORMAL_FRAME
01F0:010D          CURRENT_FRAME
01F0:010E          UPPR
01F0:010F          KEY
01F0:0110          COLOR
01F0:0111          VIOCARD
01F0:0112          NUMLINE
01F0:0113          NUMCOL
01F0:0130          CHECKBREAK
01F0:0131          CHECKEOF
01F0:0132          DIRECTVIDEO
01F0:0133          CHECKSNOW
01F0:0134          LASTMODE
01F0:0136          TEXTATTR
01F0:0138          WINDMIN
01F0:013A          WINDMAX
01F0:0144          INPUT
01F0:0244          OUTPUT
01F0:0344          SAVEINT00
01F0:0348          SAVEINT02
01F0:034C          SAVEINT1B
01F0:0350          SAVEINT23
01F0:0354          SAVEINT24
01F0:0358          SAVEINT34
01F0:035C          SAVEINT35
01F0:0360          SAVEINT36
01F0:0364          SAVEINT37
01F0:0368          SAVEINT38
01F0:036C          SAVEINT39
01F0:0370          SAVEINT3A
01F0:0374          SAVEINT3B
01F0:0378          SAVEINT3C
01F0:037C          SAVEINT3D
01F0:0380          SAVEINT3E
01F0:0384          SAVEINT3F
01F0:0388          SAVEINT75

Program entry point at 0000:0174
```

MAP file created from DEMO.PAS by TPC.EXE

The structure and content of this file are typical of all programs compiled with TPC. The file begins with a list containing the various program segments, sorted in ascending order according to their positions in the EXE file (and consequently, their order of execution in memory).

Instead of segment addresses, the starting addresses of the different segments should be accepted at distances from the start of the program. For example, the segment named SYSTEM begins at $14F0 bytes after the first program byte in the EXE file. This is also the distance between the beginning of this segment and the first byte of the program in memory at the time of its execution.

Notice that the individual segments always start at an address with an ending number of zero even when the previous segment wasn't large enough to carry up to this address. The individual segments always begin at an address divisible by 16 ($10). This means the compiler may waste up to 15 bytes filling in data between the end of the current segment and the beginning of the next segment. These fill bytes ensure that one of the segment registers can be loaded with the base address of the segment during execution of the program in memory. This is the only way to allow free and clear access to the different segments.

In addition to the individual names, TPC assigns each segment to a specific class of segments which perform certain tasks during execution.

The CODE segment stores the program code and the DATA segment stores the typed constants and variables. The STACK and HEAP segments contain the stack and heap data.

The HEAP segment is currently empty because it is only filled by New and GetMem during program execution. These procedures allocate memory areas.

For our purposes, we are only interested in the data segment because Turbo Pascal stores the desired typed constants in this segment. TPIC determines the starting address of the data segment from the segment list. This helps isolate the entries originating in the data segment from the list of the public symbols that follow the segment list. However, the addresses of these symbols in the symbol list are stored in segment/offset form, rather than as linear addresses.

If the data segment in the segment list has a starting address $1F10, as in DEMO, the addresses of the symbols in this segment from the symbol list have the form 01F1:xxxx. Here, the characters xxxx represent the offset address of the symbol in the data segment.

While the symbol list is being processed, all symbols can be filtered out of the data segment. However, it's still not known which of these symbols are variables and which are typed constants. Also, a separation should be performed to prevent too many symbols from being accepted into the constant file that will be created.

From the symbol list, the difference between the typed constants and the variables cannot be determined. So TPIC must access other information which was stored in the header of the file DEMO.EXE.

Addr.	Content	Type
$00	identification of an EXE program ($5A4D)	1 WORD
$02	file length MOD 512	1 WORD
$04	(file length DIV 512) + 1	1 WORD
$06	number of segment addresses to be passed	1 WORD
$08	size of the header in paragraphs	1 WORD
$0A	minimal number of additional paragraphs required	1 WORD
$0E	maximum number of additional paragraphs required	1 WORD
$10	content of SP register at program start	1 WORD
$12	checksum for the header of the EXE file	1 WORD
$14	content of IP register during program start	1 WORD
$16	start of the code segment in the EXE file	1 WORD
$18	address of the relocation table in the EXE file	1 WORD
$1A	overlay number	1 WORD
$1C	buffer storage	variable
$??	addresses of the segment addresses to be adjusted (relocation table)	variable
$??	program code and data	variable

An EXE file under MS-DOS

We have already mentioned that the border between the typed constants and the variables also mark the end of the EXE file, since neither the variables nor the stack and heap are stored in the EXE file. If the size of the program in the EXE file and the position where the data segment begins in the file is known, the number of bytes between the beginning of the data segment and the last stored byte in the EXE file can be calculated. The result is the number of bytes which are occupied by the typed constants in the data segment. Since they always start with the offset address 0 in the data segment, the number of bytes occupied by typed constants in the data segment also reflects the offset address in this segment where variables and typed constants meet. If this address is known, the symbols, contained within the data segment and also below this offset address, can easily be determined in the symbol list. These are the typed constants.

During the calculation of this imaginary border, TPIC accesses two pieces of information from the header of the EXE file shown above: the number of bytes stored in the EXE file (fields 1 and 2) and the size of the header of the EXE file. The latter provides the distance between the beginning of the EXE file and the beginning of the program. The difference of these two items provides the number of bytes which are occupied by the actual program (i.e., the program code and data). When the distance between the data segment DATA is subtracted from the beginning of the program, the result is the desired offset address.

We'll clarify this with an example from the DEMO program. Its header contains the following information:

Addr.	Content	Type
$00	identification of an EXE program ($5A4D)	$54AD
$02	file length MOD 512	$01B0
$04	(file length DIV 512) + 1	$0011
$06	number of segment addresses to be passed	
$08	size of the header in paragraphs	$0019

Content of the header of the DEMO.EXE file

With the information from the header of the EXE file, the following can be calculated:

```
    number of bytes in the EXE file:   ( $0011 - 1 ) * 512 + $01B0 = $21B0
-   size of the header of the EXE file:  $19 * 16             = $0190

    number of stored program bytes:                          = $2020
-   distance of DATA from the start of program:              = $1F10

    offset address of first variable:
=   $0110
```

According to the above calculation, the typed constants end at offset address $0110, where the variables start. This calculation is correct in principal, as the MAP file printed above shows. However, a small glitch, which cannot be prevented, occurs because TPC never terminates the EXE file immediately after the last typed constants. Instead, TPC fills the current paragraph. This moves the end of the stored program, under some circumstances, up to 15 bytes to the back. In the worst case, 15 variables, which consist of one byte, each are considered typed constants, and entries are prepared for them in the constant file. This small inaccuracy can be accepted since the presence of the TPIC constants for these variables doesn't affect their use.

However, among the typed constants, there are many that aren't defined by the program that will be configured, but originate in the included units. In the MAP file above, there are, for example, the typed constants, from the system unit, named OVR..., which are clearly visible. Depending on the number of included units, there may be many of these typed constants unnecessarily increasing the size of the constant file. TPIC is therefore interested in eliminating constants that don't belong to the actual program by not including them in the constant file.

This isn't easy to do because the MAP file doesn't contain any information that indicates the origins of the various constants. TPIC uses a trick here by recalling the Turbo Pascal compiler. This time, TPC compiles a second program called TPIC$$$$.PAS, generated by TPIC. This program contains the Uses command line from the original program and a blank program heading.

The TPIC$$$$.PAS source code created for the DEMO program looks like this:

```
program TPIC$$$$;
USES CRT,WIN;
begin
end.
```

The dummy program TPIC$$$$.PAS created by TPIC

TPIC lets the compiler create a MAP file for this file, in which all public symbols are recorded. This MAP file contains the typed constants and variables from the various units, but the symbols from the program to be processed are missing because they do not appear in the dummy program. The MAP file for TPIC$$$$ looks like this:

Start	Stop	Length	Name	Class
00000H	0001BH	0001CH	TPICDEMO	CODE
00020H	00786H	00767H	WIN	CODE
00790H	007FBH	0006CH	DOS	CODE
00800H	00E12H	00613H	CRT	CODE
00E20H	0183AH	00A1BH	SYSTEM	CODE
01840H	01B15H	002D6H	DATA	DATA
01B20H	05B1FH	04000H	STACK	STACK
05B20H	05B20H	00000H	HEAP	HEAP

Address	Publics by Value
0000:0000	@
0002:003C	WINSETVIEW
0002:0064	WINSTREP
0002:00A9	WINPRINT
0002:0134	WINFILL
0002:04B1	WINSCROLLUP
0002:075D	@
0079:0000	MSDOS
0079:000B	INTR
0080:0000	@
0080:016D	TEXTMODE

```
0080:0182        WINDOW
0080:01C2        CLRSCR
0080:01DC        CLREOL
0080:01F0        INSLINE
0080:01F5        DELLINE
0080:0215        GOTOXY
0080:0241        WHEREX
0080:024D        WHEREY
0080:0259        TEXTCOLOR
0080:0273        TEXTBACKGROUND
0080:028B        LOWVIDEO
0080:0291        HIGHVIDEO
0080:0297        NORMVIDEO
0080:029E        DELAY
0080:02C6        SOUND
0080:02F3        NOSOUND
0080:02FA        KEYPRESSED
0080:030C        READKEY
0080:032E        ASSIGNCRT
0184:0002        WRITE2VIEW
0184:0003        SHADOWX
0184:0004        SHADOWY
0184:001E        OVRCODELIST
0184:0020        OVRHEAPSIZE
0184:0022        OVRDEBUGPTR
0184:0026        OVRHEAPORG
0184:0028        OVRHEAPPTR
0184:002A        OVRHEAPEND
0184:002C        OVRLOADLIST
0184:002E        OVRDOSHANDLE
0184:0030        OVREMSHANDLE
0184:0032        HEAPORG
0184:0036        HEAPPTR
0184:003A        FREEPTR
0184:003E        FREEMIN
0184:0040        HEAPERROR
0184:0044        EXITPROC
0184:0048        EXITCODE
0184:004A        ERRORADDR
0184:004E        PREFIXSEG
0184:0050        STACKLIMIT
0184:0052        INOUTRES
0184:0054        RANDSEED
0184:0058        FILEMODE
0184:0059        TEST8087
0184:005A        COLOR
0184:005B        VIOCARD
0184:005C        NUMLINE
0184:005D        NUMCOL
0184:007A        CHECKBREAK
0184:007B        CHECKEOF
0184:007C        DIRECTVIDEO
0184:007D        CHECKSNOW
```

```
0184:007E        LASTMODE
0184:0080        TEXTATTR
0184:0082        WINDMIN
0184:0084        WINDMAX
0184:008E        INPUT
0184:018E        OUTPUT
0184:028E        SAVEINT00
0184:0292        SAVEINT02
0184:0296        SAVEINT1B
0184:029A        SAVEINT23
0184:029E        SAVEINT24
0184:02A2        SAVEINT34
0184:02A6        SAVEINT35
0184:02AA        SAVEINT36
0184:02AE        SAVEINT37
0184:02B2        SAVEINT38
0184:02B6        SAVEINT39
0184:02BA        SAVEINT3A
0184:02BE        SAVEINT3B
0184:02C2        SAVEINT3C
0184:02C6        SAVEINT3D
0184:02CA        SAVEINT3E
0184:02CE        SAVEINT3F
0184:02D2        SAVEINT75
```

```
Program entry point at 0000:0000
```

The MAP file of the TPIC$$$.PAS program created by TPIC

TPIC does this by comparing the first MAP file with the second MAP file, which only leaves the symbols which don't appear in the second MAP file. The typed constants from the program to be processed are almost the only thing that remains. We used the word "almost" because not all typed constants from the various units in the second MAP file are recognized.

This is related to the intelligence of the compiler's internal linker, which only accepts the symbols actually used in the program. In addition, the function and procedure calls addressed by the typed constants in the unit, called by the dummy program, are missing. Because of this, many of these constants are eliminated by the linker and do not appear in the MAP file. Therefore, they cannot be removed from the constant file that will be created.

As the listing of the constant file created for DEMO.PAS demonstrates, the typed constants can be removed from the standard units. TPIC does its job thoroughly, considering that out of the 74 data segment symbols listed in the first MAP file, only the remaining 17 symbols are accepted into the constant file.

The first of these constants (DSEG_START) indicates the starting address of the data segment in the EXE file. During later accesses of this file through the TPINST unit, this constant must be passed to the unit to permit access to the data segment in the EXE file.

A user of TPIC may wish that some typed constants from a certain unit could be passed to the constant file. Then the user would be able to configure these constants through the configuration program. TPIC provides this capability by inserting a plus character (+), followed by the name of the affected unit as a parameter during the program call. You can enter this parameter several times to exclude multiple units from being removed from the constant list.

TPIC also recognizes an additional command line parameter, which can also be used as often as necessary. This is the "/" parameter. Instead of processing the / parameter, TPIC passes it to TPIC unchanged. This allows you additional control over the compilation of the program to be processed. The call:

```
tpic oops /dSWAP +dos
```

creates a constant file for a program named OOPS.PAS, in which the typed constants from the DOS unit are also passed to this file. In addition, the parameter /dSWAP is passed to TPC during its call, which defines the constant SWAP for the conditional compilation of the program.

The source listing of TPIC.PAS in the following pages doesn't have to be documented extensively because you will encounter it more as a user than as a programmer. If you want to modify certain details for your special needs, the program uses standard algorithms, which allow quick and easy changes. The algorithms always follow the framework of standard application programming. As with all the other listings in this book, you can find this source code on the companion diskettes which accompany this book.

```
{**************************************************************************
 *   TPIC : creates a file with the addresses of all typed constants from  *
 *          the program indicated, for additional processing by TPINST     *
 **-------------------------------------------------------------------**
 *   Author        : MICHAEL TISCHER                                       *
 *   developed on  : 06/17/1989                                            *
 *   last update on : 03/05/1990                                           *
 *   call          : TPIC program name [/Parameter] [+Unit]                *
 *                    Example: TPIC DEMO +CRT,+WIN                         *
 *                     - Parameters indicated are passed to the Turbo      *
 *                       Pascal compiler during program compilation.       *
 *                     - Normally only the constants from the program      *
 *                       indicated are accepted in the constant file.      *
 *                       Constants named by units called are also listed   *
 *                       in the constant file.                             *
 *                     - The constant file created has the program's name  *
 *                       with an extension of .TCA                         *
 **************************************************************************}

{$M 20480, 0, 0 }                    { no heap, but large stack for recursions }
{$V-}                                 { ignore errors during stack processing }
{$I-}                                       { no run-time error with I/O errors }

program Tpic;

uses Dos,                                            { Turbo Pascal DOS unit }
     Swap;   { Turbo Pascal System Programming SWAP unit ( see Chapter 10 ) }

{-- declaration of global constants and variables ------------------------}

const MAX_DATA    = 600;                 { maximum number of typed constants }
      LBL_LEN     = 30;                          { maximum length of a label }
      HELPNAME    = 'TPIC$$$$';               { file name for dummy program }
      MAP_EXT     = '.MAP';                       { extension of the map file }
      EXE_EXT     = '.EXE';                       { extension of the EXE file }
      CST_EXT     = '.TCA';                  { extension of the constant file }
      PREFIX      = 'TPIC_';                      { prefix of constant name }
      DEFAULT_EXT = '.PAS';                  { extension of the source file }
      INTERNL_OPT = ' /GP ';   { internal compiler options ( for map file ) }
      COMPILER    = 'tpc.exe';                   { file name of the compiler }
      DSEG_NAME   = 'DSEG_START';       { name for beginning of data segment }

type AnyString = String[ 255 ];                              { any string }
     CharSet   = set of char;                               { for DelCInS }

     DATATyp   = record                        { describes a typed constant }
                   Name   : String[ LBL_LEN ];           { variable name }
                   Offset : word;       { offset address of the var. in DSEG }
                 end;

     DATAField = record                        { data field construction }
                   Amount : word;         { number of data records used }
                   DataA  : array [ 1..MAX_DATA ] of DATATyp;
```

```
                 end;

var Name,                                         { program name input }
    Extension,                          { extension of the source file }
    Options,                                { compiler options input }
    Units        : AnyString;                  { units to be handled }
    Field        : DATAField;        { data field for typed constants }
    LenExeHeader : word;             { size of header for the EXE file }
    StartDataSeg : word;                { beginning of data segment }
    Dummy        : boolean;          { dummy for second call of compiler }

{**************************************************************************
*  Exist : tests whether a file is available in the current directory.   *
**----------------------------------------------------------------------**
*  Input : FILE_NAME = Name of the file to be found                      *
**************************************************************************}

function Exist( File_Name : string ) : boolean;

var dummy : string;                           { stores result of FSearch }

begin
  dummy := FSearch( File_Name, '' );{ search for file in current directory }
  Exist := ( dummy <> '' );                           { file found? }
end;

{**************************************************************************
*  StUpCase : converts a string into upper case letters.                 *
**----------------------------------------------------------------------**
*  Input : SOURCE = string to be converted                               *
*  Output : converted string                                             *
**************************************************************************}

function StUpCase( Source : String ) : String;

var i : byte;                                         { loop counter }

begin
  {-- process string and convert each character separately ---------------}

  for i := 1 to length( Source ) do
    Source[ i ] := UpCase( Source[ i ] );

  StUpCase := Source;                          { return string to caller }
end;
```

```
{*****************************************************************************
 *  DelCInS : deletes a group of characters from a string.                   *
 **-------------------------------------------------------------------------**
 *  Input : SOURCE  = string to be processed                                 *
 *          CHARNUM = number of characters to be deleted                     *
 *  Output : converted string                                                *
 *****************************************************************************}

function DelCInS ( Source : String; CharNum : CharSet ) : String;

var i : BYTE;                                          { loop counter }

begin
  i := 1;                                   { start loop at first character }

  while ( i <= length( Source ) ) do        { process string to the end  }
    if ( Source[ i ] in CharNum ) then      { should character be deleted? }
      Delete( Source, i, 1 )                          { yes, delete }
    else
      Inc( i );                             { no, go to next character }

  DelCInS := Source;                                  { return result }
end;


{*****************************************************************************
 *  HtoW : converts a hexadecimal character string into binary notation      *
 *         and returns it as WORD.                                           *
 **-------------------------------------------------------------------------**
 *  Input : SOURCE = Hex string to be converted                              *
 *  Output : converted word                                                  *
 *****************************************************************************}

function HToW( Source : String ) : word;

var i   : byte;                                       { loop counter }
    Hex : word;                                    { value of the digit }

begin
  {-- remove unimportant characters -----------------------------------------}

  Source := StUpCase( DelCInS( Source, [ '$', #32 ] ) );
  Hex := 0;                                         { initialize value }

  {-- process complete string and compute value ----------------------------}

  for i := 1 to length( Source ) do
    begin
      Hex := Hex shl 4;                               { value of digit }
      if ( Source[ i ] >= 'A' ) then                  { letter? }
        inc( Hex, Ord( Source[ i ] ) - 55 )           { yes }
      else                                       { must be number }
        inc( Hex , Ord( Source[ i ] ) - 48 );
    end;
```

```
     HToW := Hex;                                   { return result }
end;

{**************************************************************************
*  LtoH : converts a Longint into a hexadecimal character string.        *
**----------------------------------------------------------------------**
*  Input : LI = Longint to convert                                       *
*          DPLACES = number of digits in result                          *
*  Output : hexadecimal character string                                 *
**************************************************************************}

function LToH( Li : longint; DPlaces : byte ) : String;

var BVal   : byte;                                { values of 4 bits }
    HexNum : char;                   { hexadecimal numbers '0'..'9','A'..'F' }
    HexStr : AnyString;                              { result string }

begin
  HexStr := '';                              { initialize result string }

  {-- loop creates the result string from right to left ------------------}

  while ( Li > 0 ) do                              { all bits processed? }
    begin                                                     { no }
      BVal := Li and $0F;                   { produce hexadecimal number }
      if ( BVal < 10 ) then            { is hexadecimal number a number? }
        HexNum := chr( BVal + 48 )     { yes, convert number to character }
      else
        HexNum := Chr( BVal + 55 );                   { calculate $A..$F }
      HexStr := HexNum + HexStr;
      Li := Li shr 4;                             { process next 4 bits }
    end;

  {-- fill result string to pre-set length -------------------------------}

  while ( length( HexStr ) < DPlaces ) do
    HexStr := '0' + HexStr;          { bring hex string to desired length }

  HexStr[ 1 ] := '$';                         { first character is $ }
  LToH := HexStr;                                   { return result }
end;

{**************************************************************************
*  Removes_Units : removes the unit-names which are passed in the        *
*                  second String from the first String                   *
**----------------------------------------------------------------------**
*  Input : SOURCE   = String from which the units are removed            *
*          REMOVEES = String with the names of the units to be removed   *
*  Output : converted string                                             *
**************************************************************************}

function Removes_Units( Source, Removees : String ) : String;
```

```
   var SPos,                               { position of the entry in SOURCE }
       EPos        : word;        { position of the first comma in REMOVEES }
       Current_Unit : string;          { destination string for processing }

 begin
   EPos := Pos( ',', Removees );              { did Removees get an entry ? }

   {-- process all entries in Removees and remove from source --------------}

   while ( EPos > 0 ) do                             { remove another unit? }
     begin                                                          { yes }
       Current_Unit := Copy( Removees, 1, EPos - 1 );{ get name of the unit }
       Delete( Removees, 1, EPos );           { remove from Removees string }
       SPos := Pos( Current_Unit, Source );    { find unit in source string }
       IF ( SPos > 0 ) then                                     { found? }
         Delete( Source, SPos, length( Current_Unit ) + 1 );   { yes, erase }
       EPos := Pos( ',',  Removees ); { another unit waiting to be removed? }
     end;

   {-- if a comma is at end of Source, it must be converted to a semicolon -}

   IF Source[ length( Source ) ] = ',' then { prep last character of Source }
     Source[ length( Source ) ] := ';';               { prepare result }
   Removes_Units := Source;                             { return result }
 end;

{**************************************************************************
*  DelComment : removes comments from a Pascal line                       *
**-----------------------------------------------------------------------**
*  Input : SOURCE = Pascal line                                           *
*  Output : the Pascal line with comments removed                         *
*  Info    : if the line has a comment start character, but no comment     *
*            end character, a comment start character is entered as last   *
*            character of the result string. Even comments stretching over *
*            several lines can be removed in this manner.                  *
***************************************************************************}

procedure DelComment( var Source : String );

var Start,                       { position of the character for comment start }
    EndC  : byte;                { position of the character for comment end }

begin
   {-- process comments in brackets ---------------------------------------}

   Start := Pos( '{', Source );   { position of the comment start character }
   if ( Start > 0 ) then                                { comment present? }
     begin                          { yes, search for comment end character }
       EndC := Pos( '}', Source ); { position of the comment end character }
       if ( EndC > 0 ) then                 { does comment end in this line? }
         Delete( Source, Start, EndC - Start + 1 )    { yes, delete comment }
       else
```

```
          Source := Copy( Source, 1, Start );        { no, delete comment end }
      end

  {-- process comments which start with '(*' ---------------------------------}

    else
      begin
        Start := Pos( '(*', Source ); { position of comment start character }
        if ( Start > 0 ) then                            { comment present }
          begin                            { yes, find comment end character }
            EndC := Pos( '*)', Source ); { position of comment end character }
            if ( EndC > 0 ) then             { does comment end in this line? }
              Delete( Source, Start, EndC - Start + 2 )      { delete comment }
            else
              Source := Copy( Source, 1, Start + 1 );   { no, delete comment }
          end;
      end;
end;

{*************************************************************************
*  Read_Command_Line : reads the command line parameters, separates them  *
*                      by file names, units and parameters and assigns    *
*                      them to the proper global variables                *
**---------------------------------------------------------------------**
*  Input : none                                                          *
*  Globals : Name/W, Extension/W, Options/W, Units/W                      *
*************************************************************************}

procedure Read_Command_Line;

var i   : byte;                                          { loop counter }
    Arg : string;   { the command line parameter currently being processed }

begin
  {-- set default values ----------------------------------------------}

  Options   := '';                               { no compiler options }
  Units     := '';                                { no units omitted }
  Extension := DEFAULT_EXT;                        { preset file extension }

  {-- read and process command line parameters -----------------------}

  for i := 1 to ParamCount do
    begin
      Arg := ParamStr( i );                    { get parameter in variable }
      case Arg[1] of                               { read first letter }
        '/' : {--------- attach compiler directive to string with options }
              Options := Options + Arg + #32;

        '+' :       {- unit, attach name separated by comma to unit string }
              Units := Units + StUpCase(Copy(Arg, 2, length(Arg)-1) + ',');
        else                                 { must be name of source file }
          Name := StUpCase( Arg );       { change name to upper case letters }
```

473

```
        end;
      end;

    {-- name of source file indicated, detach extension --------------------}

    i := Pos( '.', Name );                          { find start of extension }
    if ( i > 0 ) then                                      { found period? }
      begin                                         { yes, store extension }
        Extension := Copy( Name, i, length( Name ) - i + 1);
        Delete( Name, i, length( Name ) - i + 1 );
      end;
  end;


{******************************************************************************
 *  DelDat : deletes a file whose path and name is known                      *
 **-------------------------------------------------------------------------**
 *  Input : DATNAME = name of file to be deleted                              *
 ******************************************************************************}

procedure DelDat( DatName : string );

var Regs : Registers;                  { processor register for interrupt call }

begin
  Regs.AH := $41;                               { function number for "delete file" }
  DatName[ byte( DatName[0] )+1 ] := #0;            { attach NUL character }
  Regs.DX := Ofs( DatName )+1;                       { address of name in  }
  Regs.DS := Seg( DatName );                         { the DS:DX registers }
  MsDos( Regs );                                     { call DOS interrupt $21 }
end;


{******************************************************************************
 *  Compile_It : compiles the indicated file by calling the command line      *
 *               version of the Turbo Pascal compiler                         *
 **-------------------------------------------------------------------------**
 *  Input : NAME = name of the source file                                    *
 *        : EXE  = extension of the source file                               *
 *        : OPTS = compiler options                                           *
 *  Output : TRUE if compiler could be called, otherwise FALSE                *
 ******************************************************************************}

function Compile_It( Name, Ext, Opts : String ) : boolean;

var CPath  : string;                   { complete Turbo compiler path and name }
    Dummy : byte;                              { function result of ExecPrg }

begin
  {-- determine exact path of the command line Turbo Pascal compiler ------}

  CPath := fSearch( COMPILER, GetEnv( 'PATH' ));
  if ( CPath <> '' ) then                              { compiler found? }
    begin                                                    { yes }
      {-- call command line compiler with the ExecPrg       ------------}
```

```
      {-- function from the SWAP unit                      ------------}

      writeln;
      Dummy := ExecPrg( CPath + ' ' + Name + Ext + #32 + Opts );
      writeln;
      Compile_It := TRUE;
    end
  else                                { Turbo Pascal compiler not found }
    Compile_It := FALSE;
end;


{***************************************************************************
 *  CreateDummyPrg : creates a text file consisting of a blank program    *
 *                   heading and a USES statement from the program being   *
 *                   compiled. When this program is compiled, you can      *
 *                   determine the typed constants in the compiled program *
 *                   by comparing the program with this code.              *
 **-----------------------------------------------------------------------**
 *  Input : none                                                          *
 *  Info    : the file created has the name HELPNAME                       *
 *  Globals : Name/R, Extension/R, Units/R                                 *
 ***************************************************************************}

procedure CreateDummyPrg;

var Uses_Line,                         { line for storage of user input }
    CLine       : AnyString;                   { currently read line }
    Source_File,                       { source file with program text }
    Dest_File    : Text;             { destination file to be created }
    AuxFlg       : boolean;                        { destination flag }

begin
  {-- open source and destination file -------------------------------}

  Assign( Source_File, Name + Extension );
  Assign( Dest_File  , HELPNAME + Extension );
  Reset( Source_File );                      { open source file for reading }
  Rewrite( Dest_File );                       { create new destination file }

  {-- process source file until USES statement is found ------------------}

  AuxFlg := eof( Source_File );
  while not AuxFlg do                              { search for USES line }
    begin
      Readln( Source_File, CLine );
      AuxFlg := ( Pos( 'USES ', StUpCase( CLine ) ) > 0 ) or
                eof( Source_File );
    end;
  CLine := StUpCase( CLine );

  {-- determine names of units listed with USES statement ---}

  if ( Pos( 'USES ', CLine ) > 0 ) then               { found USES line? }
```

```
    begin                                                  { yes }
      Delete( CLine, Pos( 'USES ', CLine ), 5 );   { remove USES statement }
      Uses_Line := DelCinS( CLine, [ #32 ] );           { delete all spaces }
      DelComment( Uses_Line );                            { delete comments }
      while ( Pos( ';', CLine ) = 0 ) do { detected end of USES statement? }
        begin                              { no, continue to read until ; }
          Readln( Source_File, CLine );
          Uses_Line := Uses_Line + DelCInS( CLine, [ #32 ]);
          DelComment( Uses_Line );                   { delete commentary }
        end;
      Uses_Line := StUpCase( Uses_Line );   { convert to upper case letters }
      Uses_Line := 'USES '+                         { filter out units }
                  Removes_Units( Uses_Line, Units );
    end
  else                                         { no USES statement found }
    Uses_Line := '';


  {-- write dummy Pascal program into destination file ------------------}

  Writeln( Dest_File, 'program TPIC_' + Name + ';' );      { program name }
  Writeln( Dest_File, Uses_Line + 'begin end.');  { empty program heading }

  Close( Dest_File );                      { close source and destination file }
  Close( Source_File );
end;


{*****************************************************************************
 *  GetExeInfos: determines the address of the last program byte stored in  *
 *            the EXE file and therefore the address of the registers       *
 *            where typed constants access the variables.                   *
 *            In addition, the EXE file heading's size is calculated.       *
 **-----------------------------------------------------------------------**
 *  Input : AEND = accepts last address of the EXE file                     *
 *          SIZE = stores size of the EXE file's heading                    *
 *  Globals : Name/R                                                        *
 *****************************************************************************}

procedure GetExeInfos( var AEnd : longint; var Size : word );

type Exe_Head = record                 { construction of an EXE file heading }
               Id,                          { identification-code $5A4D }
               LengthLo,                       { file length mod 512     }
               LengthHi,                       { file length div 512 + 1 }
               SegNum,    { number of segment addresses to be relocated }
               Header   : word;     { size of the heading in paragraphs }
             end;

var EFile  : file of Exe_Head;                             { EXE file }
    ExeHdng : Exe_Head;                  { data record for EXE file heading }

begin
  {-- open file and read header information ------------------------------}
```

```
      Assign( EFile, Name + EXE_EXT );
      Reset( EFile );                          { file pointer to beginning of file }
      Read( EFile, ExeHdng);                   { store header in ExeHdng variable }

      {-- read information from EXE file heading -----------------------------}

      with ExeHdng do
        begin
          Size := Header;
          AEnd := longint( LengthHi - 1 ) * longint( 512 ) +
                  longint( LengthLo ) - longint( Header shl 4 );
        end;

      Close( EFile );                                          { close EXE file }
    end;

{*****************************************************************************
 *  ExtractTypedConst : Extracts the typical constants with length and      *
 *                      address from the map file of the source file.       *
 **-----------------------------------------------------------------------**
 *  Input : none                                                            *
 *  Output : Segment address of the data segment                            *
 *  Globals : LenExeHeader/W, Field/RW                                      *
 *****************************************************************************}

function ExtractTypedConst : word;

var EndConst    : longint;{ address as separator between constants and var }
    MapFile     : text;                     { map file created by the compiler }
    CLine,                                          { current line read }
    DataSegment : AnyString;   { segment address of the data segment (hex) }
    DSeg,                                     { segment address ( binary ) }
    DOffs       : word;                       { offset address (binary ) }
    Onward      : boolean;                      { exit condition for loop }

begin
  {-- open MAP file created by compiler & search for data segment address -}

  GetExeInfos( EndConst, LenExeHeader );                    { determine info }
  Assign( MapFile, Name + MAP_EXT );                       { open MAP file }
  Reset( MapFile );

  repeat                  { search for line with information on data segment }
    Readln( MapFile, CLine );
  until ( pos( 'DATA', CLine ) > 0 );

  {-- line found, extract starting address of the data segments ----------}

  DataSegment := Copy( CLine, 1, Pos( 'H', CLine ) - 2 );{ extract segment }
  DataSegment := DelCInS( DataSegment, [ #32 ] );                { address }
  DSeg := HToW( DATASegment );                   { segment address ( decimal ) }

  {-- process until the first entry in the map file data segment ---------}
```

477

```
      repeat                                      { find data segment }
        Readln( MapFile, CLine );
      until Pos( DataSegment + ':', CLine ) > 0;


      {-- read typed constants from the data segment -------------------------}

      Onward := TRUE;                       { exit status still not reached }
      with Field  do                        { process the global data field }
        while Onward do
          begin
            {-- get offset address of the entry and test for existence in -----}
            {-- EXE file. If so, it represents a typed constant          -----}

            DOffs := HTOW( Copy( CLine, Pos( ':', CLine ) + 1, 4 ) );
            if ( longint( DSeg ) shl 4 + longint( Doffs ) <= EndConst ) then
              begin                                { is a typed constant }
                Inc( Amount );                     { number of entries found }
                DataA[ Amount ].Offset  := DOffs;         { store address }

                {-- isolate name and store -----------------------------------}

                Delete( CLine, 1, Pos( ':', CLine ) + 5 );    { delete address }
                DataA[ Amount ].Name := DelCInS( CLine, [ #32 ] );

                {-- read next line and determine if it contains an entry ------}
                {-- from the data segment                              ------}

                Readln( MapFile, CLine );
                Onward := Pos( DataSegment + ':', CLine ) > 0;
              end
            else                         { entry after end of EXE file --> variable }
              Onward := FALSE;
          end;

    Close( MapFile );                             { close map file again }
    ExtractTypedConst := DSeg;  { return segment address of the data segment }
  end;


{*****************************************************************************
 *  Sort : Sorts the array of typed constants in ascending order by name     *
 **-------------------------------------------------------------------------**
 *  Input : none                                                             *
 *  Globals : Field/RW                                                       *
 *  Info    : Implements recursive quicksorts, and converts remaining        *
 *            recursions into iterations                                     *
 *****************************************************************************}

procedure Sort;

{-- Local recursive sort procedure, sorts the field portion between -------}
{-- the field borders left and right                              -------}
```

```
procedure PartSort( left, right  : word );

var i, j   : word;                              { left and right index }
    Middle,                                         { middle element }
    Exchge : DATATyp;              { auxiliary variable for exchange }

begin
  with Field do                    { process the global data field }
    repeat
       Middle := DataA[ ( left + right ) div 2 ];     { comparison element }
       i := left;
       j := right;

       {-- place comparison element at its final position ------------------}

       repeat
         while ( DataA[ i ].Name < Middle.Name ) do
           Inc( i );

         while ( DataA[ j ].Name > Middle.Name ) do
           Dec( j );

         if ( i <= j ) then
           begin
             Exchge := DataA[ i ];
             DataA[ i ] := DataA[ j ];
             DataA[ j ] := Exchge;
             Inc( i );
             Dec( j );
           end;
       until ( i > j );

       if left < j then             { sort left part interval with recursive }
         PartSort( left, j );                             { call }

       Left := i;                   { sort right part during next execution }

    until left >= right;                      { end status of recursion }
end;

{-- Start of the Sort procedure -----------------------------------------}

begin
  PartSort( 1, Field.Amount );                   { call of recursion }
end;
```

```
{*****************************************************************************
 *  DeleteE : deletes an entry from the field containing the names and      *
 *            addresses of the typed constants from the program in process  *
 **------------------------------------------------------------------------**
 *  Input : TY_CONAME = Name of the typical constant to be deleted          *
 *  Info  : Found constant is marked as deleted by storing 0 in Segment     *
 *  Globals : Field/RW                                                      *
 *****************************************************************************}

procedure DeleteE( Ty_CoName : String );

var middle,            { middle of the partial interval still to be searched }
    left,                         { left border of the partial interval }
    right  : word;                { right border of the partial interval }

begin
  with Field do
    begin
      left  := 1;                                  { initialize left edge }
      right := Amount;                             { initialize right edge }

      {-- search the partial interval until the element is found, or the --}
      {-- length of the partial interval is zero                        --}

      repeat
        middle := ( left + right ) div 2;   { calculate middle of interval }
        if ( DataA[ middle ].Name < Ty_CoName ) then
          left := middle + 1            { element is in the right interval }
        else if ( DataA[ middle ].Name > Ty_CoName  ) then
          right := middle - 1;            { element is in the left interval }
      until ( DataA[ middle ].Name = Ty_CoName ) or ( left > right );

      {-- delete a matching element if found                       -----}

      if ( DataA[ middle ].Name = Ty_CoName ) then        { element found? }
        DataA[ middle ].Offset := 65535;              { yes, mark as deleted }
    end;
end;


{*****************************************************************************
 *  Differnce : deletes all typed constants in the data field also found    *
 *              in the map file of the dummy program created above          *
 **------------------------------------------------------------------------**
 *  Input : none                                                           *
 *  Globals : Name/R, Extension/R, Field/RW                                *
 *****************************************************************************}

procedure Differnce;

var MapFile      : Text;        { contains map file of the destination file }
    DATASegment,                { data segment of the destination file ( hex ) }
    CLine        : AnyString;                      { currently read line }
```

```
begin
{-- open map file created by compiler, search for addr. of data segment --}

  Assign( MapFile, HELPNAME + MAP_EXT );                    { open map file }
  Reset( MapFile );           { file pointer to the beginning of the file }

  repeat                   { search for line with data segment indication }
    Readln( MapFile, CLine );
  until pos( 'DATA', CLine ) > 0;

  {-- extract data segment address, prepare and search -------------------}

  DataSegment := Copy( CLine, 1, Pos( 'H', CLine ) - 2 );{ segment address }
  DataSegment := DelCInS( DataSegment, [ #32 ] );               { extract }
  repeat                                           { find data segment }
    Readln( MapFile, CLine );
  until Pos( DataSegment + ':', CLine ) > 0;

  {-- read typed constant and delete from data field ---------------------}

  while pos( DataSegment + ':', CLine ) > 0 do         { found another? }
    begin                                                        { yes }
      Delete( CLine, 1, Pos( ':', CLine ) + 5 );       { isolate name }
      CLine := DelCInS( CLine, [ #32 ] );              { delete spaces }
      DeleteE( CLine );                        { delete entry from data field }
      Readln( MapFile, CLine );                        { read next line }
    end;
end;

{**************************************************************************
*  Create_Cst_File : creates a text file with names and addresses of all  *
*                    typed constants, stored in FIELD and undeleted       *
**----------------------------------------------------------------------**
*  Input : none                                                           *
*  Globals : Name/R, Extension/R, Field/R                                 *
**************************************************************************}

procedure Create_Cst_File;

var CFile    : Text;                               { the file to be created }
    i        : word;                                      { loop counter }
    DecAddr  : longint;          { decimal offset address in the EXE file }

begin
  Assign( CFile, Name + CST_EXT );                    { create constant file }
  Rewrite( CFile );

  Writeln(CFile,'{ Names and addresses of typed constants in file',
          #13#10, Name, Extension, ' after compilation }');

  {-- compute starting address of data segment and write it as a constant -}
  {-- named "DSEG_START" as first entry in the file                      -}
```

481

```
      DecAddr := LongInt( StartDataSeg ) shl 4 + Longint( LenExeHeader ) * 16;
      Writeln( CFile, 'const ', PREFIX, DSEG_NAME, '':40 - length( DSEG_NAME ),
                   '= ' , DecAddr:10 , '; { ', LToH( DecAddr, 6 ), ' }' );

      {-- display names and addresses of all typed constants -----------------}

      for i := 1 to Field.Amount do                 { process field with data }
        with Field.DataA[ i ] do                    { process data record I }
          if ( Offset < 65535 )   then              { delete data record? }
            begin                                    { no, display }
              Writeln( CFile, '        ', PREFIX, Name, '':40 - length( Name ),
                       '= ',  Offset:10, '; { ', LToH( Offset, 6 ), ' }'   );
            end;

      Close( CFile );                                { close constant file }
    end;

    {******************************************************************************
     *  M A I N   P R O G R A M                                                   *
     ******************************************************************************}

    begin
      {-- read command line parameter -----------------------------------------}

      writeln( #13#10'TPIC V1.0  -   (c) 1989 by MICHAEL TISCHER' );
      Read_Command_Line;

      if ( Name = '' ) then                          { file name indicated? }
        begin
          writeln( 'Attention! No filename indicated.');
          Exit;                                      { end program with error code }
        end;

      if ( Exist( Name + Extension ) = FALSE ) then  { does file exist? }
        begin
          writeln( 'Attention! File indicated not found.');
          Exit;                                      { end program with error code }
        end;

      writeln( 'Pass #1 : Compiling program' ); { compile using Turbo compiler }

      {- If a map file exists for the indicated file, delete before compiling -}

      if ( Exist( Name + MAP_EXT ) ) then            { does file already exist? }
        DelDat( Name + MAP_EXT );                    { yes, delete }
      if ( Compile_It( Name, Extension, Options + INTERNL_OPT ) = FALSE ) then
        begin
          writeln( 'Attention! command line compiler TPC.EXE not in path.');
          Exit;                                      { end program with error code }
        end;

      if ( Exist( Name + MAP_EXT ) = FALSE ) then    { create map file? }
        begin                                        { no }
```

```
        writeln( 'Attention! Error during compilation.');
        Exit;                               { end program with error code }
     end;

  writeln( 'Pass #2 : Creating dummy program ');    { create dummy program }
  CreateDummyPrg;

  writeln( 'Pass #3 : Compiling dummy program ' ); { compile dummy program }
  Dummy := Compile_It( HELPNAME, Extension, Options + INTERNL_OPT );
  if ( Exist( HELPNAME + EXE_EXT ) = FALSE ) then     { EXE file created? }
    begin                                                           { no }
       writeln( 'Attention! Error during dummy program compilation.');
       Exit;                                { end program with error code }
    end;

  {-- enter typed constants in the global variable DataA ------------------}

  writeln( 'Pass #4 : Reading typed constants' );
  Field.Amount := 0;              { initialize number of data records with 0 }
  StartDataSeg := ExtractTypedConst;

  {-- sort data fields of typed constants ( by name ) --------------------}

  writeln( 'Pass #5 : Sorting typed constants' );
  Sort;

  {-- delete Dummy program's typed constants in the data field -----------}

  writeln( 'Pass #6 : Processing dummy program ' );
  Differnce;

  {-- create info file with the addresses of the constants ---------------}

  writeln( 'Pass #7 : Creating constant file ' + Name + CST_EXT + ' ' );
  Create_Cst_File;

  DelDat( HELPNAME + Extension );                   { delete dummy files }
  DelDat( HELPNAME + MAP_EXT );
  DelDat( HELPNAME + EXE_EXT );
end.
```

12.2 The TPINST Unit

After TPIC creates a constant file, it adds this file to the configuration program. TPIC directly accesses the EXE file using the routines from the TPINST unit and the constants from the TCA file. We'll now demonstrate how the routines are constructed, and how they interact, based on the source listing of the TPINST unit.

The header of the TPINST unit lists many constants and type declarations which the programmer needs for calling the various procedures and functions from the unit. In the foreground are the three types: TPIMenu_Rec, TPIAl_Num_Rec and TPIColRec. These reflect the three kinds of interaction between computer and user.

- TPIMenu_Rec is used for the description of pulldown menus, which are constructed and controlled by the TPI_Menu procedure.

- TPIAl_Num_Rec describes an alphanumeric input field used by the TPID_Entry procedure.

- TPIColorRec selects colors from a palette of 128 possible colors. The TPIColor procedure controls this type of color selection.

TPINST accesses the KBM and WIN units listed earlier in this book. It needs these units in order to access the keyboard and screen. The mouse has no purpose in configuring a program with TPINST. You'll see a number of structural similarities between the KBM unit and the TPINST unit.

```
{*****************************************************************************
 *  TPInst : This unit makes various procedures available for the creation  *
 *           of installation programs similar to Turbo's TINST.             *
 *           Like TINST, the settings can be written directly into the EXE  *
 *           file of the program. A configuration is not required           *
 **-----------------------------------------------------------------------**
 *  Author        : MICHAEL TISCHER                                         *
 *  developed on   : 06/18/1989                                            *
 *  last update on : 03/07/1990                                            *
 *****************************************************************************}

unit TPInst;

interface

{------- include required units -------------------------------------------}

uses Crt,                                          { Turbo Pascal CRT unit }
     Kbm,        { Turbo Pascal System Programming keyboard unit ( Ch. 7 ) }
     Win;         { Turbo Pascal System Programming window unit ( Ch. 6 ) }
```

```
{-- constants, types and variables accessible to other units --------------}

const TPIMaxInst = 16;          { maximum number of entries per menu window }

const TPIWinColor   : byte = 112;              { color of the window frame }
      TPIColorHi    : byte = 15;       { color of the highlighted menu entry }
      TPIColorFirst : byte = 116;    { color of the direct selection letter }


type TPIString      = String[80];           { menu entries and window title }

     TPIMenuField = array[ 1..TPIMaxInst ] of TPIString;   { menu entries }

     TPIProcType   = procedure( Reaction : byte );    { reaction procedure }

     TPIMenu_Rec   = record {----------- data structure for menu selection }
            Left,                               { left window column }
             Top       : byte;                    { top window line }
             WTitle    : TPIString;                  { window title }
             NumEnt    : byte;            { number of menu entries }
             MnuTxt    : TPIMenuField;     { text of menu entries }
           end;

     TPIAl_Num_Rec = record {------ data structure for alphanumeric inputs }
            Left,                               { left window column }
             Top    : byte;                       { top window line }
             WTitle : TPIString;                     { window title }
             ILngth : byte;                   { length of the input }
             Text   : TPIString;             { string to be input }
           end;

     TPIColRec     = record {---------- data structure for color selection }
            Left,                               { left window column }
             Top     : byte;                      { top window line }
             WTitle  : TPIString;                    { window title }
             Color   : byte;                          { preset color }
           end;

{-- procedures and functions accessible to other units -------------------}

function  TPIOpenFile    ( Name : string; Offset : longint) : boolean;
procedure TPISaveChanges;
procedure TPICLoseFile;
procedure TPIGet         ( Address : word; ILngth : word; var Buffer );
procedure TPIPut         ( Address : word; ILngth : word; var Buffer );
procedure TPI_Menu       ( var RData : TPIMenu_Rec; Mn_React : TPIProcType);
procedure TPID_Entry     ( var RData : TPIAl_Num_Rec );
procedure TPIColor         ( var RData : TPIColRec; Mn_React : TPIProcType
);
```

The IMPLEMENTATION part of the unit defines an internal data type and some internal global variables. The type has the name SegmentTyp and comprises an almost complete 64K memory segment of the 8086/8088. The word "almost" means that 15 bytes are missing from the segment. Turbo Pascal does this through its own heap administration, since a variable of this type will be accessed through the heap. Based on the internal structure of heap administration, Turbo Pascal can allocate individual blocks of memory with up to 65,521 bytes allocated per block.

TPINST uses this type to allocate a memory block of this size through the heap. This memory block is then passed the entire data segment of the program to be configured. The unit does not know the total number of typed constants in the program. However, these constants could theoretically fill an entire 64K segment, even if this isn't possible. If the segment is less than 64K, only the occupied part is loaded (more on this later).

A global variable named DataSegment is defined to act as a pointer to the data segment, as well as other global variables.

```
implementation

{-- constants, types and variables which are only used internally ---------}

const NoSt = '                                                    ';

type SegmentTyp = array [ 0 .. 65520 ] of byte;          { the data segment }

var ExeFile       : file;                { file variable for access to EXE file }
    DataSegment   : ^SegmentTyp;                   { space for data segment }
    DataSegSize   : word;             { size of the data segment in bytes }
    DataWriteBack : word;                   { number of bytes written back }
    DataSegStart  : longint;       { start of the data segment in the EXE
file }
```

The TPIOpenFile function loads the data segment and initializes various procedures. TPIOpenFile expects the name of the EXE file to be configured as its first argument. As its second argument, TPIOpenFile accepts the offset address of the data segment, relative to the beginning of the EXE file. The caller can obtain this information from the DSEG_START constant, which appears as the first constant in the constant file.

```
{*****************************************************************************
 *  TPIOpenFile : opens task with routines from this unit and simultaneously*
 *                reads data segment of the EXE file to be installed.       *
 **-----------------------------------------------------------------------**
 *  Input : NAME   = name of the EXE file                                   *
 *          OFFSET = Offset of the data segment in the EXE file             *
 *  Output : TRUE if file opened successfully; FALSE if file was not found  *
 *  Info   : The data segment's offset address can be read from DSEG_START, *
 *           a constant found in the constant file created by TPIC.         *
 *****************************************************************************}

function TPIOpenFile( Name : string; Offset : longint) : boolean;

var OK : boolean;                                  { status after opening file }
```

```
begin
  {-- open EXE file ----------------------------------------------------}

  Assign( ExeFile, Name );
  {$I-}                                        { switch off Turbo I/O checking }
  Reset( ExeFile, 1 );                           { open file, set length = 1 }
  OK := ( IOResult = 0 );
  {$I+}                                         { switch on Turbo I/O checking }

  {-- read data segment from the EXE file into memory --------------------}

  if ( OK ) then                                { opening of file successful? }
    begin                                          { yes, read data segment }
      New( DataSegment );                      { space for copy of DSEG on the heap }
      Seek( ExeFile, Offset );                         { position file pointer }
      BlockRead( ExeFile, DataSegment^, 65521, DataSegSize);    { and read }
      DataWriteBack := 0;          { largest offset address changed up to now }
      DataSegStart  := Offset;  { store starting addr. of the data segment }
    end;

  TPIOpenFile := OK;                                        { return result }
end;
```

TPIOpenFile attempts to open the EXE file in the current directory. If the attempt is unsuccessful, TPIOpenFile returns FALSE to the caller. A successful attempt allocates a 64K buffer using the New procedure and stores the address of this buffer in the DataSegment variable. The file pointer is then directed to the beginning of the data segment in the EXE file.

The BlockRead procedure attempts to load the complete segment (65,521 bytes). Usually this attempt will fail and BlockRead will only read the range between the beginning of the data segment and the end of the EXE file. BlockRead then enters the number of bytes read into the DataSegSize variable.

The starting address of the data segment in the EXE file is then stored in the DataSegStart variable and the DataWriteBack variable is initialized with 0. This indicates that the typed constants in the data segments haven't been accessed yet. Once the function ends successfully, you can then access the various typed constants.

The constants can either be read or assigned new values using the TPIGet and TPIPut procedures. TPIGet reads the constants, expecting three arguments:

- The address of the typed constant in the form of a constant from the TCA file.

- The length of the typed constant in bytes.

- The variable in which the typed constant should be stored.

The length of the typed constant can be indicated as a constant if it is handled as a scalar type whose size is known. When dealing with scalar, subrange and structured types, we recommend reading the type declaration of the program to be configured in the configuration program, where the SizeOf function can determine the size.

The function itself consists of a Move procedure call, which moves the desired number of bytes from the data segment in memory to the indicated variable.

```
{**************************************************************************
 *  TPIGet : reads typed constant from variable in EXE file's data segment  *
 **----------------------------------------------------------------------**
 *  Input : ADDRESS = address of the typed constant (from the TCA file)   *
 *          ILNGTH  = size of the constant in bytes                       *
 *          BUFFER  = buffer/variable for storage of the constant         *
 **************************************************************************}

procedure TPIGet( Address : word; ILngth : word; var Buffer );

begin                                          { copy contents to buffer }
  Move( DataSegment^[ Address ], Buffer, ILngth );
end;
```

The TPIGet procedure works in a similar way. TPIGet loads the addressed typed constants into the data segment with the content of the variable which was passed. The new value of the constant is not written immediately into the EXE file. This occurs later, when the configuration process ends.

TPIPut does more than copy the variable contents to data segment memory using a Move call. In addition, TPIPut also controls the DataWriteBack variable, which can store the address of the last byte changed in the data segment at any time. On later calls to store the changed typed constant, only the bytes between the beginning of the data segment and the offset address in DataWriteBack must be written back to the EXE file.

An entire series of unchanged bytes are stored. Because of complexity, this must be done without creating a chained list of the addresses and sizes of manipulated typed constants.

```
{**************************************************************************
 *  TPIPut : writes a typed constant to the data segment of the EXE file    *
 **----------------------------------------------------------------------**
 *  Input : ADDRESS = address of the typed constant (from TCA file)       *
 *          ILNGTH  = size of the constant in bytes                       *
 *          BUFFER  = current "location" of the constant                  *
 **************************************************************************}

procedure TPIPut( Address : word; ILngth : word; var Buffer );

begin
  {-- write content of buffer in data segment back -----------------------}
```

488

```
    Move( Buffer, DataSegment^[ Address ], ILngth );

    {-- upper limit for changes in the data segment ------------------------}

    if ( Address + ILngth > DataWriteBack ) then
      DataWriteBack := Address + ILngth;
  end;
```

TPIPut is often called as the last link in a chain. It begins with a call to the TPI_Menu procedure. The TPI_Menu routine controls the generation of user-selectable menus, which are a major factor in the configuration process. The information required by TPI_Menu comes from a data structure of type TPIMenu_Rec, which passes the information to TPI_Menu when called. This information includes the coordinates of the upper left corner of the menu window, the menu's title, the menu's number and the menu names in an array of 16 strings. The consistent allocation of memory for 16 strings wastes a great deal of memory. But this has no negative effects in a configuration program, since little RAM is used by most of the program.

This program uses menu selection through the cursor keys. Later on, if you choose to modify these codes to your own needs, you could program direct selection keys (also called keyboard shortcuts or hotkeys). This is when pressing a single key automatically selects the menu item. The letter you wish to assign as a direct selection key must be preceded in the menu string by a number character (#). We have added the number signs to the menu items to highlight possible direct selection keys which you can modify on your own.

As a second parameter, TPI_Menu expects an argument of type TPIProcType, which is addressed in the procedure by the name Reaction. As this name suggests, TPIProcType is a procedural type, a pointer to a procedure or function. The type actually contains a pointer to a procedure, passed to a byte as a single argument. We'll take a closer look at the importance of this byte soon.

TPI_Menu calls Reaction in response to a menu selection. TPI_Menu gives the user much freedom during the use of the various menus. For example, when the TPI_Menu procedure is called, it can call a submenu from the selected menu. Since this capability is also available for the submenu Reaction procedure, a complete menu hierarchy can be implemented.

In addition, the Reaction procedure can call the TPID_Entry or TPIColor procedures to select a color or accept alphanumeric input. The Reaction procedure could even begin with a DOS command. TPI_Menu cannot and will not proceed until the DOS command has finished executing.

If the Reaction procedure returns to TPI_Menu, menu processing continues until the user selects a new menu or presses the <Escape> key. TPI_Menu then returns to its caller.

```
{**************************************************************************
*   TPI_Menu : creates a menu window and monitors the selection of a      *
*              menu, which is followed by the call of the reaction        *
*              procedure which belongs to it.                             *
**------------------------------------------------------------------------**
*   Input : RDATA     = menu data of type TPIMenu_Rec                     *
*           MN_REACT = pointer to reaction procedure                      *
*   Info  : The data is expected here as variable parameter, so the       *
*           reaction procedure of the caller can still change it during    *
*           the execution of the procedure and does not have to access     *
*           a static local copy.                                          *
**************************************************************************}

procedure TPI_Menu( var RData  : TPIMenu_Rec; Mn_React : TPIProcType );

var SWindow      : integer;                          { handle for screen window }
    StringDummy : TPIString;       { buffer for the preparation of the title }
    WWidth,                                      { width of the menu window }
    Bottom,                               { bottom screen line of menu window }
    Right,                               { right screen column of menu window }
    CurPos      : byte;                             { selected menu item }

begin
  with RData do                                { process the structure passed }
    begin
      {-- construct window and display title ----------------------------}

      Bottom := Top + NumEnt + 3;                     { determine bottom line }
      if ( WTitle <> '' ) then              { does the window have a title? }
        Stringdummy := #32 + WTitle + #32;       { yes, enclose in spaces }
      WWidth := Length( Stringdummy ) + 1;      { determine width of window }

      for Right := 1 to NumEnt do  { width of window from the longest menu }
        if ( Length( MnuTxt[ Right ] ) + 2 > WWidth ) then
          WWidth := Length( MnuTxt [ Right ] ) + 2;

      Right := Left + WWidth;                  { calculate right window column }

      SWindow := WinOpen( Left, Top, Right, Bottom );       { window         }
      WinFill( Left, Top, Right, Bottom ,#32, TPIWinColor );{ construction }
      WinFrame( Left, Top, Right, Bottom, SIN_FR, TPIWinColor );
      DisplayItCentered( Left + 1, Right, Top,
                      TPIWinColor, Stringdummy );

      {-- loop: call of the selection routine and the reaction ------------}
      {-- procedure until the termination of the menu         ------------}

      CurPos := TPIMSelect ( Left + 1, Top + 2, WWidth, NumEnt, MnuTxt, 1 );
      while ( CurPos > 0 ) do                       { was a menu selected? }
        begin                                                     { yes }
          Mn_React( CurPos );                       { call reaction procedure }
          CurPos := TPIMSelect( Left+1, Top+2, WWidth,
                            NumEnt, MnuTxt, CurPos );
```

```
        end;
    end;

  WinClose( TRUE );                                    { close window again }
end;
```

Remember that TPI_Menu's tasks are limited to administrative activities. It determines the longest of the menu names and creates the menu window and title based on this information. The TPI_MSelect function performs the actual menu selection and keyboard reading.

On return from this function, TPI_Menu receives the number of the selected menu, which it stores in the CurPos variable. If the user pressed the <Escape> key, this number is equal to 0 and TPI_Menu returns to the caller. If the user pressed the <Enter> key, TPI_Menu calls the reaction procedure for the corresponding menu and passes to it the number of the selected menu.

After the return from the procedure, TPI_Menu continues the execution of the loop. In this loop it always calls the TPI_MSelect function and the reaction procedure, until the user presses the <Escape> key.

Perhaps you noticed that TPI_Menu gets its parameters as variable parameters without trying to change the parameters. The Reaction procedure, however, should be capable of changing menu text, e.g., after selecting a menu item. This change would not have any effect within TPI_Menu if it worked with value parameters because TPI_Menu would then access a local copy of the data which cannot be manipulated by the Reaction procedure. The data access takes place internally over the pointer, which was passed and consequently reflects changes in the menu data.

This way, menus can easily be used as switches which can be toggled between two or more settings during each selection. As we will see later, the DINST configuration program for DEMO also uses this capability.

```
{*******************************************************************************
 *  TPIMSelect : displays a menu and implements menu item selection.          *
 **-------------------------------------------------------------------------**
 *  Input : XLEFT, YTOP - column, line of the first menu entry,               *
 *          MWIDTH       = width of the menu entries,                         *
 *          NUMENT       = number of the menu entries                         *
 *          RDATA        = text field for the menu entries                    *
 *          CURPOS       = current menu position                              *
 *  Output : selected menu position                                           *
 *******************************************************************************}

function TPIMSelect( XLeft, YTop, MWidth, NumEnt : byte;
```

```
                    RData                           : TPIMenuField;
                    CurPos                          : byte ) : byte;

  var i          : byte;                                     { loop counter }
     Key         : word;                                       { key code }
     SinChar     : char;                      { converted key to ASCII character }
     Stringdummy : TPIString;                     { buffer for menu text display }
     HiPos       : array[ 1..TPIMaxInst ] of byte; { selection key position }
     HiChar      : array[ 1..TPIMaxInst ] of char;    { selection key codes }
     MnuTxt      : array[ 1..TPIMaxInst ] of TPIString;      { menu text }

begin
  {-- create menu --------------------------------------------------------}

  WinHideCursor;                                             { hide cursor }
  for i := 1 to NumEnt do                         { process individual menus }
    begin
      Stringdummy := RData[ i ];                          { get menu string }
      HiPos[ i ] := Pos( '#', Stringdummy );   { find direct selection key }
      if ( HiPos[ i ] >  0 ) then                               { found? }
        begin                                                      { yes }
          HIChar[ i ] := Stringdummy[ HiPos[ i ] + 1 ];          { store }
          Delete( Stringdummy, HiPos[ i ], 1 );   { and remove from string }
          MnuTxt[ i ] := Copy( #32 + Stringdummy + NoSt, 1, MWidth - 1 );
        end
      else                              { no direct selection key found }
        begin
          HiChar[ i ] := #0;
          MnuTxt[ i ] := Copy( #32 + RData[ i ] + NoSt, 1, MWidth - 1 );
        end;

      {-- display menu entry -------------------------------------------}

      WinPrint( XLeft , YTop + i - 1, TPIWinColor, MnuTxt[ i ] );
      if ( HiPos[ i ] > 0 ) then                  { direct selection key? }
        WinPrint( XLeft + HiPos[ i ], YTop + i - 1,       { yes, highlight }
                TpiColorFirst, HiChar[ i ] );
    end;

  repeat                 { keyboard loop repeats until CR or ESC is pressed }

    {-- highlight current menu item and wait for keyboard event ----------}

    WinPrint( XLeft , YTop + CurPos - 1 , TPIColorHi, MnuTxt[ CurPos ] );
    Key := C_Input;                                  { read keyboard code }

    {-- display current menu item in normal font ------------------------}

    WinPrint( XLeft , YTop + CurPos - 1 , TPIWinColor, MnuTxt[ CurPos ] );
    if ( HiPos[ CurPos ] > 0 ) then
      WinPrint( XLeft + HiPos[ CurPos ], YTop + CurPos - 1,
              TpiColorFirst, HiChar[ CurPos ] );
```

```
   case Key of                                    { read activated key }
     ESC   : CurPos := 0;                         { ESCAPE ends input }

      CUP   : {-------------- Cursor UP, select previous menu item -------}
        if CurPos = 1 then                   { already on the first menu? }
          CurPos := NumEnt                          { yes, set to last }
        else                                                     { no }
          Dec( CurPos );                            { one menu up }

      CDOWN : {-------------- Cursor DOWN, select next menu item ----------}
        If CurPos = NumEnt then                { already on the last menu? }
          CurPos := 1                       { yes, jump back to first menu }
        else                                                     { no }
          Inc( CurPos );                          { one menu down }

      CHOME : {------------------------ Cursor HOME, select first menu ---}
        CurPos := 1;

      CEND  : {------------------------ Cursor END, select last menu -----}
        CurPos := NumEnt;

      else     {---------- test another key for direct selection key ------}
        if ( Key > 256 ) then                   { extended keyboard code? }
          begin                        { no, convert key to upper case letters }
            SinChar := Upcase ( chr( Key and 255 ) );
            for i := 1 to NumEnt do          { process direct selection keys }
              if ( SinChar = Upcase ( HiChar[ i ] ) ) then
                begin                       { direct selection key found }
                  {-- highlight new menu with color ---------------------}
                  WinPrint( XLeft , YTop + CurPos - 1 ,
                          TPIWinColor, MnuTxt[ CurPos ] );
                  it ( HiPos[ CurPos ] > 0 ) then
                    WinPrint( XLeft + HiPos[ CurPos ], YTop + CurPos - 1,
                            TpiColorFirst, HiChar[ CurPos ] );
                  Key := CR;                   { simulate <Enter> keypress }
                  CurPos := i;                  { store new menu item }
                end;
          end;
    end;
  until ( ( Key = Cr ) or ( Key = ESC ) );

  {-- menu item was selected -----------------------------------------}

  if ( Key = Cr ) then                             { was <Enter> pressed? }
    begin                            { yes, display current menu in normal color }
      WinPrint( XLeft , YTop + CurPos - 1, TPIWinColor, MnuTxt[ CurPos ] );
      if ( HiPos[ i ] > 0 ) then
        WinPrint( XLeft + HiPos[ CurPos ], YTop + CurPos - 1,
                TpiColorFirst, HiChar[ CurPos ] );
    end;
  WinLineCursor;                              { make cursor visible again }
  TPIMSelect := CurPos;       { return the number of the selected menu item }
end;
```

TPI_MSelect receives data, from TPI_Menu, which describe the active menu number, position and contents, and returns this data to the caller after the user selects a menu item or presses the <Escape> key. The first task after its call processes all menu entries, stores codes and key positions. In addition, the various menus in this loop are constructed with the potential shortcut key highlighted.

Since TPI_MSelect always receives data, any changes made to the data by the reaction procedure become visible immediately. TPI_Menu doesn't adjust the width of the menu window when changes are made: the menu window size remains constant during the execution of TPI_Menu.

In the loop that follows, TPI_MSelect continuously reads the keyboard for the <Enter> key or <Escape> key. When the user presses an applicable cursor key, the function reacts by moving the menu cursor in the direction indicated by the key.

The reaction procedure uses the TPID_Entry procedure if a selected menu item requires the entry of alphanumeric data. Alphanumeric data include path names, directory listings and date displays. The input is controlled through a structure of type TPIAl_Num_Rec, which must be passed to TPID_Entry during the call. The TPIAl_Num_Rec structure contains the coordinates of the upper left corner of the input window, the title of this window and the length of the input field. The input field length usually determines the width of the input window, but if the header is wider than the input field, the header's length then governs the window width.

The actual string is controlled by TPID_Entry from a buffer that is part of the passed structure. This buffer can contain text before the procedure is called. The text in the buffer will then appear in the input field as a default text, and the user can edit this default text.

TPID_Entry distinguishes between *insert* and *overwrite mode* during character entry. Pressing the <Insert> key toggles between insert mode and overwrite mode. The appearance of the cursor indicates which mode is currently active. TPID_Entry indicates that overwrite mode is active when the cursor appears as a thick underscore (_). If the cursor appears as a block (▮), then insert mode is active.

During character input, the TPID_Entry procedure accepts any ASCII character codes ranging from 32 to 255. The procedure allows the use of the <Delete> key, <Backspace> key, <Cursor right> and <Cursor left> keys for editing input. You can end the input and send the new data by pressing the <Enter> key. If you press the <Escape> key, any changes you might have made to the text are ignored, and the original text is retained in the input buffer.

The TPIPut procedure writes changes to text to the corresponding typed constant after the call to TPID_Entry. For example, the new text can be written to the data segment and passed to the EXE file later.

```
{*************************************************************************
*   TPID_Entry : opens screen window and inserts alphanumeric input field   *
**---------------------------------------------------------------------**
*   Input : RDATA = input data of type TPIAl_Num_Rec                     *
*   Info  : When the input is terminated with ESC, the string passed in  *
*           the data structure is returned unchanged.                    *
*************************************************************************}

procedure TPID_Entry( var RData  :  TPIAl_Num_Rec);

var Current_Pos,                        { input position in the string }
    Right       : byte;                      { right window column }
    InsrtMode   : boolean;           { insert or overwrite mode? }
    Key         : word;                    { result of the input }
    HWindow     : integer;                  { handle for window }
    InBString   : TPIString;                   { input buffer }

begin
  with RData do                    { process the data structure passed }
    begin
      {-- construct window, display title and preset text ----------------}

      if ( ILngth > Length( WTitle ) ) then      { calculate window width }
        Right := Left + ILngth + 3
      else
        Right := Left + Length( WTitle ) + 3;

      TextBackGround( 7 );                         { set display color }
      TextColor( 15 );
      HWindow := WinOpen( Left, Top, Right, Top + 2 );        { construct }
      WinFill( Left, Top, Right, Top + 2, #32, TPIWinColor );  { window   }
      WinFrame( Left, Top, Right, Top + 2, SIN_FR, TPIWinColor );
      DisplayItCentered( Left + 1, Right, Top,            { display title }
                    TPIWinColor, #32 + WTitle + #32 );
      InsrtMode := FALSE;                         { now in overwrite mode }
      InBString := copy( Text, 1, ILngth );           { store preset text }
      Cursor( Left + 2, Top + 1 );      { set cursor to beginning of input }
      write( InBString );                        { display input text }
      Current_Pos := 1;            { store current position in input field }

      repeat {----------- input loop is terminated by CR or ESC keys ------}

        Cursor( Left + Current_Pos + 1, Top + 1 );      { position cursor }
        if InsrtMode then WinBlockCursor { block cursor --> insert mode, }
                else WinLineCursor;  { line cursor --> overwrite mode }
        Key := C_Input;                                { wait for key }

        {-- read key and react accordingly ------------------------------}

        if ( ( ( Key and $ff00 ) = 0 ) and ( Key > 31 ) ) then
          begin                { key is character that can be displayed }
            write( chr( Key and 255 ) );              { display character }
            if ( not InsrtMode ) then              { insert mode active? }
```

```
        begin                            { no, overwrite mode active }
          if ( Current_Pos > length( InBString ) ) then
            InBString := InBString + chr ( Key and 255 )
          else
            InBString[ Current_Pos ] := chr ( Key and 255 );
        end
      else                               { insert mode active }
        begin
          Insert( chr ( Key and 255 ), InBString, Current_Pos );
          if ( length( InBString ) > ILngth ) then
            InBString := Copy( InBString, 1, ILngth );
          write( copy( InBString, Current_Pos + 1,
                     length( InBString ) - Current_Pos ) );
        end;
      if ( Current_Pos < ILngth ) then      { cursor at end of field? }
        Inc( Current_Pos )               { no, increment cursor position }
    end

  else                             { key < 31 or extended keyboard code }
    case Key of                                         { read key }
      CHOME    : {----------- cursor HOME, cursor in first column -}
        Current_Pos:=1;

      CEND     : {------ cursor END, cursor behind last character -}
        if ( length( InBString ) < ILngth ) then
          Current_Pos := length( InBString ) + 1
        else
          Current_Pos := length( InBString );

      CLEFT    : {-------- cursor LEFT, one character to the left -}
        if ( Current_Pos > 1 ) then
          Dec( Current_Pos );

      CRIGHT   : {------ cursor RIGHT, one character to the right -}
        if ( Current_Pos <= length( InBString ) ) and
           ( Current_Pos < ILngth ) then
          Inc( Current_Pos );

      BS       : {--- backspace, delete character left of cursor -}
        if ( Current_Pos > 1 ) then    { already on first character? }
          begin                          { no, backspace possible }
            Delete( InBString, Current_Pos - 1, 1 );
            Cursor( wherex - 1, Top + 1 );
            Dec ( Current_Pos );
            if ( Current_Pos <= length( InBString ) ) then
              write( copy( InBString, Current_Pos,
                     length( InBString ) - Current_Pos + 1 ) );
            write( #32 );
          end;

      DELETEKEY : {-- delete, delete character at current position -}
        begin                                           { delete }
          Delete( InBString, Current_Pos , 1 );
```

```
                    write( copy( InBString , Current_Pos , ILngth ) );
                    write( #32 );
                end;

            INSERTKEY :        {-- insert, switch between insert/overwrite -}
                InsrtMode := not InsrtMode;
        end;

    until ( ( Key = CR ) or  ( Key = ESC ) );

        if ( Key = CR ) then                { input ended by pressing <Enter>? }
            Text := InBString                       { yes, accept string }
    end;
    Winclose( TRUE );                               { close display screen window }
    end;
```

The TPIColor procedure selects colors in any case where a constant code represents a color. After its call, this procedure opens a screen window displaying 128 of the 256 possible text/background color combinations. The omitted colors are those in which bit 3 of the background color is set. Some video cards display these other colors as blinking colors, while other cards display these colors with high intensity backgrounds.

The colors in the window appear in a logical order: the foreground colors are arranged from top (black) to bottom (white), while background colors are arranged from left (black) to right (light gray). The upper left corner of the window displays color number 0 in each case (black text, black background).

A white frame appears around the current color combination. This frame can be moved from field to field using the cursor keys. Each time you move the white frame to another color combination, the reaction procedure, indicated by the caller of TPIColor as its second parameter, is also called.

The active color code is passed to this reaction procedure during each call. The reaction procedure uses the code to display the selected object's colors on the screen. The object should appear with the other screen elements. During program execution the object color can be selected by the user. In addition to the color selection window, a second window appears, displaying a window border, window title, a line of text in normal mode and a line of text in highlighted (or high intensity) mode. This window lets you see how your color selections will affect the appearance of the configured application. This is the best way for you to see how well certain color combinations fit together.

The content of the data structure of the type TPIColRec, which was passed during the call, determines the task of the TPIColor procedure. It contains the coordinates of the upper left corner, the header of the color selection window and the currently selected color code. If you press the <Enter> key after color selection, TPIColor enters the selected color code in that

structure. If you press the <Escape> key, any color selection is ignored and the program
defaults to the last color combination found in the data structure.

```
{*****************************************************************************
 *  TPIColor : opens a screen window from which colors can be selected from *
 *             the palette using the cursor.                                *
 **-----------------------------------------------------------------------**
 *  Input : RDATA    = color selection data of type TPIColorRec            *
 *          MN_REACT = pointer to the reaction procedure                   *
 *****************************************************************************}

procedure TPIColor ( var RData : TPIColRec; Mn_React : TPIProcType );

var HWindow : integer;                      { handle of the opened window  }
    Xpos,                                   { column of current color }
    Ypos     : byte;                        { line of current color }
    Key      : word;                        { key pressed by user }
    Dummy    : boolean;                     { dummy variable for WinInFront }


{-- PrintChar ---------------------------------------------- [ LOCAL ] --}
{-- displays character at indicated (absolute) screen position, retaining--}
{-- background color at this location                                   --}

procedure PrintChar( X, Y : byte; ConChar : char );

begin
  WinPutChar( x, y, ConChar, (WinGetCol( x, y ) and $F0) + TpiColorHi );
end;

{-- GetKey ------------------------------------------------- [ LOCAL ] --}
{-- draws frame at the selected position, deletes the frame on a keypress--}

function GetKey( X, Y : byte ) : word;

type RConChar = record        { describes the position of a frame character }
                  XOfs,                     { distance from the upper }
                  YOfs : byte;              { left frame corner       }
                  ConChar : char;           { which frame character? }
                end;

const LnDraw : array[ 1..12] of RConChar =       { the 12 characters for }
      (                                          { the color frame       }
        ( XOfs : 0 ; YOfs : 0 ;  ConChar : '⌐' ),
        ( XOfs : 1 ; YOfs : 0 ;  ConChar : '-' ),
        ( XOfs : 2 ; YOfs : 0 ;  ConChar : '-' ),
        ( XOfs : 3 ; YOfs : 0 ;  ConChar : '-' ),
        ( XOfs : 4 ; YOfs : 0 ;  ConChar : '⌐' ),
        ( XOfs : 0 ; YOfs : 1 ;  ConChar : '|' ),
        ( XOfs : 4 ; YOfs : 1 ;  ConChar : '|' ),
        ( XOfs : 0 ; YOfs : 2 ;  ConChar : 'L' ),
        ( XOfs : 1 ; YOfs : 2 ;  ConChar : '-' ),
```

```
   ( XOfs : 2 ; YOfs : 2 ;  ConChar : '-' ),
   ( XOfs : 3 ; YOfs : 2 ;  ConChar : '-' ),
   ( XOfs : 4 ; YOfs : 2 ;  ConChar : 'J' )
 );

var i,                                              { loop counter }
    WinHandle : integer;                          { window handle }
    OLine,                       { top left corner of the color window }
    Column    : byte;

begin
  Column := RData.Left + X * 3 + 1;        { calculate the top left corner }
  OLine  := RData.Top + Y + 1;             { of the color frame           }

  {-- store content of color window ---------------------------------------}

  WinHandle := WinOpen( Column, OLine, Column+5, OLine+3 );

  for i := 1 to 12 do                { process the twelve frame characters }
    with LnDraw[ i ] do              { and display                         }
      PrintChar( Column+XOfs, OLine+YOfs, ConChar );

  GetKey := C_Input;                                      { get key }

 WinClose( TRUE );                               { close window again }
end;

{-- Main part of TPIColor ------------------------------------------------}

begin
  WinHideCursor;                              { hide blinking cursor }
  with RData do             { process the data structure which was passed }
    begin
      {-- construct window for color selection --------------------------}

      HWindow := WinOpen( Left, Top, Left + 27, Top + 19);
      WinFill( Left, Top, Left + 27, Top + 19, #32, TPIColorHi );
      WinFrame( Left, Top, Left + 27, Top + 19, SIN_FR, TPIWinColor );
      DisplayItCentered( Left, Left + 27, Top,
                       TPIWinColor, #32 + WTitle + #32 );

      {-- display color palette in the window ----------------------------}

      for YPos := 0 to 15 do               { process the individual lines }
        begin
          TextColor( Ypos );                   { set foreground color }
          GotoXY( Left + 2, YPos + Top + 2 );      { position cursor }
          for XPos := 0 to 7 do        { process the 7 background colors }
            begin
              TextBackground( Xpos );            { set background color }
              Write( ' x ' );
            end;
        end;
```

```
      Xpos := Color shr 4;              { calculate position from color passed }
      Ypos := Color and 15;

      repeat                                             { keyboard loop }
        Mn_React( Xpos shl 4 + Ypos );         { call reaction procedure }
        Key := GetKey( XPos, YPos );                       { get key }

        case Key of                                        { read key }

          ESC    : {------------ Escape, end selection with preset value -}
            begin
              Xpos := Color shr 4;                 { restore default values }
              Ypos := Color and 15;
            end;

          CUP    : {---------------------------- cursor UP, one line up -}
            if ( YPos = 0 ) then
              YPos := 15                        { already up  => wrap around }
            else
              Dec ( YPos );

          CDOWN  : {------------------------- cursor DOWN, one line down -}
            if ( YPos = 15 ) then
              YPos := 0                         { already down => wrap around }
            else
              Inc ( YPos );

          CLEFT  : {----------------------- cursor LEFT, one column left -}
            if ( XPos = 0 ) then
              XPos := 7                        { already right => wrap around }
            else
              Dec ( XPos );

          CRIGHT : {--------------------- cursor RIGHT, one column right -}
            if ( XPos = 7 ) then
              XPos := 0                        { already left => wrap around }
            else
              Inc ( XPos );

          CHOME  : {---------------- cursor HOME, jump to the first field -}
            begin
              XPos := 0;
              YPos := 0;
            end;

          CEND   : {------------------ cursor END, jump to the last field -}
            begin
              XPos := 7;
              YPos := 15;
            end;

      end;
```

```
      until ( ( Key = CR ) or ( Key = ESC ) );

      Color := ( XPos shl 4 ) +  YPos;            { calculate selected color }
    end;
  WinClose( TRUE );                               { close selection window }
  WinLineCursor;
end;
```

After the constants have been changed through TPID_Entry or TPIColor, the changes are sent to the EXE file. This can either happen in the middle of program execution, or shortly before the program ends. The TPISaveChanges procedure writes all the bytes from the data segment back into the EXE file. These bytes are located between the beginning of the segment and the modified constant with the highest address.

```
{*****************************************************************************
 *   TPISaveChanges : writes the data segment and changes to the EXE file   *
 **-----------------------------------------------------------------------**
 *   Info : only the bytes between the beginning data segment and the       *
 *          constants with the highest offset addresses are written to the  *
 *          file to save time.                                              *
 *****************************************************************************}

procedure TPISaveChanges;

begin
  Seek( ExeFile, DataSegStart);          { set file pointer to data segment }
  if ( DataWriteBack <= DataSegSize ) then          { write changed part }
    BlockWrite( ExeFile, DataSegment^, DataWriteBack) { of data segment   }
  else                                                          { back }
    BlockWrite( ExeFile, DataSegment^, DataSegSize);
end;
```

Another procedure must be called before the end of the configuration program. TPICloseFile closes the EXE file again and releases the data segment memory from the heap. Neither TPIPut nor TPIGet can be called again.

```
{*****************************************************************************
 *   TPICloseFile : closes the EXE file on which installation was performed. *
 *****************************************************************************}

procedure TPICLoseFile;

begin
  close( ExeFile );                                             { close file }
  dispose( DataSegment );                  { release memory space for data segment }
end;
```

TPINST includes additional procedures and functions accessed intensively by the TPI_Menu, TPID_Entry and TPICol procedures. They are located at the beginning of the TPINST listing and are named UpCase, Cursor, C_Input and DisplayItCentered.

```
{******************************************************************************
*  UpCase : converts lower case letters into upper case letters              *
**--------------------------------------------------------------------------**
*  Input : CONCHAR = character to be converted                               *
*  Output : converted character                                              *
******************************************************************************}

function UpCase( ConChar : char ) : char;

begin
  UpCase := System.UpCase( ConChar );
end;


{******************************************************************************
*  Cursor : Sets the blinking cursor and the screen position                 *
**--------------------------------------------------------------------------**
*  Input : X = column, Y = line                                              *
*  Info    : The top left screen corner has the coordinates (0/0)            *
******************************************************************************}

procedure Cursor( X, Y : byte );

begin
  GotoXY( X, Y );                                       { set internal cursor }
  WinSetCursor( X, Y );                                 { set visible cursor }
end;


{******************************************************************************
*  C_Input : central input routine. Waits for a keyboard event from          *
*            the KBM unit                                                     *
**--------------------------------------------------------------------------**
*  Input : none                                                              *
*  Output : key code                                                         *
******************************************************************************}

function C_Input : word;

var Message : EVENT;                        { keyboard event from KBM unit }

begin
  KbmEventWait( EV_KEY_PRESSED, Message );          { wait for keyboard event }
  C_Input := Message.Key;                            { return keyboard code }
end;


{******************************************************************************
*  DisplayItCentered : displays string centered by 2 column coordinates      *
**--------------------------------------------------------------------------**
*  Input : LEFT, RIGHT = left and right column, between which the string      *
*                        should be centered                                  *
*           OLINE      = output line                                         *
*           COLOR      = color of the output text                            *
*           TEXT       = output text                                         *
******************************************************************************}
```

```
procedure DisplayItCentered ( Left, Right, OLine, Color : byte;
                              Text                       : string);

begin
  WinPrint( Left + ( Right - Left - Length ( Text ) ) div 2 , OLine,
            Color, Text );
end;
```

The configuration program DINST frequently uses all the procedures that are made available from the TPINST unit. DINST and the TPINST unit allow you to configure the DEMO program according to personal needs. The {$L} compiler directive includes the constant file DEMO.TCA in the DINST source listing during compilation. This makes the TPIC_... constants available to DINST, complete with the addresses of the typed constants.

Of the global variables, the program only recognizes the typed constant FrameMenu, which stores the frame menu data of type TPIMenu_Rec and represents the four submenus from the main menu. Many more structures of this kind are defined within the program, but FrameMenu is declared locally so that only the current procedure has access to the data. FrameMenu is an exception because the first two items in this submenu act as toggles. This means that both the procedure which constructs the submenu and the reaction procedure must have access to this data. Also, the reaction procedure cannot be a local procedure within the menu procedure because Turbo doesn't permit references to local procedures and functions through procedural types.

Turbo's strange handling of procedural types is also the reason why the reaction procedure is passed separately from the other data during the call of the TPI_Menu and TPIColor procedures. This information could have been stored in the data structures TPIMenu_Rec and TPIColRec. However, this would undermine the construction of these structures as typed constants. There are two reasons for this:

- Procedural types cannot be initialized before the start of the program.

- Turbo requires initialization of all arrays during the creation of all structures as typed constants.

```
{***********************************************************************
 *  DINST : Installation program for the DEMO.PAS source. This program  *
 *          requires the DEMO.TCA include file created by the DEMO source *
 *          when compiled with TPIC.EXE.                                 *
 **-------------------------------------------------------------------**
 *  Author         : MICHAEL TISCHER                                    *
 *  developed on   : 07/08/1989                                         *
 *  last update on : 03/07/1990                                         *
 ***********************************************************************}

program dinst;
```

```
{-- include the required units --------------------------------------------}

uses crt,                                           { Turbo Pascal CRT unit }
     dos,                                           { Turbo Pascal DOS unit }
     win,          { Turbo Pascal System Programming window unit ( Ch. 6 ) }
     tpinst; { Turbo Pascal System Programming installation unit ( Ch. 12 ) }

{-- include DEMO.TCA file which contains typed constants from DEMO.EXE ----}

{$I DEMO.TCA }

{-- global variables ------------------------------------------------------}

const DsFrameMenu : TPIMenu_Rec =                   { describes the frame menu }
  (
     Left   : 10;
     Top    : 3;
     WTitle : 'FRAME';
     NumEnt : 4;
     MnuTxt : ( '',
                '',
                '#Text window frame color',
                '#Output window frame color',
                '', '', '', '','','', '','','', '','','', '','','', '' )
  );
```

DINST contains many reaction procedures because it creates a menu tree beginning at the main menu. The ends of this tree's branches contain calls to the TPIColor procedure, which calls reaction procedures of its own. The following illustration shows this menu structure as you might encounter it.

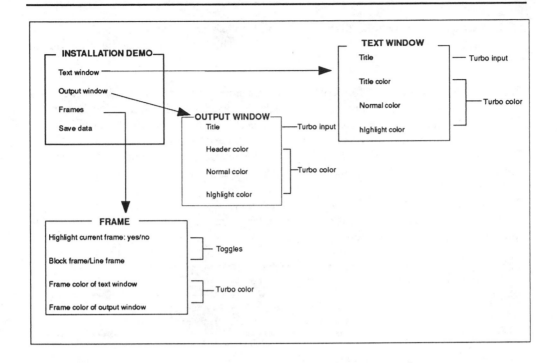

Menu structure of the DINST program

Only two procedures which operate with the menu tree aren't immediately called by TPI_Menu. These procedures are accessed by different reaction procedures called Create_a_Window and Close_the_Window, which appear as the first procedures in the program. They are the only procedures of type NEAR instead of type FAR, because they aren't referenced through procedural types.

Create_a_Window creates the window on the screen. During the color selection with TPIColor, the current reaction procedure refreshes this window to represent the current color. Remember that the window is simply displayed at the proper location on the screen, rather than as a window in the sense of our WIN unit. This isn't necessary because the color selection window always assumes that it is the current window. If the reaction procedure had its own window, a switch between the two windows would be required using the WinInFront procedure. This procedure would take time and reduce the speed with which you could move through the color selection.

Also, Create_a_Window directs its output to the screen and creates the color window for the configuration of the text and output windows. The two windows differ only in their typed constants, which determine the element colors in the DEMO program. The text and output windows are almost identical in their contents and design. During its call, Create_a_Window is passed a Boolean parameter which must contain TRUE if a duplicate

505

of the text window should be displayed. If the Boolean parameter contains FALSE, this indicates a call to one of the reaction procedures, which select a color from the output window.

Both types of windows have four colors which are stored in Create_a_Window's four local variables: FrameColor, HeaderColor, NormColor and HiColor. The display in the text window or output window determines which color is stored in which variable. Both windows have their own typed constants. The text window uses the constants Text_FrameW, TextHeaderW, TextNormW and TextHiW. The output window uses the constants Output_FrameW, OutHeaderW, OutNormW and OutHiW.

Depending on the content of the passed parameter, the TPIGet procedure decides which set of constants will be assigned to the local variables controlling window color, based on the contents of the passed parameters.

```
{****************************************************************************
 *  Create_a_Window : creates the color screen window                      *
 **----------------------------------------------------------------------**
 *  Input : TEXT = TRUE if the text window can be constructed and          *
 *                 FALSE if the output window can be constructed.          *
 ****************************************************************************}

procedure Create_a_Window ( Text : boolean);

var FrameColor,                                     { buffer for frame color }
    HeaderColor,                                   { buffer for header color }
    NormColor,                                 { buffer for normal text color }
    HiColor      : byte;                  { buffer for highlighted text color }

begin
  {-- read color values for window ---------------------------------------}

  if Text then                                              { text window? }
    begin
      TPIGet( TPIC_Text_FrameW, 1, FrameColor );            { frame color }
      TPIGet( TPIC_TextHeaderW, 1, HeaderColor );          { header color }
      TPIGet( TPIC_TextNormW, 1, NormColor);               { normal color }
      TPIGet( TPIC_TextHiW, 1, HiColor);                 { color highlight }
    end
  else                                            { no, display window }
    begin
      TPIGet( TPIC_Output_FrameW, 1, FrameColor );          { frame color }
      TPIGet( TPIC_OutHeaderW, 1, HeaderColor );           { header color }
      TPIGet( TPIC_OutNormW, 1, NormColor);                { normal color }
      TPIGet( TPIC_OutHiW, 1, HiColor);                  { color highlight }
    end;

  {-- construct window ---------------------------------------------------}

  WinFrame( 47, 15, 70, 23, DBL_FR, FrameColor );           { draw frame }
```

506

```
    WinPrint ( 48, 16, HeaderColor, '           TITLE           ' );     { display }
    WinPrint ( 48, 17, NormColor, '                         ' );         { text }
    WinPrint ( 48, 18, NormColor, ' Normal Text             ' );
    WinPrint ( 48, 19, HiColor, ' Highlighted Text     ' );
    WinPrint ( 48, 20, NormColor, '                         ' );
    WinPrint ( 48, 21, NormColor, '                         ' );
    WinPrint ( 48, 22, NormColor, '                         ' );
  end;
```

Create_a_Window creates the color window on the screen, and Close_the_Window closes it again (i.e., deletes the screen area allocated for it).

```
{*****************************************************************************
 *  Close_the_Window : close the color screen window                        *
 *****************************************************************************}

procedure Close_the_Window;

begin
  WinFill( 47, 15, 70, 23, #32, 0 );                        { paint over window }
end;
```

A call to the TPIOpenFile function attempts to open the EXE file. If the EXE file cannot be accessed, the {$F-} compiler directive ends the program with an error.

If the EXE file was accessed successfully, the program selects the main menu items from the program's menu structure. The TPI_Menu procedure then defines and enables these items.

```
{*****************************************************************************
 *      M A I N   P R O G R A M                                             *
 *****************************************************************************}

const TheMainMnu : TPIMenu_Rec =
  (
    Left   : 7;
    Top    : 1;
    WTitle : 'INSTALLATION DEMO';
    NumEnt : 4;
    MnuTxt : ( '#Text window ',
               '#Output window',
               '#Frames',
               '#Save data',
               '', '', '', '','', '','', '','', '','', '' )
  );

begin
  {-- open EXE file. If EXE file opens successfully, call main menu -------}

  if TPIOpenfile( 'demo.exe', TPIC_DSEG_START ) then
```

```
      begin                                    { DEMO.EXE could be opened }
        {-- initialize screen output -------------------------------------}

        WinWrite2View( FALSE );              { no window related text output }
        TextColor( 7 );                               { set text color }
        TextBackground( 0 );                    { set background color }
        ClrScr;                                         { clear screen }

        WinPrint( 0, 24, $70, '    DINST installs data in DEMO.EXE '+
                          '    -     (c) 1989 by MICHAEL TISCHER    ' );
        TPI_Menu( TheMainMnu, Main_Reac );             { call main menu }
        TpiCloseFile;                           { close EXE file again }
        TextColor( 7 );                          { set normal text color }
        TextBackGround( 0 );
        ClrScr;
        GotoXY( 0, 0 );
      end
    else                                     { DEMO.EXE could not be opened }
      begin
        writeln( #13#10, 'DINST  -  (c) 1989 by MICHAEL TISCHER');
        writeln( 'Attention! DEMO.EXE not found. >>> Procedure aborted <<<.');
      end;
  end.
```

The main menu uses Main_Reac as its reaction procedure. Depending on the menu number passed to Main_Reac, it calls one of three procedures responsible for controlling the text window frame, the output window frame or the frame menu. If the user selects the Save changes menu item, the TPISaveChanges procedure stores any changes made. No changes will be written to the EXE file unless you select the Save changes item—the program doesn't save changes automatically.

```
{***********************************************************************
*  Main_Reac : reaction procedure for the main menu of DINST          *
**-------------------------------------------------------------------**
*  Input : MMENU = number of the selected main menu                   *
*  Info  : Main_Reac is called as a part of the main menu by TPI_Menu *
***********************************************************************}

procedure Main_Reac( MMenu : byte );

begin
  case MMenu of                   { corresponds to the selected menu item }
    1 : TextInst;                         { call installation menu text }
    2 : OutPutInst;                     { call output installation menu }
    3 : Frame_Inst;                      { call frame installation menu }
    4 : TpiSaveChanges;                              { store changes }
  end;
end;
```

Frame_Inst controls the frame menu, which defines the first two items in this submenu. The TPIGet procedure determines the contents of the typed contents named CurrentDoubled and Frame_Line_T. TPIGet passes the Frame_Reac procedure during a subsequent call to TPI_Menu.

```
{********************************************************************
 * Frame_Inst : create menu frame attributes and call menu routine  *
 **----------------------------------------------------------------**
 * Input : none                                                     *
 ********************************************************************}

procedure Frame_Inst;

var BoolDummy : boolean;                                { dummy variable }

begin
  {-- menu data for menu window ------------------------------------------}

  with DsFrameMenu do
    begin
      {--------- select first menu entry based on CURRENTDOUBLED constant -}

      TPIGet( TPIC_CURRENTDOUBLED, 1, BoolDummy );  { read frame attribute }
      IF BoolDummy then                               { assign menu text }
        MnuTxt[1] := '#Highlight current frame: YES  '
      else
        MnuTxt[1] := '#Highlight current frame: NO';

      {---------- select second menu entry based on FRAME_LINE_T constant -}

      TPIGet( TPIC_FRAME_LINE_T, 1, BoolDummy );    { read frame attribute }
      IF BoolDummy then                               { assign menu text }
        MnuTxt[2] := '#Line frame'
      else
        MnuTxt[2] := '#Block frame';
    end;

  TPI_Menu( DsFrameMenu, Frame_Reac );  { call menu routine for selection }
end;
```

If the Frame_Reac procedure discovers that the first or second menu item was selected during this call, the menu item toggles to its alternate selection by placing the appropriate typed constant (either CurrentDoubled or Frame_Line_T) into the Boolean variable BoolDummy. This variable negates the previous selection, and TPIPut writes the current selection to the data segment. The new contents of the constant dictate the text that appears in these menu items.

```
{*****************************************************************************
 * Frame_Reac : reaction procedure for installation menu frame attribute    *
 **-----------------------------------------------------------------------**
 * Input : MITEM = number of the selected menu item                         *
 * Info    : Frame_Reac is called as part of DsFrameMenu by TPI_Menu.        *
 *****************************************************************************}

procedure Frame_Reac( MItem : byte );

const FrCText : TPIColRec =                      { frame color - text window }
  (
    Left   : 13;
    Top    : 5;
    WTitle : 'TEXT WINDOW FRAME COLOR';
    Color  : 0
  );

const FrCOutput : TPIColRec =                  { frame color - output window }
  (
    Left   : 13;
    Top    : 5;
    WTitle : 'OUTPUT WINDOW FRAME COLOR';
    Color  : 0
  );

var BoolDummy : boolean;             { for negation of a BOOLEAN constant }

begin
  case MItem of                      { case depends on menu item selected }

    1: begin {----------------- change frame attribute to CURRENTDOUBLED -}
         TPIGet( TPIC_CURRENTDOUBLED, 1, BoolDummy );     { read old value }
         BoolDummy := not BoolDummy;                             { negate }
         TPIPut( TPIC_CURRENTDOUBLED, 1, BoolDummy );        { store again }
         IF BoolDummy then                { change menu text accordingly }
           DsFrameMenu.MnuTxt[1] := '#Highlight current frame: YES  '
         else
           DsFrameMenu.MnuTxt[1] := '#Highlight current frame: NO';
       end;

    2: begin {---------- negate frame attribute 'line frame or dot frame' -}
         TPIGet( TPIC_FRAME_LINE_T, 1, BoolDummy ) ;    { read old value }
         BoolDummy := not BoolDummy;                            { negate }
         TPIPut( TPIC_FRAME_LINE_T, 1, BoolDummy );        { store again }
         IF BoolDummy then                { adjust menu text accordingly }
           DsFrameMenu.MnuTxt[2] := '#Line frame'
         else
           DsFrameMenu.MnuTxt[2] := '#Block frame '
       end;

    3: begin {------------ color selection for frame color of text window -}
         TPIGet( TPIC_TEXT_FRAMEW, 1, FrCText.Color );      { read color }
         Create_a_Window( TRUE );              { create color output window }
```

```
        TPIColor( FrCText, TextFrame_Proc );              { color selection }
        TPIPut( TPIC_TEXT_FRAMEW, 1, FrCText.Color );             { store }
        Close_the_Window;                      { close color selection window }
      end;


    4: begin {---------- color selection for frame color of output window -}
        TPIGet( TPIC_OUTPUT_FRAMEW, 1, FrCOutput.Color );    { read color }
        Create_a_Window( false );              { create color output window }
        TPIColor( FrCOutput, OutFrame_Proc );           { color selection }
        TPIPut( TPIC_OUTPUT_FRAMEW, 1, FrCOutput.Color );         { store }
        Close_the_Window;                     { close color output window }
      end;
  end;
end;
```

The two lower menu items allow color selection. The color selection constant varies:
Sometimes the Text_FrameW constant is used, while Output_FrameW is used on other
occasions. Color selection follows a specific pattern in all menu procedures. Let's look at
one specific example: the Frames menu item in DINST.

The typed constant FrCText is created with the information for the TPIColor procedure. A
call to TPIGet loads the color into the Color array in the data structure. This color is then
passed along with other data to the TPIColor procedure. A call of Create_a_Window then
passes a value of TRUE or FALSE to the procedure. TRUE changes the color of the text
window, while FALSE changes the color of the output window.

TPIColor is then called and passed the data after invoking the reaction procedure. On return
from TPIColor, TPIPut writes the selected color into the data segment on the heap. The
routine then closes the color window.

The TextFrame_Proc procedure handles the third item in the Frames menu (Text window
frame color).

```
{*************************************************************************
*  TextFrame_Proc : display the frame in the text window               *
**-------------------------------------------------------------------**
*  Input : COLOR = selected color value                                *
*  Info    : TextFrame_Proc is called as part of TPIColor (color selection)*
*************************************************************************}

procedure TextFrame_Proc( Color : byte );

begin
  WinFrame( 47, 15, 70, 23, DBL_FR, Color );              { draw new frame }
end;
```

The remaining procedures in the DINST program perform their tasks in much the same way as Frame_Int, Frame_Reac and the other reaction procedures. Now that you have some knowledge of how these programs work, you can easily implement your own configuration programs using TPIC and TPINST as a basis.

The following listing is the remaining source code of TPINST.PAS:

```
{$F+}

{***********************************************************************
 *   TextHeaderProc : display the current header in the text window    *
 **-----------------------------------------------------------------**
 *   Input : COLOR = color value selected                              *
 *   Info    : TextHeaderProc is called as part of TPIColor (color selection)*
 ***********************************************************************}

procedure TextHeaderProc( Color : byte );

begin
  WinPrint( 48, 16, Color, '         TITLE        ' );      { create window }
end;


{***********************************************************************
 *   TextNormProc : display normal text in the text window             *
 **-----------------------------------------------------------------**
 *   Input : COLOR = selected color value                              *
 *   Info    : TextNormProc is called as part of TPIColor (color selection). *
 ***********************************************************************}

procedure TextNormProc( Color : byte );

begin
  {-- create output window -------------------------------------------}

  WinPrint( 48, 17, Color, '                       ' );
  WinPrint( 48, 18, Color, ' Normal Text           ' );
  WinPrint( 48, 20, Color, '                       ' );
  WinPrint( 48, 21, Color, '                       ' );
  WinPrint( 48, 22, Color, '                       ' );
end;


{***********************************************************************
 *   TextHiProc : display highlighted text in the text window          *
 **-----------------------------------------------------------------**
 *   Input : COLOR = selected color value                              *
 *   Info    : TextHiProc is called as part of TPIColor (color selection).   *
 ***********************************************************************}

procedure TextHiProc( Color : byte );

begin
```

```
    WinPrint ( 48, 19, Color, ' Highlighted Text      ' );      { create window }
end;

{**********************************************************************
*  TextFrame_Proc : display the frame in the text window             *
**------------------------------------------------------------------**
*  Input : COLOR = selected color value                              *
*  Info    : TextFrame_Proc is called as part of TPIColor (color selection)*
**********************************************************************}

procedure TextFrame_Proc( Color : byte );

begin
   WinFrame( 47, 15, 70, 23, DBL_FR, Color );                 { draw new frame }
end;
{**********************************************************************
*  OutHeaderProc : display the current title in the output window    *
**------------------------------------------------------------------**
*  Input : COLOR = selected color value                              *
*  Info    : OutHeaderProc is called as part of TPIColor (color selection).*
**********************************************************************}

procedure OutHeaderProc( Color : byte );

begin
   WinPrint ( 48, 16, Color, '          TITLE         ' );      { create window }
end;

{**********************************************************************
*  OutNormProc : display normal text in the output window            *
**------------------------------------------------------------------**
*  Input : COLOR - color value selected                              *
*  Info    : OutNormProc is called as a part of TPIColor (color selection).*
**********************************************************************}

procedure OutNormProc( Color : byte );

begin
   WinPrint ( 48, 17, Color, '                        ' );
   WinPrint ( 48, 18, Color, ' Normal Text            ' );
   WinPrint ( 48, 20, Color, '                        ' );
   WinPrint ( 48, 21, Color, '                        ' );
   WinPrint ( 48, 22, Color, '                        ' );
end;

{**********************************************************************
*  OutHiProc : display highlighted text in the output window         *
**------------------------------------------------------------------**
*  Input : COLOR = color value selected                              *
*  Info    : OutHiProc is called as part of TPIColor (color selection).  *
**********************************************************************}

procedure OutHiProc( Color : byte );
```

513

```
begin
  WinPrint( 48, 19, Color, ' Highlighted Text      ' );      { create window }
end;

{*****************************************************************************
 * OutFrame_Proc : display the frame in the text window                      *
 **-----------------------------------------------------------------------**
 * Input : COLOR = selected color value                                      *
 * Info    : OutFrame_Proc is called as part of TPIColor (color selection).*
 ****************************************************************************}

procedure OutFrame_Proc( Color : byte );

begin
  WinFrame( 47, 15, 70, 23, DBL_FR, Color );                { draw new frame }
end;

{*****************************************************************************
 *  TextReac : reaction procedure for installation menu of the text window  *
 **-----------------------------------------------------------------------**
 *  Input : MITEM = number of the selected menu item                        *
 *  Info    : TextReac is called as part of the text menu by TPI_Menu.      *
 ****************************************************************************}

procedure TextReac( MItem : byte );

const TextHeader : TPIAl_Num_Rec =
 (
   Left  : 13;
   Top   : 5;
   WTitle : 'TEXT WINDOW TITLE';
   ILngth : 60;
   Text  : ''
 );

const ColorHeader : TPIColRec =
 (
   Left  : 13;
   Top   : 4;
   WTitle : 'TITLE  TEXT  COLOR';
   Color : 0
 );

const ColorNormal : TPIColRec =
 (
   Left  : 13;
   Top   : 4;
   WTitle : 'NORMAL TEXT WINDOW COLOR';
   Color : 0
 );

const ColorMark : TPIColRec =
```

```
 (
   Left   : 13;
   Top    : 4;
   WTitle : 'HILITE TEXT WINDOW COLOR';
   Color  : 0
 );

begin
  case MItem of                       { selection depending on menu item }

    1: begin {------------------------------------- header text window -}
         TPIGet( TPIC_TextHeader, 70, TextHeader.Text );    { read header }
         TPID_Entry( TextHeader );               { call input procedure }
         TPIPut( TPIC_TextHeader, 70, TextHeader.text );        { store }
       end;

    2: begin {--------------------- color selection of the header color -}
         Create_a_Window( TRUE );          { construct color output window }
         TPIGet( TPIC_TEXTHEADERW, 1, ColorHeader.Color );   { read color }
         TPIColor( ColorHeader, TextHeaderProc );      { color selection }
         TPIPut( TPIC_TEXTHEADERW, 1, ColorHeader.Color );      { store }
         Close_the_Window;                  { close color output window }
       end;

    3: begin {--------------- color selection of the normal output color -}
         Create_a_Window( TRUE );            { create color output window }
         TPIGet( TPIC_TEXTNORMW, 1, ColorNormal.Color );      { get color }
         TPIColor( ColorNormal, TextNormProc );      { color selection }
         TPIPut( TPIC_TEXTNORMW, 1, ColorNormal.Color );        { store }

         Close_the_Window;                   { close color output window }
       end;

    4: begin {-------------------- color selection of the highlight color -}
         Create_a_Window( TRUE );            { create color output window }
         TPIGet( TPIC_TEXTHIW, 1, ColorMark.Color );       { read color }
         TPIColor( ColorMark, TextHiProc );          { color selection }
         TPIPut( TPIC_TEXTHIW, 1, ColorMark.Color );            { store }
         Close_the_Window;                  { close color output window }
       end;
    end;
end;

{****************************************************************************
*  TextInst : create text window menu data and call menu routine           *
****************************************************************************}

procedure TextInst;

const Text_Menu : TPIMenu_Rec =
 (
   Left   : 10;
   Top    : 3;
```

```
        WTitle : 'TEXT WINDOW';
        NumEnt : 4;
        MnuTxt : ( '#Title ',                              { menu item texts }
                   'Title #Color',
                   '#Normal color',
                   'h#Ighlight color',
                   '', '', '', '','', '','', '','', '','', '' )
    );

  begin
    TPI_Menu( Text_Menu, TextReac );                   { call menu selection }
  end;

  {*************************************************************************
   *  OutReac : reaction procedure for output window installation menu     *
   **----------------------------------------------------------------------**
   *  Input : MITEM = number of the selected menu item                     *
   *  Info    : OutReac is called as a part of the OutPut_Menu from TPI_Menu. *
   *************************************************************************}

  procedure OutReac( MItem : byte );

  const TextOutput : TPIAl_Num_Rec =
   (
     Left   : 13;
     Top    : 5;
     WTitle : 'OUTPUT WINDOW TITLE';
     ILngth :  60;
     Text   : ''
   );

  const ColorOutput : TPIColRec =
   (
     Left   : 13;
     Top    : 4;
     WTitle : 'OUTPUT TITLE COLOR';
     Color  : 0
   );

  const ColorOutput_Normal : TPIColRec =
   (
     Left   : 13;
     Top    : 4;
     WTitle : 'NORMAL OUTPUT COLOR';
     Color  : 0
   );

  const Color_Highlight : TPIColRec =
   (
     Left   : 13;
     Top    : 4;
     WTitle : 'HILITE OUTPUT COLOR';
     Color  : 0
   );

  begin
    case MItem of                       { selection according to menu item chosen }
```

```
  1: begin {---------------------- text input for output window header -}
        TPIGet( TPIC_OutHeader,70,TextOutput.Text );        { read header }
        TPID_Entry( TextOutput );                    { call input procedure }
        TPIPut( TPIC_OutHeader,70,TextOutput.text );         { write input }
     end;

  2: begin {--------------------- select color of output window header -}
        TPIGet( TPIC_OutHeaderW, 1, ColorOutput.Color );    { read color }
        Create_a_Window( FALSE );              { create color output window }
        TPIColor( ColorOutput, OutHeaderProc );         { color selection }
        TPIPut( TPIC_OutHeaderW, 1, ColorOutput.Color );          { store }
        Close_the_Window;                    { close color output window }
     end;

  3: begin {-----------color selection normal text color output window -}
        TPIGet( TPIC_OutNORMW, 1, ColorOutput_Normal.Color );{ read color }
        Create_a_Window( FALSE );              { create color output window }
        TPIColor( ColorOutput_Normal, OutNormProc );    { color selection }
        TPIPut( TPIC_OUTNORMW, 1, ColorOutput_Normal.Color );    { store }

        Close_the_Window;                       { close color output window }
     end;

  4: begin {------------------- color selection for the highlight color -}
        TPIGet( TPIC_OutHIW, 1, Color_Highlight.Color );    { read color }
        Create_a_Window( FALSE );              { create color output window }
        TPIColor( Color_Highlight,
  );          { color selection }
        TPIPut( TPIC_OUTHIW, 1, Color_Highlight.Color );         { store }
        Close_the_Window;                       { close color output window }
     end;
  end;
end;

{**************************************************************************
*  OutPutInst : create output window menu data and call menu routine     *
**************************************************************************}

procedure OutPutInst;

const OutPut_Menu : TPIMenu_Rec =
  (
   Left   : 10;
   Top    : 3;
   WTitle : 'OUTPUT WINDOW';
   NumEnt : 4;
   MnuTxt : ( '#Title',
             '#Header color',
             '#Normal color',
             'h#Ighlight color',
             '', '', '', '','', '','', '','', '','', '' )
  );

begin
  TPI_Menu( OutPut_Menu, OutReac );                  { call menu selection }
end;
```

13. Multitasking

Multitasking came closer to reality when faster versions of the 80286, followed by the 80386 microprocessor, appeared on the market. Although they improved the speed of PC applications, these advances could not improve the *efficiency* of these applications because of the memory limits of 640K under MS-DOS.

Since the power and efficiency of a PC is fully realized only with multitasking, it isn't surprising that the demand for an operating system that uses multitasking is increasing. This could eventually mean the end of MS-DOS as it's used today. In the last few years more applications have tried to implement multitasking.

One example is the spreadsheet Multiplan from Microsoft. Multiplan works well because, unlike other applications, it doesn't spend execution time waiting for input. This valuable time is used more efficiently because it is spent processing other tasks rather than waiting for keyboard input.

Multiplan processes the worksheet and calculates the individual fields and displays the results while accepting input from the user. Instead of simultaneously processing several external applications, Multiplan is a parallel calculation of several processes within the program.

We'll use the multitasking unit (MT), even though it's not fully supported by MS-DOS, and a few other tricks to implement this method. The MT unit allows your Turbo Pascal programs to operate in a multitasking environment.

The MT unit enables you to divide your programs into an almost endless number of units called *tasks*. These tasks can be executed almost simultaneously. We'll present enhanced versions of the WIN and KBM units, from Chapters 6 and 7 which are specifically designed to work with the MT unit. These units give the tasks access to the screen and avoid excluding input from the keyboard and mouse.

However, merely having these units available isn't sufficient. The multitasking environment is more than the simultaneous operation of various tasks. You'll need to solve many problems before multitasking units can run properly. "Race conditions" and "interprocess communication" are two key phrases that we'll discuss in this chapter.

13.1 Multitasking with MTDEMO

We'll present an example, called MTDEMO, before discussing the theory of multitasking units. MTDEMO will clarify the multitasking unit and the units that are used with it. This program is included on the diskette accompanying this book. The files needed to execute this program are listed in the table below. Copy these into your Turbo directory and compile it into an executable file.

File	Task
MTDEMO.PAS	Demo program
MT.PAS	Multitasking unit MT
MTA.ASM	Assembler module for the multitasking unit
MTA.OBJ	MTA.ASM in assembled form
WINMT.PAS	First part of the WIN unit modified for MT
WIN2MT.PAS	Second part of the WIN unit modified for MT
KBMT.PAS	KBM unit modified for MT
KBMTA.ASM	Assembler module for the KBMT unit
KBMTA.OBJ	KBMTA.ASM in assembled form
FARJMP.PAS	"Accelerator" from Chapter 8

Files needed to convert MTDEMO.PAS into an executable EXE program

As you start MTDEMO, three windows appear on the screen representing the three tasks created by the program. They're executed simultaneously with the MT unit and each represents an application. These windows have the following responsibilities:

SHELL   Controls the other tasks based on input and commands it receives from the user.

Spreadsheet Task

This task uses the CALC command for performing complex mathematical calculations. It appears and operates similar to a spreadsheet.

Directory Task

Uses the WHERE command to search the current drive for a specified filename or extension. It displays the directories where these files are found and functions similarly to the MS-DOS utility of the same name.

When MTDEMO starts, the cursor automatically appears in the ShellTask. The other two tasks can be executed by entering a command at the SHELL. This is similar to the MS-DOS command interpreter. As usual, you enter commands following a prompt. You can use the following keys while editing your input:

<Backspace>   Erases the character preceding the cursor.

<Enter>   Completes the input.

<Esc>   Moves the cursor to the next line. No input is sent to the SHELL.

```
┌──── Spreadsheet Task ────┬──────── Directory Task ───────┐
│        A    |    B       │\PASC_EXE\DEMO.PAS             │
│  1Function Table         │\PASC_EXE\TPIC.PAS            │
│  2                       │\PASC_EXE\TPINST.PAS          │
│  3f(x)=cos(x)*sin(x)*x/-x│\TEMPO2\SAA.PAS              │
│  4      x        f(x)    │\TEMPO2\SAA2.PAS            │
│  5---------------------- │\TEMPO2\SAADEMO.PAS          │
│  6                       │                              │
│  7    19.00      0.645920│Search for: *.PAS            │
│  8    20.00      1.666124│Directory : \FL\             │
│  9    21.00     -2.100015│Found     :    6             │
│ 10    21.00     -2.100015├─────────── SHELL ───────────┤
│ 11    22.00      0.041515│                              │
│ 12    23.00      2.162412│>calc 1 3000                 │
│ 13    24.00     -1.881832│CALC started.                │
│ 14    25.00     -0.655937│                              │
│ 15    26.00      2.515417│>Where *.pas                 │
│ 16    27.00     -1.451777│                              │
│ 17    28.00     -1.379894│>                            │
│ 18    29.00      2.673391│                              │
│ 19    30.00     -0.834758│                              │
│ 20    31.00     -2.057792│                              │
│ 21    32.00      2.602227│                              │
│ 22                       │                              │
└──────────────────────────┴──────────────────────────────┘
```

An example of MTDEMO on the screen

You cannot enter normal MS-DOS commands in the SHELL, even though it's similar to the MS-DOS interpreter. These commands are not recognized by the SHELL and will result in an "Unknown command!" error. Instead, three commands are used to control the program. The first two are directed toward the two other tasks (Spreadsheet and Directory). The third command is END. Use it when you want to terminate the program.

The Spreadsheet Task (located on the left side of the screen) starts with the CALC command followed by two whole number parameters. The two parameters are the limits of a value area which CALC computes in single steps. CALC builds a Function Table in the spreadsheet. The computed value controls the Function Table and the following 14 values are used as function parameter X in the equation f(x). The equation is listed above the Function Table in the worksheet.

Please enter (note the space between the two values):

```
calc 1 3000
```

These calculations keep CALC busy for quite awhile. Even a 386 system requires time to process 3,000 values and to calculate 15 function equations involving floating point

521

operations for each value. However, since CALC is executing in a multitasking environment, you don't have to wait for this task to terminate.

Note that the cursor is blinking in the SHELL and is waiting for you to enter another task. For example, you can ask the Directory Task to locate all files, with the .PAS extension, in the current drive. Enter the following (include the space between where and *):

```
where *.pas
```

The Directory Task begins with the root directory and searches through all the subdirectories. All of the Pascal files you previously copied to the disk for compiling the MT program soon appear in the Directory window. The files that are found and the complete path name are displayed in the Directory window. While the current directory is displayed you can also see the processing of other directories, in the "Directory:" line, in the highlighted portion of the window (as shown in the illustration below). The third line of the highlighted portion of the window, "Found:", gives the number of matches MTDEMO locates in the search.

```
•••Search for: *.PAS                          •
•••Directory : \FL\                           •
••Found     :    6                            •
```

The highlighted portion of the Directory window in MTDEMO

As Directory continues its search for the specified files, the Spreadsheet Task continues to execute but at a slower rate because it's now "sharing" the processor with Directory. This is true multitasking. Although other tasks are using the processor, you can continue entering data in the SHELL window even though the other two tasks are using the processor.

As CALC and WHERE continue to execute, you can add additional commands to both tasks in the SHELL window. These commands are temporarily stored in a queue until the current task is completed. Use the "stop" command to terminate a particular task before it's completed:

```
calc stop
```
or
```
where stop
```

The two tasks stop immediately and can now accept new commands.

You can leave the MTDEMO, terminate all three tasks, and close their windows by entering the END command.

Now let's see how MTDEMO, by using the MT unit, simultaneously executes the three tasks and how SHELL passes the parameters to the other two tasks.

```
{*****************************************************************************
*    MtDemo : Demonstrates the multitasking unit MT using the               *
*             multitasking WINMT (window) and KBMT (keyboard/mouse) units.   *
**-------------------------------------------------------------------------**
*    Author        : MICHAEL TISCHER                                        *
*    developed on   : 06/30/1989                                            *
*    last update on : 03/12/1990                                            *
*****************************************************************************}

program MtDemo;

uses FarJmp,                                    { "Accelerator" from Chapter 8 }
     Dos,                                               { standard DOS unit }
     MT,                                                 { multitasking unit }
     WinMt,                                      { window unit for multitasking }
     Kbmt;                            { keyboard and mouse unit for multitasking }

type CalcCmd     = ( CALCIT, STOPc, TERMINATESc );      { Calc task command }
     CalcMessage = record                               { Calc task message }
                      CmCode : CalcCmd;                    { command code }
                      case byte of
                        0 : ( UpperLimit, BottomLimit : integer ); { CALCIT }
                    end;

     WhereCmd     = ( SEARCH, STOPw, TERMINATESw );    { Where task command }
     WhereMessage = record                             { Where task command }
                      CmCode : WhereCmd;                   { command code }
                      case byte of
                        0 : ( DirMask : string[15] );           { SEARCH }
                    end;
```

MTDEMO includes a series of units required by the main program and the various tasks. These units include MT, WinMT and Kbmt (the three multitasking units), the FarJmp unit from Chapter 8 and the standard DOS unit.

The Directory Task requires the FarJmp unit and the DOS unit requires the procedures FindFirst and FindNext to process the various directories during the search for files. When the task receives the STOP command to terminate the search, the DOS unit requires these procedures to return to the main part of the Directory Task as quickly as possible.

The USES command is followed by various internal type declarations. These describe the structure of the messages through which the Directory Task sends commands to the other two tasks. The first type, CalcCmd, reflects the various commands sent to the CALC task.

CALCIT   Prompts the CALC task to begin its calculations.

STOPc   Halts a calculation to prepare CALC for receiving the next command.

TERMINATESc
    Terminates the CALC task.

The three command codes aren't directly sent to CALC. Instead, they're part of a data structure called CalcMessage. The first field in this structure has the name CmCode and stores one of the command codes mentioned above.

The fields that follow are designed as variant records. They ensure that CalcMessage contains the command code and information required for the current task. One such variant is defined here because CalcMessage must contain information using only the CALCIT task. The two parameters the user enters (UpperLimit, BottomLimit) following the CALC command are passed in CalcMessage and the upper and lower boundaries of the region to be processed.

The types WhereCmd and WhereMessage for the Directory Task are also created similar to the types CalcCmd and CalcMessage. Here, WhereCmd uses the commands processed by Directory:

SEARCH   Initiates the search for files.

STOPw   Ends the search and prepares WHERE for receiving the next command.

TERMINATESw
    Terminates the task.

WhereMessage also contains, along with the current command code in the Variable command, a variant necessary for SEARCH. DirMask is an ASCII string containing the search criteria for the files to be found.

```
var ShellTask,                      { task descriptors for the three tasks }
    CalcTask,
    WhereTask  : TDP;
    CalcQueue,                           { queue pointer to the queue for }
    WhereQueue : QUEUEP;              { the Where and Calc tasks        }
```

The program contains only a few global variables because most of the information is in the individual tasks. Only the information which is globally available is stored here. These are three variables of the TDP (Task Descriptor Pointer) type defined by the MT unit. As we'll see, the program contains one such pointer from the MT unit when these three tasks are created. This pointer is used to identify the various tasks to the MT unit. The type of information stored by MT in a task descriptor will be examined more closely when we describe the MT unit.

The global variables create two additional variables of the type QUEUEP. Although pointers, they're not pointers to task descriptors, but pointers to queues. They're used by various tasks to exchange information. In MTDEMO the variables CalcQueue and WhereQueue are used when the two wait queues are created to send the ShellTask to its associates.

All five global variables are initialized inside the main program. Here the call of one of the public functions from the MT unit plays an important role. The MT unit provides the function MtCreateQueue to generate two queues for communication between SHELL, WHERE and CALC.

```
{********************************************************************
*                     M A I N   P R O G R A M                      *
********************************************************************}

begin
  ClrScr;

  {-- the two queues for communication with background tasks are created --}

  CalcQueue  := MtCreateQueue( 20, sizeof( CalcMessage ) );
  WhereQueue := MtCreateQueue( 20, sizeof( WhereMessage ) );

  {-- create the foreground and the two background tasks -----------------}

  ShellTask := MtCreateTask( Shell, 10,  4000, NO_ARG );
  WhereTask := MtCreateTask( Where,  5, 20000, pointer( WhereQueue ) );
  CalcTask  := MtCreateTask( Calc,   5,  4000, pointer( CalcQueue ) );

  MtaStart( 2 );                                       { start multitasking }
  WinSetCursor( 0, 0 );
end.
```

MtCreateQueue allows any number of queues as long as memory is available for the data structure required on the heap. As first parameter, MtCreateQueue expects the number of groups of data that are simultaneously placed in a queue. The value 20 is indicated for both the CALCqueue and WhereQueue. For example, as a CALC task is executed, twenty additional tasks are formulated in the ShellTask and added in sequential order to the end of the queue where they wait to be executed by CALC.

You may be wondering what happens when you enter an additional CALC command or WHERE command into a full queue. The MT unit holds the ShellTask until the next task from the queue is executed by CALC or WHERE. This will make space for the additional entry.

A second parameter, MtCreateQueue expects the size of the individual queue entries. It requires this information to allocate sufficient space for the data structures (or scalar types) on the heap. You can pass any information to tasks with a queue. A queue is only concerned with the size in bytes. It considers the stored information as a random sequence of the same size bytes. We'll provide more information on this when we describe the various tasks remaining in contact.

The function MtCreateTask, from the MT unit, is used to create the three tasks. This function expects four parameters, during its call, to describe the task to the MT unit.

First the start address is named for the task. This has to be a procedure name passed by Turbo Pascal as procedural pointer of type TS to MTCreateTask. TS represents procedures which obtain, as a single argument, a nontypical pointer from the caller. This gives the task creator the ability to send certain information to the task by passing a pointer to a certain data structure or one of the scalar data types packed in a pointer.

MtCreateTask expects a numeric value between 1 and 255 as a second parameter. These values represent the priority of the task. This parameter is important because the MT unit uses a method known as *scheduling* to give preference to tasks with the highest priority instead of allocating identical time for all tasks. Scheduling is a means of managing a multitasking system. Any tasks with lower priority are executed only when tasks with higher priority aren't available for execution.

The third parameter for MtCreateTask indicates the size of the stack at the disposal of the task. In a multitasking system, every task has its own stack so that various tasks can use the same program code. Later we'll discuss this more thoroughly and include an example.

This pointer itself is the fourth parameter which MtCreate task accepts during its call. Use the value NO_ARG, which corresponds to a NULL pointer (NIL), during the call of MtCreateTask if you don't need to use this pointer for passing information.

We'll provide more information and examples on queues, scheduling, the MT unit and tasks throughout this chapter.

Remember that the three tasks created in the main program through calls of MtCreateTask aren't started automatically. They're declared as tasks for the MT unit. Their access only begins with the start of multitasking initiated by a call of the procedure MtStart.

The three procedures SHELL, WHERE and CALC are declared as tasks. These correspond to the three tasks we've discussed. For the Scheduler to determine the priorities of the three tasks, the WhereTask and CalcTask have the value five and the ShellTask has the value ten. Therefore the ShellTask has the higher priority and WhereTask and CalcTask are "background tasks".

Note: The priorities in the MT unit are considered relative and not absolute. The specific values 5 and 10 by themselves aren't always important. What is important is that Directory and CALC have a lower priority than SHELL. The MT unit would reach the same conclusion if Directory and CALC had a value of 79 and SHELL the priority 231; only the relative relationship is important.

These priorities ensure that the CalcTask and Wheretask are executed only when SHELL is inactive, although you may have thought that SHELL is always active. This isn't necessarily true. Actually, SHELL is inactive most of the time because it's waiting for input. It's only started by the MT unit (more accurately by the KBMT unit) when a key is pressed. Until this time the MT unit controls the CalcTask and WhereTask because they're the next priority.

The value 4000, a common value, is indicated for the stack size for both CalcTask and ShellTask. This value doesn't overburden the stack by storing local variables. Although any values to 3000 may be enough, slightly higher values can be used because excess space is available since MTDEMO isn't large.

Since the WhereTask requires much more space, it is given a stack of 20,000 bytes. It searches recursively through the directory tree for specified files. Directory requires more storage on the stack than non-recursive procedures and functions for the execution of recursive procedures with local variables.

The WhereTask and CalcTask each get a pointer as parameters to their own queue. They could also obtain this information from global variables. However, in this example we want to demonstrate passing information to tasks. The ShellTask doesn't receive an argument during its call and, because of this, the constant NO_ARG is provided during the call of MtCreateTask for this parameter.

The declaration of the three tasks is immediately followed by the start of the multitasking. This also starts the ShellTask (by using the SHELL procedure) since it has the highest priority. The MtaStart procedure, responsible for starting the multitasking, passes the value two as a parameter to MTDEMO. This value sets the speed of the MT unit to switch between the various tasks. We'll discuss how important this parameter is when we describe the MT unit.

The call of MtaStart also passes control of the main program to the various tasks, which are created either through MtCreateTask or during further program execution. A return is made to the main program only when the last task created is finished. The program continues again after the MtaStart call.

The ShellTask

Let's first look at the importance of the three tasks. The commands of the ShellTask are used to coordinate how the other tasks are executed.

```
{*****************************************************************************
 * Shell : the foreground task, which has the highest priority and starts  *
 *         or stops other tasks based on input from the user.              *
 **-----------------------------------------------------------------------**
 * Input  : QueuePtr                                                        *
 *****************************************************************************}

{$F+}

procedure Shell( QueuePtr : pointer );

var WinHandle : integer;                              { window handle }
    WhereStop : WhereMessage;         { termination assignment for Where }
    CalcStop  : CalcMessage;           { termination assignment for Calc }
    CmCode,                        { strings for evaluation of command input }
    Parameter,
    InputStr  : string;
    SpacePos  : integer;               { position of the space in the string }
begin
  WinHandle := TaskWinOpen( 30, 12, 79, 24, DBL_FR, '   SHELL   ' );
  gotoxy( VL(0), VO(0) );

  repeat
    InputStr := UserInput;                     { accept input from user }
    if ( InputStr <> '' ) then                    { no empty string? }
      begin                                       { no, read command }
        SpacePos := pos( ' ', InputStr );         { search for space }
        if SpacePos = 0 then                         { not found }
          begin                 { no, enter command only without parameter }
            CmCode := InputStr;
            Parameter := '';
          end
        else                 { space found, separate command and parameter }
          begin
            CmCode := copy( InputStr, 1, SpacePos-1 );
            Parameter := copy( InputStr, SpacePos+1,
                         length( InputStr ) - SpacePos );
            while Parameter[ 1 ] = ' ' do      { remove space at beginning }
              delete( Parameter, 1, 1 );       { of the parameter          }
          end;

        {-- read command and call the proper procedure --------------------}

        if ( CmCode = 'WHERE' )
          then CmdWhere( Parameter )
          else
```

```
            if ( CmCode = 'CALC' )
              then CmdCalc( Parameter )
            else
              if ( CmCode <> 'END' ) then
                writeln( 'Unknown command!');

        writeln;
        end;
    until InputStr = 'END';

    {-- terminate program ------------------------------------------------}

    CalcStop.CmCode := TERMINATESc;        { set command code for "terminate" }
    MtWriteQueue( CalcQueue, CalcStop );              { send message to Calc }

    WhereStop.CmCode := TERMINATESw;       { set command code for "terminate" }
    MtWriteQueue( WhereQueue, WhereStop );            { send message to Where }

    WinClose( TRUE );                                 { close task window again }
  end;

  {$F-}
```

On first glance the SHELL procedure (the ShellTask) isn't different from a normal Pascal procedure and doesn't contain anything that characterizes it as a task used against other tasks. Only FAR stands out, but for a Pascal procedure called through procedural pointers, this isn't unusual. This is a characteristic of all Pascal procedures declared by the call of MtCreateTask as a task. The MT unit handles potential problems and obstacles which occur with the concurrent execution of tasks. For a programmer this is an advantage because it's possible to develop and test tasks as normal procedures before they're included in a multitasking program and are converted into a task with MtCreateTask.

Similar to other procedures, tasks can include local variables, reference global variables and call other procedures or functions. Even a recursive call of itself is valid. SHELL uses this capability by declaring local variables. Also it's able to call other procedures and functions which initiates the task.

First, with the call of the function TaskWinOpen, SHELL opens a window for itself. This function, in the MTDEMO program, accepts for all three tasks opening a window by using the various functions and procedures from the WINMT unit.

As a parameter it expects the following at its call:

• The corner coordinates of the window.

• The type of border around the window.

• An ASCII string as a window name.

529

The window name is displayed in the center of the top border in the SHELL window. It returns, to the caller, the window handle passed to it during the call by WinOpen. In this program the handle isn't required. However, this handle is used for the call of WinInFront to move a certain window into the foreground if a task opens several windows.

SHELL enters a loop after the call of TaskWinOpen. In this loop it continuously tests for a command from the keyboard. The loops ends only with the END command.

In this loop the query of the input occurs with the call of the UserInput procedure. This procedure only returns to its caller after you've acknowledged an input with <Enter>. SHELL evaluates this input and separates the actual command from the parameters. An error message appears if it isn't the WHERE, the CALC or the END command. This starts a new loop.

If, during the evaluation of the command, SHELL encounters the "WHERE" command, the CmdWhere procedure is called for further evaluation of the command. The same happens with the CmdCalc procedure when SHELL encounters the CALC command.

SHELL reacts to the END command by completing the input loop and then sending two local variables WhereStop and CalcStop to CALC and WHERE. These two variables accept commands to the two tasks. SHELL loads in the current termination code as a command. Next it sends the message with a call of the MtWriteQueue procedure from the MT unit to the affected task. The variable which contains the information to be sent and the queue pointer returned during the call of MtCreateQueue is indicated.

MtWriteQueue immediately returns to its caller if the queues of the two tasks aren't full. SHELL then erases its task window with a call of WinClose and terminates, like any normal task, with an END command. Since a task doesn't have a direct caller, terminating either the SHELL or one of the two other task procedures doesn't lead to a jump to a certain program location. The completed task is automatically removed from the list of the available tasks. This ends the multitasking environment if this task was the last one active. The program continues with the program line after the call of MtaStart.

Let's look at the various procedures and functions which are called and implemented inside SHELL. First is the function TaskWinOpen. This consists of calls to the various routines from the WIN unit.

```
{***********************************************************************
*   TaskWinOpen : creates the window for a task                       *
**-------------------------------------------------------------------**
*   Input   :  X1, Y1 = upper left corner of the task window          *
*              X2, Y2 = bottom right corner of the task window         *
*              FrType = frame type for window frame                   *
*              Title  = window title                                  *
*   Output  :  Handle for access to the task window                   *
```

```
***********************************************************************}

function TaskWinOpen( x1, y1, x2, y2, FrType : byte;
                      Title                  : string ) : integer;

begin
  TaskWinOpen := WinOpen( x1, y1, x2, y2 );                    { open window }
  WinFill(  VL(1), VO(1), VR(-1), VU(-1), ' ', $7 );                { clear }
  WinFrame( VL(0), VO(0), VR(0), VU(0), FrType, $7 );         { draw frame }
  WinPrint( ( x2-x1-length( Title )+1 ) shr 1 + x1 + 1, y1, $70, Title );
  WinSetView( VL(1), VO(1), VR(-1), VU(-1) );           { set view range }
  GotoXY( VL(0), VO(0) );  { determine output position for Write & Writeln }
end;
```

SHELL also uses the UserInput procedure to accept input from the user.

```
{***********************************************************************
* UserInput : accepts a DOS type input from the user                  *
**-------------------------------------------------------------------**
* Input    : none                                                     *
* Output   : the string which was entered                             *
***********************************************************************}

function UserInput : string;

var InputStr : string;                                  { input string }
    Ev       : EVENT;                          { keyboard/mouse event }
    i        : integer;                             { loop counter }

begin
  write( '>' );
  InputStr := '';                                  { no input occurred }

  {-- input loop terminated by <Enter> ------------------------------------}

  repeat
    WinSetCursor( WhereX, WhereY );          { set cursor to current position }
    KbmEventWait( EV_KEY_PRESSED, Ev );        { accept only keys as events }
    case Ev.Key of                                      { evaluate key }
      ESC : begin                          { ESCAPE = new beginning for input }
              write( '\', #13#10, ' ' );               { switch to next line }
              InputStr := '';                              { input empty }
            end;

      BS : if ( WhereX <> VL(1) ) then               { BS = delete character }
             begin                                   { to left of cursor     }
               write( #8#32#8 );
               dec( byte(InputStr[ 0 ]) );          { delete last character }
             end;

      else                                       { every other character }
        if ( Ev.Key > 31 ) and ( Ev.Key < 256 ) and ( WhereX < VR(-1) ) then
```

531

```
          begin    { character code between 32 and 255 and space for input }
            write( chr( Ev.Key ) );                      { display character }
            InputStr := InputStr + chr( Ev.Key );        { append to string }
          end;
    end;
  until ( Ev.Key = CR );                                    { wait for <Enter> }
  writeln;

  {-- convert string to upper case letters --------------------------------}

  for i := 1 to length( InputStr ) do
    InputStr[ i ] := UpCase( InputStr[ i ] );

  UserInput := InputStr;                                    { pass to string }
end;
```

Although the standard function ReadKey could have been used, the KbmEventWait procedure is used to query the keyboard. This procedure is unique because it doesn't require any execution time if the expected events did not occur. It's accessed only after an event from the keyboard or mouse is available. Even tasks with low priorities can access the processor with this method. This method also doesn't require input from the keyboard or mouse.

The procedures CmdWhere and CmdCalc are called inside SHELL when the procedure notes a CALC or WHERE command during the check on the input from the user. Both procedures are responsible for evaluating the parameter(s) behind the command and, if necessary, sending a message to a task which would trigger a certain action.

```
{*****************************************************************************
 *  CmdCalc : evaluates the parameters which were indicated after the Calc  *
 *            command. A message for the Calc task is created if necessary. *
 **-----------------------------------------------------------------------**
 *  Input   : Parameter = characters which followed the CALC command        *
 *  Info    : the following syntaxes are recognized:                        *
 *               CALC STOP          <<or>>                                  *
 *               CALC from to                                               *
 *****************************************************************************}

procedure CmdCalc( Parameter : string );

var CalcStart : CalcMessage;                        { assignment to Calc }
    ArgS      : string;                             { stores an argument }
    Val_Error,                            { error variable for binary conversion }
    pfr,                                              { parameter 1 }
    pto,                                              { parameter 2 }
    SpacePos  : integer;                  { character position of space }

begin
  {-- evaluate STOP parameter separately ----------------------------------}
```

```
    if ( Parameter = 'STOP' ) then                       { was STOP indicated? }
      begin                                                            { yes }
        CalcStart.CmCode := STOPc;                        { send assignment }
        MtWriteQueue( CalcQueue, CalcStart );             { to Calc          }
        writeln( 'CALC stopped.' );
        exit;
      end;

    {-- assume two numeric arguments -------------------------------------------}

    SpacePos := pos( ' ', Parameter );          { search for space as separator }
    if ( SpacePos <> 0 ) then                                           { found? }
      begin                        { yes, erase all spaces between the parameters }
        while ( Parameter[ SpacePos ] = ' ' ) and
              ( SpacePos <= length( Parameter ) ) do
          delete( Parameter, SpacePos, 1 );

        if ( SpacePos > length( Parameter ) ) then     { no second parameter? }
          SpacePos := 0;                                         { no, error }
      end;

    if ( SpacePos = 0 ) then                                          { error? }
      writeln( 'Syntax error! Call: CALC from to ' )
    else
      begin                                          { first parameter found }
        ArgS := copy( Parameter, 1, SpacePos-1 );      { get parameter "pfr" }
        val( ArgS, pfr, Val_Error );                    { convert to binary }
        if ( Val_Error = 0 ) then                  { error during conversion? }
          begin                                      { no, get second parameter }
            ArgS := copy( Parameter, SpacePos, length(Parameter)-SpacePos+1 );
            val( ArgS, pto, Val_Error );           { convert also to binary }
          end;
        if ( Val_Error <> 0 ) then             { could argument be converted? }
          writeln( 'Error! Invalid argument' )
        else                                                            { yes }
          begin
            with CalcStart do              { create assignment and send }
              begin
                CmCode      := CALCIT;
                BottomLimit := pfr;
                UpperLimit  := pto;
              end;
            MtWriteQueue( CalcQueue, CalcStart );              { send message }
            writeln( 'CALC started.' );
          end;
      end;
  end;
```

CmdCalc accepts this task for the CALC command. It checks to see if the command word "STOP" is entered as a parameter. This would cause CALC to terminate its task. If true, the MtWriteQueue procedure to CALC and CmdCalc is prematurely ended with the EXIT procedure.

533

Otherwise the parameter string passed must contain two numeric parameters and CmdCalc begins with the analysis of this parameter. Only if it actually encounters two separate parameters (numbers converted into a binary format with the VAL procedure) the command goes to CALC to process the numbers between the two values indicated and to build a Function Table.

If the analysis and conversion of the parameters fail, CmdCalc produces an error message and returns to the caller without performing any additional tasks.

CmdWhere, although operating similarly, has an easier task to accomplish. Only one parameter is expected and has to be examined for the STOP command. CmdWhere sends an error message if the user hasn't provided a character after the WHERE command. A stop or a search command is created which causes WHERE to search for the indicated files.

```
{***************************************************************************
*   CmdWhere : evaluate WHERE command and if necessary send a message    *
*             to the directory task                                       *
**-----------------------------------------------------------------------**
*   Input : Parameter = the string which followed the WHERE command       *
*   Info    : the following syntaxes are recognized:                      *
*             WHERE file mask          <<or>>                             *
*             WHERE STOP                                                   *
***************************************************************************}

procedure CmdWhere( Parameter : string );

var WhereStart : WhereMessage;                        { assignment to Where }

begin
  {-- evaluate STOP parameter separately ----------------------------------}

  if ( Parameter = 'STOP' ) then                      { was STOP indicated? }
    begin                                                          { yes }
      WhereStart.CmCode := STOPw;                   { send corresponding  }
      MtWriteQueue( WhereQueue, WhereStart );       { assignment to Where }
      writeln( 'WHERE stopped.' );
      exit;
    end;

  if ( Parameter <> '' ) then                   { was a file mask indicated? }
    begin                                                          { yes }
      WhereStart.CmCode := SEARCH;                { build start message }
      WhereStart.DirMask := Parameter;
      MtWriteQueue( WhereQueue, WhereStart );     { and send it          }
    end
  else                                            { no parameter indicated }
    writeln( 'Syntax error! Call:  WHERE file_mask' )
end;
```

The CalcTask

Now we'll discuss the second of the three tasks, the CALC procedure (identical to the task of the same name).

```
{**************************************************************************
 *  Calc : background task for spreadsheet calculations                   *
 **----------------------------------------------------------------------**
 *  Input  : QueuePtr = Pointer to the Queue, through which the task       *
 *                      gets information and assignments from other tasks  *
 **************************************************************************}

{$F+}

procedure Calc( QueuePtr : pointer );

var i            : byte;         { loop counter for construction of the screen }
    j,                          { loop counter for processing a "from-to" assignment }
    Handle       : integer;                      { handle of the task window }
    MyQueue      : QUEUEP;      { queue through which task gets assignments }
    A_NewMessage,                           { the next assignment in the queue }
    Assignment   : CalcMessage;          { assignment from another task }
    x            : real;                          { x to compute f(x) }

begin
  MyQueue := QUEUEP( QueuePtr );                     { create queue pointer }

  {-- build task window -------------------------------------------------}

  Handle := TaskWinOpen( 0, 0, 29, 24, SIN_FR, ' Spreadsheet Task ' );
  WinPrint( VL(4), VO(0), $70, '    A    |       B       ' );
  TextColor( 0 );
  TextBackGround( $7 );
  for i := 1 to 22 do
    begin
      GotoXY( VL(0), VO(i) );
      write( i:4 );
    end;
  WinPrint( VL(4), VO(1), $07, 'Function Table' );
  WinPrint( VL(4), VO(3), $07, 'f(x)=cos(x)*sin(x)*x/√x' );
  WinPrint( VL(4), VO(4), $07, '    x          f(x)    ' );
  WinPrint( VL(4), VO(5), $07, '-----------------------' );

  TextColor( $7 );
  TextBackGround( $0 );

  {-- Queue query loop --------------------------------------------------}

  repeat
    MtReadQueue( MyQueue, Assignment );     { wait for message in the queue }
    if ( Assignment.CmCode = CALCIT ) then                { evaluate command }
      begin                                               { compute! }
```

535

```
        j := Assignment.BottomLimit;                    { load initial value }

   {-- process all integer values between start and end value --------}

   while ( j <= Assignment.UpperLimit ) do        { upper limit reached? }
     begin                                          { no, another round }
       x := j;                                    { load starting value }
       for i := 7 to 21 do { process the individual spreadsheet lines }
         begin
           GotoXY( VL(4), VO(i) );
           write( x:9:2, cos(x)*sin(x)*x/sqrt(x):15:6 );
           x := x+1;                                   { compute next x }
         end;
       inc( j );                             { increment loop counter }

       {-- test if a new assignment is available and if so, process --}

       if MtPeekQueue( MyQueue, A_NewMessage ) then
         begin                       { there was a message in the queue }
           if ( A_NewMessage.CmCode = STOPc ) or
              ( A_NewMessage.CmCode = TERMINATESc ) then
             begin          { STOP or TERMINATE ---> stop immediately }
               j := Assignment.UpperLimit+1; { set termination status }
               MtReadQueue( MyQueue, Assignment );      { load message }
             end;
         end;
     end;
 until ( Assignment.CmCode = TERMINATESc );

 WinClose( TRUE );                             { close task window again }
end;

{$F-}
```

After the first call, CALC converts the nontypical pointer passed into a pointer of the type QUEUEP. It stores the pointer in the MyQueue local variable. This method better organizes the program code even though this conversion could occur during any access to this pointer without having to store it in a local variable.

Then CALC builds its screen with TaskWinOpen and the usual procedures from the WINMT unit. Then it enters into the query loop. At the beginning of this loop it reads a message from its queue with MtReadQueue in the local variable assignment. Remember that CALC, because of its low priority, is only active when SHELL is inactive. The call of MtReadQueue holds CALC until a message is available in the queue.

When MtReadQueue returns to the query loop again, CALC checks the command field, in the message received, to determine if it contains a command for calculation. In this case it loads the lower limit of the indicated area from the message into the local loop variable j and enters into a loop which continues until j has reached the indicated maximum limit.

In this loop the fifteen elements of the Function Table are recalculated and displayed in the task window. MtPeekQueue determines whether a new message (a new assignment) is already available in the queue.

In the meantime, you may have entered "calc stop" or "end" which waits in the queue. CALC checks for this message during every run through the loop to avoid waiting for the stop or end command.

If the call of MtPeekQueue returns TRUE as function result a message is waiting in the queue. This message is delivered in the indicated variable without being removed from the queue. If CALC determines that this message contains a stop or end command, it loads the loop variable j with the upper limit of the indicated area to prematurely end the output loop. Then the message, already read by MtPeekQueue, is removed from the queue with a call of MtReadQueue and simultaneously loaded into the variable assignment. Its content affects the end of the queue query loop, marked with the UNTIL command.

The queue query loop is finally terminated be receiving an end command. The task window is cleared and the task is removed from the active list.

The WhereTask

The WhereTask, located in the procedure of the same name, works in a similar way concerning the permanent query of possible stop and termination messages.

```
{**************************************************************************
 *  Where : background task for file search on active drive             *
 **----------------------------------------------------------------------**
 *  Input : QueuePtr = Pointer to the queue through which the task gets  *
 *                     information and assignments from other tasks      *
 *************************************************************************}

{$F+}

procedure Where( QueuePtr : pointer );

type DirStrTyp = string[ 64 ];              { accepts search directories }

var dummy,                          { function result from SetJmp/LongJmp }
    Found,                                      { number of files found }
    WinHandle : integer;                    { handle of the task window }
    MyQueue   : QUEUEP;                      { pointer to the task queue }
    A_NewAQ,                         { variable to permanent assignment query }
    WhatsUp   : WhereMessage;                { message from the queue }
    SearchMsk : string[12];                              { file mask }
    FoundStr  : string[5];          { number of files found as string }
    StopJmp   : JMPBUF;                    { data for SetJmp and LongJmp }
    JumpInst  : boolean;                   { was SetJmp called already? }
```

```
{-- CHECKMES : determines the receipt of a new message --[ LOCAL ]---------}
{--            and reacts according to the message.               ---------}

procedure CheckMes;

begin
  {-- test if a new assignment is available and if so, process ------------}

  if MtPeekQueue( MyQueue, A_NewAQ ) then
    begin                                  { there was a message in the queue }
      if ( A_NewAQ.CmCode = STOPw ) or
         ( A_NewAQ.CmCode = TERMINATESw ) then
        begin                    { STOP or TERMINATE ---> quit immediately }
          MtReadQueue( MyQueue, WhatsUp );                  { load message }
          LongJmp( StopJmp, 0 );           { jump to the main part of Where }
        end;
    end;

  {-- the return to the caller only occurs if neither the  ----------------}
  {-- STOPw nor TERMINATEw were received                   ----------------}

end;

{-- PRINTDIR : display of a directory name -----------------[ LOCAL ]------}

procedure PrintDir( DirStr : DirStrTyp );

var Len : integer;

begin
  Len := VR(0) - VL(12) + 1;              { compute space for directory name }
  if ( length( DirStr ) > Len ) then                     { string too long? }
    begin                                                              { yes }
      byte( DirStr[ 0 ] ) := Len-3;                       { shorten string }
      WinPrint( VL(12), VU(2), $70, '...' + DirStr );
    end
  else                                               { string not too long }
    begin
      WinFill( VL(12), VU(2), VR(0), VU(2), ' ', $70 );     { erase field }
      WinPrint( VL(12), VU(2), $70, DirStr );
    end;
end;

{-- SCAN: recursive search procedure for the file name --------[ LOCAL ]---}

procedure Scan( Where : DirStrTyp );

var DirSearch  : SearchRec;                        { for FindFirst and FindNext }

begin
  {-- search and display file(s) in indicated directory -------------------}

  PrintDir( Where );                                    { display directory }
```

```
   FindFirst( Where + SearchMsk, AnyFile, DirSearch );          { search for }
                                                                 { first file }
   while ( DosError <> 18 ) do                          { found another file? }
     begin                                                     { yes, display }
       if ( DosError <> 0 ) then                           { path not found? }
         begin                                                          { yes }
           writeln( '-- ERROR --' );
           DosError := 18;                             { set termination condition }
         end
       else                                            { another file was found }
         begin
           writeln( Where+DirSearch.name );            { display directory name }
           inc( Found );                        { increment number of entries found }
           str( Found:5, FoundStr );            { convert to ASCII and display }
           WinPrint( VL(12), VU(3), $70, FoundStr );
           CheckMes;                                    { test for new message }
           FindNext( DirSearch );                       { search for next file }
         end;
     end;

   {-- search for all subdirectories in this directory and continue the ----}
   {-- search with a recursive call of this procedure                   ----}

   FindFirst( Where + '*.*', Directory, DirSearch );        { find first file }
   while ( DosError <> 18 ) do                          { found another file? }
     begin                                                     { yes, display }
       if ( DosError <> 0 ) then                           { path not found? }
         begin                                                          { yes }
           writeln( '-- FEHLER --');
           DosError := 18;                             { set termination condition }
         end
       else                                            { another file was found }
         begin
           CheckMes;                                    { test for new message }
           if ( DirSearch.Attr = DIRECTORY ) and
              ( DirSearch.Name <> '.' ) and ( DirSearch.Name <> '..' ) then
             begin                                       { subdirectory discovered }
               Scan( Where + DirSearch.Name + '\' );          { recursive call }
               PrintDir( Where );               { display current directory again }
             end;
           FindNext( DirSearch );       { search for next file ( directory ) }
         end;
     end;
   end;
end;

{-- main part of the SCAN procedure -----------------------------------------}

begin
  {-- create screen window for directory display -------------------------}

  WinHandle := TaskWinOpen( 30, 0, 79, 11, SIN_FR, ' Directory Task ' );
  WinColor( VL(0), VU(-2), VR(0), VU(0), $70 );
  WinPrint( VL(0), VU(-2), $70, 'Search for:' );
```

```
    WinPrint( VL(0), VU(-1), $70, 'Directory :' );
    WinPrint( VL(0), VU(-0), $70, 'Found    :' );

    WinSetView( VL(0), VO(0), VR(0), VU(-3) );
    gotoxy( VL(0), VO(0) );

    MyQueue := QUEUEP( QueuePtr );

    {-- Queue query loop -------------------------------------------------}

    JumpInst := FALSE;                                { SetJmp not called yet }
    repeat
      MtReadQueue( MyQueue, WhatsUp );          { get message from the queue }
      if ( JumpInst = FALSE ) then                { SetJump installed already? }
        begin                                                       { no }
          JumpInst := TRUE;                                    { but now }
          dummy := SetJmp( StopJmp );          { jump destination for LongJmp }
        end;
      if ( WhatsUp.CmCode = SEARCH ) then                { search for files? }
        begin                                                      { yes }
          WinFill( VL(0), VO(0), VR(0), VO(0), ' ', $07 );
          SearchMsk := WhatsUp.DirMask;                    { load file mask }
          WinPrint( VL(12), VU(1), $70, SearchMsk + '        ' );
          WinPrint( VL(12), VU(3), $70, '    0' );
          Found := 0;
          Scan( '\' );                  { begin search with the root directory }
        end;
    until ( WhatsUp.CmCode = TERMINATESw );

    WinClose( TRUE );                                { close task window again }
  end;

{$F-}
```

WHERE contains three local procedures supporting the procedure during the search for all files matching the specified search criteria. The SCAN procedure is important because it performs the actual search for the files and recursively calls itself when it finds a subdirectory. Let's begin with the main part of the procedure. In many ways it's similar to the CALC procedure.

Next, the task window is created and the pointer to the queue of the task, which was passed, is loaded into a local variable after a type conversion. Then the entry into the queue query loop with MtReadQueue waits for the message if the queue occurs. Then a test is made with the JumpIst Boolean variable to determine whether SetJmp is already installed. This procedure is required to offer the task, during the recursive calls of SCAN, the ability to react to the arrival of a stop or termination assignment and to immediately return to the queue query loop again without processing all recursion levels.

Since SetJump is called once for installing the jump destination, its call is stored in the variable JumpInst. This variable is loaded with the value FALSE before the first entry into the queue query loop. SetJmp is called only during the first run through the loop. At the same time JumpInst is set to TRUE to prevent new calls of SetJmp.

You may wonder why SetJmp is called inside the loop. The answer is easy if you consider the way SetJmp works. It marks the jump destination for a call of LongJmp. When it's called, LongJmp is called from SCAN which is called from inside the queue query loop. Therefore, the destination for the jump for LongJmp must also be in this loop.

After installing SetJmp, the content of the message received is examined to determine whether it's a command to search for files. If it is, the file mask which was passed is loaded into the local variable SearchMsk. This initializes the number of found files with 0 and then calls the SCAN procedure. The root directory is passed to it as search directory. The SCAN procedure from there searches all subdirectories, their subdirectories, and so on.

SCAN always processes the directory, indicated during its call, in two runs or *loops*. During the first run it uses the standard procedures FindFirst and FindNext to search for all the files matching the search criteria. Their names are displayed in the task window. Also displayed is FOUND, which is incremented after each match.

Then the local procedure CheckMes is called. This procedure serves as reaction to stop and termination commands. If no message is present, it returns to the caller and SCAN continues searching for files.

The queue query loop is terminated when it receives an end command. This causes WHERE to close the task window and finish the procedure and, therefore, the entire task.

The first search loop is followed by a second. The second search loop detects and processes all subdirectories in the directory just processed. SCAN generates its own recursive call to include the subdirectory just detected in the search if it finds a subdirectory. Also the CheckMes procedure is called to react to stop and termination messages.

CheckMes checks for a message in the WHERE queue by using the MtPeekQueue. Once a message is found, it's inspected by the A_New AQ variable when the message is loaded into MtPeekQueue. If CheckMes actually finds a stop or end request, it loads the message into the local variable WhatsUp. This is where messages are stored by the queue query loop in the main part of WHERE.

This is the first step to pass the new message to the main part of the procedure. The second step consists of a return jump to the queue query loop with LongJmp. If an end instruction is received, the return jump immediately leads to the completion for both the loop and the entire task.

This completes our discussion of MTDEMO. You now have an understanding of how the MT unit works and what is possible with MT. In the following sections we'll discuss the theory of tasks and queues to help you write your own multitasking programs.

13.2   Theory of Multitasking

Until now our discussion centered on multitasking and the simultaneous accessing of several tasks. This is actually misleading because the multitasking isn't actually simultaneous but an illusion caused by the quick switch between the various tasks. Only multi-processor systems are capable of simultaneously accessing several programs. The existing processors can perform one command at a time and, therefore, only a single sequence of commands.

The fast switching, executed at the same time between the various applications, has been the only way to simulate multitasking. This gives users the impression that the various program units are actually being executed simultaneously similar to the way a fast moving sequence of individual pictures suggests continual movement. This technique, called *task switching,* is used by the multitasking unit presented here and by the operating systems such as Unix and OS/2.

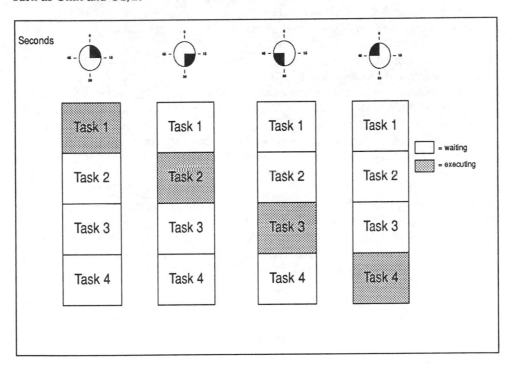

Multitasking through fast switching between various tasks

The program units performed at the same time are designated as processes or tasks. The difference between these two terms isn't very clear since different definitions appear in various publications. We'll use "task" throughout this chapter.

A fast switch between the various tasks can occur in two ways. The first is when a task always calls a specific system routine. This routine passes the execution to another task. It returns to the caller only when the other tasks also called by this routine and the original task will be selected again.

The disadvantages of this method is that the "task switching" originates from the individual tasks and requires frequent calls of the system routine for implementing fast and continuous task switching. Obviously, this increases the program code and impedes understanding the code.

The second way is used by several multitasking systems including the MT unit. This method is called "preemptive scheduling". During the task, switching triggers another task from the multitasking system and not from the active task. It simply stops the active task after a certain amount of time and continues executing the program with another task. The advantage of this method is that the speed of the task switching is always constant and are selected by the multitasking system without requiring special system calls in the tasks. However, this method is technically difficult because it requires a signal that gives the multitasking system the capability of task switching.

In the previous section you became familiar with tasks associated with the MTDEMO program. In this program every task is coded into one procedure assigned to it. However, various tasks do not always have to be represented with different procedures. The tasks will occasionally need to come in contact with other tasks. In fact, the full capabilities of the task are realized only when several tasks access the same program code. For example, in MTDEMO, for all three tasks to have open windows, they call TaskWinOpen shortly after their start. Caution must be used to avoid a memory conflict of these three units since this procedure is executed by all three tasks simultaneously.

The difference between the various tasks isn't revealed in the program code (always identical with TaskWinOpen) but in the data. First the local variables, including the passed parameters, must be mentioned and, for a function, the function result. This data is "private" since it exists for every task. The administration task assigns each task its own stack where the local variables are stored and administered.

During the task switching, the scheduler (the switch between the various tasks) also switches to the stack of the tasks to be started. The scheduler creates private local variables for each task. These variables isolate and separate it from the other tasks.

For example, TaskWinOpen manages to build three different windows at the same time. The individual task stack, where the passed parameters and the various local variables of the procedure are located, is switched with every task switching.

A similar switch isn't as easy to accomplish with global variables. They're usually task independent and are important for the entire program. They cannot be switched simply with the task switches between various data segments. We'll present various tricks and tips in this chapter to remove selected groups of global variables from general access of various tasks in order to make every task completely private.

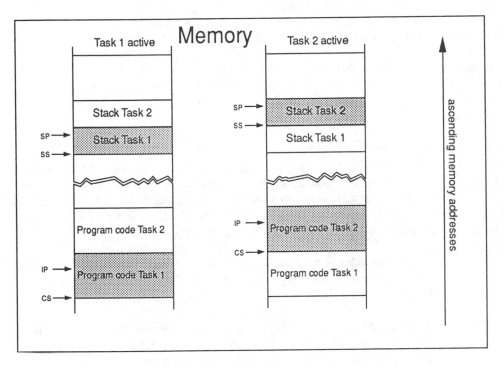

Switch of the stack and making local variables private on task levels

The switch between various stacks is only one of many tasks that the scheduler must perform in order to switch between the different tasks. Generally, during the task switching the scheduler must store the entire context of the active task and then restore the context of the task to be executed. The context of a task includes all operational items which are privately used by a task. The type of system using the multitasking system determines which operational items are included.

Besides a private stack, the context also includes the processor registers. They're stored with every task switching, similar to executing an interrupt, so that they will be available and unchanged when the task is reactivated. From this viewpoint they're simply local variables. They're resident on the processor level and not in the higher level language.

The context of a task of an MS-DOS computer also includes the interrupt vector table, the global variables of the MS-DOS kernel, the various storage locations in the BIOS variable area and the complete video RAM. This data usually isn't stored because it requires too much space. On the other hand, these variables, such as the MS-DOS kernel, aren't accessible. Some strategies are developed to use these simultaneously from various tasks without creating memory conflicts.

A multitasking system depends on the various tasks cooperating with the Interrupt Vector table, the video RAM and the BIOS variable area. They do not access overlapping areas of the screen and do not use the same interrupt vectors for storing information.

The best method in MS-DOS is to halt task switching during a DOS function. This is the only way to prevent the tasks from accessing MS-DOS simultaneously. We'll later see how these are implemented with the MT unit. Several tasks accessing MS-DOS at the same time usually leads to a system error.

A multitasking system is responsible for avoiding memory conflicts caused by the simultaneous access of various tasks to global variables and shared storage areas which are allocated through the heap. Consider an array as an example. An array in the manner of the BIOS keyboard buffer is organized as a ring buffer. Various tasks write permanent data into this buffer while removing other data from the buffer. Therefore, two indexes, indicating the write and read positions in the array, are administered in global variables.

NEXT   Accepts the index of the next array element to be read. It's advanced toward the end of the array with every read access until it passes it and is reset to the beginning of the arrays.

LAST   Accepts the index for the next array element which was newly written into the buffer and therefore should be attached behind the last element. Also, this index is incremented with every write access and, when reaching the end of the array, is reset to the beginning of the array.

Consider the WriteRp procedure as an example. It's responsible for attaching a data block to the end of the ring buffer. This is done by copying the data block into the array element, referenced by LAST, and then incrementing LAST. This pseudo-pointer is again loaded with the index of the first array element on an overflow. This listing shows how such a routine is implemented in a small program.

```
program RaceConditions;

type RData = record                     { data stored in the ring buffer }
              A,
              B,
              C  : integer;
            end;

var Next,                               { index for element to be read next }
    Last  : integer;                    { index for element to be written next }
    Rp    : array [1..100] of RData;            { the ring buffer }
```

```
    ExD    : RData;                                    { example data }

procedure WriteRp( Data : RData );

begin
  Rp[ Last ] := Data;                        { write data into ring buffer }

{-------- task switching between these two lines is very dangerous! -------}

  inc( Last );                                   { set Last to next element }
  if ( Last > 100 ) then        { Last beyond the end of the ring buffer? }
    Last := 1;                          { yes, set last again to beginning }
end;

{-----------------------------------------------------------------------}

begin
  Next := 1;                              { no more elements in ring buffer }
  Last := 1;
  WriteRp(ExD);                              { write data to ring buffer }
end.
```

Suppose that WriteRp is called by a task. The scheduler decides, after copying the data block into the ring buffer, it's time to perform a task change again. It switches to another task which interrupts the execution of WriteRp. This task now calls WriteRp on its own to add a data block to the end of the ring buffer.

Since WriteRp was interrupted during its previous call and before it could increment the LAST pointer, it writes the data block passed into the array element. The array element was loaded in the previous call. This overwrites the previous information.

After WriteRp has set the index LAST to the next element and has concluded its work, a new task change starts the original task and WriteRp again.

Since the data block was already written into the array and doesn't know it was overwritten, it sets the NEXT index to the next element. This jumps over an array element which can contain nonessential data. However, these are "critical sections" which cannot be executed simultaneously by two tasks. The resulting memory conflicts will lead to program errors.

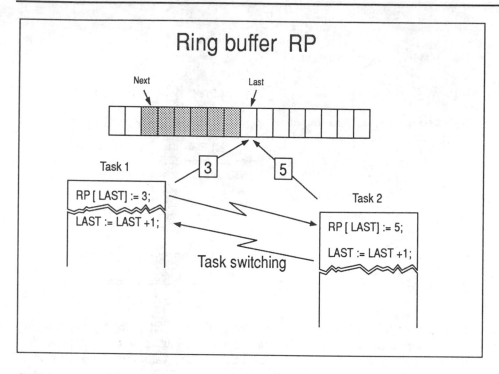

Collisions caused by race conditions, when accessing jointly used data

A lot of work was devoted to finding a way to avoid these memory conflicts, which are a result of "race conditions". The easiest solution is avoiding any data jointly used by various tasks. However, this is rarely possible. Data used jointly (in RAM or on disk) often is the main reason to implement a multitasking program.

Another possible solution is preventing task switching during the access to a jointly used set of data. At the beginning, WriteRp should call a system routine to turn off the task switching until it's turned on again. This should be done before it's completed with the call of another routine.

Actually, many race conditions are handled in this way. But this method may also prevent the execution of tasks not accessing these joint sets of data.

A more efficient method prevents tasks from simultaneously accessing certain jointly used data while allowing these tasks to access data not in conflict with each other. It's important to protect the various sets of data individually while preventing access to all data or preventing the task switching completely.

There are several tricks for doing this. For the MT unit we've selected the principle of the *semaphores*, first proposed by E.W. Dijkstra in 1965. This efficient procedure is also used by OS/2 and in an OS/2 version of Turbo Pascal.

A semaphore is simply an integer value manipulated with two system functions named Get (MtGetSem) and Release (MtReleaseSem). This kind of semaphore should be created as a global variable for each set of data in a program. Each set of data cannot be simultaneously accessed by several tasks. It acts as an exclusive access device which a task receives, with a call of the Get routine, to access the data connected to it. When this access device has examined the data, it must be returned with a call of Release so that it's available to other tasks.

We'll use semaphores in the program to access a ring buffer presented earlier.

```
program NoProblems;

uses Mt;                   { include multitasking unit with semaphore control }

type RData = record                        { data stored in the ring buffer }
             A,
             B,
             C  : integer;
           end;

var RpSem : SEMAPHORE;      { semaphore for access to Rp, Next and Last }
    Next,                              { index for element to be read next }
    Last  : integer;       { index for element to be written next }
    Rp    : array [1..100] of RData;            { the ring buffer }

    ExD   : RData;                                  { example data }

procedure WriteRp( Data : RData );

begin
  MtGetSem( RpSem );     { obtain possession of / access rights to semaphore }

  Rp[ Last ] := Data;                       { write data into ring buffer }
  inc( Last );                               { set Last to next element }
  if ( Last > 100 ) then         { is Last beyond end of ring buffer? }
    Last := 1;                        { yes, set Last to the beginning }
    MtReleaseSem( RpSem );          { access ended, release semaphore }
  end;
```

```
{------------------------------------------------------------------------}
begin
  RpSem := SEM_FREE;                               { semaphore not yet free }
  Next := 1;                           { still no elements in ring buffer }
  Last := 1;
  WriteRp( ExD );                                 { write data to ring buffer }
end.
```

Using semaphores doesn't prevent task switching. A task switch could only occur when WriteRp is executed in this program. A task could be executed which would immediately call WriteRp. This procedure is used to gain control of the semaphore and then gain access to the ring buffer. However, even if it succeeds, this wouldn't achieve anything because it could also access this data and create a memory conflict.

To prevent this, MtGetSem uses the semaphore as a counter to determine if the semaphore was already assigned. MtGetSem uses the constant SEM_FREE at the beginning of the main program to initialize the semaphore with the value one. MtGetSem decrements this value and sets it to zero. However, this occurs only when the semaphore, during the call of this routine, doesn't already contain the value 0, which signals that it was already assigned to another task. In this case, MtGetSem doesn't immediately return to the caller. Instead, it holds back the call of the task until the semaphore again assumes the value 1, when a call of MtReleaseSem releases it.

A call of MtGetSem immediately returns the indicated semaphore, which is now free (i.e., contains a value not equal to 0), to the caller. If it's controlled by another task, the caller must wait until the semaphore is released with a call of MtReleaseSem. This simple but effective method doesn't prevent the simultaneous execution of several tasks but the simultaneous access to sets of data to be successively manipulated.

This is a special application of semaphores. In this case we're using binaries because the semaphore is initialized with the value 1 (SEM_FREE) and then changes between the 0 and 1 values. A binary semaphore of this type is changed only when a task calls MtReleaseSem several times in succession without calling MtGetSem first.

Semaphores that, for example, are used for controlling queues differ from the binary semaphores. This kind of semaphore, introduced in the MTDEMO program, communicates between various tasks. As we've seen in MTDEMO, queues are created with special system routines (MtCreateQueue), written (MtWriteQueue) and read (MtReadQueue and MtPeekQueue).

By using a binary semaphore, the routines ensure that they're not executed at the same time. This would cause them to try to access the queue simultaneously. The routines are also responsible for avoiding read accesses that occur to an empty queue and write accesses to a full queue.

To do this, two semaphores called FREE and OCCUPIED are administered with each queue. These semaphores record the number of free and occupied entries in the queue. When the queue is created, FREE is initialized with the number of entries and OCCUPIED is initialized with zero.

A MtGetSem call is made to the OCCUPIED semaphore during each read access to the queue to decrement the number of occupied entries. One entry was removed by reading it. Then MtReleaseSem is called with the FREE semaphore to increment the number of available storage locations in the queue.

If the queue is empty, the task to be called is already blocked by the first MtGetSem call because the OCCUPIED semaphore contains the value zero. MtGetSem holds back one task per definition when the semaphore contains this value. The task is continued only when another task writes a message, through MtWriteQueue, into the queue. This increments the OCCUPIED semaphore through a call from MtReleaseSem because now an additional entry is ready in the queue and waits for a reader.

In a similar way, the access of a task to a full queue is blocked until an element is read through MtReadQueue. A MtGetSem is also performed on the semaphore FREE with every write access to the queue. It's decremented with every call of MtWriteQueue until reaching the value 0 when the queue is full. Another call of MtWriteQueue and a call of MtGetSem, at first blocks the task. The task remains blocked until another task calls the MtReadQueue procedure and increments the FREE semaphore again with a call in MtReleaseSem.

When discussing semaphores and queues, we're dealing with "interprocess communications", or the means for communication between various tasks working at the same time.

We've discussed "holding" or "blocking" a task. These refer to removing the active task from the list of executable tasks and making it yield to another task the scheduler selects. Along with the MtGetSem and MtReleaseSem routines, this is the only part of a multitasking system that can affect the status of a task.

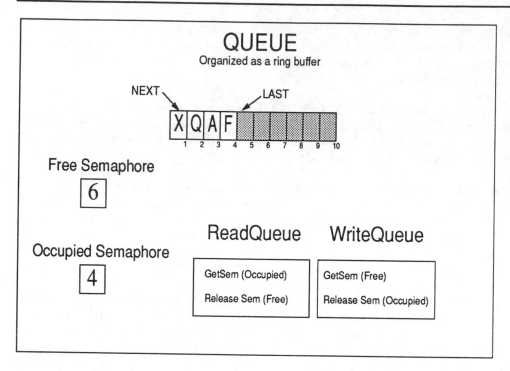

Controlling queues with semaphores

A task is always in one of three possible operating modes, designated as *process status*. After the start of the multitasking, only one task running has the attribute available. When the scheduler performs a task switch, the task is placed in the "Ready" mode. It's no longer active but available at any time to continue.

The tasks blocked by MtGetSem are placed in the "Waiting" status. They're not considered during a task switch until MtReleaseSem releases the semaphores they were waiting for and changes their status to "Ready". Under certain conditions, a task could become immediately active if it has a higher priority than the one previously active. They're now the highest priority task in the system.

The key concept for the last section of this chapter is priority, or how the scheduler determines which task starts during a task change (i.e., to place into the "Running" operating mode). The algorithm used for this determines the effectiveness of a multitasking system. Unfortunately, no universally valid algorithm has been developed because various strategies, depending on the concept of the system and its requirements, produce the best results.

Generally, the following demands are made on the scheduling algorithm related to not only the scheduler but also the full multitasking system:

- Access time for the CPU must be evenly distributed so that no equally valid task has a higher priority.

- The capability of the CPU should not be wasted by moving in unproductive loops.

- Only a small amount of time should be devoted to scheduling. Most of the capability for the CPU should be devoted to the individual tasks.

- Reaction to user input through the keyboard and mouse must be as fast as possible regardless of the execution of "background tasks".

As previously mentioned, this goal can only be achieved by implementing *preemptive scheduling*. This scheduling originates with the multitasking system instead of the individual tasks.

The *round robin scheduling* is one of the simplest and best algorithms. The scheduler allows the individual tasks to rotate, like a carousel, and then starts the task which happens to pass. Since the speed of this rotation is always constant, every task has the same execution time. Once its time is over, the task is automatically completed to make way for another task. If the task is blocked, for example by a previously assigned semaphore, the next task is immediately begun.

This method is often combined with the *priority scheduling*, in which the various tasks are assigned to various priority groups. In these priority groups, the principle of round robin scheduling is applied. The tasks in a priority group are only executed when a task in a higher level group isn't ready. These priorities are selected by the programmer (or user) as static or selected dynamically by the system. However, selecting tasks dynamically is a very complicated process since the system must analyze the frequency of task usage.

Therefore, the multitasking unit presented here supports a combination of round robin scheduling and static priority scheduling. The priorities of the individual tasks are set, in a static manner, by the programmer when a task is created through MtCreateTask. Usually you should give the highest priority to the foreground task. This is the task which accepts input from the user. By doing this, the scheduler immediately starts the task after an input is available. The other tasks should be given priority according to their importance. It's also possible for MTDEMO to assign the same priority for all background tasks so all of them have the same amount of processor time.

We have now completed our discussion of the theory of multitasking. In this section you have become familiar with the most important concepts and ideas of multitasking. Semaphores are more important and are demonstrated in the next section.

13.3   Five Philosophers and Too Much Spaghetti

As previously mentioned, E.W. Dijkstra first proposed the principle of the semaphores. He also described the "dining philosophers problem" that has become part of several training manuals.

We'll use the dining philosophers problem in the PHILO5 program to demonstrate the importance of semaphores in multitasking.

The scenario starts in a university cafeteria. Five professors from the Philosophy Department are seated at a table. Each has a full plate of spaghetti. However, there is only one fork on the left side of each plate. The philosophers soon realize one fork isn't enough for eating the spaghetti, which is buried under thick sauce.

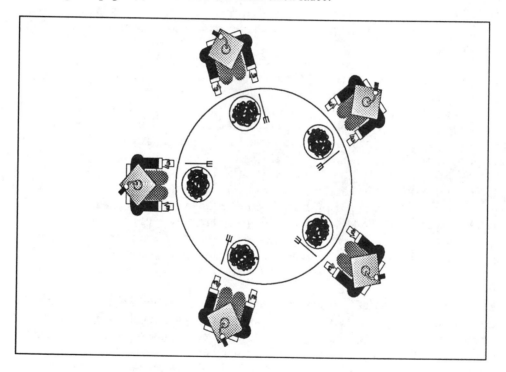

Five philosophers, five plates of spaghetti, but only five forks

In order to use two forks, each philosopher attempts to grab the fork belonging to his neighbor on the right. If successful, only two philosophers will have two forks and can eat their spaghetti at the same time. The other three philosophers can just watch and wait.

Since these five philosophers are close friends, fighting over the forks is an impossibility and we assume the three who have to wait will then use the next fork placed on the table after their associates are finished.

We need to write a procedure to imitate the life and action of each philosopher. We're reducing the life of a philosopher to eating, thinking and remaining hungry. Since all five philosophers act identically, we'll use a procedure called APhilosopher. There are five tasks operating in parallel. Several procedures and solutions may immediately come to mind. Perhaps the procedure could be created in abstract form, such as:

```
procedure APhilosopher;

begin
  while TRUE do
    begin
      I_Think;
      GrabLeftFork;
      GrabRightFork;
      I_Eat;
      PutDownLeftFork;
      PutDownRightFork;
    end;
end;
```

However this wouldn't work because all the tasks are performed simultaneously. It would fail after the left fork was taken because the fork on the right was already taken by the neighbor. Inevitably, the system would crash because each task waits for the others. A chain is formed in which the various tasks become inactive.

Since no tasks reach the PutDownLeftFork command, no task (no philosopher) can take the fork to his right because it's the left fork of his neighbor. The various tasks will never end and only an external event (for example, a system reset) stops the program.

A deadlock still occurs even if it's assumed the various tasks are performed simultaneously to the thousandth, millionth or billionths of a second. This is because the task switching is performed so fast that all five tasks (philosophers) have picked up the left fork before the first is able to grab the right fork.

The idea that if the left fork is picked up and put down after a certain period of time provided the right fork couldn't be picked up, isn't practical. Since the process is performed for all five tasks (philosophers), with the same speed, it will result in all five of them picking up their left forks and, after a short time, putting them down again. This process would be repeated continuously. Although not a deadlock, it's also not any more productive.

You could include small, random time delays into the loop so the philosophers can't pick up their left and right forks simultaneously. Although the time delays helps, the possibility of a deadlock still exists. Few problems are worse than a program functioning successfully and for an unknown reason, suddenly crashing.

We must find a solution supported with algorithms to ensure picking up the individual forks at the same time so that more than one philosopher is able to eat.

Dijkstra proposes creating two arrays each containing five elements. These elements, available globally, correspond to the five philosophers. The first array stores the current "condition" of a philosopher. The philosopher thinks, eats or remains hungry because he doesn't have the second fork.

The second array contains a binary semaphore (SEM_WAITS) for each philosopher. This semaphore at first waits because no philosopher eats. As soon as a philosopher starts to eat, the semaphore is released, only to wait again.

This somewhat unconventional way to use semaphores is shown in the program listing of PHILO5 under the name PHILO5.PAS on the companion diskettes accompanying this book.

```
{******************************************************************
 *  Philo5 : demonstrates the MT multitasking unit and the WINMT   *
 *           multitasking window unit, using the "dining philosophers *
 *           problem." This problem, described for the first time in 1965 *
 *           by the Dutch philosopher E.W. Dijkstra, occurs in the philo- *
 *           sophy department of a university. The five faculty members sit *
 *           down to dinner with five plates of spaghetti. Unfortunately, *
 *           each philosopher only has 1 utensil (a fork), and none of the *
 *           five can eat pasta with only one fork. If they share utensils *
 *           (two forks apiece), only two philosophers can eat at a time. *
 *           This creates race conditions, because one philosopher who *
 *           grabs two forks automatically excludes the neighbor to his/her *
 *           left and right from eating.                            *
 *           The following simulation shows each philosopher as a task and *
 *           displays the eat/think sequence between each philosopher. The *
 *           use of semaphores in this program alleviates race conditions, *
 *           and all five philosophers get two forks and a chance to eat. *
 **-------------------------------------------------------------**
 *  Author        : MICHAEL TISCHER                               *
 *  developed on  : 6/1/1989                                      *
 *  last update on : 3/12/1990                                    *
 ******************************************************************}

program Philo5;

uses Crt, Mt, WinMt;
```

556

```
const THECYCLES   = 5;           { number of think/eat cycles per philosopher }
      TIME_FACTOR = 5;                  { time delay for eating and thinking }

type So_It_Goes = ( THINKING, HUNGRY, EATING );{ "status" of a philosopher }

     SCORD = record                               { a screen coordinate }
               X, Y : byte;                       { column and line      }
             end;

var PStatus  : array [1..5] of So_It_Goes;    { status of the philosophers }
    ProfEats : array [1..5] of SEMAPHORE; { semaphores which indicate if a }
                                          { philosopher is currently eating }

const AAccess : SEMAPHORE = SEM_FREE;     { controls access to status array }
```

The two constants THECYCLES and TIME_FACTOR are defined at the beginning of the program. THECYCLES defines the number of think/eat cycles for each philosopher until the end of his tasks. TIME_FACTOR, used in delaying the eating and thinking, slows the individual cycles so you can follow them on the screen (the default is 5). You can use smaller values to increase or larger values to decrease the speed.

The So_It_Goes type marks the various conditions of a philosopher and the CORD type stores a screen coordinate. They're required for this program because the plates of the various philosophers and their "condition" are shown on the screen so that you can follow the program execution.

The program already knows the arrays named PStatus and ProfEats as variables and the semaphore AAccess, created as a typical constant and initialized with the value SEM_FREE. This binary semaphore controls the access to the condition array to prevent several tasks from simultaneously accessing the information stored there.

Access to ProfEats doesn't need to be protected with this semaphore. The semaphores are manipulated exclusively with the procedures MtGetSem and MtReleaseSem and the two procedures ensure that the tasks will not interfere with each other.

```
{*************************************************************************
*                   M A I N   P R O G R A M                            *
*************************************************************************}

const Plates : array [ 1..5 ] of SCORD =        { coordinates of the plates }
  ( (X : 38; Y : 7) ,
    (X : 30; Y : 10),
    (X : 46; Y : 10),
    (X : 43; Y : 13),
    (X : 33; Y : 13) );

var b : TDP;      { dummy, stores task descriptor of the five philosophers }
    i : integer;                                        { loop counter }
```

```
begin
  Randomize;                          { initialize random number generator }
  ClrScr;
  WinHideCursor;
  WinFill ( VL( 0), VO( 0), VR( 0), VO( 0), ' ', $70 );
  WinFill ( VL( 0), VU( 0), VR( 0), VU( 0), ' ', $70 );
  WinPrint( 20, 0, $70, '-  THE DINING  PHILOSOPHERS PROBLEM  -');
  WinPrint(  8, 24, $70, 'Created with the Multitasking Unit from'+
                    ' Turbo Pascal System Programming);
  for i :=1 to 5 do                          { create the five philosophers }
    begin
      b := MtCreateTask( APhilosopher, 1, 1000, ptr( 0, i ) );
      ProfEats[i] := SEM_WAITS;       { phil. does not have both forks yet }
      PStatus[i] := THINKING;                 { phil. currently thinking }

      {-- create plates ----------------------------------------------------}

      WinPrint( Plates[ i ].X+1, Plates[ i ].Y,   $7, ' ___ ');
      WinPrint( Plates[ i ].X,   Plates[ i ].Y+1, $7, '/   \');
      WinPrint( Plates[ i ].X,   Plates[ i ].Y+2, $7, '\___/');
    end;
  MtaStart( 8 );                       { start multitasking, fast task switching }

  {--- this program location occurs only after completion of all tasks ----}

  TextColor( 7 );
  TextBackGround( 0 );
  ClrScr;
  WinSetCursor(0,0);
end.
```

The screen is built in the main program. A philosopher task is created in the loop executed for each of the five philosophers. This task always starts with the APhilosopher procedure. All tasks are given the same priority. No distinction is made between the various tasks concerning the size of the available stack.

A number is passed to the various tasks as an argument. The tasks must know this number in order to display their philosopher's condition at the correct screen location. This information is passed with a pointer to the task. The function Ptr is always called to store the number of the philosopher as an offset address in a pointer whose segment address contains the value zero. This is a simple effective method for passing information to a task. The pointer of MtCreateTask requires only one or two bytes of memory.

The ProfEats array initializes the semaphore of the philosopher with the SEM_WAITS constant and the entry in the condition array with THINKING. The loop for each philosopher ends when his plate is displayed on the screen.

Immediately after creating the five philosophers, the multitasking is started with a call of MtaStart. This starts the five created tasks.

```
{*************************************************************************
*  APhilosopher : Emulates a philosopher's life (think/eat/think/eat/etc.) *
**-----------------------------------------------------------------------**
*  input : PPointer = The number of the Philosopher passed in the pointer  *
*                    offset                                                *
*************************************************************************}

{$F+}

procedure APhilosopher( PPointer : pointer );

const PhFrame : array [1..5] of SCORD =           { coordinates of each }
  ( ( X: 32; Y:  2 ),                             { philosopher windows }
    ( X: 55; Y:  9 ),
    ( X: 49; Y: 17 ),
    ( X: 17; Y: 17 ),
    ( X: 11; Y:  9 ) );

var PhiNr,                                     { number of the philosopher }
     j    : integer;                           { loop execution }

begin
  PhiNr := integer( PPointer );               { compute philosopher number }

  {-- build Philosopher window -------------------------------------------}

  WinSetView( PhFrame[ PhiNr ].X,     PhFrame[ PhiNr ].Y,
              PhFrame[ PhiNr ].X+14, PhFrame[ PhiNr ].Y+4 );
  WinFrame( VL(0), VO(0), VR(0), VU(0), DBL_FR, $07 );
  WinFill( VL(1), VO(1), VR(-1), VU(-1), ' ', $07 );
  TextColor( $0 );
  TextBackGround( $7 );
  GotoXY( VL(1), VO(0) );
  write( 'Philosopher ', PhiNr );
  WinPrint( VL(2), VO(2), $7, 'T H I N K S ');

  {-- execute the think/eat cycle ----------------------------------------}

  for j := 1 to THECYCLES do
    begin
      I_Think;
      GrabtheForks( PhiNr );
      I_Eat;
      PutDowntheForks( PhiNr );
    end;

  WinFill( VL(0), VO(0), VR(0), VU(0), ' ', $07 );        { clear window }
end;

{$F-}
```

The APhilosopher task procedure loads the number of the philosopher from the pointer into the local variable PhiNr. A window is built with coordinates from the local frame array. This array accepts the number of the philosopher and reflects his condition in the think/eat cycle. The think/eat cycle is entered through a normal FOR loop. The I_Think procedure is called to simulate how the philosopher thinks when the FOR loop is run.

A call of the GrabtheForks procedure comes next. This procedure only returns to the caller if it sent the two forks to the calling philosopher.

The next call is the I_Eat procedure. This symbolizes the enjoyment in eating the spaghetti. Then the philosopher puts the forks down with a call of PutDowntheForks. Now a new cycle starts.

The procedures I_Think and I_Eat are dummies. Each delays the program execution for a short time. Notice the time delay is randomly selected to put the factor Random into action. Replace the Random function with a constant time factor for the call of Delay if you want to study the program execution with the example of constant time thinking and eating cycles.

```
{*************************************************************************
 *  I_Think : Bridges the time period in which a philosopher thinks       *
 *************************************************************************}

procedure I_Think;

begin
  Delay( (Random(12)+6) * 50 * TIME_FACTOR );
end;


{*************************************************************************
 *  I_Eat : Bridges the time period in which a philosopher eats           *
 *************************************************************************}

procedure I_Eat;

begin
  Delay( (Random(6)+4) * 50 * TIME_FACTOR );
end;
```

The procedures GrabtheForks and PutDowntheForks are more important for successful program execution.

First let's consider the GrabtheForks procedure. A philosopher attempts to obtain the forks located to the left and right of his plate. Obviously, the procedure must know the number of the philosopher. This number is passed as an index to the procedure by the caller. Before it can access the two arrays PStatus and ProfEats, it must obtain the access semaphore to prevent a simultaneous access to these arrays by other tasks.

After the return from MtGetSem, the procedure labels the philosopher as hungry by entering the appropriate constant in his place on the array PStatus. In addition, it documents the hunger of the philosopher by displaying a message in the philosopher's window.

```
{***************************************************************************
 *  GrabtheForks : Simulates the attempt of a philosopher to grab the forks *
 *                 of his right and left neighbors                          *
 **-----------------------------------------------------------------------**
 *  Input  : I = Number of the professor who wants to take the forks        *
 *  Global : PStatus, AAccess and ProfEats                                  *
 ***************************************************************************}

procedure GrabtheForks( i: integer );

begin
  MtGetSem( AAccess );              { secure access right to condition Array }
  PStatus[ i ] := HUNGRY;                     { the Philosopher is hungry }
  WinPrint( VL(2), VO(2), $7, 'h u n g r y ');
  Test( i );              { attempt to grab the forks to the left and right }
  MtReleaseSem( AAccess );                    { release access right again    }
  MtGetSem( ProfEats[ i ] );          { wait for opportunity to eat     }
  WinPrint( VL(2), VO(2), $7, ' E A T S  ');
end;
```

After the message is displayed, a call to the Test procedure allows the philosopher to get the forks. This procedure works with the GrabtheForks procedure and the PutDowntheForks procedure. It allows the various philosophers to take the forks to the left and right of their plates whenever they desire.

This occurs only when Test determines that the specified philosopher is hungry, his neighbors aren't eating and aren't using their forks. In this case, Test enters the constant HUNGRY into the condition array for the philosopher. At the same time, his semaphore is released from the ProfEats array. It then returns to its caller.

Perhaps it doesn't make sense that Test also tests whether the philosopher is hungry. After all, this procedure is called by GrabtheForks because the philosopher is hungry and needs the help of the procedure to have two forks. But, as we'll soon see, during a call of the Test procedure by PutDowntheForks, it's uncertain whether the indicated philosopher is hungry.

After the return from Test, the GrabtheForks procedure releases the access semaphore again because it no longer accesses the condition array. The procedure doesn't know whether Test can acquire the forks for a particular professor. But this will be determined, at least indirectly, by attempting a call of MtGetSem to obtain the semaphore of the philosopher. Only when Test could actually give the forks to the philosopher, and thereby also perform a call of MtReleaseSem to the semaphore of the philosopher, can MtGetSem immediately return to the GrabtheForks procedure. If not, the active task is blocked and GrabtheForks must wait until another task releases this semaphore.

561

The PutDowntheForks procedure, called by every task to replace the forks, is responsible for this. It gives the philosopher to the left and right of the indicated philosopher the chance to pick up the forks just returned to the table, as long as the left or right neighbor is hungry and has waited for the opportunity. This procedure also releases the ProfEats semaphore of the neighbor, through which this task can terminate the previously blocked call of MtGetSem in GrabtheForks and can return to the calling procedure APhilosopher.

```
{**************************************************************************
 *  PutDowntheForks : Simulates the attempt of a philosopher to replace the *
 *                    two forks which he had previously grabbed.          *
 **-----------------------------------------------------------------------**
 *  input : I = Number of the philosopher who wants to replace the forks  *
 *  Global : PStatus, AAccess and ProfEats                                *
 **************************************************************************}

procedure PutDowntheForks( i : integer );

begin
  MtGetSem( AAccess );                        { get access right to status array }
  PStatus[ i ] := THINKING;                       { philosopher now thinks again }
  WinPrint( VL(2), VO(2), $7, 'T H I N K S ');
  test( NLeft( i ) );              { give philosophers to the left and right the }
  test( NRight( i ) );                   { chance to eat, if they're hungry }
  MtReleaseSem( AAccess );                         { release access rights again }
end;
```

The procedures GrabtheForks and PutDowntheForks working together ensure a continuous taking and releasing of the forks. The location in the GrabtheForks procedure is especially important. This is where the procedure releases the access right to the condition array, and waits through a call of GetSem until the pickup of the two forks by its philosopher.

If the sequence of the two calls were reversed, a deadlock would quickly result as soon as the preceding call of Test was unable to provide the forks for the philosopher. At that point, GrabtheForks must rely on the PutDowntheForks procedure. This releases the semaphore of the philosopher through a call of Test. PutDowntheForks can obtain the proper command only after it has acquired the access right to the condition array. It will never get this access right if GrabtheForks was blocked without having previously released the access semaphore.

This example demonstrates how important it is to maintain the same sequence during the work with several semaphores. A deadlock can easily be created because the various tasks are waiting for each other without anything happening.

The following list is of Test. Similar to PutDowntheForks, Test uses the functions NLeft and NRight to determine the number of the left and right neighbor of a certain philosopher.

```
{************************************************************************
*  NLeft : returns the number of the neighbor to the left of the specified *
*          philosopher.                                                *
**--------------------------------------------------------------------**
*  Input  : I = Number of the philosopher whose left neighbor should be  *
*               determined.                                            *
*  Output : Number of the left neighbor                                *
************************************************************************}

function NLeft( i : integer ) : integer;

begin
  if i <> 1 then                                { first philosopher? }
    NLeft := i - 1                  { no, phil. to the left has number - 1 }
  else                                                          { yes }
    NLeft := 5;                     { create connection to last philosopher }
end;

{************************************************************************
*  NRight : returns the number of the right neighbor of the indicated  *
*           philosopher.                                               *
**--------------------------------------------------------------------**
*  Input  : I = number of the philosopher, whose right neighbor should be *
*               determined.                                            *
*  Output : number of the right neighbor                               *
************************************************************************}

function NRight( i : integer ) : integer;

begin
  if i <> 5 then                                 { last philosopher? }
    NRight := i + 1                 { no, phil. to the right has number + 1 }
  else                                                          { yes }
    NRight := 1;                    { close circle to first philosopher }
end;

{************************************************************************
*  Test : permits a philosopher to eat, provided he is hungry and neither *
*         his left nor right neighbors have forks in their possession.  *
**--------------------------------------------------------------------**
*  Input  : I = number of the philosopher to be tested                 *
*  Global : PStatus, ProfEats                                          *
*  Info   : The caller must have the Semaphore in its possession before *
*           the call to prevent simultaneous access by any other task to *
*           the status array.                                          *
************************************************************************}

procedure Test( i : integer );

begin
  if ( ( PStatus[ i ] = HUNGRY ) and
       ( PStatus[ NLeft ( i ) ] <> EATING ) and
       ( PStatus[ NRight( i ) ] <> EATING ) ) then
```

563

```
        begin                      { phil. is hungry and neighbor does not eat }
          PStatus[ i ] := EATING;                          { phil eats now }
          MtReleaseSem( ProfEats[ i ] );              { release semaphore }
        end;
    end;
```

Although smaller, the listing is more complex than MTDEMO from Section 13.1 and may be difficult to follow.

Even though such a complicated handling of semaphores may not be required in your programs, once you've understood how PHILO5 works, multitasking programming will be very easy for you. Now you're prepared to work with the MT unit.

13.4 The MT Unit

You've now had experience with multitasking and using the MT unit. Next we'll present the complete MT unit including procedures and functions not yet discussed.

We'll start with how to develop the unit. You'll need to know how MT accomplishes the difficult task of multitasking. The assembler module MTA.ASMA plays an important role. It contains the routines responsible for the task switching and couldn't be developed in the Pascal language.

Unlike previous chapters which also used assembler modules, MTA.ASM has complete responsibility for operating a program in multitasking mode. The assembler module contains only the routines, which, because of inflexibility or missing optimization capabilities, cannot be implemented in Pascal.

While the actual task switcher is formulated in assembler, the scheduler uses the MtChooseNext procedure as a part of the Pascal module and is called from the assembler module. The advantage of this is that you can easily imitate the functions of the MT unit and make changes without suffering through the assembler code. This requires a complete understanding of assembler and system programming.

First we'll review the Pascal portion of the unit for anyone who isn't familiar with assembler programming.

The INTERFACE portion tells a lot about the design of the MT unit. The various types defined are required by the program for work with the public procedures and functions from the MT unit.

```
{*******************************************************************
 *  MT : A unit which permits the simultaneous execution of several *
 *       independent tasks in a Turbo Pascal program.               *
 **---------------------------------------------------------------**
 *  Author       : MICHAEL TISCHER                                  *
 *  developed on  : 06/10/1989                                      *
 *  last update on : 03/09/1990                                     *
 *******************************************************************}

unit Mt;

Interface
```

```
{== constants, public ========================================================}

const MAX_UNITS  = 5;                        { maximum number of cooperating units }
      SEM_FREE   = 1;                                    { semaphore is free }
      SEM_WAITS  = 0;                        { wait for semaphore to become free }
      NO_ARG     = ptr( 0, 0 );                  { do not pass argument to task }

{== Public type declarations required by other units for work with     =====}
{== the functions and procedures from this unit                        =====}

type SEMAPHORE = integer;                                     { a semaphore }
     SEMP      = ^SEMAPHORE;                         { pointer to a semaphore }

     QUEUEP    = ^QUEUE;                         { pointer to a queue descriptor }
     QUEUE     = record                              { queue descriptor }
                    FAccess,                             { is access free }
                    OccpdE,                     { number of occupied elements }
                    Free    : SEMAPHORE;            { number of free elements }
                    ElSize,                         { size of a queue element }
                    NumEnt  : integer;      { number of entries in the queue }
                    QBufP   : pointer;           { pointer to the queue buffer }
                    Next,                    { pointer to next element in queue }
                    Last    : integer;       { pointer to last element in queue }
                 end;

     TDP       = ^TD;                         { pointer to a task descriptor }
     TD        = record                               { task descriptor }
                    Stack     : pointer;    { memory allocated for the stack }
                    SP        : word;   { stack ptr during task interruption }
                    StackLen  : integer;        { size of the stack in bytes }
                    Priority  : byte;                    { priority level }
                    Waitfor_Sm: SEMP;       { pointer to semaphore expected }
                    Next,                    { pointer to next task descriptor }
                    Last      : TDP; { pointer to preceding task descriptor }
                    StartTime : longint;               { time of last start }
                    UnitData  : array [1..MAX_UNITS] of pointer;
                 end;

     TS        = procedure( TskPtr : pointer );{ start procedure of a task }

{---- the following types represent procedural pointers to routines  -}
{---- which must be made available to units registered as "partners" -}

UpCreate = function : pointer;
UpChange = procedure( TskPtr : pointer );
UpDelete = procedure( TskPtr : pointer; RestTasks : integer );
```

The SEMAPHORE type is represented with an INTEGER (refer to Section 13.2 for more information on semaphores). The SEMP type serving as a pointer to SEMAPHORE is very important for work with the semaphores.

The QUEUE, an elementary data type, immediately follows. Some of its fields, such as the three Semaphores AAccess, OccpdE and Free, to declare the QUEUE structure, should be familiar to you.

This is followed by the two integer variables, ElSize and NumEnt to indicate the size of the individual queue elements in bytes and their maximum number. The product of these two results in the size of the buffer allocated for the storage of individual queue entries through the heap. The component QBufP stores their start address.

The last two entries in a QUEUE structure, named Next and Last, indicate that the queue is organized like a ring buffer. Since this principle of organization was discussed in Section 13.2, we'll only mention that Next contains the index of the next element to be read and Last contains the next element to be written in the queue buffer. Since the size of the individual queue entries will become known only at run-time of the program and the queue buffer cannot be declared as a normal Pascal array, Next and Last do not act directly as index to this buffer, but serve to compute the offset address of the element to be addressed. This will become more evident during the various queue operations.

QUEUE and its pointer QUEUEP type are followed by the data structure. This is the center of the entire unit. The task descriptor TD and its pointer TDP type contain all the information the unit needs for controlling a task and its active or inactive status. A pointer beginning the private task stack is stored here. When the tasks are created, MtCreateTask allocates this pointer through the heap.

The content of the SP registers during the last task interruption is stored here. This is followed by the length of the stack. This information is needed only to release the storage allocated for the stack as the task terminates. Also stored in the task descriptors are the priority of the tasks. The scheduler requires this during its search for the next task to be executed.

Also important is the WaitFor_Sm field. It stores the address of the indicated semaphore if it contains the value 0 during the call of MtGetSem. If so, this signals it's accessed by another task.

The fields Next and Last have the same names as the fields inside the QUEUE which are used for controlling the ring buffer. However here they have another important role. They make the connection between the task descriptor of the succeeding and preceding task so that the task descriptors present a double chained list. So procedures, such as the scheduler, can easily process them.

Besides the fields Priority and WaitFor_Sm, the field StartTime provides important information for the scheduler so that it can select the next task to start. Here the scheduler stores the time of the start of the task. However, the time isn't in the format of 00/00/00 but stored with an internal counter. The scheduler stores the number of the call that led to the start of the task in this variable. If various tasks have the same priority and are ready to be carried out on the basis of this information, it can begin the task that has been waiting the longest. This uses the round robin method which was previously discussed.

As the last field a task descriptor contains an array with pointers. In turn this array contains as many elements as registered in the constant MAX_UNITS. Units in this array cooperate with the MT through a special function call. They store pointers to data blocks which they administer for every task. We'll discuss this process in more detail soon.

You may be wondering why the contents of the SP register, instead of the contents of all the other processor registers, are stored inside the task descriptor. They're also part of the task and therefore stored with every task switch. Of course the contents of these registers are stored before the start of a task switch.

However, this doesn't occur in the task descriptor. It's easier to "push" these registers on the task stack than to load them into various storage locations in a task descriptor referenced through a pointer. Only the contents of the SP register are stored inside the task descriptor. It's now able to determine when the task is reactivated and the address where the various processor registers are stored on the stack to initialize the SP register.

After the task descriptor is declared there are four procedural types. The first procedural type, TS, describes the start procedure of a task. We've seen this already with MTDEMO.

The other three types are used for the communication with registered units through a call of the function MtRegisterUnit, as colleagues of the MT unit. This function expects three procedural pointers during its call from a unit. These pointers correspond to the types UpCreate, UpChange and UpDelete.

The UpCreate type offers the unit (these units) the opportunity to store task dependent data and to initialize it. It is always called by the MT unit when a task is created with the function MtCreateTask. The returned pointer to these data is stored in the array UnitData which forms the end of a task descriptor.

To identify the current task, the MT unit delivers this pointer to the procedures of UpChange type and UpDelete. These are indicated along with the function of UpCreate type, by the caller of MtRegisterUnit. The procedure, to which UpChange points, is always called during a task switch. UpDelete is used during the call of a procedure when a task is erased or ended.

The type declarations are followed by the declarations of the public functions and procedures. You've already seen the most important of these with MTDEMO and PHILO5.

```
{== Declaration of the public procedures of the unit ====================}

function  MtCreateTask   ( Task   : TS;
                           Priory : byte;
                           SLen   : integer;
                           TskPtr : pointer   ) : TDP;
procedure MtGetSem       ( var S : SEMAPHORE );
procedure MtReleaseSem   ( var S : SEMAPHORE );
function  MtCreateQueue  ( Num, Size : integer ) : QUEUEP;
function  MtPeekQueue    ( Qp : QUEUEP; var Message ) : boolean;
procedure MtReadQueue    ( Qp : QUEUEP; var Message );
procedure MtWriteQueue   ( Qp : QUEUEP; var Message );
procedure MtDeleteQueue  ( Qp : QUEUEP );
procedure MtaStart       ( Tempo : integer );
procedure MtKillTask     ( Task : TDP );
procedure MTChangePrio   ( Task : TDP; NewPrio : byte );
procedure MtYield;
procedure MtBlock;
procedure MtContinue;


{-- Routines only intended for the call of cooperating units -------------}

function  MtRegisterUnit( Create : UPCreate;
                          Change : UPChange;
                          Delete : UPDelete ) : boolean;
procedure MtWriteQFast   ( Qp : QUEUEP; var Message );
procedure MtBlockFast;
procedure MtContinueFast;
procedure MtAtomicStart; inline( $FA );
procedure MtAtomicEnd;   inline( $FB );
```

A few functions and procedures haven't been discussed yet. We've included these in the following table.

Function	Task
MtDeleteQueue	Deletes a queue created with MtCreateQueue
MtKillTask	Deletes another task
MtChangePrio	Changes the priority of a task
MtYield	Passes the program execution voluntarily from the current task to another task
MtBlock	Blocks task switching
MtContinue	Restores task switching
MtRegisterUnit	Registers a Unit as an "associate" of the MT unit
MtWriteQFast	Fast access to a queue, which should not be exposed to interrupt handlers
MtBlockFast	MtBlock-Version for interrupt handler
MtContinueFast	MtContinue-Version for interrupt handler
MtAtomicStart	Suppresses interrupts
MtAtomicEnd	Re-enables interrupt triggering

These procedures and functions are to be used only for units used by the MT unit. They shouldn't be used in normal multitasking programs.

```
{============================================================================}
{== Implementation section                                                ==}
{============================================================================}

Implementation

{$L mta.obj}                                    { link mta assembler module }

{== Declaration of NEAR procedures from the assembler module ==============}

procedure MtaStart( Tempo : integer ) ; external;
procedure MtaYield                    ; external;
procedure MtaStop                     ; external;
procedure MtaLost                     ; external;
procedure MtaTaskEnded                ; external;
function  MtIsBlocked     : boolean   ; external;

{== Declaration of FAR procedures from the assembler module ===============}

procedure MtBlock                 ; external;
procedure MtContinue              ; external;
procedure MtBlockFast             ; external;
procedure MtContinueFast          ; external;
```

The declaration of these procedures and functions is followed by the implementation part of the unit, which starts by including the assembler module, MTA. Then the various functions and procedures from this module are defined. A differentiation is made between the routines of the NEAR type and of the FAR type.

These declarations are followed by internal constants, which, in turn, are followed by type declarations only used inside the MT unit. Therefore they're not public. Only the UNITPROC type should be emphasized. It accepts the three procedural pointers passed by a unit to the MT unit during the call of MtRegisterUnit.

```
{== Constants, internal to the module =====================================}

const MIN_STACK      = 40;              { minimum size of a task stack, must }
                                        { be sufficient for context change   }
      TP_STACK_NEED = 512;              { Turbo requires at least 512 bytes  }
      WHAT_SEMAPHORE = nil;                  { do not wait for semaphore }
      MAX_LONGINT   = 2147483647;       { largest positive value of a Longint }

{== Internal type declarations =============================================}

type PTRREC   = record                     { for access to the parts of }
                   Ofs : word;             { any pointer                }
                   Seg : word;
                 end;

     UNITPROC = record                     { unit procedures to be called }
                   CreateProc : UPCreate;           { create task }
                   ChangeProc : UPChange;           { task switch }
                   DeleteProc : UPDelete;           { delete task }
                 end;
```

The MT unit cannot do without global variables, but, in comparison with other units, there are relatively few variables and typical constants defined in the implementation part of the unit.

```
{== internal typed constants =============================================}

const FirstTask : TDP      = nil;      { pointer to first and last task   }
      LastTask  : TDP      = nil;      { Descriptor in the chain of tasks }
      NumTask   : integer = 0;             { number of tasks created    }
      NumLUnits : integer = 0;         { number of cooperating units }

{== internal global variables =============================================}

var   CurTask : TDP;                              { currently executing task }
      IdleTdp : TDP;          { pointer to task descriptor of the Idle-Tasks }
      ExitOld : pointer;          { pointer to the old Exit-procedure }
      LUnits  : array [1..MAX_UNITS] of UNITPROC;        { linked units }
```

The control of the chain of task descriptors uses the variables FirstTask and LastTask created as typical constants so they contain the value NIL at the program start. FirstTask points to the first task in the chain and LastTask points to the last task descriptor. The intervening descriptors are reached with the fields following Next or Last.

NumTask also helps the task control. This variable reflects the number of tasks created with MtCreateTask. It's initialized with 0 because a task is not created.

The constant NumLUnits follows and stores the number of the units which are registered with MtRegisterUnit as associates of the MT unit.

Next we turn to the global variables. Their content is still undefined at the start of the MT unit.

The first of these variables is CurTask. It's especially important for the task switching because it always contains the address of the task descriptor of the active task. The IdleTdp variable contains a pointer to a task descriptor. This points to the Idle task. This task is always present even though it may not be specifically created with MtCreateTask. How this task is used will be discussed with the function MtCreateTask.

ExitOld is a variable that may look familiar. It's usually given to the variables when units loaded with the address of the current End routine from the global variable ExitProc are initialized.

The last global variable of the MT unit is the array LUnits. Here the MtRegisterUnit stores the pointer to the three routines which a cooperating unit must make available to MT.

We'll now begin discussing the Pascal portion of the MT unit. Here are the public procedures and functions, and the routines excluded from the internal usage or are called with the assembler module MTA.ASM.

First is the function MtCreateTask, which usually initiates a multitasking program because only its call creates the tasks later carried out in parallel with each other.

```
{*****************************************************************************
*   MtCreateTask : creates a new task                                       *
**-----------------------------------------------------------------------**
*   input : Task   = procedure with which the execution of the task starts  *
*           Priory = priority of the task                                   *
*           SLen   = size of the task stack                                 *
*           TskPtr = pointer, passed to the starting task                   *
*   output : a pointer to the task descriptor created or NIL when           *
*            the task could not be created.                                 *
*   Info    : the start procedure of the task must be FAR !                 *
*   Global : CurTask, FirstTask, LastTask                                   *
*****************************************************************************}

function MtCreateTask( Task   : TS;
                       Priory : byte;
                       SLen   : integer;
                       TskPtr : pointer ) : TDP;
```

```
begin
  if ( NumTask = 0 ) then                            { is this the first task? }
    IdleTdp := MtBuildTask(IdleTask, 0, 0, NO_ARG); { yes, create IdleTask }
  MtCreateTask := MtBuildTask( Task, Priory, SLen, TskPtr );
end;
```

As the listing demonstrates, this procedure uses a second procedure, MtBuildTask, to create the indicated tasks. This procedure uses MtBuildTask to create not only the task indicated by the caller but also the Idle task.

The Idle task, containing a useless infinite loop, always operates on the lowest level of priority. Its purpose is to run when the scheduler cannot locate another task. When occurring, for example, in MtDemo, it leads to the start of the Idle task when the ShellTask waits for an input and neither the CALC task or the Directory Task are occupied because they're waiting for messages from their queues.

An executable task is selected since a processor is always available for use. The Idle task is started and because of its lowest priority can immediately be replaced by another task if one reaches the Ready mode.

```
{*****************************************************************************
*   IdleTask : this task, which has no function, runs on the lowest         *
*              priority level and is only called when                       *
*              no other task is available.                                  *
*****************************************************************************}

{$F+}
procedure IdleTask( TskPtr : pointer );

begin
  while ( TRUE ) do                                { useless endless loop }
    ;
end;
{$F-}
```

The function MtBuildTask creates and initializes the appropriate task descriptors for MtCreateTask.

```
{**********************************************************************
*  MtBuildTask : creates a new task                                   *
**------------------------------------------------------------------**
*  input : Task   = procedure, which begins the execution of the task *
*          Priory = priority of the task                              *
*          SLen   = size of the task stack                            *
*          TskPtr = pointer, which is passed to start of task         *
*  output : a pointer to the created task descriptor or NIL, when      *
*           the task could not be created.                            *
*  Info   : - the Start-procedure of the task must be FAR !           *
*           - this procedure is only for internal use in the MT unit.  *
*             External units must use the procedure MtCreateTask.      *
*  Global : CurTask, FirstTask, LastTask                              *
**********************************************************************}

function MtBuildTask( Task   : TS;
                      Priory : byte;
                      SLen   : integer;
                      TskPtr : pointer ) : TDP;

var NewTask : TDP;                          { pointer to new task descriptor }
    i       : integer;                                       { loop counter }

begin
  {-- create new task descriptor and attach to end of the task list -------}

  MtBlock;                                         { no task switching yet }
  New( NewTask );                              { create new task descriptor }

  if FirstTask = nil then                           { no task created yet? }
    begin                                                            { no }
      FirstTask := NewTask;                    { store pointer to first task }
      NewTask^.Last := nil;                      { there is no predecessor }
      CurTask := NewTask;          { with this task begins the multitasking }
    end
  else                                                   { not first task }
    begin
      LastTask^.Next := NewTask;              { build chaining to new task }
      NewTask^.Last := LastTask;                 { chaining to predecessor }
    end;

  LastTask := NewTask;          { the new task is the last task up to now }
  NewTask^.Next := nil;          { and has no successor yet               }

  {-- create the stack of the new task and initialize --------------------}

  if SLen < MIN_STACK then                  { minimum stack size is MIN_STACK }
    SLen := MIN_STACK;
  SLen := SLen + TP_STACK_NEED + System.StackLimit;        { TP stack needs }
  GetMem( NewTask^.Stack, SLen );                  { create memory for stack }
  NewTask^.StackLen := SLen;                 { store stack length for FreeMem() }
  NewTask^.SP := Ofs( NewTask^.Stack^ ) + SLen;        { SP to end of stack }
```

```
NewTask^.Waitfor_Sm := WHAT_SEMAPHORE; { task doesn't wait for semaphore }
NewTask^.Priority := Priory;                       { store priority }
NewTask^.StartTime := 0;                         { task was not yet started }

{-- allow external units to store information -------------------------}

for i := 1 to NumLUnits do
  NewTask^.UnitData[ i ] := LUnits[ i ].CreateProc;

{-- store the argument, the return jump address to task and various    --}
{-- processor registers on the task stack                              --}

PushStack( NewTask, PTRREC( TskPtr ).Seg );        { argument for new task }
PushStack( NewTask, PTRREC( TskPtr ).Ofs );
PushStack( NewTask, Seg( MtaTaskEnded ) ); { FAR return jump address for }
PushStack( NewTask, Ofs( MtaTaskEnded ) ); { TaskEnded                   }
PushStack( NewTask, 512);                            { flag register }
PushStack( NewTask, Seg( Task ) );          { return jump address for IRET }
PushStack( NewTask, Ofs( Task ) );
for i := 1 to 7 do                   { AX, BX, CX, DX, DI, SI & BP are 0 }
  PushStack( NewTask, 0 );
PushStack( NewTask, DSeg );          { segment addr. of the data segment }
PushStack( NewTask, 0 );                             { ES is also 0 }
```

```
{-- the task stack looks like this: ------------------------------------}
{                                                                        }
{      ┌─────────────────────────────────────┐                          }
{      │  FAR-pointer which is passed to the  │         [ SP + 1Eh ]     }
{      ├─                                    ─┤                          }
{      │  procedure [Task-Start] as Argument  │         [ SP + 1Ch ]     }
{      ├─────────────────────────────────────┤                          }
{      │  FAR-pointer to the procedure MtTask-│         [ SP + 1Ah ]     }
{      ├─                                    ─┤                          }
{      │     Ended, which ends the task       │         [ SP + 18h ]     }
{      ├─────────────────────────────────────┤                          }
{      │  content of Flag-Register for IRET   │         [ SP + 16h ]     }
{      ├─────────────────────────────────────┤                          }
{      │                                      │         [ SP + 14h ]     }
{      ├─  return-jump address for IRET      ─┤                          }
{      │                                      │         [ SP + 12h ]     }
{      ├─────────────────────────────────────┤                          }
{      │  content of AX register before INT 08│         [ SP + 10h ]     }
{      ├─────────────────────────────────────┤                          }
{      │  content of BX register before INT 08│         [ SP + 0Eh ]     }
{      ├─────────────────────────────────────┤                          }
{      │  content of CX register before INT 08│         [ SP + 0Ch ]     }
{      ├─────────────────────────────────────┤                          }
{      │  content of DX register before INT 08│         [ SP + 0Ah ]     }
{      ├─────────────────────────────────────┤                          }
{      │  content of DI register before INT 08│         [ SP + 08h ]     }
{      ├─────────────────────────────────────┤                          }
{      │  content of SI register before INT 08│         [ SP + 06h ]     }
{      ├─────────────────────────────────────┤                          }
{      │  content of BP register before INT 08│         [ SP + 04h ]     }
{      ├─────────────────────────────────────┤                          }
{      │  content of DS register before INT 08│         [ SP + 02h ]     }
{      ├─────────────────────────────────────┤                          }
{      │  content of ES register before INT 08│   <----- [ SP     ]      }
{      ├─────────────────────────────────────┤                          }
{      │                                      │                          }
{                                                                        }
{   During the next context change in this task, the registers are       }
{   loaded again from the stack and the IRET instruction makes a jump     }
{   to the procedure [ TaskStart ]. As argument this procedure finds the  }
{   pointer [ TskPtr ] on the stack.                                      }
{                                                                        }
{------------------------------------------------------------------------}

      inc( NumTask );                    { increment number of the tasks }
      MtBuildTask := NewTask;            { return pointer to task descriptor }
      MtContinue;                        { task switching possible again }
   end;
```

First MtBuildTask prevents task switching by calling MTBlock. At the time of the call this can already be in process because the call of MtCreateTask wasn't limited to the time before the start of the multitasking. The various tasks can also generate other tasks by using this function. Just like the call of MtContinue at the end of the procedure, the call of MTBlock

576

shows only the effect when the task switching is set in motion with a previous call of MtaStart. Otherwise, the call of the two procedures has no true importance.

In this case the task switching is suppressed for two reasons:

- MtBuildTask manipulates the list of the task descriptors through attachment of a new descriptor. This could lead to memory conflicts with the scheduler processing this list.

- The task switching is blocked because MtBuildTask contains calls of the procedures New and GetMem. In a multitasking environment these can be called only when the multitasking is blocked or the caller has obtained a semaphore specifically prepared through the call of MtGetSem.

The reason is related to the circumstances in which these procedures manipulate pointers such as HeapPtr and the Fragment list. As in all global variables, this may lead to problems as procedures simultaneously call and carry out several tasks.

This problem is avoided by integrating their own procedures GetMem and FreeMem, called by Turbo Pascal, instead of the old procedures in the MT unit. Before the call of the old routines, they would have to obtain a semaphore to have, for the moment, an exclusive access right to the procedures GetMem and FreeMem. Unfortunately this wouldn't work with New and Dispose. These are internally converted to calls for GetMem and FreeMem but since Turbo Pascal isn't interested in the redirected procedures, it calls the original procedures from the system unit.

The GetMem/FreeMem problem applies to all other routines of predefined units, from Turbo, accessing global variables. Although we didn't try all the routines, it's apparent for most that they probably won't access global variables because it isn't necessary. Nothing prevents the parallel use of these routines by various tasks. Use the access through a semaphore described earlier if you're unsure about the conditions.

Next is the MtBuildTask procedure. This uses New to create a new task descriptor. Then it's attached to the end of the double linked list of the task descriptors. Then the size is calculated for the space allocated for the task stacks. The value TP_STACK_NEED, corresponding to the minimum stack size the stack check routine expects, is added to the size indicated by the caller. The value from the System StackLimit variable is also included. This indicates that it's housed in the System unit. Usually this variable contains the value 0 and has no influence on the result of the formula.

The other fields in this descriptor are also loaded after GetMem allocates the task stack and its start address is stored in the Stack field in the new task descriptor. First the stack length is loaded and then the initial value for the SP register, selected in such a way that, at first, the register points to the end of the task stack.

After the fields WaitFor_SM, Priority and StartTime are also initialized, MTBuildTask calls the function UpCreate of all registered units to inform them that a new task is created. The pointer returned is stored in the various fields of the UnitData array at the end of the task descriptor.

Then MtBuildTask begins its most important task: initializing the stack. The task was already executed and turned inactive through task switching even before the first command was executed. This is connected through MtaStart with the procedures during the start of the multitasking. First the scheduler and then the task switcher are called. This executes the task selected by the scheduler. However, it always assumes that the task was suspended by a preceding task switch (which usually is true).

This means that MtBuildTask must store the various registers on the stack in the same way as the task is inactive. However, the various processor registers preceded by other values ensure that, during its start, the task begins with the start of the procedure indicated by MtCreateTask and receives the pointer intended for it as a parameter.

Therefore this pointer is examined and loaded on the task stack with the PushStack procedure from the MT unit. This procedure, similar to the machine language command PUSH, always stores a word on the top of the stack. The stack pointer, in this case available as the field SP from the task descriptor, decrements this word with the value two. On the next call it points to the preceding stack word.

Another FAR pointer is brought to the stack. However, instead of a parameter, destined for the task procedure, it contains the address of the routine to which the task procedure should jump after its completion. It corresponds to the return jump address when the processor calls a procedure with a CALL command and is automatically stored on the stack.

Since the call of this routine doesn't usually occur, MtBuildTask must provide more help. What happens after completing the task procedure, during the call of MtaTaskEnde, will be explained later. For the moment remember that, after completing the task, the control of the program execution automatically passes to the MT unit, which then deletes the task.

Behind the imaginary return jump address to the caller are the registers, stored by a task switch on the stack. This is the address where the current task was interrupted. The address is stored the same way as the return addresses are by the processor on the stack during an interrupt call. The task switcher is also called with an interrupt. This timer interrupt is usually called automatically 18.2 times per second. It's the basis for the permanent task switching and will be examined closely in the following pages.

Let's continue our discussion as MtBuildTask creates the stack. During an interrupt call, the processor stores the content of the interrupt flags and only then stores the return jump address to the interrupted program (or task) on the stack. So, MtBuildTask must also store a value on the stack. Then after the return to the interrupted program, the processor loads the value from the stack into the flag register by using the IRET command.

The value 512 indicated here is the only one in the flag register with the interrupt flag set. All other flags contain the value 0 but aren't important during the start of the task procedure. The flag register in Turbo Pascal isn't used for passing information to procedures and functions.

The address of the start procedure passed to MtBuildTask is indicated as a return jump address to the interrupted program. So, after the first task switching to this task, the execution begins with this procedure.

Various registers follow the return jump address on the stack. The task switcher, as an interrupt handler for the timer interrupt $08, stores these registers immediately after its call on the active task stack.

The value 0 is indicated for the registers AX, BX, CX, DX, DI, SI and BP because their content is undefined during a call of a procedure. This is also true for the ES register which is stored as the last register by the task switcher on the stack. Between the general registers and the ES register is the DS register, whose content is defined during a call of a procedure and must point to the data segment of the Turbo program. During the call of PushStack, the segment address of this segment is passed from the predefined DSeg variable.

The work of MtBuildTask is almost complete with storing these registers on the task stack. It increments the number of the task in the NumTask variable, loads the address of the task descriptors created as function result and returns, through MtContinue, to the caller after restarting the task switching.

Below is a listing of PushStack before discussing the procedures MtKillTask, MtiKillTask and MtDelTask. They're the counterparts of MtCreateTask and MtBuildTask.

```
{**********************************************************************
*  PushStack : stores a word on the stack of a task                  *
**----------------------------------------------------------------**
*   input : TaDes = pointer to the task descriptor                   *
*           Push  = the word to be stored on the stack               *
**********************************************************************}

procedure PushStack( TaDes : TDP; Push : word );

type WPTR = ^word;                                { pointer to a word }

begin
  with TaDes^ do          { process task descriptor, to which TaDes points }
    begin
      dec( SP, 2);                      { decrement stack pointer by 2 bytes }
      WPTR( ptr( PTRREC(Stack).Seg, SP ) )^ := Push; { store word on stack }
    end;
end;
```

A second task could use the MtKillTask procedure to delete a prematurely ended task. This is only possible when the task has a pointer to the descriptor of the other task. This descriptor cannot be its own because a task cannot erase itself with MtKillTask.

This is also the reason why MtKillTask compares the passed task descriptor with the content of the global variable CurTask. Here a pointer to the task descriptor of the active task is always stored. Only if the two pointers don't agree will MtKillTask call the MtKillTask procedure to erase the indicated task. The task switching is blocked during this event so that the task to be deleted doesn't suddenly become an active task. This could lead to serious problems when the task stack is released and the task descriptor is deleted.

```
{***************************************************************************
 *  MtKillTask: removes a task from the list of the task descriptors      *
 *              and releases the memory allocated for it again.           *
 *  input : Task : pointer to the task descriptor of the task             *
 *  Info    : - A task may not erase itself with this function            *
 *  Global : CurTask, LastTask, FirstTask                                 *
 ***************************************************************************}

procedure MtKillTask( Task : TDP );

begin
  MtBlock;                                    { suppress task switching }
  if ( Task <> CurTask ) then            { prevent, task erasing itself }
    MtiKillTask( Task );                              { erase task }
  MtContinue;                            { restore task switching again }
end;
```

When called from the assembler module, MtiKillTask is also used for the normal termination of a task procedure. It uses the MtDelTask procedure instead of erasing the task itself. First it determines whether the indicated task is the current task and if there are currently more than two active tasks. This means that at least one additional task must exist besides the indicated task and the Idle task. If true, it selects a new task with the call of MtChooseNext, because after its elimination, the active task can no longer be executed.

The active MtChooseNext task is given the priority of 0 to prevent it from being selected as a new task again. Although this ensures that the task is inferior to the Idle task, it doesn't have a lower priority because it was executed more recently than the active task.

The task is then deleted with MtDelTask. The task remaining is the Idle task. Also, the multitasking is stopped because none of the tasks previously created through MtCreateTask still exist. In this case, MtiKillTask calls MtDelTask again to erase the Idle task and then turns to the MtaStop procedure from the assembler module. This stops the multitasking and continues the program execution again after the MtaStart call.

```
{**************************************************************************
*  MtiKillTask: removes a task from the list of the task descriptors   *
*               and releases the memory allocated for it again         *
*  input : Task : pointer to the task descriptor of the task           *
*  Info    : - if a task erases itself, a new current task is          *
*                automatically selected.                               *
*             - the procedure assumes that before its call the task    *
*                switching was blocked.                                *
*  Global : CurTask, LastTask, FirstTask                               *
***************************************************************************}

procedure MtiKillTask( Task : TDP );

begin
  {-- is the current task being erased and does one task remain? ----------}
  if ( ( Task = CurTask ) and ( NumTask > 2 ) ) then
    begin                                  { yes, select new current task }
      CurTask^.Priority := 0;        { current task may not be selected }
      MtChooseNext;                       { select new current task }
    end;

    MtDelTask( Task );                                    { erase task }
    if  ( NumTask = 1 ) then          { does only IdleTask remain? }
      begin                                               { yes }
        MtDelTask( IdleTdp );                      { delete IdleTask }
        MtaStop;                         { terminate multitasking }
      end;
end;
```

MtDelTask deletes the task from the chained list of task descriptors and then calls the UpDelete procedure of the individual cooperating units to inform them the task is deleted. Then the space, allocated by MtBuildTask for the task descriptor, and the task stack are released again. The procedure is ended after the NumTask counter is decremented.

```
{**************************************************************************
*  MtDelTask: removes a task from the list of the task descriptors and  *
*             releases the memory allocated for it again               *
*  input : Task : pointer to the task descriptor of the task           *
*  Info    : - the procedure assumes that before its call the task     *
*                switching was blocked.                                *
*  Global : CurTask, LastTask, FirstTask                               *
***************************************************************************}

procedure MtDelTask( Task : TDP );

var i : integer;                                          { loop counter }

begin
  {-- delete indicated task from the list of task descriptors ------------}

  if Task = FirstTask then          { is current task first task in list? }
    FirstTask := Task^.Next                { yes, next task is now first }
```

```
    else                                  { no, connect predecessor with successor }
      Task^.Last^.Next := Task^.Next;

    if Task = LastTask then                     { was last task up to now? }
      LastTask := Task^.Last                    { yes, previous task is last }
    else                                 { no, connect successor with predecessor }
      Task^.Next^.Last := Task^.Last;

    {-- inform external units of deletion of the task ----------------------}

    for i := 1 to NumLUnits do
      LUnits[ i ].DeleteProc( Task^.UnitData[ i ], NumTask );

    FreeMem( Task^.Stack, Task^.StackLen );        { release stack memory }
    Dispose( Task );                          { release task descriptor again }
    dec( NumTask );                        { decrement number of remaining tasks }
  end;
```

Notice that multitasking doesn't have to be blocked despite the call of Dispose and FreeMem. This had to occur before the call of this procedure.

In MtiKillTask, the MtChooseNext procedure is called to select a new task. This is the procedure which the task switcher calls for selecting a new task from the assembly language module.

```
{*******************************************************************************
 *  MtChooseNext : selects the next task to be executed                      *
 **-------------------------------------------------------------------------**
 *  Info     : this procedure is called by the scheduler in the assembler    *
 *             module MTA.ASM. It assumes that the task switching was         *
 *             switched off before its call                                  *
 *  Global : CurTask : the current task                                      *
 *******************************************************************************}

procedure MtChooseNext;

const Call_Me : longint = 0;              { previous calls of this procedure }

var LookTask,                                   { currently compared task }
    MaxTask  : TDP;    { pointer to task descriptor with highest priority }
    CurPrio,                                { priority of the current task }
    MaxPrio,                                { highest priority found }
    i        : integer;                       { loop counter }
    MinTime  : longint;                       { earliest task started }

begin
  {-- find the unblocked task that currently has the highest priority and--}
  {-- has not been executed for the longest time in comparison with the  --}
  {-- other tasks of the same priority                                    --}

  MaxPrio  := -1;                         { every priority is higher than -1 }
```

```
      MinTime  := MAX_LONGINT;
      LookTask := FirstTask;                           { begin with the first task }

      for i := 1 to NumTask do          { process the chain of task descriptors }
         begin
            with LookTask^ do                     { process the task data block }
               begin
                  if ( Waitfor_Sm = WHAT_SEMAPHORE ) then      { is task free? }
                     if ( Priority > MaxPrio ) then { yes, highest current priority? }
                        begin
                           MaxPrio := Priority;               { yes, store data }
                           MaxTask := LookTask;
                           MinTime := StartTime;
                        end
                     else                    { not highest priority, but maybe equal }
                        if (Priority = MaxPrio) and
                           ((StartTime < MinTime) or
                           ((StartTime = MinTime) and (LookTask <> CurTask))) then
                           begin               { yes, and last execution was older }
                              MaxTask := LookTask;
                              MinTime := StartTime;
                           end
                  end;
            LookTask := LookTask^.Next;               { set pointer to next TD }
         end;

      if ( MaxTask <> CurTask ) then                   { perform task switch? }
         begin                                                        { yes }
            {-- notify external units of task change  -------------------------}

            for i := 1 to NumLUnits do                                { yes }
               LUnits[ i ].ChangeProc( MaxTask^.UnitData[ i ] );

            CurTask := MaxTask;                     { new current task is the task }
                                                    { with the highest priority    }
            CurTask^.StartTime := Call_Me;             { store starting time }
         end;
      inc( Call_Me );                      { increment the number of calls up to now }
   end;
```

So far we've discussed selecting a new task. This means the scheduler uses MtChooseNext to simply load the global variable CurTask with a pointer to the task descriptor of the task which shouldn't be executed. The assembler isn't concerned with what task is involved. It's more important that CurTask points to a task descriptor since the opposite of this would lead to an immediate system crash.

In this version, MtChooseNext uses the local variables MaxPrio and MinTime before entering the loop which processes all task descriptors. These variables find, in the least amount of time, a task with the highest priority and with a minimum amount of execution time. MtChooseNext does this so that even the Idle task appears to have a higher priority.

Another local variable, called LookTask, serves as run-time pointer through the list of the task descriptors and is loaded with the address of the first descriptor (i.e., Idle task) before the entry into the search loop.

Each task uses the loop to determine whether it's waiting for a semaphore. This indicates that it isn't ready for execution. If the task isn't waiting for a semaphore, the WaitFor_Sm field contains the value WHAT_SEMAPHORE in the task descriptor. MtChooseNext can begin the additional investigation of the tasks. A task is most likely to become active when it has a higher priority than the current priority. Its address, priority and last starting time are stored in local variables.

A task can, however, become active even if it has the same priority as the current priority. However, the following conditions must be met: this task isn't the active task and its last execution is earlier than the task now considered. Also, in this case, its data is stored in the local variables where the priority doesn't have to be stored again since it corresponds with the priority already stored in the MaxPrio variable.

From these two conditions, the MaxTask variable indicates, after MtChooseNext is executed, the next task to become active. If this task isn't identical to the active task, the procedure UpChange of the cooperating units are called to inform them of the task change.

At the same time the address of the new task descriptor is loaded into the global variable CurTask. This is an important step for the assembler module and for the activation of the new task. Then the task stores the starting time in the form of the call counter, incremented immediately before the procedure termination.

If the active task remains active, the new starting time isn't stored in its task descriptor because it's still executing.

The procedures and functions, through which queues and semaphores could be manipulated, are still missing. Let's look at the procedures MtGetSem and MtReleaseSem, which we used extensively in the dining philosophers example from Section 13.3.

```
{*******************************************************************************
 *  MtGetSem : brings a semaphore into possession of the caller               *
 **-------------------------------------------------------------------------**
 *  input : S = the semaphore                                                 *
 *  Info    : if the semaphore is at the time in the possession of another    *
 *            task, the task execution is stopped until the other task        *
 *            has released the semaphore through the procedure MTReleaseSem.*
 *******************************************************************************}

procedure MtGetSem( var S : SEMAPHORE );

begin
  MtBlock;                                          { block task switching }
```

```
If ( S = 0 ) then                                    { stored Wakeups? }
   begin                                { no, task must wait for release }
      if ( NumTask <> 0 ) then            { in multitasking-operation? }
         begin                                                  { yes }
            CurTask^.Waitfor_Sm := @S;              { store semaphore }
            MtaYield;  { the current task is blocked until semaphore is free }

            {-- when the task returns to this place, the semaphore has been -}
            {-- released again through a call of MtReleaseSem and the       -}
            {-- multitasking can begin again                                -}

            MtBlock;                                        { block again }
         end
      else                           { no, only the main program is active }
         repeat until ( S <> 0 );                      { wait for release }
   end;
   dec( S );                                           { decrement semaphore }
   MtContinue;                                   { start task switching again }
end;
```

MtGetSem presents the indicated semaphore to the caller and, during its start, blocks the multitasking to prevent another task from accessing the semaphore while it executes. It doesn't use a semaphore because MtGetSem would have to call itself, which leads to an endless recursion.

After MtGetSem determines if the semaphore contains the value 0 and a return to the caller isn't immediately required because the semaphore is already assigned, it uses the NumTask variable to test whether the program is already in the multitasking mode.

This condition is recognized if the global variable NumTask contains a value not equal to zero. Most likely you'll never call MtGetSem before the call of MtaStar but you'll probably use routines such as KbmEventWait. In the KBMT unit, adapted for multitasking, this procedure accesses a semaphore and will call MtGetSem when the program is still in the single task mode.

A semaphore must be used differently in this mode than in a multitasking environment. A task can't be blocked because there isn't another task forced to execute.

If the program remains in the single task mode, MtGetSem enters into a simple repeat unit loop. Here it accesses the semaphore until it no longer contains the value zero.

You may be wondering why a semaphore would be set during the single task mode since the only task (the actual program) controls the query of the semaphore. An interrupt handler could do this and, as we shall see later, the KBMT unit is designed in such a way that the handlers for the mouse and keyboard act in a similar manner.

However, in the multitasking mode the procedure waits until the semaphore is released again through a call of MtRelease. It stores the address of the semaphore in the field WaitFor_Sm in the task descriptor. This is one reason why MtGetSem obtains the semaphore to be processed as a variable parameter and not as a value parameter. Otherwise the address operator @ would return only the address of the local copy and not the actual address of the semaphore. This address is needed in MtReleaseSem in order to release the task blocked by a semaphore.

After storing the address of the semaphore in the task descriptor and placing the task into the "Waiting" status, MtGetSem calls MtaYield to pass the program execution to another task. It returns to the command which follows the call of MtaYield only when another task has released the semaphore with a call of MtReleaseSem. This changes the status of the task to "Ready" and the next task switch makes it the new active task.

Then the program execution comes to the end of MtGetSem, where the semaphore is decremented and multitasking is switched on again.

```
{***************************************************************************
 *  MtReleaseSem : releases a semaphore again                              *
 **----------------------------------------------------------------------**
 *  input : S = the semaphore                                              *
 *  Info  : if tasks with a higher priority than the current task are      *
 *          waiting for the release of the semaphore, the execution of the*
 *          current task is interrupted to activate one of these tasks.   *
 ***************************************************************************}

procedure MtReleaseSem( var S : SEMAPHORE );

var Tlp          : TDP;          { pointer into the chain of task descriptors }
    i,                                                      { loop counter }
    Prio         : integer;              { task with the highest priority }
    NotBlocked,                  { task switching before call not yet blocked? }
    Yield        : boolean;              { pass execution to other tasks? }

begin
  NotBlocked := not(MtIsBlocked);       { task switching blocked already? }
  MtBlock;                                     { block task switching }
  if ( S = 0 ) then              { maybe tasks are waiting for semaphore? }
    begin                                      { yes, find such a task }
      Tlp := FirstTask;                   { start search with first task }
      Prio := CurTask^.Priority;          { this priority must be higher }
      Yield := FALSE;                              { do not yield }
      for i := 1 to NumTask do  { process the individual tasks in the list }
        begin
          with Tlp^ do                         { process task descriptor }
            if ( Waitfor_Sm = @S ) then   { is task waiting for semaphore? }
              begin             { yes, task does not have to wait any more }
                Waitfor_Sm := WHAT_SEMAPHORE;
                if ( Priority > Prio ) then  { task with highest priority? }
```

```
                    Yield := NotBlocked;              { yes, task switching }
                end;
              Tlp := Tlp^.Next;                    { set Tlp to next task data }
          end;
        inc( S );                                   { increment semaphore }
        if ( Yield ) then                          { switch to another task? }
          MtaYield;                                           { yes }
      end
    else                              { no task is waiting for the semaphore }
      inc( S );                                      { increment semaphore }
    MtContinue;                                     { restart task switching }
  end;
```

MtReleaseSem is more complex than MtGetSem. In relation to the semaphores to be released, MtReleaseSem must process not only the current task but all tasks to find the task waiting for the semaphore, which can be changed to the "Ready" status again.

This happens only when MtReleaseSem determines that the semaphore, until now containing the value 0, may have blocked a task. Otherwise, the semaphore is simply incremented and, after the call of MtContinue, a return is made to the caller.

If the semaphore contained the value 0, all the tasks must be processed and the waiting task must be unblocked. But this task is made the active task if it has a higher priority than the task active until now. This happens only when the task switching wasn't already blocked before the call of the procedure.

This is also why MtReleaseSem calls the function MtIsBlocked. It informs MtReleaseSem, with a Boolean result, if the task switching is now blocked. This call is located at the very beginning of the procedure because it can call MtBlock at any time to block the task switching.

The function result from MtIsBlocked is canceled and stored in the local variable NotBlocked, which then assumes the value TRUE when the task switching isn't blocked. This variable is always used when the procedure, while processing the various task descriptors, finds the task waiting for the semaphore and this task also has a higher priority than the current task. So, it's inevitable that it will be activated inside MtReleaseSem through a call of MtaYield. This happens only if the task switching is not blocked before the call of MtReleaseSem.

Therefore the local variable Yield, which before the entry into the loop set to FALSE, is loaded with the content of NotBlocked. If the task switching wasn't blocked before the call of MtReleaseSem, it either keeps the value TRUE or the value FALSE. After completing the loop, this variable determines if a direct task switch can occur. If yes, the MtaYield procedure is called as an MtGetSem.

The procedures MtWriteQueue, MtQriteQFast, MtReadQueue and MtPeekQueue build on the procedures MtGetSem and MtReleaseSem, which control a queue with semaphores.

We've seen this in Section 13.2. We'll need to present the MtCreateQueue procedure before discussing these other procedures.

```
{***********************************************************************
 *   MtCreateQueue : creates a queue                                   *
 **------------------------------------------------------------------**
 *   input : NUM  = maximum number of the elements in the queue        *
 *           SIZE = size of a queue element in bytes                   *
 *   output : pointer to the queue, which is needed for all subsequent *
 *            queue operations.                                        *
 ***********************************************************************}

function MtCreateQueue( Num, Size : integer ) : QUEUEP;

var Qp : QUEUEP;                    { pointer to memory area for allocated queue }

begin
  MtBlock;                                                     { new block }
  New( Qp );                                  { allocate memory area for queue }
  MtContinue;

  with Qp^ do                                            { process the queue }
    begin
      FAccess := SEM_FREE;        { until now nobody has accessed the queue }
      OccpdE  := 0;                             { no entry into the queue }
      Free    := Num;                          { all elements are free }
      NumEnt  := Num;                               { store length }
      ElSize  := Size;                      { store size of elements }
      MtBlock;                                   { block task switching }
      GetMem( QBufP, Num * Size );           { allocate queue buffer }
      MtContinue;                            { continue task switching }
      Next := 1;                     { the pointers Next and Last point to }
      Last := 1;                     { the beginning of the queue buffer   }
    end;
  MtCreateQueue := Qp;                             { pass pointer to queue }
end;
```

The procedure creates the queue with a New call and stores the returned pointer to the queue in the local variable Qp. This is later returned to the caller as a function result. The various fields are initialized, as previously discussed in Section 13.2. The GetMem procedure is used to allocate the queue buffer through the heap.

In a similar way, deleting the queue continues with MtDeleteQueue. This releases the two allocated buffers to delete the queue. Of course MtDeleteQueue must know which queue to delete and therefore it expects, during its call, the pointer which MtCreateQueue returned when the queue was created.

```
{***************************************************************
*  MtDeleteQueue : deletes a queue previously created with MtCreateQueue  *
**-----------------------------------------------------------------**
*  input : QP = pointer to the queue                            *
*  Info   : Tasks which are still waiting for the queue to be deleted  *
*            must be deleted before the call of this procedure, or they  *
*            will never terminate.                              *
****************************************************************}

procedure MtDeleteQueue( Qp : QUEUEP );

begin
  with Qp^ do                          { process the queue data block }
    begin
      MtBlock;                         { block the call of FreeMem }
      FreeMem( QBufP, NumEnt * ElSize );   { release queue buffer }
    end;
  Dispose( Qp );                       { release queue itself }
  MtContinue;                          { permit task switching again }
end;
```

MTDEMO illustrates that MtDeleteQueue doesn't necessarily need to be called. At the end of the program, Turbo Pascal releases the complete heap and automatically deletes the queues. If you use MtDeleteQueue now, remember a task isn't waiting for the queue because it would also be waiting for a semaphore which no longer exists after the queue was deleted. So, using MtDeleteQueue could produce unpredictable effects in the program.

```
{***************************************************************
*  MtWriteQueue: write a message into a queue                   *
**-----------------------------------------------------------------**
*  input : QP      = pointer to the addressed queue            *
*          MESSAGE = pointer to the message which should be copied to the  *
*                    queue                                      *
*  Info   : - if the queue is full, the function returns to the caller  *
*            only when another task has read an element from the queue.  *
****************************************************************}

procedure MtWriteQueue( Qp : QUEUEP; var Message );

type QBUF = array [0..65000] of byte;    { image of a queue buffer }
     QBP  = ^QBUF;                       { pointer to such a buffer }

begin
  with Qp^ do                           { process the queue }
    begin
      MtGetSem( Free );                 { wait until at least one entry is free }
      MtGetSem( FAccess );              { get access right to queue }
      Move( Message, QBP(QBufP)^[ (Last-1) * ElSize ], ElSize );
      if ( Last = NumEnt ) then         { reached last element? }
        Last := 1                       { yes, set Last to next element }
      else                              { no, increment only }
```

589

```
        inc( Last );
      MtReleaseSem( OccpdE );                { one element more occupied }
      MtReleaseSem( FAccess );                 { release FAccess again }
    end;
  end;
```

MtWriteQueue operates while accessing the queue in the same way presented in Section 13.2. The QBUF and QBP types are defined for access to the queue buffer here as in all other queue procedures. QBUF forms a large byte array and QBP forms a pointer to it. The access to the addressed queue element occurs in the various routines with the Move procedure. Two steps are required for calculating the address of the indicated element.

First the nontypical pointer, which inside the QUEUE structure points to the queue buffer, is converted to a pointer of the QBP type. The address of the element (i.e., the index for access to this imaginary array) is formed by multiplying the size of a queue element with the number of the elements to be addressed. Because of this, the machine language specific address formation doesn't require the function Ptr or other tricks.

Through a call of MtGetSem, MtWriteQueue decrements the Free semaphore from the QUEUE structure. If the queue is already full now, executing the task is delayed until another task has read an element from the queue.

After the call of MtGetSem is performed and there is space for at least one element in the queue, MtWriteQueue obtains the access right to the queue by performing a MtGetSem to the FAccess semaphore.

The sequence in which the two MtGetSem calls are performed is important. If MtWriteQueue was the first to obtain the access right, and only then the Free semaphore was decremented, a deadlock of this task could result. Another task may already have access rights. This means that MtReadQueue would be unable to read a message from the queue. Consequently, MtReadQueue couldn't allocate memory for MtWrite Queue to execute.

Once MtWriteQueue has acquired the access right to the queue, the data passed is written into the entry in the queue buffer, to which the Last variable points. Then it's set to the next element. Notice the *wrap around* that occurs from the end of the queue buffer to the first element. Before the procedure returns the access right, it increments the OccpdE semaphore from the QUEUE structure, which unblocks the tasks waiting for the queue.

MtReadQueue proceeds in a similar straight line while reading an element from the queue. The OccpdE semaphore is decremented with MtGetSem and the task execution is stopped until an entry is ready in the queue. Then the procedure obtains the access right to the queue and copies the queue element to be read into the variable, which the caller indicated for this purpose as a procedure parameter.

Through incrementing the Next index, the procedure ensures that the returned queue element isn't the object of a read access to the queue again. Notice the wrap around at the end of the queue occurs again. Since another element in the queue is free, the Free semaphore is incremented with a call of MtReleaseSem and then the access right to the queue is returned.

```
{***********************************************************************
*  MtReadQueue: read a message from a queue                           *
**-------------------------------------------------------------------**
*  input : QP      = pointer to the addressed queue                   *
*          Message = pointer to buffer to which the message is copied *
*  Info   : - if the queue is empty, the function only returns to the *
*             caller when another task has written an element into    *
*             the queue.                                              *
***********************************************************************}

procedure MtReadQueue( Qp : QUEUEP; var Message );

type QBUF = array [0..65000] of byte;            { image of a queue buffer }
     QBP  = ^QBUF;                               { pointer to such a buffer }

begin
  with Qp^ do                                        { process the queue }
    begin
      MtGetSem( OccpdE );       { wait until at least one entry is occupied }
      MtGetSem( FAccess );                      { secure access right to queue }
      Move( QBP(QBufP)^[ (Next-1) * ElSize ], Message, ElSize );
      if ( Next = NumEnt ) then                     { reached last element? }
        Next := 1                          { yes, set Next to next element }
      else                                          { no, increment only }
        inc( Next );
      MtReleaseSem( Free );                      { one more element free now }
      MtReleaseSem( FAccess );                     { release FAccess again }
    end;
end;
```

MtPeekQueue proceeds somewhat differently during access to the queue because the queue element read here isn't removed from the queue as long as one is available.

```
{***********************************************************************
*  MtPeekQueue: determines if a message is in the queue. If so, return this*
*               message without removing it from the queue.           *
**-------------------------------------------------------------------**
*  input : QP      = pointer to the addressed queue                   *
*          Message = pointer to buffer where the message will be copied *
*  output : TRUE, a message was ready                                 *
*  Info   : in contrast with MTReadQueue the function returns immediately *
*           to the caller, even when no message was ready in the queue. *
***********************************************************************}

function MtPeekQueue( Qp : QUEUEP; var Message ) : boolean;
```

```
type QBUF = array [0..65000] of byte;              { image of a queue buffer }
     QBP  = ^QBUF;                                 { pointer to such a buffer }

begin
  with Qp^ do                                              { process the queue }
    begin
      MtGetSem( FAccess );                      { secure access rights to queue }
      if ( OccpdE <> SEM_WAITS ) then                    { message in queue? }
        begin                                   { yes, load into variable passed }
          Move( QBP(QBufP)^[ (Next-1) * ElSize ], Message, ElSize );
          MtPeekQueue := TRUE;                              { return message }
        end
      else                                        { no message in the queue }
        MtPeekQueue := FALSE;
      MtReleaseSem( FAccess );                        { release FAccess again }
    end;
end;
```

MtPeekQueue also demands the access right to the queue and then determines, with the OccpdE semaphore, if an element in the queue waits for a reader. If not, the variable passed by the caller for accepting the queue element isn't affected and the value FALSE is returned to the caller.

Otherwise, Move copies the queue element, to which Next points, from the queue buffer to the variable passed. The value TRUE is loaded as function result. Before MtPeekQueue is finished, it returns the access right to the queue with MtReleaseSem.

An exception among queue procedures is MtWriteQFast. This procedure isn't used for the call of normal application programs but is reserved for the interrupt handlers of the units which cooperate with the MT unit. Since an interrupt handler must always be finished quickly and cannot wait for the release of a queue element, this procedure avoids the usual testing of the various semaphores and writes directly into the queue. It does this even if another task is now accessing the queue. Only an interrupt handler, never another task, should perform write accesses to such a queue in order to avoid a memory conflict during write accesses.

The tasks waiting for an element in the queue are unblocked since access doesn't occur, through MtGetSem and MtReleaseSem, to the various semaphores. If the procedure finds such a task, the MtaLost procedure is called from the assembler module, which performs a task switch as soon as possible.

```
{****************************************************************************
 *  MtWriteQFast: writes a message into a queue, even if another           *
 *                task is currently accessing the queue.                   *
 **-----------------------------------------------------------------------**
 *  input : QP      = pointer to the addressed queue                       *
 *                    MESSAGE = message which should be copied to the queue *
 *  Info   : - if the queue is full, the last queue element is over-       *
```

```
*          written without waiting for the next read access          *
*          - this procedure should only be called by interrupt handlers  *
*              that must access the queue fast and unconditionally.    *
**********************************************************************}

procedure MtWriteQFast( Qp : QUEUEP; var Message );

type QBUF = array [0..65000] of byte;          { image of a queue buffer }
     QBP  = ^QBUF;                              { pointer to such a buffer }

var Tlp    : TDP;              { pointer into the chain of task descriptors }
    i      : integer;                             { loop counter }
    Switch : boolean;          { is TRUE, when a task is waiting for the queue }

begin
  with Qp^ do                                       { process the queue }
    begin
      MtAtomicStart;                          { no interruptions permitted }
      Move( Message, QBP(QBufP)^[ (Last-1) * ElSize ], ElSize );
      if ( Free <> 0 ) then                       { is the queue full? }
        begin                                          { no }
          if ( Last = NumEnt ) then           { reached last element? }
            Last := 1                     { yes, set Last to first element }
          else                                 { no, increment only }
            inc( Last );
          dec( Free );                       { one element less free }

          {-- if the queue was empty until now, tasks which were      ---}
          {-- waiting for this queue must be unblocked                ---}

          if ( OccpdE = 0 ) then                      { queue empty? }
            begin                             { yes, unblock waiting tasks }
              Switch := FALSE;                     { do not leave switch }
              Tlp := FirstTask;              { start search with first task }
              for i := 1 to NumTask do                 { process list }
                begin                    { is task waiting for semaphore? }
                  if ( Tlp^.Waitfor_Sm = @OccpdE ) then
                    begin                             { yes, unblock }
                      Tlp^.Waitfor_Sm := WHAT_SEMAPHORE;
                      Switch := TRUE;    { task switch as soon as possible }
                    end;
                  Tlp := Tlp^.Next;           { set pointer Tlp to next task }
                end;
              if ( Switch ) then          { task switch as soon as possible? }
                MtaLost;                    { yes, inform the assembler module }
            end;
          inc( OccpdE );                        { another element occupied }
        end;
      MtAtomicEnd;                            { interruption permitted again }
    end;
end;
```

This completes the analysis of the most important routines from the Pascal portion of the MT unit. We haven't explained the less important routines because the comments in the program listing should provide enough information for you.

```
{*******************************************************************************
 *   MtRegisterUnit : Registers a unit as associate of the MT unit            *
 **---------------------------------------------------------------------------**
 *   input : Create : procedure called during the creation of a task          *
 *           Change : procedure called during the change of a task            *
 *           Delete : procedure called during the deletion of a task          *
 *   output : TRUE, if the unit could be registered                           *
 *   Info    : a maximum of MAX_UNITS can be registered                       *
 *   Global : NumLUnits, LUnits                                               *
 *******************************************************************************}

function  MtRegisterUnit( Create : UPCreate;
                          Change : UPChange;
                          Delete : UPDelete ) : boolean;

begin
  if ( NumLUnits < MAX_UNITS ) then                  { can units be registered? }
    begin                                                                 { yes }
      inc( NumLUnits );                   { increase number of registered units }
      LUnits[ NumLUnits ].CreateProc := Create;
      LUnits[ NumLUnits ].ChangeProc := Change;
      LUnits[ NumLUnits ].DeleteProc := Delete;
      MtRegisterUnit := TRUE;                                    { everything OK }
    end
  else                                        { already MAX_UNITS are registered }
      MtRegisterUnit := FALSE;                               { return error }
end;


{*******************************************************************************
 *   MtYield : pass program execution voluntarily to another task             *
 *******************************************************************************}

procedure MtYield;

begin
  MtBlock;                                              { block task switching }
  MtaYield;                                             { activate next task }

  {-- Continue is executed automatically by MtaYield ---------------------}
end;


{*******************************************************************************
 *   MtChangePrio : changes the priority of a task                            *
 **---------------------------------------------------------------------------**
 *   input : Task     = pointer to the task descriptor of the task            *
 *           NewPrio = new priority of the task                               *
 *******************************************************************************}
```

```
procedure MTChangePrio( Task : TDP; NewPrio : byte );

begin
  Task^.Priority := NewPrio;                        { set new priority }
end;
```

The end of the MT unit, with the initialization part and the MtEnd procedure, is called as a close-up routine of the unit. It tests, based on the global variable NumTask, if various tasks are still active. If active, this means instead of ending the normal way, Turbo Pascal ended the program. Either a run-time error occurred or the user pressed <Ctrl><Break> during the standard input routine of Turbo Pascal.

If this happens, MtEnd erases all existing tasks with MtiKillTask and displays an error message.

```
{****************************************************************************
*  MtEnd : is called in the following situations:                         *
*                - normal end of a program which works with the MT unit   *
*                - program termination through activation of Ctrl-Break   *
*                - program termination through a run-time error           *
****************************************************************************}

{$F+}                                                      { must be FAR }

procedure MtEnd;

var Resultat : boolean;              { accepts function result of MtKillTask }

begin
  MtBlock;

  {-- was the program terminated through a run-time error? ---------------}

  if (NumTask <> 0 ) then                           { still tasks active? }
   begin                              { yes, error, clear all active tasks }
     CurTask := nil;                                       { no more tasks }
     while ( NumTask <> 0 ) do                    { not even one more task? }
       MtiKillTask( LastTask );                      { no! clear last task }
     writeln('Multitasking error');
   end;

  ExitProc := ExitOld;                        { re-install old Exit procedure }
end;

{$F-}

{**-----------------------------------------------------------------------**}
{** Starting code of the unit                                            **}
{**-----------------------------------------------------------------------**}

begin
```

```
   ExitOld := ExitProc;                { mark address of Exit procedure }
   ExitProc := @MtEnd;                 { define MtEnd as Exit procedure }
end.
```

The MtaStart procedure, used to start the multitasking after creating the various tasks, cannot be found in the Pascal part of the MT unit. It's in the assembler module MTA.ASM and will be discussed when we turn to the assembler portion of the unit.

Beginning the assembler module MTA.ASM is a series of declarations to declare the various constants and macros. Also a structure is declared under the name TD, whose construction resembles the task descriptors from the Pascal part of the unit. Now the assembler module can access these important data structures.

```
;******************************************************************;
;*                        M T A . A S M                          *;
;*--------------------------------------------------------------*;
;*     task       : Assembler module for the MT multitasking unit *;
;*--------------------------------------------------------------*;
;*     Author     : MICHAEL TISCHER                               *;
;*     developed on : 06/12/1989                                  *;
;*     last update : 03/08/1990                                   *;
;*--------------------------------------------------------------*;
;*     assemble   : TASM /MX MTA                                  *;
;*                  ... link with the MT unit                     *;
;******************************************************************;

;== Constants =====================================================

STACK_LEN       equ 300                 ;Length of the internal stack in words

TIMER_0_CTRL    equ 43h                 ;Timer #0, control register
TIMER_0_DATA    equ 40h                 ;Timer #0, data register
TIMER_0_LOAD    equ 36h                 ;Load command

INTR_EOI        equ 20h                 ;EOI signal for interrupt controller
INTR_PORT       equ 20h                 ;Port of the interrupt controller

;== Macros ========================================================

Block       macro
            inc  StopSwap               ;Increment block flag
            endm

Continue    macro
            dec  StopSwap               ;Decrement block flag
            endm

;== Structures ====================================================

TD          struc                       ;Task descriptor, must match the construction
                                        ;of the record with the same name from the
```

```
                                         ;MT unit
StackPtr    equ this dword               ;Points to task stack
StackOfs    dw ?                         ;Offset address of the task stack
StackSeg    dw ?                         ;Segment address of the task stack

TaskSP      dw ?                         ;SP during task interruptions
StackLen    dw ?                         ;Length of the task stack
Priority    db ?                         ;Task priority
Waitfor_Sm  dd ?                         ;Pointer to expected semaphore
Last        dd ?                         ;Pointer to previous task descriptor
Next        dd ?                         ;Pointer to next task descriptor

TD          ends
```

The various constants are used for programming the timer, which generates the cyclical signal that enables fast task switching and the programming of the interrupt controller, which, after processing the timer interrupt, must contain the message that a new call of this interrupt can occur.

The two macros Block and Continue are used for the suppression and resumption of the task switching. They increment and decrement a flag, internal to the module StopSwap. Only when this flag contains the value 0, the new handler of the timer interrupt can perform task switching; otherwise the task continues unaffected.

In the data segment, the assembler module doesn't have any variables even though it needs variables for its work. Instead it references only the CurTask and NumTask variables from the Pascal portion of the unit.

```
;== Data Segment ========------========------========---------=======================

DATA    segment word public

extrn   CurTask : dword                 ;Pointer to current task (descriptor)
extrn   NumTask : word;                 ;Number of tasks

DATA    ends
```

The variables of the assembler module are stored in the code segment. They're generally addressed from the timer interrupt because when the timer interrupt is called it's uncertain whether the DS register points to the data segment of the Turbo program.

A series of routines are declared as "public" before the variables are declared by the module in its code segment. The Pascal part of the unit calls these routines. On the other hand, the two procedures MtiKillTask and MtChooseNext are declared as "extrn" so the routine isn't blocked from calling these routines.

```
;== program ================================================================

CODE          segment byte public     ;The program segment


;-- Declaration of the public routines -----------------------------------

public        MtaStart                ;Starts the multitasking
public        MtBlock                 ;Stops the task switching
public        MtContinue              ;Starts the task switching again
public        MtBlockFast             ;The two versions of the interrupt
public        MtContinueFast          ;handler
public        MtIsBlocked             ;Task switching blocked?
public        MtaTaskEnded            ;Is called at termination of a task
                                      ;automatically
public        MtaStop                 ;Switch multitasking off again
public        MtaYield                ;Release execution (voluntarily)
                                      ;to other task
public        MtaLost                 ;Trigger task switching at next
                                      ;opportunity


;-- Declaration of the addressed routines from the MT unit ----------------

extrn         MtiKillTask  : near     ;Remove task from the list of task
                                      ;descriptors and release memory
extrn         MtChooseNext : near     ;Determines the next task to be executed
```

In the code segment, MTA must store the content of the registers SS and SP as variables at the time of the call of MtaStart. Then at the end of all tasks and before returning to the Pascal program, it can start the old Turbo stack again to ensure correct program execution.

The TurboDS variable stores the segment address of the Turbo data segment. A variable controls the task switching through the macros Block and Continue for StopSwap.

The variables Faster, Speed, Ticks, RetAdr and Lost and their significance will be discussed when we describe MtaStart and the task switcher.

```
;== Variables in the Code Segment =========================================

TurboSS    dw ?                       ;Stack segment of Turbo Pascal
TurboSP    dw ?                       ;Stack pointer of Turbo Pascal
TurboDS    dw ?                       ;Data segment of Turbo Pascal
StopSwap   db 1                       ;Is TRUE when a task cannot be
                                      ;interrupted. Must be
                                      ;initialized with TRUE.
Faster     db ?                       ;Is TRUE when system clock is accelerated
Speed      db ?                       ;Speed factor for system clock
Ticks      db ?                       ;Remaining ticks until the call of the old
                                      ;Timer interrupt handler
RetAdr     dw ?                       ;Return jump address for TaskSwitch
Lost       db 0                       ;Is TRUE when a task switch was suppressed
```

```
                                   ;by a block and must now be made up

OldTimer    equ this dword
OldTimerO   dw  ?                  ;Offset and segment address of the old
OldTimerS   dw  ?                  ;timer interrupt handler

OldDisk     equ this dword
OldDiskO    dw  ?                  ;Offset and segment address of the old
OldDiskS    dw  ?                  ;BIOS disk interrupt handler (INTR 13)

OldDos      equ this dword
OldDosO     dw  ?                  ;Offset and segment address of the old
OldDosS     dw  ?                  ;DOS function dispatcher (INTR 21)

MyStack     dw  STACK_LEN dup (?)  ;Internal stack
MyStackEnd equ this byte           ;Label marks end of stack
```

The first six variables store the addresses of the old interrupt handlers. During the call of MtaStart these interrupt handlers are replaced with $08 (Timer), $13 BIOS disk/hard disk interface and $21 (MS-DOS function dispatcher).

The two variables, which store the segment and offset address of the old handler, are preceded by a label of the dword type, through which the two are loaded quickly, with a machine language command LES and LDS, into the processor registers.

The end of the variables in the code segment form an internal stack which is always used when the module cannot use either the task stacks or the stack of the actual Turbo program.

In the user programs the MtaStart procedure, which follows the different variables, is the most important routine in the assembler module because:

•   It reveals the secret of the parameter provided during the call of this procedure.

•   It determines the speed of the task switching.

The value corresponds to a rate of 18.2 switches conforming to the call of the timer interrupt $08. A higher switch rate can be set so the various tasks appear to be executed simultaneously. However, there's a danger in increasing the speed too much. After a certain point, the entire system may crash depending on the time required by a task switch. Also, as the number of switches per second increases, the amount of time available decreases for the various tasks. So they'll take longer to execute.

You should do some experimenting on your own with the MTDEMO and PHILO5 programs. If you're using a 386 computer, operating at 25 MHz, a speed setting of up to 32 won't create problems. If your using an old PC operating at 4.77 MH, problems may occur at settings as low as four or five.

MtaStart cannot only make the task switching faster but also can make the switching slower. This helps the individual tasks, and in the screen output, clearly reveals the displacement of the tasks at a certain time. If you want to see how this affects your programs, set a value smaller than -1 during the call of MtaStart.

```
;== Procedures ================================================================

          assume cs:code, ds:data


;-----------------------------------------------------------------------------
;-- MtaStart       : Installs the scheduler as new timer interrupt and
;--                  starts the multitasking with it
;-- input          : TEMPO = speed
;--                      > 1 = Timer faster by factor TEMPO
;--                      <-1 = Timer slower by factor TEMPO
;-- call from TP: procedure MtaStart( Tempo : integer );
;-- Info           : To start multitasking, this procedure must be called
;--                  from the MT unit.

MtaStart    proc near

            mov    TurboSS,ss           ;Store Turbo stack
            mov    TurboSP,sp
            mov    TurboDS,ds           ;Store data segment

            ;-- Install new BIOS disk interrupt handler --------------

            mov    ax,3513h             ;Get interrupt vector 13h
            int    21h
            mov    OldDisk0,bx          ;Store address in variables
            mov    OldDiskS,es

            mov    cx,ds                ;Store DS in CX

            mov    ax,2513h             ;Install new handler
            mov    dx,offset NewDisk
            push   cs                   ;Load CS into DS
            pop    ds                   ;DS:DX now points to new handler
            int    21h

            ;-- Install new DOS interrupt handler --------------------

            mov    ax,3521h             ;Get interrupt vector 21h
            int    21h
            mov    OldDos0,bx           ;Store address in variables
            mov    OldDosS,es

            mov    ax,2521h             ;Install new handler
            mov    dx,offset NewDos
            push   cs                   ;Load CS into DS
            pop    ds                   ;DS:DX now points to new handler
            int    21h
```

```
          mov    ds,cx                  ;Restore DS from CX

          ;-- Evaluate speed factor ----------------------------

          mov    bp,sp                  ;Make stack addressable
          mov    cx,[bp+4]              ;get argument "Tempo"
          or     ch,ch                  ;Greater than 0?
          jne    Slower                 ;No, slower

          ;-- Accelerate the system clock ----------------------

          mov    Faster,1               ;Set flag
          cmp    cx,1                   ;Neither faster nor slower?
          je     MtaSt1                 ;Yes, timer does not have to be programmed

          mov    al,TIMER_0_LOAD        ;Send command code to timer #0
          out    TIMER_0_CTRL,al
          xor    ax,ax                  ;Calculate 65536 / CX
          mov    dx,1
          div    cx                     ;Load quotient into AX
          cli                           ;Suppress interrupts
          out    TIMER_0_DATA,al        ;Load new timer frequency: low byte
          mov    al,ah
          out    TIMER_0_DATA,al        ;High byte
          sti                           ;Re-enable interrupts

MtaSt1:   mov    dx,offset FastTimer    ;Address of the new handler
          jmp    ReplTimer

Slower:   ;-- Slow down system clock -----------------------

          neg    cx                     ;Convert CX to positive number
          mov    Faster,0               ;Set flag
          mov    dx,offset SlowTimer    ;Address of the new handler

ReplTimer: ;-- Install new timer interrupt handler ------------------

          mov    Speed,cl               ;Store speed factor
          mov    Ticks,cl

          mov    ax,3508h               ;Get interrupt vector 08h
          int    21h
          mov    OldTimerO,bx           ;Store address in variables
          mov    OldTimerS,es

          mov    cx,ds                  ;Store DS in CX
          mov    ax,2508h               ;Install new handler
          push   cs                     ;Load CS to DS
          pop    ds                     ;DS:DX now points to new handler
          int    21h
          mov    ds,cx                  ;Restore DS from CX
```

```
               call   MtChooseNext          ;Select first task

      StartTask: ;-- Start execution of task again, to whose task descriptor -----
                 ;-- CurTask points                                         -----

               mov    es,word ptr CurTask+2;Pointer to current task descriptor
               mov    bx,word ptr CurTask  ;Move to ES:BX
               cli                         ;Do not disturb
               mov    ss,es:[bx].StackSeg  ;Switch to task stack
               mov    sp,es:[bx].TaskSP
               sti
               Continue                    ;Do not suppress task switching

               pop    es                   ;Get the registers from the task stack
               pop    ds
               pop    bp
               pop    si
               pop    di
               pop    dx
               pop    cx
               pop    bx
               pop    ax
               iret                        ;Jump into the task

      MtaStart    endp
```

MtaStart must perform a few assignments before it concentrates on the speed setting passed. It stores the registers SS, SP and DS in the variables provided and then installs the two new interrupt handlers for the interrupts $13 and $21. At the same time it determines the addresses of the old handlers and stores them in the proper variables.

Then MtaStart considers the speed setting passed and tests for a negative or positive setting. MtaStart jumps to the label Slower if the setting is a negative number or continues with the normal program execution if the setting is a positive number.

It loads the Faster variable with the setting 1 to indicate that a minimum of 18.2 task switches will be carried out per second. If a setting larger than 1 is indicated, the timer is reprogrammed so that it generates not 18.2, but correspondingly more calls of the interrupt $08. Then the offset address of the new interrupt handler for the timer interrupt (of the task switcher) is loaded into the DX register and a jump performed to the ReplTimer label. The new interrupt handler is installed here.

Instead of slowing the internal clock, the timer isn't reprogrammed when a negative speed setting is indicated. After a command changed the speed setting and converted it to a positive value, only 0 is loaded into the Faster variable. This is because, besides the task switcher, portions of the operating system (perhaps the BIOS) also rely on the timer and are set for a constant frequency of 18.2 calls per second. The normal frequency is maintained with SlowTimer but an interrupt handler is installed that calls the old interrupt handler with every call. However, this occurs only after every n calls performs a task switch.

The FastTimer operates very differently when a setting equal to or larger than 1 is indicated. It performs a task switch during every call but calls the old interrupt handler only after every n calls. Therefore it's activated only 18.2 times per second.

Additionally, these different methods are the reason why switch frequencies larger and smaller than 18.2 install a different interrupt handler at the label ReplTimer, after the address of the old handler was determined.

Then the MtChooseNext procedure is called to determine which task to activate first. It also starts immediately at the label StartTask. This label is called by the two task switchers after they've selected a new task. The program loads the content of the CurTask pointer into the register pair ES:BX and loads, from the TD structure addressed in this manner, the stack address, of the task to start, into the registers SS and SP. Remember the value for SP is taken from the SP field of the task descriptor while the value for SS comes from the segment part of the stack field.

Then the macro Continue enables a task switch again. The processor registers, stored during the task switch, are loaded again from the stack and then a jump is performed, with an IRET command, to the task procedure indicated at MtCreateTask.

Beforehand, the two interrupt handlers, which proceed similarly, ensure that the task switching is now possible.

```
;----------------------------------------------------------------------
;-- SlowTimer : The new interrupt handler, when the timer interrupt was   -
;--             slowed
;-- call from TP: Not permitted !

SlowTimer   proc near

            cmp     Lost,1              ;Does a previous TaskSwitch
            je      StCall              ;have to be suppressed?

            dec     Ticks              ;Is call of the task switcher due?
            jne     STimer             ;No

            ;-- Call task switcher, if possible ----------------------

StCall:     push    ax                 ;Load counter "Ticks" again
            mov     al,Speed
            mov     Ticks,al
            pop     ax

            cmp     StopSwap,0         ;Task switching blocked?
            je      StSwitch           ;NO ---> StSwitch
```

```
            mov    Lost,1              ;Yes, the task switch cannot be
                                       ;executed
STimer:     jmp    [OldTimer]          ;Jump to old handler

StSwitch:   mov    Lost,0              ;No call suppressed
            mov    RetAdr,offset STimer  ;Return jump address for TaskSwitch

            ;-- Direct transition to TaskSwitch ---------------------------

SlowTimer   endp
```

During its call, SlowTimer verifies whether any task switches should have occurred since the last call but didn't because the task switching was blocked. If so, the Lost flag contains the value 1 and SlowTimer jumps to the StCall label where a task switching begins. Otherwise, the counter Ticks is decremented. This counter then always reaches the value 0 if a task switch is required again. Also in this case the program execution is continued with StCall.

The Ticks counter is loaded with the speed setting passed during the call of MtaStart. This ensures that a task switching, unless it's discovered before the Lost flag is set, occurs only after n calls of the interrupt handler. Since the AX register is involved in this operation and the various registers haven't yet been stored, it's pushed on the stack before this operation and then reloaded.

Usually task switching occurs only when the StopSwap flag contains the value 0 and, therefore, SlowTimer loads the Lost flag again with the value 1 when it wants to avoid task switching. Then it jumps to the old interrupt handler. At the end of the program this continues with the task interrupted through the call of the timer interrupts with an IRET command. The same also occurs when SlowTimer, at its start, determines the Lost flag isn't set and it isn't yet time for task switching.

The task switching is performed with the TaskSwitch procedure following SlowTimer in the program listing. Technically, this isn't a procedure because it cannot end with a RET command. Since it begins a new task and its stack during its execution, the RET command wouldn't find the return jump address again. It's stored on the stack of the task made inactive in the meantime. When ending, TaskSwitch jumps to the program location whose address was stored in the RetAdr variable before its "call" by the caller.

```
;-----------------------------------------------------------------------
;-- TaskSwitch : Controls preemptive switching between various
;--                tasks
;-- input     : Variable RetAdr = return jump address to caller
;-- call from TP: not permitted!

TaskSwitch proc near
```

```
        push   ax                      ;Store the registers on the stack
        push   bx                      ;of the current task
        push   cx
        push   dx
        push   di
        push   si
        push   bp
        push   ds
        push   es


;-- Store current stack pointer in the task descriptor -----------

        mov    ds,TurboDS              ;Load Turbo data segment
        mov    es,word ptr CurTask+2   ;Load pointer CurTask to ES:BX
        mov    bx,word ptr CurTask
        mov    es:[bx].TaskSP,sp

        cli                            ;Switch to own stack
        push   cs
        pop    ss
        mov    sp,offset MyStackEnd
        sti

        Block
        call   MtChooseNext            ;Select next task
        Continue

;-- Load pointer to new active task and return register from    -
;-- its task stack

        mov    ax,word ptr CurTask+2   ;Load pointer CurTask into DS:BX
        mov    bx,word ptr CurTask
        mov    ds,ax
        cli                            ;Switch to task stack
        mov    ss,[bx].StackSeg
        mov    sp,[bx].TaskSP
        sti

        pop    es                      ;Load registers from task stack
        pop    ds
        pop    bp
        pop    si
        pop    di
        pop    dx
        pop    cx
        pop    bx
        pop    ax

        jmp    [RetAdr]                ;Jump to caller

TaskSwitch endp
```

During its call, TaskSwitch stores the various processor registers on the stack of the active task and enters the content of the SP register in a field with the same name in the current task descriptor. It then installs the stack, internal to the module, so during the call of MtChooseNext, which follows, enough space is available on the stack. This obviously depends on the use of local variables in MtChooseNext. This wouldn't be assured otherwise with the Idle task.

After selecting a new task, TaskSwitch proceeds just like MtaStart. Next it installs the stack whose address is stored in CurTask. Then it returns the processor registers, from this stack, stored there when the last task was made inactive. Restarting this task isn't performed by TaskSwitch. It doesn't end with the required IRET instruction but instead jumps to its caller through the RetAdr variable.

FastTimer could also be the source of a caller of TaskSwitch. When, during the call of MtaStart, a setting equal to or larger than 1 is indicated, FastTimer acts as an interrupt handler for interrupt $08. During its call, this routine verifies whether task switching is possible at the moment and in this case calls TaskSwitch. Otherwise the Lost flag is set to 1.

In both cases the routine checks if the old interrupt handler should be called because a certain number of calls have passed. If yes, the tick counter is loaded again with its initial value and a jump performed to the old handler. The IRET command at its end ensures the start of the newly selected task.

If a call of the old handler doesn't occur, then FastTimer must inform the interrupt controller about completing the interrupt. This command is one that the old handler would have performed but isn't too difficult since only a certain command code is sent to one of the ports of the controller. The jump to the newly activated task is the result of an IRET command inside FastTimer.

```
;-------------------------------------------------------------------------
;-- FastTimer : The new interrupt handler, when the timer interrupt
;--             was accelerated
;-- call from TP: not permitted!

FastTimer   proc near

            cmp    StopSwap,0            ;Task switching blocked?
            jne    Ft                    ;Yes

            ;-- Task switching permitted, call task switcher ---------------

            mov    RetAdr,offset Ft1     ;Return jump address for taskSwitch
            jmp    taskSwitch

Ft:         mov    Lost,1               ;Make up task switch
```

```
Ft1:        push  ax                      ;Store AX on the stack
            dec   Ticks                   ;Call to old handler is due
            jne   FtEnde                  ;No ---> FtEnde

            ;-- Call old timer interrupt handler --------------------

            mov   al,Speed                ;Load Speed into Ticks
            mov   Ticks,al
            pop   ax                      ;Restore AX again
            jmp   [OldTimer]              ;Jump to old handler

            ;-- The old handler returns to the caller, jump to label -------
            ;-- FtEnde is not made

FtEnde:     ;-- Return to caller without calling the old handler ----

            mov   al,INTR_EOI             ;Send "End of Interrupt" signal (EOI)
            out   INTR_PORT,al            ;to interrupt controller
            pop   ax
            iret                          ;Back to caller

FastTimer   endp
```

The assembler module contains a series of routines for the call through an applications program and the Pascal portion of the MT unit. These routines are different from the routines which the user will never use such as, FastTimer, SlowTimer or TaskSwitch.

These other routines include MtBlock and MtContinue. We already encountered these with the Pascal portion of the unit as a way to suppress the task switching.

```
;-------------------------------------------------------------------
;-- MtBlock       : Stops the task switching until MtContinue is called
;-- call from TP: procedure MtBlock;

MtBlock     proc far

            Block                         ;Increment block flag
            mov Lost,0                    ;A task switch was not "lost"
            ret                           ;Back to caller

MtBlock     endp
```

To determine if, during the time the task switching was blocked, a task switch should have occurred, MtBlock sets the Lost flag to zero. During its next call, the new interrupt handler for the Timer interrupt, whether a SlowTimer or FastTimer, will set this flag to 1 if its work is prevented by the preceding call of MtBlock.

```
;--------------------------------------------------------------------------
;-- MtContinue   : Starts task switching again, after it had been stopped
;--                       previously by MtBlock
;-- call from TP: procedure MtContinue

MtContinue proc far

                Continue                ;Decrement block flag
                cmp    Lost,0           ;Was a task switch lost?
                je     MtC              ;No, return

                cmp    StopSwap,0       ;Is switching permissible again?
                jne    MtC              ;No ---> MtC

                ;-- A task switch should have been performed, ------
                ;-- make up for this now

                Block                   ;Block before yield
                call   MtaYield         ;Perform task switch

MtC:            ret                     ;Back to caller

MtContinue endp
```

MtContinue benefits from the way MtBlock proceeds, by verifying, after decrementing the StopSwap flag using the Continue macro, whether the Lost flag still contains the value zero. A task switch shouldn't have occurred in the meantime. If so, it returns to the caller using the fastest route possible.

Otherwise, it verifies whether StopSwap now contains the value 0 in order to permit a task switch. This isn't necessarily the case, despite the preceding "call" of Continue, since the macros Block and Continue only increment or decrement the StopSwap flag and don't simply set it to 0 or 1 because nested calls of MtBlock and MtContinue could occur. For example, this happens when a procedure in the Pascal portion of the module, which at the start calls MtBlock and at its end calls MtContinue, calls a procedure that acts the same way.

The StopSwap flag would again be set to 1 at the end of the called procedure and the task switching would start again when the calling procedure was not yet completed (i.e., had not yet reached the MtContinue call). Therefore MtBlock and MtContinue increment and decrement only the StopSwap flag, so the interrupt handler only performs a task switch when as many calls of MtContinue have occurred as have preceded the calls of MtBlock.

MtContinue cannot be sure, after decrementing StopSwap, whether this flag now contains a 0 with this process, so it must be able to verify this after previously determining that at least one task switch had to be suppressed with the preceding call of MtBlock. If task switching is again permitted, MtContinue calls MtaYield to pass program execution voluntarily to another task. Otherwise, MtContinue immediately returns to the caller.

Before presenting the MtaYield procedure, we'll discuss MtBlockFast and MtContinueFast. They operate similarly to MtBlock and MtContinue. However, an important difference exists in the way they handle suppressed task switches. Since MtBlockFast and MtContinueFast aren't affected by a suppressed task switch, they don't verify the content of the Lost flag to catch the task switch.

So MtBlockFast and MtContinueFast are ideal to use in interrupt handlers. Here the program execution doesn't pass from the interrupt handler to another task because the interrupt handler should be finished as fast as possible in order to continue executing the interrupted task. The example in this chapter is the KBM unit. This version uses this capability in its interrupt handler as an adaptation for multitasking.

```
;-----------------------------------------------------------------------
;-- MtBlockFast  : Stops the task switching until MtContinueFast is called
;-- call from TP: procedure MtBlockFast;
;-- Info         : This procedure should be used only by the
;--                interrupt handler

MtBlockFast proc  far

            Block                   ;Increment flag
            ret                     ;Back to caller

MtBlockFast endp

;-----------------------------------------------------------------------
;-- MtContinueFast: Starts the task switching again after it was stopped
;--                 by MtBlockFast
;-- call from TP: procedure MtContinueFast
;-- Info         : Unlike MtContinue a switch is not made to
;--                another task, even if it should have occurred
;--                in the meantime

MtContinueFast proc far

            Continue                ;Decrement block flag
            ret                     ;Back to caller

MtContinueFast endp
```

The MtaYield procedure is called not only from inside the assembler module but also from the Pascal portion of the unit. During the call, it assumes the task switching was already blocked and therefore calls the corresponding Pascal procedure MtYield. It calls MtBlock before turning to MtaYield.

This simulates a task switch triggered by the interrupt call of the timer. The flag register and then the return jump address to the caller are stored, in the form of a FAR pointer, on

the stack. Since the routine itself is of the NEAR type, it only finds the offset address of
the caller on the stack and therefore must get the segment address from the CS register.

```
;------------------------------------------------------------------------
;-- MtaYield : Passes program execution (voluntarily) to another task
;-- call from TP: MtaYield
;-- Info        : - Call only possible from the MT unit!
;--                - During the call of this procedure, the task switching
;--                  must already be blocked.

MtaYield proc near

            ;-- Emulate interrupt call ----------------------------------

        pop    ax                    ;Get offset addr. of the caller
        pushf                        ;Flag register to the stack

        push   cs                    ;Segment addr. for return jump on the stack
        push   ax                    ;Offset addr. for return jump to stack

        mov    RetAdr,offset MtaYRet ;Return jump address for TaskSwitch
        jmp    TaskSwitch            ;Switch to next task

MtaYRet: cli                         ;No timer call now
        mov    Lost,0                ;No switches lost
        Continue                     ;Task switching permitted again
        iret                         ;Back to caller

MtaYield   endp
```

The task switch itself occurs as usual with TaskSwitch, which returns to MtaYield after its
completion. It quickly sets the Lost flag to 0 and, using an IRET command, jumps to the
newly selected task.

A Pascal procedure can use the function MtIsBlocked to return a boolean result as function
result to the caller if it must know whether the task switching is now possible. The value
TRUE is always received by the caller when no task switches are occurring at the moment.

```
;------------------------------------------------------------------------
;-- MtIsBlocked : Inform the caller if the task switching is blocked at
;--               the moment
;-- call from TP: boolean := MtIsBlocked;

MtIsBlocked proc near

        cmp    StopSwap,0            ;Block flag deleted?

        mov    ax,1                  ;No, no task switch currently permitted
        ret                          ;Back to caller
```

610

```
NoBlock:    xor   ax,ax              ;Return 0 for FALSE
            ret                      ;Back to caller


MtIsBlocked endp
```

To complete the multitasking environment, the MtiKillTask procedure calls the MtaStop procedure from the Pascal portion of the unit. This call is done as soon as MtiKillTask has determined that the last task created with MtCreateTask was deleted. MtaStop resets the Timer to its old frequency and installs the old interrupt handler again for the $08, $13 and $21 interrupts.

```
;-----------------------------------------------------------------------
;-- MtaStop : Re-installs the old interrupt handler and programs the timer -
;-            to its old frequency again
;-- call of TP: MtaStop
;-- Info       : - Call only possible from the MT unit!
;--               - During the call of this procedure the task switching
;--                 must have been blocked already.

MtaStop     proc near

            mov   cx,ds              ;Store DS in CX

            mov   Lost,0             ;to prevent task switch

            ;-- Reactivate old DOS interrupt ---------------------------

            mov   ax,2521h           ;Install new handler
            lds   dx,OldDos          ;Load DS:DX with old handler
            int   21h

            ;-- Reactivate old BIOS disk interrupt ---------------------

            mov   ax,2513h           ;Install new handler
            lds   dx,OldDisk         ;Load DS:DX with old handler
            int   21h

            ;-- Reactivate old timer -----------------------------------

            mov   ax,2508h           ;Install old timer interrupt handler
            lds   dx,OldTimer        ;again
            int   21h

            ;-- Set old timer frequency again --------------------------

            mov   al,TIMER_0_LOAD    ;Set timer 0 again to old value
            out   TIMER_0_CTRL,al    ;to generate 18.2 ticks per
            xor   al,al              ; second
            out   TIMER_0_DATA,al
            out   TIMER_0_DATA,al
```

```
              mov    ds,cx                        ;Return DS from CX
              ret                                 ;Back to caller

MtaStop       endp
```

The last public procedure from the assembler module is MtaLost. This can only be used by the Pascal portion of the unit to register a suppressed task switch. MtaLost sets the Lost flag to one. A task switch is performed even if it was not yet time during the next call of the Timer.

```
;-------------------------------------------------------------------------
;-- MtaLost : Cause a task switch at the next opportunity (timer call)
;-- call from TP: MtaLost;
;-- Info         : - Call only possible from the MT unit!

MtaLost       proc near

              mov    Lost,1                 ;Make up task switch
              ret                           ;Back to caller

MtaLost       endp
```

The MtaTaskEnded procedure is always called, even if not from a task, because MtCreateTask has initialized the task stack, when the task was created, in such a way that MtaTaskEnded appears as the return jump address to the caller of the task.

```
;-------------------------------------------------------------------------
;-- MtaTaskEnded : Is called automatically when the end of the start
;--               procedure of a task has been reached.
;-- call from TP: not permitted!

MtaTaskEnded proc near

              Block
              cli                           ;Switch to own stack
              push   cs
              pop    ss
              mov    sp,offset MyStackEnd
              sti

              ;-- Delete task with MtiKillTask from the Pascal ----
              ;-- part of the unit

              push   word ptr CurTask + 2   ;FAR pointer to current task
              push   word ptr CurTask       ;descriptor as parameter on the stack
              call   MtiKillTask            ;Call Pascal procedure
              cmp    NumTask,0              ;Was last task deleted?
              je     StopMt                 ;Yes, back to caller of MtaStart

              jmp    StartTask              ;Start execution of new task
```

```
StopMt:      ;-- Multitasking ended, back to caller of MtaStart() ----

             cli
             mov    ds,TurboDS              ;Load Turbo data segment
             mov    ss,TurboSS              ;Install Turbo stack
             mov    sp,TurboSP
             sti

             retf   2                       ;Back to caller with FAR return
                                            ;Remove arguments for MtaStart from
                                            ;stack

MtaTaskEnded endp
```

MtaTaskEnded blocks the multitasking and switches to the internal stack of the assembler module. This occurs with the call of MtiKillTask, executed immediately afterwards in order to delete the task. Since it also releases the space allocated by the task stack, it's unwise to perform this procedure on a stack which it erases itself. Then it verifies if a task is active. If the task ended is the last task, MtiKillTask has also simultaneously deleted the Idle task and the multitasking was switched off.

When this happens, MtaTaskEnded again installs the stack, which MtaStart found during its call, and returns to the actual Pascal program behind the call of MtaStart. Since the integer value passed to MtaStart is still on the stack, the return to the Pascal program occurs with the command RET 2, which also removes this parameter from the stack.

You have encountered the two interrupt handlers, SlowTimer and FastTimer, for the timer interrupt. Here they serve as a source for the permanent task switching.

MtaStart also installs two additional interrupt handlers for the interrupts $13 and $21. These are the new interrupt handlers for the BIOS disk/hard disk unit interrupt and the MS-DOS functions dispatcher, through which all MS-DOS functions are called. Although not related to the task switching, they ensure that your multitasking programs do not crash when using the functions hiding behind these interrupts.

As we already discovered in Chapter 11, MS-DOS cannot serve several tasks simultaneously and, therefore, MS-DOS functions are called in sequential order. Most noticeable is interrupt $21 which is the doorway to the several hundred MS-DOS functions passed by all function calls.

```
;-- The new interrupt 21h handler (DOS scheduler) -------------------------

NewDos       proc far

             Block                          ;Suppress task switching
             pushf                          ;Emulate call of the old interrupt handler
             call   OldDos                  ;through INT 13h
             call   CheckLost               ;Perform blocked switches
```

```
            ret   2                    ;Back to caller, but do not get
                                       ;flag register from the stack
    NewDos   endp


;-----------------------------------------------------------------------

    CODE     ends                      ;End of code segment
             end                       ;End of program
```

This listing shows the new handler for the MS-DOS interrupt $21 which concludes MTA.ASM. Here the task switching is blocked so that MS-DOS can perform the function call without interruption and another task is unable to perform an MS-DOS function call. After the suppression, an interrupt call of the old function dispatcher is simulated by storing the Flag register on the stack and calling the old handler through a FAR call.

Then there is a call of the CheckLost routine. This routine is used for task switching which didn't occur but should have occurred when executing the MS-DOS function. After returning to the interrupt handler, it returns to the caller. It doesn't use the IRET command as usual because it would get the Flag register, from the stack again, which was stored there during the interrupt call. It shouldn't be changed after an MS-DOS function call since many MS-DOS functions report to the caller with the Carry flag if the function call succeeded or if an error occurred.

```
    ;-----------------------------------------------------------------------
    ;-- CheckLost : is called by one of the internal interrupt handlers to
    ;--             trigger a task switch, if during its execution a task switch
    ;--             had been blocked and the task switching is no longer blocked
    ;-- call of TP: not permitted!

    CheckLost  proc near

               pushf                   ;Store flag register
               Continue                ;Enable task switching
               cmp  StopSwap,0         ;Enabled now?
               jne  clEnd              ;NO ---> clEnd

               cmp  Lost,0             ;Task switching permitted, switch blocked?
               je   clEnd              ;NO ---> clEnd

               ;-- Task switching is permitted and a switch --
               ;-- was already blocked. Do this switch

               Block                   ;Must execute before MtaYield
               push   ax               ;MtaYield changes ax, then store
               call MtaYield           ;Execute task change
               pop    ax               ;and return
    clEnd:     popf                    ;Get flag register from stack
               ret                     ;Return to caller

    CheckLost  endp
```

614

CheckLost is designed so that it doesn't change any processor registers. Because of this, it stores the Flag register on the stack because some individual flags are changed by the subsequent commands. Then it performs a Continue and checks if a task switching is possible again. If not, the call of this routine is immediately completed and it returns to the caller after reloading the Flag register.

If task switching is permitted, CheckLost now determines if a task switch was suppressed in the meantime. This is easily detected on the basis of the Lost flag. If so, CheckLost calls MtaYield to trigger a task switch.

First it must block the task switching again and store the AX register on the stack of the active task because this register is changed in MtaYield. A call of MtContinue isn't necessary after the return from MtaYield because the task switching is automatically possible again.

```
;-- The new interrupt 13h handler (BIOS disk interrupt) --------------------

NewDisk     proc far

            Block                       ;Suppress task switching
            pushf                       ;Call the old interrupt handler
            call    OldDisk             ;Emulate int 13h
            call    CheckLost           ;Suppress switches

            ret     2                   ;Return to caller, but do not
                                        ; store registers on stack
NewDisk     endp
```

The new handler for the BIOS disk/hard disk interrupt performs similarly to the new MS-DOS interrupt handler. The main difference between the two routines is in the call of the old handler since its address is stored in different variables in the code segment.

This brings us to the end of the assembler module and to the end of this section. We've given you an explanation of how the MT unit functions. This helps you in using this unit now that you know the hidden execution sequences and therefore know what is and isn't possible.

In the next two sections we'll discuss the WINMT and KBMT units. They derive from the units WIN and KBM from Chapters 6 and 7.

13.5　Window Control

In Chapters 6 and 7 we explained how to use the WIN unit and the KBM unit to access the screen and keyboard. Examples such as MTDEMO and PHILO5 from the preceding sections demonstrate that multitasking programs also frequently use the screen and keyboard without the limits of a foreground task.

However, the WIN unit and the KBM unit must be modified in order to be used in the multitasking operation (i.e., to integrate them in the parallel operation of various tasks). We'll explain the reasons for this in this section and in Section 13.6.

In its current version, WIN was used by only one program. Now it must be modified to:

- Multitask (be used by several programs simultaneously).

- Allow the various tasks to coordinate the windows because these are not closed in the same sequence they were opened.

- Use Write and Writeln to have several view areas simultaneously active in different windows, in order to display information in the window of the active task.

Only one window and one list of window drivers had to be tracked before. In multitasking, this data must be made available to every task individually. This is simply multiple control of local variables in the various task stacks. As the MT unit switches with every task switch to the stack of the active task, so the new WIN unit, WINMT, switches with every task switch to the WIN data of the new task.

When it starts, the unit must be informed of a task switch. This means participating in the execution inside the MT unit. This is why the MT unit has the ability to register other units as associates. It informs these units not only of each task switch but also in creating and terminating tasks. The key to this is the MtRegisterUnit, which WINMT uses to register itself as an associate of the MT unit.

As the following program segment from the WINMT unit illustrates, this happens as the WinInit initialization routine ends. This is called from the initialization part of the WINMT unit.

```
{**********************************************************************
 *  WinInit : Initializes the WIN unit                               *
 *  Globals : VioCard/W, NumCol/W, NumLine/W, Color/W, VioSeg/W, HaPtr/W  *
 *            Line_Ofs/W                                              *
 **********************************************************************}

procedure WinInit;

const VioMode : array [0..11] of byte = ( MDA, CGA, 0, EGA, EGA_MONO, 0,
                                          VGA_MONO, VGA, 0, MCGA,
                                          MCGA_MONO, MCGA );
      EgaMode : array [0..2] of byte  = ( EGA, EGA, EGA_MONO );

var Regs : Registers;                       { processor regs for interrupt calls }

begin
  VioCard := $ff;                                   { no video card found yet }
  {-- test for VGA or MCGA card ---------------------------------------------}
  Regs.ax := $1a00;                            { call function $1A of the }
   intr($10, Regs);                            { video BIOS               }
   if Regs.al = $1a then                              { VGA or MCGA? }
     begin                                                    { yes }
       VioCard := VioMode[ Regs.bl-1 ];          { get code from table }
       Color := not( ( VioCard = MDA ) or ( VioCard = EGA_MONO ) );
     end
   else                                          { neither VGA nor MCGA }
     begin                                          { test for EGA card }
       Regs.ah := $12;                              { call function $12 }
       Regs.bl := $10;                              { subfunction $10   }
       intr($10, Regs);                             { call video BIOS }
       if Regs.bl <> $10 then                       { EGA installed? }
         begin                                              { yes }
           VioCard := EgaMode[ (Regs.cl shr 1) div 3 ];      { get code }
           Color := VioCard <> EGA_MONO;
         end;
     end;

  {-- get pointer to video RAM ----------------------------------------------}

  Regs.ah := 15;                                { get current video mode }
   intr($10, Regs);                             { call BIOS video interrupt }
   if Regs.al = 7 then                              { monochrome mode? }
     VioSeg := $b000                             { yes, video RAM at B000 }
   else                                             { no, color mode }
     VioSeg := $b800;                            { video RAM at B800 }

  if VioCard = $ff then                          { not EGA, VGA or MCGA? }
     begin                                                   { yes }
       if Regs.al = 7 then VioCard := MDA
                       else VioCard := CGA;
       NumLine := 25;                            { in 25 line text mode }
     end
   else                              { if EGA, VGA or MCGA, get number of lines }
```

```
    NumLine := BPTR( Ptr( $40, $84 ) )^ + 1;
    Color := not( ( Regs.al=0 ) or ( Regs.al=2 ) or ( Regs.al=7 ) );

    NumCol := BPTR( Ptr( $40, $4a ) )^;                    { number of columns }
    Line_Ofs := NumCol shl 1;                       { offset to start of next line }

    Regs.ah := 5;                              { select current screen page }
    Regs.al := 0;                                         { screen page 0 }
    intr($10, Regs);                                { call BIOS video interrupt }

    Regs.ah := 3;                             { get current cursor position }
    Regs.bh := 0;                                  { access to screen page 0 }
    intr($10, Regs);                               { call BIOS video interrupt }
    ATD.CurY    := Regs.dh;                           { store cursor position }
    ATD.CurX    := Regs.dl;
    ATD.CurVisi := TRUE;


  {-- divert file variable OUTPUT to internal output routine --------------}

  with TextRec( Output ) do            { manipulate the file variable OUTPUT }
      begin
         Handle   := $FFFF;        { Turbo expects this declaration like this }
         Mode     := fmClosed;                         { device still closed }
         BufSize  := SizeOf( Buffer );             { set size and address }
         BufPtr   := @Buffer;                          { of buffer          }
         OpenFunc := @OutputOpen;                 { address of Open procedure }
         Name[0]  := #0;                       { change name to empty string }
      end;
  Rewrite( Output );                              { initialize file variable }

  {-- allocate and initialize task data block for main program -----------}

  MnTaDaP   := WinTaskCreate;
  CurTaDaP := MnTaDaP;
  ATD       := MnTaDaP^.i;

  {-- WinMt included as part of the MT unit -----------------------------}

  if not( MtRegisterUnit( WinTaskCreate,
                  WinTaskChange,
                  WinTaskDelete ) ) then
  RunError;

end;


{$I win2mt.pas }
```

The MtRegisterUnit procedure is called to register the WinTaskCreate, WinTaskChange and WinTaskDelete routines from the WINMT unit. From now on they'll be called when creating or terminating a task and with every task switch.

Before discussing these routines, you should be familiar with the commands before registering the unit. This is the creation and registration of a *task data block*. Even though

618

WINMT is almost identical to WIN, a task data block wasn't mentioned in Chapter 6. This task data block is the main difference between WIN and WINMT.

A task data block such as this is created for every task with the registered function WinTaskCreate. They'll contain all data, for example in the visible area, that was previously controlled globally but now is available to every task. This task data block is declared together with the many other type declarations in the Implementation part.

```
TAINTERN =                           { record defined in the context of a  }
 record                              { task in conjunction with WinMt unit }
   CurVisi,
   Write2View      : boolean;
   WritelnX,
   WritelnY,
   WritelnCol,
   ViewX1, ViewY1,
   ViewX2, ViewY2,
   CurX, CurY      : byte;
   WritelnPtr      : VPTR;
   StrepStr        : string;
   FirstWinPtr     : WIPTR;
   CurBufPtr       : VELARPTR;
   HaPtr           : HANDPTR;
   NumWin          : integer;
   CurWinPtr       : WIPTR;
 end;

TASKDATA = record
             i               : TAINTERN;
             SaveOutput      : TextRec;
           end;

TASKDPTR = ^TASKDATA;
```

The actual task data block is the TASKDATA type. In the field it contains a TAINTERN type structure in which the different variables are controlled (i.e., the visible area and the window stack).

SaveOutput is a file variable that provides each task with a version of the OUTPUT file variable. This way the various tasks don't interfere with each other during simultaneous calls of Write and Writeln. This defines only one variable, of this type, internally and stores it in memory because this variable may not be available to all tasks.

TAINTERN contains CurVisi in addition to all variables administered globally in WIN. CurVisi is a Boolean variable. Since every task also has its own blinking cursor, it would take too long to move the cursor, with a BIOS function, more than 18 times per second to a different screen location. This only occurs with tasks in which the CurVisi variable contains the value TRUE.

This isn't true after creating the task. This variable is set only when the task makes the cursor visible with the call of WinSetCursor. If it hides the cursor with a call of WinHideCursor, the flag is set automatically to FALSE and the cursor position will not change during a switch to this task.

You can see how these task data blocks are created and administered in the example of three registered routines: WinTaskCreate, WinTaskChange and WinTaskDelete. All three are a FAR type because they're called from the MT unit with FAR pointers.

```
{**************************************************************************
 *  WinTaskCreate : creates a task while calling the MT unit            *
 **----------------------------------------------------------------------**
 *  Output: pointer to the allocated data block                        *
 *  Info  : this function can only be called when task switching is blocked *
 **************************************************************************}

{$F+}

function WinTaskCreate : pointer;

var TaDaP : TASKDPTR;

begin
  {-- new must be available for access -----------------------------------}

  New( TaDaP );
  with TaDaP^.i do
    begin
      CurVisi    :- FALSE;
      Write2View := TRUE;
      WritelnX   := 0;
      WritelnY   := 0;
      WritelnPtr := GetVioPtr( 0, 0 );
      WritelnCol := $7;
      StrepStr   := '';
      ViewX1     := 0;
      ViewY1     := 0;
      ViewX2     := NumCol - 1;
      ViewY2     := NumLine - 1;
      NumWin     := 0;
      CurWinPtr  := NIL;

      New( HaPtr );
      FillChar( HaPtr^, SizeOf(HaPtr^), 0);
    end;
  TaDaP^.SaveOutput := TEXTREC( Output );
  WinTaskCreate := pointer( TaDaP );
end;

{$F-}
```

During its call, WinTaskCreate creates a new task data block. It chains this to the new task by returning, to the caller, a pointer to this data block from the MT unit. Because of the way it's defined, this returned pointer is passed to the procedures for task switching and task termination. So, these routines can directly access the task data block of the active tasks.

WinTaskCreate not only creates the task data block, but also initializes it by loading the various fields of the TAINTERN structure with their default values and copies the current content, in the OUTPUT file variable, into the components of the task data block provided for this.

The WinTaskChange procedure is responsible for the switch between the various tasks. First it stores the task dependent data in the active task data block so they can be used when they become active again.

```
{-- mark task-dependent data for current task -------------------------}

CurTaDaP^.i := ATD;
CurTaDaP^.SaveOutput := TextRec( Output );
```

Two items are important in understanding these program lines. In the CurTaDaP variable, WinTaskChange stores the pointer passed to it. This pointer points to the active task data block. Since this variable isn't immediately loaded at the beginning of the procedure, this pointer can access the task data block which was active until now. The content of the component i from the active task data block and the different variables, such as the visible area, are stored in the global variable ATD (Actual Task Data block).

The reason for this is that all routines from the WINMT unit, which access variables such as the visible area or CurVisi, no longer can address global variables. Instead, they must obtain this data in the active task data block. To do this they would have to reference this data block during every access through the CurTaDaP pointer, which would take a long time. However, this time could be saved by allowing the routines to access the global variable ATD, which stores the task dependent variables, from the active task data block.

Instead of a data access through a FAR pointer, Turbo must access only a global variable in the data segment, whose address can be directly coded into the individual commands and which is of the NEAR type. Although this saves time, there's a small problem with this method. The active task data block must be loaded, beginning with WinTaskChange, with the content of ATD in order to permanently store the changes of the variables.

Also ATD must be loaded with the content of the new task data block when WinTaskChange is executed. Since the time required for the two copy processes is considerably less than the time required for the constant references of the different variables through FAR pointer, this method is more efficient.

```
{*****************************************************************************
 *  WinTaskChange : calls task changes from the MT unit                     *
 **------------------------------------------------------------------------**
 *  Input : ATD.HaPtr which receives the setting for the current task       *
 *  Info  : this procedure can only be called during blocked task switching *
 *****************************************************************************}

{$F+}

procedure WinTaskChange( TskPtr : pointer );

var Regs : Registers;

begin
  {-- mark task-dependent data for current task ---------------------------}

  CurTaDaP^.i := ATD;
  CurTaDaP^.SaveOutput := TextRec( Output );

  {-- load task-dependent data for new current task ----------------------}

  CurTaDaP := TASKDPTR(TskPtr);
  ATD := CurTaDaP^.i;

  TextRec( Output ) := CurTaDaP^.SaveOutput;

  with ATD do
    if ( CurVisi ) then
      begin
        Regs.ah := 2;
        Regs.bh := 0;
        Regs.dh := CurY;
        Regs.dl := CurX;
        intr($10, Regs);
      end;
end;

{$F-}
```

After WinTaskChange has updated the previously active task data block and has also loaded the new task data block into the global variable ATD, it verifies whether the new task has set the cursor. If this is so, the function $02 of the BIOS video interrupt is called in order to bring the cursor to its last position.

The command of WinTaskDelete is simple compared to WinTaskChange. It must release the storage for the task data block that is sent to it. It belongs to a task deleted in the MT unit. The MT unit also informs WinTaskDelete of the number of the still active tasks. This helps WinTaskDelete determine if the multitasking operation is now terminated since no tasks remain active.

This information is important for WinTaskDelete. The various routines can also be called from the WINMT unit in the normal program mode (single task mode) and a task data block must be available in the ATD Variable. The global variable MnTaDaP (MaiN program TAsk DAta block Pointer) exists for this purpose. It points to a task data block for the main program, which is created in the initialization routine of the unit and was active until the multitasking started with a call of MtaStart.

Inside WinTaskDelete, this data block is now activated again if all tasks were deleted and the program execution is continued in the main program after the call of MtaStart.

```
{******************************************************************************
 *  WinTaskDelete : calls the MT unit while deleting a task                   *
 ******************************************************************************}

{$F+}

procedure WinTaskDelete( TskPtr : pointer; RestTasks : integer );

begin
  {-- Dispose must not be blocked because task switching must be blocked --}
  {-- before calling this procedure                                      --}

  Dispose( TskPtr );
  if ( RestTasks = 0 ) then
    WinTaskChange( MnTaDaP );
end;

{$F-}
```

The following listing of the WINMT unit and its Include file WIN2MT shows the changes made to the previous versions of WINMT and WIN2MT.

```
{******************************************************************************
 *  WINMT : This unit contains routines for directly accessing the video     *
 *          RAM and for working with windows in a multitasking environment.  *
 **------------------------------------------------------------------------**
 *  Author          : MICHAEL TISCHER                                         *
 *  developed on     : 03/17/1989                                            *
 *  last update on   : 03/09/1990                                            *
 ******************************************************************************}
unit WinMt;
interface
  uses Dos, Crt, Mt;                                        { link units }

{-- declaration of functions and procedures that can be called from --------}
{-- other programs                                               --------}

  function  VL             ( Offset : integer ) : byte;
  function  VR             ( Offset : integer ) : byte;
  function  VO             ( Offset : integer ) : byte;
```

```
function  VU              ( Offset : integer ) : byte;
function  WinOpen         ( x1, y1, x2, y2 : byte ) : integer;
function  WinOpenShadow   ( x1, y1, x2, y2 : byte ) : integer;
function  WinInFront      ( Key : integer ) : boolean;
function  WhereX          : integer;
function  WhereY          : integer;
procedure WinClose        ( ReDraw : boolean );
procedure WinWrite2View   ( Doit : boolean );
procedure WinPutChar      ( Column, Line : byte; Character : char;
                            WColor : byte );
procedure WinSetCursor    ( Column, Line : byte );
procedure WinDefCursor    ( Start, WEnd : byte );
procedure WinHideCursor;
procedure WinBlockCursor;
procedure WinLineCursor;
procedure GotoXY          ( X, Y : integer );
procedure ClrScr;
procedure TextColor       ( Color : byte );
procedure TextBackground( Color : byte );
procedure WinSetView      ( x1, y1, x2, y2 : byte);
procedure WinGetView      ( var x1, y1, x2, y2 : byte );
procedure WinPrint        ( Column, Line, WColor : byte; WOutput : string );
procedure WinFill         ( x1, y1, x2, y2 : byte; Character : char;
                            WColor : byte );
function  WinStRep        ( Character : char; Amount : byte ) : string;
procedure WinFrame        ( x1, y1, x2, y2, WBorder, WColor : byte );
procedure WinScrollDown   ( x1, y1, x2, y2, Amount, WColor : byte );
procedure WinScrollUp     ( x1, y1, x2, y2, Amount, WColor : byte );
procedure WinScrollLeft   ( x1, y1, x2, y2, Amount, WColor : byte );
procedure WinScrollRight( x1, y1, x2, y2, Amount, WColor : byte );
procedure WinMoveUp       ( Amount : byte );
procedure WinMoveDown     ( Amount : byte );
procedure WinMoveRight    ( Amount : byte );
procedure WinMoveLeft     ( Amount : byte );
procedure WinMove         ( x, y : byte );
procedure WinColor        ( x1, y1, x2, y2, WColor : byte );

{-- public constants ---------------------------------------------------}

const {-- the following constants represent the contents of the Video card-}
      MDA       = 0;                        {   MDA and HGC              }
      CGA       = 1;
      EGA       = 2;
      EGA_MONO  = 3;                        { EGA on MDA monitor         }
      VGA       = 4;
      VGA_MONO  = 5;                        { VGA on analog mono monitor }
      MCGA      = 6;
      MCGA_MONO = 7;                        { MCGA on analog mono monitor }

      {-- constants for use with the WinFrame procedure ------------------}

      SIN_FR    = 1;                                      { single frame }
      DBL_FR    = 2;                                      { double frame }
```

624

```
        DOT_FR  = 3;                                    { dotted frame }
        FULL_FR = 4;                                    { full frame   }

        NO_CLEAR    = 255;               { for use with WinScroll procedures }
        WinOpenError = -1;                   { window could not be opened }
        MAX_COLS    = 132;             { some VGA cards support 132 columns }

        {-- colors -------------------------------------------------------}

        BLACK        =  0;
        BLUE         =  1;
        GREEN        =  2;
        CYAN         =  3;
        RED          =  4;
        MAGENTA      =  5;
        BROWN        =  6;
        LIGHTGRAY    =  7;
        DARKGRAY     =  8;
        LIGHTBLUE    =  9;
        LIGHTGREEN   = 10;
        LIGHTCYAN    = 11;
        LIGHTRED     = 12;
        LIGHTMAGENTA = 13;
        YELLOW       = 14;
        WHITE        = 15;

{-- global variables, also accessible to other programs -------------------}

var  Color      : boolean;          { TRUE if a color video card is found }
     VioCard,                          { code for the active video card }
     NumLine,                                      { number of lines }
     NumCol     : byte;                           { number of columns }

{-- public standard constants --------------------------------------------}

const Write2View : boolean = TRUE;        { consider visible area when using }
                                          { Write or Writeln commands        }

        ShadowX    : byte = 2;              { width of shadow in columns }
        ShadowY    : byte = 1;              { depth of shadow in lines   }

implementation

{-- constants internal to this module ------------------------------------}

const {-- window attributes -----------------------------------------------}

        WIN_SHADOW = 1;                        { Bit 0: window has a shadow }

{-- type declarations, internal to this module ---------------------------}

type BPTR      = ^byte;                            { pointer to a byte }

     VEL       = record                 { describes a character/attribute }
```

```
                        case boolean of        { combination in video RAM      }
                          true  : ( Character, Attribute : byte );
                          false : ( Contents          : word );
                      end;

VPTR      = ^VEL;                          { pointer to a character/attribute }

VELARRAY = array [0..9999] of VEL;                      { window buffer }

VELARPTR = ^VELARRAY;                          { pointer to a window buffer }

WIPTR     = ^WINDES;                      { pointer to a window descriptor }

WINDES    = record                                { window descriptor }
                  Attribute,                        { window attribute }
                  Handle,                      { key to accessing the window }
                  x1, y1,            { the corner coordinates of the window }
                  x2, y2,
                  ViewX1, ViewY1,        { coordinates of the visible area }
                  ViewX2, ViewY2,
                  curc, curr    : byte;{ cursor coordinates before opening }
                  lastwin,                      { link to previous window }
                  nextwin       : WIPTR;          { and to the following }
                  Buffer        : byte;    { window buffer starts here }
              end;

PTRREC    = record                          { used to access the }
                  Ofs : word;                      { components of a    }
                  Seg : word;                      { desired pointer    }
              end;

HANDLES  = array [0..7] of byte;          { bit field, accepts Handles }

HANDPTR  = ^HANDLES;                      { pointer to the Handles Array }

TAINTERN =                          { record defined in the context of a  }
 record                             { task in conjunction with WinMt unit }
   CurVisi,
   Write2View    : boolean;
   WritelnX,
   WritelnY,
   WritelnCol,
   ViewX1, ViewY1,
   ViewX2, ViewY2,
   CurX, CurY    : byte;
   WritelnPtr    : VPTR;
   StrepStr      : string;
   FirstWinPtr   : WIPTR;
   CurBufPtr     : VELARPTR;
   HaPtr         : HANDPTR;
   NumWin        : integer;
   CurWinPtr     : WIPTR;
 end;
```

```
        TASKDATA = record
                     i            : TAINTERN;
                     SaveOutput   : TextRec;
                   end;

        TASKDPTR = ^TASKDATA;

{-- global variables, internal to this module ----------------------------}

var  VioSeg     : word;                        { segment address of video RAM }
     Line_Ofs   : integer;                     { number of bytes in one line }
     ATD        : TAINTERN;            { internal data of the current task }
     MnTaDaP,                                  { task data for main program }
     CurTaDaP   : TASKDPTR;           { pointer to current task data block }

{**************************************************************************
 *  VL           : returns a coordinate relative to the left border of the   *
 *                 current window                                            *
 **----------------------------------------------------------------------**
 *  Input   : Offset = Position of left window border                        *
 *  Output  : absolute column coordinate                                     *
 **************************************************************************}

function  VL( Offset: integer ) : byte;

begin
  VL := ATD.ViewX1 + Offset;
end;

{**************************************************************************
 *  VR : returns a coordinate relative to the right border of the current    *
 *       window                                                              *
 **----------------------------------------------------------------------**
 *  Input   : Offset = distance from right window border                     *
 *  Output  : absolute column coordinate                                     *
 *  Info    : if no window is open, the entire screen is used                *
 **************************************************************************}

function VR( Offset : integer ) : byte;

begin
  VR :- ATD.ViewX2 + Offset;
end;
```

```
{*************************************************************************
 *  VO : returns a coordinate relative to the top border of the current *
 *         window                                                       *
 **--------------------------------------------------------------------**
 *  Input   : Offset = distance from top window border                  *
 *  Output  : absolute line coordinate                                  *
 *  Info    : if no window is open, the entire screen is used           *
 *************************************************************************}

function VO( Offset : integer ) : byte;

begin
  VO := ATD.ViewY1 + Offset;
end;


{*************************************************************************
 *  VU : returns a coordinate relative to the bottom border of the current *
 *         window                                                       *
 **--------------------------------------------------------------------**
 *  Input   : Offset = distance from bottom window border               *
 *  Output  : absolute line coordinate                                  *
 *  Info    : if no window is open, the entire screen is used           *
 *************************************************************************}

function VU( Offset : integer ) : byte;

begin
  VU := ATD.ViewY2 + Offset;
end;


{*************************************************************************
 *  GetVioPtr  : returns a pointer to a specific character in video RAM *
 **--------------------------------------------------------------------**
 *  Input   : Line, Column = coordinates of the character               *
 *  Output  : pointer to the character in video RAM of type VPTR        *
 *  Info    : starting point is at the upper left corner of the screen  *
 *            (coordinates 0/0)                                         *
 *************************************************************************}

function  GetVioPtr( Column, Line : byte ) : VPTR;

begin
  GetVioPtr := Ptr(VioSeg, (NumCol * Line + Column ) shl 1);
end;
```

```
{*****************************************************************************
 *  WinPutChar : puts the ASCII code of the character in the given  screen  *
 *               position                                                   *
 **------------------------------------------------------------------------**
 *  Input   : Line, Column = coordinates of the character                   *
 *            Character    = the character to be put                        *
 *            CColr         = character color                               *
 *  Info    : point of origin lies in the upper left corner (0/0)           *
 *****************************************************************************}

procedure WinPutChar( Column, Line : byte; Character : char; WColor : byte );

var OfsPos : integer;          { offset position of the character in video RAM }

begin
  OfsPos := (NumCol * Line + Column ) shl 1;
  Mem[ VioSeg : OfsPos ] := ord( Character );
  Mem[ VioSeg : OfsPos+1] := WColor;
end;


{*****************************************************************************
 *  WinSetCursor : position the blinking screen cursor                      *
 **------------------------------------------------------------------------*
 *  Input   : Line, Column = new cursor position                            *
 *  Globals : vLine/W, vColumn/W                                            *
 *****************************************************************************}

procedure WinSetCursor( Column , Line : byte);

var Regs : Registers;

begin
  Regs.ah := 2;                            { function number for set cursor }
  Regs.bh := 0;                              { place on screen page 0 }
  Regs.dh := line;                                          { row }
  Regs.dl := column;                                     { column }
  intr($10, Regs);                        { call BIOS video interrupt }

  ATD.CurY       := line;
  ATD.CurX       := column;
  ATD.CurVisi    := ( ( Column < NumCol ) and ( Line < NumLine ) );
end;


{*****************************************************************************
 *  WinDefCursor : defines the appearance of the cursor                     *
 **------------------------------------------------------------------------**
 *  Input   : Start = new start line for cursor                             *
 *            WEnd  = new end line for cursor                               *
 *****************************************************************************}

procedure WinDefCursor( Start, WEnd : byte );

var Regs : Registers;                    { processor regs. for interrupt call }
```

629

```
begin
  Regs.ah := 1;                        { define function number for Cursor }
  Regs.ch := Start;            { load start and end lines in the registers }
  Regs.cl := WEnd;
  intr($10, Regs);                            { call BIOS video interrupt }
end;


{****************************************************************************
 *  WinHideCursor : removes the cursor from the screen                     *
 ***************************************************************************}

procedure WinHideCursor;

begin
  WinSetCursor( 0, NumLine + 1 );        { move the cursor beyond the screen }
end;


{****************************************************************************
 *  WinBlockCursor : sets the cursor to block mode                         *
 ***************************************************************************}

procedure WinBlockCursor;

begin
  if ( Color ) then                               {color card active? }
    WinDefCursor( 0, 7 )                                    { yes }
  else                                     { monochrome card active }
    WinDefCursor( 0, 13 );
end;


{****************************************************************************
 *  WinLineCursor : sets cursor to line mode                               *
 ***************************************************************************}

procedure WinLineCursor;

begin
  if ( Color ) then                               {color card active? }
    WinDefCursor( 6, 7 )                                    { yes }
  else                                     { monochrome card active }
    WinDefCursor( 12, 13 );
end;


{****************************************************************************
 *  WinSetView : defines a screen region as the view region to which the   *
 *               functions VL, VR, VO and VU will relate                   *
 **------------------------------------------------------------------------**
 *  Input   : x1, y1 = coordinates of the upper left corner of the region  *
 *            x2, y2 = coordinates of the lower right corner of the region  *
 ***************************************************************************}

procedure WinSetView( x1, y1, x2, y2 : byte);
```

```
begin
  ATD.ViewX1 := x1;                              { store coordinates in the }
  ATD.ViewY1 := y1;                              { global View variables     }
  ATD.ViewX2 := x2;
  ATD.ViewY2 := y2;
end;


{**********************************************************************
 *   WinGetView : returns the current VIEW region                    *
 **-----------------------------------------------------------------**
 *   Input    : x1, y1 = coordinates of the upper left corner of the region  *
 *              x2, y2 = coordinates of the lower right corner of the region  *
 *   Info     : - the VIEW region defines the region for which the functions  *
 *                VL, VR, VO and VU are active                        *
 *              - the passed variables store the coordinates of the VIEW  *
 *                region as noted above                               *
 **********************************************************************}

procedure WinGetView( var x1, y1, x2, y2 : byte );

begin
  x1 := ATD.ViewX1;                              { get coordinates from the }
  y1 := ATD.ViewY1;                              { global View variables    }
  x2 := ATD.ViewX2;
  y2 := ATD.ViewY2;
end;


{**********************************************************************
 *   WinWrite2View: determines whether the current view region is available  *
 *                  for output                                        *
 **-----------------------------------------------------------------**
 *   Input    : DoIt = TRUE : Use view region                        *
 *                     FALSE: Use entire screen, but no scrolling past end  *
 *                            of screen                               *
 **********************************************************************}

procedure WinWrite2View( DoIt : boolean);

begin
  ATD.Write2View := DoIt;                                            { set flag }
end;


{**********************************************************************
 *   WhereX : returns the output column of the next Writeln used by the  *
 *            OUTPUT file variable                                    *
 **-----------------------------------------------------------------**
 *   Output   : see above                                            *
 **********************************************************************}

function WhereX : integer;
```

631

```
begin
  WhereX := ATD.WritelnX;                                    { return column }
end;

{*****************************************************************************
 *   WhereY : returns the output row of the next Writeln used by the        *
 *                   OUTPUT file variable                                   *
 **------------------------------------------------------------------------**
 *   Output  : see above                                                    *
 *****************************************************************************}

function WhereY : integer;

begin
  WhereY := ATD.WritelnY;                                       { return row }
end;

{*****************************************************************************
 *   TextColor : sets the foreground color for output from Writeln          *
 **------------------------------------------------------------------------**
 *   Input   : Col = the foreground color (0-15)                            *
 *****************************************************************************}

procedure TextColor( Color : byte );

begin
  ATD.WritelnCol := ( ATD.WritelnCol and $F0 ) or Color;     { insert color }
end;

{*****************************************************************************
 *   TextBackground : sets the background color for output from Writeln     *
 **------------------------------------------------------------------------**
 *   Input   : Col = the background color (0-15)                            *
 *****************************************************************************}

procedure TextBackground( Color : byte );

begin
 ATD.WritelnCol := ( ATD.WritelnCol and $0F ) or ( Color shl 4 );
end;

{*****************************************************************************
 *   ClrScr : clear screen                                                  *
 **------------------------------------------------------------------------**
 *   Input   : none                                                         *
 *   Info    : replaces the procedure of the same name from the CRT unit    *
 *****************************************************************************}

procedure ClrScr;

begin
  WinFill( 0, 0, NumCol-1, NumLine-1, ' ', ATD.WritelnCol );
end;
```

```
{****************************************************************************
 *   GotoXY : replaces the procedure of the same name from the CRT unit,    *
 *            establishes the output position for the next call of the      *
 *            diverted Writeln procedure                                    *
 **------------------------------------------------------------------------**
 *   Input   : X = output column                                            *
 *             Y = output line                                              *
 *   Info    : the screen cursor is not moved with this procedure as it is  *
 *             with the normal GotoXY procedure                             *
 ****************************************************************************}
procedure GotoXY( X, Y : integer );
begin
   ATD.WritelnX := X;              { store output position in global variables }
   ATD.WritelnY := Y;
   ATD.WritelnPtr := GetVioPtr( x, y ); { create pointer to output position }
end;


{****************************************************************************
 *   GetScr : gets a specified screen region from video RAM and stores it   *
 *            in a buffer                                                    *
 **------------------------------------------------------------------------**
 *   Input   : x1, y1 = coordinates of the upper left corner of the region  *
 *             x2, y2 = coordinates of the lower right corner of the region  *
 *             BufPtr = pointer to the buffer to which the region will be    *
 *                      copied                                              *
 *   Info    : the individual lines are stored in direct succession in the   *
 *             buffer                                                        *
 ****************************************************************************}

procedure GetScr( x1, y1, x2, y2 : byte; BufPtr : pointer );

var nbytes : integer;                      { number of bytes to copy per line }

begin
  nbytes := ( x2 - x1 + 1 ) shl 1;                        { bytes per line }
  while y1 <= y2 do                              { process each line }
    begin
      Move( GetVioPtr(x1, y1)^, BufPtr^, nbytes);
      inc( PTRREC( BufPtr ).Ofs, nbytes );
      inc( y1 );                                 { set Y1 to next line }
    end;
end;
```

```
{**************************************************************************
 *   PutScr : copies the contents of a buffer back to video RAM          *
 **----------------------------------------------------------------------**
 *   Input   : x1, y1 = coordinates of the upper left corner of the region *
 *             x2, y2 = coordinates of the lower right corner of the region *
 *             BufPtr = pointer to the buffer whose contents are to be    *
 *                      copied to video RAM                               *
 *   Info    : the buffer must be formatted in the way PutScr will deliver it *
 **************************************************************************}

procedure PutScr( x1, y1, x2, y2 : byte; BufPtr : pointer );

var nbytes : integer;                          { number of bytes to copy per line }

begin
  nbytes := ( x2 - x1 + 1 ) shl 1;                          { bytes per line }
  while y1 <= y2 do                                    { process each line }
    begin
      Move( BufPtr^, GetVioPtr(x1, y1)^, nbytes);
      inc( PTRREC( BufPtr ).Ofs, nbytes );
      inc( y1 );                                    { set Y1 to next line }
    end;
end;


{**************************************************************************
 *   WinOpen : opens a new window                                        *
 **----------------------------------------------------------------------**
 *   Input   : x1, y1 = coordinates of the upper left window corner       *
 *             x2, y2 = coordinates of the lower right window corner      *
 *   Output  : Handle for later access to the window                     *
 *   Info    : if the window cannot be opened due to insufficient memory  *
 *             on the heap, the value WinOpenError (-1) is returned as the *
 *             Handle                                                    *
 **************************************************************************}

function WinOpen( x1, y1, x2, y2 : byte ) : integer;

var i, j,                                              { loop counter }
    Key,                                            { stores the Handle }
    BufLen : integer;                        { length of the window buffer }
    WinPtr : WIPTR;                                { window descriptor }

begin
  BufLen := ( x2 - x1 + 1 ) * ( y2 - y1 + 1 ) shl 1;
  if MaxAvail >= BufLen + SizeOf( WINDES ) - 1 then
    begin                       { there is enough memory available on the heap }
      MtBlock;                        { execute GetMem without task switching }
      GetMem( WinPtr, BufLen + SizeOf( WINDES ) - 1 );
      MtContinue;                                    { re-enable task switching }
      WinPtr^.x1      := x1;                          { store window  }
      WinPtr^.x2      := x2;                          { coordinates in }
      WinPtr^.y1      := y1;                          { window        }
      WinPtr^.y2      := y2;                          { descriptor    }
```

```
        WinPtr^.curc    := ATD.CurX;                   { also store the current }
        WinPtr^.curr    := ATD.CurY;                   { cursor position        }
        WinPtr^.ViewX1  := ATD.ViewX1;                    { store the View       }
        WinPtr^.ViewY1  := ATD.ViewY1;                    { region coordinates   }
        WinPtr^.ViewX2  := ATD.ViewX2;                    { in the window        }
        WinPtr^.ViewY2  := ATD.ViewY2;                    { descriptor           }
        WinPtr^.Attribute:= 0;                     { window has no attribute yet }
        WinPtr^.LastWin := ATD.CurWinPtr;{ link to previous window descriptor }
        WinPtr^.NextWin := NIL;                     { no next window exists yet }

        GetScr( x1, y1, x2, y2, @WinPtr^.Buffer );
        ATD.CurBufPtr := VELARPTR(@WinPtr^.Buffer);{ pointer to window buffer }

        WinSetView( x1, y1, x2, y2 );      { the window is the new view region }
        if ATD.CurWinPtr <> NIL then          { did a window already exist? }
          ATD.CurWinPtr^.NextWin := WinPtr           { yes, link to new window }
        else                      { no, this is the first and only window }
          ATD.FirstWinPtr := WinPtr;              { set pointer to first window }
        ATD.CurWinPtr := WinPtr;          { set pointer to current descriptor }

        inc( ATD.NumWin );                { increment number of open windows }

        {-- look for a free Handle in the buffer, set HaPtr to it ------------}

        Key := 0;                { the Handle corresponds to the bit position }
        while (ATD.HaPtr^[ Key shr 3 ] and ( 1 shl (Key and 7) )) <> 0 do
          inc( Key );                    { Handle already assigned, test next }
        ATD.HaPtr^[ Key shr 3 ] :=
                ATD.HaPtr^[ Key shr 3 ] or ( 1 shl ( Key and 7 ));
        WinPtr^.Handle := Key;                   { store Handle in descriptor }
        WinOpen := Key;                          { pass Handle back to caller }
      end
  else               { not enough memory for window descriptor and buffer }
    WinOpen := -1;
end;

{*****************************************************************************
 *  WinClose : closes the current window                                    *
 **-----------------------------------------------------------------------**
 *  Input   : Redraw = TRUE : the contents of the screen region under the   *
 *                            window are restored to the screen             *
 *  Info    : - the calling routine is responsible for making sure that     *
 *              at least one window is open before this procedure is called *
 *****************************************************************************}

procedure WinClose( ReDraw : boolean );

var WinPtr : WIPTR;                        { pointer to the current descriptor }

begin
  with ATD.CurWinPtr^ do
    begin
      {-- the window's Handle is freed ------------------------------------}
```

```
            ATD.HaPtr^[ Handle shr 3 ] := ATD.HaPtr^[ Handle shr 3 ] and
                                           not( 1 shl ( Handle and 7 ));
        if ReDraw then                              { redraw old screen? }
          PutScr( x1, y1, x2, y2, @Buffer );                      { yes }
        WinSetView( ViewX1, ViewY1, ViewX2, ViewY2 );    { old view region }
        WinSetCursor( curc, curr );              { cursor to previous position }
        WinPtr := ATD.CurWinPtr;        { store pointer to current descriptor }
        ATD.CurWinPtr := LastWin;         { pointer to previous descriptor }
        if LastWin <> NIL then                    { no more windows open? }
          ATD.CurWinPtr^.NextWin := NIL           { yes, no more windows }
        else                                                     { no }
          ATD.FirstWinPtr := NIL;           { pointer points to nothing }
        {-- clear memory allocated to descriptor --------------------------}

        MtBlock;                   { execute FreeMem without task switching }
        FreeMem( WinPtr, (x2-x1+1) * (y2-y1+1) shl 1 + SizeOf(WINDES) - 1);
        MtContinue;                         { re-enable task switching }
        ATD.CurBufPtr := VELARPTR(@ATD.CurWinPtr^.Buffer); { ptr - win buffer }
        dec( ATD.NumWin );                { decrement number of open windows }
      end;
  end;


{*****************************************************************************
 *  WinStRep : builds a string out of the character to be repeated          *
 **-------------------------------------------------------------------------**
 *  Input    : Character = the repeating character                          *
 *             Amount  = number of repetitions, equal to the string length  *
 *  Output   : the completed string                                         *
 *****************************************************************************}

function WinStRep( Character : char; Amount : byte ) : string;

var StrepString : String;                    { the string is assembled here }

begin
  StrepString[0] := chr( Amount );
  FillChar( StrepString[1], Amount, Character );
  WinStRep := StrepString;
end;


{*****************************************************************************
 *  WinPrint : writes a string direct to video RAM                          *
 **-------------------------------------------------------------------------**
 *  Input    : Column, Line = WOutputposition                               *
 *             WColor       = Color/attribute of the character to be shown   *
 *             WOutput      = String to be output                           *
 *  Info     : - When the string passes the end of line, the output wraps   *
 *               around to the following line                               *
 *             - When the liner reaches the end of the current window, the   *
 *               window's contents to NOT scroll                            *
 *****************************************************************************}

procedure WinPrint( Column, Line, WColor : byte; WOutput : string );
```

636

```
var VioPtr : VPTR;                                    { pointer to video RAM }
    i, j   : byte;                                        { loop counter     }

begin
  VioPtr := GetVioPtr( Column, Line );          { load pointer to video RAM }
  j := length( WOutput );               { get length of string to be displayed }
  for i:=1 to j do                          { execute character in string }
    begin
      VioPtr^.Character := ord( WOutput[i] );   { character code and attri- }
      VioPtr^.Attribute := WColor;                  { bute passed to video RAM }
      inc( PTRREC( VioPtr ).Ofs, 2 );       { set pointer to next character }
    end;
end;


{**********************************************************************
 *  WinDummy : called during a Close on the diverted file variable OUTPUT  *
 **------------------------------------------------------------------**
 *  Input   : F = the file variable OUTPUT of type TextRec             *
 *  Output  : always returns the value 0 (no error)                    *
 **********************************************************************}


{$F+}                                                        { must be FAR }

function WinDummy( var f : TextRec ) : integer;
begin
  WinDummy := 0;                                              { return 0 }
end;

{$F-}


{**********************************************************************
 *  WinWriteln : called by Turbo Pascal during a WRITE or WRITELN command  *
 *               on the file variable OUTPUT                           *
 **------------------------------------------------------------------**
 *  Input   : F = the file variable OUTPUT of type TextRec             *
 *  Output  : must return the value 0 (no error)                       *
 **********************************************************************}


{$F+}                                                        { must be FAR }

function WinWriteln( var f : TextRec ) : integer;

var i    : integer;                                        { loop counter }
    ZPtr : BPTR;                              { pointer to the output character }
    Character : byte;

begin
  with f do                                      { process the file variable }
    begin
      ZPtr := BPTR( BufPtr );          { set pointer to the first character }
      if ( Write2View ) then                    { consider the view region? }
        begin                              { yes, visible area may be scrolled }
```

```
        for i := 1 to BufPos do                    { process each character }
          begin
            Character := Zptr^;              { evaluate the current character }
            case Character of
              7 : begin                                { BEL : output sound }
                    Sound( 880 );                              { sound on }
                    Delay( 750 );                          { wait 3/4 second }
                    NoSound;                                   { sound off }
                  end;

              8 : begin               { backspace (BS): one character back }
                    if ( ATD.WritelnX = ATD.ViewX1 ) then { start line?   }
                      begin                   { yes, return to previous line }
                        ATD.WritelnX := ATD.ViewX2;     { the last column }
                        dec( ATD.WritelnY );        { of the previous line }
                      end
                    else                                    { line remains }
                      dec( ATD.WritelnX );              { one column back }
                    ATD.WritelnPtr := GetVioPtr( ATD.WritelnX,
                                                 ATD.WritelnY );
                  end;

             10 : begin            { Linefeed (LF): increment output line }
                    if ( ATD.WritelnY = ATD.ViewY2 ) then
                      WinScrollUp( ATD.ViewX1, ATD.ViewY1+1, ATD.ViewX2,
                                   ATD.ViewY2, 1, ATD.WritelnCol )
                    else                      { view region must not scroll }
                      begin
                        inc ( ATD.WritelnY );          { last view line? }
                        ATD.WritelnPtr := GetVioPtr( ATD.WritelnX,
                                                     ATD.WritelnY);
                      end;
                  end;

             13 : begin                        { CR: return to start of line }
                    ATD.WritelnX := ATD.ViewX1;
                    ATD.WritelnPtr := GetVioPtr( ATD.WritelnX,
                                                 ATD.WritelnY );
                  end;
            else              { output all other characters unprocessed }
            begin
              {-- write character code and attribute to video RAM ----}
              ATD.WritelnPtr^.Character := Character;
              ATD.WritelnPtr^.Attribute := ATD.WritelnCol;
              {-- set pointer to the next character ------------------}
              inc( PTRREC( ATD.WritelnPtr ).Ofs, 2 );
              inc( ATD.WritelnX );                  { increment output column }
              if ( ATD.WritelnX > ATD.ViewX2 ) then   { ViewX2 reached? }
                begin                                              { yes }
                  ATD.WritelnX := ATD.ViewX1;    { to start of next one }
                  if ( ATD.WritelnY = ATD.ViewY2 ) then
                    begin { go to last line of view region }
                      WinScrollUp( ATD.ViewX1, ATD.ViewY1+1,ATD.ViewX2,
```

```
                                  ATD.ViewY2, 1, ATD.WritelnCol );
                        ATD.WritelnX := ATD.ViewX1;
                    end
                else { do not scroll view region }
                    inc( ATD.WritelnY );
                ATD.WRitelnPtr := GetVioPtr( ATD.WritelnX,
                                             ATD.WritelnY );
                end;
            end;
        end;
        inc( PTRREC( ZPtr ).Ofs );
    end;
end
else   { view region not reacting, just write to video RAM }
  begin
    for i := 1 to BufPos do { execute individual characters }
      begin
        case ZPtr^ of

            7 : begin                          { BEL : output sound }
              Sound( 880 );                            { sound on }
              Delay( 750 );                       { wait 3/4 second }
              NoSound;                                { sound off }
            end;

            8 : begin            { backspace (BS): one character back }
              if ( ATD.WritelnX = 0 ) then           { start line? }
                begin                 { yes, return to previous line }
                  ATD.WritelnX := NumCol -1;      { the last column }
                  dec( ATD.WritelnY );        { of the previous line }
                end
              else                                  { line remains }
                dec( ATD.WritelnX );             { one column back }
              ATD.WritelnPtr := GetVioPtr( ATD.WritelnX,
                                           ATD.WritelnY );
            end;

            10 : begin            { Linefeed (LF): increment output line }
                inc( ATD.WritelnY );
                ATD.WritelnPtr := GetVioPTr( ATD.WritelnX,
                                             ATD.WritelnY );
            end;

            13 : begin                    { CR: return to start of line }
                ATD.WritelnX := 0;
                ATD.WritelnPtr := GetVioPtr( ATD.WritelnX,
                                             ATD.WritelnY );
            end;
          else                  { send every other character unaltered }
            begin
              {-- write character code and attribute to video RAM ----}
              ATD.WritelnPtr^.Character := ZPtr^;
              ATD.WritelnPtr^.Attribute := ATD.WritelnCol;
```

639

```
                              {-- set pointer to the next character ------------------}
                              inc( PTRREC( ATD.WritelnPtr ).Ofs, 2 );
                              inc( ATD.WritelnX );              { increment output column }
                              if ( ATD.WritelnX = NumCol ) then        { EOL reached? }
                                begin                                          { yes }
                                  ATD.WritelnX := 0;                 { to start of next one }
                                  inc( ATD.WritelnY );
                                end;
                            end;
                        end;
                        inc( PTRREC( ZPtr ).Ofs );
                    end;
                end;        BufPos := 0;                    { all characters processed }
        end;

  WinWriteln := 0;                                                      { return 0 }
end;

{$F-}


{*****************************************************************************
 *  OutputOpen : Places the contents of OUTPUT file variable into WinInit    *
 *               on the initial call of Write or Writeln.                    *
 **-------------------------------------------------------------------------**
 *  Input   : F = OUTPUT file variable of type TextRec                       *
 *  Output  : must return 0 by definition (no error)                         *
 *  Globals : none                                                           *
 *****************************************************************************}

{$F+}                                                          { must be FAR }

function OutputOpen( var f : TextRec ) : integer;

begin
  with f do                                         { work with file variable }
    begin
      InOutFunc := @WinWriteln;          { set address of the output function }
      FlushFunc := @WinWriteln;             { "Flush" corresponds to "Out" }
      CloseFunc := @WinDummy;               { Close still not considered }
    end;
  OutputOpen := 0;                                             { 0 returned }
end;

{$F-}


{*****************************************************************************
 *  WinTaskCreate : creates a task while calling the MT unit                 *
 **-------------------------------------------------------------------------**
 *  Output: pointer to the allocated data block                             *
 *  Info  : this function can only be called when task switching is blocked  *
 *****************************************************************************}

{$F+}
```

```
function WinTaskCreate : pointer;

var TaDaP : TASKDPTR;

begin
 {-- new must be available for access ------------------------------------}

 New( TaDaP );
 with TaDaP^.i do
   begin
     CurVisi    := FALSE;
     Write2View := TRUE;
     WritelnX   := 0;
     WritelnY   := 0;
     WritelnPtr := GetVioPtr( 0, 0 );
     WritelnCol := $7;
     StrepStr   := '';
     ViewX1     := 0;
     ViewY1     := 0;
     ViewX2     := NumCol - 1;
     ViewY2     := NumLine - 1;
     NumWin     := 0;
     CurWinPtr  := NIL;

     New( HaPtr );
     FillChar( HaPtr^, SizeOf(HaPtr^), 0);
   end;
 TaDaP^.SaveOutput := TEXTREC( Output );
 WinTaskCreate := pointer( TaDaP );
end;

{$F-}

{*****************************************************************************
 *  WinTaskChange : calls task changes from the MT unit                     *
 **-----------------------------------------------------------------------**
 *  Input : ATD.HaPtr which receives the setting for the current task       *
 *  Info  : this procedure can only be called during blocked task switching *
 *****************************************************************************}

{$F+}

procedure WinTaskChange( TskPtr : pointer );

var Regs : Registers;

begin
 {-- mark task-dependent data for current task ---------------------------}

 CurTaDaP^.i := ATD;
 CurTaDaP^.SaveOutput := TextRec( Output );
```

641

```
      {-- load task-dependent data for new current task ----------------------}

      CurTaDaP := TASKDPTR(TskPtr);
      ATD := CurTaDaP^.i;

      TextRec( Output ) := CurTaDaP^.SaveOutput;

      with ATD do
        if ( CurVisi ) then
          begin
            Regs.ah := 2;
            Regs.bh := 0;
            Regs.dh := CurY;
            Regs.dl := CurX;
            intr($10, Regs);
          end;
    end;

    {$F-}

    {*****************************************************************************
     *  WinTaskDelete : calls the MT unit while deleting a task                  *
     *****************************************************************************}

    {$F+}

    procedure WinTaskDelete( TskPtr : pointer; RestTasks : integer );

    begin
      {-- Dispose must not be blocked because task switching must be blocked --}
      {-- before calling this procedure                                      --}

      Dispose( TskPtr );
      if ( RestTasks = 0 ) then
        WinTaskChange( MnTaDaP );
    end;

    {$F-}

    {*****************************************************************************
     *  WinInit : Initializes the WIN unit                                       *
     *  Globals : VioCard/W, NumCol/W, NumLine/W, Color/W, VioSeg/W, HaPtr/W     *
     *            Line_Ofs/W                                                      *
     *****************************************************************************}

    procedure WinInit;

    const VioMode : array [0..11] of byte = ( MDA, CGA, 0, EGA, EGA_MONO, 0,
                                              VGA_MONO, VGA, 0, MCGA,
                                              MCGA_MONO, MCGA );
          EgaMode : array [0..2] of byte  = ( EGA, EGA, EGA_MONO );

    var Regs : Registers;                     { processor regs for interrupt calls }
```

642

```
begin
  VioCard := $ff;                                      { no video card found yet }
{-- test for VGA or MCGA card -------------------------------------------------}
  Regs.ax := $1a00;                                    { call function $1A of the }
   intr($10, Regs);                                    { video BIOS              }
   if Regs.al = $1a then                                   { VGA or MCGA? }
     begin                                                       { yes }
       VioCard := VioMode[ Regs.bl-1 ];                  { get code from table }
       Color := not( ( VioCard = MDA ) or ( VioCard = EGA_MONO ) );
     end
   else                                                 { neither VGA nor MCGA }
     begin                                                 { test for EGA card }
       Regs.ah := $12;                                     { call function $12 }
       Regs.bl := $10;                                     { subfunction $10   }
       intr($10, Regs);                                    { call video BIOS   }
       if Regs.bl <> $10 then                                 { EGA installed? }
         begin                                                       { yes }
           VioCard := EgaMode[ (Regs.cl shr 1) div 3 ];          { get code }
           Color := VioCard <> EGA_MONO;
         end;
     end;

{-- get pointer to video RAM --------------------------------------------------}

  Regs.ah := 15;                                        { get current video mode }
   intr($10, Regs);                                     { call BIOS video interrupt }
   if Regs.al = 7 then                                       { monochrome mode? }
     VioSeg := $b000                                    { yes, video RAM at B000 }
   else                                                     { no, color mode }
     VioSeg := $b800;                                       { video RAM at B800 }

  if VioCard = $ff then                                 { not EGA, VGA or MCGA? }
     begin                                                          { yes }
       if Regs.al = 7 then VioCard := MDA
                       else VioCard := CGA;
       NumLine := 25;                                   { in 25 line text mode }
     end
   else                             { if EGA, VGA or MCGA, get number of lines }
    NumLine := BPTR( Ptr( $40, $84 ) )^ + 1;
  Color := not( ( Regs.al=0 ) or ( Regs.al=2 ) or ( Regs.al=7 ) );

  NumCol := BPTR( Ptr( $40, $4a ) )^;                      { number of columns }
  Line_Ofs := NumCol shl 1;                          { offset to start of next line }

  Regs.ah := 5;                                        { select current screen page }
  Regs.al := 0;                                                { screen page 0 }
  intr($10, Regs);                                     { call BIOS video interrupt }

  Regs.ah := 3;                                        { get current cursor position }
  Regs.bh := 0;                                             { access to screen page 0 }
  intr($10, Regs);                                     { call BIOS video interrupt }
  ATD.CurY    := Regs.dh;                                 { store cursor position }
```

```
   ATD.CurX    := Regs.dl;
   ATD.CurVisi := TRUE;

{-- divert file variable OUTPUT to internal output routine ---------------}

   with TextRec( Output ) do           { manipulate the file variable OUTPUT }
      begin
         Handle   := $FFFF;        { Turbo expects this declaration like this }
         Mode     := fmClosed;                        { device still closed }
         BufSize  := SizeOf( Buffer );                { set size and address }
         BufPtr   := @Buffer;                          { of buffer          }
         OpenFunc := @OutputOpen;             { address of Open procedure }
         Name[0]  := #0;                       { change name to empty string }
      end;
   Rewrite( Output );                           { initialize file variable }

{-- allocate and initialize task data block for main program ------------}

   MnTaDaP  := WinTaskCreate;
   CurTaDaP := MnTaDaP;
   ATD      := MnTaDaP^.i;

{-- WinMt included as part of the MT unit -------------------------------}

   if not( MtRegisterUnit( WinTaskCreate,
                           WinTaskChange,
                           WinTaskDelete ) ) then
      RunError;

end;

{$I win2mt.pas }

{**-----------------------------------------------------------------------**}
{** Starting code of the unit                                            **}
{**-----------------------------------------------------------------------**}
begin
   WinInit;                                 { call initialization procedure }
   end.
```

WIN2MT.PAS

Here's the listing for WIN2MT.PAS.

```
{******************************************************************
 *  WinFill : fills a given screen region with a constant character and  *
 *            its attribute                                              *
 **--------------------------------------------------------------------**
 *  Input    : x1, y1 = coordinates of the upper left corner of the region  *
 *             x2, y2 = coordinates of the lower right corner of the region *
 *             Character,                                                 *
 *             WColor  = the character and its attribute                  *
 *  Globals : none                                                       *
 ******************************************************************}

procedure WinFill( x1, y1, x2, y2 : byte; Character : char; WColor : byte );

var Line : string;                     { stores one line with the character }

begin
  Line := WinStRep( Character, x2-x1+1 );          { construct a line }
  while y1 <= y2 do                                { process each line }
    begin
      WinPrint( x1, y1, WColor, Line );               { output a line }
      inc( y1 );                              { increment line number }
    end;
end;


{******************************************************************
 *  WinFrame : creates one of four frame types around a specified screen  *
 *             region                                                    *
 **--------------------------------------------------------------------**
 *  Input    : x1, y1 = coordinates of the upper left corner of the region  *
 *             x2, y2 = coordinates of the lower right corner of the region *
 *             WBorder = one of the constants SIN_FR, DBL_FR etc.         *
 *             WColor  = color or attribute for the frame character       *
 ******************************************************************}
procedure WinFrame( x1, y1, x2, y2, WBorder, WColor : byte );
type RStruc = record                { describes the characters of a frame }
                UpperLeft,
                UpperRight,
                LowerLeft,
                LowerRight,
                Vertical,
                Horizontal  : char;
              end;
const RCharacter : array[1..4] of RStruc =       { the possible frame types }
```

```
          (
            ( UpperLeft  : '⌐'; UpperRight  : '¬'; LowerLeft   : 'L';
              LowerRight : '⌐'; Vertical    : '|'; Horizontal  : '—' ),
            ( UpperLeft  : '⌐'; UpperRight  : '¬'; LowerLeft   : 'L';
              LowerRight : '⌐'; Vertical    : '||'; Horizontal : '=' ),
            ( UpperLeft  : '▓'; UpperRight  : '▓'; LowerLeft   : '▓';
              LowerRight : '▓'; Vertical    : '▓'; Horizontal  : '▓' ),
            ( UpperLeft  : '█'; UpperRight  : '█'; LowerLeft   : '█';
              LowerRight : '█'; Vertical    : '█'; Horizontal  : '█' )
          );
var StrepBuf : string;                          { stores a horizontal line }
    Line     : byte;                                    { loop counter }

begin
  with RCharacter[ WBorder ] do
    begin
      WinPutChar( x1, y1, UpperLeft, WColor );          { output the four }
      WinPutChar( x2, y1, UpperRight, WColor );         { frame corners   }
      WinPutChar( x1, y2, LowerLeft, WColor );
      WinPutChar( x2, y2, LowerRight, WColor );

      StrepBuf := WinStRep( Horizontal, x2-x1-1 );      { output the two }
      WinPrint( x1+1, y1, WColor, StrepBuf );           { horizontal     }
      WinPrint( x1+1, y2, WColor, StrepBuf );           { lines          }

      dec( y2 );                                        { calculate last line }
      for Line:=y1+1 to y2 do                           { process each line }
        begin                                           { draw vertical line }
          WinPutChar( x1, Line, Vertical, WColor );
          WinPutChar( x2, Line, Vertical, WColor );
        end;
    end;
end;


{*******************************************************************************
 *  WinColor : fills a given screen region with a constant attribute          *
 *             without affecting the existing characters in the region        *
 **---------------------------------------------------------------------------**
 *  Input    : x1, y1 = coordinates of the upper left corner of the region    *
 *             x2, y2 = coordinates of the lower right corner of the region    *
 *             WColor = the new color                                         *
 *******************************************************************************}
procedure WinColor( x1, y1, x2, y2, WColor : byte );

var VioPtr : VPTR;                              { pointer to the video RAM }
    Line,                                       { loop counter for processing lines }
    Column,                                     { loop counter for processing columns }
    DeltaX : integer;                           { distance to next line }

begin
  VioPtr := GetVioPtr( x1, y1 );        { set pointer to the first character }
  DeltaX := Line_Ofs - ( (x2-x1) shl 1 ) - 2;   { offset from x2 to x1 }
```

646

```
      for Line:=y1 to y2 do                            { process the lines }
        begin                              { process each column within the line }
          for Column:=x1 to x2 do
            begin
              VioPtr^.Attribute := WColor;          { write color to video RAM }
              inc( PTRREC(VioPtr).Ofs, 2 );            { increase offset by 2 }
            end;
          inc( PTRREC(VioPtr).Ofs, DeltaX );
        end;
  end;

{************************************************************************
 *  WinShadow : creates a shadow for a specified screen region          *
 **-------------------------------------------------------------------**
 *  Input    : x1, y1 = coordinates of the upper left shadow corner     *
 *             x2, y2 = coordinates of the lower right shadow corner     *
 *             BufPtr = pointer to the buffer to be manipulated          *
 *  Info     : - in color mode, the shadow is created by changing the    *
 *               character attribute, in mono mode, it is made by filling *
 *               the shadow region with the character "▓"                *
 ************************************************************************}


procedure WinShadow( x1, y1, x2, y2 : byte; BufPtr : VPTR );

var Attribute : byte;                         { the attribute to be manipulated }
    Line,                                    { loop counter for processing lines }
    Column,                                 { loop counter for processing columns }
    DeltaX   : integer;                         { distance to the next line }

begin
  inc( PTRREC( BufPtr ).Ofs, ( y1 * NumCol + x1 ) shl 1 );   { load pointer }
  DeltaX := Line_Ofs - ( (x2-x1) shl 1 ) - 2;         { offset from x2 to x1 }

  if ( Color ) then                                        { color mode? }
    for Line := y1 to y2 do                            { process each line }
      begin                                          { process each column }
        for Column := x1 to x2 do
          begin
            Attribute := BufPtr^.Attribute;        { get character attribute }
            {-- change background color ----------------------------------}
            if Attribute and 128 <> 0 then           { lighter background? }
              Attribute := Attribute and 128            { yes, clear bit 7 }
            else                                    { no, normal background }
              Attribute := Attribute and 15;       { background is now black }

            {-- change foreground color ----------------------------------}
            if Attribute and 8 <> 0 then             { lighter foreground? }
              Attribute := Attribute and (255 - 8);    { yes, clear bit 3 }

            BufPtr^.Attribute := Attribute;    { attribute back to video RAM }
            inc( PTRREC(BufPtr).Ofs, 2 );     { set pointer to next character }
          end;
        inc( PTRREC(BufPtr).Ofs, DeltaX );
```

```
            end
      else                                            { no, monochrome mode }
        for Line := y1 to y2 do                         { process each line }
          begin                                       { process each column }
            for Column := x1 to x2 do
              begin
                BufPtr^.Contents := ord( '▓' ) + ( $7 shl 8 );{ set char.&color }
                inc( PTRREC(BufPtr).Ofs, 2 );   { set pointer to next character }
              end;
            inc( PTRREC(BufPtr).Ofs, DeltaX );
          end
end;


{***************************************************************************
 *   WinOpenShadow : opens a new window and accents it with a shadow       *
 **-----------------------------------------------------------------------**
 *   Input    : x1, y1  = coordinates of the upper left window corner      *
 *              x2, y2  = coordinates of the lower right window corner      *
 *   Info     : - the width and depth of the shadow are specified with the *
 *                global variables ShadowX and ShadowY                     *
 *              - the given coordinates do not include the shadow, so they *
 *                must be chosen so that the window plus the shadow will fit*
 *                on the screen                                            *
 *              - in color mode, the shadow is created by changing the     *
 *                character attribute, whereas in mono mode, the shadow    *
 *                is represented by the character '▓'                      *
 ***************************************************************************}

function WinOpenShadow( x1, y1, x2, y2 : byte ) : integer;

var  Handle : integer;                             { Handle for the open window }

begin
  Handle := WinOpen( x1, y1, x2 + ShadowX, y2 + ShadowY);
  if ( Handle <> WinOpenError ) then
    begin
      ATD.CurWinPtr^.Attribute := WIN_SHADOW;          { window has a shadow }
      WinSetView( x1, y1, x2, y2 );     { shadow is outside the view region }
      WinShadow( x2+1, y1+1, x2+ShadowX, y2+ShadowY, VPTR(ptr(VioSeg,0)) );
      WinShadow( x1+ShadowX, y2+1, x2, y2+ShadowY, VPTR(ptr(VioSeg,0)) );
    end;
  WinOpenShadow := Handle;            { return window Handle to calling routine }
end;
```

```
{**************************************************************************
*  ScrollHori : scrolls a specified screen region a specified distance from*
*               Column to the left or to the right                        *
**------------------------------------------------------------------------**
*  Input     : x1, y1    = upper left corner coordinate of the region      *
*              x2, y2    = bottom right corner coordinate of the region    *
*              Amount    = number of columns the region should be moved to *
*                          the right or left                               *
*              WColor    = color/attribute of the "clearing" column        *
*              ToTheLeft = TRUE  : region moves to the left                *
*                          FALSE : region moves to the right               *
*  Info      : - If the color constant NO_CLEAR is given, the column left  *
*                behind by the movement is not cleared.                    *
**************************************************************************}

procedure ScrollHori( x1, y1, x2, y2, Amount, WColor : byte;
                      ToTheLeft : boolean );

var frm,                                        { copy from...... }
    cpto       : VPTR;                           { ... to          }
    Byte2Copy,                                  { number of bytes per line }
    CurLine  : integer;                          { the current line }

begin
 Byte2Copy := (x2 - x1 + 1) shl 1;               { number of bytes }
 frm := GetVioPtr( x1, y1 );
 if ToTheLeft then                          { move the region to the left? }
   cpto := GetVioPtr( x1 - Amount, y1 )                           { yes }
 else                                       { move the region to the right? }
   cpto := GetVioPtr( x1 + Amount, y1 );

 for CurLine := y1 to y2 do                            { execute lines }
   begin
     Move( frm^, cpto^, Byte2Copy );                    { copy line }
     inc( PTRREC( frm ).Ofs, Line_Ofs );
     inc( PTRREC( cpto ).Ofs, Line_Ofs );
   end;

 {-- clear free blank columns ---------------------------------------------}

 if WColor <> NO_CLEAR then                       { delete blank columns? }
   if ToTheLeft then                              { yes, scroll to left? }
     WinFill( x2-Amount+1, y1, x2, y2, ' ', WColor)
   else                                           { no, scroll to right }
     WinFill( x1, y1, x1+Amount-1, y2, ' ', WColor);
end;
```

```
{***************************************************************************
 *  WinScrollDown : scrolls any screen region a specific amount down       *
 **----------------------------------------------------------------------**
 *  Input    : x1, y1 = upper left corner coordinates of the region       *
 *             x2, y2 = lower right corner coordinates of the region       *
 *             Amount = number of rows by which the region should be scrolled*
 *             WColor = color/attribute for the freed line                 *
 *  Info     : if the constant NO_CLEAR is given for WColor, the freed line *
 *             is not cleared.                                             *
 ***************************************************************************}

procedure WinScrollDown( x1, y1, x2, y2, Amount, WColor : byte );

var frm,                                            { copy from ..... }
    cpto      : VPTR;                               { ... to          }
    Byte2Copy,                              { number of bytes per line }
    CurLine : integer;                                { current line }

begin
 Byte2Copy := (x2 - x1 + 1) shl 1;                    { number of bytes }
 frm  := GetVioPtr( x1, y2 );                { pointer to line to be moved }
 cpto := GetVioPtr( x1, y2 + Amount );       { pointer to its new position }

 for CurLine := y1 to y2 do                          { process each line }
   begin
     Move( frm^, cpto^, Byte2Copy );                      { copy line }
     dec( PTRREC( frm ).Ofs, Line_Ofs );
     dec( PTRREC( cpto ).Ofs, Line_Ofs );
   end;

 if WColor <> NO_CLEAR then                        { clear blank lines? }
   WinFill( x1, y1, x2, y1+Amount-1, ' ', WColor);              { yes }
end;

{***************************************************************************
 *  WinScrollUp : scrolls a given screen region up by a given number of lines*
 **----------------------------------------------------------------------**
 *  Input    : x1, y1 = coordinates of the upper left corner              *
 *             x2, y2 = coordinates of the lower right corner             *
 *             Amount = number of lines to be scrolled                    *
 *             WColor = color or attribute of the freed lines             *
 *  Info     : if the constant NO_CLEAR is given as the color, the freed  *
 *             lines are not cleared                                      *
 ***************************************************************************}

procedure WinScrollUp( x1, y1, x2, y2, Amount, WColor : byte );

var frm,                                            { copy from ... }
    cpto     : VPTR;                                { ... to        }
    Byte2Copy,                              { number of bytes per line }
    CurLine  : integer;                             { the current line }

begin
```

```
Byte2Copy := (x2 - x1 + 1) shl 1;                        { number of bytes }
frm  := GetVioPtr( x1, y1 );                   { pointer to line to be moved }
cpto := GetVioPtr( x1, y1 - Amount );          { pointer to its new position }
for CurLine := y1 to y2 do                           { process each line }
  begin
    Move( frm^, cpto^, Byte2Copy );                        { copy line }
    inc( PTRREC( frm ).Ofs, Line_Ofs );
    inc( PTRREC( cpto ).Ofs, Line_Ofs );
  end;

if WColor <> NO_CLEAR then                            { clear blank lines? }
  WinFill( x1, y2+1-amount, x2, y2, ' ', WColor);            { yes }
end;

{*********************************************************************
*  WinScrollLeft : scrolls a given screen region to the left       *
**---------------------------------------------------------------**
*  Input   : see WinScrollUp, WinScrollDown                        *
*********************************************************************}

procedure WinScrollLeft( x1, y1, x2, y2, Amount, WColor : byte );

begin
  ScrollHori( x1, y1, x2, y2, Amount, WColor, TRUE );
end;

{*********************************************************************
*  WinScrollRight: scrolls a given screen region to the right      *
**---------------------------------------------------------------**
*  Input   : see WinScrollUp, WinScrollDown                        *
*********************************************************************}

procedure WinScrollRight( x1, y1, x2, y2, Amount, WColor : byte );

begin
  ScrollHori( x1, y1, x2, y2, Amount, WColor, FALSE );
end;

{*********************************************************************
*  WinMoveUp : moves window up on the screen                       *
*  Input   : Amount = number of lines to move the window up        *
*  Info    : the calling routine is responsible for making sure that the *
*            window will not be moved off the screen               *
*********************************************************************}

procedure WinMoveUp( Amount : byte );

var BufPtr : VPTR;                           { pointer to temporary buffer }
    WWidth,                                  { window width in columns }
    WLength,                                 { window length in columns }
    BufLen : integer;             { length of the temporary buffer in bytes }

function GetPtr( Line : integer ) : pointer;
```

```
begin
  GetPtr := @ATD.CurBufPtr^[ Line * WWidth ];
end;

begin
  with ATD.CurWinPtr^ do                  { access the current window descriptor }
    begin
      WWidth := x2 - x1 + 1;
      WLength := y2 - y1 + 1;
      BufLen := WWidth * Amount shl 1;
      MtBlock;                            { execute GetMem without task switching }
      GetMem( BufPtr, BufLen );                    { allocate temp. memory }
      MtContinue;                              { re-enable task switching }
      GetScr( x1, y1-Amount, x2, y1-1, BufPtr );
      WinScrollUp ( x1, y1, x2, y2, Amount, NO_CLEAR );
      PutScr( x1, y2-Amount+1, x2, y2, GetPtr( WLength - Amount ) );
      Move( GetPtr( 0 )^, GetPtr(Amount)^, WWidth * (WLength-Amount) shl 1);
      Move( BufPtr^, GetPtr( 0 )^, BufLen );

      {-- if the cursor was within the window, it must also be moved -------}

      if ( (x1 <= ATD.CurX ) and (x2 >= ATD.CurX ) and
           (y1 <= ATD.CurY ) and (y2 >= ATD.CurY ) ) then
        WinSetCursor( ATD.CurX , ATD.CurY - Amount );

      {-- in Write2View mode, the output position for Write and ------------}
      {-- Writeln must be moved with the window            ------------}

      if ( ATD.Write2View ) then                        { in Write2View mode? }
          dec( ATD.WritelnY, Amount );                  { pass Write position }

      dec( y1, amount );                          { update window coordinates }
      dec( y2, amount );
      MtBlock;                            { execute FreeMem without task switching }
      FreeMem( BufPtr, BufLen );                    { clear allocated buffer }
      MtContinue;                              { re-enable task switching }
      end;
  dec( ATD.ViewY1, amount );                          { move view region }
  dec( ATD.ViewY2, amount );                          { with the window  }
end;
```

```
{*****************************************************************************
*  WinMoveDown : moves the current window a specified number of lines down  *
**-------------------------------------------------------------------------**
*  Input    : Amount = number of lines to move the window down              *
*  Info     : the calling routine is responsible for making sure that the   *
*             window will not be moved off the screen                       *
*****************************************************************************}

procedure WinMoveDown( Amount : byte );

var BufPtr : VPTR;                                      { pointer to temp. buffer }
```

```
      WWidth,                                    { window width in columns }
      WLength,                                   { window length in columns }
      BufLen : integer;                    { length of temp. buffer in bytes }

{-- GetPtr returns a pointer to the start of a line in the -------[ LOCAL ]-}
{-- buffer of the current window                                          -}

function GetPtr( Line : integer ) : pointer;

begin
  GetPtr := @ATD.CurBufPtr^[ Line * WWidth ];
end;

begin
  with ATD.CurWinPtr^ do                 { access the current window descriptor }
    begin
      WWidth := x2 - x1 + 1;
      WLength := y2 - y1 + 1;
      BufLen := WWidth * Amount shl 1;
      MtBlock;                          { execute GetMem without task switching }
      GetMem( BufPtr, BufLen );                    { allocate temp. memory }
      MtContinue;                               { re-enable task switching }
      GetScr( x1, y2+1, x2, y2+Amount, BufPtr );
      WinScrollDown( x1, y1, x2, y2, Amount, NO_CLEAR );
      PutScr( x1, y1, x2, y1+Amount-1, GetPtr( 0 ) );
      Move( GetPtr(Amount)^, GetPtr( 0 )^, WWidth * (WLength-Amount) shl 1);
      Move( BufPtr^, GetPtr( WLength - Amount )^, BufLen );

      {-- if the cursor was in the window, it must also be moved -----------}

      if ( (x1 <= ATD.CurX ) and (x2 >= ATD.CurX ) and
           (y1 <= ATD.CurY ) and (y2 >= ATD.CurY ) ) then
        WinSetCursor( ATD.CurX , ATD.CurY + Amount );

      {-- in Write2View mode, the output position for Write and -----------}
      {-- Writeln must be moved with the window              -----------}

      if ( ATD.Write2View ) then                  { in Write2View mode? }
          inc( ATD.WritelnY, Amount );            { pass Write position }
      inc( y1, amount );                     { update window coordinates }
      inc( y2, amount );
      MtBlock;                          { execute FreeMem without task switching }
      FreeMem( BufPtr, BufLen );                    { free allocated buffer }
      MtContinue;                               { re-enable task switching }
    end;
  inc( ATD.ViewY1, amount );                   { move the view region (global }
  inc( ATD.ViewY2, amount );                   { variables) with the window   }
end;
```

```
{*****************************************************************************
*   WinMoveRight : moves the current window a specified number of columns    *
*                  to the right                                              *
**--------------------------------------------------------------------------**
*   Input   : Amount = number of columns to move the window                  *
*   Info    : the calling routine is responsible for making sure that the    *
*             window will not be moved off the screen                        *
*****************************************************************************}

procedure WinMoveRight( Amount : byte );

var BufPtr,                                        { pointer to temp. buffer }
    LBufPtr  : VPTR;                        { running pointer to in temp. buffer }
    Byte2Copy,                                     { number of bytes to copy }
    Line,                         { loop counter for processing the window lines }
    EndLine,                                                        { same }
    WWidth,                                       { window width in columns }
    WLength,                                      { window length in columns }
    BufLen   : integer;                      { length of temp. buffer in bytes }

function GetPtr( Line, Column : integer ) : pointer;

begin
  GetPtr := @ATD.CurBufPtr^[ Line * WWidth + Column ];
end;


begin
  with ATD.CurWinPtr^ do                  { access current window descriptor }
    begin
      WWidth := x2 - x1 + 1;
      WLength := y2 - y1 + 1;
      BufLen := WLength * Amount shl 1;
      MtBlock;                          { execute GetMem without task switching }
      GetMem( BufPtr, BufLen );                     { allocate temp. memory }
      MtContinue;                             { re-enable task switching }
      GetScr( x2+1, y1, x2+Amount, y2, BufPtr );
      ScrollHori( x1, y1, x2, y2, Amount, NO_CLEAR, FALSE );

      Byte2Copy := ( WWidth - Amount ) shl 1;
      LBufPtr := BufPtr;                  { running pointer to start of buffer }
      EndLine := WLength - 1;
      for Line:=0 to EndLine do                        { process each line }
        begin
          PutScr( x1, Line+y1, x1+Amount-1, Line+y1,
                     GetPtr( Line, 0 ) );
          Move( GetPtr( Line, Amount )^, GetPtr( Line, 0 )^, Byte2Copy );
          Move( LBufPtr^, GetPtr( Line, WWidth - Amount )^, Amount shl 1 );
          inc( PTRREC( LBufPtr ).Ofs, Amount shl 1 );
        end;

      {-- if the cursor was in the window, it must also be moved -----------}
```

```
       if ( (x1 <= ATD.CurX ) and (x2 >= ATD.CurX ) and
             (y1 <= ATD.CurY ) and (y2 >= ATD.CurY ) ) then
         WinSetCursor( ATD.CurX + Amount , ATD.CurY );

       {-- in Write2View mode, the output position for Write and ------------}
       {-- Writeln must be moved with the window        -----------}

       if ( ATD.Write2View ) then                   { in Write2View mode? }
           inc( ATD.WritelnX, Amount );             { pass Write position }

       inc( x1, amount );                       { update window coordinates }
       inc( x2, amount );
       MtBlock;                         { execute Freemem without task switching }
       FreeMem( BufPtr, BufLen );              { free allocated buffer }
       MtContinue;                         { re-enable task switching }
     end;
   inc( ATD.ViewX1, amount );                   { move view region (global }
   inc( ATD.ViewX2, amount );                   { variables) with window   }
 end;

{**************************************************************************
*  WinMoveLeft : moves the current window a specified number of columns   *
*                to the left                                              *
**----------------------------------------------------------------------**
*  Input   : Amount = number of columns to move the window                *
*  Info    : the calling routine is responsible for making sure that the  *
*            window will not be moved off the screen                      *
**************************************************************************}

procedure WinMoveLeft( Amount : byte );

var BufPtr,                                  { pointer to temp. buffer }
    LBufPtr   : VPTR;               { running pointer in the temp. buffer }
    Byte2Copy,                              { number of bytes to copy }
    Line,                   { loop counter for processing each window line }
    EndLine,                                          { same }
    WWidth,                             { window width in columns }
    WLength,                            { window length in columns }
    BufLen    : integer;            { length of temp. buffer in bytes }
{-- GetPtr returns a pointer to a certain character in the -------[ LOCAL ]-}
{-- buffer of the current window                                           -}

function GetPtr( Line, Column : integer ) : pointer;

begin
  GetPtr := @ATD.CurBufPtr^[ Line * WWidth + Column ];
end;


begin
  with ATD.CurWinPtr^ do                 { access the current window descriptor }
    begin
      WWidth  := x2 - x1 + 1;
      WLength := y2 - y1 + 1;
```

```
      BufLen  := WLength * Amount shl 1;
      MtBlock;                        { execute GetMem without task switching }
      GetMem( BufPtr, BufLen );                { allocate temp. memory }
      MtContinue;                              { continue task switching }
      GetScr( x1-Amount, y1, x1-1, y2, BufPtr );
      ScrollHori( x1, y1, x2, y2, Amount, NO_CLEAR, TRUE );
      Byte2Copy := ( WWidth - Amount ) shl 1;
      LBufPtr := BufPtr;              { running pointer to start of buffer }
      EndLine := WLength - 1;
      for Line:=0 to EndLine do                    { process each line }
        begin
          PutScr( x2-Amount+1, Line+y1, x2, Line+y1,
                    GetPtr( Line, WWidth - Amount ) );
          Move( GetPtr( Line, 0 )^, GetPtr( Line, Amount )^, Byte2Copy );
          Move( LBufPtr^, GetPtr( Line, 0 )^, Amount shl 1 );
          inc( PTRREC( LBufPtr ).Ofs, Amount shl 1 );
        end;

      {-- if the cursor was in the window, it must also be moved -----------}

      if ( (x1 <= ATD.CurX ) and (x2 >= ATD.CurX ) and
           (y1 <= ATD.CurY ) and (y2 >= ATD.CurY ) ) then
        WinSetCursor( ATD.CurX + Amount , ATD.CurY );

      {-- in Write2View mode, the output position for Write and ------------}
      {-- Writeln must be moved with the window            ------------}

      if ( ATD.Write2View ) then                  { in Write2View mode? }
          dec( ATD.WritelnX, Amount );            { pass Write position }

      dec( x1, amount );                          { update window coordinates }
      dec( x2, amount );
      MtBlock;                        { execute FreeMem without task switching }
      FreeMem( BufPtr, BufLen );               { free allocated buffer }
      MtContinue;                              { re-enable task switching }
    end;
  dec( ATD.ViewX1, amount );                    { move view region (global }
  dec( ATD.ViewX2, amount );                    { variables) with window   }
end;


{*****************************************************************************
*  WinMove : moves the current window to a specified screen position        *
**-------------------------------------------------------------------------**
*  Input   : x, y : new coordinates of the upper left window corner         *
*  Info    : the calling routine is responsible for making sure that the    *
*            window will not be moved off the screen                        *
*****************************************************************************}

procedure WinMove( x, y : byte );

var BufPtr : VPTR;                                { pointer to temp. buffer }
    DeltaX,                               { distance between old and new }
    DeltaY,                               { window positions             }
```

```
      WWidth,                                        { window width in columns }
      WLength,                                       { window length in columns }
      BufLen : integer;                     { length of temp. buffer in bytes }

begin
  with ATD.CurWinPtr^ do                  { access current window descriptor }
    begin
      WWidth := x2 - x1;
      WLength := y2 - y1;
      BufLen := ( WLength + 1 ) * ( WWidth + 1 ) shl 1;
      MtBlock;                       { execute GetMem without task switching }
      GetMem( BufPtr, BufLen );                    { allocate temp. buffer }
      MtContinue;                            { re-enable task switching }
      GetScr( x1, y1, x2, y2, BufPtr );     { copy current window to buffer }
      PutScr( x1, y1, x2, y2, @Buffer );
      DeltaX := x - x1;                             { distance in columns }
      DeltaY := y - y1;                               { distance in lines }

      {-- if the cursor was in the window, it must also be moved -----------}
      if ( (x1 <= ATD.CurX ) and (x2 >= ATD.CurX ) and
           (y1 <= ATD.CurY ) and (y2 >= ATD.CurY ) ) then
        WinSetCursor( ATD.CurX - x1 + x, ATD.CurY - y1 + y );

      {-- in Write2View mode, the output position for Write and ------------}
      {-- Writeln must be moved with the window          ------------}

      if ( ATD.Write2View ) then                   { in Write2View mode? }
        begin
          dec( ATD.WritelnX, x1 - x );
          dec( ATD.WritelnY, y1 - y );
        end;

      x1 := x;                              { set new window coordinates }
      x2 := x + WWidth - 1;
      y1 := y;
      y2 := y + WLength - 1;

      GetScr( x, y, x2, y2, @Buffer );
      PutScr( x, y, x2, y2, BufPtr );

      MtBlock;                     { execute FreeMem without task switching }
      FreeMem( BufPtr, BufLen );                    { free allocated buffer }
      MtContinue;                            { re-enable task switching }
    end;

  inc( ATD.ViewX1, DeltaX );                   { move view region (global }
  inc( ATD.ViewX2, DeltaX );                   { variables) with window   }
  inc( ATD.ViewY1, DeltaY );
  inc( ATD.ViewY2, DeltaY );
end;
```

657

```
{****************************************************************************
 *  WinInFront : moves a specified window to the foreground               *
 **------------------------------------------------------------------------**
 *  Input    : Key = window Handle that is returned by WinOpen or         *
 *                   WinOpenShadow when a window is opened                *
 *  Output   : True, if the window can be moved to the foreground,        *
 *             False, if there is not enough memory to execute the function *
 ****************************************************************************}

function WinInFront( Key : integer ) : boolean;

var DummyWD : WINDES;                                  { dummy descriptor }
    RunWiP,                          { running pointer through the window list }
    WiP     : WIPTR;                       { pointer to the window being moved }
    TempBuf,                          { temporary buffer to store a window }
    WinBuf,                                { second copy of the video RAM }
    WinNrBuf,                         { contents of the window being moved }
    VioCopy,                    { pointer to buffer with copy of the video RAM }
    WDesn,          { pointer to the buffer in which the window is disassembled}
    Design  : VPTR;                            { pointer to new screen }
    Nr,                          { number of windows to process in the list }
    TempLen,                              { length of temporary buffer }
    VioLen,                               { number of bytes in video RAM }
    AwiLen,                               { length of window to process }
    i, j    : integer;                            { loop counters }

{-- the local procedures Get and Put are used to process the various -------}
{-- buffers that recreate the video RAM                             -------}

procedure Get( x1, y1, x2, y2 : byte; VioPtr, BufPtr : pointer );

var nbytes : integer;                     { number of bytes to copy per line }

begin
  nbytes := ( x2 - x1 + 1 ) shl 1;                       { bytes per line }
  inc( PTRREC( VioPtr ).Ofs, (x1 + y1 * NumCol) shl 1 );
  while y1 <= y2 do                                 { process each line }
    begin
      Move( VioPtr^, BufPtr^, nbytes);
      inc( PTRREC( VioPtr ).Ofs, Line_Ofs );
      inc( PTRREC( BufPtr ).Ofs, nbytes );
      inc( y1 );                                 { set Y1 to next line }
    end;
end;

procedure Put( x1, y1, x2, y2 : byte; VioPtr, BufPtr : pointer );

var nbytes : integer;                     { number of bytes to copy per line }

begin
  nbytes := ( x2 - x1 + 1 ) shl 1;                       { bytes per line }
  inc( PTRREC( VioPtr ).Ofs, (x1 + y1 * NumCol) shl 1 );
  while y1 <= y2 do                                 { process each line }
```

```
      begin
        Move( BufPtr^, VioPtr^, nbytes );
        inc( PTRREC( VioPtr ).Ofs, Line_Ofs );
        inc( PTRREC( BufPtr ).Ofs, nbytes );
        inc( y1 );                                   { set Y1 to next line }
      end;
  end;

begin
  {-- set the pointer WiP to the window being processed -------------------}

  WiP := ATD.FirstWinPtr;              { WiP points to the first window }
  Nr := 0;                             { the first window is number 0 }
  while WiP^.Handle <> Key do                   { Handle not yet found? }
    begin                                                        { no }
      WiP := WiP^.NextWin;                     { set pointer to next window }
      inc( Nr );                                 { increment the number }
    end;

  if ( WiP = ATD.CurWinPtr ) then      { is the window already on top? }
    begin                                        { yes, end function }
      WinInFront := TRUE;
      exit;
    end;

  {-- allocate five buffers to store parts of the video RAM or each --------}
  {-- window                                                       --------}

  VioLen := NumLine * NumCol shl 1;        { number of bytes in video RAM }
  if MaxAvail <= VioLen * 5 then        { enough room for all 5 buffers? }
    begin                                                        { no }
      WinInFront := false;             { return error to the calling routine }
      exit;                                        { exit the function }
    end;

  {-- enough memory is available on the heap, enter cursor position and ----}
  {-- view region in the descriptor of the current window              ----}

  DummyWD := Wip^;                         { store the current descriptor }

  Wip^.curc   := ATD.CurX;
  Wip^.curr   := ATD.CurY;
  Wip^.ViewX1 := ATD.ViewX1;
  Wip^.ViewY1 := ATD.ViewY1;
  Wip^.ViewX2 := ATD.ViewX2;
  Wip^.ViewY2 := ATD.ViewY2;

  {-- set cursor position and view region for the new window --------------}

  with Wip^.NextWin^ do
    begin
      WinSetView( ViewX1, ViewY1, ViewX2, ViewY2 );
      WinSetCursor( curc, curr );
```

```
        end;

{-- enter the data for the window being moved in its current -------------}
{-- successor                                               -------------}

with Wip^.NextWin^ do
  begin
    ViewX1 := DummyWD.ViewX1;
    ViewY1 := DummyWD.ViewY1;
    ViewX2 := DummyWD.ViewX2;
    ViewY2 := DummyWD.ViewY2;
    curc   := DummyWD.curc;
    curr   := DummyWD.curr;
  end;


MtBlock;                          { execute GetMem without task switching }
GetMem( Design,  VioLen);                   { memory for the new screen }
GetMem( WDesn,   VioLen);         { memory for the disassembled window }
GetMem( VioCopy, VioLen);             { memory for the video RAM copy }
MtContinue;                                  { re-enable task switching }

{-- copy video RAM contents to buffers VioCopy and Design ----------------}

GetScr( 0, 0, NumCol-1, NumLine-1, VioCopy );
Move( VioCopy^, Design^, VioLen );            { copy of video RAM to Design }

{-- close all windows on top of the window being processed in the --------}
{-- Design buffer                                          --------}

RunWip := ATD.CurWinPtr;               { pointer to current (last) window }
for i:=ATD.NumWin-1 downto Nr+1 do                   { process each window }
  with RunWiP^ do
    begin
      Put( x1, y1, x2, y2, Design, @Buffer );
      RunWiP := LastWin;                    { pointer to previous window }
    end;

{-- store contents of window being processed in a separate buffer --------}
{-- (accessed with the pointer WinNrBuf                    --------}

with WiP^ do
  begin
    if ( ( Attribute and WIN_SHADOW ) <> 0 ) then
      begin                          { window has a shadow, do not copy shadow }
        AwiLen := (x2-x1+1-ShadowX) * (y2-y1+1-ShadowY) shl 1;   { buffer }
        MtBlock;                    { execute GetMem without task switching }
        GetMem( WinNrBuf, AwiLen );            { allocate memory for window }
        MtContinue;                            { re-enable task switching }
        Get( x1, y1, x2-ShadowX, y2-ShadowY, Design, WinNrBuf );
        Put( x1, y1, x2, y2, Design, @Buffer );            { clear window }
      end
    else                           { window has no shadow, copy entire window }
      begin
```

660

```
        AwiLen := (x2 - x1 + 1) * (y2 - y1 + 1) shl 1;     { buffer length }
        MtBlock;                       { execute GetMem without task switching }
        GetMem( WinNrBuf, AwiLen );             { allocate memory for window }
        MtContinue;                              { re-enable task switching }
        Get( x1, y1, x2, y2, Design, WinNrBuf ); { copy window to buffer }
        Put( x1, y1, x2, y2, Design, @Buffer );            { clear window }
      end;
  end;

{-- bring each window that was under the window being moved into the -----}
{-- Design buffer and store its contents                          -----}

for i:=Nr+1 to ATD.NumWin-1 do                      { process each window }
  begin
    Move( VioCopy^, WDesn^, VioLen );          { copy video RAM to WDesn }
    RunWiP := ATD.CurWinPtr;              { WiP points to the last window }

    {-- delete the windows above window i in WDesn buffer ----------------}

    for j:=ATD.NumWin-1 downto i+1 do
      with RunWiP^ do
        begin
          Put( x1, y1, x2, y2, WDesn, @Buffer );          { delete window }
          RunWiP := LastWin;                  { set WiP to previous window }
        end;

    {-- get the contents under window i from the Design buffer and then --}
    {-- copy window i to the Design buffer                            --}

    with RunWiP^ do
      begin
        Get( x1, y1, x2, y2, Design, @Buffer );{ get screen under window  }

        {-- if the window has a shadow, it must be recreated -------------}

        if ( ( Attribute and WIN_SHADOW ) <> 0 ) then
          begin                                       { recreate the shadow }
            TempLen := ( x2-x1+1-ShadowX ) * ( y2-y1+1-ShadowY ) shl 1;
            MtBlock;             { execute Getmem without task switching }
            GetMem( TempBuf, TempLen );           { allocate temp. buffer }
            MtContinue;                          { re-enable task switching }
            Get( x1, y1, x2 - ShadowX, y2 - ShadowY, WDesn, TempBuf );
            Put( x1, y1, x2 - ShadowX, y2 - ShadowY, Design, TempBuf );
            WinShadow( x2-ShadowX+1, y1+ShadowY, x2, y2, Design );
            WinShadow( x1+ShadowX, y2-ShadowY+1, x2-ShadowX, y2, Design );
          end
        else                                      { no shadow to reconstruct }
          begin
            TempLen := (x2 - x1 + 1) * (y2 - y1 + 1) shl 1;
            MtBlock;               { execute GetMem without task switching }
            GetMem( TempBuf, TempLen );            { allocate temp. buffer }
            MtContinue;                          { re-enable task switching }
            Get( x1, y1, x2, y2, WDesn, TempBuf );
```

```
               Put( x1, y1, x2, y2, Design, TempBuf );
           end;
         MtBlock;                         { execute FreeMem without task switching }
         FreeMem( TempBuf, TempLen );                          { free temp. buffer }
         MtContinue;                                    { re-enable task switching }
       end;
    end;

{-- store contents under the new window and store the window itself ------}
{-- in the Design buffer                                            ------}

with WiP^ do
  begin
    Get( x1, y1, x2, y2, Design, @Buffer );
    if ( ( Attribute and WIN_SHADOW ) <> 0 ) then
      begin                          { window has a shadow, recreate shadow }
        Put( x1, y1, x2-ShadowX, y2-ShadowY, Design, WinNrBuf );
        WinShadow( x2-ShadowX+1, y1+ShadowY, x2, y2, Design );
        WinShadow( x1+ShadowX, y2-ShadowY+1, x2-ShadowX, y2, Design );
      end
    else                                        { window has no shadow }
      Put( x1, y1, x2, y2, Design, WinNrBuf );
    end;

{-- put the descriptor of the moved window at the end of the linked ------}
{-- list of window descriptors                                     ------}

Wip^.NextWin^.LastWin := WiP^.LastWin;
if WiP = ATD.FirstWinPtr then                      { was WiP the first window? }
  ATD.FirstWinPtr := WiP^.NextWin { yes, successor is now the first window}
else                                       { no, WiP has another successor }
  Wip^.LastWin^.NextWin := WiP^.NextWin;

Wip^.NextWin := nil;                         { no more windows after WiP }
Wip^.LastWin := ATD.CurWinPtr;       { the previous top window follows WiP }
ATD.CurWinPtr^.NextWin := WiP;                        { now points to WiP }
ATD.CurWinPtr := WiP;
ATD.CurBufPtr := @Wip^.Buffer;

{-- output the assembled buffer to the screen ---------------------------}

PutScr( 0, 0, NumCol-1, NumLine-1, Design );

{-- free the allocated buffers ------------------------------------------}

MtBlock;                            { execute Freemem without task switching }
FreeMem( WinNrBuf, AwiLen );
FreeMem( Design,  VioLen);                      { memory for the new screen }
FreeMem( WDesn,   VioLen);               { memory for the assembled window }
FreeMem( VioCopy, VioLen);              { memory for the copy of video RAM }
MtContinue;                                    { re-enable task switching }

WinInFront := TRUE;                                  { everything's o.k. }
end;
```

13.6   Keyboard and Mouse Access

The changes necessary for cooperation with the MT unit differ for the keyboard and mouse KBMT unit. Unlike WINMT, several tasks do not simultaneously query the keyboard and the mouse. Even though nothing prevents the tasks from calling the routines in the KBMT, you would be unable to perform 18 task changes every second.

The effective use of the processor with KBMT is more important than the adjustment to the multitasking operation. The keyboard and mouse queries often force the processor into nonproductive waiting loops, which can only be terminated by pressing a key or moving the mouse.

By modifying the interrupt handler, MTDEMO proved that the time spent waiting for input can be used productively for other tasks. The queue created for this purpose is controlled through a routine from the MT unit. This change is supplemented through a query of this queue in the KbmGetEvent procedure. This procedure is used, for example, by the KbmEventWait procedure.

KbmGetEvent simply performs a MtReadQueue call to the keyboard and mouse queue. This call is automatically blocked by KbmEventWait until an event becomes available from the keyboard or mouse. The additional time is applied to other tasks which can be executed during this period.

Since the routines from the MT unit easily perform this, changes in this unit are limited to the routines MouEventHandler, KbHandler, KbmGetEvent and KbmPeekEvent. The listing has become slightly shorter compared with KBMT since the unit no longer controls the mouse and keyboard queue by itself.

```
{*****************************************************************************
 *   K B M T : A unit which provides easy access to mouse and keyboard in   *
 *             connection with the MT unit.                                 *
 **-----------------------------------------------------------------------**
 *   Author        : MICHAEL TISCHER                                        *
 *   developed on   : 06/01/1989                                           *
 *   last update on : 03/10/1990                                           *
 *****************************************************************************}

unit Kbmt;

interface

uses Dos, Mt, WinMt;                                    { link units }

{== Type declarations needed by procedures and functions using this unit ==}

type  KCODE    = word;              { key code, >= 256 : extended key code }
```

```
          PTRVIEW  = longint;                              { mouse pointer design }

          MSRANGE  = record                        { describes a mouse range }
                        x1,                  { upper left coordinates of the }
                        y1,                     { specified range            }
                        x2,                  { lower right coordinates of the }
                        y2 : byte;              { specified range            }
                     end;
          RNGARRAY = array [0..99] of MSRANGE;              { range array }
          RNGPTR   = ^RNGARRAY;                   { pointer to range array }

          EVENT = record                    { describes mouse or keyboard event }
                     EvntCode : integer;                       { event code }
                     Time     : longint;                  { time in ticks }

                     case byte of                    { keyboard or mouse }
                        0 : { Mouse: ( EV_MOU_...) ----------------------------}
                           ( Rel_Row,                 { mouse pointer position, }
                             RelColumn,              { relative to range        }
                             Abs_Row,              { mouse pointer position,    }
                             AbsColumn,            { relative to stored screen }
                             Range,                        { mouse range }
                             Buttons : byte );              { button status }

                        1 : { KCode: ( EV_KEY_PRESSED ) -----------------------}
                           ( Key : KCODE );                   { key pressed }

                        2 : { Keys which produce no code: ( EV_KEY_UNKNOWN ) ---}
                           ( ScanCode,                   { scan code returned }
                             Status    : byte );         { control key status }

                        3 : { Status key, no code ( EV_KEY_STATUS ) ------------}
                           ( StateKey : byte );
                  end;

          EVENTHANDLER = procedure ( var EvRec : EVENT );

{== Declaration of functions and procedures which can be called from ======}
{== other programs                                                   ======}

procedure KbmRegisterHandler  ( Event : word; Handler : EVENTHANDLER );
procedure KbmDeRegisterHandler( Event : word );
procedure KbmGetEvent         ( var EvRec : EVENT );
procedure KbmPeekEvent        ( var EvRec : EVENT );
function  MouPtrMask          ( Character, Color : word ) : PTRVIEW;
function  PtrDifChar          ( Character : byte ) : word;
function  PtrDifCol           ( Color : byte ) : word;
procedure MouDefinePtr        ( Mask : PTRVIEW );
procedure MouDefRange         ( Amount : byte; BPtr : RNGPTR );
procedure KbmEventWait        ( WaitEvent : integer; var EvRec : EVENT );
procedure MouShowMouse;
procedure MouHideMouse;
procedure MouSetMoveArea      ( x1, y1, x2, y2 : byte );
```

664

```
procedure MouSetSpeed          ( XSpeed, YSpeed : integer );
procedure MouMovePtr           ( Col, Row : byte );
procedure MouSetDefaultPtr     ( Standard : PTRVIEW );

{== Variables needed from within an application program ===================}

var MouAvail : boolean;                    { TRUE when a mouse is available }

   {-- Variables loaded every time the mouse handler is called ------------}

   CurRng,                                 { number of current range }
   CurBut,                                 { mouse button status }
   CurX,                              { current mouse pointer position }
   CurY  : byte;                      { relative to entire screen      }
   Eqp   : QUEUEP;

{== Constants needed by an application program ==============================}

const {-------------------------------------------------- Event codes ------}

         EV_NO_EVENT     =    0;                       { no event prepared }
         EV_MOU_MOVE     =    1;                          { mouse moved }
         EV_LEFT_PRESS   =    2;               { left mouse button pressed }
         EV_LEFT_REL     =    4;              { left mouse button released }
         EV_RIGHT_PRESS  =    8;              { right mouse button pressed }
         EV_RIGHT_REL    =   16;             { right mouse button released }
         EV_KEY_PRESSED  =  256;                           { key pressed }
         EV_KEY_UNKNOWN  =  512;     { key combination that produces no code }
         EV_KEY_STATUS   = 1024;          { Status key, produces no code }

         EV_MOU_ALL      =   31;                     { all mouse events }
         EV_KEY_ALL      = 1792;                  { all keyboard events }
         EV_ALL          = 1823;        { all mouse and keyboard events }

      {---------------------------------- Status key codes -------------}

         KEY_RIGHT_SHIFT =    1;
         KEY_LEFT_SHIFT  =    2;
         KEY_CTRL        =    4;
         KEY_ALT         =    8;
         KEY_SCROLL_LOCK =   16;
         KEY_NUM_LOCK    =   32;
         KEY_CAPS_LOCK   =   64;
         KEY_INSERT      =  128;

      {-------------- Constants used for describing mouse pointer --------}

         PtrSameChar = $00ff;
         PtrSameCol  = $00ff;
         PtrInvCol   = $7777;
         PtrSameColB = $807f;                 { blinking - same color      }
         PtrInvColB  = $F777;                 { blinking - different color }
```

665

```
{------------------------------------- Control key codes ------------}

      BEL      =    7;                    { Bell character  }
      BS       =    8;                    { Backspace key   }
      TAB      =    9;                    { Tab key         }
      LF       =   10;                    { Linefeed        }
      CR       =   13;                    { Return key      }
      ESC      =   27;                    { Escape key      }
      SPACE    =   32;                    { Space           }
      CTRL_A   =    1;                    { CTRL + A        }
      CTRL_B   =    2;                    { CTRL + B        }
      CTRL_C   =    3;                    { CTRL + C        }
      CTRL_D   =    4;                    { CTRL + D        }
      CTRL_E   =    5;                    { CTRL + E        }
      CTRL_F   =    6;                    { CTRL + F        }
      CTRL_G   =    7;                    { CTRL + G        }
      CTRL_H   =    8;                    { CTRL + H        }
      CTRL_I   =    9;                    { CTRL + I        }
      CTRL_J   =   10;                    { CTRL + J        }
      CTRL_K   =   11;                    { CTRL + K        }
      CTRL_L   =   12;                    { CTRL + L        }
      CTRL_M   =   13;                    { CTRL + M        }
      CTRL_N   =   14;                    { CTRL + N        }
      CTRL_O   =   15;                    { CTRL + O        }
      CTRL_P   =   16;                    { CTRL + P        }
      CTRL_Q   =   17;                    { CTRL + Q        }
      CTRL_R   =   18;                    { CTRL + R        }
      CTRL_S   =   19;                    { CTRL + S        }
      CTRL_T   =   20;                    { CTRL + T        }
      CTRL_U   =   21;                    { CTRL + U        }
      CTRL_V   =   22;                    { CTRL + V        }
      CTRL_W   =   23;                    { CTRL + W        }
      CTRL_X   =   24;                    { CTRL + X        }
      CTRL_Y   =   25;                    { CTRL + Y        }
      CTRL_Z   =   26;                    { CTRL + Z        }
      BACKTAB  =  271;                    { SHIFT + TAB     }
      ALT_Q    =  272;                    { ALT + Q         }
      ALT_W    =  273;                    { ALT + W         }
      ALT_E    =  274;                    { ALT + E         }
      ALT_R    =  275;                    { ALT + R         }
      ALT_T    =  276;                    { ALT + T         }
      ALT_Y    =  277;                    { ALT + Y         }
      ALT_U    =  278;                    { ALT + U         }
      ALT_I    =  279;                    { ALT + I         }
      ALT_O    =  280;                    { ALT + O         }
      ALT_P    =  281;                    { ALT + P         }
      ALT_A    =  286;                    { ALT + A         }
      ALT_S    =  287;                    { ALT + S         }
      ALT_D    =  288;                    { ALT + D         }
      ALT_F    =  289;                    { ALT + F         }
      ALT_G    =  290;                    { ALT + G         }
      ALT_H    =  291;                    { ALT + H         }
      ALT_J    =  292;                    { ALT + J         }
```

```
ALT_K      = 293;        { ALT + K        }
ALT_L      = 294;        { ALT + L        }
ALT_Z      = 300;        { ALT + Z        }
ALT_X      = 301;        { ALT + X        }
ALT_C      = 302;        { ALT + C        }
ALT_V      = 303;        { ALT + V        }
ALT_B      = 304;        { ALT + B        }
ALT_N      = 305;        { ALT + N        }
ALT_M      = 306;        { ALT + M        }
F1         = 315;        { F1 key         }
F2         = 316;        { F2 key         }
F3         = 317;        { F3 key         }
F4         = 318;        { F4 key         }
F5         = 319;        { F5 key         }
F6         = 320;        { F6 key         }
F7         = 321;        { F7 key         }
F8         = 322;        { F8 key         }
F9         = 323;        { F9 key         }
F10        = 324;        { F10 key        }
CDOWN      = 336;        { Cursor Down    }
CHOME      = 327;        { Cursor Home    }
CUP        = 328;        { Cursor Up      }
CPGUP      = 329;        { Page Up        }
CLEFT      = 331;        { Cursor Left    }
CRIGHT     = 333;        { Cursor Right   }
CEND       = 335;        { Cursor Right   }
CPGDN      = 337;        { Page Dn        }
INSERTKEY  = 338;        { INSERT key     }
DELETEKEY  = 339;        { DELETE key     }
SHIFT_F1   = 340;        { SHIFT + F1     }
SHIFT_F2   = 341;        { SHIFT + F2     }
SHIFT_F3   = 342;        { SHIFT + F3     }
SHIFT_F4   = 343;        { SHIFT + F4     }
SHIFT_F5   = 344;        { SHIFT + F5     }
SHIFT_F6   = 345;        { SHIFT + F6     }
SHIFT_F7   = 346;        { SHIFT + F7     }
SHIFT_F8   = 347;        { SHIFT + F8     }
SHIFT_F9   = 348;        { SHIFT + F9     }
SHIFT_F10  = 349;        { SHIFT + F10    }
CTRL_F1    = 350;        { CTRL + F1      }
CTRL_F2    = 351;        { CTRL + F2      }
CTRL_F3    = 352;        { CTRL + F3      }
CTRL_F4    = 353;        { CTRL + F4      }
CTRL_F5    = 354;        { CTRL + F5      }
CTRL_F6    = 355;        { CTRL + F6      }
CTRL_F7    = 356;        { CTRL + F7      }
CTRL_F8    = 357;        { CTRL + F8      }
CTRL_F9    = 358;        { CTRL + F9      }
CTRL_F10   = 359;        { CTRL + F10     }
ALT_F1     = 360;        { ALT + F1       }
ALT_F2     = 361;        { ALT + F2       }
ALT_F3     = 362;        { ALT + F3       }
ALT_F4     = 363;        { ALT + F4       }
```

```
            ALT_F5    = 364;                        { ALT + F5         }
            ALT_F6    = 365;                        { ALT + F6         }
            ALT_F7    = 366;                        { ALT + F7         }
            ALT_F8    = 367;                        { ALT + F8         }
            ALT_F9    = 368;                        { ALT + F9         }
            ALT_F10   = 369;                        { ALT + F10        }
            CTRL_LF   = 371;                        { CTRL + Left      }
            CTRL_RI   = 372;                        { CTRL + Right     }
            CTRL_PGDN = 374;                        { CTRL + PgUp      }
            CTRL_HOME = 375;                        { CTRL + Home      }
            ALT_1     = 376;                        { ALT + 1          }
            ALT_2     = 377;                        { ALT + 2          }
            ALT_3     = 378;                        { ALT + 3          }
            ALT_4     = 379;                        { ALT + 4          }
            ALT_5     = 380;                        { ALT + 5          }
            ALT_6     = 381;                        { ALT + 6          }
            ALT_7     = 382;                        { ALT + 7          }
            ALT_8     = 383;                        { ALT + 8          }
            ALT_9     = 384;                        { ALT + 9          }
            ALT_0     = 385;                        { ALT + 0          }
            CTRL_PGUP = 388;                        { CTRL + PgUp      }

implementation

{$L kbmta}                              { add kbma.obj assembler module }

{== Internal constants ======================================================}

const NO_MSRANGE   = 255;                  { mouse pointer not in range xy }
      EVQ_LEN      = 100;           { length of mouse or keyboard queue }

{== Internal type declarations ===============================================}

type  PTRREC   = record                    { used for access to the    }
                    Ofs : word;            { elements of any mouse      }
                    Seg : word;            { pointer                    }
                 end;

      PTRVREC  = record                        { used for access to the }
                    ScreenMask : word;         { elements of a PTRVIEW   }
                    PointrMask : word;
                 end;

      RNGBUF   = array [0..10000] of byte;              { range buffer }

      RBPTR    = ^RNGBUF;                     { pointer to a range buffer }

      EVQUEUE = array [1..EVQ_LEN] of event;         { an EvntCode queue }

      EVQUEUEPTR  = ^EVQUEUE;                   { pointer to the event queue }

      EVHANDREC = record              { element in the event handler table }
                    Call    : boolean;             { handler installed? }
```

```
                     Handler : EVENTHANDLER;              { procedure pointer }
                 end;

{== Internal global variables ===========================================}

const EvNext : integer = 0;          { pointer to next event in event queue }
      EvLast : integer = 0;          { pointer to last event in event queue }

var  NumRanges,                                         { number of ranges }
     TLine,                                        { number of text lines }
     TCol    : byte;                             { number of text columns }
     OldPtr,                                          { old pointer image }
     StdPtr   : PTRVIEW;                  { mask for default mouse pointer }
     BufPtr   : RBPTR;               { pointer to range recognition buffer }
     CurRngPtr: RNGPTR;                 { pointer to current range vector }
     BLen     : integer;                   { range buffer length in bytes }
     ExitOld  : pointer;                { pointer to old exit procedure }
     HandTab  : array [1..16] of EVHANDREC;   { table with event handlers }
     EvqPtr   : EVQUEUEPTR;                   { pointer to event queue }

     OldKbHandler : pointer;                   { address of old int09 handler }

     Time      : longint absolute $40:$6C;       { BIOS tick counter }
     BiosKbFlag : byte absolute $40:$17;         { BIOS keyboard flag }
     CurStatus  : byte;                       { current keyboard status }

{== Declarations of external functions ===================================}

{$F+}                                          { the function is FAR }
procedure NewMouHandler ; external ;           { mouse event handler }
procedure NewKbHandler  ; external ;      { new keyboard handler (Int $09) }
{$F-}                                          { FAR functions disabled }

{**********************************************************************}
{*  KbmIGetIndex : uses an event mask to retrieve the corresponding index *}
{*              from the event handler table                          *}
{**------------------------------------------------------------------*}
{*  Input  : MASK = the event mask                                    *}
{*  Output : Index between 1 and 16                                   *}
{**********************************************************************}

function KbmIGetIndex( Mask : word ) : byte ;

var i : byte;                                           { stores the index }

begin
  i := 1;
  while ( Mask <> 1 ) do                { event bit still not in bit 0 ? }
    begin                                                           { No }
      Mask := Mask shr 1;              { move mask one bit to the right }
      inc( i );                                      { increment index }
    end;
  KbmIGetIndex := i;                                     { return index }
```

669

```
end;

{*****************************************************************************}
{*   KbmRegisterHandler : registers an application program's handler       *}
{*                        for a certain event                              *}
{**-----------------------------------------------------------------------*}
{*   Input  : EVENT   = the event mask                                     *}
{*            HANDLER = the handler to be called                           *}
{*****************************************************************************}

procedure KbmRegisterHandler( Event : word; Handler : EVENTHANDLER );

var i : byte;                               { index in event handler table }

begin
  i := KbmIGetIndex( Event );                              { get index }
  HandTab[ i ].Call := TRUE;                             { call handler }
  HandTab[ i ].Handler := Handler;           { store pointer to handler }
end;

{*****************************************************************************}
{*   KbmDeRegisterHandler : removes an application program's handler for   *}
{*                          a certain event                                *}
{**-----------------------------------------------------------------------*}
{*   Input  : EVENT = the event mask                                       *}
{*****************************************************************************}

procedure KbmDeRegisterHandler( Event : word );

begin
  HandTab[ KbmIGetIndex( Event ) ].Call := FALSE;      { do not call the }
end;                                                    { handler any more }

{*****************************************************************************}
{*   KbmGetEvent : reads next event                                        *}
{**-----------------------------------------------------------------------*}
{*   Input  : EvRec = variable taken on by event record                    *}
{*   Info:    if no event exists when KbmGetEvent is called, this procedure*}
{*            waits for the next event                                      *}
{*****************************************************************************}

procedure KbmGetEvent( var EvRec : EVENT );

begin
    MtReadQueue( EQP, EvRec );                { read event from Eqp queue }
end;
```

```
{****************************************************************************}
{*  KbmPeekEvent : reads the next event from the event queue              *}
{**------------------------------------------------------------------------**}
{*  Input  : EvRec = variable from which the event record is taken        *}
{*  Info:    If no event exists when KbmPeekEvent is called, EV_NO_EVENT  *}
{*           is placed in the EVNTCODE array.                             *}
{****************************************************************************}

procedure KbmPeekEvent( var EvRec : EVENT );

begin
  if not ( MtPeekQueue( Eqp, EvRec ) ) then                 { event code? }
    EvRec.EvntCode := EV_NO_EVENT;              { no, return EV_NO_EVENT }
end;


{****************************************************************************}
{*  KbHandler : called by the Int09 handler (NewKbHandler in the          *}
{*              assembler module) when a key is pressed                    *}
{**------------------------------------------------------------------------**}
{*  Input  : KbPort = code read from keyboard port $60                    *}
{****************************************************************************}

procedure KbHandler( KbPort : byte );

var EvRec  : EVENT;                              { EVENT record to be created }
    Regs   : Registers;                             { processor register }
    NewKbS : byte;                              { new keyboard status }

begin
  EvRec.Time := Time;                                    { get clock time }
  Regs.AH := 1;                                { determine if a key has been }
  intr( $16, Regs );                           { converted to a key code   }
  if ( Regs.Flags and FZERO = 0 ) then
    begin                              { yes, character now in keyboard buffer }
      Regs.AH := 0;                             { load character from keyboard }
      intr( $16, Regs );                        { buffer via the BIOS        }
      if ( Regs.AL = 0 ) then EvRec.Key := Regs.AH + 256
                        else EvRec.Key := Regs.AL;
      EvRec.EvntCode := EV_KEY_PRESSED;                     { set event code }
      MtWriteQFast( Eqp, EvRec );                    { place event in queue }
    end
  else                                   { keystroke produced no key code }
    begin
      NewKbS := BiosKbFlag;                        { get status of control keys }
      if ( CurStatus <> NewKbS ) then                     { status change? }
        begin
          if ( CurStatus < NewKbS ) then                  { was a bit set? }
            begin                                         { yes, save event }
              EvRec.StateKey := CurStatus xor NewKbS;       { isolate flag }
              if ( EvRec.StateKey <> KEY_INSERT ) then     { not INSERT? }
                begin                                 { no, create EVENT }
                  EvRec.EvntCode := EV_KEY_STATUS;
                  MtWriteQFast( Eqp, EvRec );           { put event in queue }
```

671

```
                    end;
              end
          end
        else                                   { no, no status change }
          if ( KbPort < 128 ) then                    { make code? }
            begin                                 { yes, create event }
              EvRec.EvntCode := EV_KEY_UNKNOWN;       { unknown code }
              EvRec.ScanCode := KbPort;              { pass scan code }
              EvRec.Status   := NewKbs;    { load status in EVENT record }
              MtWriteQFast( Eqp, EvRec );        { put event in queue }
            end;
          CurStatus := NewKbS;             { store new keyboard status }
        end;
end;

{****************************************************************************}
{* MouPtrMask: creates the pointer mask and screen mask from the bit     *}
{*             for the character and the color                           *}
{**----------------------------------------------------------------------**}
{* Input  : Character = bit mask for pointer mask and screen mask        *}
{*                      character                                        *}
{*          Color     = bit mask for pointer mask and screen mask color  *}
{* Output : pointer mask and screen mask as one value of type PTRVIEW    *}
{* Info:    the constants PtrSameChar, PtrSameCol, PtrSameColB,          *}
{*          PtrInvCol and PtrInvColB as well as the results of the       *}
{*          functions PtrDifChar and PtrDifCol can be passed as the      *}
{*          color and character                                          *}
{****************************************************************************}

function MouPtrMask( Character, Color  : word ) : PTRVIEW;

var Mask : PTRVIEW;                    { the pointer/screen mask to be created }

begin
  PTRVREC( Mask ).ScreenMask := ( ( Color and $ff ) shl 8 ) +
                                  ( Character and $ff );
  PTRVREC( Mask ).PointrMask := ( Color and $ff00 ) + ( Character shr 8 );
  MouPtrMask := Mask;                       { return mask to calling routine }
end;


{****************************************************************************}
{* PtrDifChar: creates the character component of the screen mask and    *}
{*             pointer mask                                               *}
{**----------------------------------------------------------------------**}
{* Input  : ASCII code of the character to represent the mouse pointer   *}
{* Output : pointer and screen masks for this character                  *}
{* Info:    the result is further processed by the MouPtrMask procedure  *}
{****************************************************************************}

function PtrDifChar( Character : byte ) : word;

begin
  PtrDifChar := Character shl 8;
```

672

```
end;

{*******************************************************************}
{*  PtrDifCol: creates the color component of the pointer mask and screen *}
{*             mask                                                   *}
{**----------------------------------------------------------------**}
{*  Input  : color of the character that will represent the mouse pointer *}
{*  Output : pointer and screen masks for this color                 *}
{*  Info:    the result is further processed by the MouPtrMask procedure *}
{*******************************************************************}

function PtrDifCol( Color : byte ) : word;

begin
  PtrDifCol := Color shl 8;
end;

{*******************************************************************}
{*  MouDefinePtr: passes the pointer mask and screen mask to the mouse    *}
{*                driver, which then defines the appearance of the mouse  *}
{*                pointer                                             *}
{**----------------------------------------------------------------**}
{*  Input  : Mask = the pointer mask and screen mask as one parameter of  *}
{*                  type PTRVIEW                                      *}
{*  Info:    - the parameter mask is created by the MouPtrMask procedure  *}
{*           - the upper 16 bits of Mask represents the screen mask, *}
{*             the lower 16 bits represent the pointer mask           *}
{*******************************************************************}

procedure MouDefinePtr( Mask : PTRVIEW );

var Regs : Registers;               { processor register for interrupt call }

begin
  Regs.AX := $000a;          { function number for "Set text pointer type" }
  Regs.BX := 0;                                { create software pointer }
  Regs.CX := PTRVREC( Mask ).ScreenMask;        { low word is AND mask }
  Regs.DX := PTRVREC( Mask ).PointrMask;        { high word is XOR mask }
  Intr( $33, Regs);                             { call mouse driver }
end;

{*******************************************************************}
{*  MouEventHandler: called by mouse driver via the assembler routine    *}
{*                   kbma when a mouse event occurs                   *}
{**----------------------------------------------------------------**}
{*  Input  : EvFlags  = the event mask                               *}
{*           ButState = current status of mouse buttons              *}
{*           X, Y     = current position of mouse pointer in relation to  *}
{*                      the text screen                              *}
{*******************************************************************}

procedure MouEventHandler( EvFlags, ButState, x, y : integer );
```

```
var NewC,                              { new coordinates of mouse pointer }
    NewR,                              { relative to new range            }
    NewRng : byte;                          { range number where the }
    EvData : EVENT;                         { new event occurred      }
    Ticks  : longint;                 { stores the current clock time }
    i,                                        { loop counter }
    Mask   : integer;                          { bit mask }

begin
  Ticks := Time;                                        { get time }
  NewRng  := BufPtr^[ y * TCol + x ];                   { get range }
  if ( NewRng = NO_MSRANGE ) then                       { no range? }
    begin                     { yes, coordinates relate to entire screen }
      NewR := y;
      NewC := x;
    end
  else              { no, coordinates relate to upper left corner of range }
    begin
      NewR := y - CurRngPtr^[ NewRng ].y1;
      NewC := x - CurRngPtr^[ NewRng ].x1;
    end;

  {-- capture each event separately as an EVENT record --------------------}

  Mask := 1;                                     { start with event bit 0 }
    for i:=0 to 7 do  { execute individual bits in EvFlags }
      begin
        if not((EvFlags and Mask = 0) or
               ((Mask = EV_MOU_MOVE) and ((x = CurX) and (y = CurY )))) then
          begin
            with EvData do                        { create event record }
              begin
                Time     := Ticks;        { load data in the event record }
                Buttons  := ButState;
                Range    := NewRng;
                Rel_Row  := NewR;
                RelColumn := NewC;
                Abs_Row  := y;
                AbsColumn := x;
              end;
            MtWriteQFast( Eqp, EvData );      { place event record in queue }
          end;
        Mask := Mask shl 1;                        { process next event bit }
      end;

  CurX := x;                                        { new mouse position }
  CurY := y;
  CurBut := ButState;                        { store status of mouse buttons }
  CurRng := NewRng;                              { store new mouse range }
end;
```

```
{***********************************************************************}
{*  KbmIBufFill: stores the range code for a mouse range in the internal *}
{*               range buffer of this module                             *}
{**-------------------------------------------------------------------**}
{*  Input  : x1, y1 = upper left corner of the mouse range             *}
{*           x2, y2 = lower right corner of the mouse range             *}
{*           Code   = the range code                                   *}
{***********************************************************************}

procedure KbmIBufFill( x1, y1, x2, y2, Code : byte );

var Index    : integer;                 { points to field being processed }
    Column,                                       { loop counter }
    Row      : byte;

begin
  for Row  :=y1 to y2 do                         { process each line }
    begin
      Index := Row * TCol + x1;            { first index of the line }
      for Column:=x1 to x2 do         { process each column in the line }
        begin
          BufPtr^[ Index ] := Code;                 { save code }
          inc( Index );                    { set index to next field }
        end;
    end;
end;


{***********************************************************************}
{*  MouDefRange:   enables the assignment of different screen ranges   *}
{*                 which can be recognized as mouse ranges             *}
{**-------------------------------------------------------------------**}
{*  Input  : Amount = number of the screen range                       *}
{*           BPtr   = pointer to the array describing the ranges as a   *}
{*                    structure of type MSRANGE                         *}
{*  Info:    - the free remaining screen ranges are assigned the code   *}
{*             NO_MSRANGE                                               *}
{***********************************************************************}

procedure MouDefRange( Amount : byte; BPtr : RNGPTR );

var CurRng,                             { number of the current range }
    Range : byte;                               { loop counter }

begin
  CurRngPtr := BPtr;                    { mark pointer to vector and }
  NumRanges := Amount;                   { number of ranges          }
  FillChar( BufPtr^, BLen, NO_MSRANGE );  { all elements = NO_MSRANGE }
  for Range:=0 to amount-1 do            { process individual ranges }
   with BPtr^[ Range ] do
     KbmIBufFill( x1, y1, x2, y2, Range );

  CurRng := BufPtr^[ CurY * TCol + CurX ];       { send current range }
end;
```

675

```
{****************************************************************}
{*   KbmEventWait: waits for the occurrence of a certain keyboard or mouse *}
{*               event                                          *}
{**------------------------------------------------------------**}
{*   Input  : WAIT_EVENT = bit mask that specifies the desired event   *}
{*            EV_REC     = event record in which information on the event *}
{*                         will be returned.                    *}
{*   Info:    - WAIT_EVENT can be specified by combining the various  *}
{*              event constants EV_MOU_MOVE, EV_LEFT_PRESS etc. with a *}
{*              logical OR                                       *}
{*            - the procedure will only return when one of the specified *}
{*              events occurs. Non-specified events that occur in the  *}
{*              meantime are ignored                            *}
{*            - this procedure can be called recursively, so that an event *}
{*              handler can also access KbmEventWait.           *}
{****************************************************************}

procedure KbmEventWait( WaitEvent : integer; var EvRec : EVENT );

var CurEvent : EVENT;                      { stores the current event index }
    Index    : byte;                       { in the event handler table    }

begin
  repeat                                            { wait for specific event }
    KbmGetEvent( CurEvent );                           { get event code }

    {-- call handler of application program ----------------------------}

    Index := KbmIGetIndex( CurEvent.EvntCode );    { get index from table }
    if ( HandTab[ Index ].Call ) then              { handler installed? }
     HandTab[ Index ].Handler( CurEvent );                { yes, call }

  until ( CurEvent.EvntCode and WaitEvent <> 0 );
   EvRec := CurEvent;                       { pass event to calling routine }
end;


{****************************************************************}
{*   KbmIGetX: returns the text column where the mouse pointer is located *}
{**------------------------------------------------------------**}
{*   Output : column of the mouse pointer relative to the text screen  *}
{****************************************************************}

function KbmIGetX : byte;

var Regs : Registers;                    { processor register for interrupt call }

begin
  Regs.AX := $0003;                { function number for "Get mouse position" }
  Intr( $33,  Regs );                              { call mouse driver }
  KbmIGetX := Regs.CX shr 3;                   { compute and return column }
end;
```

```
{***********************************************************************}
{*   KbmIGetY: returns the text row where the mouse pointer is located   *}
{**---------------------------------------------------------------------**}
{*   Output : row of the mouse pointer, relative to the text screen      *}
{***********************************************************************}

function KbmIGetY : byte;

var Regs : Registers;                    { processor register for interrupt call }

begin
  Regs.AX := $0003;                      { function number for "Get mouse position" }
  Intr( $33, Regs );                                    { call mouse driver }
  KbmIGetY := Regs.DX shr 3;                         { compute and return row }
end;

{***********************************************************************}
{*   MouShowMouse: makes mouse pointer visible on the screen            *}
{**---------------------------------------------------------------------**}
{*   Info: calls to MouShowMouse and MouHideMouse must be balanced      *}
{***********************************************************************}

procedure MouShowMouse;

var Regs : Registers;                    { processor register for interrupt call }

begin
  Regs.AX := $0001;                      { function number for "Show Mouse" }
  Intr( $33, Regs );                                 { call mouse driver }
end;

{***********************************************************************}
{*   MouHideMouse: removes the mouse pointer from the screen            *}
{**---------------------------------------------------------------------**}
{*   Info: calls to MouShowMouse and MouHideMouse must be balanced      *}
{***********************************************************************}

procedure MouHideMouse;

var Regs : Registers;                    { processor register for interrupt call }

begin
  Regs.AX := $0002;                      { function number for "Hide Mouse" }
  Intr( $33, Regs);                                  { call mouse driver }
end;
```

```
{***********************************************************************}
{*  MouSetMoveArea: sets the area in which the mouse can move          *}
{**-----------------------------------------------------------------**}
{*  Input  :  x1, y1 = coordinates of the upper left corner of the range  *}
{*            x2, y2 = coordinates of the lower right corner of the range *}
{*  Info:     - these coordinates relate to the text screen and not to the *}
{*              virtual graphics screen of the mouse driver             *}
{***********************************************************************}

procedure MouSetMoveArea( x1, y1, x2, y2 : byte );

var Regs : Registers;                { processor register for interrupt call }

begin
  Regs.AX := $0008;                { function number for "Set vertical limits" }
  Regs.CX := integer( y1 ) shl 3;                        { convert to virtual }
  Regs.DX := integer( y2 ) shl 3;                        { mouse screen        }
  Intr( $33, Regs );                                     { call mouse driver  }
  Regs.AX := $0007;                { function number for "Set horizontal limits" }
  Regs.CX := integer( x1 ) shl 3;                        { convert to virtual }
  Regs.DX := integer( x2 ) shl 3;                        { mouse screen        }
  Intr( $33, Regs );                                     { call mouse driver  }
end;


{***********************************************************************}
{*  MouSetSpeed: sets the relationship between mouse movement and the  *}
{*               resulting movement of the mouse pointer               *}
{**-----------------------------------------------------------------**}
{*  Input  : XSpeed = speed in X direction                             *}
{*           YSpeed = speed in Y direction                             *}
{*  Info:    - both parameters are expressed in Mickeys (8 pixels)     *}
{***********************************************************************}

procedure MouSetSpeed( XSpeed, YSpeed : integer );

var Regs : Registers;                { processor register for interrupt call }

begin
  Regs.AX := $000f;     { function number for "Set mickeys to pixel ratio" }
  Regs.CX := XSpeed;
  Regs.DX := YSpeed;
  Intr( $33, Regs);                                      { call mouse driver }
end;


{***********************************************************************}
{*  MouMovePtr: moves the mouse pointer to a new screen position       *}
{**-----------------------------------------------------------------**}
{*  Input  : COL = the new screen column of the mouse pointer          *}
{*           ROW = the new screen row of the mouse pointer             *}
{*  Info:    - the coordinates relate to the text screen and not to the *}
{*             virtual graphics screen of the mouse driver             *}
{***********************************************************************}
```

```pascal
procedure MouMovePtr( Col, Row : byte );

var Regs   : Registers;              { processor register for interrupt call }
    NewRng : byte;                               { range to move mouse to }

begin
  Regs.AX := $0004;      { function number for "Set mouse pointer position" }
  CurX := col;                                   { store coordinates      }
  CurY := row;                                   { in global variables    }
  Regs.CX := integer( col ) shl 3;        { convert coordinates and        }
  Regs.DX := integer( row ) shl 3;        { store in global variables      }
  Intr( $33, Regs );                            { call mouse driver       }

  CurRng := BufPtr^[ Row * TCol + Col ];                { get new range }
end;

{****************************************************************************}
{*  MouSetDefaultPtr : defines appearance of the mouse pointer           *}
{**----------------------------------------------------------------------**}
{* Input  : Standard = pointer and screen mask                           *}
{* Info   : - parameters must be created using the MouPtrMask function    *}
{****************************************************************************}

procedure MouSetDefaultPtr( Standard : PTRVIEW );

begin
  StdPtr := Standard;                      { mark bit mask in global var }
  MouDefinePtr( Standard );                { display pointer in new form }
end;

{****************************************************************************}
{*  KbmEnd: called to end use of the functions and procedures of the     *}
{*          mouse module                                                 *}
{**----------------------------------------------------------------------**}
{*  Info:  - this procedure does not have to be explicitly called from    *}
{*           the application program since the procedure KbmInit defines  *}
{*           it as the Exit procedure                                    *}
{****************************************************************************}

{$F+}                            { must be FAR to be called as Exit procedure }

procedure KbmEnd;

var Regs : Registers;                { processor register for interrupt call }

begin
  MouHideMouse;                             { hide mouse pointer from screen }
  Regs.AX := 0;                                     { reset mouse driver }
  Intr( $33, Regs );                                { call mouse driver }

  FreeMem( BufPtr, BLen );                              { release memory }
  SetIntVec( $09, OldKbHandler );           { restore old kbd handler }
```

```
    ExitProc := ExitOld;                      { re-install old exit procedure }
  end;

  {$F-}                                          { disable FAR procedure }

  {***************************************************************************}
  {*  KbmInit: initialization procedure                                     *}
  {**-----------------------------------------------------------------------}
  {*  Input  : Columns = number of screen columns                          *}
  {*           Lines_  = number of screen lines                            *}
  {***************************************************************************}

  procedure KbmInit( Columns, Lines_ : byte );

  var Regs    : Registers;                { processor register for interrupt call }
      i       : byte;                     { loop counter as index in HandTab }

  begin

    {-- install new keyboard handler -----------------------------------------}

    Regs.ah := 2;                                 { convey control key status }
    intr( $16, Regs );                           { call BIOS keyboard interrupt }
    CurStatus := BiosKbFlag;                      { load BIOS keyboard status }

    GetIntVec( $09, OldKBHandler );            { Get address of int 09h handler }
    SetIntVec( $09, @NewKbHandler );               { install new handler }

    TLine := Lines_;                          { Store number of columns and }
    TCol  := Columns;                         { rows in global variables    }

    {-- allocate and fill buffer for mouse range ---------------------------}

    BLen := TLine * TCol;                    { number of characters on screen }
    GetMem( BufPtr, BLen );                  { allocate internal range buffer }
    KbmIBufFill( 0, 0, TCol-1, TLine-1, NO_MSRANGE );

    Regs.AX := 0;                                 { initialize mouse driver }
    Intr( $33, Regs );                            { call mouse driver }
    MouAvail := ( Regs.AX = $ffff );               { mouse available? }
    CurRng := NO_MSRANGE;                         { mouse pointer in no range }

    {-- allocate and initialize event queue -------------------------------}

    new( EvqPtr );                          { allocate event pointer on the heap }
    CurX    := TCol + 1;                        { position outside the screen }

    for i := 1 to 16 do                 { still no user event handler installed }
      HandTab[ i ].Call := FALSE;

    if ( MouAvail ) then                        { is there a mouse installed? }
      begin                                                        { Yes }
        MouSetMoveArea( 0, 0, TCol-1, TLine-1 );     { set range of movement }
```

```
    CurX    := KbmIGetX;                      { load current mouse position }
    CurY    := KbmIGetY;                      { in global variables        }
    StdPtr  := MouPtrMask( PTRSAMECHAR, PTRINVCOL ); { default pointer }
    OldPtr  := PTRVIEW( 0 );

    {-- install NewMouHandler mouse event handler  --------------------}

    Regs.AX := $000C;            { function number for "Set Mouse Handler" }
    Regs.CX := EV_MOU_ALL;                         { load event mask }
    Regs.DX := Ofs( NewMouHandler );     { offset address of handler }
    Regs.ES := Seg( NewMouHandler );     { segment address of handler }
    Intr( $33,  Regs );                         { call mouse driver }
  end;
  Eqp := MTCreateQueue( EVQ_LEN, sizeof( EVENT ) );
end;

{**----------------------------------------------------------------------**}
{** Starting code of unit                                                **}
{**----------------------------------------------------------------------**}

begin
  KbmInit( NumCol, NumLine );                       { initialize unit }
  ExitOld := ExitProc;                 { mark address of Exit procedure }
  ExitProc := @KbmEnd;                 { define KbmEnd as Exit procedure }
end.

;****************************************************************************;
;*                        K B M T A . A S M                               *;
;*------------------------------------------------------------------------*;
;*    Task             : Assembler module for the KBMT unit              *;
;*------------------------------------------------------------------------*;
;*    Author           : MICHAEL TISCHER                                 *;
;*    developed on      : 06/01/1989                                      *;
;*    last update       : 06/03/1989                                      *;
;*------------------------------------------------------------------------*;
;*    assembly          : TASM /MX KBMTA                                  *;
;*                        ... KBMT unit will access assembled OBJ file    *;
;****************************************************************************;

;== Constants ============================================================

STACK_LEN  equ 1024

;== Data segment =========================================================

DATA    segment word public

extrn  OldKbHandler : dword        ;Address of old Int 09 handler
DATA    ends

;== Program ==============================================================
```

```
CODE      segment byte public          ;Program segment

          assume CS:CODE               ;CS points to the code segment. Contents
                                       ;of DS, SS and ES are unknown

public    NewMouHandler                ;gives the Turbo Pascal program the
public    NewKbHandler                 ;option of supplying the address of the
                                       ;assembler handler

extrn     MtBlockFast     : far        ;MT unit procedures
extrn     MtContinueFast  : far

extrn     MouEventHandler : near       ;Turbo Pascal event handler to be called
extrn     KbHandler       : near       ;Keyboard handler to be called

;-- Stack and stack variables used by mouse handler -----------------------

MouSp     dw ?                         ;SP on calling NewMouHandler
MouSS     dw ?                         ;SS on calling NewMouHandler
MouStack  db STACK_LEN dup (?)         ;Stack for mouse handler
MouSEnd   equ this byte

;-- Stack and stack variables used by keyboard handler --------------------

InKb      db 0                         ;Displays recursion

KbSP      dw ?                         ;SP on calling NewKbHandler
KbSS      dw ?                         ;SS on calling NewKbHandler
KbStack   db STACK_LEN dup (?)         ;Stack for keyboard handler
KbSEnd    equ this byte


;--------------------------------------------------------------------------
;-- NewMouHandler: Event handler first called by the mouse driver, used for
;--                calling the Turbo Pascal MouEventHandler procedure
;-- Call from TP : Not allowed!

NewMouHandler proc far

          call  MtBlockFast            ;Suppress task switching

          ;-- Save current stack and initialize new stack -----------------

          mov   MouSP,sp
          mov   MouSS,ss
          cli                          ;Please do not disturb
          push  cs                     ;Set SS to CS
          pop   ss
          mov   sp,offset MouSEnd
          sti                          ;Come in, please

          push ax                      ;Get processor registers
          push bx
          push cx
```

```
        push dx
        push di
        push si
        push bp
        push es
        push ds

;-- Place arguments for calling the Turbo Pascal function -------
;-- onto the stack
;-- Call:
;--    MouEventHandler (EvFlags, ButStatus, x , y : integer );

        push ax                 ;Place event flags on the stack
        push bx                 ;Place mouse button status on the stack

        mov  di,cx              ;Place horizontal coordinate in DI
        mov  cl,3               ;Loop counter for coordinate number

        shr  di,cl              ;Divide DI (horizontal coord.) by 8
        push di                 ;and place on the stack

        shr  dx,cl              ;Divide DX (vertical coord.) by 8
        push dx                 ;and place on the stack

        mov  ax,DATA            ;Move segment address of data segment
        mov  ds,ax              ;AX into the DS register

        call MouEventHandler    ;Call the Turbo Pascal procedure

;-- Get needed registers from stack ----------------------------

        pop  ds
        pop  es
        pop  bp
        pop  si
        pop  di
        pop  dx
        pop  cx
        pop  bx
        pop  ax

;-- Toggle back to old stack -----------------------------------

        cli                     ;No interruptions, please
        mov  ss,MouSS           ;Load SS and SP
        mov  sp,MouSP
        sti

;-- Emulate interrupt call to procedure ------------------------

        pop  ax                 ;Get return address from stack
        pop  bx
```

683

```
              pushf                    ;Place flag register on stack
              push  bx                 ;Place ret. addr. on stack
              push  ax

              cli                      ;Disable interrupts
              call  MtContinueFast     ;Re-enable task switching
              iret                     ;Return to mouse driver

NewMouHandler endp

;--------------------------------------------------------------------------
;-- NewKbHandler: New keyboard handler, called by interrupt 09h to call the
;--               Turbo Pascal KbHandler procedure
;-- Call from TP :Not allowed!

NewKbHandler proc far

              cmp   InKb,0             ;Recursive call?
              je    KbNoRecur          ;No--> call Turbo handler

              ;-- Recursion. Call direct from old handler and return to caller

              push  ax                 ;Load Turbo data segment in order to
              push  ds                 ;enable the pointer with the address
              mov   ax,DATA            ;to the old keyboard handler
              mov   ds,ax

              assume ds:DATA
              pushf                    ;Emulate interrupt call
              call  [OldKbHandler]     ;Call old handler

              pop   ds                 ;Return registers
              pop   ax
              iret                     ;Return to caller

              assume ds:nothing

              ;-- Save current stack and install new stack ------------------

KbNoRecur:    call  MtBlockFast        ;Suppress task switching

              mov   InKb,1             ;Now in KbHandler
              mov   KbSP,sp
              mov   KbSS,ss
              push  cs                 ;Set SS to CS
              pop   ss
              mov   sp,offset KbSEnd

              sti                      ;Enable interrupt call

              push ax                  ;Get processor registers
              push bx
              push cx
```

```
            push dx
            push di
            push si
            push bp
            push es
            push ds

            in    al,60h            ;Read scan code from keyboard and
            xor   ah,ah             ;push onto stack as argument for
            push  ax                ;calling KbHandler

            mov   ax,DATA           ;Segment address of data segment AX
            mov   ds,ax             ;Place AX in the DS register

            assume ds:data

            pushf                   ;Simulate interrupt call to old
            call [OldKbHandler]     ;interrupt handler

            ;-- Place arguments needed for calling Turbo Pascal function ----
            ;-- on the stack
            ;-- Call:
            ;--    KbHandler( KbPort : byte );

            call  KbHandler         ;Call Turbo Pascal procedure

            assume ds:nothing

            ;-- get needed registers from stack ---------------------------

            pop   ds
            pop   es
            pop   bp
            pop   si
            pop   di
            pop   dx
            pop   cx
            pop   bx
            pop   ax

            ;-- toggle to old stack ---------------------------------------

            cli                     ;No interrupts
            mov   ss,KbSS           ;Reload SS and SP
            mov   sp,KbSP

            call  MtContinueFast    ;Re-enable task switching
            mov   InKb,0            ;No longer in keyboard handler
            iret                    ;Return to interrupted program

NewKbHandler endp

;----------------------------------------------------------------------------
```

```
CODE     ends              ;End of code segment
         end               ;End of program
```

14. Object Oriented Programming (OOP)

The OOP hysteria and the hype that preceded object oriented programming in 1989 and 1990 have died down somewhat. These have given way to the disappointing realization that you can use this technology to keep up with, but not surpass, the growing complexity of modern software. OOP programming also has its price, as Turbo Vision, the object oriented library from Turbo Pascal 6.0, convincingly demonstrates.

Only a handful of Pascal programmers make full use of the object oriented options of Turbo Pascal 5.5 and 6.0, although their number should increase in the years to come. This is reason enough for us to concern ourselves with the object oriented language extensions that Borland has given us, beginning with Turbo Pascal Version 5.5.

Unfortunately, there is no clear-cut standard, because while C has already established a standard for itself in the form of C++, no such standard for Pascal exists.

In 1988, one of the goals of SAA (System Application Architecture) was to standardize mainframes, workstations and PCs. This standardization allows users to control any application on any system. This permits unlimited data exchange between these systems, simplified user interfaces, abbreviated learning time for users and friendlier applications.

This chapter demonstrates object oriented programming techniques in Turbo Pascal. We've included a pair of source codes for creating an SAA unit, and the source code of a demonstration program, which creates a dialog box on the screen. This box includes many objects you might need for creating your own dialog boxes.

You may need to refer to the *OOP Guide* you received with Turbo Pascal Version 5.5, or the chapter on object oriented programming included in the Version 6.0 *User's Guide*, if you're unfamiliar with the techniques and principals of object oriented programming. This guide provides descriptions of many fundamental concepts of object oriented programming. Our own SAA unit presented here makes extensive use of these capabilities, but it's beyond the scope of this book to thoroughly explain OOP programming. Keep your documentation close at hand throughout this chapter.

Common User Interface (CUI)

The Common User Interface (CUI) portion of the SAA standard determines how the user selects program commands and options, and enters data needed by various parts of a program.

One of the results of the CUI standard was the development of software using the mouse as an effective input device. Developers and users discovered that it was easier and quicker to select information with the mouse than entering it from the keyboard. Most application software packages on the market today feature mouse support, including PCTOOLS, Microsoft Windows and Microsoft Word.

The CUI standard has copied the split screen and work area from Microsoft Windows and Microsoft Word into a menu bar where individual commands are displayed in a main menu. These commands may also have submenus containing a different set of commands. You should be familiar with menus and submenus from the integrated development environment of Turbo Pascal.

A dialog box appears, if a command is called, which requires additional data input (refer to the demo dialog box illustration). The dialog box contains several input fields to accept information from the user. Further input options are available, depending on the type of information to be entered (alphanumeric text, Yes/No query or selection from a list).

At the end of this chapter and on the companion diskettes which accompany this book you'll find a source code called SAADEMO.PAS. The compiled version of SAADEMO generates the following dialog box :

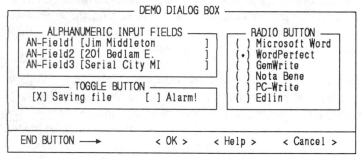

An example of a dialog box

Any number of dialog boxes can be created and the input accepted by the user. We chose implementing dialog control because it's handled extremely well in object oriented programming.

14.1   CUI Standard Dialog Boxes

A *dialog box* is a window displaying a number of dialog buttons or input fields. These buttons and fields allow you to communicate with the program.

Toggle buttons

The *toggle buttons* are identified by two square brackets [ ], expecting a yes or no response, followed by an option. When the option isn't active or the answer is no, the space between the brackets is empty. An X appears when the option is active or the answer is yes.

Radio buttons

The *radio buttons* are only in groups and are usually inside a box. They're built like toggle buttons but the options are enclosed by parentheses ( ) instead of square brackets. A small dot (•) appears next to an active option.

End buttons

The third group of switches are called *end buttons*. Every dialog box is required by the CUI standard to contain two end buttons. This lets you select and close the dialog box after completing or cancelling the data input.

A few suggestions and rules must be followed for the end buttons:

*   A less than character and greater than character < > enclose the text representing the command (e.g., <OK> or <Cancel>).

*   End buttons should always be located at the bottom right corner of the dialog box.

*   A horizontal line should separate them from the other switches.

*   They can be selected with the mouse or the keyboard.

*   Use the <Enter> key as a keyboard equivalent of OK and the <Esc> key to terminate the dialog box without accepting input, since you, as a developer, can determine the key that represents the end button option.

A proper SAA dialog box provides a third end button for "Help," usually invoked by pressing one of the function keys. It displays important information regarding the dialog box and its individual fields. Unlike <Cancel> and <OK>, which close the dialog box, <Help> returns to the dialog box.

By placing the mouse pointer at the desired location and clicking the mouse button, all of the options are easily selected. It's not necessary to have the pointer directly between the two enclosing characters; any area between the left character and the last letter is acceptable.

Open dialog box

The Open dialog box also contains a series of options. However, unlike a radio button, the Open dialog box usually contains additional options than those listed. These are selected by using the cursor keys or mouse to scroll through the list until the desired option(s) appear on the screen. This advantage allows more options to be available. You can select other files, change directories or change devices.

Open boxes are difficult to program. Because of this, they're the only standard SAA field types that aren't discussed in this chapter. The various techniques of object oriented programming are better demonstrated with simple field types.

In a dialog box, only one field accepts input from the keyboard at one time. Therefore, you must be able to move the cursor easily and quickly between the fields. To avoid applications using different keys, the CUI standard assigns the <Tab> and <Shift><Tab> keys for cursor movement between the fields.

How these elements can be implemented with programming will be discussed in the following section. If you've never used applications with dialog boxes, refer to the example SAADEMO.PAS, which uses dialog boxes for data input. The SAADEMO.PAS source contains many of the elements of SAA dialog control.

To experience the capabilities of a SAA dialog control system, use Turbo Pascal to convert this program into an executable EXE file. The following table lists the files required for the program to compile.

File	Assignment
SAADEMO.PAS	The demo program
SAA.PAS	Main part of the SAA unit
SAA2.PAS	Include file for SAA.PAS
WIN.TPU	Compiled screen/window unit (Chapter 6)
KBM.TPU	Compiled mouse/keyboard unit (Chapter 7)
KBMA.OBJ	Assembled form of the assembler module KBMA.ASM for the KBM unit

Files required for compiling SAADEMO.PAS into an executable EXE program

14.2 Development of Dialog Control

There must be a central control device to coordinate the activity of the individual fields in a dialog box. Without this control, it's impossible to determine if a selected key is meant for one field or another.

A *scheduler* must be used as a central control device to accept input from the keyboard or mouse and pass them to the proper fields. For the scheduler to be effective it must:

- Inform a field that it's active and that another field is now inactive.

- Pass information to various fields.

- Determine if the field accepts keyboard or mouse input.

You must determine whether the scheduler and the various fields should be implemented as one unit or remain separate. By remaining separate, you are able to implement the scheduler and the various fields as independent units, interconnected only through various procedures and functions. Therefore, they won't interfere with each other. This makes development easier and leaves space to develop other types of dialog fields.

The CUI standard also prefers this method. It requires a dialog field to be related to the information it accepts. There are no limits to creativity when the window applications define their own dialog fields. The predefined field types that appear must be saved so that you can use the new field types automatically. All this is implemented in the usual way. That is the only requirement the CUI standard demands of our creativity.

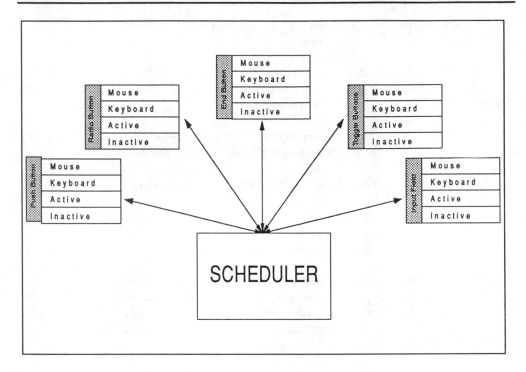

Communication between the scheduler and the various input fields

You may be wondering why object oriented programming techniques are required and what is considered an object.

Actually, everything in the dialog box is an object. This includes the scheduler and the various types of input fields.

These are the only two object types:

SAASched Scheduler control.

SAAT Abstract object type used for implementing existing field types (not for creating the dialog boxes themselves).

The SAAT object uses the inheritance principle in developing all of the CUI field types as a hierarchical system.

In the first level, all types of fields are a direct result of the SAAT type. From this type you can create additional objects in the second level. For example, you can develop an alphanumeric date field as an input field to automatically convert the input to an internal date format stored in the object.

The hierarchy equips all field types with different variables, methods, procedures and functions required for communication between the scheduler and the field. Every field requires a method for sending keyboard and mouse events. Also, the field must be notified if it's an active or inactive field.

All objects are of the SAAT type for the scheduler. Other object types developed in other units, the SAA unit or other programs cannot access the scheduler. The various field types implement individual routines for accepting keyboard and mouse events, depending on their method of operation. Therefore, the scheduler isn't allowed to access the routines from the SAAT type, which are dummy routines anyway.

Late binding is needed here. Late binding determines what type of object is actually accessed and is produced only at the time of the call of the communication routine in the scheduler. Instead of the universally valid routine from SAAT, the routine of this object type is addressed. This is only possible if the various communication routines are virtual methods. Unlike the static methods, virtual methods use late binding at run-time. This makes creating various field types and reducing errors in the dialog control much easier.

A structure, with pointers to routines of the object, must be passed to the scheduler and stored in a list. This ensures that, when the dialog box is created, the scheduler is operating normally in calling the communication routine of the field type. Turbo Pascal proceeds in this manner but the assignment is sent to the compiler. The resulting increase in program code size is negligible, and makes the program subject to fewer errors.

Another advantage is implementing the individual field types as object classes. An object automatically accesses only the variables of the currently addressed object. It's easier to accept several fields of the same type in a dialog box. The usual programming style could be used under more difficult conditions but the dialog control remains clearer.

It's possible the scheduler requires a second scheduler. If <Help> was selected in the dialog box, various end buttons will be needed in the help window on the screen. Since the scheduler is an object, a second scheduler can be implemented by creating and executing the new object type.

By creating a new object type scheduler, with enhanced features, this also allows extending the scheduler. It's possible to design a scheduler quickly and automatically by providing the end buttons <OK> and <Cancel> and inserting them into the dialog box, without the caller of the scheduler.

The various field types and schedulers are good examples of how object oriented programming enhances the dialog box and reduces the complexity of the program code.

14.3 The SAA Unit

The scheduler and program code for the various standard field types are in two units. The amount of data needed for creating this unit required us to split the SAA source into two files: SAA.PAS and SAA2.PAS. Compiling SAA.PAS includes SAA2.PAS in the process, thus combining the two sources into a single executable file.

SAA uses the predefined CRT unit, the WIN unit from Chapter 6 and the KBM unit from Chapter 7. SAA must access many of the routines and variables mentioned in these units (please refer to Chapters 6 and 7 for more information about the WIN and KBM unit, and your Turbo Pascal Reference Guide for more information about the CRT unit).

```
{*****************************************************************************
 *   SAA: A unit containing routines for implementing SAA dialog boxes.     *
 **-----------------------------------------------------------------------**
 *   Author          : MICHAEL TISCHER                                      *
 *   developed on     : 07/13/1989                                          *
 *   last update on   : 03/12/1990                                          *
 *****************************************************************************}

unit SAA;

interface

{*****************************************************************************
 * Imported units                                                           *
 *****************************************************************************}

uses Crt,                                       { Turbo Pascal CRT unit }
     Win,          { Turbo Pascal System Programming window unit ( Ch. 6 ) }
     Kbm;          { Turbo Pascal System Programming keyboard and mouse unit}
                   ( Ch. 7 ) }
```

Untyped constants

The various typed and untyped constants, which are accessible to other programs and units, are located in the interface part at the beginning of the unit. The first ten constants are very important for the development of proprietary dialog objects. They provide the codes which the communication routines of a dialog object return to the scheduler.

```
{***************************************************************************
* Declarations of typed and untyped constants, accessible from other units *
* or programs                                                              *
***************************************************************************}

const {-- Return codes of individual objects to scheduler ----------------}
      {-- for use with external subclasses              ----------------}

          RC_ACCEPTED  = 0;        { Return code : Accept keyboard/mouse event }
          RC_NEXT      = 1;        { Return code : Activate next object        }
          RC_PREV      = 2;        { Return code : Activate previous object    }
          RC_ACT_ME_T  = 3;        { Return code : Activate me w/ a keypress   }
          RC_ACT_ME_M  = 4;        { Return code : Activate me w/ the mouse    }
          RC_NOT_MINE  = 32;       { Return code : Key/mouse event not for me  }
          RC_TERMINATE = 127;      { Return code : End scheduler               }
```

The constants preceded by the RC_ prefix inform the scheduler whether the called object has processed the information and how it was passed. In the best case, the value RC_ACCEPTED would be returned by the two communication routines for the acceptance of mouse and keyboard events. This indicates that the key was accepted or the mouse event was processed. If the RC_ACCEPTED value is returned, the scheduler terminates its activity and waits for the next event from the mouse or keyboard.

The scheduler becomes active when the return message from an object contains the constants RC_NEXT or RC_PREV. The current object is now inactive. The object immediately preceding or following the dialog box becomes active.

The constant RC_NOT_MINE indicates that the current object couldn't use the key or mouse event that was passed and must now find an object ready to process this event. In this case, the scheduler checks all objects until one returns, either the RC_ACT_ME_T or RC_ACT_ME_M code, or it determines that the dialog objects cannot use the event.

The scheduler obtains the RC_TERMINATE code when an object, based on a mouse or keyboard event, terminates input and closes the dialog box. In such a case, one of three constants is passed, in addition to RC_TERMINATE, to indicate what caused the input to terminate.

```
          {-- Predefined exit codes for called procedures --------------------}

          RS_OK       = 0;          { Exit code Scheduler : End with OK     }
          RS_A_BREAK  = 1;          { Exit code Scheduler : End with break  }
          RS_HELP     = 256;        { Exit code Scheduler : Get help        }
```

These codes, preceded by the prefix RS_, are returned by the scheduler to the routine which caused its call. This completes the discussion on untyped public constants.

Typed constants

The typed constants determine the color codes for the screen elements in a dialog box, provided some form of color video card is in use. The predefined field types relate to these constants during the screen output. Their dialog objects should use these constants the same way so object colors remain consistent.

```
{-- Predefined color values for screen layout ----------------------}

CO_HOT      : byte = CYAN shl 4 + YELLOW;    { hotkey of an object }
CO_NORM     : byte = CYAN shl 4 + BLACK;     { normal line display }
CO_FRAME    : byte = CYAN shl 4 + WHITE;      { SAA window frame }
CO_WIN      : byte = CYAN shl 4 + BLACK;      { window background }
CO_ACT      : byte = CYAN;                     { current end button }
CO_INVERS   : byte = CYAN;        { current entry in selection window }
```

The SAA unit automatically switches to the proper monochrome attribute if it detects a monochrome card. This will be explained later in this chapter.

The programs and units can modify their programs, just as the SAA unit can reload these constants, to change dialog box appearance.

```
{******************************************************************************
 * Declarations of different objects and corresponding types                  *
 ******************************************************************************}

{** Common SAA objects. Ancestor objects for all SAA objects **************}

type SAAT       =
        object
        {-- Variables ----------------------------------------------------}

        RCode,                          { internal return code for scheduler }
        MCode    : word;     { internal message code for called procedure }
        IsActive,                                        { object active? }
        Hkeys    : boolean;                            { hotkey pressed? }

        {-- Statistical methods ------------------------------------------}

        constructor Init;                       { initialization procedure }
        procedure ReturnCode( var RC, XC : word );
        procedure WriteIt( X, Y : byte;
                           Text : string;
                           HKey : boolean );

        {-- Virtual methods ----------------------------------------------}

        procedure Open; virtual;                    { open an SAA object }
        procedure DispHKey; virtual;                   { display hotkeys }
        procedure SetActive( message : word ); virtual;        { activate }
```

```
        procedure SetPassive; virtual;              { deactivate SAA object }
        procedure Get_AKey( Key : word ); virtual;        { keyboard event }
        procedure GetMouse( NewX, NewY,                     { mouse event }
                            OldX, OldY : byte;              { received    }
                            FrstEv,
                            Pressed    : boolean;
                            Time       : longint ); virtual;
    end;

    SAAPtr       = ^SAAT;                      { pointer to common SAA objects }
```

When the object types are in the foreground, the constants are usually followed by the public type declarations.

The abstract SAAT type contains only the variables and method declarations which a dialog object requires the scheduler to use in the dialog box. This is in accordance with object hierarchy. Objects that follow will use all other variables and declarations.

The above routine declares an ancestor object. Unlike other Pascal types, the Turbo Pascal 5.5 type called Object passes object data to descendant objects (inheritance). The ancestor object contains important information that can be inherited by descendant objects.

The SAAT type contains a total of four variables. The first two are RCode and MCode. These variables store the code returned to the caller by the object after the call of its communication routines. RCode must accept one of the RC_... constants and MCode must accept one of the RS_... constants.

Note: MCode must only be loaded when the value RC_TERMINATE is entered in the RCode. At that time the content of MCode is returned to the caller of the scheduler.

The use of the IsActive Boolean variable allows an object to determine whether it's the active dialog object. This is important information for the majority of dialog objects. They must react differently to key and mouse events, when active or waiting to become active. We'll present examples during the analysis of the various objects and their methods.

An object stores the information that indicates whether a hotkey is available by using the HKeys variable (also a Boolean type). You may be familiar with hotkeys from the integrated development environment of Turbo Pascal. Press a hotkey combination to select individual commands from the various menus. Pressing <Alt> displays the hotkey characters. Pressing <Alt> and the desired key selects the appropriate object.

Every dialog object is represented by a hotkey in the CUI standards of the dialog control. The only faster method to activate an object is to use a mouse.

In addition to the four variables and communication routines presented in the preceding section, a series of methods are defined in the SAAT objects.

The following methods aren't required by either the scheduler or the individual dialog objects:

- Those the object itself requires.

- Those that differ from one object to another.

- Those which the scheduler always calls, in relation to the SAAT object, and not for the objects which proceed from it.

Init is used to initialize the object. It's called by a program to create an object and place it in a dialog box. Init also loads various parameters into the object. These parameters reflect the specific characteristics of the object, in relation to its object type.

The toggle buttons require different information than that is required for the alphanumeric input fields. This is why every kind of dialog object has its own individual Init method to accept parameters required by the object.

Theoretically, a program could enter the required information directly into the proper object variables. Because of the principle of data compression, every object should have an individual Init routine available. This already occurred for the standard dialog types defined in the SAA unit.

Init is considered a constructor and not a normal procedure or function. This is so that when objects are created through the heap, the Init method is called at the same time.

The ReturnCode procedure is the second static method defined by SAAT. This procedure works exclusively with the scheduler. After the call of a communication routine, the scheduler uses the ReturnCode procedure to query the internal variables RCode and MCode to start the object.

The objects use the WriteIt procedure to display strings containing the hotkeys on the screen.

Note: The hotkey of an object is directly integrated into the text. Any object can be coded to accept a hotkey to select an alphanumeric input field, or to activate the object (toggle buttons and radio buttons). This hotkey, which must be a letter or a number, must be preceded by a number sign (#) in the string. This makes it visible for the various routines.

The objects require the WriteIt procedure as a static method to display a string on the screen without displaying the pound sign as well. Through this method the hotkey can be highlighted in color. All other methods of the SAAT objects are virtual. They're called by the scheduler for communication with the object.

The Open and the DispHKey methods represent procedures similar to other methods. The Open procedure is responsible for bringing the object to the screen when building the dialog box. This always occurs when opening a dialog box, unlike the Init constructor, which only needs one call.

The DispHKey procedure is only called once during an input to a dialog box. It tells the object to highlight its hotkey in color on the screen. To do this, it uses the static WriteIt method, as described above.

As a rule, the hotkeys of the various objects aren't displayed until you press <Alt> to trigger the scheduler into calling the DispHKey method of all objects.

The four virtual methods, SetActive, SetPassive, Get_AKey and GetMouse, should already be familiar to you, since they correspond to the four communication procedures presented in the preceding section. They're an important link between the scheduler and the objects. This method will be discussed in more detail with the scheduler and the various predefined dialog objects.

Next let's consider the methods of the SAAT object type. These are typically dummy methods.

```
{*****************************************************************************
* Implementation of objects :  S A A T                                     *
*****************************************************************************}


{*****************************************************************************
*  Init : Initialization of SAA objects                                    *
*****************************************************************************}

constructor SAAT.Init;

begin
  RCode := RC_ACCEPTED;                  { initialize return code with 0 }
  MCode := 0;                          { initialize message code with 0 }
  HKeys := false;                           { still no hotkey display }
end;
```

```
{***************************************************************************
*  Open : opens an SAA object.                                             *
**-------------------------------------------------------------------------**
*  Info : blank superclass procedure needed, just as virtual methods and   *
*         functions are needed in subclasses.                              *
***************************************************************************}

procedure SAAT.Open;

begin
end;


{***************************************************************************
*  DispHKey : "displays" the hotkeys of an SAA object                      *
***************************************************************************}

procedure SAAT.DispHKey;

begin
  HKeys := true;                              { display text with hotkeys }
end;


{***************************************************************************
*  SetActive : activates an SAA object.                                    *
**-------------------------------------------------------------------------**
*  Input    : MESSAGE = bases of activation through the scheduler          *
***************************************************************************}

procedure SAAT.SetActive( message : word );

begin
  IsActive := true;                              { set active flag to TRUE }
end;


{***************************************************************************
*  SetPassive : deactivates an SAA object.                                 *
***************************************************************************}

procedure SAAT.SetPassive;

begin
  IsActive := false;                            { set active flag to FALSE }
end;


{***************************************************************************
*  Get_AKey : receives a keyboard event from scheduler.                    *
**-------------------------------------------------------------------------**
*  Input    : KEY = key value                                              *
***************************************************************************}

procedure SAAT.Get_AKey( Key : word );

begin
```

700

```
  RCode := RC_NOT_MINE;               { superclass cannot handle the key }
end;

{**************************************************************************
*  GetMouse : receives a mouse event from scheduler.                      *
**----------------------------------------------------------------------**
*  Input    : NEWX, NEWY = column, row of new mouse position              *
*             OLDX, OLDY = column, row of previous mouse position         *
*             FRSTEV     = first call for object?                         *
*             PRESSED    = left mouse button pressed?                     *
*             TIME       = time period of mouse event                     *
**************************************************************************}

procedure SAAT.GetMouse( NewX, NewY, OldX, OldY : byte;
                         FrstEv, Pressed        : boolean;
                         Time                   : longint );

begin
  RCode := RC_NOT_MINE;          { superclass cannot handle any mouse events }
end;
```

As the listing above shows, the various methods of the object class SAAT are dummies. These methods load only the various object variables and then return to the caller. The WriteIt and ReturnCode methods are more active.

```
{**************************************************************************
*  WriteIt : screen display for all SAA object texts.                     *
**----------------------------------------------------------------------**
*  Input    : X, Y = column, row of output                                *
*             TEXT = output text                                          *
*             HKEY = hotkey pressed?                                       *
**********************************************************************AAAAAAAA*}

procedure SAAT.WriteIt( X, Y : byte; Text : String; HKey : boolean );

var Position : byte;         { position of hotkey characters in output text }

begin
  Cursor( X, Y );                            { cursor to beginning of input }
  Position := Pos( '#', Text );
  if ( Position <> 0 ) then                                   { hotkey found }
    begin                               { yes, string appears divided }
      Delete( Text, Position, 1 );                            { delete # }
      WinPrint( X, Y, CO_NORM, Text );                   { display text }
      if ( Hkey ) then               { hotkey displayed in another color? }
        WinPrint( X + Position - 1, Y, CO_HOT, Text[ Position ] );
    end
  else                            { if no hotkey, then display entire text }
    WinPrint( X, Y, CO_NORM, Text );                      { display text }
end;
```

701

WriteIt checks the string passed as a hotkey marker, in the form of a number sign (#). If a number sign is not found, the string displays normally and the procedure terminates. If WriteIt finds a number sign character, it's removed from the string and brought to the screen. If the hotkey should be highlighted with color (HKey = true), the hotkey is displayed separately in the color provided.

```
{***************************************************************************
*  ReturnCode : returns object message to scheduler.                       *
*--------------------------------------------------------------------------*
*  Input    : RC = variable containing the return code taken from          *
*                   Get_AKey or GetMouse                                    *
*             X  = variable in which the Exit code is entered               *
*  Info     : the Exit code in XC is only valid when the preceding call     *
*              from GetMouse or Get_AKey was set with the RC_TERMINATE code. *
***************************************************************************}


procedure SAAT.ReturnCode( var RC, XC : word );

begin
  RC := Rcode;                                { return code for scheduler }
  XC := Mcode;                      { message code for called procedure }
  RCode := RC_ACCEPTED;             { default for subsequent calls from }
  Mcode := 0;                       { GetMouse and Get_AKey loads        }
end;
```

The scheduler uses the ReturnCode method to read the result of the virtual methods Get_AKey and GetMouse. These methods must store the RCode and MCode object variables. The ReturnCode method returns the two parameters to the caller and initializes them so that RC_ACCEPTED is returned during the next call. This is done, unless another code is specifically loaded into the RCode object variable. Since RC_ACCEPTED is the most frequently returned message, this saves work for the various GetMouse and Get_AKey methods.

You may have noticed the WriteIt method, for positioning of the cursor, which uses a procedure called Cursor. This procedure wasn't defined in the WIN unit or as a part of the object. It belongs to the five procedures because they're available to the scheduler and the various objects. They're the only routines in the SAA unit which are defined outside the objects.

Experienced OOP programmers should notice that these routines could have been defined as methods in an abstract object. They could then form the basis for the scheduler as well as the dialog objects. In the SAA unit these routines are normal procedures and functions.

The internal starting position for Write and Writeln commands and the position of the blinking cursor can be defined after the Cursor procedure combines the routines GotoXY and WinSetCursor from the WIN unit.

```
{**************************************************************************
*  Cursor : sets the internal display position for Write and Writeln, as  *
*           well as the position for the blinking screen cursor.          *
**-----------------------------------------------------------------------**
*  Input  : X = Column, Y = Row                                           *
*  Info   : The WIN unit distinguishes between the visible cursor and the *
*           text display position. This procedure positions BOTH cursors. *
**************************************************************************}

procedure Cursor( X, Y : byte );

begin
  GotoXY( X, Y );                              { set internal cursor }
  WinSetCursor( X, Y );                        { set visible cursor }
end;
```

The TBColor procedure combines two additional routines from the WIN unit (TextColor and TextBackground). These routines were made available by the standard CRT unit.

TBColor expects a color code consisting of background and foreground colors. For example, when Write and Writeln write into the video RAM, TBColor splits the data into two components and defines their colors. The data is then displayed in color through Write and Writeln.

```
{**************************************************************************
*  TBColor : sets the text and background colors.                         *
**-----------------------------------------------------------------------**
*  Input  : CVal = color value                                            *
*  Info   : Low  = text color, High = background color                    *
A A***********************************************************************}

procedure TBColor( CVal : byte );

begin
  TextColor( CVal and 15 );                    { set text color }
  TextBackground( CVal shr 4 );                { set background color }
end;
```

The HotKeyCode function is used to determine the hotkeys. It expects a string as a parameter and returns the key code of the hotkey, in this string, if a function result was available.

```
{**************************************************************************
*  HotKeyCode : establishes codes for hotkeys.                            *
**-----------------------------------------------------------------------**
*  Input  : TEXT = string which supplies the hotkey codes.                *
*  Output : Key code of the hotkeys                                       *
*  Info   : The hotkey is the first character in the string preceded by a *
*           #. To select the object, the <Alt> key must be pressed at the *
*           same time as the hotkey.                                       *
```

```
********************************************************************}

function HotKeyCode( Text : string ) : word;

const AltTab : array[ 0.. 42 ] of word     { table containing hotkey codes }
              = ( 385, 376, 377, 378, 379, 380, 381, 382,  { 0 - 7 }
                  383, 384, 0, 0, 0, 0, 0, 0, 0,            { 8 - @ }
                  286, 304, 302, 288, 274, 289, 290, 291,   { A - H }
                  279, 292, 293, 294, 306, 305, 280, 281,   { I - P }
                  272, 275, 287, 276, 278, 303, 273, 301,   { Q - X }
                  277, 300 );

var Where: byte;                 { position of #, PAlt code position in table }

begin
  {-- convey hotkey characters as string --------------------------------}

  Where:= Pos( '#', Text );                         { search for mark in text }
  if ( Where<> 0  ) then                                  { hotkey found? }
    begin                                { other characters following the # }
      Where:= Ord( Upcase( Text [ Where+ 1 ] ) ) - $30; { table pos. char. }
      HotKeyCode := AltTab[ Where ];                { read hotkey from table }
    end
  else
    HotKeyCode := 0;                                 { no hotkey in input text }
end;
```

The WithinRange function can be called to determine if the mouse pointer is in a certain area. It expects the coordinates, which will be tested, and the coordinates of the top left and bottom right corner of the area. WithinRange returns the value TRUE, if the coordinates given are within the area.

```
{**************************************************************************
 *  WithinRange : test for cursor position within specified rectangle.    *
 **--------------------------------------------------------------------**
 *  Input   : X, Y   = column, row of cursor                              *
 *            XL, YT = column, row of upper left corner of test range     *
 *            XR, YB = column, row of lower right corner of test range     *
 *  Output  : TRUE if cursor is within rectangle, otherwise FALSE          *
 **************************************************************************}

function WithinRange( X, Y, XL, YT, XR, YB : byte ) : boolean;

begin
  WithinRange := ( X >= XL ) and ( X <= XR ) and ( Y >= YT ) and ( Y <= YB );
end;
```

The final routine, which is not directly connected with an object, is the LeftPressed function. This KBM unit function determines whether you pressed down the left mouse button.

```
{****************************************************************************
*  LeftPressed : tests for a pressed left mouse button.                    *
**------------------------------------------------------------------------**
*  Input   : Buttons = Mouse button status                                 *
*  Output  : TRUE if left mouse button is pressed, otherwise FALSE         *
*  Info    : Uses mouse button codes as declared in KBM unit.              *
****************************************************************************}

function LeftPressed( Buttons : word ) : boolean;

begin
  LeftPressed := ( ( Buttons and Left_MouseB ) = Left_MouseB );
end;
```

The description of the SAA unit will be continued with the scheduler. Its operations are crucial to the caller of dialog boxes and the dialog objects. To see this refer to the definition of the object scheduler, which already reveals much about the work of the scheduler.

```
type SAASched    =
       object                                        { object scheduler }
         {-- Variables -------------------------------------------------}

         XL,                        { left window column, screen window  }
         YO,                        { top window row, screen window      }
         XR,                        { right window column, screen window }
         YU          : byte;        { bottom window row, screen window   }
         MouseX,                    { mouse position on exit from schedulers }
         MouseY      : byte;
         NumObj      : byte;            { number of displayed objects }
         WinHandle   : integer;             { screen window handler }
         First,                     { pointer to head of object list }
         Last      : SAAListPtr;     { pointer to end of object list }

         {-- Static methods -------------------------------------------}

         constructor Init( Cl1,                    { initialization }
                           Ro1,                    { of scheduler   }
                           Cl2,
                           Ro2 : byte );
         procedure Add( AnObject : SAAPtr );        { display an object }
         procedure Open;                            { open SAA window }
         function Run( StartPos  : word ) : word;            { run }
         procedure Close;                       { close SAA window }
         destructor Done;                         { release memory }
       end;

     SAASchedPtr = ^SAASched;                   { pointer to scheduler }
```

Every scheduler contains the following information as object variables:

- Upper left corner coordinates of the dialog window.

- Lower right corner coordinates of the dialog window.

- Any additional coordinates which store the position of the mouse pointer when exiting the scheduler.

This list is required when leaving the scheduler to respond to a help request and then to continue processing the dialog box through the scheduler. At that time the mouse pointer is automatically moved to the position that it occupied before leaving the scheduler.

In the object variable NumObj, the scheduler stores the number of the dialog fields it administers. The WinHandle variable accepts the handle of the dialog window. This is returned during the call of the WinOpenShadow procedure from the WIN unit.

The variables First and Last control the dialog objects in the form of a double chained list. These variables point to the beginning and end of this chain. Both are of type SAAListPtr, which is defined by the scheduler.

```
SAAListPtr  = ^SAAList;                        { pointer to object list }

SAAList     = record                  { enter object list in scheduler }
              OP     : SAAPtr;                       { pointer to object }
              Next,                              { pointer to next entry }
              Prev   : SAAListPtr;           { pointer to previous entry }
              end;
```

SAAListPtr isn't a direct pointer to a dialog object. Instead, it points to a structure of type SAAList. It makes the individual links of the chained list available and contains, along with a pointer to the dialog object, pointers to the preceding and following SAAList structure.

The scheduler can easily reach and access every object in the dialog box through the First and Last object variables and the pointers stored in the individual links. This chain must be created first. The methods, executed in the object declarations of the scheduler, are used for this. Remember, since a late binding isn't required for these routines, all methods are static.

Always use the Init method when working with the scheduler and creating a dialog box. The Init method initializes the scheduler in relation to a dialog object. However, the scheduler doesn't expect any dialog object information during the call of this method. It only stores the corner coordinates of the dialog window in the appropriate object variables.

Next we need to add dialog fields to the empty dialog box. The scheduler allows the Add method to be available in order to add the dialog fields. This augments the scheduler by one dialog field. The Add method expects a pointer to the object of the type SAAPtr, which it stores in the chained list of objects.

You should now have some understanding of the beginning of the dialog object hierarchy. The scheduler uses the SAAPtr to store a pointer to an object of SAAT type. Through this pointer the scheduler can reference everything following the object.

Note: The sequence in which the individual dialog objects are registered through Add are important in processing the dialog box. The sequence dictates fields to be activated when you press the <Tab> or <Shift><Tab> keys. <Tab> moves the registration from the first field to the second, from the second to the third, etc. <Shift><Tab> moves the registration from the first field to the last field in the box, etc. The CUI standard allows movement in a dialog box with these keys from top to bottom and from left to right. The individual objects should be registered with the scheduler in this sequence.

Although not always necessary, we recommend starting the dialog input after registering the individual objects. The scheduler can be created with Init and Add during the program start and called later when you have selected the correct command.

Init and Add calls don't have to be repeated for every dialog input. Once created, the scheduler is available during the entire program and can be used as often as you like for dialog input.

Input process

The input process occurs in two steps. First, the Open method must be called to display the dialog box and its fields. Only then is the Run call able to accept input. The number of the field where the dialog input starts must be passed to this method. When the scheduler receives this information, you're no longer able to use the field registered with Add to start the dialog input.

Run returns the code indicating the end of the input as the result of a function. This code is returned as a message of type RC_TERMINATE. The object loads this code into its MCode object variable. Until this point, only the end buttons allow an end to dialog box input. The code returned informs you which of the end buttons was selected.

Since Run doesn't automatically close the dialog box, you can return to the box before it disappears. Instead, the dialog box remains on the screen. If an input error occurs, you can return to the dialog box by recalling Run without leaving the dialog box.

You should use the Close method call to close the dialog box. However, this method removes only the dialog box from the screen. The Done method removes the scheduler and objects from the screen. This terminates any tasks running through the scheduler. If you recall the scheduler, you must also recall Init to initialize the scheduler and Add to display the objects.

The following program code illustrates the methods of a scheduler:

```
{********************************************************************************
 * Implementation of objects :  S A A S c h e d                                 *
 ********************************************************************************}


{********************************************************************************
 *  Init : initializes a SAA scheduler.                                         *
 **----------------------------------------------------------------------------**
 *  Input    : Cl1, Ro1 = upper left window corner,                             *
 *             Cl2, Ro2 = lower right window corner                             *
 ********************************************************************************}

constructor SAASched.Init( Cl1, Ro1, Cl2, Ro2 : byte );

begin
  NumObj := 0;                          { no objects displayed up until now }
  First := nil;                          { initialize list in specified }
  Last := nil;                           { scheduler objects as blank   }
  XL := Cl1;                                  { left column frame }
  YO := Ro1;                                     { top row frame }
  XR := Cl2;                                 { right column frame }
  YU := Ro2;                                { bottom row frame }
  MouseX := ( XR + XL ) div 2;              { position mouse in   }
  MouseY := ( YU + YO ) div 2;              { center of SAA window }
end;
```

The Init method initializes the object variables so that no dialog objects are registered. The dialog box occupies the area indicated by the caller on the display.

The Add method is more complex in program logic. It has several responsibilities:

- Creates an entry of SAAList type.

- Fills SAAList type with the pointer to the dialog object that was passed.

- Attaches this to the end of the list of the dialog objects.

```
{********************************************************************************
 *  Add : displays an object for scheduler.                                     *
 **----------------------------------------------------------------------------**
 *  Input    : ANOBJECT = pointer to an inserted object                         *
 ********************************************************************************}

procedure SAASched.Add( AnObject : SAAPtr );

var ListP : SAAListPtr;                    { help pointer to list insertion }

begin
  new( ListP );                            { reserve memory for new list entry }
```

```
   Inc( NumObj );                        { increment number of displayed objects }
   ListP^.OP := AnObject;                    { direct pointer to new object }
   if ( First = nil ) then                        { ListP still empty? }
     begin                                    { yes, alternate handling }
       ListP^.Next := nil;             { next object still not available }
       ListP^.Prev := nil;           { previous object still not available }
       First := ListP;          { ListP is first entry in the object list }
       Last  := ListP;               { ListP is also last single entry }
     end
   else                                          { ListP is not empty }
     begin
       ListP^.Next := nil;               { still no entries following }
       ListP^.Prev := Last;              { preceding was last entry }
       Last^.Next := ListP;      { old last entry has another following it }
       Last := ListP;                     { ListP is new last entry }
     end;
 end;
```

Initial access to the various dialog objects occurs in the Open method. A window for the dialog box opens. This window is filled with spaces and surrounded with a simple frame. Then the list with the registered objects is processed and a call to the Open method of the object brings the object to the screen.

```
{*****************************************************************************
 *   Open : opens an SAA window.                                            *
 *****************************************************************************}

procedure SAASched.Open;

var Pos : SAAListPtr;                       { help pointer to object list }

begin
  WinHandle := WinOpenShadow( XL, YO, XR, YU );          { open SAA window }
  WinFill( XL, YO, XR, YU, #32, CO_WIN );                  { fill window }
  WinFrame( XL, YO, XR, YU, SIN_FR, CO_FRAME );            { draw frame }
  Pos := First;                      { position to beginning of object list }
  while ( Pos <> nil ) do                        { execute entire ListP }
    begin
      Pos^.OP^.Open;                   { call open procedure for objects }
      Pos^.OP^.SetPassive;                        { deactivate objects }
      Pos := Pos^.Next;                      { continue with next object }
    end;
end;
```

In addition, the SetPassive procedure is called inside this loop to ensure every dialog object remains inactive.

The Run method is the most complex and comprehensive method of the object type scheduler. It coordinates the selection of the dialog objects and the information input within these objects.

First it processes the chained list of the objects until it has reached the object specified by its caller as the Start object. It uses the SetActive method to activate this object.

Even though the RC_NEXT code was sent as the reason for activating the object, it isn't significant in the SetActive method. The object assumes that it was activated by its predecessor, which returned the <Tab> key code to the scheduler.

Then the mouse pointer is set to the position which was determined with the object variables MouseX and MouseY in the scheduler. This coordinate is also loaded into the local variables OldX and OldY. We'll discuss the roles of these variables in a moment.

The scheduler enters a loop after leaving the Repeat command. It leaves this loop only when receiving the RC_TERMINATE code from an object.

```
{***************************************************************************
 *  Run : controls and governs input in a SAA dialog box.               *
 *-------------------------------------------------------------------------*
 *  Input   : StartPos = number of the first active object              *
 *  Output  : return code of the scheduler                              *
 ***************************************************************************}

function SAASched.Run( StartPos : word ) : word;

var HPtr,                        { pointer for executing the object list }
    ActOb        : SAAListPtr;      { pointer to current active object }
    NewAction,                   { test for new readable mouse event }
    Action    : Event;              { keyboard or mouse event }
    OldX,
    OldY      : byte;            { buffer for cursor, mouse position }
    Answer,
    ExitCode  : word;            { return code of object on the scheduler }

begin
  {-- Pass pointer to current object and activate object ------------------}

  ActOb := First;                { pointer to the first object on the list }
  for Answer := 1 to StartPos-1 do          { pointer to starting object }
    ActOb := ActOb^.Next;
  ActOb^.OP^.SetActive( RC_NEXT );                { activate current object }

  Answer := RC_ACCEPTED;                    { initialize object return codes }
  ExitCode := 0;

  MouMovePtr( MouseX, MouseY );                     { set mouse pointer }
  OldX := MouseX;                        { note current mouse position }
  OldY := MouseY;

  {-- Scheduler work loop -------------------------------------------------}

  repeat
```

710

```
MouShowMouse;                                        { display mouse pointer }
KBMEventWait( EV_ALL, Action );       { wait for keyboard or mouse event }
MouHideMouse;                                          { hide mouse pointer }

with Action do                          { convey keyboard or mouse event }
  begin
    {-- <Alt> key pressed = display hotkeys --------------------------}

    if ( EvntCode = EV_KEY_STATUS ) and ( StateKey = KEY_ALT ) then
      begin                          { <Alt><hotkeys> display all objects }
        OldX := WhereX;                           { store cursor column }
        OldY := WhereY;                              { store cursor row }

        HPtr := First;                   { pointer to start of object list }
        while ( HPtr <> nil ) do                  { execute entire list }
          begin
            HPtr^.OP^.DispHKey;                        { display hotkey }
            HPtr := HPtr^.Next;               { pointer to next object }
          end;

        Cursor( OldX, OldY );            { cursor returned to old position }
      end

    {-- Normal keystroke ---------------------------------------------}

    else if ( EvntCode = EV_KEY_PRESSED ) then          { key pressed? }
      begin        { yes, send key to active object and evaluate reaction }
        ActOb^.OP^.Get_AKey( Key );
        ActOb^.OP^.ReturnCode( Answer, ExitCode );

        {-- Convert return message of active object ------------------}

        if ( Answer = RC_NEXT ) then          { next object activated? }
          begin                                                 { yes }
            ActOb^.OP^.SetPassive;           { deactivate old object }
            if ( ActOb^.Next = nil ) then             { end of list? }
              ActOb := First          { yes, continue from top of list }
            else
              ActOb := ActOb^.Next;   { no, continue with next object }
            ActOb^.OP^.SetActive( RC_NEXT );    { activate new object }
          end

        else if ( Answer = RC_PREV ) then { previous object activated? }
          begin                                                 { yes }
            ActOb^.OP^.SetPassive;           { deactivate old object }
            if ( ActOb^.Prev = nil ) then            { start of list? }
              ActOb := Last           { yes, continue from end of list }
            else
              ActOb := ActOb^.Prev;{ no, continue with previous object }
            ActOb^.OP^.SetActive( RC_PREV );  { activate newest object }
          end

        else if ( Answer = RC_NOT_MINE ) then    { key not acceptable? }
```

711

```
            begin                                    { no, search for addresses }
              HPtr := First;            { start search at beginning of list }
              repeat
                HPtr^.OP^.Get_AKey( Key );                          { send key }
                HPtr^.OP^.Returncode( Answer, ExitCode );
                if ( Answer = RC_NOT_MINE ) then
                   HPtr := HPtr^.Next;              { not found, continue }
              until ( Answer <> RC_NOT_MINE ) or ( HPtr = nil );

              if ( HPtr <> nil ) then                        { answer found? }
                begin                                                  { yes }
                  ActOb^.OP^.SetPassive;          { deactivate old object }
                  ActOb := HPtr;                { point to new active object }
                  if ( Answer = RC_ACT_ME_T ) then
                     ActOb^.OP^.SetActive( RC_ACT_ME_T );        { activate }
                end;
          end;
      end

  {-- Mouse event, left mouse button was pressed --------------------}

  else if ( EvntCode = EV_LEFT_PRESS ) then
    begin
      OldX := AbsColumn;              { mouse not moved, but the left    }
      OldY := Abs_Row;               { button has been pressed          }
      HPtr := First;

      {-- Search for mouse event addresses ------------------------}

      repeat
        HPtr^.OP^.GetMouse( AbsColumn, Abs_Row, OldX, OldY,
                            true, LeftPressed( Buttons ), Time );
        HPtr^.OP^.Returncode( Answer, ExitCode );
        if ( Answer = RC_NOT_MINE ) then             { event occurred? }
          HPtr := HPtr^.Next;                        { no, continue }
      until ( Answer <> RC_NOT_MINE ) or ( HPtr = nil );

      if ( HPtr <> nil ) then                        { nothing found? }
        begin                                                  { yes }
          if ( Answer = RC_ACT_ME_M ) then
            begin        { object would like to be activated by mouse }
              ActOb^.OP^.SetPassive;          { deactivate old object }
              ActOb := HPtr;                { direct to new active object }
              ActOb^.OP^.SetActive( RC_ACT_ME_M );          { Activate }
              MouShowMouse;                   { display mouse pointer }

              {-- Mouse loop, as long as left mouse button is pressed }

              repeat                              { mouse action loop }
                Delay( MouseDelay );                  { mouse delay }
                OldX := AbsColumn;        { mark old mouse position }
                OldY := Abs_Row;
```

```
                         {-- If no event is ready for, display until the user -}
                         {-- presses the mouse button again                    -}

                         KBMPeekEvent( NewAction );                { read event }
                         if ( NewAction.EvntCode <> EV_NO_EVENT ) then
                            KBMGetEvent( NewAction );               { get event }

                         if ( ( NewAction.EvntCode = EV_MOU_MOVE ) or
                              ( NewAction.EvntCode = EV_LEFT_REL ) )  then
                           begin                       { new sensible mouse event }
                             OldX := AbsColumn;            { mark mouse position }
                             OldY := Abs_Row;
                             Action := NewAction;             { use new event }
                           end;

                         HPtr^.OP^.GetMouse( AbsColumn, Abs_Row, OldX, OldY,
                                             false, LeftPressed( Buttons ),
                                             Time );
                         HPtr^.OP^.Returncode( Answer, ExitCode );
                       until ( EvntCode = EV_LEFT_REL ) or
                             ( Answer = RC_TERMINATE );

                     if ( Answer = RC_TERMINATE ) then    { scheduler ended? }
                        MouHideMouse;
                   end;
                end;
              end;
            end;
        until ( Answer = RC_TERMINATE );

        Run := ExitCode;                         { end code for called procedure }
        ActOb^.OP^.SetPassive;                   { deactivate last active object }
        MouseX := OldX;                               { stores mouse column }
        MouseY := OldY;                                  { stores mouse row }
     end;
```

The scheduler displays the mouse pointer in this loop. The mouse pointer disappears again after receiving an event from the KbmEvenWait procedure. This has a very basic background. Usually an access to the screen of the GetMouse or Get_AKey method of the current object occurs because of user input or a mouse event. Since the mouse pointer must be hidden in this case, this task can be removed from the various objects by performing it in the scheduler.

All Get_AKey and GetMouse methods assume that the mouse pointer is hidden during their calls. This leaves them free to perform any screen manipulations.

The scheduler starts to evaluate the event after receiving it from KbmGetEvent. If, at that time, the scheduler determines that you pressed the <Alt> key, the scheduler sends the hotkeys of the various objects to the screen. The scheduler processes the list of the objects in a loop and calls the DispHKey method for every object.

The scheduler proceeds in a completely different way when receiving a normal key. The key must be sent to the active object. Next it uses the Get_AKey and ReturnCode methods to evaluate how the object reacts.

If it determines from the result of the ReturnCode that the object returned the RC_NEXT or RC_PREV code, a call of the SetPassive method deactivates the current object. The ActOb pointer, which always points to the current object, is set to the object following or preceding the current object. Which object depends on the code received. A call to the SetActive method activates the object indicated by the ActOb pointer.

However, if the current object can't process the key, the scheduler receives the RC_NOT_MINE message. In this case, the scheduler calls the Get_AKey method for all registered objects with the character that it received. It does this until an object processes the key or determines that no object can use this key.

If the scheduler cannot find an object it continues to process the object through the next loop. If it still cannot find an object, which can use this key, the current object is made inactive and the scheduler activates a new object.

The scheduler passes the RC_ACT_ME_T code when it calls the SetActive method. This is done so the object recognizes that it has requested to become active.

If no messages were left by the objects for the scheduler, an RC_ACCEPTED or an RC_TERMINATE message is produced. In either case the scheduler remains inactive. In the case of RC_TERMINATE, it simply terminates the query loop. It starts a new loop execution when receiving an RC_ACCEPTED message.

If it receives a key from a mouse event and not from KbmEventWait, the scheduler becomes active only when the left mouse button is pressed. All other mouse events will not affect it. Neither the movement of the mouse nor pressing the right (or middle) mouse button causes an object to execute.

In this case, however, the scheduler processes all registered objects and calls their GetMouse method until it finds an object to be activated by the mouse event. If it cannot find an object, the mouse event remains unused and the scheduler continues in its processing loop with the query of an event.

If an object has stored the RC_ACT_ME_M code in its RCode object variable, the scheduler deactivates the previously active object.

The scheduler uses a call of the SetActive method to activate the object. It passes the code RC_ACT_ME_M to the SetActive method to ensure that the object knows it was activated by a mouse event. Then the scheduler starts executing a special mouse loop. It leaves this loop only when the left mouse button is released or if the scheduler receives the RC_TERMINATE message from the current object.

Since an event is always created and processed when the left mouse button is pressed, the scheduler must use its own query loop. This is true even if the mouse wasn't moved. The reason is in the alphanumeric input fields.

For example, move the mouse pointer over a character in an alphanumeric input field. Press and hold the left mouse button. This activates the input field and highlights the field beneath the mouse pointer.

As you move the mouse pointer, the input cursor follows through in the input field. This results in a new input position in the input field as the mouse pointer is moved.

The CUI standard requires a command to scroll the field when the mouse pointer reaches the left or right border of the input field. This is only possible with fields not occupying the full width of the screen. This process should continue as long as the mouse pointer is at either side of the input field and you hold down the left mouse button.

Since the mouse pointer may remain in the same location on the screen, the KBM unit doesn't create any events which can be queried through the KbmEventWait procedure. The scrolling of the input field is only possible when the mouse is moved.

The special mouse loop uses the KbmPeekEvent procedure to determine whether an event is available. If it's available it's accepted and evaluated by KbmGetEvent from the KBM unit.

If the KbmPeekEvent call determines that no event is available, the last event is re-evaluated and, in the case of an alphanumeric input field, continues scrolling.

You may need to include a time delay in this mouse loop. The speed at which the event is repeated might make the entries in the input field unreadable on a high-speed computer.

Working with two different constants you can achieve a delay in the scheduler, and a field dependent delay in the alphanumeric input field.

Use the MouseDelay constant at the beginning of the loop and MouseInpWait constants to regulate the processing speed of mouse events.

MouseInpWait is used inside the alphanumeric input fields as the field is scrolled to the left or right. It also ensures that the scrolling isn't repeated too quickly and the character in the input field doesn't flash across the screen. You can use MouseInpWait to set the mouse delay when developing new field types.

```
{*****************************************************************************
* Constants, accessible to other programs and units                        *
*****************************************************************************}

const MouseDelay   = 5;                        { normal delay rate for mouse }
      MouseInpWait = 20;                        { delay rate for mouse input }

      Left_MouseB = 1;              { comparison for test of left mouse button }
```

The end of the mouse query loop also marks the end of the scheduler's large processing loop. The scheduler actually ends only when the RC_TERMINATE message is passed by the current object.

It then loads the End code queried during the call of the ReturnCode method as the function result for the caller. The current object becomes inactive. Finally, the scheduler stores the current mouse position in the Object variable.

The Run method finishes execution and returns to its caller. It can recognize, from the returned function result, which end button terminated the input.

It depends on which end button was selected, but under certain conditions it will recall the Run method of the scheduler. Alternatively, it will remove the scheduler from the screen by calling the Close method.

Both the window and all of its objects disappear from the screen. WinClose deletes the dialog box.

```
{*****************************************************************************
*  Close : closes an SAA window.                                            *
*****************************************************************************}

procedure SAASched.Close;

begin
  WinClose( true );                      { close window and restore background }
end;
```

Even after calling both the Close method and Run, the scheduler can return to the screen at any time to accept input. The one exception is calling the Done method. This method releases the individual entries in the chained list of objects. Once Done is called, Init and Add must re-register the entries before the scheduler can be accessed again.

```
{*****************************************************************************
*  Done : releases reserved memory from the scheduler.                      *
*****************************************************************************}

destructor SAASched.Done;
```

```
begin
  {-- Execute list of objects and release allocated memory ---------------}

  Last := First;                     { both pointer to beginning of list }
  while ( First <> nil ) do          { as long as list still isn't empty }
    begin
      First := First^.Next;            { a pointer to the next element }
      Dispose( Last );                          { release memory }
      Last := First;                 { set both pointers to rest of list }
    end;
end;
```

You should now be familiar with dialog control, the scheduler and the SAAT object. We still need to discuss the various dialog objects, defined as the SAAT object types, in the SAA unit. While the object declarations relating to it begin the SAA.PAS file, the methods of the various objects are in the SAA2.PAS Include file.

SAA2.PAS includes the methods of the toggle buttons, radio buttons, end buttons and the alphanumeric input fields. In the following pages we'll discuss how to create these objects.

The simplest object to create is a single toggle button consisting of the button and related option. It only needs two conditions. These are toggled back and forth by using the mouse or keyboard.

However, a toggle button requires, for its control, an entire series of Object variables of the SAAT object type. In addition, text is also stored to the screen location where the hotkey starts. The text follows the button and may include a hotkey for activating the button.

The code of this hotkey is stored as the variable hotkey. The most important information is ON or OFF (or the current condition of the button) stored in the Boolean variable PushSet.

```
{** SAA object toggle button ************************************************}

    SAAPushB   =
      object ( SAAT )                               { subclass of SAAT }
      {-- Variables ----------------------------------------------------}

        X,                                   { screen column button }
        Y       : byte;                      { screen row button }
        Text    : string[ 40 ];                    { button text }
        Hotkey  : word;                       { code for hotkey }
        PushSet : boolean;                    { toggle button set? }

      {-- Static methods -----------------------------------------------}

      constructor Init( Cl, Ro  : byte;          { initialization of }
                        Name    : string;        { toggle buttons    }
                        Default : boolean );
```

```
{-- Virtual methods ------------------------------------------------}

    procedure Open; virtual;                        { toggle button design }
    procedure DispHKey; virtual;          { display toggle button hotkey }
    procedure SetActive( message : word ); virtual;      { activate it }
    procedure Get_AKey( Key : word ); virtual;        { keyboard event }
    procedure GetMouse( NewX, NewY,            { receive mouse event }
                        OldX, OldY : byte;
                        FrstEv,
                        Pressed    : boolean;
                        Time       : longint ); virtual;
end;
```

Unlike the other dialog objects presented in the following pages, the SAAPushB object type doesn't add to the methods already controlling the object. With SAAPushB's simple structure, it uses predefined methods and redefines them for its own purposes.

A toggle button, like all other dialog objects, provides a special form of Init to accept the required information to initialize a toggle button. These include the screen location of the Button, its text and its preset condition.

Note: The screen coordinates of dialog objects refer to the distance of the object from the upper left corner of the dialog box, not to the absolute location on the screen. Objects may not be affected by dialog box movement.

To ensure that the coordinates relate to the current window and the dialog box, methods such as Open, Get_AKey and GetMouse must reference the screen with functions VL, VO, VR and VU from the WIN unit.

Virtual method declaration is similar to the declaration in the SAAT object type. Any differences would be immediately returned as errors by Turbo Pascal. However, the various methods in the object declarations of SAAPushB must be redeclared because SAAPushB replaces the previous methods with its own methods.

Next we'll consider the Init methods used to initialize a toggle button. The initialization routine of the object type is called with SAAT.Init, derived from the object type SAAPushB. This is an important step to enhance an object hierarchy. It isolates an object type from possible changes in the previous levels.

All dialog types coming from this object use this capability to prevent possible changes in defining SAAT. SAAPushB isn't alone in calling the initialization routine from the SAAT object.

After calling this method, the initialization routine loads the parameters passed into the variables provided. The HotKeyCode function helps the routine determine the keycode of the hotkey, which the caller indicated in the button text that was passed.

718

```
{**********************************************************************
 * Implementation of object :  S A A P u s h B                        *
 **********************************************************************}

{**********************************************************************
 *  Init : initializes SAA object toggle buttons.                     *
 **------------------------------------------------------------------**
 *  Input    : Cl, Ro  = column, row of toggle button                 *
 *             NAME     = text of toggle button                       *
 *             DEFAULT  = default value of toggle button              *
 **********************************************************************}

constructor SAAPushB.Init( Cl, Ro  : byte; Name : string;
                           Default : boolean );

begin
  SAAT.Init;                                { initialize superclass }
  X := Cl;                                  { display text column }
  Y := Ro;                                    { display text row }
  Text := Name;                             { button display text }
  PushSet := Default;                          { button status }
  HotKey := HotKeyCode( Text );          { filter hotkey from text }
end;
```

Any methods already declared by SAAT and not formulated as dummies are used by the initialization routines of the various dialog types. Also, all virtual DispHKey methods use their predecessors from the SAAT object type, to set the corresponding object variable. They're also used to accept other commands which may become necessary due to future updates of the SAAT object type.

The method displays its hotkey by calling the WriteIt method inherited from SAAT.

```
{**********************************************************************
 *  DispHKey : displays the hotkey of a toggle button.                *
 **********************************************************************}

procedure SAAPushB.DispHKey;

begin
  SAAT.DispHKey;                          { call superclass procedure }
  WriteIt( VL( X )+4, VO( Y ), Text, Hkeys );       { display text }
end;
```

The Open method uses the WriteIt method to send a toggle button to the screen. This method also sends the brackets and text and places the X in the brackets, indicating an active button as a default.

```
{***************************************************************************
*   Open : opens the object toggle button.                                *
***************************************************************************}

procedure SAAPushB.Open;

begin
  SAAT.Open;                                          { open common object }
  WriteIt( VL( X ), VO( Y ), '[ ] ' + Text, Hkeys );      { display text }
  if PushSet then                                     { toggle button marked? }
    WinPrint( VL( X )+1, VO( Y ), CO_NORM, 'X' )         { yes, display X }
end;
```

The blinking cursor doesn't have to be set in the Init, the DispHKey or the Open methods. It's only needed when the toggle button is activated. The SetActive method handles the responsibility of setting the blinking cursor. SetActive calls its predecessor method from the object hierarchy and moves the cursor to the character between the object's two brackets.

```
{***************************************************************************
*   SetActive : activates a toggle button object.                         *
**----------------------------------------------------------------------**
*   Input    : MESSAGE = reason for activation by scheduler               *
***************************************************************************}

procedure SAAPushB.SetActive( message : word );

begin
  SAAT.SetActive( message );              { superclass activation procedure }
  Cursor( VL( X + 1 ), VO( Y ) );                  { cursor for marking }
end;
```

The Get_AKey and GetMouse methods are more comprehensive than the previously introduced methods of SAAPushB. These methods react to the previous events instead of simply loading some fixed variables.

Get_AKey tests whether the hotkey of the toggle button was received by SAAPushB. If the hotkey is received, it triggers the method to send a RC_ACT_ME_T message which instructs the scheduler to activate the object, provided it was not already active. Simultaneously, the status of the buttons is switched, which involves manipulating the object variable PushSet and the character between the two brackets to the new button status.

```
{***************************************************************************
*   Get_AKey : receives keyboard event from scheduler.                    *
**----------------------------------------------------------------------**
*   Input    : KEY = key value                                            *
***************************************************************************}

procedure SAAPushB.Get_AKey( Key : word );
```

```
begin
  {-- test hotkey for object ---------------------------------------------}

  if ( Key = Hotkey ) then
    begin
      RCode := RC_ACT_ME_T;                           { activate object }
      PushSet := not PushSet;                         { invert marking }
      if PushSet then                          { toggle button marked? }
        WinPrint( VL( X )+1, VO( Y ), CO_NORM, 'X' )
      else
        WinPrint( VL( X )+1, VO( Y ), CO_NORM, ' ' )
    end

  {-- Other keys can only be used with the active object ------------------}

  else if ( IsActive ) then
    begin
      {-- Display key code -----------------------------------------------}

      case Key of
        TAB     : RCode := RC_NEXT;                { activate next object }
        BACKTAB : RCode := RC_PREV;            { activate previous object }
        CDOWN,
        CLEFT   : PushSet:= false;                     { delete marking }
        CUP,
        CRIGHT  : PushSet := true;                        { set marking }
        SPACE   : PushSet := not PushSet;              { invert marking }
        else      RCode := RC_NOT_MINE;     { key not intended for object }
      end;

      {-- Display button with new marking --------------------------------}

      if PushSet then                          { toggle button marked? }
        WinPrint( VL( X )+1, VO( Y ), CO_NORM, 'X' )
      else
        WinPrint( VL( X )+1, VO( Y ), CO_NORM, ' ' )
    end

  {-- Object inactive and not a hotkey - not acceptable ------------------}

  else
    RCode := RC_NOT_MINE;                             { object inactive }
end;
```

If a key other than the hotkey is received, the method continues evaluating the key, if the object is active. This can easily be determined with the IsActive object variable. If the object isn't active, the RC_NOT_MINE code is returned and the key isn't accepted. Otherwise, the key is evaluated with a case statement.

The <Tab> and <Shift><Tab> keys instruct the object to send an RC_NEXT or RC_PREV message to the scheduler. These messages prompt the scheduler to activate the dialog object preceding or following it.

The status of the toggle buttons is changed with the cursor keys. The predefined RC_ACCEPTED code is returned to the scheduler only when a cursor key, the <Tab> or <Shift><Tab> keys are pressed. Another code cannot be accepted into the RCode object variable.

This is a technique which can be observed with many other dialog objects. RCode is loaded, with a certain value, when the message RC_ACCEPTED should not be returned to the scheduler. The case statement reads the key when no specified keys were received and rejects invalid keys.

After the evaluation of the key, the button is set to its new status by placing either a space or an uppercase X between the two brackets (either [ ] or [X]). Although resulting in more interaction with the button than necessary, this method takes little time and uses simple logic.

In querying the mouse, the GetMouse method must proceed from Get_AKey. This can be seen in the variety of the parameters which the method accepts from the scheduler.

The GetMouse method uses the coordinates of the current mouse position for its first parameter. These coordinates refer to the entire screen, not just the upper left corner of the dialog box. You will need to move the mouse pointer out of the dialog box.

The GetMouse method also has an additional mouse coordinate to reflect the mouse location during the previous call of this method. The GetMouse method can always determine, through the OldX and OldY parameters, the mouse pointer location during the previous call. This permits the method to find out whether the mouse pointer moved and the distance whether it moved.

Note: Using the Run method of the scheduler, the GetMouse method of an object can only be called in a special mouse loop. The scheduler enters this loop only after you press the left mouse button.

Two Boolean type parameters, FrstEv (to inform the method about its assignment) and Pressed, follow the two coordinate indications.

There is an important difference, if the method was called at the beginning of the mouse loop; if a mouse event falls into the activity range of an object; or if the method is called later in the scheduler's mouse loop, after the object declared itself responsible for the first event.

If the method is called at the beginning of the loop, it only informs the scheduler whether it wants to become active with the RC_ACT_ME_M event or remain inactive with RC_NOT_MINE.

The method must process the event if called later in the mouse loop. The Pressed parameter helps the method determine whether the left mouse button is still pressed.

The last parameter is called Time. It reflects the time of the event as returned to a caller (e.g., by KbmEventWait of the KBM unit). This information is important in reading and reacting to double clicks used in dialog box control.

```
{**************************************************************************
*  GetMouse : receives mouse event from scheduler.                       *
**----------------------------------------------------------------------**
*  Input   : NEWX, NEWY = column, row of new mouse position              *
*            OLDX, OLDY = column, row of previous mouse position         *
*            FRSTEV     = first call for object?,                        *
*            PRESSED    = left mouse button pressed?                     *
*            TIME       = time period of mouse event                     *
**************************************************************************}

procedure SAAPushB.GetMouse( NewX, NewY, OldX, OldY : byte;
                             FrstEv, Pressed       : boolean;
                             Time                  : longint );
var Action : boolean;                        { object action flag necessary }

begin
  if FrstEv then                  { event does not depend on object, test }
    if WithinRange( NewX, NewY, VL( X ), VO( Y ),
                 VL( X ) + Length( Text ) + 1, VO( Y ) ) then
      begin
        RCode := RC_ACT_ME_M;                { "activate me" in scheduler }
        Action := true;                      { action within the object }
      end
    else
      begin
        RCode := RC_NOT_MINE;                { "not for me" in scheduler }
        Action := false;                     { no action i object }
      end
  else
    begin
      RCode := RC_ACCEPTED;               { "key accepted" in scheduler }
      Action := ( NewY <> OldY ) and ( NewY = VO( Y ) ) and Pressed;
    end;
  if ( Action ) then
    begin                         { mouse event for object, execute action }
      PushSet := not PushSet;                            { invert flag }
      MouHideMouse;                              { hide mouse pointer }
      if PushSet then                   { toggle button marked? }
        WinPrint( VL( X )+1, VO( Y ), CO_NORM, 'X' )
      else
```

```
        WinPrint( VL( X )+1, VO( Y ), CO_NORM, ' ' );
      MouShowMouse;                              { show mouse pointer again }
    end;
  end;
end;
```

The GetMouse method of the object class toggle button checks whether this is the first call in the mouse loop. This method is responsible for discovering a relationship between itself and the mouse event. The object related WithinRange procedure helps GetMouse determine whether the mouse pointer is in the screen area it controls. If so, it returns the code RC_ACT_ME_M and switches the toggle buttons by loading the local variable Action with the value TRUE.

If the call of WithinRange indicates that the mouse event was not meant for the toggle button, the code RC_NOT_MINE is returned and the Action flag is set to FALSE to prevent changing the buttons.

The message RC_ACCEPTED is returned to the scheduler, if this isn't the first call of the method. In this case (the event processed with switching the buttons only occurs when the left mouse button remains pressed), the mouse pointer is in line with the buttons, but it wasn't in line with the buttons in the preceding call.

Unlike the Get_AKey method, the mouse pointer must be removed from the screen when output occurs in the GetMouse method. This doesn't automatically occur in the scheduler's mouse loop, which is permanent and isn't executed exactly when an event is actually available (unlike the main operating loop of the scheduler). If the mouse pointer was automatically hidden before the GetMouse method was called, the result is a distracting flicker of the mouse pointer and output doesn't occur in GetMouse.

Radio buttons as dialog objects

The radio buttons as dialog objects are more complex than the toggle buttons. They actually involve two objects consisting of several buttons. A group of radio buttons should be represented by a descendant object of the SAAT type.

This is why an object is defined with the SAARButtons type. This type has only one static method (Init) to initialize the object.

```
{** SAA object radio buttons *********************************************}

  SAARButtons =
    object                              { data block for a radio button }
    {-- Variables -------------------------------------------------}

    X,                                              { screen column }
    Y    : byte;                                       { screen row }
    Text : string[ 40 ];                              { button text }
```

```
{-- Static methods ----------------------------------------------}

constructor Init( XL,                           { initialize data block }
                  YT   : byte;
                  Name : string );
end;
```

As usual, the Init procedure, acting as constructor, is responsible for loading the object variables describing the object.

```
{***********************************************************************
* Implementation of objects :  S A A R a d i o B                      *
***********************************************************************}


{***********************************************************************
*  Init : initializes individual radio buttons.                       *
**-------------------------------------------------------------------**
*  Input   : XL, YT = column, row,                                    *
*            NAME   = text of buttons                                 *
***********************************************************************}

constructor SAARButtons.Init( XL, YT : byte; Name : string );

begin
  X := XL;                                      { column of left character }
  Y := YT;                                      { row of button }
  Text := Name;                                 { button text }
end;
```

An object of the toggle button type must control the various buttons of the object SAARButtons type. Therefore, they're placed in a dummy array, called SAARButtonF, and can accept up to 500 individual buttons.

```
type SAARButtonF = array[ 1 .. 500 ] of SAARButtons;     { radio button }
                                                         { data block   }
```

This array isn't used during the declaration of toggle buttons, or in the dialog object radio button. It only offers a possibility to define a pointer to an array with a certain number of buttons.

```
type SAARButtPtr = ^SAARButtonF;       { pointer to radio button data block }
```

Through the pointer type SAARButtPtr, access to the individual buttons occurs exclusively in the various methods of accessing the dialog object radio button. The array contains only the amount of buttons that are displayed on the screen. We assumed that an array of 500 buttons is more than sufficient for most developers.

The pointer is fixed on an array in the object for the dialog type radio button, called SAARadioB, and is derived from the SAAT basic object. In addition, the object stores the numbers of the buttons and the current buttons in the range from 1 to n.

```
SAARadioB   =
  object ( SAAT )                                      { subclass of SAAT }
    {-- Variables -------------------------------------------------------}

    NumBut    : byte;                              { number of buttons }
    RDataPtr  : SAARButtPtr;             { pointer to button data block }
    CurBut    : byte;                              { current buttons }

    {-- Static methods --------------------------------------------------}

    constructor Init( Number  : byte;         { initialization of    }
                      RData    : pointer;     { radio button objects }
                      Current  : byte );
    procedure DispButton( Pos : byte );

    {-- Virtual methods -------------------------------------------------}

    procedure Open; virtual;                      { create radio buttons }
    procedure DispHKey; virtual;   { display hotkey for radio buttons }
    procedure SetActive( message : word ); virtual;       { activate }
    procedure Get_AKey( Key : word ); virtual;        { keyboard event }
    procedure GetMouse( NewX, NewY,            { receive mouse event }
                        OldX, OldY : byte;
                        FrstEv,
                        Pressed    : boolean;
                        Time       : longint ); virtual;
  end;
```

In addition to the required Init constructor and virtual communication methods, a radio button also contains the DispButton method. This method, reserved for internal use in the object, displays an individual button on the screen.

Note: The Init method expects an untyped pointer, as a pointer to the array, with the various buttons. Then the caller doesn't have to construct a type conversion to type SAAEButtPtr, or store the individual buttons in an array of 500 elements of type SAARButtonF.

```
{********************************************************************
*  Init : initializes radio button SAA objects.                   *
**----------------------------------------------------------------**
*  Input   : NUMBER  = number of buttons in object               *
*            RDATA   = pointer to the RData field                *
*            CURRENT = number of active buttons                  *
********************************************************************}

constructor SAARadioB.Init( Number  : byte; RData : pointer;
```

```
                              Current : byte );

begin
  SAAT.Init;                                    { initialize superclasses }
  NumBut := Number;                          { number of buttons in object }
  RDataPtr := RData;                  { pointer to array [ 1.. Number ] of RData }
  CurBut := Current;                        { point to currently active button }
end;
```

The DispButton method is the workhorse of the above methods. It's always called where a complete radio button, the hotkey of a button or the dot between parentheses (•) must be displayed. The execution speed stays the same, since these methods display the button as a whole. Also, the scheduler spends most of its time waiting for input, costing only a few clock cycles.

```
{*********************************************************************
*  DispButton : displays a button marker.                          *
**---------------------------------------------------------------**
*  Input   : POS = position in RData block                         *
*********************************************************************}

procedure SAARadioB.DispButton( Pos : byte );

var HelpP : SAARButtPtr;                    { help pointer for RData block }

begin
  MouHideMouse;                               { hide mouse pointer }
  with RDataPtr^[ Pos ] do                    { row to be displayed }
    begin
      WriteIt( VL( X ), VO( Y ), '( ) '+ Text, Hkeys );    { display button }
      if ( Pos = CurBut ) then                          { button current? }
        WinPrint( VL( X )+1, VO( Y ), CO_NORM, #7 );        { yes, mark it }
      Cursor( VL( X + 1 ), VO( Y ) );            { set cursor to marking }
    end;
  MouShowMouse;                               { re-display mouse pointer }
end;
```

One method used frequently by DispButton is the Open method for the radio button, which displays the various buttons on the screen.

```
{*********************************************************************
*  Open : opens a radio button object.                             *
*********************************************************************}

procedure SAARadioB.Open;

var i : byte;                                           { loop counter }

begin
  SAAT.Open;                                    { call superclass }
  for i := 1 to NumBut do                        { display all buttons }
    DispButton( i );
end;
```

The DispHKey method acts in a similar way while displaying the hotkeys. DispButton must also be called for each button that's assigned a hotkey.

```
{***************************************************************************
 *  DispHKey : displays hotkeys for radio buttons.                         *
 ***************************************************************************}

procedure SAARadioB.DispHKey;

var i : byte;                                            { loop counter }

begin
  SAAT.DispHKey;                              { call superclass procedure }
  for i := 1 to NumBut do                        { display all buttons }
    DispButton( i );
end;
```

Our DispButton method, workhorse, is called inside SetActive. This time it only sets the mouse pointer to the current button.

```
{***************************************************************************
 *  SetActive : activates a radio button object.                           *
 **-------------------------------------------------------------------**
 *  Input    : MESSAGE = base for activating scheduler                     *
 ***************************************************************************}

procedure SAARadioB.SetActive( message : word );

begin
  SAAT.SetActive( message );          { call superclass activation procedure }
  DispButton( CurBut );                      { place cursor in current row }
end;
```

The Get_AKey method operates basically the same way for radio buttons as it does for toggle buttons. The main difference is that with radio buttons the Get_AKey method must consider several buttons instead of only one.

Get_AKey reads the hotkeys of all the radio buttons. The reading continues until the method activates the object or ignores the passed key.

Another difference between the object type toggle buttons is the reaction after pressing a cursor key. The cursor keys move between the various radio buttons belonging to this object, instead of selecting a single button.

```
{***************************************************************************
 *  Get_AKey : receives keyboard event from scheduler.                     *
 **-------------------------------------------------------------------**
 *  Input    : KEY = key value                                             *
 ***************************************************************************}
```

```
procedure SAARadioB.Get_AKey( Key : word );

var ButtonPtr : SAARButtPtr;                        { pointer to button data }
    DummyPos,                                            { loop counter }
    Old        : byte;                          { buffer for old active button }

begin
  {-- Hotkey tests for a radio button ------------------------------------}

  DummyPos := 1;
  while  ( DummyPos <= NumBut ) and
         ( Key <> HotKeyCode( RDataPtr^[ DummyPos ].Text ) ) do
    Inc( DummyPos );
  if ( DummyPos <= NumBut ) then              { appropriate end button found }
    begin
      Old := CurBut;                                  { mark old button }
      CurBut := DummyPos;                             { direct to new button }
      DispButton( Old );                     { display old button as normal }
      DispButton( CurBut );                          { new display button }
      RCode := RC_ACT_ME_T;                          { activate object }
    end

  {-- Other keyboard events must only be possible on the active object ----}

  else if ( IsActive ) then
    begin
      {-- <Tab> key => "activate next object" message --------------------}

      if ( Key = Tab ) then
        RCode := RC_NEXT

      {-- <BackTab> key => "activate previous object" message ------------}

      else if ( Key = BACKTAB ) then
        RCode := RC_PREV

      {-- <Cursor Dn> key => select next radio button --------------------}

      else if ( Key = CDOWN ) then
        begin
          Dummypos := CurBut;                         { mark old button }
          if ( CurBut = NumBut ) then                     { last row? }
            CurBut := 1                    { then continue with first row }
          else
            Inc( CurBut );                 { otherwise continue with next row }
          DispButton( DummyPos );                   { deactivate old button }
        end

      {-- <Cursor Up> key => select previous radio button ----------------}

      else if ( Key = CUP ) then
        begin
```

```
            DummyPos := CurBut;                              { mark old button }
            if ( CurBut = 1 ) then                               { first row? }
              CurBut := NumBut                   { then continue with last row }
            else
              Dec( CurBut );                { otherwise continue with previous row }
            DispButton( DummyPos );                   { deactivate old button }
          end

      {-- Key could not be accepted by object ----------------------------}

        else
          RCode := RC_NOT_MINE;
        DispButton( CurBut );                             { display new row }
      end

    {-- Object inactive and no hotkey pressed, key not accepted -------------}

      else
        RCode := RC_NOT_MINE;
  end;
```

Although the GetMouse method considers the changed conditions, it doesn't operate much differently from its toggle button equivalent.

```
{*****************************************************************************
 *  GetMouse : receives mouse event from scheduler.                         *
 **-----------------------------------------------------------------------**
 *  Input   : NEWX, NEWY = column, row of new mouse position               *
 *            OLDX, OLDY = column, row of previous mouse position          *
 *            FRSTEV     = first call for object?,                         *
 *            PRESSED    = left mouse button pressed?                      *
 *            TIME       = time period for mouse event                     *
 *****************************************************************************}

procedure SAARadioB.GetMouse( NewX, NewY, OldX, OldY : byte;
                              FrstEv, Pressed        : boolean;
                              Time                   : longint );

var Action : boolean;                             { object action flag needed }
    Pos,                                          { counter for button number }
    Old    : byte;                            { memory for old active button }

begin
  if ( Pressed ) then                               { mouse button pressed? }
    begin
      if FrstEv then                 { event does not depend on object, test }
        begin
          Pos := 1;                     { number of buttons to be compared }
          while ( ( VO( RDataPtr^[ Pos ].Y ) <> NewY ) or
                  ( VL( RDataPtr^[ Pos ].X ) > NewX ) or
                  ( VL( RDataPtr^[ Pos ].X ) +
                    Length( RDataPtr^[ Pos ].Text ) + 3 < NewX ) )
```

730

```
                  and ( Pos < NumBut ) do
               Inc( Pos );                           { increment position number }
           if ( VO( RDataPtr^[ Pos ].Y ) = NewY ) and
              ( VL( RDataPtr^[ Pos ].X ) <= NewX ) and
              ( VL( RDataPtr^[ Pos ].X ) +
                Length( RDataPtr^[ Pos ].Text ) + 3 >= NewX ) then
             begin                                   { new current button found }
               RCode := RC_ACT_ME_M;              { "activate me" in scheduler }
               Action := true;                     { action within the object }
             end
           else
             begin
               RCode := RC_NOT_MINE;                 { "not for me" in scheduler }
               Action := false;                        { no action in object }
             end
         end
       else            { events following caused in mouse movement w/ button }
         begin
           RCode := RC_ACCEPTED;                   { "key accepted" in scheduler }
           Action := ( NewY <> OldY );     { action only when status changes }
         end;
       if ( Action ) then
         begin                          { mouse event for object, execute action }
           Pos := 1;                        { number of buttons to be compared }
           while ( VO( RDataPtr^[ Pos ].Y ) <> NewY ) and
                 ( Pos < NumBut ) do
             Inc( Pos );                           { increment position number }
           if ( VO( RDataPtr^[ Pos ].Y ) = NewY ) then
             begin
               Old := CurBut;                               { mark old button }
               CurBut := Pos;                  { direct to new current button }
               DispButton( Old );            { display old button as normal }
               DispButton( CurBut );             { display new current button }
             end;
         end;
     end
   else if ( FrstEv ) then
     RCode := RC_NOT_MINE                      { event not intended for object }
   else
     Rcode := RC_ACCEPTED;                  { event accepted without reaction }
  end;
```

End buttons as dialog objects

The end buttons, which closely resemble the radio buttons, are the only buttons that we haven't yet discussed out of the three predefined button types.

A separate object named SAAEButtons is defined here, describing one end button. This object registers the screen location of the button, the button text on the screen, the hotkey for the button and the return code. After you select this button, the scheduler returns this code to its caller.

A constructor is available to initialize a single end button with the Init method.

```
{******************************************************************
* Implementation of objects :   S A A E n d B                    *
******************************************************************}


{******************************************************************
*   Init : initializes one end button.                           *
**--------------------------------------------------------------**
*   Input    : XL, YT = column, row of left button border        *
*              KEYC   = shortcut key                             *
*              RCODE  = return code for scheduler                *
*              NAME   = button text                              *
******************************************************************}

constructor SAAEButtons.Init( XL, YT : byte; KeyC : word;
                              RCode  : word; Name  : string );

begin
  X := XL;                               { column of left border }
  Y := YT;                                     { row of button }
  KeyCode := KeyC;                           { default end key }
  Returncode := RCode;{ end code for scheduler when end button is selected }
  Text := Name;                                 { button text }
end;
```

The individual end buttons are placed in SAAEButtonF type array. The SAAEButtPtr type
is defined as a pointer to an array of this type.

```
type SAAEButtonF = array[ 1 .. 500 ] of SAAEbuttons;{ array w/ end buttons }
type SAAEButtPtr = ^SAAEButtonF;          { pointer to array w/ end buttons }
```

A pointer is used because the buttons are stored in an array separate from the actual end
button object. This should be familiar to you from the radio button objects. In addition, the
object stores the number of the buttons, the number of the currently selected button and the
default button for ending input (usually the <Enter> key).

The end button object number is loaded as the number of the current button through the
Open method. It must be loaded before opening the buttons. This ensures that a certain end
button is active as the dialog box opens.

```
    SAAEndB      =
      object ( SAAT )                          { a group of end buttons }

        {-- Variables -------------------------------------------------}

        RDataPtr   : SAAEButtPtr;                    { pointer to data }
        NumBut,                              { number of end buttons }
        Default,                        { number of default end buttons }
        Current    : byte;                        { current end button }
```

```
      {-- Static methods -----------------------------------------------}

      procedure DispButton( No    : byte;              { display end button }
                            Mouse : boolean );
      constructor Init( Defaultkey,                    { end button object }
                        NumKey    : byte;              { initialization    }
                        RData     : pointer );

      {-- Virtual methods ----------------------------------------------}

      procedure Open; virtual;                  { create and display object }
      procedure DispHKey; virtual;              { display end button hotkeys }
      procedure SetActive( message : word ); virtual;{ activate end bttn }
      procedure Get_AKey( Key : word ); virtual;        { keyboard event }
      procedure GetMouse( NewX, NewY,                  { return mouse event }
                          OldX, OldY : byte;
                          FrstEv,
                          Pressed    : boolean;
                          Time       : longint ); virtual;

   end;
```

Another similarity between radio buttons and end buttons is in implementing a DispButton
method for the end button object class. Along with the number of the button to be
displayed, the caller must also indicate whether the button was selected with the mouse. End
buttons selected by the mouse pointer are marked in color, which isn't the case in other
button types.

```
{*******************************************************************************
 *  DispButton : displays text of an end button                               *
 **-------------------------------------------------------------------------**
 *  Input   : NO    = position in RData block                                 *
 *            MOUSE = row selected by mouse?                                   *
 *  Info    : When a button is selected by the mouse, the button changes to   *
 *            inverse video.                                                   *
 *******************************************************************************}

procedure SAAEndB.DispButton( No : byte; Mouse : boolean );

var Dummy : string[ 80 ];                            { help string for output }

begin
  with RDataPtr^[ No ] do                            { row to be shown }
    begin
      {-- Button selected by mouse -----------------------------------------}

      if ( Mouse ) then
        begin
          Dummy := Text;                             { copy text for editing }
          if ( pos( '#', Dummy ) > 0 ) then          { marking received? }
```

733

```
              Delete( Dummy, Pos( '#', Dummy ), 1 );        { yes, delete it }
          WinPrint( VL( X ), VO( Y ), CO_ACT, '< ' + Dummy + ' >' );
        end

    {--- No input currently resulting from button selection w/ mouse ----}

    else if ( No = Current ) then
      begin
        WinPrint( VL( X ), VO( Y ), CO_HOT, '<' );    { highlighted edges }
        WriteIt( VL( X ) + 1, VO( Y ), ' '+Text+' ', Hkeys);
        if ( Pos( '#', Text ) > 0 ) then              { text highlighted? }
          WinPrint( VL( X ) + Length(Text) + 2, VO( Y ), CO_HOT, '>' )
        else                                          { no markers in text }
          WinPrint( VL( X ) + Length(Text) + 3, VO( Y ), CO_HOT, '>' );
      end

    {-- Display normal button ------------------------------------------}

    else
      WriteIt( VL( X ), VO( Y ), '< ' + Text + ' >', Hkeys );
    Cursor( VL( X ) + pos( '#', text ) + 1, VO( Y ) );    { set cursor }
  end;
end;
```

The Init, DispHKey and Open methods are similar to the corresponding methods for the radio button object class.

```
{*****************************************************************************
* DispHKey : displays through hotkey an end button object.                  *
*****************************************************************************}

procedure SAAEndB.DispHKey;

var i : byte;                                          { loop counter }

begin
  SAAT.DispHKey;                           { call superclass procedure }
  for i := 1 to NumBut do                     { display all buttons }
    DispButton( i, false );
end;

{*****************************************************************************
* Init : initializes the end button object.                                 *
**-------------------------------------------------------------------------**
* Input    : DEFAULTKEY = default end key                                   *
*            NUMKEY     = number of end keys                                 *
*            RDATA      = pointer to start of RData block                    *
*****************************************************************************}

constructor SAAEndB.Init( DefaultKey, NumKey : byte; RData : pointer );

begin
```

```
      SAAT.Init;                          { call superclass initialization procedure }
      RDataPtr := SAAEButtPtr( RData );            { direct pointer to RData block }
      NumBut := NumKey;                              { mark amount of RData }
      Default := DefaultKey;                        { direct to default end key }
   end;

   (*****************************************************************************
   *  Open : opens an end button type object.                                 *
   ****************************************************************************)

   procedure SAAEndB.Open;

   var i : byte;                                        { loop counter }

   begin
      SAAT.Open;                             { call superclass open function }
      Current := Default;              { current end button is default button }
      for i := 1 to NumBut do                      { execute all buttons }
         DispButton( i, false );                      { display buttons }
   end;
```

The SetActive method already shows a considerable difference between radio buttons and end buttons. This originates in button selection using the <Tab> and <Shift><Tab> keys. You cannot activate the end buttons using these keys, but you can select one of the end or other buttons. Thus, if the dialog box opens with the first end button selected, pressing <Tab> selects the next end button. Pressing <Shift><Tab> selects the preceding button.

The SetActive method of this object class evaluates the code passed to determine why the object was activated.

```
   {*****************************************************************************
   *  SetActive : activates the end button object.                            *
   **-----------------------------------------------------------------------**
   *  Input    : MESSAGE = activation base through the scheduler              *
   ****************************************************************************)


   procedure SAAEndB.SetActive( message : word );

   var Dummy : byte;                          { buffer for old active button }

   begin
      SAAT.SetActive( message );           { superclass activation procedure }
      if ( message <> RC_ACT_ME_M ) then       { activation through keyboard? }
         begin                          { yes, then display new current button }
            Dummy := Current;                     { mark old current button }
            if ( message = RC_NEXT ) then          { call followed by <Tab>? }
               Current := 1                  { yes, set first button as current }
            else if ( message = RC_PREV ) then         { call using <BackTab>? }
               Current := NumBut;            { yes, set last button as current }
            if ( Dummy <> Current ) then         { current button been changed? }
```

```
        DispButton( Dummy, false );            { display old button as normal }
      DispButton( Current, false );              { cursor on current button }
    end;
  end;
```

SetActive remains inactive if it determines that the object should be activated by a mouse event. It determines this after calling the method with the same name from the basic object SAAT.

The GetMouse method has performed all the necessary functions. If the activation was the result of a keyboard event, GetMouse checks whether an RC_NEXT or an RC_PREV message was received.

An RC_NEXT message indicates that <Tab> was pressed and the previous object activates the end button. In this case the next end button is selected as the current end button.

If SetActive receives an RC_PREV message, a jump from a following object to the end button can only occur with <Shift><Tab>. In this example, the previous end button is selected as the current button.

For the <Tab> and <Shift><Tab> keys in the Get_AKey method, executing the object type end button must be interpreted the same way. When a jump cannot be executed to a preceding or following end button, A PC_PREV or PC_NEXT message is sent. Therefore, the change to another dialog object is inevitable.

When the input is completed and either <Enter> or the corresponding key for the button is pressed, the routine RC_TERMINATE sends a message and ends the input.

The key corresponding to a button was defined through a call of the Init method of the button. When this key is pressed, the return code of the button is returned to the caller of the scheduler. In this case it's the <Enter> key.

```
{*****************************************************************************
 *  Get_AKey : receives keyboard event from scheduler.                      *
 **-----------------------------------------------------------------------**
 *  Input    : KEY = key value                                              *
 *****************************************************************************}

procedure SAAEndB.Get_AKey( Key : word );

var OlderButton : byte;                        { buffer for old button }
    Pos         : byte;                { position pointer in RData block }

begin
  {-- <Tab> key -----------------------------------------------------------}

  if ( Key = TAB ) then
```

```
    if ( Current = NumBut ) then                          { end of object? }
       begin                                    { yes, continue to next object }
          RCode := RC_NEXT;       { <Tab> =  "next object active" in scheduler }
          OlderButton := Current;                          { mark old button }
          Current := Default;               { default button is again current }
          DispButton( OlderButton, false );   { display old button as normal }
          DispButton( Current, false );                 { mark default button }
       end
    else
       begin                               { no, jump to next end button only }
          OlderButton := Current;                          { mark old button }
          inc( Current );                         { increment current button }
          DispButton( OlderButton, false );   { display old button as normal }
          DispButton( Current, false );                 { mark default button }
       end

{-- <BackTab> key -----------------------------------------------------}

else if ( Key = BACKTAB ) then
    if ( Current = 1 ) then                               { start of objects? }
       begin                                { yes, continue to previous object }
          RCode := RC_PREV;          { "previous object active" in scheduler }
          OlderButton := Current;                          { mark old button }
          Current := Default;               { default button is again current }
          DispButton( OlderButton, false );   { display old button as normal }
          DispButton( Current, false );                 { mark default button }
       end
    else
       begin                               { no, jump to previous end button }
          OlderButton := Current;                          { mark old button }
          dec( Current );                         { decrement current button }
          DispButton( OlderButton, false );    { display old button as normal }
          DispButton( Current, false );                 { mark default button }
       end

{-- <Enter> key -----------------------------------------------------}

else if ( Key = CR ) then                        { end with current button }
    begin
       RCode := RC_TERMINATE;                                   { terminate }
       Mcode := RDataPtr^[ Current ].Returncode;         { set return code }
    end

{-- Test for button activation through hotkey or direct access ----------}

else
    begin
       {-- Check for hotkey or shortcut key ------------------------------}

       Pos := 1;                                   { use as position counter }
       while ( HotKeyCode( RDataPtr^[ Pos ].Text ) <> Key ) and
             ( RDataPtr^[ Pos ].Keycode <> Key ) and
             ( Pos < NumBut ) do               { end of list still not reached }
```

```
        Inc( Pos );

    {-- Hotkey selection -----------------------------------------------}

    if ( HotKeyCode( RDataPtr^[ Pos ].Text ) = Key ) then       { hotkey? }
      begin
        OlderButton := Current;                      { mark old current button }
        Current := Pos;              { current button corresponds to hotkey }
        DispButton( OlderButton, false ); { display old button as normal }
        DispButton( Current, false );                 { mark default button }
        if ( IsActive ) then                        { object already active? }
          RCode := RC_ACCEPTED                 { yes, handle key internally }
        else
          RCode := RC_ACT_ME_T;            { no, object will be activated }
      end

    {-- Select using direct key selection ------------------------------}

    else if ( RDataPtr^[ Pos ].Keycode = Key ) then           { end key? }
      begin
        OlderButton := Current;                      { mark old current button }
        Current := Pos;              { current button corresponds to hotkey }
        DispButton( OlderButton, false ); { display old button as normal }
        DispButton( Current, false );                 { mark default button }
        RCode := RC_TERMINATE;                              { terminate }
        Mcode := RDataPtr^[ Pos ].ReturnCode;          { return code }
      end

    {-- Key not intended for object ------------------------------------}

    else
        RCode := RC_NOT_MINE;                    { key not intended for object }
    end;
  end;
```

This method operates differently with end buttons than with previous GetMouse methods. It's responsible for ensuring that after the left mouse button is pressed, the end button is highlighted in color where the mouse is currently located.

When the left mouse button is released an RC_TERMINATE message for the current end button is created (provided the pointer is at an end button). If not, the event is cancelled.

```
{**************************************************************************
*   GetMouse : receives mouse event from scheduler.                      *
**------------------------------------------------------------------------**
*   Input    : NEWX, NEWY = column, row of new mouse position            *
*              OLDX, OLDY = column, row of previous mouse position       *
*              FRSTEV     = first call for object?                       *
*              PRESSED    = left mouse button pressed?                   *
*              TIME       = time period of mouse event                   *
***************************************************************************}
```

```
procedure SAAEndB.GetMouse( NewX, NewY, OldX, OldY : byte;
                            FrstEv, Pressed        : boolean;
                            Time                   : longint );

var Pos    : byte;                              { position in RData field }

begin
  if ( Pressed ) then                           { mouse button still pressed? }
    begin
      if ( OldX <> NewX ) or ( OldY <> NewY ) or ( FrstEv ) then
        begin               { when position on one button, display as inverse }
          Pos := 1;                             { check for button in RData field }
          while ( Pos <= NumBut) and
              ( ( OldY <> VO( RDataPtr^[ Pos ].Y ) ) or
                ( OldX < VL( RDataPtr^[ Pos ].X ) ) or
                ( OldX > VL( RDataPtr^[ Pos ].X ) +
                      Length( RDataPtr^[ Pos ].Text ) + 3 ) )
              do     { execute all end buttons until appropriate one found }
            Inc( Pos );
          if ( Pos <= NumBut ) then             { old end button found }
            DispButton( Pos, false );           { display button as normal }
          Pos := 1;                             { display 2nd new button as inverse }
          while ( Pos <= NumBut) and
              ( ( NewY <> VO( RDataPtr^[ Pos ].Y ) ) or
                ( NewX < VL( RDataPtr^[ Pos ].X ) ) or
                ( NewX > VL( RDataPtr^[ Pos ].X ) +
                      Length( RDataPtr^[ Pos ].Text ) + 3 ) )
              do     { execute all end buttons until appropriate one found }
            Inc( Pos );
          if ( Pos <= NumBut ) then             { new end button found }
            begin
              DispButton( Pos, true );          { display button as inverse }
              if FrstEv then                    { first call for mouse event }
                Rcode := RC_ACT_ME_M            { activate object }
              else
                Rcode := RC_ACCEPTED;           { mouse event accepted }
            end
          else if FrstEv then                   { first call for mouse event }
            Rcode := RC_NOT_MINE   { mouse event not intended for object }
          else
            Rcode := RC_ACCEPTED;               { mouse event accepted }
        end
      else
        Rcode := RC_ACCEPTED;                   { mouse event accepted }
    end
  else                              { mouse exits when terminated by a button }
    begin
      Pos := 1;                                 { search for button in RData field }
      while ( Pos <= NumBut) and
            ( ( NewY <> VO( RDataPtr^[ Pos ].Y ) ) or
              ( NewX < VL( RDataPtr^[ Pos ].X ) ) or
              ( NewX > VL( RDataPtr^[ Pos ].X ) +
```

```
                        Length( RDataPtr^[ Pos  ].Text ) + 3 ) )
        do               { execute all end buttons until appropriate one found }
      Inc( Pos );
    MouHideMouse;                                    { hide mouse pointer }
    if ( Pos <= NumBut ) then                        { end button found }
      begin
        RCode := RC_TERMINATE;                              { terminate }
        Mcode := RDataPtr^[ Pos ].ReturnCode;            { return code }
        DispButton( Pos, false );            { hide button under mouse }
      end
    else
      DispButton( Current, false );        { pointer on current button }
    MouShowMouse;                          { display mouse pointer again }
  end;
end;
```

Alphanumeric input fields

As you're already aware from the integrated development environment of Turbo Pascal, the object SAAIn can be used for creating alphanumeric input fields. Since you're now familiar with developing various communication methods of dialog objects, we'll discuss only the object declarations and their specific characteristics.

The following is the object declaration of SAAIn. It originates from the basic object SAAT and does not require the support of other objects.

```
SAAIn        =
  object ( SAAT )                                 { subclass of SAAT }
    {-- Variables -------------------------------------------------}

    InpTitle  : String[ 40 ];              { title above the input }
    Content   : String[ 255 ];                      { input text }
    CurPos    : word;                  { cursor position in input text }
    ScrnCur,                           { cursor column on the screen }
    ColumnOne,                   { column of first character entered }
    Column,                                     { title column }
    Row,                                         { title row }
    VWidth,                            { visible screen width }
    TWidth,                            { total width of input }
    Wait      : byte;            { delay counter for mouse event }
    InsertM   : boolean;                    { insert mode active? }

    {-- Static methods -------------------------------------------}

    procedure Print( TColor : byte );          { display input text }
    constructor Init( Cl, Ro,          { initialize input text field }
                      GWidth,
                      BWidth : byte;
                      PreText,
                      Default : string );
```

740

```
{-- Virtual methods -------------------------------------------}

function IsItValid( Key : word ) : boolean; virtual;     { valid? }
procedure Open; virtual;                       { create input field }
procedure DispHKey; virtual;                      { display hotkey }
procedure SetActive( message : word ); virtual;  { activate input }
procedure SetPassive; virtual;            { deactivate input field }
procedure Get_AKey( Key : word ); virtual;        { keyboard event }
procedure GetMouse( NewX, NewY,              { receive mouse event }
                    OldX, OldY : byte;
                    FrstEv,
                    Pressed    : boolean;
                    Time       : longint ); virtual;
function Result : string; virtual;

end;
```

The control of an alphanumeric input field requires a series of variables as demonstrated by declaring the object type. Some variables are loaded through the Init constructor and reflect the specific characteristics of the input field. Other variables are required for the control of inputs and mouse events with the Get_AKey and GetMouse methods.

The Init static method and the Print procedure are defined. The Print procedure sends the input field to the screen area which was assigned to it.

Note: The Print procedure may not display the entire input string on the screen. According to SAAIn, input fields cannot be longer than the width in the dialog box.

As a virtual method, SAAIn enhances the previous methods from the SAAT object declaration with two additional methods. These methods, IsItValid and Result, accept different commands.

The Result method acts as the caller of a dialog box to locate the entered string. It should not be directly accessed by object variable Content because the string is stored there in a special format. This format displays the string in its full length. Any remaining characters from the end of the string to the allocated end of the string is filled with fill characters (ASCII code 255). A fill character appears as a normal space on the screen.

The Result method removes the fill characters and doesn't pass the input string to the caller as it's stored in the Content object variable. The caller obtains a string which corresponds exactly to the actual input. The Result method is virtual because other input fields can be developed from the SAAIn object, which, during the call of Result, perform conversions proceeding beyond converting input strings.

This concept was also used in developing the IsItValid function. An SAAIn object (or one of its descendants) determines the characters which can be entered in the input field with the

IsItValid function. This is implemented with the Get_AKey method which the object calls when it receives a normal ASCII character, and compares this with the IsItValid function. The character is stored in the input buffer only when IsItValid returns the value TRUE. Otherwise the character is ignored.

Here are the various methods required for the SAAIn objects:

```
{*******************************************************************************
 * Implementation of object :  S A A I n                                       *
 *******************************************************************************}


{*******************************************************************************
 *  IsItValid : tests a key to see whether it is a valid input key.            *
 **---------------------------------------------------------------------------**
 *  Input    : KEY  = key value to be tested                                   *
 *  Output   : TRUE if key is valid, otherwise FALSE                           *
 *  Info     : By changing this virtual method into a subclass of SAAIn,       *
 *             it can be adapted for input objects for numeric values, etc.    *
 *******************************************************************************}

function SAAIn.IsItValid( Key : word ) : boolean;

begin
  IsItValid := ( byte( Key and 255 ) in [ 8, 32..126, 128..175, 224..254 ] )
end;


{*******************************************************************************
 *  Print : displays the visible part of the input field.                     *
 **---------------------------------------------------------------------------**
 *  Input    : COLOR = displays the color of the input text                    *
 *******************************************************************************}

procedure SAAIn.Print( TColor : byte );

begin
  WinPrint( VL( ColumnOne ), VO( Row ), TColor,            { display text }
            Copy( Content + WinStRep( #255, 255 - Length( Content ) ),
            Curpos - ScrnCur + 1, VWidth ) );
  Cursor( VL( ColumnOne ) + ScrnCur - 1, VO( Row ) );      { set cursor }
end;


{*******************************************************************************
 *  Init : initializes SAA object input.                                       *
 **---------------------------------------------------------------------------**
 *  Input    : Cl, Ro = column, row                                            *
 *             GWIDTH = total width of text input                              *
 *             BWIDTH = width of visible region                                *
 *             PRETEXT = title text                                            *
 *             DEFAULT = default text for entry                                *
 *******************************************************************************}
```

```
constructor SAAIn.Init( Cl, Ro, GWidth, BWidth : byte;
                        PreText, Default        : String );

begin
  SAAT.Init;                                    { superclass initialization }
  InpTitle := PreText;                            { title text for input }
  Content := Default;                       { point to object default text }
  Column := Cl;                                       { column of title }
  Row := Ro;                                             { row of title }
  ColumnOne := Column + Length( InpTitle );       { column 1 of input line }
  if ( Pos( '#', InpTitle ) = 0 ) then                        { hotkey? }
   dec( ColumnOne );                          { no, decrement by one column }
  VWidth := BWidth;                         { input field width on screen }
  TWidth := GWidth;                            { length of input string }
end;

{*****************************************************************************
*  Open : opens the input object.                                          *
*****************************************************************************}

procedure SAAIn.Open;

begin
  SAAT.Open;                                     { call superclass procedure }
  InsertM := false;                               { disable insert mode }
  CurPos := 1;                          { default to cursor position at start }
  ScrnCur := 1;                     { cursor position at start of screen range }
  WriteIt( VL( Column ), VO( Row ),                { display input title }
           InpTitle + '[' + WinStRep( #32, VWidth ) + ']', HKeys );
  Print( CO_NORM );                              { display input contents }
  Content := Content + WinStRep( #255, TWidth - Length( Content ) );
end;                                      { fill length of string with #255 }

{*****************************************************************************
*  DispHKey : displays hotkeys for an input type.                          *
*****************************************************************************}

procedure SAAIn.DispHKey;

begin
  SAAT.DispHKey;                                 { call superclass procedure }
  WriteIt( VL( Column ), VO( Row ), InpTitle, HKeys );    { display title }
end;

{*****************************************************************************
*  SetActive : activates an input object.                                  *
**-------------------------------------------------------------------------**
*  Input    : MESSAGE = base for activation from scheduler                 *
*****************************************************************************}

procedure SAAIn.SetActive( message : word );

begin
```

```
      SAAT.SetActive( message );               { superclass activation procedure }
      Print( CO_ACT );                         { display input contents, set cursor }
      if ( insertM ) then                                    { insert mode enabled? }
        WinBlockCursor;                  { cursor appears as block in insert mode }
    end;

    {**************************************************************************
     *  SetPassive : deactivates an input object.                            *
     **************************************************************************}

    procedure SAAIn.SetPassive;

    begin
      SAAT.SetPassive;                       { superclass deactivation procedure }
      Print( CO_NORM );                      { display input contents, set cursor }
      WinLineCursor;                         { change cursor to normal appearance }
    end;

    {**************************************************************************
     *  Get_AKey : receives keyboard event from scheduler.                   *
     **-------------------------------------------------------------------**
     *  Input    : KEY = key value                                           *
     **************************************************************************}

    procedure SAAIn.Get_AKey( Key : word );

    var i : byte;                                              { loop counter }

    begin
      {-- Test of hotkey for object ----------------------------------------}

      if ( Key = HotkeyCode( InpTitle ) ) then
        RCode := RC_ACT_ME_T

      {-- Other keys only enabled by active object -------------------------}

      else if ( IsActive ) then        { otherwise, keys only when object active }
        case Key of                                             { process key }
          {-- <Tab> key => "activate next object" ----------------------------}

          TAB :
            RCode := RC_NEXT;

          {-- <BackTab> key => "activate previous object" --------------------}

          BACKTAB :
            RCode := RC_PREV;

          {-- <Insert> key ---------------------------------------------------}

          INSERTKEY :
            begin
              InsertM := not InsertM;                       { invert Insert mode }
```

744

```
            if ( insertM ) then                    { Insert mode active? }
              WinBlockCursor                     { yes, then block cursor }
            else
              WinLineCursor;             { no, then normal line cursor }
            RCode := RC_ACCEPTED;        { "key accepted" in scheduler }
          end;


  {-- <Home> key ------------------------------------------------------}

  CHOME :
    begin
        if ( ScrnCur = 1 ) then             { cursor on first character? }
          begin                           { yes, display text from start }
            CurPos := 1;                          { set cursor to start }
            ScrnCur := 1;             { cursor to start of screen range }
            Print( CO_ACT );                 { display text from start }
          end
        else                          { no, set cursor to first character }
          begin
            CurPos := CurPos - ScrnCur + 1;       { new cursor position }
            ScrnCur := 1;             { visible cursor to start of input }
          end;
        RCode := RC_ACCEPTED;           { "key accepted" in scheduler }
      end;

  {-- <End> key -------------------------------------------------------}

  CEND :
    begin
        if ( ScrnCur = VWidth ) then            { cursor on last character }
          begin                         { yes, display last section of text }
            CurPos := TWidth;                           { cursor back }
            ScrnCur := VWidth;            { cursor to end of screen field }
            Print( CO_ACT );                          { display text }
          end
        else                                    { set cursor only back }
          begin
            Curpos := Curpos - ScrnCur + VWidth;          { set cursor }
            ScrnCur := VWidth;                    { cursor displayed }
          end;
        RCode := RC_ACCEPTED;           { "key accepted" in scheduler }
      end;

  {-- <Ctrl><Home> key ------------------------------------------------}

  CTRL_HOME :
    begin
        Content := WinStRep( #255, TWidth );        { make Content blank }
        CurPos := 1;                          { set cursor to the start }
        ScrnCur := 1;              { cursor to start of screen range }
        Print( CO_ACT );                 { print input field as blank }
        RCode := RC_ACCEPTED;           { "key accepted" in scheduler }
```

```
      end;


{-- <Cursor Right> key ----------------------------------------------}

CRIGHT :
  begin
    if ( CurPos < TWidth ) then
      begin                        { only sensible when still not at end }
        if ( ScrnCur = VWidth ) then          { cursor to end of field }
          begin                                  { scroll screen range }
            WinScrollLeft( VL( ColumnOne ) + 1, VO ( Row ),
                           VL( ColumnOne ) + VWidth - 1,
                           VO( Row ), 1, CO_ACT );
            Inc( CurPos );                 { increment position in text }
            WinPrint( VL( ColumnOne ) + ScrnCur - 1, VO( Row ),
                      CO_ACT, Content[ CurPos ] );        { character }
          end
        else
          begin                                      { move cursor only }
            Inc( ScrnCur );              { increment screen position }
            Inc( Curpos );               { increment cursor position }
          end
      end;
    RCode := RC_ACCEPTED;               { "key accepted" in scheduler }
  end;

{-- <Cursor Left> key -----------------------------------------------}

CLEFT :
  begin
    if ( CurPos > 1 ) then
      begin                     { only makes sense if not at start yet }
        if ( ScrnCur = 1 ) then              { cursor to start of field }
          begin                                  { scroll screen range }
            WinScrollRight( VL( ColumnOne ), VO( Row ),
                            VL( ColumnOne ) + VWidth - 2,
                            VO( Row ), 1, CO_ACT );
            Dec( CurPos );                   { decrement text position }
            WinPrint( VL( ColumnOne ), VO( Row ), CO_ACT,
                      Content[ CurPos ] );       { display character }
          end
        else
          begin                                      { move cursor only }
            Dec( ScrnCur );              { increment screen position }
            Dec( Curpos );               { increment cursor position }
          end;
      end;
    RCode := RC_ACCEPTED;               { "key accepted" in scheduler }
  end;

{-- <Delete> key ----------------------------------------------------}
```

746

```
DELETEKEY :
  begin
    Delete( Content, CurPos, 1 );     { delete character under cursor }
    Content := Content + #255;                  { fill up contents again }
    WinScrollLeft( VL( ColumnOne ) + ScrnCur, VO( Row ),
                   VL( ColumnOne ) + VWidth - 1,        { scroll rest }
                   VO( Row ), 1, CO_ACT );
    WinPrint( VL( ColumnOne ) + VWidth - 1, VO( Row ), CO_ACT,
              Content[ Curpos - ScrnCur + VWidth ] );
    RCode := RC_ACCEPTED;                   { "key accepted" in scheduler }
  end;


{-- <Backspace> key -------------------------------------------------}

BS :
  begin
    if ( Curpos > 1 ) then          { action only when cursor is not  }
      begin                         { at the first character position }
        Dec( Curpos );                     { decrement cursor position }
        Delete( Content, CurPos, 1 );       { delete left of cursor }
        Content := Content + #255;               { refill contents }
        if ( ScrnCur > 1 ) then      { cursor cannot be moved left? }
          begin
            WinScrollLeft( VL( ColumnOne ) + ScrnCur - 1,
                           VO( Row ), VL( ColumnOne ) + VWidth - 1,
                           VO( Row ), 1, CO_ACT );
            Dec( ScrnCur );
            WinPrint( VL( ColumnOne ) + VWidth - 1, VO( Row ),
                      CO_ACT, Content[ Curpos - ScrnCur + VWidth ] );
          end;
      end;
    RCode := RC_ACCEPTED;                   { "key accepted" in scheduler }
  end;


{-- Specific characters instead of control keys --------------------}

else
  if ( Key < 256 ) and IsItValid( Key ) then
    begin
      {-- Handle the key in insert mode --------------------------}

      if ( insertM ) then                       { insert mode enabled? }
        begin
          if ( ( CurPos < TWidth ) and ( ScrnCur < VWidth ) ) then
            begin
              Delete( Content, TWidth, 1 );       { delete character }
              Insert( chr( Key and 255 ), Content, Curpos );
              WinScrollRight( VL( ColumnOne ) + ScrnCur - 1,
                              VO( Row ), VL( ColumnOne ) + VWidth - 2,
                              VO( Row ), 1, CO_ACT );
              WinPrint( VL( ColumnOne ) + ScrnCur - 1, VO( Row ),
                        CO_ACT, chr( Key and 255 ) );
              inc( CurPos );
```

```
                            inc( ScrnCur );
                    end
            end

        {-- Handle key in overwrite mode ------------------------------}

          else
            begin
              Content [ CurPos ] := chr( Key and 255 );       { character }
              WinPrint( VL( ColumnOne ) + ScrnCur - 1, VO( Row ),
                        CO_ACT, Content[ Curpos ] );            { display }
              if ( CurPos < TWidth ) then             { last character? }
                begin                          { no, move cursor one char. right }
                  Inc( Curpos );               { increment cursor position }
                  if ( ScrnCur = VWidth ) then             { end of field }
                    begin                          { scroll field to left }
                      WinScrollLeft( VL( ColumnOne ) + 1,VO( Row ),
                                     VL( ColumnOne ) + VWidth - 1,
                                     VO( Row ), 1, CO_ACT );

                      WinPrint( VL( ColumnOne ) + VWidth - 1, VO( Row ),
                                CO_ACT, Content[Curpos - ScrnCur + VWidth]);
                    end
                  else
                    Inc( ScrnCur );            { increment screen position }
                end;
            end;
          RCode := RC_ACCEPTED;               { "key accepted" in scheduler }
        end

    {-- Key cannot be accepted from object ------------------------------}

      else
        RCode := RC_NOT_MINE;                 { key unsuitable for input object }
    end

  {-- Object inactive and NOT a hotkey, therefore cannot be accepted ------}

  else
    RCode := RC_NOT_MINE;                     { "key not for object" in scheduler }

  if ( RCode = RC_ACCEPTED ) then                              { key accepted? }
    Cursor( VL( ColumnOne ) + ScrnCur - 1, VO( Row ) );        { yes, cursor }
end;

{*****************************************************************************
 *  GetMouse : receives mouse event from scheduler.                          *
 **-------------------------------------------------------------------------**
 *   Input   : NEWX, NEWY = column, row of new mouse position                *
 *             OLDX, OLDY = column, row of previous mouse position           *
 *             ERSTEV     = first call for object?                           *
 *             PRESSED    = left mouse button pressed?                       *
 *             TIME       = time period for mouse event                      *
```

```
*******************************************************************************}

procedure SAAIn.GetMouse( NewX, NewY, OldX, OldY : byte;
                          FrstEv, Pressed        : boolean;
                          Time                   : longint );

var Action : boolean;                          { object action flag necessary }
    Pos    : byte;

begin
  if FrstEv then                      { event not depending on object, testing }
    if ( NewY = VO( Row ) ) and ( NewX >= VL( ColumnOne ) ) and
       ( NewX <= VL( ColumnOne ) + VWidth ) then
      begin
        RCode := RC_ACT_ME_M;                   { "activate me" from scheduler }
        Wait := MouseInpWait;                          { initialize delay }
        Action := true;                             { action within the object }
      end
    else
      begin
        RCode := RC_NOT_MINE;              { "not meant for me" in scheduler }
        Action := false;                           { no action for object }
      end
  else
    begin
      RCode := RC_ACCEPTED;                   { "key accepted" in scheduler }
      Action := true;                             { action within the object }
    end;
  if ( Action ) then
    begin                           { mouse event for object, so execute action }
      if ( NewX < VL( ColumnOne ) ) then
        begin        { mouse position to left of input, scroll to the right }
          Dec( Wait );                               { decrement delay counter }
          if ( Wait = 0 ) then                            { action or delay }
            begin
              if ( ScrnCur > 1 ) then   { cursor previously in input field? }
                begin                   { no, move cursor one character back }
                  Dec( ScrnCur );                     { visible cursor back }
                  Dec( CurPos );                      { internal cursor back }
                end
              else if ( CurPos > 1 ) then       { cursor to start of input? }
                begin                  { cursor already at start of input field }
                  WinScrollRight( VL( ColumnOne ), VO( Row ),
                                  VL( ColumnOne ) + VWidth - 2, VO( Row ),
                                  1, CO_ACT );                    { scroll }
                  Dec( CurPos );                     { internal cursor back }
                  WinPrint( VL( ColumnOne ), VO( Row ),     { display new }
                            CO_ACT, Content[ CurPos ] );    { first char. }
                end;
              Wait := MouseInpWait;                      { set new delay }
            end;
        end
      else if ( NewX > VL( ColumnOne ) + VWidth - 1 ) then
```

```
             begin          { mouse position to right of input, scroll to the left }
               Dec( Wait );                            { decrement delay counter }
               if ( Wait = 0 ) then                           { action or delay }
                 begin
                   if ( ScrnCur < VWidth ) then { cursor behind in input field? }
                     begin              { no, move first cursor one character back }
                       Inc( ScrnCur );               { visible cursor as before }
                       Inc( CurPos );               { internal cursor as before }
                     end
                   else if ( CurPos < TWidth ) then   { cursor at end of input? }
                     begin
                       WinScrollLeft( VL( ColumnOne ) + 1, VO( Row ),
                                    VL( ColumnOne ) + VWidth - 1, VO( Row ),
                                    1, CO_ACT );                      { scroll }
                       Inc( CurPos );                 { reset internal cursor }
                       WinPrint( VL( ColumnOne ) + VWidth - 1, VO( Row ),
                               CO_ACT, Content[ CurPos ] );   { display char. }
                     end;
                   Wait := MouseInpWait;                       { set new delay }
                 end;
             end
           else
             begin                          { mouse position within input field }
               Wait := MouseInpWait;                { re-initialize delay counter }
               Pos := NewX - VL( ColumnOne ) + 1;   { cursor position on screen }
               CurPos := CurPos - ScrnCur + Pos;       { position of input text }
               ScrnCur := Pos;                       { point to screen position }
             end;
           Cursor( VL( ColumnOne ) + ScrnCur - 1, VO( Row ) );        { cursor }
         end;
end;

{*******************************************************************************
 *  Result : returns a prepared string.                                       *
 **---------------------------------------------------------------------------**
 *  Output  : Specified string                                                *
 *  Info    : If contents are read directly, the input contains fill char-    *
 *            acters (#255). These are used for absolute results.             *
 *******************************************************************************}

function SAAIn.Result : string;

var Stringdummy : string[ 255 ];                      { buffer for result }
    i           : byte;                               { loop counter }

begin
  i := TWidth;                                 { position on last character }
  while ( Content[ i ] = #255 ) and ( i >= 0 ) do      { fill character }
    Dec( I );                                       { decrement position }
  if ( i > 0 ) then                                 { no blank input? }
    begin
      Stringdummy := Copy( Content, 1, i );             { copy out input }
      for i := 1 to length( Stringdummy ) do            { execute input }
```

```
        if ( Stringdummy[ i ] = #255 ) then    { replace fill characters }
            Stringdummy[ i ] := #32;           { in input with spaces    }
      Result := Stringdummy;                            { pass result }
    end
  else
    Result := '';                                  { blank input field }
end;
```

This concludes the description of the SAA unit.

Now that you know how objects and dialog boxes are brought to the screen, let's look at a program that pulls it all together.

14.4   An SAA Demo Program

To conclude this book, we've listed a short program called SAADEMO.PAS, which creates a dialog box and objects based on information in the SAA unit. After SAADEMO.PAS is compiled, the executable program SAADEMO.EXE displays a dialog box using object data from the SAA unit.

Now that you've read descriptions of how the dialog box and many of its objects were implemented, you may want to try augmenting the various objects. For instance, you could convert the alphanumeric input field into a purely numeric input field, so the field would accept only numbers. You can further enhance it so it offers the caller of the dialog box the opportunity to convert the input directly into binary numbers.

If this seems too easy, modify the scheduler so that it automatically brings the three end buttons (Help, OK and Cancel) into the dialog box without the caller clearly declaring them as objects and having to register them with Add.

These are only two examples of enhancing our SAA unit. We wish you the best on your experiments with OOP.

```
{*****************************************************************************
 *  SAADemo : Demo program using the SAA unit. This program generates       *
 *            a dialog box, radio buttons and other dialog objects.          *
 **-----------------------------------------------------------------------**
 *  Author        : MICHAEL TISCHER                                          *
 *  developed on   : 08/21/1989                                             *
 *  last update    : 03/13/1990                                             *
 *****************************************************************************}

program SAADemo;

{*****************************************************************************
 * Imported units                                                           *
 *****************************************************************************}

uses Win,          { Turbo Pascal System Programming window unit ( Ch. 6 ) }
     KBM,   { Turbo Pascal System Programming keyboard/mouse unit ( Ch. 7 ) }
     SAA;          { Turbo Pascal System Programming SAA unit ( Ch. 14 ) }


{-- Global variables ------------------------------------------------------}

var MainSched,                         { scheduler for the main dialog box }
    HelpSched : SAASched;                 { scheduler for the help window }

{-- Objects for the main dialog box ---------------------------------------}

    MEndButs : array[1..3] of SAAEButtons;          { three end buttons }
```

```
    MEndBut   : SAAEndB;                                  { the end button object }
    MANField1,                              { three alphanumeric input fields }
    MANField2,
    MANField3 : SAAIn;
    MRaButs   : array [1..6] of SAARButtons;              { 6 radio buttons }
    MRaBut    : SAARadioB;
    MPB1,                                            { 2 toggle buttons }
    MPB2      : SAAPushB;

{-- Objects for the help window -------------------------------------------}

    HEndButs : array[1..3] of SAAEButtons;        { the three end buttons }
    HEndBut  : SAAEndB;                            { the end button object }


{***************************************************************************
*  Help : controls the help text window.                                  *
**-----------------------------------------------------------------------**
*  Input   : none                                                         *
*  Globals : HelpSched/R                                                  *
***************************************************************************}

procedure Help;

var EndIt  : boolean;                                { return to caller }
    HPage : integer;                              { displayed help page }
    SBuf  : string[5];                         { string conversion buffer }

begin
  {-- scheduler opens help screen and controls window --------------------}

  HelpSched.Open;
  WinFrame( VL(24), VO(0), VR(0), VU(0), SIN_FR, CO_FRAME );
  WinPrint( VL(24), VO(0), CO_FRAME, #194 );
  WinPrint( VL(24), VU(0), CO_FRAME, #193 );
  WinPrint( VL( 2), VO(7), CO_HOT, 'This is a help screen.' );
  WinPrint( VL(13), VO(1), CO_FRAME, 'Page' );

  {-- Read loop. Displays options to the user, and available buttons ------}

  HPage := 1;                           { start with the first help page }
  EndIt  := false;                            { can't go past the first }

  repeat
    str( HPage:5, SBuf );
    WinPrint( VL(18), VO(1), CO_NORM, SBuf );
    case HelpSched.Run(1) of                  { convey pressed button }
      0 : if ( HPage < 1000 ) then                     { next page }
           inc( HPage );
      1 : if ( HPage > 1 ) then                   { previous pages }
           dec( HPage );
      2 : EndIt := true;                     { select < CANCEL > button }
    end;
  until EndIt;                            { until < CANCEL > is selected }
```

```
    HelpSched.Close;                                { close help window }
  end;

  {*****************************************************************************
  *                     M A I N   P R O G R A M                               *
  *****************************************************************************}

  begin
    {-- create screen ------------------------------------------------------}

    if ( color ) then                              { color card installed? }
      TextBackground( BLUE )                        { yes, blue background }
    else
      TextBackGround( BLACK );                       { no, black background }
    clrscr;                              { clear screen in new background color }

    {-- scheduler initializes help window and its objects ------------------}

    HEndButs[1].Init( 26,  6, ESC,      2, '#Cancel ' );  { place three end }
    HEndButs[2].Init( 26,  7, ord('+'), 0, '+ Page');      { buttons in the  }
    HEndButs[3].Init( 26,  8, ord('-'), 1, '- Page' );     { help window     }
    HEndBut.Init( 2, 3, @HEndButs );          { initialize end button objects }

    HelpSched.Init( 37, 1, 75, 11 );             { initialize the scheduler }
    HelpSched.Add( @HEndBut );                     { display the end button }

    {-- Initialize the different objects used in the main dialog box --------}

    MEndButs[1].Init( 28, 12, CR,   RS_OK,    '#OK' );       { the three    }
    MEndButs[2].Init( 39, 12, F1,   RS_HELP,  '#Help' );     { end buttons  }
    MEndButs[3].Init( 52, 12, ESC, RS_A_BREAK, '#Cancel' );
    MEndBut.Init( 1, 3, @MEndButs );                  { the end button object }

    MANField1.Init( 4, 3, 70, 22, 'AN-Field#1 ', 'Jim Middleton' );{ the    }
    MANField2.Init( 4, 4, 25, 22, 'AN-Field#2 ', '201 Bedlam E.' );{ 3 AN   }
    MANField3.Init( 4, 5, 22, 22, 'AN-Field#3 ', 'Serial City MI' );{ fields }

    MRaButs[1].Init( 43, 3, 'Microsoft #Word' );              { initialize }
    MRaButs[2].Init( 43, 4, 'Word#Perfect' );                 { the six    }
    MRaButs[3].Init( 43, 5, '#GemWrite' );                    { radio      }
    MRaButs[4].Init( 43, 6, '#Nota Bene' );                   { buttons    }
    MRaButs[5].Init( 43, 7, 'P#C-Write' );                    { used here  }
    MRaButs[6].Init( 43, 8, '#Edlin' );
    MRaBut.Init( 6, @MRaButs, 2 );               { the radio button object }

    MPB1.Init(  5, 8, 'Saving file', true );             { initialize two }
    MPB2.Init( 26, 8, 'Alarm!', false );                 { toggle buttons }

    {-- Scheduler initializes and executes main dialog box -----------------}

    with MainSched do                            { use main scheduler }
      begin
```

```
        Init( 5, 6, 70, 19 );                        { initialize scheduler }
        Add( @MANField1 );                           { display the different }
        Add( @MANField2 );                           { dialog objects         }
        Add( @MANField3 );
        Add( @MPB1 );
        Add( @MPB2 );
        Add( @MRaBut );
        Add( @MEndBut );
        Open;                                         { open dialog window }


        WinPrint( VL( 25 ), VO( 0 ), CO_HOT, ' DEMO DIALOG BOX ' );

        WinFrame( VL( 2 ), VO( 2 ), VL( 39), VO( 6 ), SIN_FR, CO_FRAME );
        WinPrint( VL( 7 ), VO( 2 ), CO_FRAME,
          ' ALPHANUMERIC INPUT FIELDS ' );

        WinFrame( VL( 2 ), VO( 7 ), VL( 39), VO( 9 ), SIN_FR, CO_FRAME );
        WinPrint( VL( 13 ), VO( 7 ), CO_FRAME, ' TOGGLE BUTTON ' );

        WinFrame( VR(-24), VO( 2 ), VR( -3), VO( 9 ), SIN_FR, CO_FRAME );
        WinPrint( VR(-20), VO( 2 ), CO_FRAME, ' RADIO BUTTON ' );

        WinPrint( VL( 0 ), VU( -2 ), CO_FRAME,
                  #195 + WinStRep( #196, VR( -1 ) - VL( 0 ) ) + #180 );
        WinPrint( VL(3), VU(-1), CO_FRAME, 'END BUTTON ƒƒƒ'#16 );

        {-- Scheduler input loop ------------------------------------------}

        while run( 1 ) = RS_HELP do                      { HELP been called? }
          Help;                              { yes, open and display help window }

        Close;                       { if user selects OK or CANCEL, close dialog }
        Done;                        { box and end scheduler                     }
      end;

   HelpSched.Done;                                             { end help window }

   {-- clear screen and end program ---------------------------------------}

   TextColor( LIGHTGRAY );                               { foreground color }
   TextBackGround( BLACK );                              { background color }
   ClrScr;
   WinSetCursor( 0, 0 );
end.
```

Appendix A: IBM ASCII Table

Dec	Hex	Char	Dec	Hex	Char	Dec	Hex	Char	Dec	Hex	Char
0	00		32	20		64	40	@	96	60	`
1	01	☻	33	21	!	65	41	A	97	61	a
2	02	●	34	22	"	66	42	B	98	62	b
3	03	♥	35	23	#	67	43	C	99	63	c
4	04	♦	36	24	$	68	44	D	100	64	d
5	05	♣	37	25	%	69	45	E	101	65	e
6	06	—	38	26	&	70	46	F	102	66	f
7	07	•	39	27	'	71	47	G	103	67	g
8	08	◘	40	28	(	72	48	H	104	68	h
9	09	o	41	29	)	73	49	I	105	69	i
10	0A	j	42	2A	*	74	4A	J	106	6A	j
11	0B	k	43	2B	+	75	4B	K	107	6B	k
12	0C	l	44	2C	,	76	4C	L	108	6C	l
13	0D	m	45	2D	–	77	4D	M	109	6D	m
14	0E	♫	46	2E	.	78	4E	N	110	6E	n
15	0F	☼	47	2F	/	79	4F	O	111	6F	o
16	10	►	48	30	0	80	50	P	112	70	p
17	11	◄	49	31	1	81	51	Q	113	71	q
18	12	↕	50	32	2	82	52	R	114	72	r
19	13	‼	51	33	3	83	53	S	115	73	s
20	14	¶	52	34	4	84	54	T	116	74	t
21	15	﹁	53	35	5	85	55	U	117	75	u
22	16	▬	54	36	6	86	56	V	118	76	v
23	17	↕	55	37	7	87	57	W	119	77	w
24	18	↑	56	38	8	88	58	X	120	78	x
25	19	↓	57	39	9	89	59	Y	121	79	y
26	1A	→	58	3A	:	90	5A	Z	122	7A	z
27	1B	←	59	3B	;	91	5B	[	123	7B	{
28	1C	∟	60	3C	<	92	5C	\	124	7C		
29	1D	↔	61	3D	=	93	5D	]	125	7D	}
30	1E	▲	62	3E	>	94	5E	^	126	7E	~
31	1F	▼	63	3F	?	95	5F	_	127	7F	

Dec	Hex	Char	Dec	Hex	Char	Dec	Hex	Char	Dec	Hex	Char
128	80	Ä	160	A0	⌐	192	C0	¿	224	E0	α
129	81	Å	161	A1	╟	193	C1	▓	225	E1	▓
130	82	Ç	162	A2	¢	194	C2	¬	226	E2	Γ
131	83	É	163	A3	£	195	C3	√	227	E3	╜
132	84	Ñ	164	A4	§	196	C4	–	228	E4	╢
133	85	Ö	165	A5	•	197	C5	≈	229	E5	╣
134	86	Ü	166	A6	¶	198	C6	Δ	230	E6	π
135	87	á	167	A7	β	199	C7	«	231	E7	τ
136	88	à	168	A8	¿	200	C8	»	232	E8	Φ
137	89	â	169	A9	⌐	201	C9	╔	233	E9	╡
138	8A	ä	170	AA	¬	202	CA	╩	234	EA	╪
139	8B	π	171	AB	½	203	CB	╦	235	EB	σ
140	8C	å	172	AC	¼	204	CC	╠	236	EC	▓
141	8D	ç	173	AD	╚	205	CD	=	237	ED	╞
142	8E	é	174	AE	Æ	206	CE	╬	238	EE	∈
143	8F	è	175	AF	Ø	207	CF	╧	239	EF	∩
144	90	ê	176	B0	∞	208	D0	╨	240	F0	℞
145	91	ë	177	B1	±	209	D1	╤	241	F1	▮
146	92	ì	178	B2	≤	210	D2	π	242	F2	╧
147	93	î	179	B3	│	211	D3	╙	243	F3	│
148	94	î	180	B4	¥	212	D4	╘	244	F4	⌠
149	95	ï	181	B5	μ	213	D5	╒	245	F5	⌡
150	96	ñ	182	B6	δ	214	D6	÷	246	F6	╪
151	97	ó	183	B7	Σ	215	D7	╫	247	F7	╕
152	98	ò	184	B8	╕	216	D8	ÿ	248	F8	°
153	99	ô	185	B9	π	217	D9	≡	249	F9	╚
154	9A	ö	186	BA	║	218	DA	┌	250	FA	·
155	9B	⊤	187	BB	╗	219	DB	█	251	FB	├
156	9C	ú	188	BC	╝	220	DC	▄	252	FC	ⁿ
157	9D	ù	189	BD	Ω	221	DD	▌	253	FD	²
158	9E	û	190	BE	æ	222	DE	▐	254	FE	■
159	9F	ü	191	BF	ø	223	DF	▀	255	FF	

Appendix B: References

Borland/Heimsoeth: Turbo Pascal 5.0 Handbook

Borland/Heimsoeth: Turbo Pascal 5.5 Handbook

Borland/Heimsoeth: Turbo Pascal 6.0 Handbook

IBM: AT Technical Reference Manual, IBM 1984

Rector/Alexy: The 8086/8088 Book, TEWI 1982

Schaepers, Arne: Turbo Pascal 4.0/5.0, Volume 2, Addison/Wesley 1989

Schaepers, Arne: Turbo Pascal 5.0, Addison/Wesley 1989

Tischer, Michael: PC System Programming for Developers, Abacus 1989

Wilton, R.: Programmer's Guide to PC & PS/2 Video Systems, Microsoft Press 1987

Appendix C: Program List (alphabetical)

\PAS directory

ALIGN.PAS	2.3	Illustrates the alignment of variables to byte or word limits
CLOCK.PAS	11.1	ISR program, used to display the time on the screen permanently
DEMO.PAS	12.1	Demo program which can be configured with the help of DINST
DINST.PAS	12.2	Configuration of the DEMO program with the help of routines from the TPINST unit
EMS.PAS	9.2	Unit for accessing the EMS memory
EMSDEMO.PAS	9.2	Sample program for working with the EMS unit
EXT.PAS	9.1	Unit for accessing extended memory
EXTDEMO.PAS	9.1	Sample program for working with the EXT unit
FARJMP.PAS	8.1	Unit for jumping over function and procedure limits
FASTKB.PAS	5.1	Programming the keyboard controller as an example of hardware close programming
FJDEMO.PAS	8.1	Example using the FARJMP unit
HEAP5.PAS	2.6.1	Demonstrates Heap management under Versions 5.0 and 5.5
HEAP6.PAS	2.6.2	Demonstrates Heap management under Version 6.0
KBM.PAS	7.2	Unit for comfortably prompting mouse and keyboard

KBMDEMO.PAS	7.2	Sample program for using KBM unit
KBMT.PAS	13.6	Multitasking version of the KBM unit
MT.PAS	13.4	Multitasking unit used for dividing a program into single tasks that are executed parallel to each other
MTDEMO.PAS	13.1	Demo program for using multitasking unit
PHILO5.PAS	13.3	Classic example of a multitasking problem: five philosophers who would like to eat a plate of spaghetti, but don't have enough forks
PROT.PAS	4.2	Unit for automatically logging all output using READ and WRITE
PROTDEMO.PAS	4.2	Sample program for working with the PROT unit
SAA.PAS	14.3	The SAA unit for working with dialog boxes in accordance to the CUA standard
SAA2.PAS	14.3	Second part of the SAA unit
SAADEMO.PAS	14.4	Example of using the SAA unit to build dialog boxes
SWAP.PAS	10.1	SWAP unit used for swapping a program from the memory in order to make room for another program temporarily
SWAPDEMO.PAS	10.1	Sample program for using the SWAP unit
TPIC.PAS	12.1	Utility program for the TPINST unit, with whose help the variables can be determined in a program to be configured
TPINST.PAS	12.2	Unit for external configuration of compiled TP programs
TSR.PAS	11.2	TSR unit for programming TSR programs with the help of Turbo Pascal
TSRDEMO.PAS	11.2	A TSR program as an example of using the TSR unit
WIN.PAS	6.2	A unit for quick screen access and window management
WIN2.PAS	6.2	Second part of the WIN unit

WIN2MT.PAS	13.5	Second part of the multitasking version of the WIN unit
WINDEMO.PAS	6.2	Sample program which demonstrates the use of the WIN unit
WINMT.PAS	13.5	First part of the multitasking version of the MT unit

\ASM Directory

KBMA.ASM	7.2	Assembler routines for the KBM unit (Readout of the mouse and keyboard)
KBMTA.ASM	13.6	Assembler routines for the multitasking version of the KBM unit
MTA.ASM	13.4	Assembler routines in the core of the multitasking unit MT, which take over task control and task rotation
SWAPA.ASM	10.1	Assembler routines for the SWAP unit, which can be used to swap a program to the EMS memory or the disk
TSRA.ASM	11.2	Assembler routines for context exchange in the TSR unit

\OBJ Directory

KBMA.OBJ	7.2	Assembled form of KMBA.ASM
KBMTA.OBJ	13.6	Assembled form of KBMTA.ASM
MTA.OBJ	13.4	Assembled form of MTA.ASM
SWAPA.OBJ	10.1	Assembled form of SWAPA.ASM
TSRA.OBJ	11.2	Assembled form of TSRA.ASM

Appendix D: Program List (chapter)

EMSDEMO.PAS	9.2	Sample program for working with the EMS unit
SWAP.PAS	10.1	SWAP unit used for swapping a program from the memory in order to make room for another program temporarily
SWAPA.ASM	10.1	Assembler routines for the SWAP unit, which can be used to swap a program to the EMS memory or the disk
SWAPDEMO.PAS	10.1	Sample program for using the SWAP unit
CLOCK.PAS	11.1	ISR program, used to display the time on the screen permanently
TSR.PAS	11.2	TSR unit for programming TSR programs with the help of Turbo Pascal
TSRDEMO.PAS	11.2	A TSR program as an example of using the TSR unit
TSRA.ASM	11.2	Assembler routines for context exchange in the TSR unit
DEMO.PAS	12.1	Demo program which can be configured with the help of DINST
TPIC.PAS	12.1	Utility program for the TPINST unit, with whose help the variables can be determined in a program to be configured
DINST.PAS	12.2	Configuration of the DEMO program with the help of routines from the TPINST unit
TPINST.PAS	12.2	Unit for external configuration of compiled TP programs
MTDEMO.PAS	13.1	Demo program for using multitasking unit
PHILO5.PAS	13.3	Classic example of a multitasking problem: five philosophers who would like to eat a plate of spaghetti, but don't have enough forks
MT.PAS	13.4	Multitasking unit used for dividing a program into single tasks that are executed parallel to each other
MTA.ASM	13.4	Assembler routines in the core of the multitasking unit MT, which take over task control and task rotation
WIN2MT.PAS	13.5	Second part of the multitasking version of the WIN unit

Index

D

N

O

P

Abacus
pc catalog
Order Toll Free 1-800-451-4319

5370 52nd Street SE • Grand Rapids, MI 49512
Phone: (616) 698-0330 • Fax: (616) 698-0325

Productivity Series books are for users who want to become more productive with their PC.

Tips & Tricks for your PC Printer

Describes how printers work, basic printer configurations using DIP switches, using MS-DOS commands for simple printer control. Includes utilities on a 5.25" companion diskette to demonstrate popular software commands. Useful printer accessories, font editor and printing tricks and tips. 400 pp. with companion disk containing essential printer utilities.
ISBN 1-55755-075-1. $34.95
Canada: 53903 $45.95

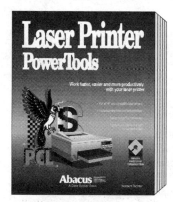

Laser Printer PowerTools

shows you how to harness all the capabilities built into your HP-compatible laser printer quickly and easily. You'll learn about both the built-in and add-on fonts, the whys and hows of printing graphics, understanding the Printer Control Language (PCL) and how to set up dozens of applications to get the most from your laser printer. The companion disk includes programs for printing ASCII files, initializing margins and fonts; printing soft fonts, using Word printer drivers, converting ASCII files to print characters. It also includes many sample files you can use to get the most out of your printer.

350 page book with companion disk.
ISBN 1-55755-095-6 $34.95
Canada: 53925 $45.95

To order direct call Toll Free 1-800-451-4319

In US and Canada add $5.00 shipping and handling. Foreign orders add $13.00 per item. Michigan residents add 4% sales tax.

Word 5.0 Know-How
This new book is written for users who demand professional results. You'll find dozens of in-depth techniques for producing high quality documents with the least amount of effort. You'll see how to easily select special purpose fonts, combine graphics with your text, work with multiple columns and use Word 5.0 for desktop publishing.
550 page book with companion disk.
ISBN 1-55755-088-3. $24.95
Canada: 54385 $33.95

Microsoft Word 5.0/5.5 PowerTools allows you to tap into Word 5.0 and Word 5.5's powerful built-in functions, quickly and easily. Contains over 150 special macros from both Word 5.0 and 5.5. Makes Word simple to use, which saves you valuable time and effort.
Microsoft Word 5.0/5.5 PowerTools also includes a collection of ready-to-run editing utilities and provides powerful style sheets to improve your document design. You'll find helpful macros and utilities for casual correspondence, generating professional form letters and more.

Microsoft Word 5.0/5.5 PowerTools with companion diskette.
ISBN 1-55755-101-4. $34.95
Canadian $45.95.

Word for Windows Know-How

Microsoft Word for Windows is considered the premier wordprocessor among Windows users. This book is not only a guide to using Word for Windows, it also presents many important techniques for exploiting all of the powerful features in this package. Learn about working with macros; handling graphics; printer formatting and more. Includes complete details on the new Word BASIC and companion disk that contains style sheets, Word BASIC examples, macros and much more.

ISBN 1-55755-093-X. $34.95
Canada: 53924 $45.95

Word for Windows Powertools

contains many tools including ready-to-use style templates and printer files for beginners and advanced users who demand professional results. All of these tools can be easily integrated with your other Windows applications. You'll learn important elements of programming in WordBASIC and Word's macro language.

Word for Windows Powertools comes with companion disk containing many style sheets and more.

ISBN 1-55755-103-0. Suggested retail price $34.95.
Canada: 53924 $45.95

Upgrading & Maintaining your PC

Your PC represents a major investment. This book shows you how to turn your PC into a high performance computing machine. It describes what you'll see when you open the "hood" and how all of the parts work together. Whether you want to add a hard drive, increase your memory, upgrade to a higher resolution monitor, or turn your XT into a fast AT or 386 screamer, you'll see how to do it easily and economically, without having to be an electronics wizard.
ISBN 1-55755-092-1. $24.95
Canada: 53926 $33.95

Batch files make your computer sessions easier. **Batch File Powertools** shows you how to use powerful, easy-to-learn techniques for many DOS applications. You'll boost your computing productivity with these techniques for making truly powerful batch files. **Batch File Powertools** includes dozens of new batch commands for writing time-saving, easy-to-use "power" batch files.

Batch File Powertools includes BatchBASIC on the companion disk. BatchBASIC adds dozens of new commands to DOS to help increase your computing productivity. The companion disk also contains dozens of practical examples.
ISBN 1-55755-102-2. $34.95
Canada: $45.95

Stepping up to DR DOS 5.0

DR DOS 5.0 is a new alternative operating system to MS-DOS. Its many new features overcome some of the limitations that users find in MS-DOS.

This fast paced guide shows you the most important features of DR DOS 5.0. It presents practical examples to get you going quickly with DR DOS 5.0. It takes you step-by-step through the world of DR DOS 5.0. You'll find clear explanations and many "hands on" examples on using DR DOS. Learn the information you'll need to become more productive with DR DOS. 210 pages.

ISBN 1-55755-106-5. $14.95
Canada: 57913 $19.95

Novell NetWare Simplified

answers many questions about file servers and workstations using the most popular LAN system. **Novell NetWare Simplified** is your first step to understanding and using Novell NetWare more effectively.

Some of the topics include:
- Installing extra printers and PC workstations.
- Memory requirements for each user.
- Sending messages through your systems.
- Developing a user-friendly menu system and more.

ISBN 1-55755-105-7. $24.95
Canada: 57910 $3395

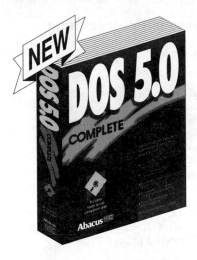

DOS 5.0 Complete

Not just another reference book - **DOS 5.0 Complete** is a practical user's guide to learning and using Microsoft's new DOS. It's an encyclopedia of DOS knowledge not only for the computer whiz but for the everyday user.

DOS 5.0 Complete is loaded with helpful hints for outfitting any computer with MS-DOS 5.0. From installing DOS 5.0 to using the new features for file, directory and storage maintenance you'll find techniques and hints here.

DOS 5.0 Complete has dozens of easy to follow examples. This book explains AUTOEXEC.BAT and CONFIG.SYS. The detailed explanations make this the most authoritative DOS book available. The friendly, easy to understand writing style insures that even beginners will grasp the fundamentals quickly and easily. And you'll find a complete DOS command reference.

Topics include:

- Learn the "ins and outs" of using the new MS-DOS 5.0
- Boost your productivity with these practical techniques
- Discover ways to solve your own DOS problems
- Save valuable time with the ready-to-run companion disk.
- Browse the extensive MS-DOS reference section
- Using DOS' new memory management features
- Using the improved SHELL ;for performing your computer housekeeping ;chores
- Using the new DOSKEY utility for faster command line editing and macro power.
- Using EDIT, the new full-screen editor
- Using QBASIC, DOS' new BASIC programming language
- Complete DOS command reference.

DOS 5.0 Complete includes a companion disk with example batch files, detailed explanations, and powerful tips and tricks to help you get the most out of MS-DOS 5.0. **DOS 5.0 Complete** will become THE source for reference information about DOS 5.0.

DOS 5.0 Complete
Authors: Michael Tornsdorf, Helmut Tornsdorf
ISBN 1-55755-109-X.
Suggested retail price $34.95 with companion disk.

Virus Secure for Windows

Eliminate potential valuable data loss and minimize your risks with Virus Secure.

Don't give viruses the chance to ruin your data when you're using Windows. Avoid virus infection and potential valuable data loss. **Virus Secure for Windows** provides complete data protection for your hard and/or floppy disks from computer virus infection. **Virus Secure** is written by virus authority Ralf Burger (author of <u>Computer Viruses and Data Protection</u>). This is security that will keep your data alive and your PC operations productive.

Virus Secure can be run by both beginning and experienced users. Beginners will like the clear user interface and detailed error system. Experts will like the numerous options offered by **Virus Secure.** Beginning and advanced users will learn how to protect their diskettes and hard drives from unwanted data loss caused by viruses.

Virus Secure can detect over 200 known viruses and has built-in power for recognizing new or unknown viruses. It can also distinguish "normal" changes from "unusual" changes that viruses can make. **Virus Secure** can also be expanded. You can easily expand the recognition of viruses using a standard word processor. **Virus Secure** allows you to stay up to date as new viruses appear in the PC community.

Item #S108, ISBN 1-55755-108-1. Retail price $95.00.
System requirements: PC AT, 386 or compatible, hard drive and Windows 3.0.
Windows not included.

Author Ralf Burger

Windows is a trademark of Microsoft Corporation.

In US and Canada add $5.00 shipping and handling. Foreign orders add $13.00 per item.
Michigan residents add 4% sales tax.

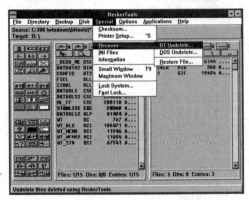